D0241917

LONGMAN *Pocket* ENGLISH DICTIONARY

Pearson Education Limited
Edinburgh Gate, Harlow, Essex CM20 2JE, England
and associated companies throughout the world

© Pearson Education Limited 2001

Visit our website: http://www.longman.com/dictionaries

All rights reserved; no part of this publication may be reproduced, stored in a retrieval system, or transmitted in any form or by any means, electronic, mechanical, photocopying, recording or otherwise, without the prior written permission of the Publishers.

First published 2001

005 007 008 006 004

Words that the editors have reason to believe constitute trademarks have been described as such. However, neither the presence nor the absence of such a description should be regarded as affecting the legal status of any trademark.

ISBN 0 582 488974

Set in 7pt MetaPlus Normal by Peter Wray
Printed in Spain by Cayfosa-Quebecor, Barcelona

ACKNOWLEDGEMENTS

Director Della Summers
Editorial Director & Publisher Pierre-Henri Cousin
Editor & Project Manager Wendy Lee
Pronunciation Editor Dinah Jackson
Design Alex Ingr
Cover design Abbey Design, Harlow, Essex
Proofreader Lynda Carey

and the Longman Dictionaries team

Using the Dictionary

- The *Longman Pocket English Dictionary* is the ideal handy dictionary for intermediate students of English.
- The meanings of over 16 000 words and phrases are explained clearly and simply using the Longman Defining Vocabulary of just 2000 English words. Any additional words, that you may not know, are written in SMALL CAPITAL LETTERS. These additional words are explained in their own alphabetical position. Example sentences and phrases, based on real sentences and phrases in books and newspapers, show how the words are used in natural, everyday English.
- Special language notes explain how to use some of the most important English words without making mistakes. The *Longman Pocket Dictionary* also helps with grammar points such as irregular verbs and adjectives, and with prepositions – showing which preposition links the word with the following word or words: for example, *Are you afraid **of** the dark?*
- Sometimes words with the same spelling are different in meaning, grammar, or pronunciation. These words are explained in separate entries. For example: **love**[1] is a verb and **love**[2] is a noun; **row**[1] means a line, **row**[2] means a quarrel.
- You sometimes want to know about other words you could use instead of the one you are looking at, or to find out which words mean the opposite. The *Longman Pocket Dictionary* gives you this information too. Where these words are useful, they are listed at the end of an entry. The dictionary also has 15 pages of colour pictures showing words connected with common, everyday situations.
- By giving you the basic building blocks to work with, the *Longman Pocket Dictionary* helps you to build up your word power, so that you can produce English sentences which are not only accurate but also sound natural.

Pronunciation Table

Consonants		Vowels	
Symbol	**Keyword**	**Symbol**	**Keyword**
p	pan	iː	beat
b	ban	ɪ	bit
t	tip	e	bet
d	dip	æ	bat
k	cap	ɑː	bar
g	gap	ɒ	block
tʃ	church	ɔː	bought
dʒ	judge	ʊ	book
f	few	uː	boot
v	view	ʌ	but
θ	throw	ɜː	burn
ð	though	ə	brother
s	sip	eɪ	bay
z	zip	əʊ	bone
ʃ	fresh	aɪ	by
ʒ	measure	aʊ	bound
h	hot	ɔɪ	boy
m	sum	ɪə	beer
n	sun	eə	bare
ŋ	sung	ʊə	poor
l	lot	eɪə	player
r	rot	əʊə	lower
j	yet	aɪə	tire
w	wet	aʊə	flower
		ɔɪə	employer

/ˈ/ shows main stress
/ˌ/ shows secondary stress
/ʳ/ at the end of a word means that /r/ is usually pronounced when the next word begins with a vowel sound
/ᵊ/ means that /ə/ may or may not be used

Irregular Verbs

verb	present participle	past tense	past participle
arise	arising	arose	arisen
be	being	was	been
bear	bearing	bore	borne
beat	beating	beat	beaten
become	becoming	became	become
begin	beginning	began	begun
bend	bending	bent	bent
beset	besetting	beset	beset
bet	betting	betted *or* bet	betted *or* bet
bind	binding	bound	bound
bite	biting	bit	bitten
bleed	bleeding	bled	bled
bless	blessing	blessed *or* blest	blessed *or* blest
blow	blowing	blew	blown
break	breaking	broke	broken
breed	breeding	bred	bred
bring	bringing	brought	brought
broadcast	broadcasting	broadcast	broadcast
build	building	built	built
burn	burning	burned *or* burnt	burned *or* burnt
bust	busting	busted *or* bust	busted *or* bust
buy	buying	bought	bought
cast	casting	cast	cast
catch	catching	caught	caught
choose	choosing	chose	chosen
cling	clinging	clung	clung
come	coming	came	come
cost	costing	cost	cost
creep	creeping	crept	crept
cut	cutting	cut	cut
deal	dealing	dealt	dealt
die	dying	died	died
dig	digging	dug	dug
dive	diving	dived	dived
do	doing	did	done
draw	drawing	drew	drawn
dream	dreaming	dreamed *or* dreamt	dreamed *or* dreamt
drink	drinking	drank	drunk
drive	driving	drove	driven
dwell	dwelling	dwelled *or* dwelt	dwelled *or* dwelt
eat	eating	ate	eaten
fall	falling	fell	fallen
feed	feeding	fed	fed
feel	feeling	felt	felt
fight	fighting	fought	fought

verb	present participle	past tense	past participle
find	finding	found	found
fly	flying	flew	flown
forbid	forbidding	forebade	forbidden
foresee	foreseeing	foresaw	foreseen
forget	forgetting	forgot	forgotten
freeze	freezing	froze	frozen
get	getting	got	got
give	giving	gave	given
go	going	went	gone
grind	grinding	ground	ground
grow	growing	grew	grown
hang	hanging	hung *or* hanged	hung *or* hanged
have	having	had	had
hear	hearing	heard	heard
hide	hiding	hid	hidden
hit	hitting	hit	hit
hold	holding	held	held
hurt	hurting	hurt	hurt
keep	keeping	kept	kept
kneel	kneeling	knelt	knelt
knit	knitting	knitted *or* knit	knitted *or* knit
know	knowing	knew	known
lay	laying	laid	laid
lead	leading	led	led
lean	leaning	leaned *or* leant	leaned *or* leant
leap	leaping	leaped *or* leapt	leaped *or* leapt
learn	learning	learned *or* learnt	learned *or* learnt
leave	leaving	left	left
lend	lending	lent	lent
let	letting	let	let
lie[1]	lying	lay	lain
lie[2]	lying	lied	lied
lose	losing	lost	lost
make	making	made	made
mean	meaning	meant	meant
meet	meeting	met	met
mislead	misleading	misled	misled
misspell	misspelling	misspelled *or* misspelt	misspelled *or* misspelt
mistake	mistaking	mistook	mistaken
misunderstand	misunderstanding	misunderstood	misunderstood
mow	mowing	mowed *or* mown	mowed *or* mown
outdo	outdoing	outdid	outdone
outgrow	outgrowing	outgrew	outgrown
overcome	overcoming	overcame	overcome
overdo	overdoing	overdid	overdone
overhear	overhearing	overheard	overheard

verb	present participle	past tense	past participle
oversleep	oversleeping	overslept	overslept
overtake	overtaking	overtook	overtaken
overthrow	overthrowing	overthrew	overthrown
panic	panicking	panicked	panicked
pay	paying	paid	paid
picnic	picnicking	picknicked	picknicked
put	putting	put	put
quit	quitting	quit	quit
read	reading	read	read
rebuild	rebuilding	rebuilt	rebuilt
redo	redoing	redid	redone
repay	repaying	repaid	repaid
resit	resitting	resat	resat
rewind	rewinding	rewound	rewound
rewrite	rewriting	rewrote	rewritten
ride	riding	rode	ridden
ring	ringing	rang	rung
rise	rising	rose	risen
run	running	ran	run
saw	sawing	sawed	sawn
say	saying	said	said
see	seeing	saw	seen
seek	seeking	sought	sought
sell	selling	sold	sold
send	sending	sent	sent
set	setting	set	set
sew	sewing	sewed	sewn
shake	shaking	shook	shaken
shear	shearing	sheared	shorn
shed	shedding	shed	shed
shine	shining	shone	shone
shoot	shooting	shot	shot
show	showing	showed	shown
shrink	shrinking	shrank	shrunk
shut	shutting	shut	shut
sing	singing	sang	sung
sink	sinking	sank	sunk
sit	sitting	sat	sat
sleep	sleeping	slept	slept
slide	sliding	slid	slid
sling	slinging	slung	slung
slit	slitting	slit	slit
smell	smelling	smelt	smelt
sow	sowing	sowed	sown
speak	speaking	spoke	spoken
speed	speeding	speeded *or* sped	speeded *or* sped
spell	spelling	spelled *or* spelt	spelled *or* spelt

verb	present participle	past tense	past participle
spend	spending	spent	spent
spill	spilling	spilled *or* spilt	spilled *or* spilt
spin	spinning	spun	spun
spit	spitting	spat	spat
split	splitting	split	split
spoil	spoiling	spoilt	spoilt
spring	springing	sprang	sprung
stand	standing	stood	stood
steal	stealing	stole	stolen
stick	sticking	stuck	stuck
sting	stinging	stung	stung
stink	stinking	stank	stunk
stride	striding	strode	stridden
strike	striking	struck	struck
strive	striving	strove	striven
swear	swearing	swore	sworn
sweep	sweeping	swept	swept
swell	swelling	swelled	swollen
swim	swimming	swam	swum
swing	swinging	swung	swung
take	taking	took	taken
teach	teaching	taught	taught
tear	tearing	tore	torn
tell	telling	told	told
think	thinking	thought	thought
throw	throwing	threw	thrown
thrust	thrusting	thrust	thrust
tie	tying	tied	tied
tread	treading	trod	trodden
undergo	undergoing	underwent	undergone
understand	understanding	understood	understood
undertake	undertaking	undertook	undertaken
undo	undoing	undid	undone
unwind	unwinding	unwound	unwound
uphold	upholding	upheld	upheld
upset	upsetting	upset	upset
wake	waking	waked *or* woke	woken
wear	wearing	wore	worn
weave	weaving	wove	woven
weep	weeping	wept	wept
wet	wetting	wet *or* wetted	wet *or* wetted
win	winning	won	won
wind	winding	wound	wound
withhold	withholding	withheld	withheld
withdraw	withdrawing	withdrew	withdrawn
withstand	withstanding	withstood	withstood
wring	wringing	wrung	wrung
write	writing	wrote	written

Aa

a /ə; *strong* eɪ/ *indefinite article*
1 one; any ▶ *I gave him a pencil.* ▶ *A bird has two legs.*
2 for each; in each ▶ *The sweets cost 10 cents a bag.* ▶ *three times a year*

An is used instead of **a** before a word that starts with the sound of **a, e, i, o,** or **u**.
LOOK AT: **an**

abandon /əˈbændən/ *verb*
to leave someone or something ▶ *The baby was abandoned by its mother.* ▶ *We abandoned our holiday because we had no money.*

abbey /ˈæbɪ/ *noun*
a large church ▶ *Westminster Abbey*

abbreviation /əˌbriːvɪˈeɪʃən/ *noun*
a short way of writing or saying a word or name ▶ *Mr is the abbreviation for Mister.*

ABC /ˌeɪ biː ˈsiː/ *noun*
the English alphabet ▶ *She's learning her ABC.*

abdomen /ˈæbdəmən/ *noun*
the front part of your body below your waist

abduct /əbˈdʌkt/ *verb*
to take someone away illegally and by using force ▶ *Police believe that the woman has been abducted.*

ability /əˈbɪlətɪ/ *noun (no plural)*
the power or knowledge to do something ▶ *Doctors now have the ability to keep people alive for much longer.*

ablaze /əˈbleɪz/ *adjective*
burning with a lot of flames ▶ *Soon the whole building was ablaze.*

able /ˈeɪbəl/ *adjective*
having the power or the knowledge to do something ▶ *Is he able to swim?* ▶ *I'm afraid I won't be able to come.*
OPPOSITE: **unable**

abnormal /æbˈnɔːməl/ *adjective*
not normal, especially in a way that is strange or dangerous ▶ *The doctors found some abnormal cells in her body. (adverb: **abnormally**)*

aboard /əˈbɔːd/ *preposition, adverb*
on or onto a ship or plane ▶ *Are all the passengers aboard?*

abolish /əˈbɒlɪʃ/ *verb*
to end something or get rid of it by law ▶ *The new government abolished the tax on wine.*

abolition /ˌæbəˈlɪʃən/ *noun (no plural)*
ending or getting rid of something by law ▶ *the abolition of taxes*

abortion /əˈbɔːʃən/ *noun*
an operation to stop a baby developing inside its mother, by removing the baby so that it dies ▶ *She was told about the dangers of having an abortion.*

about /əˈbaʊt/ *preposition, adverb*
1 concerning ▶ *What are you talking about?* ▶ *a book about birds*
2 a little more or less than ▶ *Come at about 6 o'clock.*
3 here and there ▶ *The children were kicking a ball about.* ▶ *They walked about the town.*
4 be about to do something to be just going to do something ▶ *I was about to come and see you.*
5 how about/what about used when you are suggesting something ▶ *What about some lunch?* ▶ *How about going to the cinema?*

above /əˈbʌv/ *adverb, preposition*
1 at a higher place; higher than, over ▶ *The picture is on the wall above my desk.* ▶ *the blue sky above*
2 more than a certain number or amount ▶ *children above the age of five*
OPPOSITE (**1** and **2**): **below**

3 above all more than anything else; most important of all ▶ *I want you to remember this above all.*

abroad /əˈbrɔːd/ *adverb*
in or to a foreign country ▶ *My brother is studying abroad.* ▶ *He wants to go abroad.*

abrupt /əˈbrʌpt/ *adjective*
1 sudden ▶ *an abrupt knock at the door*
2 not polite ▶ *an abrupt answer to his question*
*(adverb: **abruptly**)*

absence /ˈæbsəns/ *noun (no plural)*
not being there ▶ *Her absence was noticed by her friends.*
OPPOSITE: **presence**

absent /ˈæbsənt/ *adjective*
not there; not present ▶ *He was absent from work last Tuesday.*

absentee /ˌæbsənˈtiː/ *noun*
a person who is not where they usually are or where they should be ▶ *There were several absentees.*

absenteeism /ˌæbsənˈtiːɪzəm/ *noun (no plural)*
regular absence from work or school without a good reason ▶ *Absenteeism at the factory is becoming a real problem.*

absent-minded /ˌæbsənt ˈmaɪndɪd/ *adjective*
not noticing things that are happening around you, and often forgetting things

absolute /ˈæbsəluːt/ *adjective*
complete ▶ *Are you telling me the absolute truth?*

absolutely /ˌæbsəˈluːtlɪ/ *adverb*
1 very; completely ▶ *It's absolutely beautiful.* ▶ *You must keep it absolutely secret.*
2 used to show that you agree with someone ▶ *"Do you think I'm right?" "Absolutely!"*

absorb /əbˈsɔːb/ *verb*
1 to take in liquid slowly
2 to learn and understand something thoroughly ▶ *I haven't really absorbed all the information yet.*

absorbent /əbˈsɔːbənt/ *adjective*
able to take in liquid ▶ *This material is quite absorbent.*

absorbing /əbˈsɔːbɪŋ/ *adjective*
very interesting ▶ *an absorbing book*

abstain /əbˈsteɪn/ *verb*
1 to not do something even though you want to ▶ *Patients were advised to abstain **from** drinking alcohol.*
2 to deliberately not vote ▶ *Four members of the committee abstained.*

abstract /ˈæbstrækt/ *adjective*
based on ideas rather than specific examples or real events ▶ *Beauty is an abstract idea.*

absurd /əbˈsɜːd/ *adjective*
very silly ▶ *The story was so absurd that no one believed it.*
*(adverb: **absurdly**)*

abundant /əˈbʌndənt/ *adjective*
existing in large quantities ▶ *an abundant supply of fresh fruit*

abuse¹ /əˈbjuːz/ *verb (present participle **abusing**, past **abused**)*
to call someone rude and insulting names, or speak rudely to them

abuse² /əˈbjuːs/ *noun (no plural)*
1 rude and insulting things said to someone ▶ *He shouted abuse at me.*
2 bad treatment or wrong use ▶ *the problem of drug abuse*

abusive /əˈbjuːsɪv/ *adjective*
using words that are rude and insulting ▶ *an abusive letter*

academic /ˌækəˈdemɪk/ *adjective*
concerning the work done in schools, colleges, or universities ▶ *academic subjects*

academy /əˈkædəmɪ/ *noun (plural **academies**)*
a school or college where students

learn a special subject or skill ▶ *a military academy*

accelerate /ək'seləreɪt/ *verb (present participle **accelerating**, past **accelerated**)*
to make a car go faster ▶ *I accelerated and passed the lorry in front.*

accelerator /ək'seləreɪtəʳ/ *noun*
the thing that you press with your foot in a car to make it go faster

accent /'æksənt/ *noun*
a way of speaking, that shows that a person comes from a particular place ▶ *Maria speaks English with an Italian accent.*
COMPARE: **dialect**

accept /ək'sept/ *verb*
1 to receive or take something that is offered to you ▶ *Will you accept my offer?* ▶ *I accepted another piece of cake.*
2 to agree to do something ▶ *David asked three friends to his party, and they all accepted.*

acceptable /ək'septəbəl/ *adjective*
of good enough quality ▶ *Your work is not acceptable.*
OPPOSITE: **unacceptable**

acceptance /ək'septəns/ *noun (no plural)*
agreement to receive or take something that is offered to you ▶ *her acceptance of the offer*

accepted /ək'septɪd/ *adjective*
agreed by most people to be right ▶ *the accepted rules of the game*

access /'ækses/ *noun (no plural)*
a way to get to a place, a person, or a thing ▶ *There is no access **to** the street through that door.* ▶ *Students need access to books.*

accessible /ək'sesəbəl/ *adjective*
easy to reach, find, or use ▶ *The national park is not accessible by road.* ▶ *the wide range of information that is accessible on the Internet*

accessory /ək'sesərɪ/ *noun (plural **accessories**)*
something such as a belt or jewellery that you wear because it looks nice with your clothes ▶ *a dress with matching accessories*

accident /'æksɪdənt/ *noun*
1 something, often bad, that happens by chance ▶ *John's had an accident – he's been hit by a car.* ▶ *I'm sorry I broke the cup. It was an accident.*
2 by accident by chance; not on purpose ▶ *I did it by accident.*

accidental /ˌæksɪ'dentl/ *adjective*
by chance; not on purpose ▶ *an accidental meeting (adverb: **accidentally**)*

accommodate /ə'kɒmədeɪt/ *verb (present participle **accommodating**, past **accommodated**)*
1 to give someone a place to live or stay in
2 to have space for something ▶ *You could accommodate another four children in your class.*

accommodation /əˌkɒmə'deɪʃən/ *noun (no plural)*
somewhere to live or stay ▶ *I must find some accommodation.*

> Remember that the noun **accommodation** has no plural: *Accommodation will be provided for the students.* ▶ *Do you have any accommodation?*

accompany /ə'kʌmpənɪ/ *verb (past **accompanied**)*
1 to go with someone ▶ *He accompanied me to the doctor's.*
2 to play music while someone else is singing or playing another instrument ▶ *Maria sang, and I accompanied her on the piano.*

accomplish /ə'kʌmplɪʃ/ *verb*
to do or finish something ▶ *We accomplished a lot during the day.*

accomplished /ə'kʌmplɪʃt/ *adjective*

A

very good at doing something ▶ *an accomplished musician*

accomplishment /əˈkʌmplɪʃmənt/ *noun*
something that you achieve or are able to do well ▶ *Passing the exam was quite an accomplishment.*

accord /əˈkɔːd/ *noun (no plural)*
of your own accord without being asked ▶ *She went of her own accord.*

accordance /əˈkɔːdəns/ *noun (no plural)*
in accordance with something done in a way that follows a particular system or rule ▶ *Safety checks were made in accordance with the rules.*

accordingly /əˈkɔːdɪŋlɪ/ *adverb*
in a way that is suitable for a particular situation ▶ *He broke the law and was punished accordingly.*

according to /əˈkɔːdɪŋ tuː/ *preposition*
from what is said or written ▶ *According to the map, we're very close to the sea.*

account[1] /əˈkaʊnt/ *noun*
1 a story or description ▶ *an exciting account **of** the match*
2 a list of payments owed to someone
3 an amount of money kept in a bank ▶ *He paid the money into his bank account.*
4 on account of because of ▶ *We stayed at home on account of the bad weather.*
5 take something into account to consider something before making a decision ▶ *You must take the price into account when choosing which one to buy.*
6 accounts *plural noun* lists of money that a person or company spends and earns

account[2] *verb*
account for to give the reason for something ▶ *I can't account for her strange behaviour.*

accountable /əˈkaʊntəbəl/ *adjective*
responsible for the effects of your actions, and willing to explain or be criticized for them ▶ *At what age is a person legally accountable **for** their actions?*

accountancy /əˈkaʊntənsɪ/ *noun (no plural)*
the job of being an accountant

accountant /əˈkaʊntənt/ *noun*
a person whose job is to keep lists of money spent and money earned, for people or companies

accumulate /əˈkjuːmjʊleɪt/ *verb (present participle **accumulating**, past **accumulated**)*
1 to gradually get more and more of something ▶ *During his life, he had accumulated a huge collection of paintings.*
2 to gradually increase ▶ *Her problems started to accumulate after the baby was born.*

accuracy /ˈækjʊrəsɪ/ *noun (no plural)*
the quality of being exactly right or correct

accurate /ˈækjʊrət/ *adjective*
right; correct ▶ *Is this watch accurate? (adverb: **accurately**)*
OPPOSITE: **inaccurate**

accusation /ˌækjʊˈzeɪʃən/ *noun*
an act of saying that someone has done something wrong ▶ *accusations **of** cheating*

accuse /əˈkjuːz/ *verb (present participle **accusing**, past **accused**)*
to say that someone has done something wrong ▶ *The teacher accused Paul **of** cheating.*
COMPARE: **blame**

accusing /əˈkjuːzɪŋ/ *adjective*
showing that you think someone has done something wrong ▶ *"Where have you been?" asked Jenny in an accusing voice. (adverb: **accusingly**)*

accustomed to /ə'kʌstəmd tuː/ *adjective*
used to something ▶ *I'm not accustomed to this sort of behaviour.*

ace[1] /eɪs/ *adjective*
excellent ▶ *He's an ace goalkeeper.*

ace[2] *noun*
one of four playing cards in a pack, that can have either the highest or the lowest value in a game of cards ▶ *the ace of diamonds*

ache[1] /eɪk/ *verb (present participle **aching**, past **ached**)*
to be painful; to hurt ▶ *Her head ached.*

ache[2] *noun*
a continuing pain ▶ *a stomach ache*

achieve /ə'tʃiːv/ *verb (present participle **achieving**, past **achieved**)*
to succeed in doing something by working ▶ *He achieved top marks in the examination.*

achievement /ə'tʃiːvmənt/ *noun*
something that you have worked hard for and done well

acid /'æsɪd/ *noun*
a powerful liquid that can burn things

acid rain /ˌæsɪd 'reɪn/ *noun (no plural)*
rain which causes damage to trees and plants because it contains acid put into the air by factories

acknowledge /ək'nɒlɪdʒ/ *verb (present participle **acknowledging**, past **acknowledged**)*
1 to agree that something is true ▶ *Do you acknowledge that you were wrong?*
2 to write to someone to say that you have received something ▶ *Please acknowledge my letter.*

acknowledgement /ək'nɒlɪdʒmənt/ *noun*
1 something that someone says, writes, or does to thank someone or to show that they have received something ▶ *I haven't received an acknowledgement **of** my letter yet.*
2 something that shows you admit or accept that something is true or that a situation exists ▶ *an acknowledgement **of** defeat*

acne /'æknɪ/ *noun (no plural)*
a skin problem which is common among young people and causes small spots to appear on the face

acorn /'eɪkɔːn/ *noun*
a small nut which grows on OAK trees

acquaintance /ə'kweɪntəns/ *noun*
a person you know slightly because you have met him or her a few times
COMPARE: **friend**

acquainted /ə'kweɪntɪd/ *adjective*
be acquainted with to know someone ▶ *Are you acquainted with Mr Smith?*

acquire /ə'kwaɪə^r/ *verb (present participle **acquiring**, past **acquired**)*
to get or buy something ▶ *How did you acquire this money?*

acre /'eɪkə^r/ *noun*
a measure of land; 4,047 square metres

acrobat /'ækrəbæt/ *noun*
a person who performs in a CIRCUS and does difficult tricks with their body

acronym /'ækrənɪm/ *noun*
a word that is made from the first letters of a group of words. For example, TEFL is an acronym for Teaching English as a Foreign Language

across /ə'krɒs/ *adverb, preposition*
from one side of a place to the other; on the other side of something ▶ *They swam across the river.* ▶ *the house across the street*

act[1] /ækt/ *verb*
1 to do something or behave in a certain way ▶ *You're acting like a fool.*

A

2 to pretend to be someone else, in a play or film
3 act as to be in place of someone or something ▶ *This room acts as her office.*

act² *noun*
1 an action ▶ *an act of bravery*
2 something pretended ▶ *She seems happy, but it's just an act.*
3 a part of a play

acting /ˈæktɪŋ/ *noun (no plural)*
the work done by an ACTOR or ACTRESS

action /ˈækʃən/ *noun*
1 something that you do ▶ *His quick action saved her life.* ▶ *The government must take action to help the poor.*
2 in action doing something ▶ *photographs of the players in action during the match*
3 out of action not working ▶ *My car is out of action.*

action replay /ˌækʃən ˈriːpleɪ/ *noun*
an interesting part of a sports event that is shown again on television immediately after it happens ▶ *The action replay showed that the ball crossed the line.*

activate /ˈæktɪveɪt/ *verb (present participle* ***activating****, past* ***activated****)*
to make something start to work ▶ *Pressing this button will activate the car alarm.*

active /ˈæktɪv/ *adjective*
1 always doing things ▶ *He is an active member of the club.* ▶ *an active old lady*
OPPOSITE: **inactive**
2 doing the action. In the sentence "John kicked the ball", "kicked" is an active verb
OPPOSITE (**2**): **passive**

actively /ˈæktɪvlɪ/ *adverb*
in a way that involves doing things to try to make something happen ▶ *The government has actively encouraged immigration.*

activist /ˈæktɪvɪst/ *noun*
a person who works hard to change society or a political situation they do not agree with ▶ *a political activist*

activity /ækˈtɪvətɪ/ *noun*
1 *(plural* ***activities****)* something you do, especially to enjoy yourself ▶ *Dancing is her favourite activity.*
2 *(no plural)* being active ▶ *The classroom was full of activity – every child was busy.*

actor /ˈæktəʳ/ *noun*
a man or woman who acts in plays or films

actress /ˈæktrəs/ *noun (plural* ***actresses****)*
a woman who acts in plays or films

actual /ˈæktʃʊəl/ *adjective*
real and clear ▶ *We think he stole the money, but we have no actual proof.*

actually /ˈæktʃʊəlɪ/ *adverb*
1 really; in fact ▶ *Do you actually believe that?* ▶ *I've spoken to him on the telephone, but I've never actually met him.*
2 used to say in a polite way that someone has a wrong idea ▶ *Actually, the film starts at 3 o'clock, not 4.*

acute /əˈkjuːt/ *adjective*
1 very serious or bad ▶ *patients who suffer acute pain*
2 (used about angles) less than 90°

ad /æd/ *noun*
an advertisement

AD /ˌeɪ ˈdiː/
after the birth of Christ, used in dates ▶ *the year AD 700*

adamant /ˈædəmənt/ *adjective*
determined not to change your opinion or decision ▶ *She was adamant that she would stay.*

adapt /əˈdæpt/ *verb*
1 to change something to make it more suitable ▶ *a kitchen adapted for blind people*
2 to become used to something

A

► *The children have adapted* ***to*** *their new school.*

adaptable /ə'dæptəbəl/ *adjective*
(used about a person) able to become used to new things easily

adaptation /ˌædæp'teɪʃən/ *noun*
a play or film that is based on a book ► *The film is a modern adaptation of "Romeo and Juliet".*

adapter /ə'dæptəʳ/ *noun*
something that you use to connect two pieces of equipment when you cannot connect them together directly ► *an electrical adapter*

add /æd/ *verb*
1 to put something together with something else ► *If you add 2 and 7, you get 9.* ► *To make the cake, mix the butter and sugar, and then add the flour.*
2 add up to put numbers or amounts together to find a total ► *Add up these numbers.* ► *I can't add up* (=I am not good at putting numbers together and finding the total).
COMPARE (**2**): **subtract**
3 to say something more

adder /'ædəʳ/ *noun*
a snake with a dangerous bite

addict /'ædɪkt/ *noun*
someone who is not able to stop taking harmful drugs

addicted /ə'dɪktɪd/ *adjective*
not able to stop doing something, especially taking a harmful drug ► *He was addicted* ***to*** *heroin.* ► *My children are completely addicted* ***to*** *computer games.*

addictive /ə'dɪktɪv/ *adjective*
making you addicted to something ► *a highly addictive drug*

addition /ə'dɪʃən/ *noun*
1 *(no plural)* adding numbers or amounts together
COMPARE: **subtraction**
2 someone or something added ► *an addition to the family* (=a new baby)
3 in addition to as well as ► *In addition to English, the children also learn German and Spanish.*

additional /ə'dɪʃənəl/ *adjective*
added to what is already there ► *We always need additional staff over the New Year.*

address¹ /ə'dres/ *noun (plural* ***addresses****)*
the name of the place where you live ► *Please write your name and address.*

address² *verb*
1 to write an address on something ► *She addressed the letter to Mrs Wilson.*
2 to speak to someone ► *The captain addressed his team.*

adept /'ædept/ *adjective*
good at doing something that needs care or skill ► *I'm not very adept* ***at*** *typing.*

adequate /'ædɪkwət/ *adjective*
enough ► *an adequate amount of food*
OPPOSITE: **inadequate**

adjacent /ə'dʒeɪsənt/ *adjective*
next to something ► *buildings adjacent* ***to*** *the palace*

adjective /'ædʒɪktɪv/ *noun*
a word that describes someone or something. In the phrase "a beautiful song", "beautiful" is an adjective

adjoining /ə'dʒɔɪnɪŋ/ *adjective*
next to and connected to another building, room, etc. ► *She hurried into the adjoining room.*

adjust /ə'dʒʌst/ *verb*
to make a small change in something or to move it slightly to make it better

adjustable /ə'dʒʌstəbəl/ *adjective*
able to be changed or moved slightly to make it better ► *adjustable car seats*

A

adjustment /ə'dʒʌstmənt/ *noun*
a small change that you make in something to make it better ▶ *We had to make a few adjustments to our original plan.*

administer /əd'mɪnɪstəʳ/ *verb*
1 to organize or manage something ▶ *A special committee will administer the scheme.*
2 to give someone a drug or medical treatment ▶ *Only doctors and nurses can administer drugs.*

administration /əd,mɪnɪ'streɪʃən/ *noun (no plural)*
looking after or managing a business or an organization

administrative /əd'mɪnɪstrətɪv/ *adjective*
connected with organizing or managing the work in a company or an organization ▶ *The company has 13 administrative staff.*

administrator /əd'mɪnɪstreɪtəʳ/ *noun*
a person whose job is to help organize a particular area of work in a company or an organization

admirable /'ædmərəbəl/ *adjective*
good and deserving your respect ▶ *He had many admirable qualities, especially honesty. (adverb:* ***admirably****)*

admiral /'ædmərəl/ *noun*
the most important officer in the navy

admiration /,ædmə'reɪʃən/ *noun (no plural)*
thinking a person or thing is very good, nice to look at, etc.

admire /əd'maɪəʳ/ *verb (present participle* ***admiring****, past* ***admired****)*
1 to respect and approve of someone or something
2 to think a person or thing is very nice to look at ▶ *I was just admiring your new car.*

admission /əd'mɪʃən/ *noun*
1 agreeing that something unpleasant about yourself is true, or saying that you have done something wrong ▶ *an admission* ***of*** *guilt*
2 *(no plural)* permission to go into a place ▶ *Admission was free for children.*

admit /əd'mɪt/ *verb (present participle* ***admitting****, past* ***admitted****)*
1 to agree that something unpleasant about yourself is true ▶ *She admitted she was lazy.*
OPPOSITE: **deny**
2 to let someone into a place ▶ *This ticket admits two people* ***to*** *the football match.*

adolescence /,ædə'lesəns/ *noun (no plural)*
the time when a young person is developing into an adult, usually between the ages of 13 and 18 ▶ *Adolescence is a difficult time for young people.*

adolescent /,ædə'lesənt/ *noun*
a boy or girl between about 13 and 16 years old

adopt /ə'dɒpt/ *verb*
to take a child into your family and treat him or her as your own

adoption /ə'dɒpʃən/ *noun (no plural)*
the act of taking a child into your family and treating him or her as your own

adorable /ə'dɔːrəbəl/ *adjective*
very attractive ▶ *What an adorable little girl!*

adore /ə'dɔːʳ/ *verb (present participle* ***adoring****, past* ***adored****)*
to love someone or something very much ▶ *She adored her son.* ▶ *I adore chocolate.*

adrenalin /ə'drenəlɪn/ *noun (no plural)*

a substance that your body produces when you are frightened, excited, or angry, and which gives you more energy

adult /ˈædʌlt, əˈdʌlt/ *noun*
a grown-up person ▶ *a group of three adults and four children*

adultery /əˈdʌltərɪ/ *noun (no plural)*
the act of having sex when you are married, with someone who is not your husband or wife ▶ *She accused her husband of adultery.*

advance¹ /ədˈvɑːns/ *verb (present participle* ***advancing****, past* ***advanced****)*
to move forward ▶ *The army advanced towards the town.*
COMPARE: **retreat**

advance² *noun*
in advance before something happens or before you do something ▶ *You must pay in advance.*

advanced /ədˈvɑːnst/ *adjective*
of a high or difficult level ▶ *advanced English classes*

advantage /ədˈvɑːntɪdʒ/ *noun*
something that helps a person ▶ *It is an advantage to speak several languages.*
OPPOSITE: **disadvantage**

advent /ˈædvent/ *noun (no plural)*
the time when something important first starts to exist ▶ *Since the advent* ***of*** *computers, offices have changed completely.*

adventure /ədˈventʃəʳ/ *noun*
an exciting thing that happens to someone

adventurous /ədˈventʃərəs/ *adjective*
liking a life full of adventures

adverb /ˈædvɜːb/ *noun*
a word which tells us how, when, or where something is done. In the sentence "She spoke loudly", "loudly" is an adverb

adverse /ˈædvɜːs/ *adjective*
bad and causing problems ▶ *The illness has had an adverse effect on her school work.* ▶ *Adverse weather conditions caused the accident.*

advert /ˈædvɜːt/ *noun*
an advertisement

advertise /ˈædvətaɪz/ *verb (present participle* ***advertising****, past* ***advertised****)*
to put notices in a public place to give people information about something ▶ *The company has spent a lot of money advertising its new shampoo.*

advertisement /ədˈvɜːtɪsmənt/ *noun*
a notice or a short film offering something for sale ▶ *a newspaper advertisement* ▶ *an advertisement for a new soap*

advertising /ˈædvətaɪzɪŋ/ *noun (no plural)*
the business of advertising things on television, in public places, etc.

advice /ədˈvaɪs/ *noun (no plural)*
a suggestion about what someone should do ▶ *If you take my advice, you'll go home.* ▶ *That's good advice.*

advisable /ədˈvaɪzəbəl/ *adjective*
that should be done in order to avoid problems ▶ *It's advisable* ***to*** *book your ticket early.*

advise /ədˈvaɪz/ *verb (present participle* ***advising****, past* ***advised****)*
to tell someone what you think they should do ▶ *She advised me to go home.*

adviser /ədˈvaɪzəʳ/ *noun*
a person whose job is to give advice to a company, government, etc. ▶ *a financial adviser*

advocate¹ /ˈædvəkeɪt/ *verb (present participle* ***advocating****, past* ***advocated****)*
to say that you support a particular plan or method ▶ *We have never advocated the use of violence.*

A

A

advocate² /'ædvəkət/ *noun*
a person who supports a particular plan or method ▶ *He was an advocate **of** fascism.*

aerial /'eərɪəl/ *noun*
a wire, on top of a building or piece of apparatus, which sends out or receives radio or television signals

aerobic /eə'rəʊbɪk/ *adjective*
(used about exercise) making your heart and lungs stronger ▶ *an aerobic workout*

aerobics /eə'rəʊbɪks/ *noun (no plural)*
a form of very active exercise done to music

aeroplane /'eərəpleɪn/ *noun*
a large flying machine with wings, in which people can travel

aerosol /'eərəsɒl/ *noun*
a container from which a liquid can be SPRAYED

affair /ə'feəʳ/ *noun*
1 a sexual relationship between two people, especially one which is secret because they are married to other people ▶ *Her husband was having an affair.*
2 an event ▶ *The party was a noisy affair.*
3 affairs *plural noun* things connected with a particular subject ▶ *government affairs*

affect /ə'fekt/ *verb*
to make a difference to someone or something ▶ *The hot weather affected his health* (=made him ill).

affection /ə'fekʃən/ *noun (no plural)*
the feeling of liking and caring for another person

affectionate /ə'fekʃənət/ *adjective*
feeling or showing love *(adverb: **affectionately**)*

affinity /ə'fɪnətɪ/ *noun*
a feeling that you like and understand a person or animal ▶ *He had a remarkable affinity **with** horses.* ▶ *She felt a natural affinity **for** these people.*

affirmative /ə'fɜːmətɪv/ *adjective*
saying or meaning "yes" ▶ *an affirmative reply*
OPPOSITE: **negative**

afflict /ə'flɪkt/ *verb*
be afflicted by something to be badly affected by a serious disease or problem ▶ *a country that is afflicted by disease and famine*

affliction /ə'flɪkʃən/ *noun*
something that makes people suffer ▶ *Bad eyesight is a common affliction.*

affluent /'æfluənt/ *adjective*
rich ▶ *an affluent suburb of Paris*

afford /ə'fɔːd/ *verb*
to have enough money to pay for something ▶ *We can't afford a holiday.*

affordable /ə'fɔːdəbəl/ *adjective*
not too expensive, so that most people have enough money to buy it ▶ *It was difficult to find affordable accommodation.*

affront /ə'frʌnt/ *noun*
something that someone says or does that offends or upsets you ▶ *The people saw the remark as an affront **to** their religion.*

afraid /ə'freɪd/ *adjective*
feeling fear ▶ *Are you afraid **of** the dark?*
SAME MEANING: **scared**

afresh /ə'freʃ/ *adverb*
start afresh to start again from the beginning ▶ *You'd better start afresh on a clean piece of paper.*

after /'ɑːftəʳ/ *preposition, conjunction*
1 later than; following ▶ *My birthday is the day after tomorrow.* ▶ *We were very worried after we'd heard the news.*
OPPOSITE: **before**

A

2 behind; trying to catch ▶ *The child ran after her dog.*
3 after all in spite of what you did or thought before ▶ *I thought it was a mistake, but it was right after all.*
4 after that next; then ▶ *What did she do after that?*
5 be after something to be trying to get something ▶ *I think he's after more money.*

aftereffects /ˈɑːftərɪˌfekts/ *plural noun*
the unpleasant results that stay after the end of the condition or event that caused them ▶ *the aftereffects **of** the war*

afternoon /ˌɑːftəˈnuːn/ *noun*
the time between the middle of the day and evening ▶ *Good afternoon, Mrs Brown* (=said as a greeting).

aftershave /ˈɑːftəʃeɪv/ *noun*
a liquid with a nice smell that a man puts on his face after he has SHAVED ▶ *Are you wearing aftershave?*

afterthought /ˈɑːftəθɔːt/ *noun*
something that you do after doing other things, because you forgot to do it earlier ▶ *She invited me to the party, but only as an afterthought.*

afterwards /ˈɑːftəwədz/ *adverb*
later; after something has happened ▶ *We saw the film, and afterwards walked home together.*

again /əˈgen/ *adverb*
1 one more time; once more ▶ *Come and see us again soon.*
2 again and again many times
3 now and again sometimes, but not very often ▶ *My aunt visits us now and again.*

against /əˈgenst, əˈgeɪnst/ *preposition*
1 not agreeing with someone or something ▶ *I'm against killing animals for their fur.*
2 on the other side in a game or match ▶ *We're playing against the village team.*
3 close to; touching ▶ *Put the ladder against the wall.*
4 in order to stop something happening ▶ *government action against the job losses*
5 against the law not allowed by the law ▶ *It's against the law to drive too fast.*

age /eɪdʒ/ *noun*
1 the number of years someone has lived or something has been ▶ *What age is he?* ▶ *He is ten years of age.*
2 *(no plural)* one of the periods of a person's life ▶ *old age* ▶ *at a young age*
3 *(no plural)* being old ▶ *The wine improves with age.*
4 a period of time in history
5 ages a long time ▶ *We talked for ages.*

aged /eɪdʒd/ *adjective*
being of a particular age ▶ *children aged six and under*
COMPARE: **old**

agency /ˈeɪdʒənsɪ/ *noun (plural **agencies**)*
a business that arranges services for people ▶ *We found the flat through an agency.*

agenda /əˈdʒendə/ *noun*
a list of the things that people are going to discuss at a meeting ▶ *The next item on the agenda is this year's budget.*

agent /ˈeɪdʒənt/ *noun*
a person who looks after business for someone else ▶ *our company's agent in New York*

aggravate /ˈægrəveɪt/ *verb (present participle **aggravating**, past **aggravated**)*
to annoy someone ▶ *He really aggravates me sometimes.*

aggression /əˈgreʃən/ *noun (no plural)*

A

angry or violent behaviour or feelings ▶ *You need to learn how to control your aggression.*

aggressive /əˈgresɪv/ *adjective* behaving angrily, as if you want to fight or attack someone ▶ *He is very aggressive when he plays football.* (*adverb:* ***aggressively***)

agile /ˈædʒaɪl/ *adjective* able to move quickly and easily ▶ *In spite of her size, Sara is very agile.*

agitated /ˈædʒɪteɪtɪd/ *adjective* very worried or upset ▶ *You really shouldn't get so agitated.*

ago /əˈgəʊ/ *adverb* in the past ▶ *We came to live here six years ago.* ▶ *a few minutes ago*

Ago is used with the past tense of verbs, but you cannot use it with past tenses which are formed with **have**. Compare these sentences: *He arrived a month ago.* ▶ *He has been here since last month.*
LOOK AT: **before, since**

agonize /ˈægənaɪz/ *verb (present participle* ***agonizing****, past* ***agonized****)* to think and worry for a long time about something you have to do ▶ *Don't agonize for too long about any of the questions.*

agonizing /ˈægənaɪzɪŋ/ *adjective*
1 very painful ▶ *an agonizing injury*
2 making you feel very worried or nervous ▶ *Waiting for the results was agonizing.*

agony /ˈægənɪ/ *noun (no plural)* very bad pain

agree /əˈgriː/ *verb (past* ***agreed****)*
1 to have the same opinion as someone else ▶ *I agree* ***with*** *you.* ▶ *We all agreed.*
OPPOSITE: **disagree**
2 agree to something to say yes to something ▶ *He agreed to the plan.*
3 agree with something to believe that something is right; to approve of something
OPPOSITE (3): **disagree**

agreeable /əˈgriːəbəl/ *adjective* pleasant or enjoyable ▶ *a very agreeable young man*

agreed /əˈgriːd/ *adjective*
1 accepted by everyone ▶ *The agreed price for the bike was £50.*
2 be agreed on something to accept something ▶ *Are we all agreed on the date for the next meeting?*

agreement /əˈgriːmənt/ *noun*
1 an arrangement or a promise between people or countries ▶ *Britain has trade agreements with many other countries.*
2 *(no plural)* having the same opinion as someone else ▶ *They finally reached agreement on the price.*
OPPOSITE: **disagreement**
3 in agreement having the same opinion ▶ *We are all in agreement.*

agricultural /ˌægrɪˈkʌltʃərəl/ *adjective* used in farming or to do with farming

agriculture /ˈægrɪkʌltʃəʳ/ *noun (no plural)* the science of growing crops and raising animals

ahead /əˈhed/ *adverb*
1 forward ▶ *Walk straight ahead until you reach the river.*
2 at a distance in front of someone or something ▶ *I saw her ahead of me.*

aid[1] /eɪd/ *noun (no plural)* help ▶ *aid for poor countries*

aid[2] *verb* to help someone
SAME MEANING: **assist**

AIDS /eɪdz/ *noun (no plural)* a very serious disease which destroys the body's ability to fight illnesses

ailment /ˈeɪlmənt/ *noun* an illness that is not very serious

► *He misses too much work because of minor ailments.*

aim[1] /eɪm/ *verb*
1 to point something and get ready to throw it or fire it towards a person or thing ► *to aim a gun **at** someone*
2 to want to do something ► *We aim to win.*
COMPARE (**2**): **intend**

aim[2] *noun*
1 an act of pointing something and getting ready to throw it or fire it towards a person or thing
2 something you want to do

ain't /eɪnt/
a short form of "am not", "is not", "are not", "has not", or "have not" that many people think is not correct ► *It ain't true!*

air[1] /eəʳ/ *noun*
1 *(no plural)* the gas surrounding the Earth, which people breathe
2 an appearance ► *an air **of** excitement*
3 by air in an aircraft ► *We travelled by air.*
4 the air the space above you ► *He threw his hat into the air.*

air[2] *verb*
to make a room or clothes fresh by letting in air

air-conditioning /'eə kən,dɪʃənɪŋ/ *noun (no plural)*
machines for keeping the air in a building cool

aircraft /'eəkrɑːft/ *noun (plural **aircraft**)*
a flying machine

airfare /'eəfeəʳ/ *noun*
the price of a plane trip ► *I couldn't afford the airfare to go and see him.*

airfield /'eəfiːld/ *noun*
a place where aircraft land

airforce /'eəfɔːs/ *noun*
soldiers who use aircraft for fighting
COMPARE: **army, navy**

air hostess /'eə ,həʊstɪs/ *noun (plural **air hostesses**)*
a woman whose job is to look after the passengers on a plane

airless /'eələs/ *adjective*
without any fresh air ► *an airless room*
OPPOSITE: **airy**

airline /'eəlaɪn/ *noun*
a company which carries people or goods by plane

airmail /'eəmeɪl/ *noun (no plural)*
letters and parcels sent by aircraft

airport /'eəpɔːt/ *noun*
a place where aircraft are kept and where they arrive and leave

air raid /'eə reɪd/ *noun*
an attack by soldiers in aircraft

airstrip /'eə,strɪp/ *noun*
a long, narrow piece of land that planes can fly to and from

airtight /'eətaɪt/ *adjective*
completely closed so that air cannot get in or out ► *an airtight jar*

airy /'eərɪ/ *adjective (**airier, airiest**)*
having fresh air inside ► *an airy room*
OPPOSITE: **airless**

aisle /aɪl/ *noun*
a narrow passage between rows of seats

ajar /ə'dʒɑːʳ/ *adjective*
(of a door or window) not quite closed

alarm[1] /ə'lɑːm/ *noun*
1 *(no plural)* a feeling of fear or danger
2 something, such as a bell, that warns people of danger ► *a fire alarm*

alarm[2] *verb*
to worry someone or make them afraid

alarm clock /ə'lɑːm ,klɒk/ *noun*
a clock that makes a noise at the time you want to wake up

A

album /'ælbəm/ *noun*
1 a book with empty pages where you can put photographs, stamps, etc.
2 a record with several songs on each side ▶ *a Michael Jackson album*

alcohol /'ælkəhɒl/ *noun (no plural)*
a strong liquid, in beer and other drinks, which makes you feel drunk

alcoholic /ˌælkə'hɒlɪk/ *adjective*
containing alcohol ▶ *an alcoholic drink*

alert /ə'lɜːt/ *adjective*
awake and quick to notice things

A level /'eɪ ˌlevəl/ *noun*
ADVANCED LEVEL; an examination in a particular subject that students in England, Wales, and Northern Ireland take when they are 18 ▶ *I have A levels in French and English.*

algebra /'ældʒɪbrə/ *noun (no plural)*
a kind of MATHEMATICS in which you use letters to represent numbers

alias[1] /'eɪlɪəs/ *preposition*
used to give another name that someone uses, after giving their real name ▶ *the writer Eric Blair, alias George Orwell*

alias[2] *noun (plural* ***aliases****)*
a false name, usually used by a criminal ▶ *Bates sometimes uses the alias John Smith.*

alibi /'ælɪbaɪ/ *noun*
proof that someone was not at the place where a crime happened ▶ *He has an alibi for the night of the murder.*

alien /'eɪlɪən/ *noun*
a creature from another world ▶ *a spaceship full of aliens*

alienate /'eɪlɪəneɪt/ *verb (present participle* ***alienating****, past* ***alienated****)*
to make someone feel that they do not belong to your group ▶ *We don't want to alienate young people.*

alight /ə'laɪt/ *adjective*
burning; on fire ▶ *The house was alight.*

alike /ə'laɪk/ *adjective, adverb*
the same in some way ▶ *They were all dressed alike in white dresses.*

alive /ə'laɪv/ *adjective*
living; not dead ▶ *Is his grandfather still alive?*

all /ɔːl/ *adjective, adverb*
1 the whole amount of ▶ *Don't eat all that bread!*
2 every one of ▶ *all the children*
3 completely ▶ *He was dressed all in black.*
4 all over everywhere ▶ *I've been looking all over for you.*
5 not at all not in any way ▶ *I'm not at all hungry.* ▶ *She didn't understand it at all.*

all clear /ˌɔːl 'klɪəʳ/ *noun*
permission to begin doing something ▶ *We have to wait for the all clear from the safety committee before we can start.*

allegation /ˌælɪ'geɪʃən/ *noun*
a statement that someone has done something bad or illegal, but for which there is no proof ▶ *allegations that the police had tortured prisoners*

allege /ə'ledʒ/ *verb (present participle* ***alleging****, past* ***alleged****)*
to say that something is true without showing proof ▶ *Baldwin is alleged to have killed two people.*

allegiance /ə'liːdʒəns/ *noun*
loyalty or support given to a leader, country, belief, etc. ▶ *allegiance* ***to*** *the king*

allergic /ə'lɜːdʒɪk/ *adjective*
1 caused by an allergy ▶ *an allergic rash*
2 becoming ill when you eat, drink, or touch a particular thing ▶ *I'm allergic* ***to*** *cats.*

allergy /'ælədʒɪ/ *noun (plural* ***allergies****)*

an illness that causes you to become ill every time you eat, drink, or touch a particular thing

alley /'ælɪ/ *noun*
a very narrow road in a town

alliance /ə'laɪəns/ *noun*
an agreement between countries or groups to work together for a purpose

alligator /'ælɪgeɪtəʳ/ *noun*
a large animal with a long body and short legs which lives on land and in rivers in some countries

allocate /'æləkeɪt/ *verb (present participle* ***allocating****, past* ***allocated****)*
to decide to use an amount of money, time, etc. for a particular purpose ▶ *We have been allocated £5,000 for new computers.*

allow /ə'laʊ/ *verb*
to let someone do something ▶ *You're not allowed to go in there.*
OPPOSITE: **forbid**

allowance /ə'laʊəns/ *noun*
1 money that someone gives you regularly or for a special reason ▶ *His father gives him a small monthly allowance.* ▶ *a travel allowance*
2 make allowances for to consider someone's behaviour or work in a sympathetic way because they have a problem or disadvantage ▶ *Her mum died last week – we have to make allowances for her just now.*

all right *(also* ***alright****)* /ˌɔːl 'raɪt/ *adjective, adverb*
1 well; not hurt ▶ *Do you feel all right?*
2 good enough; quite good ▶ *The film was all right, but I've seen better ones.*
3 yes; I agree ▶ *"Shall we go to town?" "All right – let's go now."*

all-round /'ɔːl raʊnd/ *adjective*
good at doing many different things, especially in sports ▶ *an all-round athlete*

allude /ə'luːd/ *verb (present participle* ***alluding****, past* ***alluded****)*
to mention something, without saying it directly or clearly ▶ *I think he was alluding* ***to*** *your problems at work.*

ally /'ælaɪ/ *noun (plural* ***allies****)*
someone who helps you work or fight against someone else

almost /'ɔːlməʊst/ *adverb*
nearly ▶ *It's almost 9 o'clock.*

alone /ə'ləʊn/ *adjective, adverb*
1 not with other people ▶ *He lives alone.*
COMPARE: **lonely**
2 only ▶ *She alone knows the truth.*
3 leave someone or something alone to stop touching or disturbing someone or something ▶ *Leave the dog alone!*

along /ə'lɒŋ/ *preposition, adverb*
1 following the length of; from end to end of something long and thin ▶ *We walked along the road.* ▶ *the houses along the street*
2 forward ▶ *Move along, please!*
3 with you ▶ *Can I bring my friend along?*

alongside /əˌlɒŋ'saɪd/ *preposition, adverb*
by the side of something

aloud /ə'laʊd/ *adverb*
in a voice that is easy to hear ▶ *She read the story aloud.*

alphabet /'ælfəbet/ *noun*
the letters of a language in a special order ▶ *The English alphabet begins with A and ends with Z.*

alphabetical /ˌælfə'betɪkəl/ *adjective*
in the same order as the letters of the alphabet ▶ *The words in this dictionary are in alphabetical order.*

already /ɔːl'redɪ/ *adverb*
1 before now ▶ *He has seen that film twice already.*
2 by this or that time ▶ *It was already*

raining when we started our journey.
LOOK AT: **just, yet**

alright /ɔːlˈraɪt/ *adjective, adverb*
another word for **all right**

also /ˈɔːlsəʊ/ *adverb*
as well; too

When there is only one verb, put **also** before the verb, unless it is the verb **be**, which must have **also** after it: *He enjoys football and cricket, and he also likes tennis.* ▶ *She likes music and she is also interested in sport.* When there are two verbs, put **also** after the first one: *I would also like to come.* ▶ *It is an expensive sport which can also be dangerous.*

altar /ˈɔːltəʳ/ *noun*
a raised table in a religious place, where things are offered to a god

alter /ˈɔːltəʳ/ *verb*
to change ▶ *She altered her plans.*

alteration /ˌɔːltəˈreɪʃən/ *noun*
a change

alternate /ɔːlˈtɜːnət/ *adjective*
first one, then another ▶ *He works on alternate Saturdays* (=he works one Saturday, does not work the next, and so on).

alternative¹ /ɔːlˈtɜːnətɪv/ *noun*
something you can do or use instead of something else ▶ *You must go – there is no alternative.*

alternative² *adjective*
different from something else ▶ *an alternative plan*

alternatively /ɔːlˈtɜːnətɪvlɪ/ *adverb*
used to suggest something different from what you have just said ▶ *I could call you, or alternatively I could come to your house.*

although /ɔːlˈðəʊ/ *conjunction*
even if; in spite of something ▶ *Although they are poor, they are happy.*

altitude /ˈæltɪtjuːd/ *noun*
the height of something above sea level ▶ *Breathing is more difficult at high altitudes.*

alto /ˈæltəʊ/ *noun*
a female singer with a low voice, or a male singer with a high voice

altogether /ˌɔːltəˈgeðəʳ/ *adverb*
counting everyone or everything; completely ▶ *Altogether there were 12 people on the bus.* ▶ *He's not altogether sure what to do.*

aluminium /ˌæljʊˈmɪnɪəm/ *noun (no plural)*
a silver metal that is light and easy to bend

always /ˈɔːlweɪz/ *adverb*
1 at all times ▶ *He always arrives late.*
OPPOSITE: **never**
2 for ever ▶ *I shall always remember you.*

When there is only one verb, put **always** before the verb, unless it is the verb **be**, which must have **always** after it: *We always enjoy our holidays.* ▶ *It is always nice to see you.* When there are two verbs, put **always** after the first one: *You must always be careful when you cross the road.* ▶ *She is always complaining.*

am¹ /ˌeɪ ˈem/
in the morning ▶ *I got up at 8 am*

am² /əm; *strong* æm/ *verb*
the part of the verb **be** that we use with **I** ▶ *I am very sorry.* ▶ *Am I late for dinner?* ▶ *I'm* (=I am) *very late, aren't I?*

amateur /ˈæmətəʳ/ *adjective*
doing something for pleasure rather than for money ▶ *an amateur golfer*
COMPARE: **professional**

amaze /əˈmeɪz/ *verb (present participle* ***amazing****, past* ***amazed****)*
to surprise someone very much

amazement /əˈmeɪzmənt/ *noun (no plural)*
very great surprise ▶ *His mouth opened in amazement.*

amazing /əˈmeɪzɪŋ/ *adjective*
very surprising and exciting ▶ *What amazing news!*
SAME MEANING: **incredible**

ambassador /æmˈbæsədəʳ/ *noun*
an important person who represents his or her government in another country

ambiguous /æmˈbɪgjʊəs/ *adjective*
having more than one possible meaning ▶ *His comment was rather ambiguous.*

ambition /æmˈbɪʃən/ *noun*
1 *(no plural)* a strong wish to be successful
2 something you very much want to do ▶ *Her ambition was to be a famous singer.*

ambitious /æmˈbɪʃəs/ *adjective*
wanting very much to be successful

ambivalent /æmˈbɪvələnt/ *adjective*
not sure whether you like or want something ▶ *I feel somewhat ambivalent **about** moving abroad.*

ambulance /ˈæmbjʊləns/ *noun*
a special vehicle for carrying people who are ill or wounded

ambush[1] /ˈæmbʊʃ/ *noun (plural **ambushes**)*
a sudden attack by people who have been waiting and hiding ▶ *Two soldiers were killed in an ambush near the border.*

ambush[2] *verb*
to suddenly attack someone from a place where you have been hiding

amend /əˈmend/ *verb*
to make small changes or improvements to something that has been written ▶ *The law has been amended several times.*

amendment /əˈmendmənt/ *noun*
a change made in a law or document ▶ *We made a few amendments to the contract.*

amends /əˈmendz/ *noun*
make amends to do something to show that you are sorry for hurting or upsetting someone ▶ *I tried to make amends by inviting him to lunch.*

amenity /əˈmiːnətɪ/ *noun (plural **amenities**)*
something that is available for you to use in a place, which makes visiting or living there enjoyable and pleasant ▶ *The hotel's amenities include a pool and two bars.*

American /əˈmerɪkən/ *adjective*
of, about, or from the United States ▶ *American cars*

American football /əˌmerɪkən ˈfʊtbɔːl/ *noun (no plural)*
a game played in the US, in which two teams, wearing special clothes to protect them, carry, kick, or throw a ball

amicable /ˈæmɪkəbəl/ *adjective*
done in a friendly way, without arguing ▶ *an amicable divorce (adverb: **amicably**)*

amiss /əˈmɪs/ *adjective*
be amiss if something is amiss, there is a problem ▶ *I checked the house, but nothing was amiss.*

ammunition /ˌæmjʊˈnɪʃən/ *noun (no plural)*
something that you can shoot from a weapon

amnesty /ˈæmnəstɪ/ *noun (plural **amnesties**)*
a period of time when a government lets some people leave prison or does not punish people ▶ *The new government announced an amnesty for political prisoners.*

among /əˈmʌŋ/ *(also **amongst** /əˈmʌŋst/) preposition*

1 in the middle of a lot of people or things ▶ *houses among the trees*
2 between three or more people ▶ *The money was shared among the children*
LOOK AT (**2**): **between**
3 in a particular group of people ▶ *a common problem among young people*

amount /əˈmaʊnt/ *noun*
a sum of money or a quantity of something ▶ *a large amount **of** gold*

amp /æmp/ *noun*
a measure of electricity

ample /ˈæmpəl/ *adjective*
as much as you need and more
COMPARE: **enough**

amplifier /ˈæmplɪfaɪəʳ/ *noun*
a piece of electronic equipment that you use to make music louder

amputate /ˈæmpjʊteɪt/ *verb (present participle **amputating**, past **amputated**)*
to cut off a part of someone's body for medical reasons ▶ *After the accident, the doctors had to amputate her leg.*

amuse /əˈmjuːz/ *verb (present participle **amusing**, past **amused**)*
to make someone laugh or smile

amusement /əˈmjuːzmənt/ *noun*
1 *(no plural)* enjoyment
2 an enjoyable thing to do

amusement park /əˈmjuːzmənt ˌpɑːk/ *noun*
a large park where people can enjoy themselves, for example by riding on big machines such as ROLLER COASTERS

amusing /əˈmjuːzɪŋ/ *adjective*
making you laugh or smile ▶ *an amusing story*
SAME MEANING: **funny**

an /ən; *strong* æn/ *indefinite article*
used instead of **a** before a word that starts with the sound of **a, e, i, o,** or **u** ▶ *an apple* ▶ *an orange*

You use **an** instead of **a** before words beginning with a vowel sound: *a dog* ▶ *a girl* ▶ *a house*, but *an umbrella* ▶ *an elephant* ▶ *an object*. Remember that there is sometimes a difference in the way a word is spelt and the way it sounds. Use **an** before words which begin with a vowel sound but are not spelt with **a, e, i, o,** or **u** at the beginning: *An MG* (=/ˌemˈdʒiː/) *is a type of car.* In the same way, use **a**, not **an**, with words which are spelt with a vowel at the beginning but do **not** begin with a vowel sound: *a European* (/ˌjʊərəˈpiːən/) *country*
LOOK AT: **a**

anaesthetic /ˌænəsˈθetɪk/ *noun*
something which is given to people by doctors to stop them feeling pain, especially by making them sleep

anaesthetist /əˈniːsθətɪst/ *noun*
a doctor whose job is to give anaesthetics to people in hospitals

anagram /ˈænəgræm/ *noun*
a word or phrase that you make by changing the order of the letters in another word or phrase ▶ *"Dear" is an anagram of "read".*

analogy /əˈnælədʒɪ/ *noun (plural **analogies**)*
a way of explaining one thing by showing how it is similar to another thing ▶ *He made an analogy between the brain and a computer.*

analyse /ˈænəlaɪz/ *verb (present participle **analysing**, past **analysed**)*
to look at something very carefully to find out what it is made of or to understand it ▶ *We need to analyse this problem carefully before deciding what to do.*

analysis /əˈnæləsɪs/ *noun (plural **analyses** /əˈnæləsiːz/)*
a careful examination of something

analyst /ˈænəlɪst/ *noun*
a person whose job is to look at a subject very carefully in order to understand it and explain it to other people ▶ *a political analyst*

anarchist /ˈænəkɪst/ *noun*
a person who believes that there should be no government or laws

anarchy /ˈænəkɪ/ *noun (no plural)*
a situation in which people do not obey the rules or laws and no one has control ▶ *efforts to prevent the country from sliding into anarchy*

anatomy /əˈnætəmɪ/ *noun (no plural)*
the scientific study of the structure of the body

ancestor /ˈænsestəʳ/ *noun*
a person in your family who lived a long time before you were born
COMPARE: **descendant**

ancestry /ˈænsəstrɪ/ *noun (no plural)*
your ancestors, or the place they came from ▶ *He is of Welsh ancestry.*

anchor /ˈæŋkəʳ/ *noun*
a heavy weight dropped down from a ship to the bottom of the sea to stop the ship from moving

ancient /ˈeɪnʃənt/ *adjective*
very old ▶ *ancient history* ▶ *an ancient building*

and /ən, ənd; *strong* ænd/ *conjunction*
a word used to join two words, expressions, or parts of a sentence ▶ *I went to the station and bought my ticket.* ▶ *I had a drink and a piece of cake.*

anecdote /ˈænɪkdəʊt/ *noun*
an interesting or a funny story about something that really happened ▶ *He told a funny anecdote about his work.*

angel /ˈeɪndʒəl/ *noun*
a messenger from God, usually shown in pictures as a person with wings

anger /ˈæŋgəʳ/ *noun (no plural)*
the feeling of being very annoyed

angle /ˈæŋgəl/ *noun*
the shape made when two straight lines meet each other

angler /ˈæŋgləʳ/ *noun*
a person who goes fishing using a rod

angling /ˈæŋglɪŋ/ *noun (no plural)*
the activity of fishing with a rod

angry /ˈæŋgrɪ/ *adjective (**angrier, angriest**)*
feeling very annoyed ▶ *I'm very angry with them. (adverb: **angrily**)*
SAME MEANING: **cross**

anguish /ˈæŋgwɪʃ/ *noun (no plural)*
great suffering or pain

angular /ˈæŋgjʊləʳ/ *adjective*
having sharp corners

animal /ˈænɪməl/ *noun*
something alive that is not a person or a plant ▶ *Dogs, goats, and lions are animals.*

animated /ˈænɪmeɪtɪd/ *adjective*
1 showing a lot of interest and energy ▶ *an animated discussion*
2 (used about films, cartoons, etc.) having drawings of people or things that seem to move and talk

animation /ˌænɪˈmeɪʃən/ *noun (no plural)*
1 the process of making animated films
2 energy and excitement

ankle /ˈæŋkəl/ *noun*
the bottom part of your leg just above your foot, which can bend

annexe /ˈæneks/ *noun*
a separate building that has been added to a larger one ▶ *a hospital annexe*

annihilate /əˈnaɪəleɪt/ *verb (present participle **annihilating**, past **annihilated**)*
to destroy something or defeat

A

someone completely ▶ *In 1314, the English army was annihilated by the Scots.*

anniversary /ˌænɪˈvɜːsərɪ/ *noun (plural* ***anniversaries****)*
the same date each year that something important happened in the past: *We were married on April 7th 1973, so every year we have a party on our anniversary* (=April 7th).

An **anniversary** is a day when you remember something special or important which happened on the same date in an earlier year: *Their wedding anniversary is June 12th* (=they got married on June 12th). ▶ *Today is the 50th anniversary of the end of the war.*
A person's **birthday** is the date on which they were born: *My birthday is October 20th* (=I was born on October 20th).

announce /əˈnaʊns/ *verb (present participle* ***announcing****, past* ***announced****)*
to say something in public ▶ *The captain announced that the plane was going to land.*

announcement /əˈnaʊnsmənt/ *noun*
something written or spoken to tell people important news ▶ *a wedding announcement in the newspaper*

announcer /əˈnaʊnsəʳ/ *noun*
a person whose job is to broadcast information to people, on radio or television, or at a station, airport, etc.

annoy /əˈnɔɪ/ *verb*
to make someone slightly angry ▶ *It really annoys me when he rings while we're eating.*

annoyance /əˈnɔɪəns/ *noun (no plural)*
the feeling of being slightly angry ▶ *I tried not to show my annoyance.*

annoyed /əˈnɔɪd/ *adjective*
slightly angry ▶ *Are you annoyed* ***with*** *me just because I'm a bit late?* ▶ *She was really annoyed* ***at*** *the way he just ignored her.*

annual /ˈænjʊəl/ *adjective*
happening every year ▶ *an annual event*

anonymous /əˈnɒnɪməs/ *adjective*
having a name that other people do not know ▶ *The person who complained wishes to remain anonymous. (adverb:* ***anonymously****)*

anorak /ˈænəræk/ *noun*
a short, warm coat with a cover for your head

anorexia /ˌænəˈreksɪə/ *noun (no plural)*
a mental illness that makes someone stop eating because they think they are fat ▶ *Many teenage girls suffer from anorexia.*

anorexic /ˌænəˈreksɪk/ *adjective*
very thin and ill because of a mental illness that makes someone stop eating because they think they are fat

another /əˈnʌðəʳ/ *adjective, pronoun*
1 one more ▶ *Would you like another cup of tea?*
2 a different one ▶ *This plate is broken – can you get me another one?*

answer[1] /ˈɑːnsəʳ/ *verb*
1 to say or write something after you have been asked a question ▶ *"Did you do it?" "No, I didn't," she answered.*
SAME MEANING: **reply**
2 answer the door to open the door when someone knocks on it
3 answer the telephone to pick up the telephone when it rings

answer[2] *noun*
1 something that you say or write after you have been asked a question ▶ *My answer is "No".*
2 the correct result of a sum, or the correct name or fact for a question ▶ *Do you know the answer?*

► *That's the wrong answer.*

answering machine /'ɑːnsərɪŋ məʃiːn/ *noun*
a machine which answers your telephone and records messages when you are out

ant /ænt/ *noun*
a small insect that lives in a large group

Antarctic /æn'tɑːktɪk/ *noun*
the Antarctic the most southern part of the world, where it is very cold
COMPARE: **Arctic**

antelope /'æntɪləʊp/ *noun (plural* ***antelope*** *or* ***antelopes****)*
a wild animal that runs very fast and has horns on its head

antenna /æn'tenə/ *noun (plural* ***antennae*** /æn'teniː/*)*
one of two long, thin parts on an insect's head that it uses to feel things

anthem /'ænθəm/ *noun*
a song that is sung at special religious, sports, or political ceremonies

anthropology /ˌænθrə'pɒlədʒɪ/ *noun (no plural)*
the scientific study of people, their customs, beliefs, etc.

antibiotic /ˌæntɪbaɪ'ɒtɪk/ *noun*
a type of drug used to fight illness in a person's body ► *The doctor gave me an antibiotic for my sore throat.*

anticipate /æn'tɪsɪpeɪt/ *verb (present participle* ***anticipating****, past* ***anticipated****)*
to expect something to happen ► *We anticipate a few problems.*

anticipation /ænˌtɪsɪ'peɪʃən/ *noun (no plural)*
a hopeful or slightly nervous feeling that you have when something exciting is going to happen ► *The audience waited in eager anticipation.*

anticlimax /ˌæntɪ'klaɪmæks/ *noun (plural* ***anticlimaxes****)*
something that is not as exciting as you expected ► *The end of the exams is always an anticlimax.*

anticlockwise /ˌæntɪ'klɒkwaɪz/ *adjective, adverb*
in the opposite direction to the way the hands of a clock move round
OPPOSITE: **clockwise**

antics /'æntɪks/ *plural noun*
funny, silly, or annoying behaviour ► *We laughed at the children's antics.*

antidote /'æntɪdəʊt/ *noun*
1 something that makes a bad situation better ► *Laughter can be an antidote* ***to*** *stress.*
2 a substance that stops a poison harming or killing someone ► *The snake's bite is deadly, and there is no known antidote.*

antique /æn'tiːk/ *noun*
an object which is old and worth a lot of money ► *an antique table*

antiseptic /ˌæntɪ'septɪk/ *noun, adjective*
a chemical substance that kills harmful BACTERIA, especially on wounds or infected parts of the body

antisocial /ˌæntɪ'səʊʃəl/ *adjective*
upsetting or annoying other people ► *Kids as young as eight are turning to vandalism, petty crime, and other forms of antisocial behaviour.*

antler /'æntlə[r]/ *noun*
one of the two horns on the head of a male DEER

anxiety /æŋ'zaɪətɪ/ *noun (no plural)*
a feeling of worry

anxious /'æŋkʃəs/ *adjective*
worried

any[1] /'enɪ/ *adjective*
1 it does not matter which one ► *You can buy them in any big shop.* ► *on any day of the week*
2 used in questions, and sentences

A

with "not", to mean "some" ► *Do you have any bread?* ► *There isn't* (=is not) *any in the cupboard.*

> Use **any**, not **some**, in questions and in NEGATIVE sentences: *I must buy some coffee.* ► *Is there any coffee?* ► *There isn't any coffee.* But when you are asking for something or offering something, you use **some**: *Would you like some coffee?* ► *Can I have some coffee, please?*

any[2] *adverb*
used in questions, and sentences with "not", to mean "at all" ► *Don't* (=do not) *drive any faster.* ► *Are you feeling any better?*

anybody /ˈenɪˌbɒdɪ/ *(also* ***anyone*** */ˈenɪwʌn/) pronoun*
any person ► *Has anybody seen my pen?* ► *She liked John, but she wouldn't talk to anybody else* (=any other person or people).

> Use **anybody** or **anyone**, not **somebody** or **someone**, in questions and in NEGATIVE sentences: *There was somebody waiting outside.* ► *Is there anybody there?* ► *There wasn't anybody at home.*

anyhow /ˈenɪhaʊ/ *adverb*
another word for **anyway**

anyone /ˈenɪwʌn/ *pronoun*
another word for **anybody**

anything /ˈenɪθɪŋ/ *pronoun*
1 used in questions and sentences with "not" to mean "something" ► *Do you want anything?* ► *She didn't want anything else* (=any other things) *to eat.*

> Use **anything**, not **something**, in questions and in NEGATIVE sentences: *I must get something to drink.* ► *Have you got anything to drink?* ► *I don't want anything to drink.*

2 it does not matter what thing ► *Please tell me if there's anything I can do to help.*

anyway /ˈenɪweɪ/ *(also* ***anyhow*** */ˈenɪhaʊ/) adverb*
1 in spite of something else ► *The dress cost a lot of money, but I bought it anyway.*
2 used when you are saying something which supports what you have just said ► *I don't want to go – anyway, I haven't been invited.*
SAME MEANING (**2**): **besides**

anywhere /ˈenɪweəʳ/ *adverb*
in, at, or to any place ► *I can't find my key anywhere.* ► *Have you been anywhere else* (=to any other places)*?*

apart /əˈpɑːt/ *adverb*
1 separately; away from another, or others ► *The two villages are 6 miles apart.*
2 apart from except ► *All the children like music, apart from Joseph.*

apartment /əˈpɑːtmənt/ *noun*
a part of a building, on one floor, where someone lives
SAME MEANING: **flat**

apathetic /ˌæpəˈθetɪk/ *adjective*
not interested in anything and not willing to make any effort ► *People here are too apathetic to organize a strike.*

apathy /ˈæpəθɪ/ *noun (no plural)*
the feeling of not being interested in anything and being unwilling to make any effort to change things ► *public apathy about the coming election*

ape /eɪp/ *noun*
a large animal like a monkey, but with a very short tail or no tail at all

apologetic /əˌpɒləˈdʒetɪk/ *adjective*
saying that you are sorry about something you have done ► *He was really apologetic about forgetting my birthday.* (adverb: ***apologetically***)

apologize /ə'pɒlədʒaɪz/ *verb (present participle **apologizing**, past **apologized**)*
to say that you are sorry about something you have done ▸ *He apologized **for** his bad behaviour.*

apology /ə'pɒlədʒɪ/ *noun (plural **apologies**)*
something that you say or write to show that you are sorry about something you have done

apostrophe /ə'pɒstrəfɪ/ *noun*
the sign (') used in writing, to show that letters have been left out, e.g. "don't" instead of "do not", or with "s" to show that someone owns something as in *Karen's book* or *ladies' hats*

appal /ə'pɔːl/ *verb (present participle **appalling**, past **appalled**)*
if something appals you, it shocks you because it is so unpleasant ▸ *The idea of killing animals appals me.*

appalling /ə'pɔːlɪŋ/ *adjective*
very bad ▸ *an appalling accident* ▸ *an appalling film*

apparatus /ˌæpə'reɪtəs/ *noun (no plural)*
tools or other things needed for a special purpose ▸ *There is sports apparatus in the gym.*

apparent /ə'pærənt/ *adjective*
clearly able to be seen or understood ▸ *It was apparent that he knew nothing about how to repair cars.*
SAME MEANING: **obvious**

apparently /ə'pærəntlɪ/ *adverb*
used when you are saying that something seems to be true ▸ *They've been married for 20 years, and apparently they're very happy.*

appeal¹ /ə'piːl/ *verb*
1 to ask for something strongly; to beg for ▸ *She appealed **to** me **for** help.*
2 appeal to someone to please or interest someone ▸ *That type of holiday doesn't appeal to me.*

appeal² *noun*
an act of asking for something ▸ *an appeal **for** money*

appealing /ə'piːlɪŋ/ *adjective*
attractive or interesting ▸ *That's an appealing idea.*

appear /ə'pɪəʳ/ *verb*
1 to seem ▸ *She appears to be unhappy.*
2 to come into sight suddenly ▸ *Her head appeared round the door.*
OPPOSITE (**2**): **disappear**

appearance /ə'pɪərəns/ *noun*
1 the sudden arrival or coming into sight of a person or thing
2 the way a person looks to other people ▸ *his neat appearance*

appendices /ə'pendɪsiːz/
a plural of **appendix**

appendicitis /əˌpendɪ'saɪtɪs/ *noun (no plural)*
an illness in which your appendix hurts a lot

appendix /ə'pendɪks/ *noun (plural **appendixes** or **appendices** /-dɪsiːz/)*
1 a small organ inside your body, near your stomach
2 a part at the end of a book that has additional information ▸ *There is a list of dates in the appendix.*

appetite /'æpɪtaɪt/ *noun*
the wish for food ▸ *I lost my appetite when I was ill.*

applaud /ə'plɔːd/ *verb*
to hit your hands together many times to show that you liked or enjoyed something ▸ *Everyone applauded when the music ended.*
SAME MEANING: **clap**

applause /ə'plɔːz/ *noun (no plural)*
hitting your hands together many times to show that you liked or enjoyed something ▸ *the sound of applause*

A

apple /'æpəl/ *noun*
a round, hard, juicy fruit which is usually red or green

apple pie /ˌæpəl 'paɪ/ *noun*
a type of sweet cake with cooked apples in the middle

appliance /ə'plaɪəns/ *noun*
an instrument or piece of equipment for doing something useful ▶ *kitchen appliances such as washing machines*

applicable /ə'plɪkəbəl/ *adjective*
concerning a particular person or situation ▶ *Question 8 on the form is only applicable to married people.*

applicant /'æplɪkənt/ *noun*
a person who has formally asked for a job, a place at a college, etc. ▶ *We have had an increase in the number of applicants this year.*

application /ˌæplɪ'keɪʃən/ *noun*
a written paper asking for something ▶ *an application for a job*

application form /ˌæplɪ'keɪʃən fɔːm/ *noun*
a printed piece of paper on which you write the answers to questions about yourself, and why you should get a job, a place at a college, etc. ▶ *It took hours to fill in the application form.*

apply /ə'plaɪ/ *verb (past* ***applied****)*
1 to ask for something ▶ *I want to apply* ***for*** *the job.*
2 to be important or useful to a particular person ▶ *The rules apply* ***to*** *everyone.*
3 to put something on a surface ▶ *to apply make-up* ***to*** *your face*

appoint /ə'pɔɪnt/ *verb*
to give someone a job ▶ *I appointed her as my secretary.*

appointment /ə'pɔɪntmənt/ *noun*
1 a time arranged for seeing someone ▶ *I made an appointment to see the doctor.*
2 a job

appreciate /ə'priːʃɪeɪt/ *verb (present participle* ***appreciating****, past* ***appreciated****)*
to be grateful for something
▶ *I appreciate your help.*

appreciation /əˌpriːʃɪ'eɪʃən/ *noun (no plural)*
the feeling of being grateful to someone because they have helped you ▶ *I gave her some flowers to show my appreciation.*

appreciative /ə'priːʃətɪv/ *adjective*
showing that you have enjoyed something or feel grateful for it ▶ *The audience was very appreciative.*

apprehensive /ˌæprɪ'hensɪv/ *adjective*
worried or nervous about something you have to do in the future ▶ *I'm apprehensive* ***about*** *taking my driving test.*

apprentice /ə'prentɪs/ *noun*
someone who is learning a job, especially a job you do with your hands

approach¹ /ə'prəʊtʃ/ *verb*
1 to come near ▶ *A man approached me and asked the time.*
2 to begin to deal with something ▶ *Is this the best way to approach the problem?*

approach² *noun (plural* ***approaches****)*
1 a way of doing something or dealing with a problem ▶ *Mr James had an exciting approach to teaching science.*
2 when something comes nearer

approachable /ə'prəʊtʃəbəl/ *adjective*
friendly and easy to talk to ▶ *Dr Grieg seems very approachable.*
OPPOSITE: **unapproachable**

appropriate /ə'prəʊprɪət/ *adjective*
right; suitable *(adverb:* ***appropriately****)*
OPPOSITE: **inappropriate**

approval /ə'pruːvəl/ *noun (no plural)*
the judgement or opinion that someone or something is good
OPPOSITE: **disapproval**

approve /ə'pruːv/ *verb (present participle* ***approving****, past* ***approved****)*
to think that something is good
► *I don't approve* ***of*** *smoking.*
OPPOSITE: **disapprove**

approx. /ə'prɒks/
a short way of writing and saying the word **approximately**

approximate /ə'prɒksɪmət/ *adjective*
not exact ► *Our approximate time of arrival is 2 o'clock* (=it might be just before or just after 2).

approximately /ə'prɒksɪmətlɪ/ *adverb*
a little more or less than an exact amount, number, time, etc.
► *Approximately a quarter of the students are from Japan.*
SAME MEANING: **roughly**

apricot /'eɪprɪkɒt/ *noun*
a round, soft, yellow fruit

April /'eɪprəl/ *noun*
the fourth month of the year

apron /'eɪprən/ *noun*
a large piece of cloth that you put on top of your other clothes, to keep your clothes clean when you are cooking

aptitude /'æptɪtjuːd/ *noun*
a natural ability to do something well
► *They tested our aptitude for computing.*

aquarium /ə'kweərɪəm/ *noun*
a large, glass box in which live fish are kept

Arabic /'ærəbɪk/ *noun (no plural)*
the language of Arab people, or the religious language of ISLAM

arbitrary /'ɑːbɪtrərɪ/ *adjective*
not based on any practical or good reasons ► *Age limits for films are rather arbitrary.*

arc /ɑːk/ *noun*
a part of a circle, or any curved line

arcade /ɑː'keɪd/ *noun*
1 a building where there are many shops ► *a new shopping arcade*
2 a large room or building where people go to play VIDEO GAMES, etc.

arch /ɑːtʃ/ *noun (plural* ***arches****)*
a curved shape like the curved part of a bridge

archaeological /ˌɑːkɪə'lɒdʒɪkəl/ *adjective*
of or about archaeology ► *an archaeological dig*

archaeologist /ˌɑːkɪ'ɒlədʒɪst/ *noun*
a person who studies very old things made by people who lived a long time ago

archaeology /ˌɑːkɪ'ɒlədʒɪ/ *noun (no plural)*
the study of very old things made by people who lived a long time ago

archaic /ɑː'keɪ-ɪk/ *adjective*
very old-fashioned ► *the archaic language of Shakespeare*

archbishop /ˌɑːtʃ'bɪʃəp/ *noun*
an important Christian leader; a chief BISHOP

archery /'ɑːtʃərɪ/ *noun (no plural)*
the sport of shooting ARROWS from a BOW

architect /'ɑːkɪtekt/ *noun*
a person whose job is planning and drawing buildings
COMPARE: **builder**

architectural /ˌɑːkɪ'tektʃərəl/ *adjective*
of or about architecture

architecture /'ɑːkɪtektʃəʳ/ *noun (no plural)*
1 the shape and style of buildings
► *modern architecture*
2 the job of planning and drawing buildings ► *He studies architecture.*

A

Arctic /ˈɑːktɪk/ *noun*
the Arctic the most northern part of the world, where it is very cold
COMPARE: **Antarctic**

ardent /ˈɑːdənt/ *adjective*
admiring or supporting something very strongly ▶ *an ardent fan of Manchester United*

arduous /ˈɑːdjʊəs/ *adjective*
needing a lot of effort and hard work ▶ *an arduous task*

are /əʳ; *strong* ɑːʳ/ *verb*
the part of the verb **be** that is used with **we, you** and **they** ▶ *Who are you?* ▶ *We're* (=we are) *Jane's friends.* ▶ *They aren't very tall, are they?*

area /ˈeərɪə/ *noun*
1 a part of a country, region, or city ▶ *He lives in the Glasgow area* (=near Glasgow).
2 the measure of a surface ▶ *The square has an area of 9 square centimetres.*

area code /ˈeərɪə ˌkəʊd/ *noun*
the part of a telephone number that you have to add when you are telephoning a different town or country
SAME MEANING: **dialling code**

arena /əˈriːnə/ *noun*
a building with a large, flat area inside with seats all around it, used for watching something such as a sports game ▶ *The concert will be at Wembley arena.*

aren't /ɑːnt/
1 are not ▶ *Bob and Sue aren't coming to the party.* ▶ *Aren't you a clever girl?*
2 used in questions instead of **am not** ▶ *I'm your best friend, aren't I?*

argue /ˈɑːgjuː/ *verb (present participle* ***arguing****, past* ***argued****)*
to fight or disagree in words ▶ *They often argued about money.*

argument /ˈɑːgjʊmənt/ *noun*
a disagreement; a quarrel ▶ *They had an argument.*

argumentative /ˌɑːgjʊˈmentətɪv/ *adjective*
liking to argue ▶ *Don't be so argumentative.*

arise /əˈraɪz/ *verb (present participle* ***arising****, past tense* ***arose*** */əˈrəʊz/, past participle* ***arisen*** */əˈrɪzən/)*
to happen or appear ▶ *A problem has arisen.*

aristocracy /ˌærɪˈstɒkrəsɪ/ *noun*
the people belonging to the highest social class in some countries, who usually have a lot of land, money, and power

aristocrat /ˈærɪstəkræt/ *noun*
a person from an important, old family

arithmetic /əˈrɪθmətɪk/ *noun (no plural)*
sums done with numbers, including addition, division, etc.

arm¹ /ɑːm/ *noun*
the part of your body between your shoulder and your hand

arm² *verb*
to give someone weapons

armchair /ˈɑːmtʃeəʳ/ *noun*
a comfortable chair with places to rest your arms on

armed /ɑːmd/ *adjective*
carrying a weapon, especially a gun ▶ *an armed robber*
OPPOSITE: **unarmed**

armed forces /ˌɑːmd ˈfɔːsɪz/ *plural noun*
all the soldiers of a country who fight on land, at sea, or in planes

armour /ˈɑːməʳ/ *noun (no plural)*
a covering of metal worn as protection by soldiers in the past

armoured /ˈɑːməd/ *adjective*
protected against bullets or other

weapons by a strong layer of metal ▶ *an armoured car*

armpit /ˈɑːmpɪt/ *noun*
the place under your arm where your arm joins your body

arms /ɑːmz/ *plural noun*
weapons such as guns and bombs

army /ˈɑːmɪ/ *noun (plural **armies**)*
a large number of soldiers fighting together
COMPARE: **airforce, navy**

aroma /əˈrəʊmə/ *noun*
a strong, pleasant smell ▶ *the aroma of baking bread*

arose /əˈrəʊz/
the PAST TENSE of the verb **arise**

around /əˈraʊnd/ *(also **round**) preposition, adverb*
1 with a movement or shape like a circle ▶ *We sat around the fire.*
2 on all sides of something ▶ *a wall around the garden*
3 in or to different places ▶ *They walked around the town.*
4 not exactly; about ▶ *at around 10 o'clock*
5 to face another way ▶ *She walked away, and then turned around and came back.*

arrange /əˈreɪndʒ/ *verb (present participle **arranging**, past **arranged**)*
1 to put things in a way which makes them look neat or attractive ▶ *She arranged the flowers in a vase.*
2 to make plans for something ▶ *I have arranged a meeting for tomorrow.*

arrangement /əˈreɪndʒmənt/ *noun*
a plan or an agreement that something will happen

arrears /əˈrɪəz/ *plural noun*
be in arrears to owe someone money and not make a payment when you should ▶ *The family are in arrears with the rent.*

arrest[1] /əˈrest/ *verb*
to make someone a prisoner because they are believed to have done something wrong

arrest[2] *noun*
an act of arresting someone ▶ *The police made three arrests yesterday.*

arrival /əˈraɪvəl/ *noun (no plural)*
getting to a place ▶ *We are sorry for the late arrival of your train.*
OPPOSITE: **departure**

arrive /əˈraɪv/ *verb (present participle **arriving**, past **arrived**)*
to get to a place ▶ *She arrived home very late.* ▶ *We arrived in London on Tuesday.*

arrogant /ˈærəgənt/ *adjective*
too proud

arrow /ˈærəʊ/ *noun*
1 a sharp stick that is used as a weapon and shot from a BOW
2 a sign which points to where something is

arson /ˈɑːsən/ *noun (no plural)*
the crime of deliberately burning something, especially a building ▶ *He was accused of arson.*

art /ɑːt/ *noun*
1 *(no plural)* the skill of drawing and painting ▶ *He's very good at art.*
2 something which you need skill to do ▶ *the art of cooking*
3 the arts music, writing, painting, films, etc.

artery /ˈɑːtərɪ/ *noun (plural **arteries**)*
one of the tubes in your body that carry blood from your heart around your body

arthritis /ɑːˈθraɪtɪs/ *noun (no plural)*
a disease that makes your hands, arms, legs, etc. painful and difficult to move

artichoke /ˈɑːtɪtʃəʊk/ *noun*
a green vegetable that looks like a flower

article /ˈɑːtɪkəl/ *noun*
1 a thing ▶ *articles of clothing*

A

2 a piece of writing in a newspaper ▶ *an article about ships*
3 the words **a** or **an** (=indefinite article), or **the** (=definite article)

articulate[1] /ɑːˈtɪkjʊlət/ *adjective*
able to express your thoughts and feelings clearly ▶ *He's clever, but not very articulate.*

articulate[2] /ɑːˈtɪkjʊleɪt/ *verb (present participle* ***articulating****, past* ***articulated****)*
to be able to say what you think or feel ▶ *Some people can find it hard to articulate their feelings.*

artificial /ˌɑːtɪˈfɪʃəl/ *adjective*
not real ▶ *artificial flowers*

artist /ˈɑːtɪst/ *noun*
a person whose job is painting pictures
SAME MEANING: **painter**

artistic /ɑːˈtɪstɪk/ *adjective*
able to make attractive, interesting things, for example by drawing or painting

as /əz; *strong* æz/ *adverb, preposition, conjunction*
1 when; while ▶ *We sang as we worked.*
2 because ▶ *I can't come as I'm busy.*
3 being a particular thing for a time ▶ *She's working as a teacher for a few months.* ▶ *We can use this box as a table.*
4 **as ... as** (used when comparing things) ▶ *I'm not as old as you.* ▶ *It's just as good as the other one.*
5 **as well** also ▶ *Can I have some as well?*

a.s.a.p. /ˌeɪ es eɪ ˈpiː/ *adverb*
a short way of writing or saying the words **as soon as possible** ▶ *I will let you know a.s.a.p.*

ascend /əˈsend/ *verb*
to move up or towards the top of something ▶ *The plane ascended rapidly.*
OPPOSITE: **descend**

ascent /əˈsent/ *noun*
the activity of moving up or climbing to the top of something ▶ *a successful ascent of Mount Everest*
OPPOSITE: **descent (1)**

ash /æʃ/ *noun (plural* ***ashes****)*
the grey powder that is left after something has burned

ashamed /əˈʃeɪmd/ *adjective*
feeling bad about something you have done wrong ▶ *She was very ashamed that she had stolen the money.*
LOOK AT: **embarrassed**

ashore /əˈʃɔːʳ/ *adverb*
onto the land ▶ *Pull the boat ashore!*

ashtray /ˈæʃtreɪ/ *noun*
a small dish in which you put the ash from cigarettes

aside /əˈsaɪd/ *adverb*
to or towards one side; away

ask /ɑːsk/ *verb*
1 to say something that is a question ▶ *"Who are you?" she asked.*
2 to try to get something from someone ▶ *They asked me the time.* ▶ *She asked me* ***for*** *some money.*
3 **ask someone to something** to invite someone to a place or an event

asleep /əˈsliːp/ *adjective*
1 sleeping
OPPOSITE: **awake**
2 **fast asleep** sleeping deeply

asparagus /əˈspærəgəs/ *noun (no plural)*
a long, thin, green plant which is eaten as a vegetable

aspect /ˈæspekt/ *noun*
a particular part of a situation ▶ *One of the most serious aspects of the problem is the lack of money.*

asphyxiate /æsˈfɪksɪeɪt/ *verb (present participle* ***asphyxiating****, past* ***asphyxiated****)*
to stop someone breathing, often causing them to die ▶ *The thick*

smoke asphyxiated three children in an upstairs bedroom.

aspirin /ˈæsprɪn/ *noun*
a medicine taken to make a pain in your body go away

ass /æs/ *noun (plural* ***asses****)*
an animal like a small horse, with long ears

assailant /əˈseɪlənt/ *noun*
a person who attacks another person ▶ *He did not know his assailant.*

assassin /əˈsæsɪn/ *noun*
someone who kills an important person for political reasons

assassinate /əˈsæsɪneɪt/ *verb (present participle* ***assassinating****, past* ***assassinated****)*
to kill an important person for political reasons
COMPARE: **murder**

assassination /əˌsæsɪˈneɪʃən/ *noun*
the killing of an important person for political reasons ▶ *the assassination of President Kennedy*

assault¹ /əˈsɔːlt/ *verb*
to attack or hit someone

assault² *noun*
an attack

assemble /əˈsembəl/ *verb (present participle* ***assembling****, past* ***assembled****)*
to gather together in a group

assembly /əˈsemblɪ/ *noun (plural* ***assemblies****)*
a group of people gathered together for a special purpose or meeting

assert /əˈsɜːt/ *verb*
1 assert your rights/authority to say strongly that you have rights or authority ▶ *My father decided to assert his authority by refusing to let me go out.*
2 assert yourself to say what you think, or ask for what you want, in a confident and determined way

assertive /əˈsɜːtɪv/ *adjective*
behaving in a confident and determined way ▶ *You must be more assertive if you want people to listen to you.*

assess /əˈses/ *verb*
to examine something and make a decision about it ▶ *First we must assess the cost of repairing the damage.*

asset /ˈæset/ *noun*
a person or thing that helps you to succeed ▶ *Tom is a real asset to the team.*

assignment /əˈsaɪnmənt/ *noun*
a piece of work that someone gives you to do ▶ *a homework assignment*

assist /əˈsɪst/ *verb*
to help someone
SAME MEANING: **aid**

assistance /əˈsɪstəns/ *noun (no plural)*
help

assistant /əˈsɪstənt/ *noun*
a person who helps someone in their job

associate /əˈsəʊʃɪeɪt/ *verb (present participle* ***associating****, past* ***associated****)*
1 to connect two things or ideas in your mind
2 to spend time with someone or be connected with them ▶ *I don't wish to associate* ***with*** *him.*

association /əˌsəʊsɪˈeɪʃən/ *noun*
a group of people joined together for one purpose

assortment /əˈsɔːtmənt/ *noun*
a mixture of various different types of thing ▶ *an assortment of chocolates*

assume /əˈsjuːm/ *verb (present participle* ***assuming****, past* ***assumed****)*
to think that something is true even though no one has said so ▶ *I assumed she was his mother, but in fact she's his aunt.*

A

assumption /ə'sʌmpʃən/ *noun*
something that you think is true although you have no proof ▶ *We made the assumption that people would come by car.* ▶ *We're working on the assumption that prices will continue to rise.*

assurance /ə'ʃʊərəns/ *noun*
a definite statement or promise ▶ *Can you give me an assurance that the plane is safe?*

assure /ə'ʃɔːʳ/ *verb (present participle* ***assuring****, past* ***assured****)*
to tell someone that something is true

asterisk /'æstərɪsk/ *noun*
the sign *

asthma /'æsmə/ *noun (no plural)*
an illness that makes it difficult for you to breathe ▶ *Both sisters suffer from asthma.*

astonish /ə'stɒnɪʃ/ *verb*
to surprise someone very much

astonished /ə'stɒnɪʃt/ *adjective*
very surprised ▶ *I was astonished at how easy it was.*

astonishing /ə'stɒnɪʃɪŋ/ *adjective*
very surprising ▶ *an astonishing £50,000 profit (adverb:* ***astonishingly****)*

astonishment /ə'stɒnɪʃmənt/ *noun (no plural)*
great surprise

astound /ə'staʊnd/ *verb*
to shock and surprise someone very much

astounding /ə'staʊndɪŋ/ *adjective*
very surprising and shocking ▶ *The news was astounding.*

astray /ə'streɪ/ *adverb*
1 go astray to become lost ▶ *My letter went astray in the post.*
2 lead someone astray to encourage someone to do bad things ▶ *Don't let the older girls lead you astray.*

astride /ə'straɪd/ *adverb, preposition*
with one leg on either side of something ▶ *He was sitting astride his horse.*

astrologer /ə'strɒlədʒəʳ/ *noun*
a person who studies the PLANETS and stars, believing that they can influence people's characters and change what happens in their lives

astrology /ə'strɒlədʒɪ/ *noun (no plural)*
the study of the PLANETS and stars, in the belief that they can influence people's characters and change what happens in their lives

astronaut /'æstrənɔːt/ *noun*
a person who travels in space

astronomer /ə'strɒnəməʳ/ *noun*
a person who studies the sun, moon, and stars

astronomy /ə'strɒnəmɪ/ *noun (no plural)*
the study of the sun, moon, and stars

astute /ə'stjuːt/ *adjective*
clever and quick to understand how to gain advantage from a situation ▶ *an astute politician*

at /ət; *strong* æt/ *preposition*
1 in a particular place ▶ *He left his bag at the station.* ▶ *She is at work.*
2 at a particular time ▶ *It gets cold at night.* ▶ *at one o'clock*
3 towards someone or something ▶ *Look at me!*
4 used to show how much, how old, or how fast ▶ *He got married at 21.* ▶ *driving at 90 miles an hour* ▶ *at a cost of £9.50*

ate /et, eɪt/
the PAST TENSE of the verb **eat**

atheist /'eɪθɪ-ɪst/ *noun*
a person who does not believe in God

athlete /'æθliːt/ *noun*
someone who is good at sports in which they have to run, jump, or throw things

athletic /æθ'letɪk/ *adjective*
physically strong and good at sport

athletics /æθ'letɪks/ *noun (no plural)*
a general name for sports in which people run, jump, or throw things to see who is the best

atlas /'ætləs/ *noun (plural **atlases**)*
a book of maps

ATM /ˌeɪ tiː 'em/ *noun*
an AUTOMATED TELLER MACHINE; a machine in the wall outside a bank where the customers of the bank can get money
SAME MEANING: **cash dispenser, cashpoint**

atmosphere /'ætməsfɪəʳ/ *noun (no plural)*
1 the air surrounding the Earth
2 a feeling that a place or group of people gives you ▶ *the exciting atmosphere of a football match*

atom /'ætəm/ *noun*
the smallest part of a chemical

atomic /ə'tɒmɪk/ *adjective*
1 of or about atoms ▶ *atomic structure*
2 using the power that is produced by splitting atoms ▶ *atomic weapons*

atomic energy /əˌtɒmɪk 'enədʒɪ/ *noun (no plural)*
power from the forces in an atom, used to make electricity

atrocious /ə'trəʊʃəs/ *adjective*
very bad ▶ *Your spelling is atrocious! (adverb: **atrociously**)*

atrocity /ə'trɒsətɪ/ *noun (plural **atrocities**)*
a very cruel and violent action
▶ *Both sides in the war committed atrocities.*

attach /ə'tætʃ/ *verb*
to fix something to something else

attached /ə'tætʃt/ *adjective*
be attached to to like someone or something very much ▶ *I was quite attached to that old car.*

attachment /ə'tætʃmənt/ *noun*
1 a strong feeling of liking or loving someone or something ▶ *He had a close attachment to his family.*
2 a document or FILE that you send with an E-MAIL

attack¹ /ə'tæk/ *verb*
to fight against someone or harm them ▶ *The newspaper attacked* (=wrote things against) *the new tax.*
COMPARE: **defend**

attack² *noun*
a violent act to try to harm someone
▶ *an attack **on** the soldiers*

attacker /ə'tækəʳ/ *noun*
a person who physically attacks another person ▶ *Her attacker ran off.*

attempt¹ /ə'tempt/ *verb*
to try to do something

attempt² *noun*
an act of trying ▶ *She made an attempt to speak their language.*

attend /ə'tend/ *verb*
to be present at an event ▶ *to attend a meeting*

attendance /ə'tendəns/ *noun (no plural)*
being present ▶ *His attendance **at** school is bad* (=he does not go often enough).

attendant /ə'tendənt/ *noun*
a person whose job is to look after a place or person

attention /ə'tenʃən/ *noun (no plural)*
1 looking at and listening to someone or something ▶ *May I have your attention* (=will you listen to me, please)?
2 attract someone's attention to make someone notice you
3 pay attention to someone to listen to someone very carefully

attentive /ə'tentɪv/ *adjective*
listening or watching carefully
▶ *The students were very attentive. (adverb: **attentively**)*

A

attic /ˈætɪk/ *noun*
a room at the top of a house, inside the roof, often used for storing things
SAME MEANING: **loft**

attitude /ˈætɪtjuːd/ *noun*
the way you think or feel about something ▶ *her attitude* ***towards*** *her job*

attract /əˈtrækt/ *verb*
1 to make someone or something come near ▶ *Many people visited the sea, attracted by the fine weather.*
2 to cause interest and admiration ▶ *It was his sense of humour that first attracted me* ***to*** *him.*

attraction /əˈtrækʃən/ *noun*
1 something that people like to see or do because it is interesting or enjoyable ▶ *Buckingham Palace is one of London's most popular tourist attractions.*
2 *(no plural)* the feelings you have for someone when you are interested in them in a sexual way ▶ *There was a strong physical attraction between us.*

attractive /əˈtræktɪv/ *adjective*
pleasing, especially to look at
OPPOSITE: **unattractive**

aubergine /ˈəʊbəʒiːn/ *noun*
a large vegetable with a dark purple skin

auburn /ˈɔːbən/ *noun, adjective*
a reddish-brown colour

auction /ˈɔːkʃən/ *noun*
a meeting where things are sold to the person who offers the most money

audible /ˈɔːdɪbəl/ *adjective*
loud enough to be heard ▶ *His words were clearly audible.*

audience /ˈɔːdɪəns/ *noun*
all the people watching a play, listening to music, etc.

audio /ˈɔːdɪəʊ/ *adjective*
for recording and broadcasting sounds ▶ *an audio tape* ▶ *an audio signal*

audiovisual /ˌɔːdɪəʊˈvɪʒʊəl/ *adjective*
having recorded pictures and sound ▶ *audiovisual equipment for language teaching*

audition /ɔːˈdɪʃən/ *noun*
a short performance by an actor or a singer to test whether they are good enough to be in a play or concert ▶ *I have an audition for a part in "Annie" tomorrow.*

auditorium /ˌɔːdɪˈtɔːrɪəm/ *noun*
the part of a theatre where people sit to watch a performance

August /ˈɔːgəst/ *noun*
the eighth month of the year

aunt /ɑːnt/ *noun*
the sister of one of your parents, or the wife of your uncle

au pair /əʊ ˈpeəʳ/ *noun*
a young woman who stays with a family in a foreign country and looks after their children ▶ *I worked for a year as an au pair.*

aural /ˈɔːrəl/ *adjective*
connected with hearing and listening ▶ *aural skills*

austere /ɔːˈstɪəʳ/ *adjective*
plain and simple ▶ *The room was very austere.*

austerity /ɔːˈsterɪtɪ/ *noun (no plural)*
bad economic conditions in which people do not have enough money to live ▶ *the austerity of the post-war years*

authentic /ɔːˈθentɪk/ *adjective*
not copying or pretending to be something else ▶ *The restaurant serves authentic Chinese food.* ▶ *Is it an authentic Van Gogh painting?*

author /ˈɔːθəʳ/ *noun*
a person who has written a book

authoritarian /ɔːˌθɒrɪˈteərɪən/ *adjective*
forcing people to obey strict rules or laws and not allowing them any freedom ▶ *an authoritarian regime*

authority /ɔːˈθɒrətɪ/ *noun*
1 *(no plural)* the power to make people do what you want ▶ *The teacher has authority to punish any pupil.*
2 *(plural **authorities**)* a person or group in control of or governing something

authorize /ˈɔːθəraɪz/ *verb (present participle **authorizing**, past **authorized**)*
to give someone official permission to do something ▶ *You can't go in unless I authorize it.*

autobiography /ˌɔːtəbaɪˈɒgrəfɪ/ *noun (plural **autobiographies**)*
a book that someone has written telling the story of their own life
COMPARE: **biography**

autograph /ˈɔːtəgrɑːf/ *noun*
a famous person's name, written by them
COMPARE: **signature**

automatic /ˌɔːtəˈmætɪk/ *adjective*
working by itself ▶ *automatic doors* (=doors which open and close without being touched)

autopsy /ˈɔːtɒpsɪ/ *noun (plural **autopsies**)*
an official examination of a dead body to discover why the person died ▶ *Doctors performed an autopsy on the body.*

autumn /ˈɔːtəm/ *noun, adjective*
the season before winter in cool countries, when the leaves fall off the trees

auxiliary /ɔːgˈzɪljərɪ/ *adjective*
giving additional help or support to others ▶ *auxiliary nurses*

auxiliary verb /ɔːgˌzɪljərɪ ˈvɜːb/ *noun*
a verb used with another verb to make questions, NEGATIVE sentences, and tenses. In English, the auxiliary verbs are "be", "do", and "have".
COMPARE: **modal verb**

availability /əˌveɪləˈbɪlətɪ/ *noun (no plural)*
the possibility of being able to get, buy, or use something ▶ *I rang to ask about the availability of tickets.*

available /əˈveɪləbəl/ *adjective*
able to be seen, used, bought, etc. ▶ *Is the doctor available?*
OPPOSITE: **unavailable**

avalanche /ˈævəlɑːntʃ/ *noun*
a large amount of snow or a lot of rocks falling down a mountain

avenue /ˈævənjuː/ *noun*
a road in a town, especially one with trees on both sides
COMPARE: **street**

average[1] /ˈævərɪdʒ/ *adjective*
1 usual; ordinary ▶ *The average child enjoys listening to stories.*
2 got by adding several amounts together, and then dividing the total by the number of amounts you have added ▶ *The average age of the children is 12.* ▶ *What is the average rainfall in this area?*

average[2] *noun*
the amount you get by adding several numbers together, and then dividing the total by the number of amounts. For example, the average of 3, 5, and 7 is 5

avert /əˈvɜːt/ *verb*
to stop something unpleasant from happening ▶ *How can we avert the crisis?*

aviation /ˌeɪvɪˈeɪʃən/ *noun (no plural)*
the activity of flying or making planes ▶ *an expert in aviation*

avid /ˈævɪd/ *adjective*
liking and doing something a lot ▶ *Doug's an avid fan of American football.*

avocado /ˌævəˈkɑːdəʊ/ *noun*
a green, PEAR-shaped fruit with a large stone in the middle and a skin which you cannot eat

avoid /ə'vɔɪd/ *verb*
to keep away from a person, place, or thing ▶ *Are you trying to avoid me?*

await /ə'weɪt/ *verb*
to wait for someone or something

awake /ə'weɪk/ *adjective*
not sleeping ▶ *The baby is awake.*
OPPOSITE: **asleep**

award[1] /ə'wɔːd/ *noun*
a prize or an amount of money, given for a special reason ▶ *an award **for** bravery*

award[2] *verb*
to give someone a prize or an amount of money for a special reason

aware /ə'weəʳ/ *adjective*
knowing about something ▶ *I was not aware **of** the problem.*
OPPOSITE: **unaware**

awash /ə'wɒʃ/ *adjective*
covered with water ▶ *The streets were awash **with** flood water.*

away /ə'weɪ/ *adverb*
1 to another place ▶ *Go away!* ▶ *He turned round and walked away.*
2 distant from a place ▶ *Do you live far away?* ▶ *The nearest town is 3 miles away.*
3 not at home or at work ▶ *I'll be away for a few days.*
4 put something away to put something in a safe place

awe /ɔː/ *noun (no plural)*
a feeling of great admiration and sometimes fear ▶ *She gazed with awe at the breathtaking landscape.* ▶ *He was slightly in awe of his boss.*

awesome /'ɔːsəm/ *adjective*
very impressive, often in a way that is frightening ▶ *an awesome task*

awful /'ɔːfəl/ *adjective*
1 very bad or frightening ▶ *an awful accident*
2 not pleasing; not liked ▶ *That's an awful book.*
SAME MEANING (**1** and **2**): **dreadful, terrible**

awfully /'ɔːfəlɪ/ *adverb*
very ▶ *She's awfully clever.*
SAME MEANING: **terribly**

awkward /'ɔːkwəd/ *adjective*
1 not skilful in handling things; not moving in an easy way ▶ *He's very awkward – he keeps dropping things.*
2 not easy to handle ▶ *The cup is an awkward shape.*
3 making you feel uncomfortable ▶ *There was an awkward silence, when no one knew what to say.*

awoke /ə'wəʊk/
the PAST TENSE of the verb **awake**

awoken /ə'wəʊkən/
the PAST PARTICIPLE of the verb **awake**

axe /æks/ *noun*
a tool with a metal blade fixed onto a handle, used for cutting down trees

axis /'æksɪs/ *noun (plural **axes** /'æksiːz/)*
a line at the side or bottom of a GRAPH, where you write the measurements

axle /'æksəl/ *noun*
the bar that connects two wheels on a vehicle

Bb

BA /ˌbiː 'eɪ/ *noun*
BACHELOR OF ARTS; a university degree in a subject such as history or literature ▶ *She has a BA in French.*

baby /'beɪbɪ/ *noun (plural **babies**)*
a very young child

babyish /'beɪbɪ-ɪʃ/ *adjective*
like a baby ▶ *Don't be so babyish!*

babysit /'beɪbɪsɪt/ *verb (present participle **babysitting**, past **babysat** /'beɪbɪsæt/)*
to care for a child while his or her parents are away

babysitter /ˈbeɪbɪˌsɪtəʳ/ *noun*
a person who is paid to care for a child when the child's parents are away

bachelor /ˈbætʃələʳ/ *noun*
a man who is not married and has never been married
COMPARE: **spinster**

back[1] /bæk/ *noun*
1 the part of your body that is behind you and goes from your neck to your legs ▶ *I lay on my back.* ▶ *Her back aches.*
2 the part that is furthest from the front ▶ *Write this exercise at the back of your book.* ▶ *There's a hut at the back of* (=behind) *the house.*
OPPOSITE (**1** and **2**): **front**
3 back to front with the back where the front should be ▶ *You're wearing your hat back to front.*
4 behind someone's back without someone knowing ▶ *You shouldn't talk about people behind their backs.*
5 turn your back on someone to refuse to help or be friendly with someone ▶ *Now that he's famous, he's turned his back on his friends.*

back[2] *adverb*
1 in the direction that is behind you; away from the front ▶ *Stand back from the fire; it's very hot.*
2 to a place where something or someone was before ▶ *Put the book back on the shelf when you've finished it.* ▶ *When do you come back from your holiday?*
3 in reply ▶ *I wrote to her, and she wrote back to me the next day.*

back[3] *adjective*
at the back ▶ *the back seat of a car*
OPPOSITE: **front**

back[4] *verb*
1 to make a vehicle move in the direction that is behind you ▶ *She backed the car into the street.*
2 back away from someone or something to move away from someone or something because you are afraid of them
3 back someone up to support someone by agreeing that what they are saying is true

backache /ˈbækeɪk/ *noun (no plural)*
pain in your back ▶ *I've got terrible backache.*

backbone /ˈbækbəʊn/ *noun*
the line of bones going from your neck to your bottom
SAME MEANING: **spine**

backfire /ˌbækˈfaɪəʳ/ *verb (present participle* ***backfiring****, past* ***backfired****)*
to have the opposite result to the one you wanted ▶ *The plan backfired when I realized I didn't have enough money.*

background /ˈbækgraʊnd/ *noun*
the area that is behind the main objects or people in a picture ▶ *This is a photo of Mary, with our house in the background.*

backing /ˈbækɪŋ/ *noun (no plural)*
money or support that a person or an organization gives you in order to help you achieve something ▶ *The government gives financial backing to many small businesses.*

backlog /ˈbæklɒg/ *noun*
work that still needs to be done and should have been done earlier ▶ *a huge backlog of orders*

backpack /ˈbækpæk/ *noun*
a bag that you carry on your back
SAME MEANING: **rucksack**

backpacking /ˈbækˌpækɪŋ/ *noun (no plural)*
an occasion when you go walking and camping, carrying a backpack ▶ *We're going backpacking in Nepal.*

backside /ˈbæksaɪd/ *noun*
the part of your body that you sit on

backstage /ˌbækˈsteɪdʒ/ *adverb, adjective*

B

in the area behind the stage in a theatre ▶ *We're hoping to go backstage and talk to the actors.*

backstroke /'bækstrəʊk/ *noun (no plural)*
a way of swimming which you do lying on your back in the water ▶ *Can you do backstroke?*

back-to-back /ˌbæk tə 'bæk/ *adjective, adverb*
with the backs of two people or things facing each other ▶ *Stand back-to-back and we'll see who's tallest.*

backup /'bækʌp/ *noun*
a copy of a document, especially a computer FILE, that you can use if you lose or damage the original one ▶ *Do you have a backup of this file?*

backward /'bækwəd/ *adjective*
1 in the direction that is behind you ▶ *a backward movement*
OPPOSITE: **forward**
2 slow to learn things

backwards /'bækwədz/ *adverb*
1 in the direction that is behind you ▶ *The train is going backwards.*
2 starting at the end; in the opposite way to the usual way. For example, if you count backwards from 5, you say 5, 4, 3, 2, 1.
OPPOSITE (**1** and **2**): **forwards**
3 **backwards and forwards** moving many times, first in one direction and then in the opposite direction ▶ *He travels backwards and forwards between London and New York.*

backyard /ˌbæk'jɑːd/ *noun*
a small area of land behind a house and belonging to it

bacon /'beɪkən/ *noun (no plural)*
meat from the back or sides of a pig, that is prepared in salt, cooked, and eaten hot
COMPARE: **ham**

bacteria /bæk'tɪərɪə/ *plural noun*
living things which are so small that you cannot see them, but which live in dirt and old food and can make people ill

bad /bæd/ *adjective (**worse** /wɜːs/, **worst** /wɜːst/)*
1 not good or nice ▶ *bad news* ▶ *bad behaviour* ▶ *a bad smell*
2 not able to do something well ▶ *I'm really bad **at** maths.* ▶ *a bad doctor*
OPPOSITE (**1** and **2**): **good**
3 serious or severe ▶ *He's got a very bad cold.*
4 very old and no longer good to eat ▶ *That meat is bad, so don't eat it.*
5 **go bad** to become old and not good to eat ▶ *This meat has gone bad.*
6 **be bad for someone** to cause harm to someone ▶ *Smoking is bad for you.*
7 **not bad** quite good

badge /bædʒ/ *noun*
something that you wear on your clothes to show your name, your job, the name of your school, etc.
COMPARE: **brooch**

badger /'bædʒəʳ/ *noun*
a wild animal with black and white fur, that lives in a hole and comes out at night

badly /'bædlɪ/ *adverb*
1 not well; not nicely ▶ *She sang very badly.*
OPPOSITE: **well**
2 very much ▶ *to want something badly*
3 severely ▶ *badly hurt*

badminton /'bædmɪntən/ *noun (no plural)*
a game like tennis, in which you hit a special type of very light ball with feathers on it

bad-tempered /ˌbæd 'tempəd/ *adjective*
becoming angry very easily ▶ *You're very bad-tempered today.* ▶ *a bad-tempered man*

baffle /ˈbæfəl/ *verb (present participle **baffling**, past **baffled**)*
to cause someone to be unable to understand something ▶ *I was completely baffled by his explanation.*

bag /bæg/ *noun*
a container made of cloth, paper, plastic, or leather which opens at the top and which you use for carrying things ▶ *a bag of shopping*

bagel /ˈbeɪgəl/ *noun*
a type of bread in the shape of a ring

baggage /ˈbægɪdʒ/ *noun (no plural)*
all the bags that you take with you when you travel
SAME MEANING: **luggage**

baggy /ˈbægɪ/ *adjective (**baggier**, **baggiest**)*
(used about clothes) very loose ▶ *baggy trousers*

bail¹ /beɪl/ *noun (no plural)*
money that you pay to a court so that a prisoner does not have to stay in prison before the TRIAL starts ▶ *They released him on £10,000 bail this morning.*

bail² *verb*
bail someone out to help someone who is in trouble, especially by giving them money ▶ *She asked her dad to bail her out.*

bait /beɪt/ *noun (no plural)*
food that you use to attract fish or animals so that you can catch them

bake /beɪk/ *verb (present participle **baking**, past **baked**)*
to cook something using dry heat in a closed box called an OVEN ▶ *I'm baking a cake.*
COMPARE: **roast**

baked beans /ˌbeɪkt ˈbiːnz/ *plural noun*
round, white beans cooked with TOMATOES and sold in tins

baker /ˈbeɪkəʳ/ *noun*
1 a person whose job is making bread and cakes
2 baker's a shop that sells bread and cakes ▶ *I'm going to the baker's to get some bread.*

bakery /ˈbeɪkərɪ/ *noun (plural **bakeries**)*
a building where bread and cakes are baked for selling

balance¹ /ˈbæləns/ *verb (present participle **balancing**, past **balanced**)*
to keep yourself or something else steady, especially in a difficult position ▶ *to balance a book on your head*

balance² *noun (no plural)*
1 the ability to stay steady without falling to one side or the other ▶ *My balance isn't very good so I can't ride a bicycle.*
2 keep your balance to stay steady without falling to one side or the other
3 lose your balance to fall when you are trying to remain steady in a difficult position ▶ *I lost my balance and fell when I was walking on the ice.*

balanced /ˈbælənst/ *adjective*
1 giving equal and fair attention to all sides ▶ *He has a very balanced attitude to the situation.*
2 including a good mixture of all the things that are needed ▶ *a balanced diet*

balcony /ˈbælkənɪ/ *noun (plural **balconies**)*
1 a place above the ground on the outside of a building, where people can sit ▶ *Our flat has a large balcony.*
2 the upstairs part of a theatre or cinema where people sit ▶ *We had seats in the balcony.*

bald /bɔːld/ *adjective*
with no hair on the head ▶ *a bald old man*

B

bale /beɪl/ *noun*
a large quantity of goods or material tied tightly together ▶ *a bale of hay*

ball /bɔːl/ *noun*
1 a round object that you use in some games for throwing or kicking
2 a thing with a round shape ▶ *a ball of wool*
3 a large, important party at which people dance ▶ *The queen attended a ball.*

ballad /ˈbæləd/ *noun*
a song that tells a story, especially about love

ballerina /ˌbæləˈriːnə/ *noun*
a female ballet dancer

ballet /ˈbæleɪ/ *noun*
a kind of dance in which the dancers sometimes stand on the ends of their toes and move to music in a way that tells a story

balloon /bəˈluːn/ *noun*
a rubber bag that can be filled with air or gas so that it floats in the air

ballot[1] /ˈbælət/ *noun*
a system of voting, especially in secret

ballot[2] *verb*
to find out what people think by letting them vote, especially in secret ▶ *All members will be balloted before any action is taken.*

ballpark /ˈbɔːlpɑːk/ *adjective*
(used about numbers, amounts, etc.) not exactly correct but close enough ▶ *a ballpark figure of, say, £2 million.*

ballpoint /ˈbɔːlpɔɪnt/ *(also **ballpoint pen** /ˌbɔːlpɔɪnt ˈpen/) noun*
a pen full of ink, with a very small, metal ball at the end you write with
SAME MEANING: **Biro**

ballroom /ˈbɔːlrʊm/ *noun*
a large room where formal dances take place

bamboo /bæmˈbuː/ *noun (no plural)*
a tall, hard grass that is like wood and is sometimes used for making furniture

ban[1] /bæn/ *verb (present participle **banning**, past **banned**)*
to make a rule or law saying that something is not allowed ▶ *Smoking is banned in school.*
COMPARE: **forbid, prohibit**

ban[2] *noun*
an order which says you must not do a particular thing ▶ *There is a ban **on** smoking.*

banal /bəˈnɑːl/ *adjective*
ordinary and not interesting ▶ *a banal conversation*

banana /bəˈnɑːnə/ *noun*
a long fruit with a yellow skin

band /bænd/ *noun*
1 a narrow piece of material used for holding things together ▶ *Put a rubber band around these books.*
2 a group of people who are together for some purpose ▶ *a band of thieves*
3 a group of people who play music together

bandage[1] /ˈbændɪdʒ/ *noun*
a long piece of cloth that is tied on to your body to cover a wound
COMPARE: **plaster**

bandage[2] *verb (present participle **bandaging**, past **bandaged**)*
to tie a bandage on a part of someone's body

bandit /ˈbændɪt/ *noun*
a robber with a gun who is part of a group and attacks travellers in quiet country places

bang[1] /bæŋ/ *noun*
1 a loud noise like the noise made by a gun
2 a blow ▶ *a bang on the head*

bang[2] *verb*
1 to hit something ▶ *He fell and banged his head.* ▶ *to bang a drum*
2 to shut something with a loud noise ▶ *Don't bang the door!*

bangle /ˈbæŋgəl/ *noun*
a piece of jewellery worn around a woman's arm or ankle

banish /ˈbænɪʃ/ *verb*
to send someone away from their own country as a punishment

banister /ˈbænɪstəʳ/ *noun*
a type of fence along the outer edge of stairs to prevent people falling

banjo /ˈbændʒəʊ/ *noun*
a musical instrument with four or more strings and a round body

bank[1] /bæŋk/ *noun*
1 an organization which looks after people's money for them by keeping it safe, and which sometimes lends people money
2 the raised land along the side of a lake or river

bank[2] *verb*
1 to put or keep money in a bank ▶ *to bank your wages*
2 bank on someone or something to depend on someone or something ▶ *You can never bank on her to help you.*

bank account /ˈbæŋk əˌkaʊnt/ *noun*
an arrangement you make to leave your money in a bank until you need it ▶ *How much money do you have in your bank account?* ▶ *to open a bank account*

banker /ˈbæŋkəʳ/ *noun*
a person who owns or controls a bank

bank holiday /ˌbæŋk ˈhɒlɪdeɪ, -dɪ/ *noun*
a special day which is not a Saturday or Sunday, when everyone has a holiday and all the banks and most of the shops are shut

banking /ˈbæŋkɪŋ/ *noun (no plural)*
the business done by a bank

bank note /ˈbæŋk nəʊt/ *noun*
a piece of paper money
COMPARE: **coin**

bankrupt /ˈbæŋkrʌpt/ *adjective*
not able to pay the money owed to people

bankruptcy /ˈbæŋkrʌptsɪ/ *noun (plural* ***bankruptcies****)*
a situation in which a company or person is not able to pay the money owed to people ▶ *A series of business failures led to bankruptcy.*

banner /ˈbænəʳ/ *noun*
a long piece of cloth with writing on it, that is usually carried by people ▶ *crowds waving banners that read "Welcome Home"*

banquet /ˈbæŋkwɪt/ *noun*
a special, important meal where there are a lot of people

baptism /ˈbæptɪzəm/ *noun*
the ceremony in which someone, usually a baby, becomes a member of the Christian church

baptize /bæpˈtaɪz/ *verb (present participle* ***baptizing****, past* ***baptized****)*
to make someone a member of the Christian church by performing a special ceremony

bar[1] /bɑːʳ/ *noun*
1 a place where people go to buy and drink alcohol
2 a solid piece of something, longer than it is wide ▶ *a bar of soap* ▶ *a bar of chocolate*
3 a long piece of wood or metal for keeping a door, etc. shut or for preventing people from entering or leaving a room ▶ *a window with bars across it*
4 behind bars in PRISON

bar[2] *verb (present participle* ***barring****, past* ***barred****)*
1 to close something firmly with a long piece of wood or metal ▶ *She barred the door.*
2 to block something ▶ *The soldiers barred the road to the city.*

B

barbaric /bɑːˈbærɪk/ *adjective*
violent and cruel ▶ *This was a barbaric crime.*

barbecue /ˈbɑːbɪkjuː/ *noun*
1 a meal that is cooked outside on a type of fire and usually eaten outside
COMPARE: **picnic**
2 a type of fire for cooking food outside

barbed wire /ˌbɑːbd ˈwaɪəʳ/ *noun (no plural)*
wire with short, sharp points in it ▶ *a barbed wire fence*

barber /ˈbɑːbəʳ/ *noun*
1 a person whose job is to cut men's hair
COMPARE: **hairdresser**
2 barber's a shop where men can go to have their hair cut ▶ *to go to the barber's*

bar code /ˈbɑː kəʊd/ *noun*
a row of black lines printed on products sold in a shop, that a computer reads when you buy the product

bare /beəʳ/ *adjective*
1 not covered by anything ▶ *bare feet* (=without shoes and socks)
2 empty ▶ *a bare room* (=with no furniture)

barefoot /ˌbeəˈfʊt/ *adjective, adverb*
not wearing any shoes or socks ▶ *to walk barefoot*

barely /ˈbeəlɪ/ *adverb*
just; almost not ▶ *He had barely enough money to buy food.*
SAME MEANING: **hardly**

bargain[1] /ˈbɑːgɪn/ *verb*
to talk or argue about the price of something that you are buying or selling

bargain[2] *noun*
1 something which you can buy for a little money but is worth more ▶ *These shoes are a bargain at only £10.*
2 an agreement in which two people or groups each promise to do something ▶ *to make a bargain with someone*

barge /bɑːdʒ/ *noun*
a large boat with a flat bottom, used for carrying things such as coal on rivers

bark[1] /bɑːk/ *verb*
to make the sound made by a dog

bark[2] *noun*
1 *(no plural)* the strong, hard skin that covers the outside of a tree
2 the sound a dog makes

barley /ˈbɑːlɪ/ *noun (no plural)*
a type of grass that is grown on farms and is used for making beer

barmaid /ˈbɑːmeɪd/ *noun*
a woman whose job is to serve drinks in a BAR or PUB

barman /ˈbɑːmən/ *noun (plural* ***barmen*** */-mən/)*
a man whose job is to serve drinks in a BAR or PUB

barn /bɑːn/ *noun*
a large building on a farm, used as a place for keeping animals and crops

barometer /bəˈrɒmɪtəʳ/ *noun*
an instrument that tells you if the weather is going to change

barracks /ˈbærəks/ *plural noun*
a building that soldiers live in

barrage /ˈbærɑːʒ/ *noun*
a lot of complaints, questions, sounds, etc. that happen very quickly after each other ▶ *We faced a barrage* ***of*** *criticism after announcing the winner.*

barrel /ˈbærəl/ *noun*
1 a large, round container with flat ends, used for keeping liquids such as oil and beer
2 the part of a gun that is like a tube

barren /ˈbærən/ *adjective*
(used about land, earth, etc.) not able to grow plants and seeds very well ▶ *a barren desert*

barricade[1] /ˈbærɪkeɪd/ *noun*
something that is temporarily built across a road, door, etc. to prevent people from going through

barricade[2] *verb (present participle* ***barricading****, past* ***barricaded****)*
to put something across a road, door, etc. to prevent people from going through ▶ *The kids had barricaded themselves into their bedroom.*

barrier /ˈbærɪəʳ/ *noun*
a fence or wall ▶ *The police put a barrier across the road.*

barrow /ˈbærəʊ/ *noun*
a small cart that you pull or push by hand and use for carrying things

barter /ˈbɑːtəʳ/ *verb*
to pay for goods or services by giving other goods or services instead of using money ▶ *They bartered food for coal.*

base[1] /beɪs/ *noun*
1 the bottom of something; the part something stands on ▶ *Stand the bottle on its base.*
2 the place where something is controlled from ▶ *The company has offices all over the world, but their base is in London.*

base[2] *verb (present participle* ***basing****, past* ***based****)*
1 be based somewhere to have your main home, office, etc. in a place ▶ *We're based in the city, but we spend a lot of time in the country.*
2 base something on something to develop something from something that already exists, or from something that has already happened ▶ *a book based on her experiences during the war*

baseball /ˈbeɪsbɔːl/ *noun (no plural)*
a ball game in which two teams in turn try to hit a ball with a round stick and then run round a specially shaped field

basement /ˈbeɪsmənt/ *noun*
a part of a house, shop, or building which is below the level of the street ▶ *They live in the basement.*
COMPARE: **cellar**

bases /ˈbeɪsiːz/
the plural of **basis**

bash /bæʃ/ *verb*
to hit something or someone hard ▶ *I bashed my leg on the table.*

bashful /ˈbæʃfəl/ *adjective*
embarrassed and shy ▶ *Why are you looking so bashful?*

basic /ˈbeɪsɪk/ *adjective*
simple and more important than anything else ▶ *basic skills such as reading and writing*

basically /ˈbeɪsɪklɪ/ *adverb*
1 used to introduce a simple explanation of something ▶ *Basically, the team didn't play well enough.*
2 in the most important ways ▶ *Norwegian and Danish are basically the same.*

basics /ˈbeɪsɪks/ *plural noun*
the most important skills or facts of something ▶ *I don't even know the basics of first aid.*

basin /ˈbeɪsən/ *noun*
1 a round dish
2 a large bowl fixed to the wall for washing your hands
COMPARE (**2**): **sink**

basis /ˈbeɪsɪs/ *noun (plural* ***bases*** */ˈbeɪsiːz/)*
the part of something from which something else develops ▶ *These ideas formed the basis of the plan.*

bask /bɑːsk/ *verb*
to lie somewhere warm and enjoy doing this ▶ *The cat was basking* ***in*** *the sun.*

basket /ˈbɑːskɪt/ *noun*
1 a container made of thin pieces of shaped wood which you use for carrying things

B

2 when a player gets the ball into the net at BASKETBALL

basketball /ˈbɑːskɪtbɔːl/ *noun (no plural)*
a game in which two teams try to throw a ball through a round net which is high above the ground

bass[1] /beɪs/ *adjective*
playing low musical notes ▶ *He plays the bass guitar.*

bass[2] /beɪs/ *noun (plural **basses**)*
a singer or an instrument that sings or plays notes that are the lowest in the range

bass[3] /bæs/ *noun (plural **bass** or **basses**)*
a fish used for food

bassoon /bəˈsuːn/ *noun*
a long, wooden musical instrument that makes a low sound

bat[1] /bæt/ *noun*
1 a piece of wood used for hitting the ball in some games ▶ *a baseball bat*
2 a small animal with wings that flies at night and hangs upside down when it sleeps

bat[2] *verb (present participle **batting**, past **batted**)*
to hit a ball with a special piece of wood

batch /bætʃ/ *noun (plural **batches**)*
a number of people or things arriving or being dealt with together ▶ *to cook a batch of cakes* ▶ *a batch of new students*

bath[1] /bɑːθ/ *noun (plural **baths** /bɑːðz, bɑːθs/)*
1 a large container that you fill with water and then sit in to wash your body
2 baths a swimming pool ▶ *Shall we go to the baths?*
3 have a bath to wash yourself in a bath ▶ *I have a bath every day.*

bath[2] *verb*
1 to wash someone in a bath ▶ *to bath a baby*
2 to wash yourself in a bath ▶ *She baths every morning.*

> Do not confuse the verb **bath** (=to wash in a bath) with the verb **bathe** (=to swim): *to bathe in the sea.* The verb **bath** is not used often. People usually use the expression "have a bath" instead: *He had a bath and washed his hair.* Do not use "have a bath" instead of **bathe**.

bathe /beɪð/ *verb (present participle **bathing** /ˈbeɪðɪŋ/, past **bathed** /beɪðd/)*
to swim for pleasure in a river or the sea
LOOK AT: **bath**

bather /ˈbeɪðəʳ/ *noun*
a person who is swimming for pleasure in a river or the sea

bathing suit /ˈbeɪðɪŋ ˌsuːt/ *noun*
a piece of clothing that you wear when you swim

bathrobe /ˈbɑːθrəʊb/ *noun*
a type of loose coat that you put on after you have had a bath

bathroom /ˈbɑːθrʊm/ *noun*
a room in a house where people wash their bodies or have baths

battalion /bəˈtæljən/ *noun*
a large group of soldiers that consists of several smaller groups

batter /ˈbætəʳ/ *verb*
to hit someone or something hard, again and again

battered /ˈbætəd/ *adjective*
old and damaged ▶ *a battered old book*

battery /ˈbætərɪ/ *noun (plural **batteries**)*
a box that produces or stores electricity, like the ones used in radios, etc. or the one in a car

battle /ˈbætl/ *noun*
a fight between soldiers, ships, or

aircraft ▶ *one of the most important battles of the war*
COMPARE: **war**

battlefield /ˈbætlfiːld/ *noun*
a place where a battle has been fought

battleship /ˈbætlʃɪp/ *noun*
a very large ship used in wars

bawl /bɔːl/ *verb*
to shout or cry loudly ▶ *Can't you stop that child bawling!*

bay /beɪ/ *noun*
a part of the sea that curves inwards so that it is enclosed by land

bazaar /bəˈzɑːʳ/ *noun*
1 a market or a group of shops, especially in the Middle East
2 a sale to collect money for an organization such as a church or school ▶ *the annual church bazaar*

BC /ˌbiː ˈsiː/
before the birth of Christ, used in dates ▶ *It was built in the year 2000 BC.*

be /bɪ; *strong* biː/ *verb*

present tense

singular	*plural*
I **am** (I**'m**)	We **are** (We**'re**)
You **are** (You**'re**)	You **are** (You**'re**)
He/She/It **is** (He**'s**/She**'s**/It**'s**)	They **are** (They**'re**)

past tense

singular	*plural*
I **was**	We **were**
You **were**	You **were**
He/She/It **was**	They **were**

present participle	**being**
past participle	**been**
negative short forms	**aren't, isn't, wasn't, weren't**

(you can find each of these words in its own place in the dictionary)

1 used to describe or give information about people or things ▶ *His name is Peter.* ▶ *My mother is a teacher.* ▶ *The milk is on the table.* ▶ *I'm* (=I am) *very happy.* ▶ *"How old are you?" "I'm 16."* ▶ *"What's* (=what is) *your name?" "It's* (=it is) *Emma."* ▶ *It was my birthday yesterday.*
2 used with other verbs to show that something is happening now ▶ *"What are you doing?" "I am painting a picture."*
3 used with other verbs to show that something happens to a person or thing ▶ *She is paid to clean their house* (=they pay her to clean their house). ▶ *He was attacked by a dog.* ▶ *The house was built 50 years ago.*
4 there is *(plural* ***there are****)* used to say that someone or something is in a place ▶ *Look – there's* (=there is) *Sue!* ▶ *There are too many people at the party.* ▶ *How many children are there in your class?* ▶ *There was a loud noise.*

beach /biːtʃ/ *noun (plural* ***beaches****)*
a shore covered in sand or stones where people go to swim

beacon /ˈbiːkən/ *noun*
a light that flashes to guide boats or planes

bead /biːd/ *noun*
a small ball of glass with a small hole for string or wire to pass through ▶ *She wore a string of beads round her neck.*

beady /ˈbiːdɪ/ *adjective (****beadier, beadiest****)*
(used about eyes) small and dark ▶ *an old woman with beady eyes*

beak /biːk/ *noun*
the hard, pointed mouth of a bird

beam[1] /biːm/ *noun*
1 a large, long, heavy piece of wood used to support the roof of a building
2 a line of light shining from a bright

B

object ▸ *the sun's beams* ▸ *a beam of light*

beam² *verb*
to smile in a very happy way ▸ *She beamed with pleasure.*

bean /biːn/ *noun*
1 a seed or seed container of a plant which is eaten as a vegetable ▸ *green beans*
2 a seed of a plant which is used for making food or drink ▸ *coffee beans*

bear¹ /beəʳ/ *noun*
a large and sometimes fierce wild animal with a thick coat

bear² *verb (past tense **bore** /bɔːʳ/, past participle **borne** /bɔːn/)*
1 to carry or support the weight of something ▸ *These pillars bear the weight of the roof.*
2 to accept something bad without complaining ▸ *The pain was too much for me to bear.*
3 can't bear (used to show that you dislike someone or something very much) ▸ *I can't bear loud music.*

bearable /ˈbeərəbəl/ *adjective*
difficult but not too bad to be accepted or dealt with ▸ *His letters made her loneliness bearable.*
OPPOSITE: **unbearable**

beard /bɪəd/ *noun*
hair on a man's face below his mouth
COMPARE: **moustache**

bearing /ˈbeərɪŋ/ *noun*
1 have a bearing on something to affect something ▸ *Recent events have had a bearing on his decision.*
2 lose your bearings to become lost ▸ *The boat lost its bearings in the fog.*

beast /biːst/ *noun*
1 a wild and dangerous animal
2 an unkind or cruel person ▸ *You beast – I hate you!*

beat¹ /biːt/ *verb (past tense **beat**, past participle **beaten** /ˈbiːtn/)*
1 to defeat someone; to have a better result than someone ▸ *We beat the other team at football.*
2 to hit someone or something many times ▸ *to beat a drum*
3 to move regularly ▸ *Her heart was beating fast.*
4 to beat someone up to hit someone until they are hurt

beat² *noun*
a single stroke or movement as part of a regular group ▸ *a beat of your heart*

beaten¹ /ˈbiːtn/
the PAST PARTICIPLE of the verb **beat**

beaten² *adjective*
off the beaten track far away from places that people usually visit ▸ *We want to stay somewhere off the beaten track.*

beautician /bjuːˈtɪʃən/ *noun*
a person who gives beauty treatment to your face and body

beautiful /ˈbjuːtɪfəl/ *adjective*
1 very attractive and nice to look at ▸ *a beautiful woman* ▸ *a beautiful view*
2 very pleasing or nice ▸ *What a beautiful day!* ▸ *beautiful music*

> The adjectives **beautiful** and **pretty** can be used to describe women, children, and things, but they are never used to describe men. A man who is nice to look at can be described as **handsome**.

beautifully /ˈbjuːtɪfəlɪ/ *adverb*
very well; in a way which looks or sounds good ▸ *She speaks French beautifully.*

beauty /ˈbjuːtɪ/ *noun*
1 *(no plural)* being beautiful ▸ *a place of great beauty*
2 *(plural **beauties**)* something or someone beautiful ▸ *His mother was a great beauty.*

became /bɪˈkeɪm/
the PAST TENSE of the verb **become**

because /bɪˈkɒz/ *conjunction*
1 (used when you are giving a reason for something) ▶ *I missed the train because I was late.*
2 because of for this reason ▶ *We stayed at home because of the rain.*

beckon /ˈbekən/ *verb*
to make a sign with your finger asking someone to come to you

become /bɪˈkʌm/ *verb (present participle* ***becoming****, past tense* ***became*** /bɪˈkeɪm/, *past participle* ***become****)*
1 to begin to be something ▶ *The prince became king when his father died.* ▶ *The actor became famous in the 1960s.*
2 What has become of ...? a question you ask when you want to know what has happened to a person or thing, or where someone or something is ▶ *What has become of that friend of yours who went to live in Australia?*

bed /bed/ *noun*
1 a piece of furniture you sleep on ▶ *What time did you go to bed last night* (=go to your bed to sleep)*?*
2 the base or bottom of something ▶ *the bed of a river*
3 make a bed to tidy a bed and make it ready for sleeping in
4 go to bed with someone to have sex with someone

bed and breakfast /ˌbed ən ˈbrekfəst/ *noun*
a family house where you can pay to be a guest for the night. You can have breakfast there, but no other meals ▶ *We stayed in a bed and breakfast.*

bedclothes /ˈbedkləʊðz/ *plural noun*
all the covers put on a bed to keep you warm

bedding /ˈbedɪŋ/ *noun (no plural)*
all the covers put on a bed

bedroom /ˈbedrʊm/ *noun*
a room for sleeping in

bedside /ˈbedsaɪd/ *noun*
the area next to a bed ▶ *His mother stayed at his bedside all night.*

bedsit /bedˈsɪt/ *noun*
a room used for both living and sleeping in ▶ *Many students live in bedsits.*

bedspread /ˈbedspred/ *noun*
a cloth cover for a bed, used to keep you warm or to make the bed look attractive
COMPARE: **duvet**

bedtime /ˈbedtaɪm/ *noun*
the time when you usually go to bed ▶ *It's past my bedtime.*

bee /biː/ *noun*
a stinging, flying insect that makes HONEY

beef /biːf/ *noun (no plural)*
the meat from cattle

beefburger /ˈbiːfbɜːgəʳ/ *noun*
meat that has been cut into very small pieces and then made into a round, flat shape before being cooked
SAME MEANING: **hamburger**

beehive /ˈbiːhaɪv/ *noun*
another word for **hive**

been /biːn, bɪn/
1 the PAST PARTICIPLE of the verb **be** ▶ *It has been very cold this week.*
2 have been somewhere to have gone and come back from a place ▶ *She's been away on holiday* (=but now she's back). ▶ *Have you ever been to Scotland?*
LOOK AT: **gone**

beep /biːp/ *verb*
to make a short, high noise ▶ *The computer beeps when you make a mistake.*

beeper /ˈbiːpəʳ/ *noun*
a small machine that you carry with you which makes a sound to tell you to telephone someone
SAME MEANING: **pager**

B

B

beer /bɪəʳ/ *noun*
1 *(no plural)* an alcoholic drink made from grain
2 a glass or bottle of this drink
▶ *Can I have two beers, please?*

beetle /ˈbiːtl/ *noun*
an insect whose outside wings make a hard cover for its body

beetroot /ˈbiːtruːt/ *noun*
a round, red vegetable that grows under the ground

before¹ /bɪˈfɔːʳ/ *adverb*
at some earlier time ▶ *I have never seen you before* (=this is the first time I have seen you).

before² *preposition, conjunction*
1 earlier than ▶ *You must leave before 8 o'clock.* ▶ *Finish your work before you go.* ▶ *the day before yesterday*
OPPOSITE: **after**
2 before that used when you want to show that something happens or happened earlier than something else ▶ *She was a teacher, and before that she worked in an office.*

> **Before** means "earlier than something else": *She left before I arrived.* ▶ *Clean your teeth before you go to bed.* **Ago** means "in the past": *We went to Scotland three years ago.* ▶ *Our second visit to America was in 1993, and our first visit was three years before* (=in 1990). ▶ *It happened many years ago.* ▶ *It happened before the war.*
> LOOK AT: **ago**

beforehand /bɪˈfɔːhænd/ *adverb*
before something else happens
▶ *She knew I was coming because I telephoned her beforehand.*

beg /beg/ *verb (present participle **begging**, past **begged**)*
1 to ask people in the street for money or food
2 to ask someone very strongly to do something ▶ *I begged her not to go.*
3 I beg your pardon a phrase used when you are sorry because you have done something wrong, or when you did not hear what someone said and you want them to say it again ▶ *I beg your pardon, but could you repeat that?*

began /bɪˈgæn/
the PAST TENSE of the verb **begin**

beggar /ˈbegəʳ/ *noun*
a person who asks people in the street for money or food

begin /bɪˈgɪn/ *verb (present participle **beginning**, past tense **began** /bɪˈgæn/, past participle **begun** /bɪˈgʌn/)*
1 to start ▶ *The film begins at 2 o'clock.*
OPPOSITE: **end**
2 to start something ▶ *When do you begin your new job?* ▶ *It's beginning to rain.*
3 to begin with at first ▶ *To begin with, I didn't like school, but now I enjoy it.*

> Remember that the PAST TENSE is beg**a**n, and the PAST PARTICIPLE is beg**u**n.

beginner /bɪˈgɪnəʳ/ *noun*
a person who is starting to do or learn something ▶ *a swimming class for beginners*

beginning /bɪˈgɪnɪŋ/ *noun*
the start ▶ *the beginning **of** the year*
OPPOSITE: **end**

begrudge /bɪˈgrʌdʒ/ *verb (present participle **begrudging**, past **begrudged**)*
to feel upset because someone else has something you would like ▶ *I don't begrudge him his success.*

begun /bɪˈgʌn/
the PAST PARTICIPLE of the verb **begin**

behalf /bɪˈhɑːf/ *noun*
on behalf of someone instead of someone; for someone ▶ *I have come*

on behalf of my brother, as he's ill. ▶ *I paid the money on your behalf* (=for you).

behave /bɪˈheɪv/ *verb (present participle* ***behaving****, past* ***behaved****)*
1 to act in a particular way ▶ *The children behaved very badly.*
2 **behave yourself** to act in a way which will not annoy or offend other people

behaviour /bɪˈheɪvjəʳ/ *noun (no plural)*
the way a person acts ▶ *What bad behaviour!*

behind /bɪˈhaɪnd/ *preposition, adverb*
at the back (of) ▶ *He hung his coat on the nail behind the door.* ▶ *My brother went in front, and I walked behind.* ▶ *She hid behind a tree.*

beige /beɪʒ/ *noun, adjective*
a very light brown colour ▶ *a beige dress*

being[1] /ˈbiːɪŋ/
the PRESENT PARTICIPLE of the verb **be**

being[2] *noun*
a person ▶ *a being from another world*

belated /bɪˈleɪtɪd/ *adjective*
happening or done late ▶ *Myra sent me a belated birthday card.*

belch /beltʃ/ *verb*
to let air come out noisily from your stomach through your mouth
SAME MEANING: **burp**

belief /bɪˈliːf/ *noun*
1 *(no plural)* the feeling that something is true or exists ▶ *a belief in God*
2 an opinion or idea which you think is true ▶ *religious beliefs*

believable /bɪˈliːvəbəl/ *adjective*
easy to believe ▶ *His story is very believable.*
OPPOSITE: **unbelievable**

believe /bɪˈliːv/ *verb (present participle* ***believing****, past* ***believed****)*
1 to think that something is true ▶ *I don't believe the things you say.*
2 to think that someone is telling the truth ▶ *Don't you believe me?*
3 to have an opinion ▶ *I believe we will be successful.*
4 **believe in something** to be sure that something exists ▶ *Do you believe in God?*
5 **believe in someone** to trust someone and be sure they will succeed ▶ *The soldiers all believe in their leader.*

believer /bɪˈliːvəʳ/ *noun*
someone who believes that a particular idea or thing is good ▶ *He's a great believer in eating lots of fruit and vegetables.*

bell /bel/ *noun*
a round, hollow, metal object that makes a musical sound when it is hit ▶ *church bells*

bellow /ˈbeləʊ/ *verb*
to shout something in a loud, deep voice ▶ *"Go away!" he bellowed angrily.*

belly /ˈbelɪ/ *noun (plural* ***bellies****)*
your stomach ▶ *I've got a pain in my belly.*

belly button /ˈbelɪ ˌbʌtn/ *noun*
the small hole in your stomach
SAME MEANING: **navel**

belong /bɪˈlɒŋ/ *verb*
1 **belong to someone** to be owned by someone ▶ *Who does this coat belong to* (=who is the owner)?
2 **belong to something** to be a member of a group or club

belongings /bɪˈlɒŋɪŋz/ *plural noun*
your own property ▶ *Please take all your belongings with you when you leave the plane.*

beloved /bɪˈlʌvɪd/ *adjective*
loved very much ▶ *She was the beloved wife of Tom Smith.*

below /bɪ'ləʊ/ *adverb, preposition*
1 at a lower place; lower than; under ▶ *The children threw sticks from the bridge into the river below.* ▶ *My brother is in the class below mine.*
2 less than a particular amount ▶ *children below the age of five.*
OPPOSITE (**1** and **2**): **above**

belt /belt/ *noun*
a piece of cloth or leather that you wear around the middle of your body

bemused /bɪ'mjuːzd/ *adjective*
slightly confused ▶ *She looked bemused by what he was saying.*

bench /bentʃ/ *noun (plural **benches**)*
a long, wooden seat ▶ *a bench in the park*

bend[1] /bend/ *verb (past **bent** /bent/)*
1 *(also **bend down, bend over**)* to move the top part of your body down towards the ground ▶ *She bent down to pick up a book from the floor.*
2 to move something into a curved position ▶ *to bend your knees*

bend[2] *noun*
a curve ▶ *a bend in the road*

beneath /bɪ'niːθ/ *preposition*
below; under ▶ *Shall we sit beneath these trees?* ▶ *beneath a sunny sky*

beneficial /ˌbenɪ'fɪʃəl/ *adjective*
helpful or useful ▶ *It might be beneficial to talk to someone about your problems.*

benefit[1] /'benɪfɪt/ *verb*
to be useful or helpful to someone ▶ *The plants benefited from* (=were helped by) *the rain.*

benefit[2] *noun*
1 an advantage ▶ *the benefits of a good education*
2 for someone's benefit to help someone ▶ *I did it for your benefit.*

benign /bɪ'naɪn/ *adjective*
not likely to hurt you or to cause CANCER ▶ *a benign tumour*
OPPOSITE: **malignant**

bent /bent/
the PAST TENSE and PAST PARTICIPLE of the verb **bend**

bereaved /bɪ'riːvd/ *adjective*
having a relative or close friend who has recently died ▶ *a support group for bereaved parents*

bereavement /bɪ'riːvmənt/ *noun*
the situation when a relative or close friend has recently died ▶ *He is away from work because of a family bereavement.*

beret /'bereɪ/ *noun*
a flat, round hat made of woollen cloth

berry /'berɪ/ *noun (plural **berries**)*
a small, soft fruit that grows on a bush or tree

berserk /bɜː'sɜːk/ *adjective*
go berserk to become very angry and violent in a crazy way ▶ *He went berserk and started hitting Sue.*

beset /bɪ'set/ *verb (present participle **besetting**, past **beset**)*
be beset by something to have a lot of problems, difficulties, etc. to deal with ▶ *The company has been beset by financial difficulties.*

beside /bɪ'saɪd/ *preposition*
next to someone or something ▶ *Come and sit beside me.*

besides /bɪ'saɪdz/ *adverb*
a word used when you are giving another reason or fact to support what you are saying ▶ *I can't go out tonight because I'm too tired – besides, I haven't got any money.*
SAME MEANING: **anyway**

besiege /bɪ'siːdʒ/ *verb (present participle **besieging**, past **besieged**)*
1 be besieged by people to be surrounded by a lot of people ▶ *a rock star besieged by fans*
2 be besieged with something to receive a lot of something ▶ *The radio station was besieged with letters of complaint.*

best[1] /best/ *adjective*
1 the SUPERLATIVE of **good** ▶ *It was the best film I've ever seen.*
OPPOSITE: **worst**
2 best wishes a phrase used at the end of a letter when the person you are writing to is not a close friend ▶ *Have a happy Christmas, with best wishes from Mrs Jones and family.*

best[2] *adverb*
1 the SUPERLATIVE of **well** ▶ *the best-dressed person in the room*
OPPOSITE: **worst**
2 most ▶ *The blue dress suits you best.* ▶ *Which one do you like best?*
OPPOSITE: **least**

best[3] *noun (no plural)*
1 the best the most good person or thing ▶ *You're the best!* ▶ *She wants her children to have the best of everything* (=the best things possible).
2 do your best to try as hard as you can to succeed in something ▶ *It doesn't matter if you didn't win – you did your best.*

best man /ˌbest 'mæn/ *noun (plural* ***best men*** */ˌbest 'men/)*
a male friend who is chosen to help and support a man who is getting married ▶ *Will you be best man at my wedding?*
COMPARE: **bridesmaid**

best-seller /ˌbest'seləʳ/ *noun*
a book that a lot of people have bought

bet[1] /bet/ *verb (present participle* ***betting****, past* ***bet*** *or* ***betted****)*
to risk money on the result of a future event ▶ *He bet me £1 that the team would win.* ▶ *to bet money on a horse* (=in a race)
COMPARE: **gamble**

bet[2] *noun*
an agreement to risk money on the result of a future event ▶ *a bet of £1*

betray /bɪ'treɪ/ *verb*
to harm someone who trusts you by breaking a promise made to them ▶ *I asked you not to tell anyone, but you betrayed me.*

betrayal /bɪ'treɪəl/ *noun*
the act of harming someone who trusts you by breaking a promise made to them

better[1] /'betəʳ/ *adjective*
1 the COMPARATIVE of **good** ▶ *This book is better than the other one.*
2 not as ill as before ▶ *I hope you are feeling better.*
OPPOSITE (**1** and **2**): **worse**

better[2] *adverb*
1 the COMPARATIVE of **well** ▶ *He can sing better than me.*
OPPOSITE: **worse**
2 more ▶ *I like him better than his brother.*
3 had better should; ought to ▶ *You'd* (=you had) *better go home.* ▶ *I'd* (=I had) *better not miss my train.*

better off /ˌbetər 'ɒf/ *adjective*
1 more successful, richer, or having more advantages than you did before ▶ *Most businesses in the area are better off than they were ten years ago.*
OPPOSITE: **worse off**
2 be better off doing something used to give advice about what someone should do ▶ *You'd be better off taking a taxi to the airport.*

between /bɪ'twiːn/ *adverb, preposition*
1 *(also* ***in between****)* in the space in the middle of two people or things ▶ *There is a fence between his garden and our garden.* ▶ *April comes between March and May.*
2 in the period before one time and after another ▶ *The shop is open between 9 o'clock and 5 o'clock.*
3 more than one number or amount but less than another number or

amount ▶ *children aged between five and ten*
4 joining two places ▶ *the train between Cambridge and London* ▶ *flights between Paris and Geneva*
5 used when saying how things are shared or divided ▶ *You and I can share the cost between us.*

Use **between** when you are talking about something which is done or shared by two people or things. Use **among** when you are talking about something which is done or shared by more than two people or things: *She divided the cake between the two children.* ▶ *The money was divided among his brothers and sisters.*

beverage /ˈbevərɪdʒ/ *noun*
a drink ▶ *We do not sell alcoholic beverages.*

beware /bɪˈweəʳ/ *verb*
used to tell someone to be careful of something because it is dangerous ▶ *Beware **of** the dog!*

bewildered /bɪˈwɪldəd/ *adjective*
confused and not sure what to do or think ▶ *The children looked bewildered and scared.*

beyond /bɪˈjɒnd/ *adverb, preposition*
past; on the other side of something ▶ *beyond the mountains*

bias /ˈbaɪəs/ *noun (plural **biases**)*
an opinion about whether something is good or bad that unfairly influences how you deal with it ▶ *The judge's decision definitely shows a bias against women.*

biased /ˈbaɪəst/ *adjective*
showing that your personal opinions have unfairly affected your judgement ▶ *Some newspapers are biased in favour of the government.*

bib /bɪb/ *noun*
a piece of material that is tied under a child's chin to keep its clothes clean when it is eating

bible /ˈbaɪbəl/ *noun*
1 the Bible the holy book of the Christian religion
2 a useful and important book on a particular subject ▶ *a textbook that is the medical student's bible*

biblical /ˈbɪblɪkəl/ *adjective*
from or in the Bible

bibliography /ˌbɪblɪˈɒgrəfɪ/ *noun (plural **bibliographies**)*
a list of books about a particular subject

bicker /ˈbɪkəʳ/ *verb*
to argue about something that is not very important ▶ *The kids were bickering about who was the fastest runner.*

bicycle /ˈbaɪsɪkəl/ *noun*
a machine with two wheels. You sit on it and move your legs to make it go forward ▶ *to travel by bicycle*
SAME MEANING: **bike, cycle**

bid[1] /bɪd/ *verb (present participle **bidding**, past **bid**)*
to make an offer of money in order to buy something ▶ *He bid £10 for the bicycle.*

bid[2] *noun*
an offer of an amount of money to buy something

big /bɪg/ *adjective (**bigger, biggest**)*
large in size ▶ *They live in a big house.*
OPPOSITE: **little, small**

bigheaded /ˌbɪgˈhedɪd/ *adjective*
thinking that you are more successful or intelligent than other people

bigot /ˈbɪgət/ *noun*
a person who has strong and unreasonable opinions about people who belong to a different race, religion, or political group

bigoted /ˈbɪgətɪd/ *adjective*
having strong and unreasonable opinions about people who belong to a different race, religion, or political

group ► *a bigoted old man*

bike /baɪk/ *noun*
a machine with two wheels. You sit on it and move your legs to make it go forward ► *to travel by bike*
SAME MEANING: **bicycle, cycle**

biker /'baɪkəʳ/ *noun*
a person who rides a MOTORCYCLE, especially as part of a group

bikini /bɪ'kiːnɪ/ *noun*
a garment with two pieces, one covering the breasts and one covering the bottom, which women and girls wear when they swim

bilingual /baɪ'lɪŋgwəl/ *adjective*
1 able to speak two languages equally well ► *He's bilingual in French and German.*
2 spoken or written in two languages ► *a bilingual dictionary*

bill /bɪl/ *noun*
1 a piece of paper showing the amount you must pay for something ► *How much was the electricity bill this month?*
2 a plan for a new law ► *The government is considering the new education bill.*

billboard /'bɪlbɔːd/ *noun*
a big sign next to a road that is used to advertise things

billiards /'bɪljədz/ *noun (no plural)*
a game in which you hit balls across a table with long sticks

billion /'bɪljən/ *adjective, noun*
the number 1,000,000,000,000 (=a million million), or, especially in America, 1,000,000,000 (=a thousand million)

billow /'bɪləʊ/ *verb*
to rise into the air in large amounts ► *Smoke billowed out of the chimneys.*

bin /bɪn/ *noun*
a large container used for holding things that are to be thrown away or have been thrown away
COMPARE: **dustbin**

bind /baɪnd/ *verb (past* ***bound*** */baʊnd/)*
to tie something with rope or string

binge[1] /bɪndʒ/ *noun*
a short period of time when you eat too much food or drink too much alcohol ► *He's gone out on a binge with his mates.*

binge[2] *verb (present participle* ***binging****, past* ***binged****)*
to eat a lot of food or drink a lot of alcohol in a short period of time

bingo /'bɪŋgəʊ/ *noun (no plural)*
a game played with numbers in order to win prizes

binoculars /bɪ'nɒkjʊləz/ *plural noun*
a pair of special glasses which make things in the distance look bigger
COMPARE: **telescope**

biodegradable /ˌbaɪəʊdɪ'greɪdəbəl/ *adjective*
able to be destroyed by natural processes, in a way that does not harm the environment ► *Plastic is not biodegradable.*

biographer /baɪ'ɒgrəfəʳ/ *noun*
a person who writes someone's biography

biography /baɪ'ɒgrəfɪ/ *noun (plural* ***biographies****)*
the story of a person's life written by someone else
COMPARE: **autobiography**

biological /ˌbaɪə'lɒdʒɪkəl/ *adjective*
of or about BIOLOGY ► *The company does biological research.*

biologist /baɪ'ɒlədʒɪst/ *noun*
a person who studies biology

biology /baɪ'ɒlədʒɪ/ *noun (no plural)*
the scientific study of living things

bird /bɜːd/ *noun*
an animal with wings and feathers ► *Most birds can fly.*

B

bird of prey /ˌbɜːd əv 'preɪ/ *noun (plural **birds of prey**)*
a bird that kills and eats other birds and small animals ▶ *The eagle is a bird of prey.*

Biro /'baɪrəʊ/ *noun trademark*
a pen which has a very small metal ball at the end you write with
SAME MEANING: **ballpoint**

birth /bɜːθ/ *noun*
1 the act of a baby being born ▶ *the birth of a baby* ▶ *the number of births and deaths this year*
2 give birth to have a baby ▶ *She gave birth to a baby boy last night.*

birth control /'bɜːθ kənˌtrəʊl/ *noun (no plural)*
ways of limiting the number of children you have

birthday /'bɜːθdeɪ/ *noun*
the day of the year on which a person was born ▶ *My birthday is on January 6th.*
LOOK AT: **anniversary**

birthmark /'bɜːθmɑːk/ *noun*
an unusual mark on someone's skin that is there when they are born

birthplace /'bɜːθpleɪs/ *noun*
the place where someone was born ▶ *Stratford-upon-Avon is the birthplace of William Shakespeare.*

biscuit /'bɪskɪt/ *noun*
a dry, thin cake, usually sweet ▶ *a packet of biscuits*

bisexual /baɪ'sekʃʊəl/ *adjective*
sexually attracted to men and women

bishop /'bɪʃəp/ *noun*
a Christian priest who looks after the churches and the people in a large area
COMPARE: **vicar**

bit¹ /bɪt/
the PAST TENSE of the verb **bite**

bit² *noun*
1 a small piece or amount ▶ *I must do a bit **of** work.* ▶ *He ate every bit of food* (=all the food). ▶ *Would you like another bit of cake?*
2 a bit slightly ▶ *I'm sorry I'm a bit late.* ▶ *It's a bit too cold to go outside.*
3 for a bit for a short time ▶ *Why don't you go and lie down for a bit?*
4 bit by bit slowly, a little at a time ▶ *Bit by bit, they discovered the truth.*

bite¹ /baɪt/ *verb (present participle **biting**, past tense **bit** /bɪt/, past participle **bitten** /'bɪtn/)*
1 to cut or wound something with the teeth ▶ *That dog bit me.* ▶ *Does your dog bite?*
2 (used about an insect) to hurt you by pricking your skin

bite² *noun*
1 an act of biting ▶ *Do you want a bite of my apple?*
2 a wound made by biting ▶ *She was covered in insect bites.*

bitten /'bɪtn/
the PAST PARTICIPLE of the verb **bite**

bitter /'bɪtəʳ/ *adjective*
1 having a sharp, sour taste ▶ *bitter fruit*
2 angry ▶ *a bitter quarrel*
3 very cold ▶ *a bitter wind*

bitterly /'bɪtəlɪ/ *adverb*
very ▶ *It's bitterly cold outside.* ▶ *We were bitterly disappointed to lose.*

bizarre /bɪ'zɑːʳ/ *adjective*
very unusual and strange ▶ *a bizarre coincidence (adverb: **bizarrely**)*

black¹ /blæk/ *adjective*
1 of the colour of the sky at night ▶ *black shoes*
2 with dark-coloured skin ▶ *a black family*
3 (used about tea and coffee) without milk ▶ *I'd like my coffee black.*
4 black and blue having dark marks on your skin as a result of being hurt ▶ *Her arm was black and blue after the accident.*
5 black and white containing only the

colours black, white, and grey ▶ *an old black and white film*

black² *noun*
1 *(no plural)* the colour of the sky at night ▶ *He was dressed in black.*
2 a person with dark-coloured skin

blackberry /ˈblækbərɪ/ *noun (plural* ***blackberries****)*
a small, dark fruit that grows on bushes

blackbird /ˈblækbɜːd/ *noun*
a bird which is very common in Europe. The male is black and has a yellow beak.

blackboard /ˈblækbɔːd/ *noun*
a dark board on the wall at the front of a class that the teacher writes on

blackcurrant /ˈblæk-kʌrənt/ *noun*
a small, round, dark fruit that grows on bushes

black eye /ˌblæk ˈaɪ/ *noun*
an area of dark skin around someone's eye where they have been hit ▶ *How did you get that black eye?*

black magic /ˌblæk ˈmædʒɪk/ *noun (no plural)*
a type of magic used to do bad or evil things

blackmail¹ /ˈblækmeɪl/ *noun (no plural)*
a situation in which you make someone do what you want by saying that you will tell secrets about them ▶ *"End your relationship with her, and I might be prepared to forget about it." "That's blackmail!"*

blackmail² *verb*
to make someone do what you want by saying that you will tell secrets about them

black market /ˌblæk ˈmɑːkɪt/ *noun*
a system of buying and selling things illegally ▶ *They buy drugs on the black market.*

blackout /ˈblækaʊt/ *noun*
a short period of time when you suddenly cannot see, hear, or feel anything, for example because you are ill or have hit your head ▶ *I had a blackout and couldn't remember anything.*

blacksmith /ˈblækˌsmɪθ/ *noun*
a person who works with iron and makes shoes for horses

bladder /ˈblædəʳ/ *noun*
the part of your body where URINE stays before it leaves your body

blade /bleɪd/ *noun*
1 the flat, sharp part of anything that is used for cutting ▶ *the blade of a knife*
2 a long, flat leaf of grass

blame¹ /bleɪm/ *verb (present participle* ***blaming****, past* ***blamed****)*
1 blame someone for something to say that someone is the cause of something bad ▶ *The policeman blamed the car driver for causing the accident.*
COMPARE: **accuse**
2 be to blame for something to be responsible for something bad ▶ *He is to blame for the accident.*

blame² *noun (no plural)*
take the blame for something to accept that you are responsible for something bad

bland /blænd/ *adjective*
1 not interesting or exciting ▶ *the usual selection of bland entertainment*
2 having very little taste ▶ *a rather bland white sauce*

blank /blæŋk/ *adjective*
1 without anything on ▶ *a blank piece of paper* (=one without writing on it) ▶ *a blank cassette* (=one without any sounds on it)
2 not showing any expression ▶ *She looked at him with a blank face.*

blanket /ˈblæŋkɪt/ *noun*
a thick, woollen cloth, used as a cover on a bed to keep you warm

B

B

blare /bleəʳ/ *verb (present participle* ***blaring****, past* ***blared****)*
to make a loud and unpleasant noise ▸ *The radio was blaring.*

blast¹ /blɑːst/ *noun*
1 a sudden, strong movement of wind or air ▸ *There was a blast of wind as she opened the door.*
2 a loud sound like the sound made by some instruments which you blow ▸ *The driver gave a blast on his horn.*
3 an explosion ▸ *Many people were killed in the blast.*
4 at full blast as loud as possible ▸ *The television was at full blast.*

blast² *verb*
1 to break something by using an explosion ▸ *They blasted away the rock.*
2 blast off to leave the ground at the beginning of a space flight ▸ *The spaceship blasted off.*

blast-off /ˈblɑːst ɒf/ *noun*
the moment when a spaceship, etc. leaves the ground

blatant /ˈbleɪtənt/ *adjective*
easy to notice, in a way that is shocking ▸ *a blatant lie (adverb:* ***blatantly****)*

blaze¹ /bleɪz/ *noun*
1 a very large, strong fire ▸ *The fire burned slowly at first, but soon became a blaze.*
2 brightly shining light or colour ▸ *The flowers were a blaze of colour.*

blaze² *verb (present participle* ***blazing****, past* ***blazed****)*
to burn strongly ▸ *The fire was blazing.*

blazer /ˈbleɪzəʳ/ *noun*
a short coat that people often wear as part of a uniform ▸ *She was wearing her school blazer.*

bleach¹ /bliːtʃ/ *verb*
1 to make something white ▸ *Did you bleach this tablecloth?*
2 to make something lighter ▸ *Her hair was bleached by the sun.*

bleach² *noun (no plural)*
a liquid or powder used to make things clean or lighter in colour

bleak /bliːk/ *adjective*
unpleasantly cold ▸ *a bleak winter's day*

bleary-eyed /ˌblɪərɪ ˈaɪd/ *adjective*
looking tired or as if you have been crying ▸ *She came down to breakfast looking bleary-eyed.*

bleat¹ /bliːt/ *verb*
to make the sound made by a sheep or goat

bleat² *noun*
the sound made by a sheep or goat

bleed /bliːd/ *verb (past* ***bled*** */bled/)*
to lose blood ▸ *His nose was bleeding.*

bleeding /ˈbliːdɪŋ/ *noun (no plural)*
the flow of blood from a wound ▸ *She pressed on the wound to stop the bleeding.*

bleep /bliːp/ *verb*
to make a high electronic sound ▸ *The alarm clock was bleeping.*

bleeper /ˈbliːpəʳ/ *noun*
a small machine that you carry with you which makes a sound to tell you to telephone someone
SAME MEANING: **pager**

blemish /ˈblemɪʃ/ *noun (plural* ***blemishes****)*
a small mark that spoils something ▸ *My new dress had a small blemish on the collar.*

blend¹ /blend/ *verb*
1 to mix things together ▸ *Blend the sugar and eggs together.*
2 to go well together ▸ *The colours in the room blend nicely.*

blend² *noun*
a mixture produced by blending things together ▸ *my favourite blend of coffee*

blender /'blendəʳ/ *noun*
a small electric machine used for mixing foods or liquids together

bless /bles/ *verb (past* ***blessed*** *or* ***blest*** /blest/*)*
1 to ask God's favour and protection for something ▶ *The priest blessed the new ship.*
2 Bless you! something you say to someone when they SNEEZE

blew /bluː/
the PAST TENSE of the verb **blow**

blind¹ /blaɪnd/ *adjective*
not able to see because you have something wrong with your eyes ▶ *She was born blind.*

blind² *noun*
a piece of material that you can pull down to cover a window
COMPARE: **curtain**

blindfold¹ /'blaɪndfəʊld/ *verb*
to cover someone's eyes with material so that they cannot see

blindfold² *noun*
a piece of material used to cover someone's eyes so they cannot see

blinding /'blaɪndɪŋ/ *adjective*
very bright ▶ *There was a blinding flash as the car exploded.*

blink /blɪŋk/ *verb*
to shut and open your eyes quickly
COMPARE: **wink**

bliss /blɪs/ *noun (no plural)*
complete happiness ▶ *A hot bath and a glass of wine is my idea of bliss.*

blister /'blɪstəʳ/ *noun*
a swelling under your skin, filled with liquid, usually caused by rubbing or burning ▶ *My new shoes have given me blisters.*

blitz /blɪts/ *noun (plural* ***blitzes****)*
a short period when you use a lot of effort to do something ▶ *We had a blitz on cleaning the house.*

blizzard /'blɪzəd/ *noun*
a very bad storm with snow and with very strong winds
COMPARE: **hurricane**

bloated /'bləʊtɪd/ *adjective*
feeling very full and uncomfortable ▶ *I'd eaten so much I felt bloated.*

blob /blɒb/ *noun*
a drop of thick liquid ▶ *a blob* ***of*** *paint*

block¹ /blɒk/ *noun*
1 a solid mass or piece of wood, stone, etc.
2 a large building divided into separate parts ▶ *a block of flats* ▶ *an office block*
3 a large building or group of buildings between two streets ▶ *She lives two blocks away.*

block² *verb*
to stop someone or something from moving beyond a certain point ▶ *A row of police cars was blocking the road.*

blockade /blɒ'keɪd/ *noun*
a situation in which an army or a navy surrounds a place to stop people getting in or out

blockage /'blɒkɪdʒ/ *noun*
something that blocks a tube or pipe

blockbuster /'blɒk,bʌstəʳ/ *noun*
a book or film that is very successful ▶ *the latest Hollywood blockbuster*

block capitals /,blɒk 'kæpɪtlz/ *plural noun*
letters in their large form, for example A, B, C, instead of a, b, c

bloke /bləʊk/ *noun*
a man

blond /blɒnd/ *adjective*
(used of hair) light yellow in colour

blonde¹ /blɒnd/ *adjective*
(used of a woman) having light-coloured hair

blonde² *noun*
a woman with light-coloured hair ▶ *a beautiful blonde*

B

blood /blʌd/ *noun (no plural)*
the red liquid that flows through your body

bloodbath /ˈblʌdbɑːθ/ *noun*
a situation in which a lot of people are killed violently in one place

bloodcurdling /ˈblʌdˌkɜːdlɪŋ/ *adjective*
very frightening ▶ *a bloodcurdling scream*

bloodshed /ˈblʌdʃed/ *noun (no plural)*
the killing of people, especially during a war ▶ *The army has surrendered to avoid further bloodshed.*

bloodshot /ˈblʌdʃɒt/ *adjective*
slightly red

bloodstream /ˈblʌdstriːm/ *noun*
the blood flowing around your body ▶ *The drugs get into your bloodstream very quickly.*

bloodthirsty /ˈblʌdˌθɜːstɪ/ *adjective*
enjoying violence

blood vessel /ˈblʌd ˌvesəl/ *noun*
one of the tubes in your body that blood flows through

bloody /ˈblʌdɪ/ *adjective (**bloodier, bloodiest**)*
1 covered in blood ▶ *Her hands were all bloody.*
2 involving actions that kill or wound a lot of people ▶ *a bloody battle*

bloom[1] /bluːm/ *noun*
1 a flower
2 in full bloom having a lot of open flowers ▶ *The trees are in full bloom.*

bloom[2] *verb*
to open out into flowers ▶ *These roses bloom in the summer.*

blossom /ˈblɒsəm/ *noun (no plural)*
the flowers of a fruit tree ▶ *apple blossom*

blot[1] /blɒt/ *noun*
a dirty mark made by a drop of liquid ▶ *an ink blot*

blot[2] *verb (present participle **blotting**, past **blotted**)*
to dry wet ink with special paper

blotch /blɒtʃ/ *noun (plural **blotches**)*
a mark on something ▶ *There were red blotches on his face.*

blotting paper /ˈblɒtɪŋ ˌpeɪpəʳ/ *noun (no plural)*
a special, soft paper used to dry wet ink

blouse /blaʊz/ *noun*
a shirt for women or girls

blow[1] /bləʊ/ *verb (past tense **blew** /bluː/, past participle **blown** /bləʊn/)*
1 to send out air through your mouth ▶ *Don't blow too hard or you will break the whistle.*
2 to move something with a current of air ▶ *The wind blew his hat off.*
3 (used of wind) to move and make a noise ▶ *The wind was blowing all night.*
4 to send air into something so that it makes a sound ▶ *The guard blew his whistle to call for help.*
5 blow something out to stop something like a candle burning by using a movement of air ▶ *Blow out the candles on your birthday cake!*
6 blow something up (**a**) to fill something with air ▶ *Can you help me blow up the balloons?*
(**b**) to destroy something by making it explode ▶ *The bridge was blown up in the war.*
7 blow your nose to push air out through your nose to clear it

blow[2] *noun*
1 a hard stroke with your hand or a weapon ▶ *a blow on the head*
2 a shock and disappointment ▶ *The news of her death was a terrible blow to us all.*

blow-dry /ˈbleʊ draɪ/ *verb (past **blow-dried**)*
to dry your hair using a HAIRDRYER

blown /bləʊn/
the PAST PARTICIPLE of the verb **blow**

blue /bluː/ *adjective, noun*
the colour of the sky when there are no clouds ▶ *a blue dress* ▶ *the blue of her eyes*

blue-collar /ˌbluː ˈkɒləʳ/ *adjective*
doing jobs such as repairing machines and making things in factories ▶ *blue-collar workers*
COMPARE: **white-collar**

blues /bluːz/ *plural noun*
1 a slow, sad style of music that came from the southern US ▶ *a blues singer*
2 the blues sad feelings

bluff /blʌf/ *verb*
to pretend that you know something or can do something, especially when you want someone to believe you

blunder /ˈblʌndəʳ/ *noun*
a careless or stupid mistake that causes serious problems

blunt /blʌnt/ *adjective*
1 (used of a knife) not able to cut very well
2 (used of a pencil) with a rounded end which needs to be sharpened
OPPOSITE (**1** and **2**): **sharp**

blur /blɜːʳ/ *noun*
something that you cannot see or remember clearly ▶ *The crash is all a blur in my mind.*

blurred /blɜːd/ *adjective*
not easy to see or remember ▶ *The photograph was rather blurred.*

blurt /blɜːt/ *verb*
blurt something out to say something suddenly and without thinking, especially something you should have tried to keep quiet or secret ▶ *Peter blurted out the news before we could stop him.*

blush /blʌʃ/ *verb*
to become red in the face, usually from shame or EMBARRASSMENT

blustery /ˈblʌstərɪ/ *adjective*
very windy ▶ *a blustery winter day*

board[1] /bɔːd/ *noun*
1 a long, thin, flat piece of wood
2 a flat surface used for a special purpose ▶ *a chopping board* ▶ *The teacher wrote the answers on the board.*
3 a group of people who run a company
4 on board on a ship, plane, train, bus, etc. ▶ *Is everyone on board yet?*

board[2] *verb*
1 to get on a ship, plane, train, bus, etc. ▶ *Passengers should board the train now.*
2 to sleep and eat in someone else's home and pay them money

boarder /ˈbɔːdəʳ/ *noun*
a pupil who lives at school and goes home in the holidays

boarding school /ˈbɔːdɪŋ ˌskuːl/ *noun*
a school, usually private, at which pupils live

boardroom /ˈbɔːdrʊm/ *noun*
a room where the people who run a company have meetings

boast /bəʊst/ *verb*
to talk too proudly about yourself ▶ *He boasted that he could run very fast.*
SAME MEANING: **brag**

boastful /ˈbəʊstfəl/ *adjective*
talking too proudly about yourself ▶ *He's very boastful about the money he earns.*

boat /bəʊt/ *noun*
a small, open ship ▶ *a fishing boat* ▶ *We're going by boat.*

bob /bɒb/ *verb (present participle **bobbing**, past **bobbed**)*
to move quickly up and down ▶ *The small boat bobbed up and down on the lake.*

B

bobbed /bɒbd/ *adjective*
(used about hair) the same length all the way around your head

bodily /ˈbɒdɪlɪ/ *adjective*
of the body ▶ *He did not suffer any bodily harm.*

body /ˈbɒdɪ/ *noun (plural* ***bodies****)*
1 the whole of a person or an animal
2 the central part of a person or an animal, not the head, arms, or legs ▶ *He had a cut on his leg and two more on his body.*
3 a dead person or animal ▶ *Her body was found in the woods.*

bodybuilding /ˈbɒdɪˌbɪldɪŋ/ *noun (no plural)*
the activity of doing physical exercises to make your muscles bigger and stronger

bodyguard /ˈbɒdɪgɑːd/ *noun*
a person whose job is to protect someone important

bog¹ /bɒg/ *noun*
an area of soft, wet, muddy ground

bog² *verb*
get bogged down to be unable to make any progress because you have become too involved in dealing with a particular problem ▶ *Let's not get bogged down with minor details.*

bogus /ˈbəʊgəs/ *adjective*
false, but pretending to be real ▶ *a bogus doctor*

boil /bɔɪl/ *verb*
1 to make water or another liquid so hot that it starts to steam ▶ *Boil some water to make a cup of coffee.*
2 to become very hot and start to steam ▶ *The water began to boil.*
3 to cook food in boiling water ▶ *Boil the eggs for five minutes.*

boiler /ˈbɔɪləʳ/ *noun*
a piece of equipment that heats a large amount of water for people to use

boiling /ˈbɔɪlɪŋ/ *adjective*
very hot ▶ *a boiling hot day*

boiling point /ˈbɔɪlɪŋ ˌpɔɪnt/ *noun*
the temperature at which a liquid gets so hot that it starts changing into steam ▶ *The boiling point of water is 100° centigrade.*

boisterous /ˈbɔɪstərəs/ *adjective*
noisy, cheerful, and full of energy ▶ *a boisterous four-year-old*

bold /bəʊld/ *adjective*
not afraid to do dangerous things ▶ *He was very bold and tried to stop the thief.*

bollard /ˈbɒlɑːd/ *noun*
a short, thick post that is fixed in the ground to stop cars going onto a piece of land or road

bolt¹ /bəʊlt/ *noun*
1 a piece of metal or wood used for keeping a door closed
2 a screw with no point which fastens into a NUT and holds two things together

bolt² *verb*
1 to fasten something with a bolt ▶ *Bolt the door, please.*
2 to run away suddenly ▶ *The horse bolted and threw its rider to the ground.*

bomb¹ /bɒm/ *noun*
a container full of a substance that will explode, used as a weapon

bomb² *verb*
to drop bombs on a place ▶ *The airforce bombed two towns.*

bombard /bɒmˈbɑːd/ *verb*
1 to attack a place with guns and bombs ▶ *The city was bombarded from all sides.*
2 to ask someone too many questions, give them too much information, etc. to deal with ▶ *The radio station has been bombarded with enquiries.*

bomber /ˈbɒməʳ/ *noun*
1 a plane that drops bombs
2 a person who puts a bomb somewhere

bond[1] /bɒnd/ *noun*
a shared feeling or interest that makes people feel love and loyalty towards each other ▶ *There's a strong bond between the two brothers.*

bond[2] *verb*
1 to develop a special loving relationship with someone ▶ *It takes time to bond* ***with*** *a new baby.*
2 to join or glue things together firmly

bone /bəʊn/ *noun*
one of the hard, white parts in a person's or an animal's body ▶ *He fell and broke a bone in his leg.*

bone-dry /ˌbəʊn ˈdraɪ/ *adjective*
completely dry ▶ *After the long, hot summer, the ground was bone-dry.*

bonfire /ˈbɒnfaɪəʳ/ *noun*
a big fire in the open air

bonfire night /ˈbɒnfaɪə ˌnaɪt/ *noun*
November 5th, when people in Britain light fires in the open air and have FIREWORKS

bonnet /ˈbɒnɪt/ *noun*
1 a soft hat that you tie under your chin
2 the part of a car's body that covers the engine

bonus /ˈbəʊnəs/ *noun (plural* ***bonuses****)*
1 money that is added to someone's usual pay ▶ *All members of staff get a Christmas bonus.*
2 something good that you did not expect ▶ *Getting a free printer with the computer was a bonus.*

bony /ˈbəʊnɪ/ *adjective (****bonier, boniest****)*
(used of a person's body) so thin that you can see the bones ▶ *bony fingers*

boo[1] /buː/ *verb*
to shout "boo" at someone, especially in a theatre, to show that you did not like their performance

boo[2] *interjection*
1 something you say loudly when you want to surprise someone who does not know you are there
2 something you shout at someone, especially in a theatre, to show that you do not like their performance

booby prize /ˈbuːbɪ praɪz/ *noun*
a prize given as a joke to the person who finishes last in a competition

booby trap /ˈbuːbɪ træp/ *noun*
a bomb or another dangerous thing that is hidden in something that seems harmless

book[1] /bʊk/ *noun*
1 a set of sheets of paper fastened together and with writing on them, for reading ▶ *What book are you reading?*
2 a set of sheets of paper fastened together for writing on ▶ *Write a poem in your exercise book* (=a book to do your school work in).

book[2] *verb*
to arrange to have something that you want to use later ▶ *I've booked tickets for tomorrow night's show.*

bookcase /ˈbʊk-keɪs/ *noun*
a piece of furniture with shelves for books

booking /ˈbʊkɪŋ/ *noun*
an arrangement that you make to have a hotel room, a seat on a plane, etc. at a particular time in the future ▶ *Can I make a booking for this evening?*

booklet /ˈbʊklɪt/ *noun*
a small book that contains information ▶ *a booklet that gives advice to patients with the disease*

bookmaker /ˈbʊkˌmeɪkəʳ/ *noun*
a person whose job is to serve people who want to BET on the result of a game or competition

bookmark /ˈbʊkmɑːk/ *noun*
a piece of paper that you put in a book so that you can find the page you want

B

B

bookshop /ˈbʊkʃɒp/ *noun*
a shop that sells books

book token /ˈbʊk ˌtəʊkən/ *noun*
a card that is given to you as a gift so that you can buy books with it ▶ *My uncle gave me a £10 book token for my birthday.*

boom /buːm/ *noun*
a loud, deep sound

boost¹ /buːst/ *noun*
something that helps you become more successful or feel more confident and happy ▶ *The queen's visit gave a great boost to local people.*

boost² *verb*
to increase the value or amount of something ▶ *The hot weather boosted sales of ice cream.*

boot /buːt/ *noun*
1 a shoe that covers your foot and ankle
2 the part of a car's body where bags, boxes, etc. can be carried

booth /buːð/ *noun*
a small, enclosed area, often used for doing something privately ▶ *a telephone booth* ▶ *a voting booth*

booze /buːz/ *noun (no plural)*
alcoholic drink

border /ˈbɔːdəʳ/ *noun*
1 an edge ▶ *white plates with a blue border*
2 the dividing line between two countries
SAME MEANING (**2**): **frontier**

bore¹ /bɔːʳ/ *verb (present participle* ***boring****, past* ***bored****)*
1 to make someone feel uninterested ▶ *He bored me with his stamp collection.*
2 to make a deep, round hole in something, especially rock or stone ▶ *This machine can bore through solid rock.*

bore² *noun*
an uninteresting or a dull person or thing

bore³
the PAST TENSE of the verb **bear**

bored /bɔːd/ *adjective*
feeling tired and uninterested ▶ *She was bored with her job.*
COMPARE: **fed up**
LOOK AT: **boring**

boredom /ˈbɔːdəm/ *noun (no plural)*
the feeling of being bored

boring /ˈbɔːrɪŋ/ *adjective*
not interesting; dull ▶ *a boring film*

> Do not confuse the adjectives **boring** and **bored**. If something is **boring**, it is not interesting: *a boring lesson.* **Bored** is used to describe the way you feel when something is boring: *The children were bored with the game and did not want to play any more.*

born /bɔːn/ *adjective*
be born to come into the world; to be given life ▶ *The baby was born yesterday.*

borne /bɔːn/
the PAST PARTICIPLE of the verb **bear**

borrow /ˈbɒrəʊ/ *verb*
to use something which belongs to someone else. You usually ask permission and say when you will return the thing ▶ *Can I borrow your bicycle until Saturday?*

> Compare the verbs **borrow** and **lend**. If you **lend** something to a person, you let them use it for a while. If you **borrow** something from someone, you take it from them, knowing that you will give it back to them later. The verb **lend** often has two objects (to lend something to somebody), but **borrow** just has one (to borrow something): *Will you lend* ***me*** *some money?* ▶ *Can I borrow some money?*

bosom /ˈbʊzəm/ *noun*
a woman's breast or breasts

boss[1] /bɒs/ *noun (plural **bosses**)*
a person who is in charge and tells other people what work to do

boss[2] *verb*
boss someone about to tell someone what to do, usually by giving them too many orders ▶ *My brother's always bossing me about.*

bossy /ˈbɒsɪ/ *adjective (**bossier, bossiest**)*
liking to give orders to other people ▶ *a bossy older sister*

botany /ˈbɒtənɪ/ *noun (no plural)*
the scientific study of plants

both /bəʊθ/ *adjective, pronoun, adverb*
this one and that one; the two ▶ *Hold the dish with both hands.* ▶ *We both like dancing.*

bother[1] /ˈbɒðəʳ/ *verb*
1 to interrupt someone and annoy them ▶ *I'm sorry to bother you, but I need some help.* ▶ *Don't bother your father now – he's very busy.*
2 to worry someone ▶ *I always know when something is bothering him.*
3 can't be bothered to not want to do something because it is too much effort ▶ *I can't be bothered to go out tonight.*
4 not bother not to make the effort to do something ▶ *Don't bother to dry the plates.* ▶ *He didn't even bother to say goodbye.*

bother[2] *noun (no plural)*
something that causes difficulty ▶ *We had a little bother when the policeman stopped us.*

bottle[1] /ˈbɒtl/ *noun*
a tall, round glass or plastic container, with a narrow neck
COMPARE: **jar**

bottle[2] *verb (present participle **bottling**, past **bottled**)*
to put something into bottles ▶ *This is where they bottle the milk.*

bottle bank /ˈbɒtl bæŋk/ *noun*
a place where old glass bottles are taken so that the glass can be used again

bottled /ˈbɒtld/ *adjective*
kept or sold in bottles

bottleneck /ˈbɒtlnek/ *noun*
a place in a road where the traffic cannot pass easily, so that cars are delayed

bottom /ˈbɒtəm/ *noun*
1 the lowest part of something ▶ *at the bottom **of** the page*
2 the base of something ▶ *The price is on the bottom **of** the box.*
3 the lowest position in something, e.g. a class ▶ *He's not very good at maths – he's always at the bottom **of** the class.*
OPPOSITE: (**1, 2,** and **3**): **top**
4 the part of the body that you sit on ▶ *He fell on his bottom.*

bought /bɔːt/
the PAST TENSE and PAST PARTICIPLE of the verb **buy**

boulder /ˈbəʊldəʳ/ *noun*
a large rock

boulevard /ˈbuːlvɑːd/ *noun*
a wide road in a town or city, usually with trees along the sides

bounce /baʊns/ *verb (present participle **bouncing**, past **bounced**)*
1 to spring back after hitting something or falling on something ▶ *The baby was bouncing on the bed.*
2 to throw something, e.g. a ball, against something, so that it springs back ▶ *He bounced the ball against the wall.*

bouncer /ˈbaʊnsəʳ/ *noun*
a person whose job is to keep people who behave badly out of a club or bar

bouncy /ˈbaʊnsɪ/ *adjective (**bouncier, bounciest**)*

able to spring back easily after hitting something or after being hit by something ▶ *a bouncy ball* ▶ *a bouncy bed*

bound[1] /baʊnd/ *verb*
to jump around ▶ *The young animals were bounding about the field.*

bound[2] *noun*
a big jump

bound[3]
the PAST TENSE and PAST PARTICIPLE of the verb **bind**

boundary /ˈbaʊndərɪ/ *noun (plural **boundaries**)*
the dividing line between two places ▶ *the boundary between the two gardens*
COMPARE: **border**

bound to /ˈbaʊnd tuː/ *adjective*
be bound to to be certain to do something or be certain to happen ▶ *You're bound to pass the exams – you've worked very hard.*

bouquet /bəʊˈkeɪ/ *noun*
a number of flowers fastened together that you give to someone

bout /baʊt/ *noun*
a short period of illness ▶ *a bout **of** flu*

boutique /buːˈtiːk/ *noun*
a small shop that sells fashionable clothes

bow[1] /baʊ/ *verb*
to bend the top part of your body forward to show respect ▶ *Everyone bowed to the President.*

bow[2] /baʊ/ *noun*
an act of bending your body or your head forward to show respect

bow[3] /bəʊ/ *noun*
1 a piece of wood held in a curve by a string, used for shooting arrows
2 a long, thin piece of wood with tight strings fastened along it, used for playing musical instruments like the VIOLIN
3 a knot used for tying shoes ▶ *She tied the ribbon in a bow.*

bowel /ˈbaʊəl/ *noun*
the part inside your body that carries solid waste food away from the stomach and out of the body

bowl /bəʊl/ *noun*
a deep, round dish or container ▶ *Fill the bowl with water.*
COMPARE: **plate**

bow-legged /ˌbəʊ ˈlegɪd/ *adjective*
having legs that curve outwards at the knees

bowling /ˈbəʊlɪŋ/ *noun (no plural)*
an indoor game in which you roll a heavy ball along a wooden track in order to knock over pieces of wood

bow tie /ˌbəʊ ˈtaɪ/ *noun*
a man's tie fastened in the shape of a BOW

box[1] /bɒks/ *noun (plural **boxes**)*
a container with straight sides, usually made of cardboard or wood ▶ *a box of matches*

box[2] *verb*
to fight with tightly closed hands, usually for sport

boxer /ˈbɒksəʳ/ *noun*
a man who fights with tightly closed hands, for sport

boxer shorts /ˈbɒksə ʃɔːts/ *plural noun*
loose cotton underwear for men

boxing /ˈbɒksɪŋ/ *noun (no plural)*
the sport of fighting with tightly closed hands

Boxing Day /ˈbɒksɪŋ ˌdeɪ/ *noun*
the day after Christmas

box office /ˈbɒks ˌɒfɪs/ *noun*
a place in a theatre or cinema where you can buy tickets

boy /bɔɪ/ *noun*
a male child ▶ *They have five children: three boys and two girls.*

boycott /ˈbɔɪkɒt/ *verb*
to refuse to buy or use something, as

a protest ▶ *The US has threatened to boycott French wine.*

boyfriend /ˈbɔɪfrend/ *noun*
a boy or man you have a romantic relationship with ▶ *Can my boyfriend come to the party?*

boyhood /ˈbɔɪhʊd/ *noun (no plural)*
the time during a man's life when he is a boy

boyish /ˈbɔɪ-ɪʃ/ *adjective*
looking or behaving like an attractive young man ▶ *a slim, boyish figure*

bra /brɑː/ *noun*
a piece of clothing that women wear under other clothes to support their breasts

brace /breɪs/ *noun*
a wire which some children wear inside their mouths to make their teeth straight

bracelet /ˈbreɪslɪt/ *noun*
a band or chain that you wear as an ornament round your wrist

braces /ˈbreɪsɪz/ *plural noun*
cloth bands that you wear over your shoulders to hold up your trousers

brackets /ˈbrækɪts/ *plural noun*
the small, curved lines ( ) that you sometimes use in writing to add information ▶ *Put the dates in brackets.*
SAME MEANING: **parentheses**

brag /bræg/ *verb (present participle* ***bragging,*** *past* ***bragged)***
to talk too proudly about things you have done or about your possessions ▶ *He bragged that he had passed the exam easily.* ▶ *He was bragging* ***about*** *his new expensive car.*
SAME MEANING: **boast**

braid /breɪd/ *noun (no plural)*
threads woven together and used to decorate clothes ▶ *gold braid*

braille /breɪl/ *noun (no plural)*
a type of printing that blind people can read by touching the page

brain /breɪn/ *noun*
the part inside your head with which you think

brainwash /ˈbreɪnwɒʃ/ *verb*
to force someone to believe something that is not true by telling them many times that it is true ▶ *People are brainwashed into believing that being fat is some kind of crime.*

brainwave /ˈbreɪnweɪv/ *noun*
a very good idea that you have suddenly

brainy /ˈbreɪnɪ/ *adjective (****brainier, brainiest****)*
clever and quick at doing school work
SAME MEANING: **bright**

brake[1] /breɪk/ *noun*
the part of a bicycle, car, train, etc. that you use to stop it or make it go more slowly

brake[2] *verb (present participle* ***braking,*** *past* ***braked)***
to make a bicycle, car, train, etc. stop or go more slowly by using the brake ▶ *The driver braked quickly to avoid an accident.*

bran /bræn/ *noun (no plural)*
the crushed skin of wheat and other grain, often used in bread

branch /brɑːntʃ/ *noun (plural* ***branches)***
1 a part of a tree that grows from a trunk
COMPARE: **twig**
2 one part or one office of a business ▶ *The bank has branches in all the big towns.*

brand /brænd/ *noun*
the name of a particular kind of goods made by one company ▶ *What brand of soap do you like?*

brandish /ˈbrændɪʃ/ *verb*
to wave a weapon around in a dangerous and threatening way ▶ *He ran into the room brandishing a knife.*

B

brand-new /ˌbrænd ˈnjuː/ *adjective*
completely new; never used before
▶ *a brand-new car*

brandy /ˈbrændɪ/ *noun*
1 *(no plural)* a strong alcoholic drink
2 *(plural* ***brandies****)* a glass of this drink ▶ *Can I have two brandies, please?*

brash /bræʃ/ *adjective*
behaving too confidently and speaking too loudly ▶ *a brash young salesperson*

brass /brɑːs/ *noun (no plural)*
a very hard, yellow metal which shines brightly, made by mixing COPPER and ZINC ▶ *ornaments made of brass*

brat /bræt/ *noun*
a badly behaved child ▶ *a spoilt brat*

bravado /brəˈvɑːdəʊ/ *noun (no plural)*
behaviour that is intended to show that you are brave and confident, even when you are not

brave /breɪv/ *adjective*
not afraid or not showing fear
▶ *a brave fireman (adverb:* ***bravely****)*

bravery /ˈbreɪvərɪ/ *noun (no plural)*
willingness to do dangerous things without feeling afraid ▶ *The fireman was praised for his bravery.*
SAME MEANING: **courage**
OPPOSITE: **cowardice**

bravo /ˈbrɑːvəʊ/ *interjection*
a word you shout to show that you like or approve of something

brawl /brɔːl/ *noun*
a noisy fight

breach /briːtʃ/ *noun (plural* ***breaches****)*
the act of breaking a law, rule, or agreement ▶ *If he leaves, he will be in breach of his contract.*

bread /bred/ *noun (no plural)*
a food made by mixing flour, water, and YEAST and then baking it ▶ *a loaf of bread*

breadth /bredθ/ *noun (no plural)*
the distance from one side of something to the other ▶ *What's the breadth of this river?*

breadwinner /ˈbredˌwɪnəʳ/ *noun*
the person in a family who earns most of the money that the family needs ▶ *Mum was the breadwinner after dad became ill.*

break[1] /breɪk/ *verb (past tense* ***broke*** */brəʊk/, past participle* ***broken*** */ˈbrəʊkən/)*
1 to make something separate into pieces ▶ *He broke the window with his football.*
2 to separate into pieces ▶ *The plate fell on the floor and broke.*
3 to make something not work
▶ *Don't play with the radio – you'll break it!*
4 break down (used about cars or machines) to stop working ▶ *My car broke down on the way to work.*
5 break in to get inside a place using force ▶ *Someone broke in through the window* (=broke the window to get inside the building).
6 break into something to get inside a place, e.g. a building or something that is locked, by using force ▶ *The thief broke into my drawer and stole my money.*
7 break the law to do something that the law says you must not do
8 break out (used especially about fighting or fire) to start suddenly
▶ *The fire broke out at 2 o'clock in the morning.*
9 break a promise not to do something that you promised you would do
10 break up (**a**) to finish a relationship with a boyfriend or girlfriend ▶ *John and Sarah broke up last week.*
(**b**) to stop going to school because the holidays are starting ▶ *We break up next week.*

break² *noun*
1 an opening in something made by breaking it ▶ *a break in the clouds*
2 a short rest ▶ *Let's have a break.*

breakable /ˈbreɪkəbəl/ *adjective*
likely to break

breakage /ˈbreɪkɪdʒ/ *noun*
something that has been broken ▶ *All breakages must be paid for.*

breakdown /ˈbreɪkdaʊn/ *noun*
when a car or machine stops working

breakfast /ˈbrekfəst/ *noun*
the first meal of the day

break-in /ˈbreɪk ɪn/ *noun*
the act of breaking a door or window in order to enter a building and steal things ▶ *There was a break-in at the hotel over the weekend.*

breakthrough /ˈbreɪkθruː/ *noun*
an important new discovery or development ▶ *a breakthrough in the treatment of cancer*

breakup /ˈbreɪkʌp/ *noun*
1 the process of ending a marriage or romantic relationship
2 the process of separating an organization or a country into smaller parts ▶ *the fighting that followed the breakup of Yugoslavia*

breast /brest/ *noun*
1 one of the two parts on the front of a woman's body that can produce milk
2 the top part of the front of a person's body
SAME MEANING (**2**): **chest**

breaststroke /ˈbrestˌstrəʊk/ *noun (no plural)*
a way of swimming by pulling the water back with your arms

breath /breθ/ *noun*
1 the air that you take in and let out through your nose and mouth ▶ *He took a deep breath and jumped into the water.*
2 a breath of fresh air a bit of clean air outside ▶ *Let's go to the park for a breath of fresh air.*
3 hold your breath to stop breathing for a little while, especially when you want to swim underwater ▶ *How long can you hold your breath?*
4 be out of breath not to be able to breathe easily for a little while, e.g. after running

breathe /briːð/ *verb (present participle* ***breathing****, past* ***breathed****)*
to take air into your body and let it out through your nose and mouth

breather /ˈbriːðəʳ/ *noun*
a short rest ▶ *Let's stop for a breather.*

breathless /ˈbreθləs/ *adjective*
having difficulty breathing, especially after exercise

breathtaking /ˈbreθˌteɪkɪŋ/ *adjective*
very beautiful, impressive, exciting, or surprising ▶ *a breathtaking view of the Grand Canyon*

breed¹ /briːd/ *verb (past* ***bred*** */bred/)*
1 (used about animals) to produce young ▶ *Some animals will not breed in cages.*
COMPARE: **mate**
2 to keep animals so that they will produce young ones ▶ *He breeds cattle.*

breed² *noun*
a type of animal ▶ *a breed of cattle*

breeze /briːz/ *noun*
a light wind ▶ *a cool breeze*

breezy /ˈbriːzɪ/ *adjective (****breezier, breeziest****)*
with quite a strong wind ▶ *a warm but rather breezy day*

brew /bruː/ *verb*
1 to make tea, leaving it in the pot until the taste develops ▶ *Let the tea brew for a few minutes.*
2 to make beer

B

B

3 be brewing to be going to happen ▶ *I think a storm is brewing.*

brewery /ˈbruːərɪ/ *noun (plural* ***breweries****)*
a place where beer is made, or a company that makes beer

bribe[1] /braɪb/ *verb (present participle* ***bribing****, past* ***bribed****)*
to offer to give someone money or a present if they help you by doing something that is not honest or legal ▶ *He tried to bribe the policeman to let him go.*

bribe[2] *noun*
money or a present which you give to someone if they help you by doing something that is not honest or legal ▶ *A policeman should never take bribes.*

bribery /ˈbraɪbərɪ/ *noun (no plural)*
the act of offering money or a present to someone, or accepting money or a present from them if they help you by doing something that is not honest or legal

brick /brɪk/ *noun*
a block of baked clay, used for building

bridal /ˈbraɪdl/ *adjective*
connected with a bride or a wedding ▶ *a bridal shop*

bride /braɪd/ *noun*
a woman who is going to get married, or who has just got married

bridegroom /ˈbraɪdgruːm/ *noun*
a man who is going to get married, or who has just got married
SAME MEANING: **groom**

bridesmaid /ˈbraɪdzˌmeɪd/ *noun*
a girl or woman who helps a bride at her wedding
COMPARE: **best man**

bridge /brɪdʒ/ *noun*
a road or railway line built over something ▶ *a bridge across the river*

bridle /ˈbraɪdl/ *noun*
leather bands put on a horse's head to control its movement

brief /briːf/ *adjective*
lasting a short time ▶ *a brief meeting (adverb:* ***briefly****)*

briefcase /ˈbriːfkeɪs/ *noun*
a thin, flat case for carrying papers or books
COMPARE: **suitcase**

briefs /briːfs/ *plural noun*
underwear that you wear between your waist and the top of your legs ▶ *a pair of cotton briefs*

brigade /brɪˈgeɪd/ *noun*
a large group of soldiers who are part of an army

bright /braɪt/ *adjective*
1 sending out a strong, shining light ▶ *bright sunlight*
2 having a strong, clear colour ▶ *My favourite colour is bright yellow.*
3 quick at learning things; clever ▶ *a bright child*
SAME MEANING (3): **brainy**

brighten /ˈbraɪtn/ *verb*
brighten up (used about the weather) to become more sunny or lighter and better ▶ *It should brighten up later.*

brilliant /ˈbrɪljənt/ *adjective*
1 very clever ▶ *a brilliant idea* ▶ *a brilliant student*
2 Brilliant! something you say when you think something is very good ▶ *"I got the job." "Brilliant!"*
3 (used about colours and light) very bright

brim /brɪm/ *noun*
1 the edge of a cup, glass, or bowl
2 the part of a hat that stands out around the sides

bring /brɪŋ/ *verb (past* ***brought*** */brɔːt/)*
1 to carry something to someone or towards a place ▶ *Bring me the ball.*

▶ *You can take that book home, but bring it back* (= return it) *tomorrow, please.*
COMPARE: **take**
LOOK AT: **fetch**
2 to take someone with you to a place ▶ *Bring your brother to the party.*
3 bring someone up to care for and educate a child

brink /brɪŋk/ *noun*
be on the brink of something if you are on the brink of something exciting or terrible, it will happen soon ▶ *The country is on the brink of war.*

brisk /brɪsk/ *adjective*
quick and active ▶ *a brisk walk*

bristle /ˈbrɪsəl/ *noun*
one of many short, stiff hairs, wires, etc. growing or placed together ▶ *the bristles on a toothbrush*

British /ˈbrɪtɪʃ/ *adjective*
of, about, or from Great Britain

brittle /ˈbrɪtl/ *adjective*
hard, but easily broken ▶ *brittle glass*

broach /brəʊtʃ/ *verb*
to mention a subject that may be embarrassing or unpleasant ▶ *Parents often find it hard to broach the subject of sex.*

broad /brɔːd/ *adjective*
wide ▶ *broad shoulders*
OPPOSITE: **narrow**

broadcast[1] /ˈbrɔːdkɑːst/ *verb (past* ***broadcast****)*
to send out PROGRAMMES by radio or television to the public ▶ *The new programme will be broadcast at 7 o'clock.*

broadcast[2] *noun*
a PROGRAMME that is sent out on the radio or television ▶ *a news broadcast*

broaden /ˈbrɔːdn/ *verb*
1 to make something include more kinds of things or people ▶ *The course will broaden your knowledge of computers.*
2 broaden out to become wider ▶ *The river broadens out here.*

broadly /ˈbrɔːdlɪ/ *adverb*
in a general way ▶ *I broadly agree with what you are saying.*

broadminded /ˌbrɔːdˈmaɪndɪd/ *adjective*
willing to accept behaviour or ideas that are different from your own

broccoli /ˈbrɒkəlɪ/ *noun (no plural)*
a green vegetable with green or purple flowers that you cook

brochure /ˈbrəʊʃəʳ/ *noun*
a thin book that gives information or advertises something ▶ *a holiday brochure*

broke /brəʊk/
the PAST TENSE of the verb **break**

broken[1] /ˈbrəʊkən/
the PAST PARTICIPLE of the verb **break**

broken[2] *adjective*
1 in pieces ▶ *a broken window*
2 not working ▶ *a broken clock*

broken-hearted /ˌbrəʊkən ˈhɑːtɪd/ *adjective*
very sad, especially because someone you love has died or left you

broker[1] /ˈbrəʊkəʳ/ *noun*
a person whose job is to buy and sell property, insurance, etc. for other people

broker[2] *verb*
to arrange the details of a deal, plan, etc. so that everyone can agree to it ▶ *an agreement brokered by the UN*

bronze /brɒnz/ *noun (no plural)*
a hard metal, made by mixing COPPER and TIN

brooch /brəʊtʃ/ *noun (plural* ***brooches****)*
an ornament that women sometimes pin on their clothes
COMPARE: **badge**

B

B

brood /bruːd/ *verb*
to think about something angrily or sadly for a long time ▶ *You can't just sit there brooding over your problems.*

broom /bruːm/ *noun*
a brush with a long handle

brothel /ˈbrɒθəl/ *noun*
a house where men pay to have sex with women

brother /ˈbrʌðəʳ/ *noun*
a boy or man with the same parents as another person ▶ *Peter is my brother.*
COMPARE: **sister**

brother-in-law /ˈbrʌðər ɪn lɔː/ *noun (plural **brothers-in-law**)*
1 the brother of your wife or husband
2 the husband of your sister

brought /brɔːt/
the PAST TENSE and PAST PARTICIPLE of the verb **bring**

brow /braʊ/ *noun*
the part of your face between your eyes and your hair

brown¹ /braʊn/ *adjective, noun*
a dark colour like coffee or earth ▶ *a brown chair* ▶ *the brown of her eyes*

browse /braʊz/ *verb (present participle **browsing**, past **browsed**)*
1 to spend time looking at things in a shop without buying anything and without hurrying
2 to look through a book or magazine without reading it carefully
3 to look for information on the INTERNET

browser /ˈbraʊzəʳ/ *noun*
computer SOFTWARE that you use to look at information on the INTERNET

bruise¹ /bruːz/ *noun*
a mark left on your skin after a blow or when you have fallen down

bruise² *verb (present participle **bruising**, past **bruised**)*
to mark someone's skin with a bruise ▶ *She fell and bruised her knee*

brunette /bruːˈnet/ *noun*
a woman who has dark brown hair

brunt /brʌnt/ *noun*
bear the brunt of something to suffer the worst part of something unpleasant ▶ *The south coast bore the brunt of the storm.*

brush¹ /brʌʃ/ *noun (plural **brushes**)*
a group of strong hairs on the end of a handle that can be used for cleaning, painting, tidying your hair, etc.

brush² *verb*
to clean or tidy something with a brush ▶ *Have you brushed your hair?*

brussels sprout /ˌbrʌsəlz ˈspraʊt/ *noun*
a small, round, green vegetable

brutal /ˈbruːtl/ *adjective*
very cruel and violent ▶ *a brutal murder (adverb: **brutally**)*

brute¹ /bruːt/ *noun*
1 a cruel, violent man
2 a large, strong animal

brute² *adjective*
brute force, brute strength physical strength that is used instead of gentle, clever methods ▶ *He uses brute force to get what he wants.*

BSc /ˌbiː es ˈsiː/ *noun*
BACHELOR OF SCIENCE; a university degree in a science subject ▶ *He has a BSc in Chemistry.*

bubble¹ /ˈbʌbəl/ *noun*
a hollow ball of liquid containing air or gas ▶ *soap bubbles*

bubble² *verb (present participle **bubbling**, past **bubbled**)*
to make balls of air or gas ▶ *The water was bubbling gently in the pan.*

bubbly /ˈbʌblɪ/ *adjective (**bubblier**, **bubbliest**)*
1 full of bubbles

2 cheerful and full of energy ▶ *a bubbly personality*

buck /bʌk/ *noun*
a male deer or rabbit

bucket /ˈbʌkɪt/ *noun*
a container made of metal or plastic, with a handle, for holding or carrying water

buckle /ˈbʌkəl/ *noun*
a fastener used for joining the ends of a belt

bud /bʌd/ *noun*
a young flower or leaf before it opens

Buddhism /ˈbʊdɪzəm/ *noun (no plural)*
the religion based on the teachings of Buddha

Buddhist /ˈbʊdɪst/ *noun*
a person who follows the teachings of Buddha

buddy /ˈbʌdɪ/ *noun (plural* ***buddies****)*
a friend

budge /bʌdʒ/ *verb (present participle* ***budging****, past* ***budged****)*
to make something heavy move a little ▶ *I can't budge this rock.*

budget[1] /ˈbʌdʒɪt/ *noun*
a plan of how to spend money ▶ *a government's budget*

budget[2] *verb*
to plan how much money you have to spend on certain things

budgie /ˈbʌdʒɪ/ *noun*
a small, brightly coloured bird, usually kept in a cage as a pet

buffet /ˈbʊfeɪ/ *noun*
a meal in which people serve themselves at a table and then move away to eat

bug /bʌg/ *noun*
1 a small insect
2 a very small living thing that can get into your body and make you feel unwell ▶ *I can't go to school this week because I've got a bug.*

buggy /ˈbʌgɪ/ *noun (plural* ***buggies****)*
a small, folding chair on wheels, in which you can push a small child
SAME MEANING: **pushchair**

bugle /ˈbjuːgəl/ *noun*
a musical instrument that is played by blowing and is used especially by the army

build[1] /bɪld/ *verb (past* ***built*** */bɪlt/)*
to make something by putting pieces together ▶ *The house is built of brick.*

build[2] *noun (no plural)*
the size and shape of someone's body ▶ *Maggie is tall with a slim build.*

builder /ˈbɪldəʳ/ *noun*
a person whose job it is to make houses and other buildings
COMPARE: **architect**

building /ˈbɪldɪŋ/ *noun*
something with a roof and walls, e.g. a house or an office

building society /ˈbɪldɪŋ səˌsaɪətɪ/ *noun (plural* ***building societies****)*
a type of bank where you can save money or borrow money to buy a house

built /bɪlt/
the PAST TENSE and PAST PARTICIPLE of the verb **build**

bulb /bʌlb/ *(also* ***light bulb****) noun*
the glass part of an electric light that shines when it is turned on

bulge[1] /bʌldʒ/ *verb (present participle* ***bulging****, past* ***bulged****)*
to swell out ▶ *His pocket was bulging with sweets.*

bulge[2] *noun*
a swelling shape

bulk /bʌlk/ *noun*
1 the bulk of something the main or largest part of something ▶ *The bulk of the work has already been done.*
2 in bulk in large quantities ▶ *It's cheaper to buy things in bulk.*

bulky /ˈbʌlkɪ/ *adjective (**bulkier, bulkiest**)*
having a large, difficult shape
▶ *I can't carry that box – it's too bulky.*

bull /bʊl/ *noun*
the male of the cow family

bulldog /ˈbʌldɒg/ *noun*
a short, strong dog with a thick neck and short legs

bulldozer /ˈbʊldəʊzəʳ/ *noun*
a powerful machine that moves earth to make land flat

bullet /ˈbʊlɪt/ *noun*
a piece of metal that is fired from a gun

bulletin /ˈbʊlətɪn/ *noun*
a short news report ▶ *Our next bulletin is at 6 o'clock.*

bulletin board /ˈbʊlətɪn ˌbɔːd/ *noun*
a place on a computer system where a group of people can leave and read messages

bullock /ˈbʊlək/ *noun*
a young male cow which cannot be the father of young ones

bully¹ /ˈbʊlɪ/ *noun (plural **bullies**)*
a person who likes to hurt weaker people or make them afraid

bully² *verb (past **bullied**)*
to hurt people who are not as strong as you, or make them afraid

bum /bʌm/ *noun*
the part of your body that you sit on

bump¹ /bʌmp/ *verb*
1 to knock something by accident
▶ *I bumped my knee on the chair.*
▶ *He bumped into a tree and hit his head.*
2 bump into someone to meet someone by chance ▶ *I bumped into John in town.*

bump² *noun*
a round swelling on your body where you have knocked it ▶ *He had a bump on his head.*

bumper /ˈbʌmpəʳ/ *noun*
a bar at the front and back of a car to protect it from knocks

bumpy /ˈbʌmpɪ/ *adjective (**bumpier, bumpiest**)*
rough; not smooth ▶ *a bumpy road*

bun /bʌn/ *noun*
a small, round, sweet cake

bunch /bʌntʃ/ *noun (plural **bunches**)*
several things of the same kind fastened together ▶ *a bunch **of** flowers*

bundle /ˈbʌndl/ *noun*
a number of things held together so that you can carry them or put them somewhere ▶ *a bundle **of** clothes*

bung /bʌŋ/ *verb*
to put something somewhere
▶ *Just bung your coat on the chair.*

bungalow /ˈbʌŋgələʊ/ *noun*
a house that is all on the same level as the ground

bunk /bʌŋk/ *noun*
a narrow bed which is fixed to the wall on a ship or train

bunk bed /ˈbʌŋk bed/ *noun*
one of two beds that are put one on top of another and used especially for children to sleep in

bunker /ˈbʌŋkəʳ/ *noun*
a strongly built room or building where people can shelter from bombs

buoy /bɔɪ/ *noun*
a floating object used to show ships where there are rocks

burden /ˈbɜːdn/ *noun*
something heavy that you have to carry ▶ *The donkey carried its burden up the mountain.*

bureau /ˈbjʊərəʊ/ *noun (plural **bureaux** /ˈbjʊərəʊz/)*
1 an office or organization that collects or provides information
▶ *an employment bureau*

2 a government department, or part of one ▶ *the Federal Bureau of Investigation*
3 a piece of furniture with drawers and a sloping lid that you can open and use as a desk

bureaucracy /bjʊə'rɒkrəsɪ/ *noun (no plural)*
an official system that annoys and confuses people because it has too many rules

bureaucratic /ˌbjʊərə'krætɪk/ *adjective*
involving a lot of official rules and processes in a way that annoys people

bureaux /'bjʊərəʊz/
the plural of **bureau**

burger /'bɜːgəʳ/ *noun*
meat that has been cut into very small pieces and then made into a round, flat shape before being cooked

burglar /'bɜːgləʳ/ *noun*
a person who enters buildings, usually by force, to steal things
COMPARE: **robber, thief**

burglary /'bɜːglərɪ/ *noun (plural **burglaries**)*
the crime of entering a building, usually by force, and stealing things

burgle /'bɜːgəl/ *verb (present participle **burgling**, past **burgled**)*
to enter a building, usually by force, and steal things from it

burial /'berɪəl/ *noun*
the ceremony at which a dead person is put into the ground

burn[1] /bɜːn/ *verb (past **burned** or **burnt** /bɜːnt/)*
1 to damage or destroy something with fire, or to be damaged or destroyed in this way ▶ *We burned the old furniture.*
2 to hurt yourself or a part of your body with something very hot ▶ *I've burned my fingers.*
3 **burn down** (used about a building) to be destroyed completely by fire ▶ *The cinema burned down last year.*

burn[2] *noun*
a wound or mark on your body caused by fire or by touching something very hot ▶ *a burn on his arm*

burnt /bɜːnt/
the PAST TENSE and PAST PARTICIPLE of the verb **burn**

burp /bɜːp/ *verb*
to let air come out noisily from your stomach through your mouth
SAME MEANING: **belch**

burrow /'bʌrəʊ/ *noun*
a hole in the ground made as a home by some small animals, e.g. rabbits

burst /bɜːst/ *verb (past **burst**)*
1 to break apart because of too much pressure inside ▶ *The bag will burst if you put any more things in it.*
2 to make something break apart by putting too much pressure inside it ▶ *Don't put any more air in the tyre or you'll burst it* (=make it explode).
3 **burst into tears** to start crying suddenly
4 **burst out laughing** to start laughing loudly and suddenly

bury /'berɪ/ *verb (past **buried**)*
1 to put a dead body into the ground
2 to put or hide something in the ground ▶ *The dog buried the bone.*

bus /bʌs/ *noun (plural **buses**)*
a large vehicle that takes people from one place to another ▶ *Let's go into town by bus.*

bus driver /'bʌs ˌdraɪvəʳ/ *noun*
a person whose job is driving buses

bush /bʊʃ/ *noun (plural **bushes**)*
a small tree

bushy /'bʊʃɪ/ *adjective (**bushier, bushiest**)*
growing thickly ▶ *a bushy tail*

B

busily /ˈbɪzɪlɪ/ *adverb*
done with great activity and interest ▶ *busily planning the wedding*

business /ˈbɪznəs/ *noun*
1 *(plural* ***businesses****)* a company that provides a service or sells things to earn money ▶ *He has a furniture business in town.*
2 *(no plural)* making, buying, and selling things ▶ *Business is good this year* (=we are earning a lot of money).
3 **mind your own business** a rude way of telling someone that you are not going to answer their questions about a particular matter ▶ *"Who are you going to the party with?" "Mind your own business."*
4 **none of your business** a rude way of telling someone that something is not their concern ▶ *It's none of your business how she spends her money.*

businesslike /ˈbɪznəslaɪk/ *adjective*
sensible and practical in the way you do things ▶ *a businesslike manner*

businessman /ˈbɪznəsmən/ *noun (plural* ***businessmen*** */-mən/)*
a man who works in business, especially one who owns a company or helps to run it

businesswoman /ˈbɪznəsˌwʊmən/ *noun (plural* ***businesswomen*** */-ˌwɪmɪn/)*
a woman who works in business, especially one who owns a company or helps to run it

bus stop /ˈbʌs stɒp/ *noun*
a place where buses stop for people to get off and on

bust¹ /bʌst/ *verb (past* ***bust*** *or* ***busted****)*
to break something ▶ *Someone's bust the photocopier again!*

bust² *noun*
1 a woman's breasts, or the measurement around a woman's breasts and back
2 a MODEL of someone's head, shoulders, and upper chest ▶ *a bust of Shakespeare*

bust³ *adjective*
1 **go bust** a business that goes bust has to close because it has lost so much money
2 not working ▶ *This TV is bust.*

bustle¹ /ˈbʌsəl/ *noun*
busy and noisy activity

bustle² *verb (present participle* ***bustling****, past* ***bustled****)*
to move around and do things in a quick, busy way ▶ *Linda was bustling around in the kitchen.*

busy /ˈbɪzɪ/ *adjective (****busier, busiest****)*
1 working; not free; having a lot to do ▶ *He is busy at the moment, I'm afraid.* ▶ *He's busy writing letters.*
2 full of activity ▶ *a busy day* ▶ *a busy street*

but /bət; *strong* bʌt/ *conjunction*
a word you use when you are saying that although one thing is true, another thing which is opposite to it is also true ▶ *They are poor, but happy.* ▶ *I'd like to come, but I can't.*

butcher /ˈbʊtʃəʳ/ *noun*
1 a person who sells meat
2 **butcher's** a shop that sells meat

butt¹ /bʌt/ *noun*
1 the person that other people often make jokes about ▶ *Why am I always the butt of their jokes?*
2 the end of a cigarette after it has been smoked

butt² *verb*
butt in to interrupt a conversation ▶ *Sorry, I didn't mean to butt in.*

butter /ˈbʌtəʳ/ *noun (no plural)*
yellow fat made from milk ▶ *bread and butter*

butterfly /ˈbʌtəflaɪ/ *noun (plural* ***butterflies****)*
an insect that has delicate wings with

bright colours on them
COMPARE: **moth**

buttocks /ˈbʌtəks/ *plural noun*
the part of your body that you sit on

button /ˈbʌtn/ *noun*
1 a small, round object that you push through a hole to fasten clothes ▶ *Do your buttons up; it's cold.*
2 a round object that you push to start or stop a machine

buttonhole /ˈbʌtnhəʊl/ *noun*
the hole that a button goes through

buy /baɪ/ *verb (past **bought** /bɔːt/)*
to get something by paying money for it ▶ *I bought a new radio.*
COMPARE: **sell**

buyer /ˈbaɪəʳ/ *noun*
a person who is buying something, especially something expensive ▶ *We've found a buyer for our house.*

buzz /bʌz/ *verb*
1 to make a low, steady noise like the sound a bee makes
2 buzz off a rude way of telling someone to go away ▶ *Buzz off and leave me alone!*

buzzer /ˈbʌzəʳ/ *noun*
a piece of electric equipment that makes a sudden sound to tell you that something has happened

by¹ /baɪ/ *preposition*
1 near; beside ▶ *He was standing by the window.*
2 past ▶ *He walked by me without saying hello.*
3 used to show who or what does something ▶ *The house was damaged by fire.* ▶ *a story by a famous writer*
4 used to show how something is done ▶ *I earned some money by delivering newspapers.*
5 no later than ▶ *Please do it by tomorrow.*
6 used to show what vehicle, etc. you travel on ▶ *Are you going by car or by train?*

by² *adverb*
past ▶ *I sat and watched people go by.* ▶ *Hundreds of cars drove by.*

bye /baɪ/ *(also **bye-bye** /ˌbaɪ ˈbaɪ/) interjection*
a word you say when you leave someone, or when they leave you

byte /baɪt/ *noun*
a unit for measuring the amount of information a computer can use ▶ *There are one million bytes in one megabyte.*

Cc

C a short way of writing the words **Celsius** or **centigrade**

cab /kæb/ *noun*
1 the part of a lorry where the driver sits
2 a car with a driver who will take you somewhere if you pay.
SAME MEANING (**2**): **taxi**

cabbage /ˈkæbɪdʒ/ *noun*
a large, round vegetable with thick, green leaves

cabin /ˈkæbɪn/ *noun*
1 a room on a ship or plane
2 a small, wooden house

cabinet /ˈkæbɪnət/ *noun*
1 a piece of furniture with shelves or drawers ▶ *a medicine cabinet*
2 the small group of people in a government who have the most power

cable /ˈkeɪbəl/ *noun*
1 a thick rope, usually made of metal
2 a wire that carries electricity or telephone calls

cable television /ˌkeɪbəl ˈteləvɪʒən/ *(also **cable TV** /ˌkeɪbəl tiː ˈviː/ or **cable**) noun (no plural)*
a system of broadcasting television

by sending SIGNALS through cables under the ground ▶ *The hotel has cable TV.* ▶ *The game was on cable.*

cactus /ˈkæktəs/ *noun (plural* ***cacti*** */ˈkæktaɪ/ or* ***cactuses****)*
a plant with sharp prickles and a thick stem that grows in hot, dry places

cafe /ˈkæfeɪ/ *noun*
a place where you can buy drinks and simple meals
COMPARE: **restaurant**

cafeteria /ˌkæfəˈtɪərɪə/ *noun*
a restaurant where you collect your own food and take it to a table to eat it ▶ *a self-service cafeteria*

caffeine /ˈkæfiːn/ *noun (no plural)*
the substance in coffee, tea, and some other drinks that makes people feel more awake

cage /keɪdʒ/ *noun*
a box with metal bars, in which birds or animals can be kept

cake /keɪk/ *noun*
a sweet, cooked food made of flour, fat, sugar, and eggs ▶ *to bake a cake*

calcium /ˈkælsɪəm/ *noun (no plural)*
a substance that helps bones and teeth to grow strongly ▶ *Milk contains a lot of calcium.*

calculate /ˈkælkjʊleɪt/ *verb (present participle* ***calculating****, past* ***calculated****)*
to use numbers to find the answer to a sum ▶ *Have you calculated the cost of the journey?*

calculation /ˌkælkjʊˈleɪʃən/ *noun*
the result of using numbers to find the answer to a sum

calculator /ˈkælkjʊleɪtəʳ/ *noun*
a small machine that you can use to add, subtract, etc.

calendar /ˈkæləndəʳ/ *noun*
a list of the days, weeks, and months of the year

calf /kɑːf/ *noun (plural* ***calves*** */kɑːvz/)*
1 a young cow
2 the part of your leg between your knee and your ankle

call¹ /kɔːl/ *verb*
1 to give someone a name ▶ *They called their baby John.*
2 to shout ▶ *to call for help*
3 **call on** to visit someone ▶ *He called on me last Tuesday.*
4 to telephone someone ▶ *I called my sister today.*
5 to ask someone to come to you ▶ *Mother called the doctor.*

call² *noun*
1 a shout ▶ *a call for help*
2 a visit ▶ *a call from the doctor*
3 an act of talking to someone on the telephone ▶ *There's a call for you, Mr Brown.*

call box /ˈkɔːl bɒks/ *noun (plural* ***call boxes****)*
a public telephone box

caller /ˈkɔːləʳ/ *noun*
a person who makes a telephone call ▶ *There was one caller, but he didn't give me his name.*

calm /kɑːm/ *adjective*
quiet; peaceful ▶ *The sea was calm after the storm.* ▶ *He was calm when I told him the bad news. (adverb:* ***calmly****)*

calorie /ˈkælərɪ/ *noun*
a unit that measures the amount of energy a particular food can produce ▶ *Don't eat high-calorie food if you're trying to lose weight.*

calves /kɑːvz/
the plural of **calf**

camcorder /ˈkæmˌkɔːdəʳ/ *noun*
a machine that you use to take VIDEO films

came /keɪm/
the PAST TENSE of the verb **come**

camel /ˈkæməl/ *noun*
a large animal with one or two HUMPS

on its back, used to carry things and people in deserts

camera /'kæmərə/ *noun*
a machine for taking photographs, or making films or television programmes

cameraman /'kæmərəmæn/ *noun (plural **cameramen** /-men/)*
a person whose job is to operate the camera when people are making a film or television programme

camouflage /'kæməflɑːʒ/ *noun (no plural)*
clothes or colours that hide people, animals, or things by making them look the same as the things around them ▶ *All the soldiers were in camouflage.*

camp¹ /kæmp/ *noun*
a place with tents or huts where people live for a short time

camp² *verb*
to live in a tent for a short time

campaign /kæm'peɪn/ *noun*
1 a planned set of battles and movements of soldiers in a war
2 a set of planned activities done to get a result ▶ *a campaign to stop people smoking*

camping /'kæmpɪŋ/ *noun (no plural)*
living in a tent for a short time, especially when you are on holiday ▶ *The children liked camping.*

campsite /'kæmpsaɪt/ *noun*
a large field where people can stay in tents to have a holiday

campus /'kæmpəs/ *noun (plural **campuses**)*
the land belonging to a university, college, or school

can¹ /kən; *strong* kæn/ *verb*
to know how to; to be able to ▶ *"Can she swim?" "No, she can't* (=cannot)."

can² /kæn/ *noun*
a container made of metal ▶ *Have we got any cans **of** soup?*
SAME MEANING: **tin**
COMPARE: **box**

canal /kə'næl/ *noun*
a man-made river used for taking goods from one town to another

canary /kə'neərɪ/ *noun (plural **canaries**)*
a small, yellow bird with a sweet song

cancel /'kænsəl/ *verb (present participle **cancelling**, past **cancelled**)*
to stop some planned event ▶ *We had to cancel the match because so many people were ill.*

cancellation /ˌkænsə'leɪʃən/ *noun*
a situation in which someone decides that they will not do something they were going to do, or that a planned event will not happen ▶ *airport delays and flight cancellations*

cancer /'kænsəʳ/ *noun (no plural)*
a serious illness in which a growth spreads in the body

candidate /'kændɪdət/ *noun*
1 a person who hopes to be picked for a job or position
2 a person who takes an examination

candle /'kændl/ *noun*
a piece of WAX with a string in the middle which burns to give light

candlestick /'kændlˌstɪk/ *noun*
an object used to hold a candle

cane¹ /keɪn/ *noun*
a hollow stick from some plants, like sugar

cane² *verb (present participle **caning**, past **caned**)*
to hit someone with a stick

cannabis /'kænəbɪs/ *noun (no plural)*
an illegal drug that people smoke
SAME MEANING: **marijuana**

canned /kænd/ *adjective*
sold in cans ▶ *canned food*
SAME MEANING: **tinned**

cannon /'kænən/ *noun*
a large gun

C

cannot /ˈkænət, ˈkænɒt/
can not ▶ *I cannot understand why she is so angry.*

canoe /kəˈnuː/ *noun*
a narrow, light boat for one or two people

canoeing /kəˈnuːɪŋ/ *noun (no plural)*
the sport or activity of using a canoe ▶ *We could go canoeing this weekend.*

can opener /ˈkæn ˌəʊpənəʳ/ *noun*
a tool for opening cans of food

can't /kɑːnt/
can not ▶ *I'm sorry I can't come to your house tomorrow.*

canteen /kænˈtiːn/ *noun*
a place where people in a factory, school, or office can eat meals

canvas /ˈkænvəs/ *noun (no plural)*
strong cloth used to make tents, bags, etc.

canvass /ˈkænvəs/ *verb*
to try to persuade people to vote for your political party in an election ▶ *Someone came to the house canvassing for the Labour Party.*

canyon /ˈkænjən/ *noun*
a deep, narrow valley with steep sides ▶ *the Grand Canyon*

cap /kæp/ *noun*
1 a soft hat
2 a covering for the end of a bottle or tube

capable /ˈkeɪpəbəl/ *adjective*
1 good at something ▶ *She's a very capable student*
2 capable of able to do something ▶ *I knew he wasn't capable of murder.*
OPPOSITE (**2**): **incapable**

capacity /kəˈpæsətɪ/ *noun*
1 *(no plural)* the amount that something can contain ▶ *That bowl has a capacity of 2 pints.*
2 *(plural **capacities**)* an ability to do something ▶ *Paul has a great capacity **for** working hard.*

cape /keɪp/ *noun*
a loose piece of clothing that you wrap around your shoulders and arms
COMPARE: **cloak**

capital /ˈkæpɪtl/ *noun*
1 the chief city of a country, where the government is
2 *(also **capital letter**)* a large letter that you use at the beginning of a sentence ▶ *A, D, P are capital letters; a, d, p are small letters.*

capitalism /ˈkæpɪtlɪzəm/ *noun (no plural)*
an economic system in which businesses and industry are owned by private owners and not by the government

capital letter /ˌkæpɪtl ˈletəʳ/
another way of saying **capital** (**2**)

capital punishment /ˌkæpɪtl ˈpʌnɪʃmənt/ *noun (no plural)*
the act of killing someone as official punishment for a serious crime

capsize /kæpˈsaɪz/ *verb (present participle **capsizing**, past **capsized**)*
if a boat capsizes, or if you capsize it, it turns over in the water

captain /ˈkæptɪn/ *noun*
1 the person who controls a ship or an aircraft
2 an officer in the army or the navy
3 the leader of a team or group

caption /ˈkæpʃən/ *noun*
a few words that are written under a photograph or drawing to explain what it is

captive /ˈkæptɪv/ *noun*
a prisoner

captivity /kæpˈtɪvətɪ/ *noun (no plural)*
being a prisoner ▶ *animals kept in captivity*

capture /ˈkæptʃəʳ/ *verb (present participle **capturing**, past **captured**)*
to take someone as a prisoner ▶ *They captured four enemy soldiers.*

car /kɑːʳ/ *noun*
a vehicle on wheels that is driven by an engine and that people can travel in

carat /ˈkærət/ *noun*
a unit for measuring how pure gold is, or how heavy jewels are ▶ *an 18-carat gold ring*

caravan /ˈkærəvæn/ *noun*
a little house on wheels that can be pulled by a car

carbohydrate /ˌkɑːbəʊˈhaɪdreɪt/ *noun*
a substance in some foods that gives your body energy ▶ *Bread and rice contain a lot of carbohydrates.*

carbon /ˈkɑːbən/ *noun (no plural)*
a chemical ELEMENT that is found in coal and petrol

carbon dioxide /ˌkɑːbən daɪˈɒksaɪd/ *noun (no plural)*
the gas produced when people and animals breathe out, or when CARBON is burned in air

card /kɑːd/ *noun*
1 a piece of stiff, thick paper with a picture on the front and a message inside ▶ *a birthday card* ▶ *a Christmas card*
2 a small piece of stiff paper with pictures and numbers, used for various games ▶ *It's my turn to deal the cards.*

cardboard /ˈkɑːdbɔːd/ *noun (no plural)*
stiff, thick paper used for making boxes, book covers, etc.

cardigan /ˈkɑːdɪgən/ *noun*
a piece of clothing like a JUMPER which opens with buttons down the front

care[1] /keəʳ/ *verb (present participle* ***caring****, past* ***cared****)*
1 to feel interest or worry ▶ *Does she care* ***about*** *her work?* ▶ *I don't care what you do!*
2 care for someone to look after someone ▶ *Her son cared for him when he was ill.*
3 care for something to like or want something ▶ *Would you care for a cup of tea, Mrs Brown?*

care[2] *noun*
1 *(no plural)* the act of looking after a person or thing ▶ *a high standard of medical care* ▶ *Take care of your brother while I am away.*
2 take care to be careful ▶ *When you are crossing the road, take care!*
3 something that makes you sad ▶ *The holiday gave her a chance to forget her cares for a while.*

career /kəˈrɪəʳ/ *noun*
a number of jobs one after another, in which you move on to a more important job as you get older and learn more ▶ *a career in banking*

carefree /ˈkeəfriː/ *adjective*
without any problems or worries ▶ *a carefree childhood*

careful /ˈkeəfəl/ *adjective*
thinking seriously as you do something, so that you do not make a mistake ▶ *Be careful with that hot pan! (adverb:* ***carefully****)*
OPPOSITE: **careless**

careless /ˈkeələs/ *adjective*
not thinking seriously about what you do ▶ *Careless driving causes accidents. (adverb:* ***carelessly****)*
OPPOSITE: **careful**

caretaker /ˈkeəˌteɪkəʳ/ *noun*
a person whose job is to look after a building, especially a school

cargo /ˈkɑːgəʊ/ *noun (plural* ***cargoes****)*
something carried on a ship or plane ▶ *a cargo* ***of*** *oil*

caring /ˈkeərɪŋ/ *adjective*
kind and providing care and support for others ▶ *a warm and caring person*

carnival /ˈkɑːnɪvəl/ *noun*
a big, public party in the streets of a

C

town, with dancing, drinking, and entertainment ▶ *the Venice carnival*

carnivore /ˈkɑːnɪvɔːʳ/ *noun*
an animal that eats meat

carol /ˈkærəl/ *noun*
a Christmas song

car park /ˈkɑː pɑːk/ *noun*
a building or a piece of land where cars can be parked

C

carpenter /ˈkɑːpɪntəʳ/ *noun*
a person who makes things out of wood as a job

carpentry /ˈkɑːpəntrɪ/ *noun (no plural)*
the art of making things out of wood

carpet /ˈkɑːpɪt/ *noun*
a covering for floors and stairs, usually made of wool
COMPARE: **mat**

carriage /ˈkærɪdʒ/ *noun*
1 one of the parts of a train, in which people sit
2 a vehicle pulled by horses instead of a motor

carrier bag /ˈkærɪə ˌbæg/ *noun*
a bag made of plastic or paper, used for carrying things that you have bought in a shop

carrot /ˈkærət/ *noun*
a long, orange root that is eaten as a vegetable

carry /ˈkærɪ/ *verb (past* ***carried****)*
1 to take something somewhere ▶ *He carried the food to the table.*
2 carry on to continue ▶ *Carry on* ***with*** *your homework.* ▶ *They carried on talking.*
3 carry something out to do or finish something ▶ *The soldiers carried out their orders.*

cart /kɑːt/ *noun*
a wooden vehicle pulled by horses and used for carrying things

carton /ˈkɑːtn/ *noun*
a cardboard box for holding food or drink ▶ *a carton* ***of*** *apple juice*

cartoon /kɑːˈtuːn/ *noun*
1 a film that is made with characters that are drawn, rather than real actors ▶ *a Walt Disney cartoon*
2 a drawing, especially in a magazine or newspaper, that makes a joke about something or tells a story

carve /kɑːv/ *verb (present participle* ***carving****, past* ***carved****)*
1 to cut wood, stone, etc. into shapes ▶ *He carved the figure of a woman from a piece of wood.*
2 to cut cooked meat into pieces ▶ *She carved the chicken.*

carving /ˈkɑːvɪŋ/ *noun*
an object that has been made by cutting wood, stone, etc. ▶ *a wooden carving*

case /keɪs/ *noun*
1 one example of something ▶ *This is a typical case* ***of*** *lack of proper planning.*
2 a question that is decided in a court of law ▶ *a case* ***of*** *murder*
3 a large bag for carrying clothes in, for example on holiday ▶ *I'll just take my case up to my room.*
4 in case because something might happen ▶ *I'll take some biscuits in case we get hungry.*
5 in that case as this is true ▶ *"It's raining." "In that case, we'll need coats."*

cash[1] /kæʃ/ *noun (no plural)*
coins and paper money ▶ *Have you any cash?*

cash[2] *verb*
to get cash in return for a cheque ▶ *I cashed a cheque at the bank this morning.*

cash desk /ˈkæʃ desk/ *noun*
the place in a shop where you pay

cash dispenser /ˈkæʃ dɪˌspensəʳ/ *noun*
a machine in the wall outside a bank, where you can get money from your account

SAME MEANING: **ATM, cashpoint**

cashier /kæ'ʃɪəʳ/ *noun*
a person who takes and gives out money in a bank or shop

cashpoint /'kæʃpɔɪnt/ *noun*
a machine in the wall outside a bank, where you can get money from your account
SAME MEANING: **ATM, cash dispenser**

cash register /'kæʃ ˌredʒɪstəʳ/ *noun*
a machine in a shop that shows how much you should pay

casino /kə'siːnəʊ/ *noun*
a place where people try to win money by playing games with numbers, cards, etc.

cassette /kə'set/ *noun*
a small, plastic container holding a TAPE that plays music when fitted into a special machine

cassette recorder /kə'set rɪˌkɔːdəʳ/ *(also* ***cassette player*** /kə'set ˌpleɪəʳ/*)* *noun*
a machine which plays and records sounds on CASSETTES

cast¹ /kɑːst/ *verb (past* ***cast****)*
to give an actor a particular part in a film or play ► *As usual, Hugh Grant was cast as the typical Englishman.*

cast² *noun*
all of the actors in a film or play ► *The film has a brilliant cast.*

castle /'kɑːsəl/ *noun*
a large, strong building made so that no one can attack the people inside

casual /'kæʒʊəl/ *adjective*
1 not planned or arranged ► *a casual meeting*
2 casual clothes clothes that you wear at home, not at work or school

casualty /'kæʒʊəltɪ/ *noun (plural* ***casualties****)*
1 a person who is hurt in an accident, a war, etc. ► *There have been 20 casualties following an accident on the motorway.*
2 *(no plural)* the part of a hospital where people are taken when they need urgent treatment

cat /kæt/ *noun*
a small animal that people often keep as a pet

catalogue /'kætəlɒg/ *noun*
1 a list of things in a special order ► *a catalogue of all the books in the library*
2 a book containing details of things you can buy from a shop or business

catapult /'kætəpʌlt/ *verb*
to make someone or something move through the air very quickly ► *The car stopped suddenly, catapulting the boy through the window.*

catastrophe /kə'tæstrəfɪ/ *noun*
a terrible event that causes a lot of damage or death ► *the danger of a nuclear catastrophe*

catch¹ /kætʃ/ *verb (past* ***caught*** /kɔːt/*)*
1 to stop something that is moving in the air and hold it ► *The dog caught the ball in its mouth.*
2 to run after something and take hold of it ► *We ran after the dog and caught it.*
3 to get something ► *I caught the train.* ► *She caught a cold.*
4 catch up to get to the same place as someone else ► *I tried, but I couldn't catch up with you.*

catch² /kætʃ/ *noun*
the act of catching something ► *That was a good catch!*

catching /'kætʃɪŋ/ *adjective*
(used about illnesses) easily passed from one person to another

category /'kætɪgərɪ/ *noun (plural* ***categories****)*
a group of people or things that are like one another ► *different categories* ***of*** *books*

cater /'keɪtəʳ/ *verb*
cater for to provide a particular group

of people with what they need or want ▶ *We chose the hotel because it caters for small children.*

caterpillar /'kætəˌpɪləʳ/ *noun*
the young form of some insects, that looks like a worm with many legs

cathedral /kə'θiːdrəl/ *noun*
an important, large church

C

Catholic /'kæθəlɪk/ *noun*
a Christian belonging to the church whose leader is the POPE

cattle /'kætl/ *plural noun*
large animals kept for their meat, milk, and skins

caught /kɔːt/
the PAST TENSE and PAST PARTICIPLE of the verb **catch**

cauliflower /'kɒlɪˌflaʊəʳ/ *noun*
a vegetable with green leaves around the outside and a hard, white centre

cause[1] /kɔːz/ *verb (present participle **causing**, past **caused**)*
to make something happen; be the reason for something ▶ *The heavy rain caused the flood.*

cause[2] *noun*
1 a person or thing that makes something happen; a reason for something ▶ *The heavy rain was the cause **of** the flood.*
2 an idea you believe in or care about very strongly ▶ *They were all fighting for the same cause.*

caution /'kɔːʃən/ *noun (no plural)*
great care ▶ *Drive with caution.*

cautious /'kɔːʃəs/ *adjective*
taking care to avoid danger *(adverb: **cautiously**)*
OPPOSITE: **reckless**

cavalry /'kævəlrɪ/ *noun (no plural)*
soldiers who fought on horses in the past

cave /keɪv/ *noun*
a hollow place under the ground or in the side of a mountain or rock

caveman /'keɪvmæn/ *noun (plural **cavemen** /-men/)*
a person who lived many thousands of years ago, when people lived in caves

cavity /'kævɪtɪ/ *noun (plural **cavities**)*
a hole in a tooth

CD /ˌsiː 'diː/ *noun*
a COMPACT DISC; a type of record with very high-quality sound, played on a special machine

CD player /ˌsiː 'diː ˌpleɪəʳ/ *(also **compact disc player**) noun*
a special machine for playing CDs

CD-ROM /ˌsiː diː 'rɒm/ *noun*
COMPACT DISC READ-ONLY MEMORY; a CD with a lot of information stored on it, which you look at using a computer

cease /siːs/ *verb (present participle **ceasing**, past **ceased**)*
to stop ▶ *Her mother never ceases telling you about her troubles.*

ceasefire /'siːsfaɪəʳ/ *noun*
an agreement for both sides in a war to stop fighting

ceaseless /'siːsləs/ *adjective*
never stopping

ceiling /'siːlɪŋ/ *noun*
the roof of a room

celebrate /'selɪbreɪt/ *verb (present participle **celebrating**, past **celebrated**)*
to show that you are happy about something by having a special meal or party

celebration /ˌselɪ'breɪʃən/ *noun*
a special meal or party that you have because something good has happened ▶ *There was great celebration when the baby was born.*

celebrity /sə'lebrətɪ/ *noun (plural **celebrities**)*
a famous person, especially an actor or entertainer ▶ *There were lots of TV celebrities at the party.*

celery /ˈseləri/ *noun (no plural)*
a vegetable with long, firm, pale green stems that you eat in a SALAD

cell /sel/ *noun*
1 a small room in which a prisoner is kept
2 a very small part of a living substance

cellar /ˈseləʳ/ *noun*
a room under the ground in a house, used especially for storing things in
COMPARE: **basement**

cello /ˈtʃeləʊ/ *noun*
a musical instrument like a large VIOLIN, which you hold between your knees

Celsius /ˈselsɪəs/ *noun (no plural)*
a system for measuring temperature, in which water freezes at 0° and boils at 100°
SAME MEANING: **centigrade**

cement /sɪˈment/ *noun (no plural)*
a powder that becomes hard like stone when mixed with water, used in building

cemetery /ˈsemɪtrɪ/ *noun (plural* ***cemeteries****)*
an area of land where dead bodies are put into the ground

censor /ˈsensəʳ/ *verb*
to look at books, films, etc. and remove anything that might offend or harm people ▶ *It was obvious that the television reports were being censored.*

censorship /ˈsensəʃɪp/ *noun (no plural)*
the practice of looking at books, films, etc. and removing anything that might offend or harm people ▶ *She believes that censorship is wrong.*

census /ˈsensəs/ *noun (plural* ***censuses****)*
an occasion on which official information is gathered about the number of people in a country, their ages, jobs, etc.

cent /sent/ *noun*
a small coin used in some countries

centenary /senˈtiːnərɪ/ *noun (plural* ***centenaries****)*
the day or year exactly one hundred years after an important event ▶ *We celebrated the club's centenary in 1999.*

centigrade /ˈsentɪgreɪd/ *noun*
a system for measuring temperature, in which water freezes at 0° and boils at 100°
SAME MEANING: **Celsius**

centimetre /ˈsentɪˌmiːtəʳ/ *noun*
a measure of length ▶ *There are 100 centimetres in a metre.* ▶ *3 centimetres (3cm)*

central /ˈsentrəl/ *adjective*
in the middle of something

central heating /ˌsentrəl ˈhiːtɪŋ/ *noun (no plural)*
a system for heating buildings, in which pipes carry the heat to every part of the building ▶ *Most of these houses have central heating.*

centre /ˈsentəʳ/ *noun*
1 the middle of something
2 a place where a lot of people come with a special purpose ▶ *The doctors worked at the Health Centre.* ▶ *Have you seen the new shopping centre?*

century /ˈsentʃərɪ/ *noun (plural* ***centuries****)*
a period of 100 years ▶ *This house was built in the 19th century.*

ceramics /səˈræmɪks/ *noun*
1 *(no plural)* the art of making pots, bowls, etc. from clay
2 *plural noun* artistic objects made from clay ▶ *an exhibition of ceramics*

cereal /ˈsɪərɪəl/ *noun*
a crop such as wheat, rice, or maize, used as food

ceremony /ˈserɪmənɪ/ *noun (plural* ***ceremonies****)*
a number of special actions done and

C

special words spoken in a particular order to mark an important public, social, or religious event ▶ *the wedding ceremony*

certain /'sɜːtn/ *adjective*
1 sure ▶ *I am certain he told me to come at 2 o'clock.*
OPPOSITE: **uncertain**
SAME MEANING: **positive**
2 some ▶ *You cannot smoke in certain restaurants.*

C

certainly /'sɜːtnlɪ/ *adverb*
1 without doubt ▶ *You've certainly got a lot of books.*
2 of course ▶ *"Will you help me, please?" "Certainly."*

certificate /sə'tɪfɪkət/ *noun*
an important written paper ▶ *Your birth certificate tells people when you were born.*

chain[1] /tʃeɪn/ *noun*
a number of metal rings joined together ▶ *She wore a gold chain around her neck.*

chain[2] *verb*
to tie something with a chain ▶ *Who chained the poor dog to the fence?*

chair /tʃeəʳ/ *noun*
a piece of furniture you sit on, with four legs and a back
COMPARE: **sofa, stool**

chairman /'tʃeəmən/ *noun (plural **chairmen** /-mən/)*
a person who controls a meeting

chairperson /'tʃeəˌpɜːsən/ *noun*
a person who controls a meeting ▶ *They elected a new chairperson.*

chairwoman /'tʃeəˌwʊmən/ *noun (plural **chairwomen** /-ˌwɪmɪn/)*
a woman who controls a meeting

chalk /tʃɔːk/ *noun*
1 *(no plural)* a soft, white substance found in the ground
2 a piece of this substance used for writing or drawing

challenge[1] /'tʃælɪndʒ/ *verb (present participle **challenging**, past **challenged**)*
1 to offer to fight or play a game against someone ▶ *Their school challenged ours to a football match.*
2 to test or question someone ▶ *I did not think he was right, so I challenged him.*

challenge[2] *noun*
1 an offer to fight or play against someone
2 a test of ability ▶ *To build a bridge in a month was a real challenge.*

challenging /'tʃælɪndʒɪŋ/ *adjective*
difficult but interesting or enjoyable ▶ *Teaching is a very challenging job.*

champagne /ʃæm'peɪn/ *noun (no plural)*
an alcoholic drink with BUBBLES in it

champion /'tʃæmpɪən/ *noun*
a person who is the best at something, especially a sport or game

championship /'tʃæmpɪənʃɪp/ *noun*
a competition to find who is the best at something ▶ *Our team won the swimming championships.*

chance /tʃɑːns/ *noun*
1 *(no plural)* something unexpected ▶ *I met him by chance.*
2 something that may happen ▶ *There is a chance that I will be chosen for the team.*
3 a time when something may be done ▶ *I haven't had a chance to read my letter.*
4 a risk ▶ *He is taking a chance by driving without insurance.*

chancellor /'tʃɑːnsələʳ/ *noun*
1 the head of a university or government ▶ *the Chancellor of York University* ▶ *The German Chancellor has arrived in Britain.*
2 *(also **Chancellor of the Exchequer** /ɪks'tʃekəʳ/)* in Britain, the government minister who is in charge of the money the government spends

chandelier /ʃændəˈlɪəʳ/ *noun*
a large decoration made of glass, that holds lights or candles and hangs from the ceiling

change[1] /tʃeɪndʒ/ *verb (present participle* ***changing****, past* ***changed****)*
1 to make something different or become different ▶ *This town has changed since I was a child.* ▶ *We've changed the house a lot since we moved in.*
2 to take or put something in the place of something else ▶ *She took the dress back to the shop and changed it (for another).*
3 to put on different clothes ▶ *He changed when he arrived home from school.*
4 change your mind to make a new decision which is opposite to the one before ▶ *I was going out this evening, but I've changed my mind.* (=I'm going to stay at home instead).

change[2] *noun*
1 something that has become different ▶ *You will see many changes in the village since last year.*
2 *(no plural)* money that you get back when you give too much for something ▶ *I gave him £1 and he gave me 20 pence change.*
3 for a change as something different from usual ▶ *Let's go out to a restaurant tonight for a change.*

channel /ˈtʃænl/ *noun*
a narrow piece of flowing water ▶ *The English Channel is between France and England.*

chant[1] /tʃɑːnt/ *noun*
words or phrases that are repeated again and again ▶ *a football chant*

chant[2] /tʃɑːnt/ *verb*
to repeat a word or phrase again and again ▶ *an angry crowd chanting slogans*

chaos /ˈkeɪɒs/ *noun (no plural)*
absence of order or control ▶ *After the bomb exploded the town was in chaos.*

chaotic /keɪˈɒtɪk/ *adjective*
very disorganized and confusing
▶ *The whole holiday was chaotic.*

chap /tʃæp/ *noun*
a man ▶ *Frank seems a friendly chap.*

chapel /ˈtʃæpəl/ *noun*
a small church, or part of a church

chaperone /ˈʃæpərəʊn/ *noun*
an older person who in the past went to places with a young person, especially an unmarried woman, to protect and take care of them
▶ *Your aunt will go with you as your chaperone.*

chaplain /ˈtʃæplɪn/ *noun*
a priest who works for the army, a hospital, or a college ▶ *the college chaplain*

chapter /ˈtʃæptəʳ/ *noun*
a part of a book ▶ *Open your books at Chapter 3.*

character /ˈkærɪktəʳ/ *noun*
1 what a person or thing is like ▶ *He has a strong but gentle character.*
▶ *The new buildings have changed the character of the village.*
2 a person in a book, film, or play

characteristic[1] /ˌkærɪktəˈrɪstɪk/ *noun*
a quality or feature that someone or something typically has ▶ *the characteristics of a good manager*

characteristic[2] *adjective*
typical of a particular person or thing
▶ *Mark, with characteristic kindness, offered to help. (adverb:* ***characteristically****)*

charcoal /ˈtʃɑːkəʊl/ *noun (no plural)*
a black substance made of burned wood, used for burning as FUEL or for drawing

charge[1] /tʃɑːdʒ/ *verb (present participle* ***charging****, past* ***charged****)*
1 to ask money for something ▶ *He only charged me £2 for the book.*

C

2 to say that a person has done something wrong ► *He was charged* ***with*** *stealing a car.*
3 to run or hurry ► *The little boy charged into the room.*

charge² *noun*
1 a price asked for something ► *a charge* ***for*** *the use of the telephone*
2 a statement that a person has done wrong ► *a charge* ***of*** *stealing*
3 a hurried attack
4 be in charge/take charge to be in a position of control and responsibility ► *I don't know. Ask Mr Davis. He's in charge.*

charisma /kəˈrɪzmə/ *noun (no plural)* a natural ability to make people like you ► *He is a man of great charisma.*

charismatic /ˌkærɪzˈmætɪk/ *adjective* having a natural ability to make people like you ► *The president is a very charismatic leader.*

charity /ˈtʃærətɪ/ *noun*
1 *(no plural)* goodness and kindness ► *She helped him out of charity.*
2 *(plural* ***charities****)* a group of people who collect money from the public and then give money, food, etc. to those who need it

charm¹ /tʃɑːm/ *verb* to please you very much

charm² *noun*
1 *(no plural)* pleasing behaviour ► *He had great charm – everyone liked him.*
2 a thing that is said to bring good luck

charming /ˈtʃɑːmɪŋ/ *adjective* beautiful; pleasing

chart /tʃɑːt/ *noun*
1 a map, especially of an area of sea
2 a large piece of paper with information on it in pictures and writing

charter /ˈtʃɑːtəʳ/ *noun* a statement of the beliefs, duties, and purposes of an organization ► *the charter of the United Nations*

charter flight /ˈtʃɑːtə ˌflaɪt/ *noun* a flight that you buy from a travel company, and that is often cheaper than a flight you buy directly from an AIRLINE ► *We managed to get a charter flight to Istanbul.*

chase¹ /tʃeɪs/ *verb (present participle* ***chasing****, past* ***chased****)* to follow someone or something quickly ► *The boy chased the dog.*

chase² *noun* following someone or something quickly ► *He caught it after a long chase.*

chat¹ /tʃæt/ *verb (present participle* ***chatting****, past* ***chatted****)* to talk in a friendly way

chat² *noun* a friendly talk ► *to have a chat*

château /ˈʃætəʊ/ *noun (plural* ***châteaux*** */-təʊz/ or* ***châteaus****)* a castle or large country house in some countries

chat show /ˈtʃæt ʃəʊ/ *noun* a television or radio show on which someone talks to famous or interesting people ► *Brosnan appeared as a guest on her chat show.*

chatter /ˈtʃætəʳ/ *verb* to talk quickly, especially about unimportant things ► *They just sat and chattered.*

chatty /ˈtʃætɪ/ *adjective (****chattier, chattiest****)* friendly and easy to talk to ► *She was very chatty on the telephone.*

chauffeur /ˈʃəʊfəʳ/ *noun* a person whose job is to drive another person's car, and take that person to the places they want to go ► *My chauffeur drove me to the airport.*

cheap /tʃiːp/ *adjective*

costing only a little money ▶ *A bicycle is much cheaper than a car.*
OPPOSITE: **expensive**

cheat[1] /tʃiːt/ *verb*
to deceive; to do something which is not honest ▶ *He didn't play the game fairly – he cheated.* ▶ *They cheated him out of £500.*

cheat[2] *noun*
a person who is not fair or honest

check[1] /tʃek/ *verb*
1 to make sure that something has been done well or is in good order ▶ *You should check your bicycle before you ride it.*
2 check in to report your arrival somewhere ▶ *You must check in at the airport an hour before the plane leaves.*

check[2] *noun*
1 a careful look to make sure that something is correct or as you want it to be ▶ *a police check on cars and lorries*
2 a pattern of different coloured squares ▶ *The material had checks on it.*

checked /tʃekt/ *adjective*
having a regular pattern of different coloured squares ▶ *a checked shirt*

checklist /ˈtʃekˌlɪst/ *noun*
a list that helps to remind you of all the things you have to do

checkout /ˈtʃekaʊt/ *noun*
a desk in a shop, where you pay for goods

checkpoint /ˈtʃekpɔɪnt/ *noun*
a place where an official person stops people and vehicles to examine them ▶ *There are several checkpoints along the border.*

checkup *(also* ***check-up****)* /ˈtʃek ʌp/ *noun*
an occasion when a doctor or DENTIST examines you to see if you are healthy ▶ *When was the last time you had a checkup?*

cheek /tʃiːk/ *noun*
one of the two parts on each side of your face under your eyes

cheeky /ˈtʃiːkɪ/ *adjective (**cheekier, cheekiest**)*
not polite or respectful ▶ *Don't be so cheeky.*

cheer[1] /tʃɪəʳ/ *verb*
1 *(also* ***cheer up****)* to make someone happy ▶ *The children's laughter cheered the old woman.*
2 to shout because you are pleased ▶ *The crowd cheered when the film stars arrived.*

cheer[2] *noun*
a shout of happiness or support ▶ *Let's give three cheers for the winning team.*

cheerful /ˈtʃɪəfəl/ *adjective*
smiling and happy *(adverb: **cheerfully**)*

cheerleader /ˈtʃɪəˌliːdəʳ/ *noun*
a member of a group of young women that encourages the crowd at a sports event to cheer for a particular team

cheers /tʃɪəz/ *interjection*
used just before you drink a glass of alcohol with someone, to show friendly feelings

cheese /tʃiːz/ *noun*
a solid food made from milk

cheesecake /ˈtʃiːzkeɪk/ *noun*
a sweet cake made with soft, white cheese and often fruit ▶ *strawberry cheesecake*

chef /ʃef/ *noun*
a person whose job is to cook food in a restaurant, especially the most important cook in a restaurant

chemical[1] /ˈkemɪkəl/ *noun*
a substance, especially one made by or used in chemistry

chemical[2] *adjective*
made by chemistry

C

chemist /ˈkemɪst/ *noun*
1 a person who makes and sells medicines
COMPARE: **pharmacist**
2 chemist's a shop where medicines, toiletries, and some goods for the house can be bought
COMPARE: **pharmacy**
3 a person who studies chemistry

chemistry /ˈkemɪstrɪ/ *noun (no plural)*
the science which studies substances like gas, metals, liquids, etc., what they are made of, and how they behave

cheque /tʃek/ *noun*
a printed piece of paper which you write on to pay for things; it can be exchanged for money at the bank

chequebook /ˈtʃekbʊk/ *noun*
a small book of cheques

cherry /ˈtʃerɪ/ *noun (plural **cherries**)*
a small, round fruit with red or black skin, which grows on trees

chess /tʃes/ *noun (no plural)*
a game that you play by moving different shaped pieces on a board of black and white squares

chest /tʃest/ *noun*
1 the front of your body between your shoulders and your stomach
SAME MEANING: **breast (2)**
2 a large box for storing things in

chest of drawers /ˌtʃest əv ˈdrɔːz/ *noun (plural **chests of drawers**)*
a large piece of furniture with drawers

chew /tʃuː/ *verb*
to break up food in your mouth with your teeth

chewing gum /ˈtʃuːɪŋ gʌm/ *noun (no plural)*
a type of sweet that you chew but do not swallow

chic /ʃiːk/ *adjective*
fashionable and showing good style
▶ *We had lunch at a chic little cafe.*

chick /tʃɪk/ *noun*
a young bird, especially a young chicken

chicken /ˈtʃɪkɪn/ *noun*
a bird that people keep for its eggs and meat

chicken pox /ˈtʃɪkɪn ˌpɒks/ *noun (no plural)*
an illness that causes a fever and red spots on the skin, especially caught by children ▶ *Ruth's got chicken pox.*

chief¹ /tʃiːf/ *adjective*
most important

chief² *noun*
a leader; the head of a group or tribe
▶ *the chief of police*

chiefly /ˈtʃiːflɪ/ *adverb*
mostly ▶ *He kept animals – chiefly cattle, with some pigs.*

child /tʃaɪld/ *noun (plural **children** /ˈtʃɪldrən/)*
1 a young person older than a baby but not yet fully grown
2 a son or daughter ▶ *They have three children.*
LOOK AT: **son**

childbirth /ˈtʃaɪldbɜːθ/ *noun (no plural)*
the act during which a baby is born
▶ *Childbirth is very painful.*

childcare /ˈtʃaɪldkeəʳ/ *noun (no plural)*
an arrangement in which someone looks after children when their parents are at work

childhood /ˈtʃaɪldhʊd/ *noun*
the time when you are a child

childish /ˈtʃaɪldɪʃ/ *adjective*
silly and suitable only for a child
▶ *a childish game (adverb: **childishly**)*

childless /ˈtʃaɪldləs/ *adjective*
having no children ▶ *childless couples*

childminder /ˈtʃaɪldˌmaɪndəʳ/ *noun*
a person who is responsible for

looking after young children when their parents are at work

childminding /'tʃaɪld,maɪndɪŋ/ *noun (no plural)*
the job of looking after young children when their parents are at work ► *I do a little childminding.*

children /'tʃɪldrən/
the plural of **child**

chill[1] /tʃɪl/ *verb*
1 to make something cold ► *Chill the champagne before you serve it.*
2 *(also **chill out**)* to relax and rest ► *We stayed till about 3 am, then went back to our place to chill.*

chill[2] *noun*
a feeling of coldness ► *There was a chill in the air.*

chilli /'tʃɪlɪ/ *noun*
1 *(plural **chillies**)* a small, thin, red or green vegetable with a very hot taste
2 *(no plural)* a dish made with beans, meat, and chillies

chilly /'tʃɪlɪ/ *adjective (**chillier, chilliest**)*
cold enough to make you feel uncomfortable ► *It's a bit chilly today.*

chime /tʃaɪm/ *verb (present participle **chiming**, past **chimed**)*
to make a sound like a bell ► *The clock chimed 3 o'clock.*

chimney /'tʃɪmnɪ/ *noun*
a pipe that allows smoke to go up and out of a building

chimpanzee /,tʃɪmpæn'ziː/ *noun*
an African animal like a monkey, but without a tail

chin /tʃɪn/ *noun*
the part of your face below your mouth

china /'tʃaɪnə/ *noun (no plural)*
1 cups, plates, etc. that are made from fine baked earth
2 the special kind of white earth from which cups, plates, etc. are made

chip[1] /tʃɪp/ *noun*
1 a small piece broken off something ► *a cup with a chip out of it*
2 a long, thin piece of potato cooked in oil
SAME MEANING (**2**): **(French) fry**
COMPARE (**2**): **crisp**
3 a very small piece of metal or plastic used in computers to store information and make the computer work

chip[2] *verb (present participle **chipping**, past **chipped**)*
to break a small piece off something hard ► *He chipped the cup when he dropped it.*

chirp /tʃɜːp/ *noun*
a short, high sound made by some birds and insects

chirpy /'tʃɜːpɪ/ *adjective (**chirpier, chirpiest**)*
cheerful ► *You're very chirpy this morning.*

chisel /'tʃɪzəl/ *noun*
a metal tool with a sharp end, used for cutting and shaping wood or stone

chocolate /'tʃɒklət/ *noun*
1 *(no plural)* a sweet, hard, brown food made from COCOA
2 a small sweet covered in chocolate ► *a box of chocolates*

choice /tʃɔɪs/ *noun*
1 a decision about what you want ► *I've got to make a choice between the two jobs.*
2 the result of deciding what you want ► *Her choice of dress surprised me.*
3 a variety of things from which you can choose ► *There's a wide choice of colours.*

choir /'kwaɪəʳ/ *noun*
a number of people who sing together ► *the school choir*

choke /tʃəʊk/ *verb (present participle **choking**, past **choked**)*

C

C

to be unable to breathe because of something in your throat ▶ *to choke on a piece of meat*

choose /tʃuːz/ *verb (present participle* ***choosing****, past tense* ***chose*** */tʃəʊz/, past participle* ***chosen*** */ˈtʃəʊzən/)*
to decide from a number of things or people the one you want ▶ *She chose to study chemistry.*

choosy /ˈtʃuːzɪ/ *adjective (****choosier, choosiest****)*
liking only certain things ▶ *I'm very choosy about my food.*

chop[1] /tʃɒp/ *verb (present participle* ***chopping****, past* ***chopped****)*
to cut something with an axe or a sharp knife

chop[2] *noun*
a piece of meat with a bone, cut from the side of an animal's body

chopper /ˈtʃɒpəʳ/ *noun*
a HELICOPTER

chopsticks /ˈtʃɒpstɪks/ *plural noun*
a pair of thin sticks used for eating food in East Asia

chord /kɔːd/ *noun*
two or more musical notes that you play at the same time ▶ *I can play a few chords on the guitar.*

chore /tʃɔːʳ/ *noun*
a job that you have to do, especially a boring one in the house or garden ▶ *household chores*

choreographer /ˌkɒrɪˈɒgrəfəʳ/ *noun*
a person whose job is to arrange how dancers should move during a performance

choreography /ˌkɒrɪˈɒgrəfɪ/ *noun (no plural)*
the art of arranging how dancers should move during a performance

chorus /ˈkɔːrəs/ *noun (plural* ***choruses****)*
1 a group of singers
2 a part of a song that is repeated

chose /tʃəʊz/
the PAST TENSE of the verb **choose**

chosen /ˈtʃəʊzən/
the PAST PARTICIPLE of the verb **choose**

Christ /kraɪst/
Jesus Christ, the man who Christians believe is the son of God

christen /ˈkrɪsən/ *verb*
to put holy water on someone to make them a member of the Christian church, and to give them a name ▶ *They christened the baby John.*

christening /ˈkrɪsənɪŋ/ *noun*
the Christian ceremony at which a baby is given its name

Christian /ˈkrɪstʃən, -tɪən/ *noun*
a person who follows the teachings of Jesus Christ

Christianity /ˌkrɪstɪˈænɪtɪ/ *noun (no plural)*
the religion based on the teachings of Jesus Christ

Christian name /ˈkrɪstʃən ˌneɪm/ *noun*
a person's first name, not their family name

Christmas /ˈkrɪsməs/ *noun*
December 25th, the day of the year when Christians thank God for the birth of Jesus. People get together with their families and friends and eat and drink special things.

Christmas Eve /ˌkrɪsməs ˈiːv/ *noun*
December 24th, the day before Christmas Day

Christmas stocking /ˌkrɪsməs ˈstɒkɪŋ/ *noun*
a long sock that children leave out on the night before Christmas to be filled with presents

chrome /krəʊm/ *noun (no plural)*
a hard, shiny, silver metal that is used for covering objects ▶ *The door has chrome handles.*

chronic /ˈkrɒnɪk/ *adjective*
serious and likely to continue for a

long time ▶ *There is a chronic shortage of nurses.*

chronological /ˌkrɒnəˈlɒdʒɪkəl/ *adjective*
arranged in the same order as events happened ▶ *The children had to put the events of the war in chronological order.*

chubby /ˈtʃʌbɪ/ *adjective (**chubbier, chubbiest**)*
slightly fat ▶ *He was a chubby little baby.*

chuck /tʃʌk/ *verb*
to throw something ▶ *I chucked the ball over the fence.*

chuckle /ˈtʃʌkəl/ *verb (present participle **chuckling**, past **chuckled**)*
to laugh quietly ▶ *He chuckled at the funny story.*

chunk /tʃʌŋk/ *noun*
a large piece of something solid ▶ *I cut off a chunk **of** cheese.*

church /tʃɜːtʃ/ *noun (plural **churches**)*
a building in which Christians meet and pray

churchyard /ˈtʃɜːtʃjɑːd/ *noun*
a piece of land around a church, where dead people are buried

cider /ˈsaɪdəʳ/ *noun*
1 *(no plural)* a drink containing alcohol that is made from apples
2 a glass of this drink ▶ *Can I have two ciders, please?*

cigar /sɪˈgɑːʳ/ *noun*
a thick, brown stick of tobacco leaves rolled together for smoking

cigarette /ˌsɪgəˈret/ *noun*
a thin stick made of tobacco cut into small pieces and rolled in white paper for smoking

cinema /ˈsɪnəmə/ *noun*
a building in which you can see films

circle¹ /ˈsɜːkəl/ *noun*
1 a round shape; a ring ▶ *They sat in a circle round the fire.*
2 a group of people who like the same things ▶ *a large circle of friends*

circle² *verb (present participle **circling**, past **circled**)*
to draw a circle round something ▶ *Circle the correct answer.*

circuit /ˈsɜːkɪt/ *noun*
1 a track where people race cars, bicycles, etc. ▶ *The racing cars go three times round the circuit.*
2 the complete circle that an electric current flows around ▶ *an electric circuit*

circular /ˈsɜːkjʊləʳ/ *adjective*
round; moving in a direction that takes you back to where you started ▶ *It's a circular path so we don't have to come back the same way.*

circulate /ˈsɜːkjʊleɪt/ *verb (present participle **circulating**, past **circulated**)*
to go round and round ▶ *Blood circulates round your body.*

circulation /ˌsɜːkjʊˈleɪʃən/ *noun (no plural)*
the movement of blood round your body

circumcise /ˈsɜːkəmsaɪz/ *verb (present participle **circumcising**, past **circumcised**)*
to cut off the skin at the end of a boy's or man's PENIS, or to cut off part of a girl's sex organs

circumcision /ˌsɜːkəmˈsɪʒən/ *noun*
the act of cutting off the skin at the end of a boy's or man's PENIS, or cutting off part of a girl's sex organs

circumference /səˈkʌmfərəns/ *noun*
the length around the outside edge of a round object

circumstances /ˈsɜːkəmstənsɪz/ *plural noun*
1 in/under the circumstances after what has happened ▶ *In the circumstances, I think I should stay at home.*

C

2 in/under no circumstances never ▶ *Under no circumstances will I vote for him.*

circus /'sɜːkəs/ *noun (plural **circuses**)*
a show given by people and trained animals, often in a large tent

citizen /'sɪtɪzən/ *noun*
a person who lives in a country or town and has special rights there

C

citizenship /'sɪtɪzənʃɪp/ *noun (no plural)*
the legal right to belong to a particular country ▶ *Peter has British citizenship.*

citrus fruit /'sɪtrəs ˌfruːt/ *noun*
a fruit such as an orange or a LEMON

city /'sɪtɪ/ *noun (plural **cities**)*
a very large town

civil /'sɪvəl/ *adjective*
1 not connected with military or religious organizations ▶ *The company makes civil aircraft.* ▶ *We were married in a civil ceremony, not in church.*
2 related to laws that deal with people's rights, not laws that are related to crimes ▶ *a civil case*

civilian /sɪ'vɪljən/ *noun*
a person who is not in the armed forces

civilization /ˌsɪvɪlaɪ'zeɪʃən/ *noun*
a way of life in which people have laws, government, and education

civilize /'sɪvɪlaɪz/ *verb (present participle **civilizing**, past **civilized**)*
to change the way that people live together, by making laws and having government and education

civilized /'sɪvɪlaɪzd/ *adjective*
1 a civilized society is well organized and has laws and customs ▶ *Care for the elderly is essential in a civilized society.*
2 behaving politely and sensibly ▶ *Can't we discuss this in a civilized way?*

civil rights /ˌsɪvəl 'raɪts/ *plural noun*
the legal rights that every person has

civil servant /ˌsɪvəl 'sɜːvənt/ *noun*
a person who works for the government in the civil service

civil service /ˌsɪvəl 'sɜːvɪs/ *noun*
all the people who work for a government except the army, navy, and airforce

civil war /ˌsɪvəl 'wɔːʳ/ *noun*
a war between two groups of people who live in the same country

claim¹ /kleɪm/ *verb*
1 to ask for something that you say is yours ▶ *I claimed the coat that the teacher found.*
2 to say something is true ▶ *He claimed that he hadn't done it, but I didn't believe him.*

claim² *noun*
1 something that you ask for ▶ *They made a claim for higher pay.*
2 something that you say is true ▶ *I don't believe his claim about how rich he is.*

clairvoyant /kleə'vɔɪənt/ *noun*
a person who says they can see what will happen in the future

clamber /'klæmbəʳ/ *verb*
to climb over something with difficulty, using your hands and feet ▶ *I clambered over the rocks.*

clammy /'klæmɪ/ *adjective (**clammier, clammiest**)*
wet and sticky in an unpleasant way ▶ *clammy hands*

clamour /'klæməʳ/ *verb*
to demand something loudly ▶ *All the reporters were clamouring **for** his attention.*

clamp /klæmp/ *verb*
1 to hold something tightly in a particular position so that it does not move ▶ *He clamped his hand over her mouth.*
2 to fasten a piece of equipment onto

the wheel of a car that has been parked illegally, so that it cannot be moved ▶ *Her car has been clamped again.*

3 clamp down on something to become very strict in order to stop people from doing something ▶ *The police are clamping down on drivers who go too fast.*

clang /klæŋ/ *noun*
the sound of one piece of metal hitting another ▶ *There was a clang as he dropped the tools.*

clap /klæp/ *verb (present participle **clapping**, past **clapped**)*
to make a sound by hitting your hands together, usually to show that you like something ▶ *When the singer finished, we clapped.*
COMPARE: **applaud**

clarify /ˈklærɪfaɪ/ *verb (past **clarified**)*
to make something easier to understand by explaining it in more detail ▶ *Can you clarify exactly what you mean?*

clarinet /ˌklærɪˈnet/ *noun*
a wooden musical instrument like a long, black tube, which you play by blowing into it

clash¹ /klæʃ/ *verb*
1 to fight or disagree ▶ *The police clashed **with** the angry crowd.*
2 (used about colours) to look wrong together ▶ *His shirt clashed **with** his coat.*
3 to happen at the same time ▶ *I couldn't go to the wedding as it clashed **with** my holiday.*

clash² *noun (plural **clashes**)*
1 a fight or disagreement ▶ *a clash **with** the police*
2 a loud noise of metal on metal ▶ *the clash of weapons*

clasp¹ /klɑːsp/ *verb*
to hold something tightly ▶ *He clasped my arm with fear.*
SAME MEANING: **grip**

clasp² *noun*
something that fastens two things together ▶ *He has a gold clasp on his belt.*

class /klɑːs/ *noun (plural **classes**)*
1 a group of people who learn together ▶ *She was in a class of 30 students.*
2 a group of people or things of the same kind ▶ *Cats belong to one class of animals, fish to another.*

classic /ˈklæsɪk/ *noun*
a book or film which is very good and of lasting importance ▶ *That film's a classic.*

classical /ˈklæsɪkəl/ *adjective*
(used about music) serious and of lasting importance ▶ *I prefer classical music to modern music.*

classified /ˈklæsɪfaɪd/ *adjective*
officially secret ▶ *I can't tell you where they live – that's classified information.*

classify /ˈklæsɪfaɪ/ *verb (past **classified**)*
to put things into groups according to their type, size, age, etc. ▶ *They classified Bill **as** a problem child.*

classmate /ˈklɑːsmeɪt/ *noun*
a person who is in the same class as you at school ▶ *His classmates don't like him.*

classroom /ˈklɑːsrʊm/ *noun*
a room in which a class meets for a lesson ▶ *Which classroom are we in?*

classwork /ˈklɑːswɜːk/ *noun (no plural)*
school work that you do in class, not at home ▶ *Do exercises 1 to 4 as classwork.*

clatter /ˈklætəʳ/ *noun*
the loud noise of hard things knocking together ▶ *The pans fell with a clatter.*

clause /klɔːz/ *noun*
a group of words that contains a verb

C

▶ *The sentence "As I was walking home, I met my friend" contains two clauses. "As I was walking home" is one clause, and "I met my friend" is another.*
COMPARE: **sentence**

claustrophobia /ˌklɔːstrəˈfəʊbɪə/ *noun (no plural)*
the fear of being in a small space ▶ *People who suffer from claustrophobia hate going in caves.*

claustrophobic /ˌklɔːstrəˈfəʊbɪk/ *adjective*
afraid of being in a small space

claw[1] /klɔː/ *noun*
1 one of the sharp, hard points on the foot of a bird or animal
2 the hand of a CRAB or LOBSTER

claw[2] *verb*
to tear something with the claws ▶ *The cat clawed the chair.*

clay /kleɪ/ *noun (no plural)*
soft, sticky earth from which people make pots and bricks

clean[1] /kliːn/ *adjective*
1 not dirty ▶ *Haven't you got a clean shirt?*
2 not yet used ▶ *a clean piece of paper*

clean[2] *verb*
to make something clean ▶ *Have you cleaned the kitchen?*

cleaner /ˈkliːnəʳ/ *noun*
a person who cleans houses or other buildings as their job

cleanliness /ˈklenlɪnəs/ *noun (no plural)*
the state of being clean ▶ *Cleanliness is very important in the kitchen.*

cleanse /klenz/ *verb (present participle* ***cleansing****, past* ***cleansed****)*
to make something such as a wound or your skin completely clean ▶ *Cleanse the wound with antiseptic.*

clean-shaven /ˌkliːn ˈʃeɪvən/ *adjective*
not having a BEARD

clear[1] /klɪəʳ/ *adjective*
1 easy to understand ▶ *It was clear that he wanted to be alone.*
SAME MEANING: **plain**
2 easy to see or hear ▶ *a clear voice*
OPPOSITE (**1** and **2**): **unclear**
3 easy to see through ▶ *clear water*
4 free from anything that blocks or covers ▶ *The road's clear.*

clear[2] *verb*
1 to take away something that is not wanted ▶ *to clear plates from a table*
2 clear up (**a**) to tidy or put things in order ▶ *Can you clear up before he arrives, please?*
(**b**) to get better ▶ *I hope the weather clears up before Sunday.*

clear-cut /ˌklɪə ˈkʌt/ *adjective*
certain or definite ▶ *There's no clear-cut answer to your question.*

clearing /ˈklɪərɪŋ/ *noun*
a small area in a forest where there are no trees

clearly /ˈklɪəlɪ/ *adverb*
1 in a clear way ▶ *Please speak more clearly – we can't hear you.*
2 without any doubt ▶ *Clearly he's very clever!*

cleavage /ˈkliːvɪdʒ/ *noun*
the space between a woman's breasts ▶ *She wore a dress that showed her cleavage.*

clench /klentʃ/ *verb*
to close your hands or your mouth tightly, especially because you are angry ▶ *He clenched his fists and started banging the door.* ▶ *Clenching her teeth, she said "Go away!"*

clergy /ˈklɜːdʒɪ/ *plural noun*
priests and other religious leaders ▶ *Catholic clergy are not allowed to marry.*

clergyman /ˈklɜːdʒɪmən/ *noun (plural* ***clergymen*** */-mən/)*
a male member of the clergy

clerical /ˈklerɪkəl/ *adjective*
connected with office work ▶ *We need some more clerical staff.*

clerk /klɑːk/ *noun*
a person who works in an office and writes letters

clever /ˈklevəʳ/ *adjective*
quick at learning and understanding things *(adverb:* ***cleverly****)*

cliché /ˈkliːʃeɪ/ *noun*
an expression that is used too often and no longer has any real meaning ▶ *His speech was full of clichés like "We must take one day at a time".*

click¹ /klɪk/ *noun*
a short, sharp sound ▶ *There was a loud click as she took the photograph.*

click² *verb*
to make a short, sharp sound ▶ *The door clicked shut.*

client /ˈklaɪənt/ *noun*
a person who pays a professional person for help or advice

clientele /ˌkliːənˈtel/ *noun*
the people who regularly go to a shop or restaurant ▶ *The shop's clientele is mainly women.*

cliff /klɪf/ *noun*
an area of high, steep rock, often close to the sea

climate /ˈklaɪmət/ *noun (no plural)*
the weather that a place regularly has

climax /ˈklaɪmæks/ *noun (plural* ***climaxes****)*
the most important or exciting part of something ▶ *The competition reaches its climax tomorrow.*

climb¹ /klaɪm/ *verb*
to go up ▶ *The two boys climbed the tree.* ▶ *The road climbed steeply up the hill.*

climb² *noun*
an upward journey ▶ *a long climb up the hill*

climber /ˈklaɪməʳ/ *noun*
a person who climbs mountains or rocks as a sport

climbing /ˈklaɪmɪŋ/ *noun (no plural)*
the sport of climbing mountains or rocks ▶ *We go climbing most weekends.*

cling /klɪŋ/ *verb (past* ***clung*** */klʌŋ/)*
to hold on tightly ▶ *The baby monkey clung to its mother.*

clingfilm /ˈklɪŋfɪlm/ *noun (no plural)*
thin, clear plastic that is used for wrapping food

clinic /ˈklɪnɪk/ *noun*
a place where people go to see a doctor

clinical /ˈklɪnɪkəl/ *adjective*
connected with medical treatment and tests ▶ *The drug needs to have clinical trials.*

clip¹ /klɪp/ *noun*
a small metal object used for fastening things ▶ *The letters were held together with a paper clip.*

clip² *verb (present participle* ***clipping****, past* ***clipped****)*
1 to hold things with a clip ▶ *Could you clip those letters together, please?*
2 to cut something with a sharp instrument ▶ *He clipped his fingernails.*

clippers /ˈklɪpəz/ *plural noun*
a tool used for cutting small pieces off something ▶ *a pair of nail clippers*

clipping /ˈklɪpɪŋ/ *noun*
a piece of writing that you cut from a newspaper or magazine ▶ *I found a newspaper clipping about Madonna.*

clique /kliːk/ *noun*
a small group of people who know each other well and are not very friendly to other people ▶ *Jane has become part of their clique.*

cloak /kləʊk/ *noun*
a loose piece of clothing that you

wrap around your body, on top of other clothes, to keep you warm
COMPARE: **cape**

cloakroom /ˈkləʊkrʊm/ *noun*
1 a room where you leave hats, coats, etc.
2 a TOILET

C

clock /klɒk/ *noun*
a machine that tells you what the time is
COMPARE: **watch**

clockwise /ˈklɒkwaɪz/ *adverb*
in the same direction as the hands of a clock
OPPOSITE: **anticlockwise**

clockwork /ˈklɒkwɜːk/ *noun*
like clockwork in exactly the way that you planned ▶ *Production at the factory has been going like clockwork.*

clog[1] /klɒg/ *(also* ***clog up****) verb (present participle* ***clogging****, past* ***clogged****)*
to block something ▶ *Leaves had clogged the drains.*

clog[2] *noun*
a shoe made of wood or with a wooden SOLE

clone[1] /kləʊn/ *noun*
an exact copy of a plant or an animal that a scientist develops from one of its cells

clone[2] *verb (present participle* ***cloning****, past* ***cloned****)*
to produce an exact copy of a plant or an animal from one of its cells
▶ *Scientists have successfully cloned a sheep.*

close[1] /kləʊs/ *adjective*
1 near ▶ *I live close to the shops.*
▶ *They were standing close together* (=very near each other).
2 liking or loving someone
▶ *Peter and John are close friends.*
3 careful ▶ *We kept a close watch on the children.*

close[2] /kləʊz/ *verb (present participle* ***closing****, past* ***closed****)*
1 to shut something ▶ *Please close the door.*
2 (used about a shop, a bank, etc.) to stop being available for business
▶ *What time does the bank close?*
OPPOSITE (**1** and **2**): **open**

close[3] /kləʊz/ *noun*
the end of something ▶ *at the close of the day*

closed /kləʊzd/ *adjective*
1 shut ▶ *Keep your eyes closed.*
▶ *The window was closed because it was raining.*
2 not ready for business ▶ *The shops are closed on Sundays.*
OPPOSITE (**1** and **2**): **open**

closely /ˈkləʊslɪ/ *adverb*
1 very carefully ▶ *The teacher was watching the students closely.*
2 people who are closely related are members of the same family, for example brothers or sisters
3 if people work closely together, they work together and help each other a lot ▶ *We have worked closely with the police to solve this crime.*

close-up /ˈkləʊs ʌp/ *noun*
a photograph of a person that you take when you are standing very near to them ▶ *a close-up of the actor's face*

closing /ˈkləʊzɪŋ/ *adjective*
final ▶ *In the closing chapter of the book, Max dies.*

closure /ˈkləʊʒəʳ/ *noun*
the act of closing a factory, company, school, etc. permanently ▶ *Workers are angry at the closure of their factory.*

clot /klɒt/ *noun*
a place where blood or another liquid has become almost solid ▶ *She has a blood clot in her leg.*

cloth /klɒθ/ *noun*
1 *(no plural)* a soft substance made of

wool, cotton, etc. ▶ *She bought some cloth to make some new dresses.*
SAME MEANING: **material**
2 a piece of cloth used for a particular purpose ▶ *A red tablecloth covered the table.* ▶ *He dried the dishes with a dishcloth.*
LOOK AT: **clothes**

clothe /kləʊð/ *verb (present participle* ***clothing****, past* ***clothed****)*
to provide clothes for someone ▶ *She earns barely enough to feed and clothe her children.*

clothed /kləʊðd/ *adjective*
fully clothed, partly clothed with all your clothes on or with only some of your clothes on ▶ *She got into bed fully clothed.*

clothes /kləʊðz/ *plural noun*
things that you wear on your body ▶ *I need some new clothes.*

> **Cloth** is NOT the singular of **clothes** (look at the entry for **cloth** above). The word **clothes** is always plural and does not have a singular form. People usually use the name of the thing they are talking about when there is only one: *a shirt* ▶ *a dress*

clothesline /ˈkləʊðzlaɪn/ *noun*
a rope that you hang clothes on outside so that they will dry

clothes peg /ˈkləʊðz peg/ *noun*
a small object that you use to fasten clothes to a clothesline

clothing /ˈkləʊðɪŋ/ *noun (no plural)*
things that are used as clothes ▶ *warm winter clothing*

cloud /klaʊd/ *noun*
a mass of very small drops of water floating in the sky

cloudy /ˈklaʊdɪ/ *adjective (****cloudier, cloudiest****)*
having lots of clouds ▶ *a cloudy day*

clove /kləʊv/ *noun*
1 one of the parts that a GARLIC plant is made up of ▶ *Chop up two cloves of garlic.*
2 a small, dried, black flower with a strong, sweet smell, used in cooking

clover /ˈkləʊvəʳ/ *noun (no plural)*
a small plant with white or purple flowers and three round leaves on each stem

clown /klaʊn/ *noun*
a person who wears funny clothes and tries to make people laugh

club /klʌb/ *noun*
1 a group of people who have joined together and meet each other because they share an interest ▶ *a gardening club*
2 a large, heavy stick

clubbing /ˈklʌbɪŋ/ *noun (no plural)*
the activity of going to a club to dance ▶ *When we were in Ibiza, we went out clubbing every night.*

clue /kluː/ *noun*
something that helps you find the answer to a difficult question ▶ *The police have found a clue which will help them to catch the robber.*

clump /klʌmp/ *noun*
a group of trees, bushes, plants, etc. that are close together ▶ *a clump of trees*

clumsy /ˈklʌmzɪ/ *adjective (****clumsier, clumsiest****)*
likely to move in an awkward way or drop things ▶ *You are clumsy! You've knocked over my cup of coffee!* *(adverb:* ***clumsily****)*

clung /klʌŋ/
the PAST TENSE and PAST PARTICIPLE of the verb **cling**

cluster /ˈklʌstəʳ/ *verb*
to form a group ▶ *Everyone clustered around the television.*

clutch /klʌtʃ/ *verb*
to take hold of something tightly ▶ *She clutched her baby in her arms.*

C

clutter[1] /ˈklʌtəʳ/ *(also* ***clutter up****)* *verb*
to make something untidy by covering or filling it with things ▶ *Books and papers cluttered his desk.*

clutter[2] *noun (no plural)*
a lot of things scattered in an untidy way ▶ *Please tidy up this clutter before you leave.*

cm
a short way of writing the words **centimetre** or **centimetres** ▶ *10cm*

Co. /kəʊ/
a short way of writing and saying the word **company** ▶ *Hilton, Brooks & Co.*

c/o
a short way of writing the words **care of**; used as part of an address when you send a letter to someone who will give it to the person you are writing to ▶ *Michael Miles, c/o Mrs C. Brown, 219 Park Lane, London*

coach[1] /kəʊtʃ/ *noun (plural* ***coaches****)*
1 a bus, or part of a train, that can carry many people
2 a covered vehicle with four wheels, pulled by horses
3 a person who gives special lessons ▶ *football coach*

coach[2] *verb*
to give someone special lessons ▶ *He coached her for the English examination.*

coal /kəʊl/ *noun (no plural)*
a hard, black material dug out of the ground and burned to give heat

coarse /kɔːs/ *adjective*
rough; not smooth or fine

coast /kəʊst/ *noun*
the land next to the sea ▶ *a town on the coast*

coastal /ˈkəʊstəl/ *adjective*
on the land near the sea, or in the sea near the land ▶ *the coastal regions of Italy* ▶ *coastal waters*

coastguard /ˈkəʊstˌgɑːd/ *noun*
a person whose job is to help boats and swimmers that are in danger

coastline /ˈkəʊstlaɪn/ *noun*
the edge of the land ▶ *From the ship, they saw the rocky coastline.*

coat /kəʊt/ *noun*
1 a piece of clothing that you wear over your other clothes to keep you warm when you go outside
2 an animal's fur, wool, or hair
3 a covering of something spread over a surface ▶ *a coat* ***of*** *paint*

coat hanger /ˈkəʊt ˌhæŋəʳ/ *noun*
a specially shaped piece of wood or plastic with a hook on top, used for hanging up clothes

coax /kəʊks/ *verb*
to persuade someone by kindness or care ▶ *She coaxed him to take the medicine.*

cobweb /ˈkɒbweb/ *noun*
the thin net which a SPIDER spins to catch flies and insects

cocaine /kəʊˈkeɪn/ *noun (no plural)*
a drug that prevents pain, or that is taken illegally for pleasure

cock /kɒk/ *noun*
a male bird, especially a male chicken

cockerel /ˈkɒkərəl/ *noun*
a young male chicken

cockpit /ˈkɒkˌpɪt/ *noun*
the part of a plane where the pilot sits

cockroach /ˈkɒkˌrəʊtʃ/ *noun (plural* ***cockroaches****)*
a large, black or brown insect that lives where food is kept

cocktail /ˈkɒkteɪl/ *noun*
an alcoholic drink made from a mixture of different drinks

cocky /ˈkɒkɪ/ *adjective (****cockier, cockiest****)*
too confident about yourself, in a way that annoys other people ▶ *He's very talented, but far too cocky.*

cocoa /'kəʊkəʊ/ *noun (no plural)*
1 a brown powder made from the seeds of a tree, from which chocolate is made
2 a hot drink made from this powder

coconut /'kəʊkənʌt/ *noun*
a large nut with hard, white flesh and a hollow centre filled with milky juice

cod /kɒd/ *noun (plural **cod**)*
a sea fish used for food

code /kəʊd/ *noun*
a way of using words, letters, numbers, etc. to keep messages secret ▶ *The letter was written in code and I could not understand it.*

co-ed /ˌkəʊ 'ed/ *adjective*
(used about schools and colleges) CO-EDUCATIONAL; having both male and female students

coerce /kəʊ'ɜːs/ *verb (present participle **coercing**, past **coerced**)*
to force someone to do something by threatening them ▶ *They coerced him into confessing.*

coffee /'kɒfɪ/ *noun*
1 *(no plural)* (a drink made from) a brown powder from the seeds of the coffee tree
2 a cup of this drink ▶ *Two coffees, please!*

coffee table /'kɒfɪ ˌteɪbəl/ *noun*
a low table in a LIVING ROOM

coffin /'kɒfɪn/ *noun*
a box in which a dead body is put

coil[1] /kɔɪl/ *verb*
1 to twist a rope, wire, or pipe round and round
2 to go round in a circle ▶ *The snake coiled round the tree.*

coil[2] *noun*
a set of rings joined to each other; a continuous circular shape ▶ *a coil of rope*

coin /kɔɪn/ *noun*
a piece of money made of metal
COMPARE: **bank note**

coincide /ˌkəʊɪn'saɪd/ *verb (present participle **coinciding**, past **coincided**)*
if one event coincides with another, the two things happen at the same time ▶ *My birthday coincides **with** her visit.*

coincidence /kəʊ'ɪnsɪdəns/ *noun*
a number of events happening together by chance, which are often surprising ▶ *What a coincidence that I was in London at the same time as you!*

cold[1] /kəʊld/ *adjective*
having little heat ▶ *a cold drink*
OPPOSITE: **hot**

cold[2] *noun*
1 an illness of the nose and throat ▶ *I've got a cold*
2 *(no plural)* cold weather ▶ *I don't like the cold.*
OPPOSITE (**2**): **heat**

cold-blooded /ˌkəʊld 'blʌdɪd/ *adjective*
cruel and showing no feelings ▶ *This was a cold-blooded murder.*

collaborate /kə'læbəreɪt/ *verb (present participle **collaborating**, past **collaborated**)*
to work together to produce or achieve something ▶ *Two companies collaborated **on** this project.*

collaboration /ˌkəˌlæbə'reɪʃən/ *noun (no plural)*
the act of working together to produce or achieve something

collage /'kɒlɑːʒ/ *noun*
a picture that you make by sticking pieces of paper and cloth onto a surface ▶ *The children made a collage of their visit to the zoo.*

collapse /kə'læps/ *verb (present participle **collapsing**, past **collapsed**)*
to break into pieces; to fall down ▶ *The roof of the old house collapsed.* ▶ *The old man collapsed in the street.*

C

C

collar /ˈkɒləʳ/ *noun*
1 the part of a shirt or coat that goes round your neck ▶ *The collar of his shirt was dirty.*
2 a leather or metal band put round the neck of an animal

collarbone /ˈkɒləbəʊn/ *noun*
one of two bones that go from the base of your neck to your shoulders ▶ *I broke my collarbone playing rugby.*

colleague /ˈkɒliːg/ *noun*
a person who you work with ▶ *This is Ian, a colleague of mine.*

collect /kəˈlekt/ *verb*
1 to come together or bring things together in the same place ▶ *A crowd had collected to watch the ceremony.* ▶ *I collect stamps.*
2 to come to take someone or something away ▶ *He collected the children from school.*
3 to get money from people ▶ *I'm collecting* ***for*** *the blind.*

collection /kəˈlekʃən/ *noun*
a group of things which have been brought together ▶ *a large collection* ***of*** *stamps*

collective[1] /kəˈlektɪv/ *adjective*
shared or done by all the members of a group together ▶ *It was a collective decision to give you the money.* *(adverb:* ***collectively****)*

collective[2] *noun*
a business owned and controlled by the people who work in it

college /ˈkɒlɪdʒ/ *noun*
a place where people study after they have left school
COMPARE: **university**

collide /kəˈlaɪd/ *verb (present participle* ***colliding****, past* ***collided****)*
to bang together with great force ▶ *The two trains collided.*

collision /kəˈlɪʒən/ *noun*
a violent crash ▶ *a collision between two trains*

colon /ˈkəʊlɒn/ *noun*
the sign (:) which comes before the first example in the text after 'colour' below

colonel /ˈkɜːnl/ *noun*
an officer in the army

colony /ˈkɒlənɪ/ *noun (plural* ***colonies****)*
a country that is under the control of another country

colossal /kəˈlɒsəl/ *adjective*
very big ▶ *Global warming is a colossal problem.*

colour[1] /ˈkʌləʳ/ *noun*
the quality that makes things look green, red, yellow, etc. ▶ *"What colour is her hair?" "It's black."*

> The word **colour** is not usually used in sentences describing the colour of something: *Her dress is red.* ▶ *He has brown hair.*

colour[2] *verb*
to put colour on to something ▶ *Sarah is colouring the picture in her book.*

colour-blind /ˈkʌlə ˌblaɪnd/ *adjective*
not able to see the difference between particular colours

coloured /ˈkʌləd/ *adjective*
having a colour such as blue, red, or yellow ▶ *A black dress looks good with a coloured scarf.*

colourful /ˈkʌləfəl/ *adjective*
bright; having lots of colours ▶ *colourful clothes*

colouring /ˈkʌlərɪŋ/ *noun (no plural)*
the colour of someone's hair, skin, eyes, etc. ▶ *She has the same pale colouring as her sister.*

colourless /ˈkʌləlәs/ *adjective*
not having any colour ▶ *Water is a colourless liquid.*

column /ˈkɒləm/ *noun*
1 a large post used to support a part of a building

2 something long and narrow ▶ *Can you add up this column of figures?*

coma /ˈkəʊmə/ *noun*
a condition in which someone is not conscious for a long time, usually as the result of an accident or illness
▶ *Ben was in a coma for six days.*

comb¹ /kəʊm/ *noun*
a thin piece of plastic, metal, etc. with teeth, that you use to make your hair tidy

comb² *verb*
to tidy your hair with a comb ▶ *Have you combed your hair?*

combat¹ /ˈkɒmbæt/ *noun (no plural)*
fighting during a war ▶ *Many soldiers were killed in combat.*

combat² *verb (present participle* ***combating*** *or* ***combatting****, past* ***combated*** *or* ***combatted****)*
to try to stop something bad from happening or getting worse ▶ *What is the best way to combat crime?*

combination /ˌkɒmbɪˈneɪʃən/ *noun*
a mixture of separate people or things joined together ▶ *His character is a combination* ***of*** *strength and kindness.*

combine /kəmˈbaɪn/ *verb (present participle* ***combining****, past* ***combined****)*
to join or mix together ▶ *The two small shops combined to make one large one.*

come /kʌm/ *verb (present participle* ***coming****, past tense* ***came*** */keɪm/, past participle* ***come****)*
1 to move towards the person speaking ▶ *Come here, Mary. I want to speak to you!* ▶ *I'm going out. Are you coming with me?*
2 come about to happen ▶ *This situation should never have come about.*
3 come across someone or something to find someone or something by chance ▶ *I came across an old friend I hadn't seen for years.*
4 come from to have been born or have lived a long time in a place
▶ *I come from Glasgow.*
5 Come on! Hurry up!
6 come off to become unfastened
▶ *My shoe has come off.*

comeback /ˈkʌmbæk/ *noun*
make a comeback to return after a long time and become popular or successful again ▶ *a fashion that made a brief comeback in the 1980s*

comedian /kəˈmiːdɪən/ *noun*
a person whose job is to tell jokes and make people laugh

comedy /ˈkɒmədɪ/ *noun (plural* ***comedies****)*
a funny play, film, etc.; something that makes you laugh
COMPARE: **tragedy**

comet /ˈkɒmɪt/ *noun*
a very bright object in the sky, like a star with a tail ▶ *A comet flew across the sky.*

comfort¹ /ˈkʌmfət/ *noun (no plural)*
a state in which you are free from pain, trouble, etc. ▶ *He lived in comfort* (=he had enough money to live well).

comfort² *verb*
to give help to someone or show them kindness when they are in pain or trouble ▶ *She comforted the unhappy child.*

comfortable /ˈkʌmftəbəl/ *adjective*
1 pleasant to wear, sit in, or be in
▶ *This is a very comfortable chair.*
OPPOSITE: **uncomfortable**
2 with no pain or worries ▶ *We're not rich but we are quite comfortable.*
(adverb: ***comfortably****)*

comic¹ /ˈkɒmɪk/ *adjective*
making people laugh; funny

comic² *noun*
a small book for children, with pictures that tell the story

C

comical /'kɒmɪkəl/ *adjective*
funny in a strange or an unexpected way ▶ *He looked comical with his hands waving in the air.*

comic strip /'kɒmɪk strɪp/ *noun*
a set of pictures in a newspaper or magazine that tell a short, funny story

C

coming /'kʌmɪŋ/ *adjective*
happening soon ▶ *We will be very busy over the coming months.*

comma /'kɒmə/ *noun*
the sign (,) used in writing to divide up a sentence

command¹ /kə'mɑːnd/ *verb*
1 to order someone to do something ▶ *I command you to go!*
2 to be in charge of people ▶ *A general commands a large number of soldiers.*

command² *noun*
1 an order
2 *(no plural)* power ▶ *The officer is in command of his men.*

commander /kə'mɑːndəʳ/ *noun*
an officer who is in charge of a military organization or group

commemorate /kə'meməreɪt/ *verb (present participle* ***commemorating,*** *past* ***commemorated)***
to show that an event or a person is remembered with respect ▶ *a monument commemorating those who died in the war*

commence /kə'mens/ *verb (present participle* ***commencing,*** *past* ***commenced)***
to begin ▶ *The evening performance will commence at 8 o'clock.*
SAME MEANING: **start**

commendable /kə'mendəbəl/ *adjective*
deserving praise and admiration ▶ *It is commendable that you want to help.*

comment¹ /'kɒment/ *verb*
to make a remark about something, or give an opinion about something ▶ *He commented* ***on*** *the bad road.*

comment² *noun*
an opinion or a remark about something ▶ *He's always making rude comments* ***about*** *his boss.*

commentary /'kɒməntərɪ/ *noun (plural* ***commentaries)***
a spoken description of something that is happening

commentate /'kɒmənteɪt/ *verb (present participle* ***commentating,*** *past* ***commentated)***
to describe an event on television or radio while it is happening ▶ *John McEnroe is here to commentate on the event for the BBC.*

commentator /'kɒmənteɪtəʳ/ *noun*
someone who describes an event while it is happening ▶ *a radio commentator*

commerce /'kɒmɜːs/ *noun (no plural)*
business; buying and selling goods

commercial /kə'mɜːʃəl/ *adjective*
related to the buying and selling of goods

commercialized /kə'mɜːʃəlaɪzd/ *adjective*
too concerned with making money ▶ *The holiday resort has become too commercialized.*

commission¹ /kə'mɪʃən/ *noun*
1 an official group of people whose job is to find out about something or control an activity ▶ *The International Whaling Commission decides the limits on catching whales.*
2 *(no plural)* money that a person or an organization is paid when they sell something ▶ *The bank charges commission for cashing traveller's cheques.*

commission² *verb*
to ask someone to do a particular piece of work for you ▶ *The*

government commissioned the report.

commit /kəˈmɪt/ *verb (present participle* ***committing****, past* ***committed****)*
to do something wrong ▶ *He said he hadn't committed the murder.*

commitment /kəˈmɪtmənt/ *noun*
1 a promise to do something ▶ *They made a commitment to work together.*
2 *(no plural)* determination to work hard and continue with something ▶ *You need commitment to succeed in this sport.*

committed /kəˈmɪtɪd/ *adjective*
willing to work hard at something ▶ *He seems committed* ***to*** *his work.*

committee /kəˈmɪtɪ/ *noun*
a group of people chosen to study something, plan, and make decisions ▶ *The club committee arranges all the football matches.*

common /ˈkɒmən/ *adjective*
1 found everywhere; usual ▶ *Red buses are quite common in London.* OPPOSITE: **rare, uncommon**
2 shared by several people; belonging to or used by several people ▶ *The park is common property – everyone can use it.*

commonly /ˈkɒmənlɪ/ *adverb*
often ▶ *People with this illness commonly complain of headaches.*

commonplace /ˈkɒmənpleɪs/ *adjective*
not unusual ▶ *Divorce is now commonplace.*

common sense /ˌkɒmən ˈsens/ *noun (no plural)*
the ability to behave in a sensible way and make practical decisions ▶ *Just use your common sense.*

Commonwealth /ˈkɒmənwelθ/ *noun*
a group of independent countries which used to be part of the British Empire (=under the control of Britain)

commotion /kəˈməʊʃən/ *noun (no plural)*
sudden noise or activity

communicate /kəˈmjuːnɪkeɪt/ *verb (past participle* ***communicating****, past* ***communicated****)*
to speak or write to someone ▶ *If you know English, you can communicate* ***with*** *a lot of people.* ▶ *We communicated by letter.*

communication /kəˌmjuːnɪˈkeɪʃən/ *noun*
1 *(no plural)* the act of speaking or writing to someone and being understood by them ▶ *Communication between people who speak different languages is difficult.*
2 communications *plural noun* roads, railways, radio, telephones, and all other ways of moving or sending information between places

Communism /ˈkɒmjʊnɪzəm/ *noun (no plural)*
a political system based on the idea that people are equal and that the state should own companies

Communist /ˈkɒmjʊnɪst/ *noun*
a person who believes in Communism

community /kəˈmjuːnətɪ/ *noun (plural* ***communities****)*
all the people living in one place ▶ *All children in our community go to the same school.*

commute /kəˈmjuːt/ *verb (present participle* ***commuting****, past* ***commuted****)*
to regularly travel a long distance to work ▶ *My dad commutes from Oxford to London every day.*

commuter /kəˈmjuːtəʳ/ *noun*
a person who travels a long way to work each day

compact /kəmˈpækt, ˈkɒmpækt/ *adjective*

small and taking up very little space ▶ *the compact design of modern computers*

compact disc /ˌkɒmpækt 'dɪsk/ *noun* a type of record with very high-quality sound, played on a special machine

compact disc player /ˌkɒmpækt 'dɪsk ˌpleɪəʳ/ *(also **CD player**) noun* a special machine for playing COMPACT DISCS

C

companion /kəm'pænjən/ *noun* a person you are with, often a friend ▶ *He was my travelling companion for many months.*

companionship /kəm'pænjənʃɪp/ *noun (no plural)* friendship from people who you spend time with ▶ *I missed the companionship of work.*

company /'kʌmpənɪ/ *noun*
1 *(no plural)* a person or people you are with ▶ *I had no company on the journey.*
2 *(plural **companies**)* a group of people doing business; a firm ▶ *I work for a mining company.*

comparable /'kɒmpərəbəl/ *adjective* similar in size or importance ▶ *He was offered a comparable job at another branch of the company.*

comparative /kəm'pærətɪv/ *noun, adjective* a word or a form of a word that shows that something is bigger, smaller, better, worse, etc. than something else; for example, "bigger" is the comparative form of "big"
COMPARE: **superlative**

comparatively /kəm'pærətɪvlɪ/ *adverb* compared with something else ▶ *Houses in that area are comparatively cheap.*

compare /kəm'peəʳ/ *verb (present participle **comparing**, past **compared**)* to decide in what way things are alike or different ▶ *People are always comparing me **to** my sister.* ▶ *We compared the prices in the shop **with** the prices at the market.*

comparison /kəm'pærɪsən/ *noun* an act of judging two things and saying whether they are alike or different ▶ *My shoes are small in comparison with my sister's.*

compartment /kəm'pɑːtmənt/ *noun*
1 a room in a train
2 a separate part of a container ▶ *a special compartment **for** meat*

compass /'kʌmpəs/ *noun (plural **compasses**)* an instrument with a metal needle that always points north

compassion /kəm'pæʃən/ *noun (no plural)* sympathy for people who are suffering

compassionate /kəm'pæʃənət/ *adjective* feeling sympathy for people who are suffering

compatible /kəm'pætəbəl/ *adjective*
1 having similar ideas or interests, and able to have a good relationship
2 able to exist or be used together without problems ▶ *Is the new software compatible **with** the old version?*
OPPOSITE (**1** and **2**): **incompatible**

compel /kəm'pel/ *verb (present participle **compelling**, past **compelled**)* to force someone to do something ▶ *The floods compelled us to turn back.*

compelling /kəm'pelɪŋ/ *adjective* very interesting or exciting ▶ *a compelling TV drama*

compensate /'kɒmpənseɪt/ *verb (present participle **compensating**, past **compensated**)* to do something good so that the bad effects of something else seem less important ▶ *He bought his kids presents to compensate **for** being away so much.*

compensation /ˌkɒmpən'seɪʃən/ *noun*
1 *(no plural)* money that someone is given because they have been injured or badly treated, or have lost something ▶ *The holiday company had to pay the Taylors £1,500 compensation.*
2 something that makes a bad situation seem better ▶ *Being unemployed has its compensations, like not having to get up early.*

compete /kəm'piːt/ *verb (present participle **competing**, past **competed**)*
to try to win a race, prize, etc.
▶ *Five children competed in the race.*

competence /'kɒmpɪtəns/ *noun (no plural)*
the ability to do a job correctly
OPPOSITE: **incompetence**

competent /'kɒmpɪtənt/ *adjective*
good at your work or able to do a job well ▶ *a highly competent doctor*
OPPOSITE: **incompetent**

competition /ˌkɒmpə'tɪʃən/ *noun*
a test of who is best at something
▶ *She came first in a drawing competition.*

competitive /kəm'petɪtɪv/ *adjective*
determined to be more successful than other people ▶ *Boys are usually more competitive than girls.*

competitor /kəm'petɪtəʳ/ *noun*
a person who tries to win something

compilation /ˌkɒmpɪ'leɪʃən/ *noun*
a collection of songs or pieces of writing that were originally sold as part of different records or books
▶ *The new CD is a compilation of David Bowie's hit singles.*

compile /kəm'paɪl/ *verb (present participle **compiling**, past **compiled**)*
to make a book, list, etc., using different pieces of information
▶ *They compiled a list of the most popular activities.*

complacent /kəm'pleɪsənt/ *adjective*
too pleased with what you have achieved so that you no longer try to improve ▶ *You should do well in your exams, but you mustn't get complacent.*

complain /kəm'pleɪn/ *verb*
to say that something is not very good, or that you are unhappy or annoyed with something ▶ *We complained **about** the bad food.*

complaint /kəm'pleɪnt/ *noun*
something said which expresses annoyance or unhappiness about something ▶ *We made a complaint **about** the food.*

complete¹ /kəm'pliːt/ *adjective*
1 whole; with nothing left out
▶ *a complete set of stamps*
OPPOSITE: **incomplete**
2 total ▶ *a complete waste of time*

complete² *verb (present participle **completing**, past **completed**)*
to finish something ▶ *to complete a piece of work*

completely /kəm'pliːtlɪ/ *adverb*
totally ▶ *Have you completely finished your work?*

complex¹ /'kɒmpleks/ *adjective*
consisting of many connected parts, especially in a way that is difficult to understand or explain ▶ *the complex nature of the human mind* ▶ *a highly complex issue*

complex² *noun (plural **complexes**)*
a group of buildings used for a similar purpose ▶ *a new shopping complex*

complexion /kəm'plekʃən/ *noun*
the natural colour and appearance of the skin on your face ▶ *a pale complexion*

C

complicate /ˈkɒmplɪkeɪt/ *verb (present participle **complicating**, past **complicated**)*
to make something more difficult to do or understand ▶ *Bad weather complicated the attempt to rescue the climbers.*

complicated /ˈkɒmplɪkeɪtɪd/ *adjective*
difficult to understand; not simple ▶ *A car engine is a complicated machine.*

complication /ˌkɒmplɪˈkeɪʃən/ *noun*
a problem that makes something more difficult to do or understand ▶ *We don't expect any further complications in the travel arrangements.*

compliment[1] /ˈkɒmplɪmənt/ *noun*
something nice said about someone
OPPOSITE: **insult**

compliment[2] /ˈkɒmplɪment/ *verb*
to say something nice to someone because they have done something you think is clever or good ▶ *She complimented Mary **on** her excellent Spanish.*

comply /kəmˈplaɪ/ *verb (past **complied**)*
to obey an order or a request ▶ *Anyone who fails to comply **with** the law will have to pay a £100 fine.*

component /kəmˈpəʊnənt/ *noun*
one of the different parts of a machine

compose /kəmˈpəʊz/ *verb (present participle **composing**, past **composed**)*
1 to write or make up a song, poem, or a piece of music
2 be composed of to be formed from different parts ▶ *The course will be composed of three parts ...*

composer /kəmˈpəʊzəʳ/ *noun*
a person who writes music

composition /ˌkɒmpəˈzɪʃən/ *noun*
a story, poem, piece of music, etc. that you have written

compound /ˈkɒmpaʊnd/ *noun*
a group of buildings and the land around them

comprehension /ˌkɒmprɪˈhenʃən/ *noun*
1 a test of how well students understand written or spoken language
2 *(no plural)* the ability to understand something ▶ *The students want to improve their reading comprehension skills.*

comprehensive /ˌkɒmprɪˈhensɪv/ *adjective*
including everything that is needed ▶ *a comprehensive range of books*

comprehensive school /ˌkɒmprɪˈhensɪv ˌskuːl/ *noun*
a SECONDARY school which teaches pupils of all abilities
COMPARE: **grammar school**

comprise /kəmˈpraɪz/ *verb (present participle **comprising**, past **comprised**)*
1 be comprised of to consist of particular parts, groups, or people ▶ *The committee is comprised of eight members.*
2 to form part of a larger group ▶ *Women comprise over 75% of our staff.*

compromise[1] /ˈkɒmprəmaɪz/ *noun*
a situation in which people or groups accept less than they really want, especially in order to end an argument ▶ *Talks will continue until a compromise is reached.*

compromise[2] *verb (present participle **compromising**, past **compromised**)*
to accept less than you really want, especially in order to end an argument ▶ *President Chirac has said*

that he would be ready to compromise.

compulsory /kəm'pʌlsərɪ/ *adjective*
that must be done because of a rule or law ► *Science is compulsory at our school.*

computer /kəm'pjuːtəʳ/ *noun*
a machine that stores information and can work out answers to sums very quickly ► *a personal computer*

computer game /kəm'pjuːtə ˌgeɪm/ *noun*
a game played on a computer

computer programmer /kəmˌpjuːtə 'prəʊgræməʳ/ *noun*
a person who prepares lists of rules that are put into a computer to make the computer give the right information or do the right job

con /kɒn/ *verb (present participle* ***conning****, past* ***conned****)*
to trick someone in order to get something you want ► *They conned me* ***into*** *paying for all the tickets.*

conceal /kən'siːl/ *verb*
to hide something ► *He tried to conceal the book under his jacket.* ► *Sue tried hard to conceal her disappointment from the others.*

concede /kən'siːd/ *verb (present participle* ***conceding****, past* ***conceded****)*
1 concede defeat to admit that you are not going to win a game, an argument, etc.
2 to admit that something is true, although you do not want to ► *She reluctantly conceded that I was right.*

conceited /kən'siːtɪd/ *adjective*
too proud of how good, clever, or attractive you are ► *He's so conceited about his looks.*

conceivable /kən'siːvəbəl/ *adjective*
possible ► *It is conceivable that the experts are wrong.*

conceive /kən'siːv/ *verb (present participle* ***conceiving****, past* ***conceived****)*
to become PREGNANT

concentrate /'kɒnsəntreɪt/ *verb (present participle* ***concentrating****, past* ***concentrated****)*
to keep your thoughts or attention on one thing ► *Are you concentrating* ***on*** *your work?*

concentrated /'kɒnsəntreɪtɪd/ *adjective*
(used about liquids) thick and strong because most of the water has been removed

concentration /ˌkɒnsən'treɪʃən/ *noun*
1 *(no plural)* the ability to think very carefully about something for a long time ► *The work requires a lot of concentration.* ► *The moment they lose concentration, they forget everything I have told them to do.*
2 a large amount of something in the same place ► *The area has a high concentration of wildlife.*

concept /'kɒnsept/ *noun*
a general idea ► *Many films have been based on the concept of time travel.*

conception /kən'sepʃən/ *noun (no plural)*
the act of becoming PREGNANT

concern[1] /kən'sɜːn/ *noun*
worry ► *He shows no concern for his children.*

concern[2] *verb*
1 to be about something ► *The story concerns a man who lived in Russia a long time ago.*
2 to be of importance or interest to someone ► *This letter concerns you.*
3 to worry someone ► *Her refusal to eat concerns us.*

concerned /kən'sɜːnd/ *adjective*
1 anxious or worried ► *I'm very concerned* ***about*** *my mother's illness.*

C

C

▶ *She was concerned for their safety.*
2 as far as I'm concerned in my opinion

concerning /kən'sɜːnɪŋ/ *preposition*
about ▶ *Concerning your letter, I am pleased to inform you that ....*
SAME MEANING: **regarding**

concert /'kɒnsət/ *noun*
an occasion when music is played in public for a lot of people

concession /kən'seʃən/ *noun*
something that you agree to in order to end an argument ▶ *She wasn't prepared to make any concessions.*

concise /kən'saɪs/ *adjective*
short and clear, without using too many words ▶ *He gave a concise explanation of the problem.*

conclude /kən'kluːd/ *verb*
(present participle ***concluding****, past* ***concluded****)*
1 to finish something ▶ *She concluded her speech with a joke.*
2 to decide that something is true from what you have learned ▶ *When I had heard the story, I concluded that he had told me the truth.*

conclusion /kən'kluːʒən/ *noun*
a judgement or decision that you reach after some thought ▶ *My conclusion was that the boy had told me the truth.*

conclusive /kən'kluːsɪv/ *adjective*
proving that something is definitely true ▶ *There is now conclusive evidence that smoking causes cancer.* *(adverb:* ***conclusively****)*
OPPOSITE: **inconclusive**

concrete /'kɒŋkriːt/ *noun (no plural)*
a grey powder mixed with sand and water, which becomes very hard and is used for building

concussion /kən'kʌʃən/ *noun (no plural)*
slight damage to your brain caused when you hit your head on something

condemn /kən'dem/ *verb*
to send someone to prison for a crime

condemnation /ˌkɒndem'neɪʃən/ *noun*
a statement of very strong disapproval ▶ *There has been widespread condemnation of the bombing.*

condensation /ˌkɒnden'seɪʃən/ *noun (no plural)*
small drops of water that appear on a cold surface when steam or hot air touches it

condescending /ˌkɒndɪ'sendɪŋ/ *adjective*
showing that you think you are better or more important than other people ▶ *He was laughing at her in that condescending way he has.*

condition /kən'dɪʃən/ *noun*
1 the state of someone or something ▶ *The car is in very good condition.* ▶ *Weather conditions are bad today.*
2 something that must happen before something else happens ▶ *One of the conditions* ***of*** *being given the job was that I had to learn English.* ▶ *I was given the job* ***on condition*** *that I learned English.*

conditional /kən'dɪʃənəl/ *adjective*
a conditional part of a sentence begins with "if" or "unless"

conditioner /kən'dɪʃənəʳ/ *noun*
a liquid that you put on your hair after you have washed it to keep it in good condition

condom /'kɒndəm/ *noun*
a thin piece of rubber that a man wears over his PENIS during sex

condone /kən'dəʊn/ *verb*
(present participle ***condoning****, past* ***condoned****)*
to approve of or allow behaviour that most people think is wrong ▶ *I cannot condone the use of violence.*

conduct[1] /kən'dʌkt/ *verb*
to lead or guide someone ▶ *He conducted us on a tour of the castle.*

conduct[2] /'kɒndʌkt/ *noun (no plural)*
the way you behave
SAME MEANING: **behaviour**

conductor /kən'dʌktəʳ/ *noun*
1 a person who controls a group of people playing music
2 a person who sells tickets on a bus or train

cone /kəʊn/ *noun*
1 a round shape that is pointed at one end, like the end of a sharp pencil
2 a thing that grows on the branches of CONIFER trees, which contains seeds

confederation /kənˌfedə'reɪʃən/ *(also **confederacy** /kən'fedərəsɪ/) noun*
an official group of people, organizations, or states that have joined together to achieve an aim

confer /kən'fɜːʳ/ *verb (present participle **conferring**, past **conferred**)*
to discuss something with other people so that everyone can express their opinion ▶ *I will have to confer **with** my colleagues about this.*

conference /'kɒnfərəns/ *noun*
a meeting of people to find out what they think about a subject ▶ *a doctors' conference*

confess /kən'fes/ *verb*
to tell someone about things you have done wrong ▶ *When the police questioned the man, he confessed.*

confession /kən'feʃən/ *noun*
a speech or piece of writing saying what you have done wrong ▶ *He made a confession.*

confetti /kən'fetɪ/ *noun (no plural)*
small pieces of paper that you throw over a man and woman who have just got married

confide /kən'faɪd/ *verb (present participle **confiding**, past **confided**)*
to tell a secret to someone you trust ▶ *She chose to confide **in** her sister.*

confidence /'kɒnfɪdəns/ *noun (no plural)*
a calm, unworried feeling that you are sure that you can do something ▶ *She plays the piano well, but doesn't have the confidence to play to others.*

confident /'kɒnfɪdənt/ *adjective*
feeling sure or safe ▶ *I was confident that I had passed the examination.*

confidential /ˌkɒnfɪ'denʃəl/ *adjective*
intended to be kept secret ▶ *confidential information*

confine /kən'faɪn/ *verb*
be confined to to happen in only one place, or to affect only one group of people ▶ *This illness is not confined to older people.*

confirm /kən'fɜːm/ *verb*
to say for certain that something is true or will happen ▶ *Please confirm your telephone message by writing to me.*

confirmation /ˌkɒnfə'meɪʃən/ *noun (no plural)*
something that shows other things to be true

confiscate /'kɒnfɪskeɪt/ *verb (present participle **confiscating**, past **confiscated**)*
to take something away from someone, either because they are not allowed to have it or as a punishment ▶ *The police confiscated his gun.*

conflict[1] /'kɒnflɪkt/ *noun*
a fight or an argument ▶ *a conflict **between** two countries*

conflict[2] /kən'flɪkt/ *verb*
to disagree ▶ *The two stories conflicted, so I did not know what to believe.*

conform /kən'fɔːm/ *verb*
1 to behave in the way that most other people behave ▶ *There's always*

C

pressure on kids to conform.
2 to obey or follow an established rule, pattern, etc. ▶ *Seatbelts must conform **to** official safety standards.*

confront /kən'frʌnt/ *verb*
1 to deal with a problem or difficult situation rather than ignore it ▶ *We want to help you to confront your problems.*
2 to try to make someone admit they have done something wrong ▶ *Richard confronted his sister about her lies.*

confrontation /ˌkɒnfrən'teɪʃən/ *noun*
a situation in which there is a lot of angry disagreement ▶ *I try to avoid confrontations.*

confuse /kən'fjuːz/ *verb (present participle **confusing**, past **confused**)*
to mix ideas in your mind so that you feel unsure about something ▶ *I confused the two boys, because they look so alike.*

confused /kən'fjuːzd/ *adjective*
unable to understand something clearly ▶ *I'm totally confused.* ▶ *If you're confused **about** anything, call me.*

confusing /kən'fjuːzɪŋ/ *adjective*
difficult to understand ▶ *This map is really confusing.*

confusion /kən'fjuːʒən/ *noun (no plural)*
a state of mind in which you are uncertain what to think or do ▶ *The room was **in** complete confusion.*

congestion /kən'dʒestʃən/ *noun (no plural)*
a situation in which there are too many vehicles on a road ▶ *There is a lot of congestion on the roads today.*

congratulate /kən'grætʃʊleɪt/ *verb (present participle **congratulating**, past **congratulated**)*
to say you are pleased about a happy event ▶ *I congratulated them **on** the birth of their baby.*

congratulations /kənˌgrætʃʊ'leɪʃənz/ *interjection*
an expression of happiness or admiration for something someone has done ▶ *Congratulations **on** the birth of your baby!*

congregation /ˌkɒŋgrɪ'geɪʃən/ *noun*
the people who are in a church for a religious ceremony

conifer /'kəʊnɪfəʳ/ *noun*
a tree that keeps its leaves in winter and has CONES containing its seeds

conjunction /kən'dʒʌŋkʃən/ *noun*
a word such as "and" or "but" that joins two parts of a sentence

conjure /'kʌndʒəʳ/ *verb (present participle **conjuring**, past **conjured**)*
to make something appear as if by magic ▶ *The magician conjured the rabbit out of the hat.*

conjurer *(also **conjuror**)* /'kʌndʒərəʳ/ *noun*
a person whose job is to do magic tricks

conman /'kɒnmæn/ *noun (plural **conmen** /-men/)*
a person who tries to get money by tricking people

connect /kə'nekt/ *verb*
to join two or more places or things ▶ *Will you connect this wire **to** the television?*

connected /kə'nektɪd/ *adjective*
1 related ▶ *Police think the killings may be connected **with** each other in some way.* ▶ *The two ideas are closely connected.*
2 joined together ▶ *The computer is connected **to** a laser printer.*

connection /kə'nekʃən/ *noun*
the joining of two or more things; something that joins two or more

things ▶ *The television is not working; is there a loose connection?*

conquer /ˈkɒŋkəʳ/ *verb*
to defeat someone in war ▶ *to conquer the enemy*

conquest /ˈkɒŋkwest/ *noun*
the defeat or control of a group of people ▶ *the conquest of the British army*

conscience /ˈkɒnʃəns/ *noun*
the feeling inside you that tells you whether something is right or wrong ▶ *His conscience troubled him after he took the money.*

conscientious /ˌkɒnʃɪˈenʃəs/ *adjective*
showing a lot of care and attention in the way you do things ▶ *a conscientious worker*

conscious /ˈkɒnʃəs/ *adjective*
awake and knowing what is happening around you ▶ *He is badly hurt but still conscious.*
OPPOSITE: **unconscious**

consciousness /ˈkɒnʃəsnəs/ *noun (no plural)*
the condition of being awake and understanding what is happening ▶ *She lost consciousness at 6 o'clock and died two hours later.* ▶ *Will he ever regain consciousness?*

consecutive /kənˈsekjʊtɪv/ *adjective*
happening one after the other ▶ *It rained for three consecutive days.*

consensus /kənˈsensəs/ *noun (no plural)*
general agreement between everyone in a group ▶ *The consensus of opinion is that Miller should resign.*

consent[1] /kənˈsent/ *verb*
to agree to something ▶ *With great sadness, her father consented **to** her marriage.*

consent[2] *noun (no plural)*
agreement ▶ *We need your parents' written consent.*

consequence /ˈkɒnsɪkwəns/ *noun*
something that happens as a result of something else ▶ *As a consequence of being in hospital, Jane decided that she wanted to become a nurse.*

consequently /ˈkɒnsɪkwəntlɪ/ *adverb*
happening as a result of something else

conservation /ˌkɒnsəˈveɪʃən/ *noun (no plural)*
the saving and protecting of animals or plants ▶ *There is a need for the conservation **of** trees, or there will soon be no forests left.*

conservationist /ˌkɒnsəˈveɪʃənɪst/ *noun*
a person who works to protect the environment

conservative /kənˈsɜːvətɪv/ *adjective*
preferring to do things in the way they are already done, rather than make changes ▶ *a very conservative attitude to education*

conservatory /kənˈsɜːvətərɪ/ *noun (plural **conservatories**)*
a room with glass walls and a glass roof, joined to the side of a house

consider /kənˈsɪdəʳ/ *verb*
to think about something ▶ *I'm considering changing my job.*

considerable /kənˈsɪdərəbəl/ *adjective*
great or large in amount ▶ *I spent a considerable amount of time trying to persuade him to come.* (adverb: ***considerably***)

considerate /kənˈsɪdərət/ *adjective*
thinking about other people's feelings and needs
OPPOSITE: **inconsiderate**

consideration /kənˌsɪdəˈreɪʃən/ *noun (no plural)*
1 thought and attention ▶ *They gave the plan careful consideration.*
2 thought for other people's feelings

C

C

▶ *You show no consideration **for** anyone but yourself!*

considering /kən'sɪdərɪŋ/ *preposition, conjunction*
used before a fact that you know has had an effect on a particular situation ▶ *Considering (that) we missed the bus, we're actually not too late.* ▶ *Considering the strength of the opposition, we did very well.*

consist /kən'sɪst/ *verb*
consist of to be made up of ▶ *The course consists of some classwork and some practice in the factory.*

consistency /kən'sɪstənsɪ/ *noun*
1 *(no plural)* the fact of always happening or behaving in the same way ▶ *There's no consistency **in** the way they apply the rules.*
OPPOSITE: **inconsistency**
2 the thickness of a mixture ▶ *a dessert with a nice, creamy consistency*

consistent /kən'sɪstənt/ *adjective*
1 always happening or behaving in the same way ▶ *Joe's work has shown consistent improvement this term.*
2 be consistent with something to say the same thing or follow the same principles as something else ▶ *His story is not consistent with the facts.*
*(adverb: **consistently**)*
OPPOSITE (1 and 2): **inconsistent**

consolation /ˌkɒnsə'leɪʃən/ *noun*
something that makes you feel better when you are sad or disappointed ▶ *My only consolation is that everyone else finds the work hard too.*

console[1] /kən'səʊl/ *verb (present participle **consoling**, past **consoled**)*
to help to make someone who is sad or disappointed feel better ▶ *No one could console her when her son died.*

console[2] /'kɒnsəʊl/ *noun*
a piece of equipment with buttons on it that you connect to a computer and use when you play a game on the computer ▶ *a games console*

consonant /'kɒnsənənt/ *noun*
a written letter, or the sound of a letter, which is not **a**, **e**, **i**, **o**, or **u**.
COMPARE: **vowel**

conspicuous /kən'spɪkjʊəs/ *adjective*
very easy to notice because of being different from other people or things ▶ *Being so tall makes him very conspicuous.*

conspiracy /kən'spɪrəsɪ/ *noun (plural **conspiracies**)*
a secret plan made by two or more people to do something harmful or illegal ▶ *a conspiracy to overthrow the king*

constable /'kʌnstəbəl/ *noun*
a police officer of the lowest rank

constant /'kɒnstənt/ *adjective*
happening all the time ▶ *constant rain (adverb: **constantly**)*

consternation /ˌkɒnstə'neɪʃən/ *noun (no plural)*
a feeling of shock or worry

constipated /'kɒnstɪpeɪtɪd/ *adjective*
unable to empty your BOWELS

constipation /ˌkɒnstɪ'peɪʃən/ *noun (no plural)*
the condition of being unable to empty your BOWELS

constituency /kən'stɪtʃʊənsɪ/ *noun (plural **constituencies**)*
an area of the country that chooses one member of parliament

constituent /kən'stɪtʃʊənt/ *noun*
a person who votes and lives in a particular constituency

constitute /'kɒnstɪtju:t/ *verb (present participle **constituting**, past **constituted**)*
to be or form something ▶ *His action constitutes a criminal offence.* ▶ *the people that constitute the committee*

onstitution /ˌkɒnstɪˈtjuːʃən/ *noun*
a set of laws governing a country, club, etc.

onstitutional /ˌkɒnstɪˈtjuːʃənəl/ *adjective*
written in or concerning the set of laws governing a country, club, etc.

onstraint /kənˈstreɪnt/ *noun*
something that stops you doing the things you want to do ▶ *the constraints that were placed on Victorian women*

onstruct /kənˈstrʌkt/ *verb*
to build or make something ▶ *to construct a bridge*

onstruction /kənˈstrʌkʃən/ *noun*
1 *(no plural)* building ▶ *a construction company*
2 something that is built

onstructive /kənˈstrʌktɪv/ *adjective*
intended to be helpful, or likely to produce good results ▶ *constructive criticism*

onsul /ˈkɒnsəl/ *noun*
a person who lives in a foreign city and whose job is to help people from his or her own country

onsult /kənˈsʌlt/ *verb*
to talk to someone or look at a book in order to get information ▶ *I consulted George **about** buying a car.*

onsultant /kənˈsʌltənt/ *noun*
1 a person with a lot of experience in a particular subject whose job is to give advice about it ▶ *a marketing consultant*
2 a SENIOR hospital doctor who knows a lot about a particular area of medicine

onsultation /ˌkɒnsəlˈteɪʃən/ *noun*
1 a discussion in which people who are affected by a decision can say what they think should be done ▶ *It was all done without any consultation.* ▶ *The plan was drawn up in consultation with the mayor.*
2 a meeting in which you get advice from someone such as a doctor

consume /kənˈsjuːm/ *verb (present participle **consuming**, past **consumed**)*
to eat or use something ▶ *The country consumes much more than it produces.*

consumer /kənˈsjuːməʳ/ *noun*
a person who buys things or uses a service that a company provides
▶ *Consumers are now more aware of their rights.*

consumption /kənˈsʌmpʃən/ *noun (no plural)*
the eating or using of something
▶ *The car's petrol consumption was very high.*

contact[1] /ˈkɒntækt/ *verb*
to talk or write to someone ▶ *She contacted me as soon as she arrived.*

contact[2] *noun (no plural)*
the touching or coming together of two things or people ▶ *The fire started when two wires came into contact.* ▶ *They have little contact **with** other people.*

contact lens /ˈkɒntækt ˌlenz/ *noun (plural **contact lenses**)*
a very small, plastic LENS that you put in your eye instead of wearing glasses

contagious /kənˈteɪdʒəs/ *adjective*
(used about diseases and illnesses) able to be passed from one person to another

contain /kənˈteɪn/ *verb*
to have something inside ▶ *I found a book containing all the information I needed.*

container /kənˈteɪnəʳ/ *noun*
something you can put things into, for example a box, bottle, etc.

contaminate /kənˈtæmɪneɪt/ *verb (present participle **contaminating**, past **contaminated**)*

C

to add a substance to something that makes it dirty or dangerous ▶ *The water was contaminated with chemicals.*

contamination /kənˌtæmɪˈneɪʃən/ *noun (no plural)*
the act of adding a substance to something, that makes it dirty or dangerous

C

contemplate /ˈkɒntəmpleɪt/ *verb (present participle **contemplating**, past **contemplated**)*
to think about something, especially in a serious way or for a long time ▶ *She even contemplated killing herself.*

contemporary[1] /kənˈtempərərɪ/ *adjective*
1 modern and belonging to the present time ▶ *She is one of this country's best contemporary artists.*
2 happening or existing in the same period of time ▶ *This information comes from a contemporary record of those events.*

contemporary[2] *noun (plural **contemporaries**)*
a person living at the same time as someone else ▶ *Many of Darwin's contemporaries did not agree with his theories.*

contempt /kənˈtempt/ *noun (no plural)*
a feeling that someone or something does not deserve any respect ▶ *He showed complete contempt **for** the people who worked for him.*

contend /kənˈtend/ *verb*
contend with something to deal with something that is causing problems and making it difficult to do something else ▶ *The players had to contend with very windy conditions.*

contender /kənˈtendəʳ/ *noun*
a person who is competing for a title, prize, job, etc.

content /kənˈtent/ *adjective*
satisfied and happy ▶ *She's not very content at work.*

contented /kənˈtentɪd/ *adjective*
satisfied and happy ▶ *My father seems more contented in his new job*
OPPOSITE: **discontented**

contents /ˈkɒntents/ *plural noun*
the things that are inside something ▶ *The contents of the box fell onto the floor.*

contest /ˈkɒntest/ *noun*
a fight or competition

contestant /kənˈtestənt/ *noun*
a person who enters a competition

context /ˈkɒntekst/ *noun*
1 the situation within which something happens ▶ *You need to consider these events in their historical context.*
2 the words that come before and after a word or phrase, that help you understand its meaning ▶ *Can you guess the meaning of this word from its context?*

continent /ˈkɒntɪnənt/ *noun*
one of the large areas of land on Earth, such as Africa, Europe, Australia, etc.

continental /ˌkɒntɪˈnentl/ *adjective*
of or from all of Europe except Britain ▶ *Continental breakfasts are very different from British breakfasts.*

continual /kənˈtɪnjʊəl/ *adjective*
happening often or all the time ▶ *continual arguments*

continue /kənˈtɪnjuː/ *verb (present participle **continuing**, past **continued**)*
1 to go on ▶ *She continued to look at them in silence.*
2 to start again after stopping ▶ *The play will continue in 15 minutes.*
3 to go further in the same direction ▶ *The road continues on down the valley.*

continuity /ˌkɒntɪˈnjuːətɪ/ *noun (no plural)*
the state of continuing for a long period of time without change

continuous /kənˈtɪnjʊəs/ *adjective*
never stopping ▶ *a continuous noise (adverb: **continuously**)*

contraception /ˌkɒntrəˈsepʃən/ *noun (no plural)*
methods of stopping a woman becoming PREGNANT

contraceptive /ˌkɒntrəˈseptɪv/ *noun*
a device or drug that stops a woman becoming PREGNANT

contract /ˈkɒntrækt/ *noun*
a written agreement to do work or sell goods at an agreed price

contractor /kənˈtræktəʳ/ *noun*
a person or company that does work for another company ▶ *a building contractor*

contradict /ˌkɒntrəˈdɪkt/ *verb*
1 if one statement contradicts another, the two are different and cannot both be true ▶ *Their stories contradicted each other.*
2 to say that something that someone has just said is not true ▶ *Don't contradict your mother!*

contradiction /ˌkɒntrəˈdɪkʃən/ *noun*
a difference between two statements or facts, that shows they cannot both be true ▶ *There were some obvious contradictions in what he said.*

contradictory /ˌkɒntrəˈdɪktərɪ/ *adjective*
if two statements are contradictory, they are different and cannot both be true

contrary¹ /ˈkɒntrərɪ/ *noun (no plural)*
the opposite ▶ *"You must be tired." "On the contrary – I feel wide awake."*

contrary² *adjective*
not agreeing with something ▶ *He passed the examination, contrary to what I expected.*

contrast¹ /kənˈtrɑːst/ *verb*
to compare two things and find the differences between them ▶ *In the book, the writer contrasts two different ways of planning a garden.*

contrast² /ˈkɒntrɑːst/ *noun*
a difference ▶ *I've never seen such a contrast **between** two brothers.*

contribute /kənˈtrɪbjuːt/ *verb (present participle **contributing**, past **contributed**)*
to give money or help ▶ *We all contributed money to buy Richard's present.*

contribution /ˌkɒntrɪˈbjuːʃən/ *noun*
money or help that is offered or given ▶ *Peter collected all the contributions to the school magazine.*

control¹ /kənˈtrəʊl/ *verb (present participle **controlling**, past **controlled**)*
to have power over someone or something; to decide or guide the way something or someone works ▶ *He wasn't a bad teacher, but he couldn't control the class.*

control² *noun (no plural)*
1 the state of having the power to decide or guide the way something or someone works ▶ *He wasn't in control of the car.* ▶ *The horse got out of control and the rider fell to the ground.*
2 lose control of something to stop being able to make something do what you want ▶ *He lost control of the car and it crashed.*

control tower /kənˈtrəʊl ˌtaʊəʳ/ *noun*
a high building from which people direct aircraft landing at and taking off from an airport

controversial /ˌkɒntrəˈvɜːʃəl/ *adjective*
causing a lot of disagreement and arguments ▶ *the controversial subject of abortion*

C

C

controversy /ˈkɒntrəvɜːsɪ, kənˈtrɒvəsɪ/ *noun (plural **controversies**)*
disagreement and arguments about something ▶ *The controversy **over** the nuclear energy programme is likely to continue.*

convenience /kənˈviːnɪəns/ *noun*
usefulness; helpfulness; easiness ▶ *My mother likes the convenience of living close to the shops.*

convenient /kənˈviːnɪənt/ *adjective*
suited to your needs; local to where you are ▶ *The school is in a convenient place, near my home.*
OPPOSITE: **inconvenient**

convent /ˈkɒnvənt/ *noun*
a place where women who lead a religious life (NUNS) live; a school or college run by these women
COMPARE: **monastery**

conventional /kənˈvenʃənəl/ *adjective*
of the usual type that has existed or has been used for a long time ▶ *Conventional medicine could not help her, so she tried homeopathy.* ▶ *My parents have very conventional views on sex.*

conversation /ˌkɒnvəˈseɪʃən/ *noun*
a talk between two or more people ▶ *I had a long conversation **with** your teacher.*

conversion /kənˈvɜːʃən/ *noun*
a change from one use to another, or from one religion to another

convert /kənˈvɜːt/ *verb*
to change something into something else ▶ *That building has been converted **into** a school.*

convey /kənˈveɪ/ *verb*
to express your feelings, ideas, or thoughts to other people ▶ *Mark's eyes clearly conveyed his disappointment.*

convict¹ /kənˈvɪkt/ *verb*
to decide in a law court that someone is guilty of something ▶ *He was convicted of murder.*

convict² /ˈkɒnvɪkt/ *noun*
a person who has been sent to prison for doing something wrong

conviction /kənˈvɪkʃən/ *noun*
1 the official decision that someone is guilty of a crime ▶ *Bradley had two previous convictions **for** drug offences.*
2 a very strong belief or opinion ▶ *religious convictions*

convince /kənˈvɪns/ *verb (present participle **convincing**, past **convinced**)*
1 to make a person believe something ▶ *He convinced me that I should study law.*
2 be convinced that to be completely certain about something ▶ *I was convinced that he was telling the truth.*

convincing /kənˈvɪnsɪŋ/ *adjective*
making you believe that something is true ▶ *a convincing argument*

convoy /ˈkɒnvɔɪ/ *noun*
a group of vehicles or ships travelling together

cook¹ /kʊk/ *verb*
to make food ready to eat by heating it ▶ *He's cooking dinner for me tonight.*

cook² *noun*
a person who prepares food for eating ▶ *Sarah is a very good cook.*

cooker /ˈkʊkəʳ/ *noun*
a machine for cooking food ▶ *a gas cooker*

cookery /ˈkʊkərɪ/ *noun (no plural)*
the study or activity of preparing food for eating ▶ *cookery lessons*

cooking /ˈkʊkɪŋ/ *noun (no plural)*
1 the activity of preparing food ▶ *Cooking is fun.*
2 food made in a particular way or by a particular person ▶ *Sue's cooking is always good.*

cool[1] /kuːl/ *adjective*
1 a little cold ▶ *The room was cool after the sun had gone down.*
2 calm ▶ *Don't get excited about the examination – keep cool.*

cool[2] *verb*
1 to make or become a little colder ▶ *Leave the cake to cool.*
2 cool down (**a**) to become a little colder
(**b**) to become calmer ▶ *I'll discuss it with her again when she's cooled down a bit.*

cooped up /ˌkuːpt ˈʌp/ *adjective*
kept for too long in a place that is too small ▶ *He kept his dogs cooped up in a kennel.*

cooperate /kəʊˈɒpəreɪt/ *verb (present participle* ***cooperating****, past* ***cooperated****)*
to work together with someone else to get something done ▶ *If we all cooperate, we'll finish this by 5 o'clock.*

cooperation /kəʊˌɒpəˈreɪʃən/ *noun (no plural)*
willingness to work together ▶ *Thank you for your cooperation.*

ooperative /kəʊˈɒpərətɪv/ *adjective*
willing to help other people
OPPOSITE: **uncooperative**

oordinate /kəʊˈɔːdɪneɪt/ *verb (present participle* ***coordinating****, past* ***coordinated****)*
to organize all the different things and people involved in an activity ▶ *I'm responsible for coordinating training courses.*

op /kɒp/ *noun*
a police officer

ope /kəʊp/ *verb (present participle* ***coping****, past* ***coped****)*
to deal with something successfully ▶ *How do you cope* ***with*** *all this work?*

opper /ˈkɒpə^{r}/ *noun (no plural)*
a red-gold metal

copy[1] /ˈkɒpɪ/ *verb (past* ***copied****)*
1 to make or do something exactly the same as something else ▶ *Could you copy this down in your books, please?*
2 to cheat by writing exactly the same thing as someone else ▶ *The teacher saw him copying in the history test.*

copy[2] *noun (plural* ***copies****)*
1 something that is made to look the same as something else ▶ *Please send a copy* ***of*** *this letter to Mr Brown.*
2 one magazine, book, or newspaper from the many that have been produced ▶ *Have you got another copy* ***of*** *this book?*

coral /ˈkɒrəl/ *noun (no plural)*
a hard pink, white, or red substance that is formed from the bones of very small sea animals

cord /kɔːd/ *noun*
a thin rope

core /kɔː^{r}/ *noun*
the hard, central part of certain fruits, which contains the seeds ▶ *an apple core*

coriander /ˌkɒrɪˈændə^{r}/ *noun (no plural)*
a plant with leaves and seeds that you add to food to give it a pleasant, fresh taste

cork /kɔːk/ *noun*
1 *(no plural)* a light substance that comes from the outside part of the stem of a tree
2 a piece of this, used to fill the holes in the tops of bottles

corkscrew /ˈkɔːkskruː/ *noun*
a tool you use to pull a cork out of a bottle

corn /kɔːn/ *noun (no plural)*
the seed of grain plants, including wheat and maize

corner /ˈkɔːnə^{r}/ *noun*
the place where two lines, walls, streets, etc. meet each other ▶ *The*

C

*table stood in the corner **of** the room.* ▶ *His house is on the corner of School Road and Green Street.*

cornflakes /ˈkɔːnfleɪks/ *plural noun*
a breakfast food made from crushed corn and usually eaten with milk and sugar

coronation /ˌkɒrəˈneɪʃən/ *noun*
a ceremony in which someone officially becomes a king or queen

corporal /ˈkɔːpərəl/ *noun*
a soldier who has a low rank in the army

corporation /ˌkɔːpəˈreɪʃən/ *noun*
a group of people who run a town, business, etc.

corpse /kɔːps/ *noun*
the dead body of a person

correct[1] /kəˈrekt/ *adjective*
right; with no mistakes ▶ *a correct answer (adverb: **correctly**)*
OPPOSITE: **incorrect**

correct[2] *verb*
1 to make something right ▶ *Please correct this mistake.*
2 to show the mistakes in something ▶ *I've corrected your homework.*

correction /kəˈrekʃən/ *noun*
a change that makes something right or better ▶ *He made several corrections to the letter.*

correspond /ˌkɒrɪˈspɒnd/ *verb*
to write to someone and receive letters from them ▶ *to correspond **with** a friend*

correspondence /ˌkɒrɪˈspɒndəns/ *noun (no plural)*
letters

correspondent /ˌkɒrɪˈspɒndənt/ *noun*
1 someone who writes and receives letters
2 someone who works for a newspaper or television company and reports news from another country

corridor /ˈkɒrɪdɔːʳ/ *noun*
a long, narrow part of a building, with doors into rooms on each side of it ▶ *Go down the corridor to the third room on the left.*
SAME MEANING: **passage**

corrupt[1] /kəˈrʌpt/ *adjective*
dishonest ▶ *a corrupt judge* ▶ *a corrupt political system*

corrupt[2] *verb*
to encourage someone to behave in a way that is not honest or moral ▶ *I think that television corrupts the young.*

corruption /kəˈrʌpʃən/ *noun (no plural)*
dishonest behaviour by politicians or people who work for the government ▶ *The police are being investigated for corruption.*

cosmetic /kɒzˈmetɪk/ *adjective*
intended to make your skin or body more beautiful ▶ *He had cosmetic surgery to make his nose smaller.*

cosmetics /kɒzˈmetɪks/ *plural noun*
substances that you put on the skin of your face to make you look prettier

cost[1] /kɒst/ *noun*
1 the money that you have to pay when you buy something ▶ *We gave her some money to cover the cost **of** the books she had to buy.*
2 something needed, given, or lost in order to get something else ▶ *War is never worth the terrible cost **in** human life.*
3 at all costs no matter what has to be given or lost ▶ *We must avoid war at all costs.*

cost[2] *verb (past **cost**)*
1 to have a particular amount as a price ▶ *"How much did that bag cost?" "It cost £5!"*
2 cost an arm and a leg to be very expensive
3 cost a bomb to be very expensive

co-star[1] /ˈkəʊ stɑːʳ/ *noun*

one of two or more famous actors that work together in a film or play

co-star² *verb (present participle **co-starring**, past **co-starred**)*
to be working in a film or play with other famous actors ▶ *Meryl Streep co-stars with Clint Eastwood in "The Bridges of Madison County".*

costly /ˈkɒstlɪ/ *adjective (**costlier, costliest**)*
costing a lot of money ▶ *The ring was very costly.*
SAME MEANING: **dear, expensive**

costume /ˈkɒstjuːm/ *noun*
clothes worn for a special reason, or to represent a country or time in history ▶ *They all wore national costume.*

cosy /ˈkəʊzɪ/ *adjective (**cosier, cosiest**)*
warm and comfortable ▶ *a cosy little house*

cot /kɒt/ *noun*
a bed with high sides, for a baby
COMPARE: **cradle**

cottage /ˈkɒtɪdʒ/ *noun*
a small, attractive house in the country

cotton /ˈkɒtn/ *noun (no plural)*
1 a plant grown in hot countries for the fine, white threads that cover its seeds
2 thread or cloth made from the cotton plant ▶ *a cotton dress*

cotton wool /ˌkɒtn ˈwʊl/ *noun (no plural)*
a soft mass of white material, used especially for cleaning your skin

couch /kaʊtʃ/ *noun (plural **couches**)*
a long seat on which you can sit or lie
SAME MEANING: **settee, sofa**

cough¹ /kɒf/ *noun*
a sudden, rough sound made when you send air out of your throat and mouth suddenly ▶ *The child had a bad cough.*

cough² *verb*
to push air out from your throat and mouth with a sudden, rough sound ▶ *The child was coughing all night.*

could /kəd; *strong* kʊd/ *verb*
1 the word for **can** in the past ▶ *Before I had a bicycle, I couldn't* (=could not) *visit my friend.*
2 used in sentences like these ▶ *She would help us if she could, but she can't.*
3 used as a polite way of asking someone something ▶ *Could you help me, please?*

couldn't /ˈkʊdnt/
could not ▶ *I couldn't see because it was dark.*

could've /ˈkʊdəv/
could have ▶ *I could've killed him!*

council /ˈkaʊnsəl/ *noun*
a group of people who are chosen to make decisions and laws in a town or city ▶ *The town council will decide where to plant the trees.*

councillor /ˈkaʊnsələʳ/ *noun*
someone chosen to advise people and make decisions and laws in a town or city

counselling /ˈkaʊnsəlɪŋ/ *noun (no plural)*
the act of giving people PROFESSIONAL advice about their problems ▶ *a counselling service for drug users*

counsellor /ˈkaʊnsələʳ/ *noun*
a person whose job is to give people advice about their problems ▶ *a marriage counsellor*

count¹ /kaʊnt/ *verb*
1 to say numbers in the right order ▶ *to count from 1 to 100*
2 to find out how many there are ▶ *She counted the books – there were 14 of them.*
3 to have value or importance ▶ *He said that I had no experience, so my opinion doesn't count.*
4 count against someone to help

someone lose or fail in something ▶ *My lack of experience may count against me.*

count² *noun*
1 the total reached by adding everything together ▶ *At the last count, I'd visited 15 countries.*
2 lose count to stop remembering how many ▶ *I've lost count of how many times he's said he's leaving her.*

countable /ˈkaʊntəbəl/ *adjective*
in grammar, a countable noun has a singular and a plural form. "Table" (plural "tables") and "man" (plural "men") are examples of countable nouns
OPPOSITE: **uncountable**

countdown /ˈkaʊntdaʊn/ *noun*
the act of counting numbers backwards to zero before something happens ▶ *They began the countdown to take-off.*

counter /ˈkaʊntəʳ/ *noun*
1 a long table where you go and buy things in a shop
2 a small, round piece of plastic or wood, used in playing games

countless /ˈkaʊntləs/ *adjective*
very many ▶ *She's had countless boyfriends.*

country /ˈkʌntrɪ/ *noun*
1 *(plural **countries**)* an area ruled by one government ▶ *France and Germany are European countries.*
2 *(no plural)* the land that is not a town ▶ *He lives in the country.*

country music /ˈkʌntrɪ ˌmjuːzɪk/ *(also **country and western** /ˌkʌntrɪ ən ˈwestən/) noun (no plural)*
a type of popular music from the southern and western US

countryside /ˈkʌntrɪsaɪd/ *noun (no plural)*
land outside towns and cities

county /ˈkaʊntɪ/ *noun (plural **counties**)*
a part of a country ▶ *Devon is a county in the southwest of England.*

coup /kuː/ *noun*
1 a situation in which a group of people suddenly take control of a country, especially by using force
2 an impressive achievement ▶ *Winning that contract was a real coup.*

couple /ˈkʌpəl/ *noun*
1 two things usually thought of together ▶ *I waited for a couple **of** hours.*
2 two people, usually a man and a woman, who are married, live together, or have a close relationship ▶ *We've invited three other couples to dinner.*

coupon /ˈkuːpɒn/ *noun*
a piece of paper that can be exchanged for goods or money ▶ *Collect three coupons for a free pen.*

courage /ˈkʌrɪdʒ/ *noun (no plural)*
willingness to do dangerous things without feeling afraid ▶ *The soldier showed great courage in the battle.*
SAME MEANING: **bravery**

courageous /kəˈreɪdʒəs/ *adjective*
brave ▶ *a courageous person*

courgette /kʊəˈʒet/ *noun*
a long vegetable with a dark green skin

courier /ˈkʊrɪəʳ/ *noun*
1 a person whose job is to deliver letters and packages
2 a person whose job is to help people who are on holiday with a travel company

course /kɔːs/ *noun*
1 the way that something happens, or the time when something is happening ▶ *During the course of the journey, we saw a lot of new places.*
2 the path or direction that something takes ▶ *The course of the river was marked on the map.* ▶ *The*

plane had to change course and go another way.
3 one part of a meal ▶ *We have three courses: soup, meat and vegetables, and fruit.*
4 a set of lessons ▶ *What course are you taking at college?*
5 **of course** certainly ▶ *Of course I'll still love you when you're old.*

coursebook /ˈkɔːsbʊk/ *noun*
a book written to be used by students as part of a particular course of study

court /kɔːt/ *noun*
1 a place where a person is questioned about a crime, and where other people decide whether the person is guilty or not
2 an open space where games are played ▶ *a tennis court*
3 a king or queen and all the people who live with them

courteous /ˈkɜːtɪəs/ *adjective*
polite *(adverb:* ***courteously****)*

courtesy /ˈkɜːtəsɪ/ *noun (no plural)*
polite behaviour

courtroom /ˈkɔːtrʊm/ *noun*
the room where someone is judged in a law court

courtyard /ˈkɔːtjɑːd/ *noun*
an open space inside or in front of a large building

cousin /ˈkʌzən/ *noun*
the child of your aunt or uncle

cover¹ /ˈkʌvəʳ/ *verb*
1 to put something over something else ▶ *She covered the table with a cloth.*
2 to be over a particular area or surface ▶ *The town covers 5 square miles.*
3 to include or deal with something ▶ *His talk covered British history between the wars.*
4 **cover something up** (**a**) to place something over something else to protect or hide it ▶ *Cover the furniture up before you start painting.* (**b**) to hide something ▶ *She tried to cover up her fear.*

cover² *noun*
1 something that you put over something else ▶ *a cushion cover*
2 the outside of a book
3 **take cover** to shelter or hide from something

coverage /ˈkʌvərɪdʒ/ *noun (no plural)*
the amount of attention given to a news story by television, radio, or the newspapers ▶ *Her death attracted widespread media coverage.*

covering /ˈkʌvərɪŋ/ *noun*
something that covers something else ▶ *a light covering of snow*

cover-up /ˈkʌvər ʌp/ *noun*
an attempt to stop people finding out the truth ▶ *The government says there has not been a cover-up.*

cow /kaʊ/ *noun*
a large female animal that farmers keep for milk

coward /ˈkaʊəd/ *noun*
someone who avoids pain or danger because they are not brave

cowardice /ˈkaʊədɪs/ *noun (no plural)*
behaviour that shows you are not brave ▶ *She accused him of cowardice.*
OPPOSITE: **bravery**

cowardly /ˈkaʊədlɪ/ *adjective*
showing too much fear; unwilling to do dangerous things ▶ *cowardly behaviour*
OPPOSITE: **brave**

cowboy /ˈkaʊbɔɪ/ *noun*
a man who rides a horse and looks after cattle in America

crab /kræb/ *noun*
a sea animal with ten legs and a hard shell

crack¹ /kræk/ *verb*
1 to break so that lines appear on the

C

surface ▶ *That glass will crack if you pour boiling water into it.*
2 to make a sharp noise, like thunder or a gun

crack² *noun*
1 a thin line on the surface of something ▶ *There's a crack in this cup!*
2 a sharp noise ▶ *a crack of thunder*
3 a sudden, hard hit ▶ *a crack on the head*

crackdown /ˈkrækdaʊn/ *noun*
an official attempt to stop a particular crime or bad behaviour from happening ▶ *The government announced a crackdown **on** drugs.*

cracked /krækt/ *adjective*
damaged with thin lines on the surface ▶ *a cracked mirror*

crackle /ˈkrækəl/ *verb (present participle **crackling**, past **crackled**)*
to make a lot of short noises that sound like wood burning on a fire ▶ *This radio's crackling.*

cradle /ˈkreɪdl/ *noun*
a bed for a baby, which can be moved from side to side
COMPARE: **cot**

craft /krɑːft/ *noun*
1 a job or trade needing skill, especially skill with your hands ▶ *He knew the craft of making furniture.*
2 *(plural **craft**)* a boat or plane

craftsman /ˈkrɑːftsmən/ *noun (plural **craftsmen** /-mən/)*
someone whose job needs a lot of skill, especially skill with their hands

crafty /ˈkrɑːftɪ/ *adjective (**craftier**, **craftiest**)*
clever at making other people believe things that are not true

cram /kræm/ *verb (present participle **cramming**, past **crammed**)*
to force people or things into a small space ▶ *Lots of people were crammed **into** the bus.*

cramp /kræmp/ *noun (no plural)*
a bad pain in your muscles

cramped /kræmpt/ *adjective*
not big enough for everyone or everything ▶ *Six of us lived in a tiny, cramped apartment.*

crane /kreɪn/ *noun*
a tall machine for lifting heavy things

crash¹ /kræʃ/ *noun (plural **crashes**)*
1 a loud noise, like something large falling over ▶ *The car hit the tree with a crash.*
2 an accident in which vehicles hit each other ▶ *a car crash*

crash² *verb*
1 to move noisily ▶ *The injured elephant crashed through the forest.*
2 to make a sudden, loud noise ▶ *The thunder crashed and the rain poured down.*
3 (of a car) to have an accident ▶ *The car crashed into the tree.*

crash course /ˈkræʃ kɔːs/ *noun*
a short course in which you study the most important things about a subject very quickly ▶ *I had a crash course in French before I went to live in Paris.*

crash helmet /ˈkræʃ ˌhelmɪt/ *noun*
a hard hat that you wear to protect your head when you ride a MOTORBIKE

crash-land /ˈkræʃ lænd/ *verb*
to land a plane when it is in trouble

crass /kræs/ *adjective*
stupid and rude in a way that upsets or offends people ▶ *crass remarks*

crate /kreɪt/ *noun*
a big, wooden box ▶ *a crate of fruit*

crater /ˈkreɪtəʳ/ *noun*
a large hole in the ground or at the top of a VOLCANO ▶ *Hot lava flowed from the crater.*

crawl /krɔːl/ *verb*
to move along the floor on your hands and knees ▶ *The baby crawled towards his father.*

crayon /'kreɪən/ *noun*
a soft, coloured pencil

craze /kreɪz/ *noun*
something that is very popular for a short time ▶ *the latest fashion craze*

crazy /'kreɪzɪ/ *adjective* (***crazier, craziest***)
1 mad; foolish ▶ *He's crazy to drive his car so fast.*
2 **be crazy about** to like someone or something very much ▶ *He's crazy about her.*

creak /kri:k/ *verb*
to make the sound that a door makes when it has not been oiled ▶ *The door creaked as she opened it.*

cream[1] /kri:m/ *noun (no plural)*
1 the fatty part of milk that you can eat with other foods
2 a thick liquid that you put on your skin ▶ *face cream*

cream[2] *adjective, noun*
a yellowish-white colour

creamy /'kri:mɪ/ *adjective* (***creamier, creamiest***)
containing or looking like cream ▶ *creamy soup*

crease[1] /kri:s/ *noun*
a line on cloth, paper, etc. where it has been folded

crease[2] *verb (present participle* ***creasing****, past* ***creased****)*
to put a crease or creases in a piece of cloth, paper, etc. ▶ *Try not to crease your jacket.*

create /krɪ'eɪt/ *verb (present participle* ***creating****, past* ***created****)*
to make something new ▶ *Work on the new road will create a lot of difficulties for traffic.*

creation /krɪ'eɪʃən/ *noun*
something that is made

creative /krɪ'eɪtɪv/ *adjective*
good at thinking of new ideas or ways of doing things ▶ *one of Japan's most talented and creative film directors*

creativity /ˌkri:eɪ'tɪvətɪ/ *noun (no plural)*
the ability to use your imagination or skill to produce new ideas or things

creator /krɪ'eɪtəʳ/ *noun*
a person who makes or invents something ▶ *Walt Disney, the creator of Mickey Mouse*

creature /'kri:tʃəʳ/ *noun*
an animal or insect

crèche /kreʃ/ *noun*
a place where babies are looked after while their parents are at work

credibility /ˌkredə'bɪlətɪ/ *noun (no plural)*
the quality of being believed and trusted by other people ▶ *The scandal has damaged the government's credibility.*

credit[1] /'kredɪt/ *noun (no plural)*
1 attention and approval for something good that has been done ▶ *We both made the machine, but James was given the credit for it.*
2 a way of buying things in which you pay for them later ▶ *We bought the furniture on credit.*
3 **in credit** (used about a bank account) containing money

credit[2] *verb*
to add money to a bank account
OPPOSITE: **debit**

credit card /'kredɪt ˌkɑ:d/ *noun*
a small, plastic card that allows you to buy things without using coins and notes. You pay for the goods later.

creep /kri:p/ *verb (past* ***crept*** */krept/)*
to move slowly and quietly

creeps /kri:ps/ *plural noun*
give someone the creeps to make someone feel nervous or frightened ▶ *That man gives me the creeps!*

creepy /'kri:pɪ/ *adjective* (***creepier, creepiest***)
slightly frightening ▶ *a creepy ghost story*

C

cremate /krɪ'meɪt/ *verb (present participle* ***cremating,*** *past* ***cremated)***
to burn the body of a dead person

cremation /krɪ'meɪʃən/ *noun*
the act of burning the body of a dead person ▶ *a cremation service*

crept /krept/
the PAST TENSE and PAST PARTICIPLE of the verb **creep**

C

crescent /'kresənt/ *noun*
a curved shape that is wider in the middle and pointed at the ends ▶ *a crescent moon*

crest /krest/ *noun*
1 a group of feathers that stick up on the top of a bird's head
2 the top of something ▶ *the crest* ***of*** *a hill*

crevice /'krevɪs/ *noun*
a narrow crack, especially in rock

crew /kruː/ *noun*
the people who work on a ship or plane

cricket /'krɪkɪt/ *noun*
1 *(no plural)* a ball game played by two teams of 11 players each
2 a small, brown insect that jumps and makes a loud noise

cried /kraɪd/
the PAST TENSE and PAST PARTICIPLE of the verb **cry**

cries /kraɪz/
the plural of **cry**

crime /kraɪm/ *noun*
1 an action that is wrong and can be punished by the law ▶ *Killing people is a serious crime.*
COMPARE: **sin**
2 commit a crime to do something wrong that can be punished by the law

criminal /'krɪmɪnəl/ *noun*
someone who has done something very wrong and against the law
▶ *The prison contains 325 criminals.*

crimson /'krɪmzən/ *adjective, noun*
a deep red colour, like the colour of blood

cringe /krɪndʒ/ *verb (present participle* ***cringing,*** *past* ***cringed)***
to feel embarrassed by something
▶ *I just cringe* ***at*** *the thought of some of the things we used to wear.*

cripple /'krɪpəl/ *verb (present participle* ***crippling,*** *past* ***crippled)***
to hurt someone so that they cannot use their arms or legs ▶ *She was crippled in the car accident.*

crisis /'kraɪsɪs/ *noun (plural* ***crises*** */'kraɪsiːz/)*
a time when something serious, very worrying, or dangerous happens

crisp¹ /krɪsp/ *adjective*
1 (used about food) firm and dry; easily broken ▶ *Keep the biscuits in a tin so that they stay crisp.*
2 (used about food) firm and fresh
▶ *crisp apples*

crisp² *noun*
a very thin, round piece of potato which you buy in a packet and eat cold ▶ *a packet of crisps*
COMPARE: **chip**

crispy /'krɪspɪ/ *adjective (**crispier, crispiest**)*
(used about food) pleasantly hard
▶ *crispy bacon*

criteria /kraɪ'tɪərɪə/ *plural noun*
facts or standards used to help you decide something ▶ *What are the criteria for selecting the winner?*

critic /'krɪtɪk/ *noun*
a person whose job is to write about art, music, films, etc. and say whether they are good or bad

critical /'krɪtɪkəl/ *adjective*
looking for faults ▶ *She was very critical* ***of*** *my work.*

criticism /'krɪtɪsɪzəm/ *noun*
a reason for not liking something or not feeling happy about something
▶ *I listened to all her criticisms in silence.*

criticize /'krɪtɪsaɪz/ *verb (present*

participle ***criticizing***, *past* ***criticized***)
to say what is wrong with something; to find faults in something ▶ *She's always criticizing me.*

croak /krəʊk/ *verb*
to make a deep, low sound in your throat ▶ *"Where are you?" she croaked.*

crockery /'krɒkərɪ/ *noun (no plural)*
plates, cups, and dishes that we eat and drink from

crocodile /'krɒkədaɪl/ *noun*
a large animal with a long body, a hard skin, and sharp teeth, which lives in or near rivers in hot countries

crook /krʊk/ *noun*
a dishonest person

crooked /'krʊkɪd/ *adjective*
1 bent or curved ▶ *a crooked road*
2 dishonest

crop /krɒp/ *noun*
1 a plant such as wheat, fruit, or vegetables that a farmer grows
2 an amount of vegetables, wheat, etc. that is cut or gathered at one time ▶ *a crop of apples*

cross[1] /krɒs/ *noun (plural* ***crosses****)*
a shape (X) with four arms that meet in the centre

cross[2] *verb*
to go over from one side of something to the other ▶ *They crossed the road.*

cross[3] *adjective*
angry ▶ *Why are you cross* ***with*** *me?*

cross-country /ˌkrɒs 'kʌntrɪ/ *adjective*
across fields and not along roads ▶ *cross-country running*

cross-examine /ˌkrɒs ɪg'zæmɪn/ *verb (present participle* ***cross-examining****, past* ***cross-examined****)*
to ask someone questions about something they have just said to see if they are telling the truth, especially in a law court ▶ *The lawyer cross-examined the witness for an hour.*

cross-eyed /ˌkrɒs 'aɪd/ *adjective*
having eyes that look in towards your nose

crossing /'krɒsɪŋ/ *noun*
a special place where you may cross the road

cross-legged /ˌkrɒs 'legɪd/ *adverb, adjective*
sitting with your knees wide apart and your feet crossed ▶ *We sat cross-legged on the floor.*

cross-reference /ˌkrɒs 'refərəns/ *noun*
a note in a book that tells you where to look in the same book for more information

crossroads /'krɒsrəʊdz/ *noun (plural* ***crossroads****)*
a place where several roads meet each other

cross-section /'krɒs ˌsekʃən/ *noun*
1 a drawing of what something looks like inside by showing it as if it has been cut into two pieces ▶ *a cross-section of the ship, showing all the levels*
2 a group of people or things that is typical of a larger group ▶ *The students here are a cross-section of the local community.*

crossword /'krɒswɜːd/ *noun*
a game in which you have to guess words, the letters of which fit into a pattern of squares down and across the page

crouch /kraʊtʃ/ *verb*
to make your body come close to the ground by bending your knees ▶ *She crouched by the fire to get warm.*

crow /krəʊ/ *noun*
a large, black bird with a low, hard cry

crowd[1] /kraʊd/ *noun*
a large number of people ▶ *There was a crowd* ***of*** *people waiting at the station.*

crowd² *verb*
to come together in a large group ▶ *They all crowded round the teacher.*

crowded /ˈkraʊdɪd/ *adjective*
full of people ▶ *I don't like the market; it is too crowded.*

crown /kraʊn/ *noun*
a special hat made of gold, beautiful stones, etc., worn by a king or queen

crucial /ˈkruːʃəl/ *adjective*
very important ▶ *It is crucial that we act quickly. (adverb:* ***crucially****)*

crucifix /ˈkruːsɪfɪks/ *noun*
(plural ***crucifixes****)*
a cross with a figure of Jesus on it

crude /kruːd/ *adjective*
1 raw; in the state in which something is usually found or exists ▶ *Crude oil has to be made pure before it can be used by man.*
2 rude ▶ *a crude joke*

cruel /ˈkruːəl/ *adjective*
liking to hurt other people or animals ▶ *He is cruel to animals (adverb:* ***cruelly****)*
OPPOSITE: **kind**

cruelty /ˈkruːəltɪ/ *noun (no plural)*
actions that cause pain to a person or an animal ▶ *cruelty to animals*

cruise¹ /kruːz/ *noun*
a sea journey for pleasure

cruise² *verb (present participle* ***cruising****, past* ***cruised****)*
(used about a boat or vehicle) to move in an unhurried way

crumb /krʌm/ *noun*
a little piece of something such as bread or cake

crumble /ˈkrʌmbəl/ *verb (present participle* ***crumbling****, past* ***crumbled****)*
to break up into little pieces ▶ *The walls of that old house are crumbling.*

crumple /ˈkrʌmpəl/ *verb (present participle* ***crumpling****, past* ***crumpled****)*
to make paper or clothing full of irregular folds by pressing or crushing it ▶ *Don't sit on that shirt or you'll crumple it.*

crunch /krʌntʃ/ *verb*
1 to crush food noisily with your teeth
2 to make a noise that sounds like something being crushed ▶ *The stones crunched under the car tyres.*

crunchy /ˈkrʌntʃɪ/ *adjective*
*(****crunchier, crunchiest****)*
(used about food) pleasantly hard
▶ *a crunchy biscuit*

crush /krʌʃ/ *verb*
to hurt or damage something by pressing it heavily

crust /krʌst/ *noun*
the hard part on the outside of bread

crutch /krʌtʃ/ *noun (plural* ***crutches****)*
a piece of wood or metal that supports a person who cannot walk well ▶ *to walk on crutches*

cry¹ /kraɪ/ *verb (past* ***cried****)*
1 to shout ▶ *The boy cried for help.*
2 to produce tears from your eyes usually because you are sad ▶ *She began to cry when she heard of her friend's death.*

cry² *noun (plural* ***cries****)*
a loud shout; a call ▶ *They heard a cry for help.*

cryptic /ˈkrɪptɪk/ *adjective*
having a meaning that is not clear ▶ *a cryptic message*

crystal /ˈkrɪstl/ *noun*
1 a type of rock that is transparent
2 *(no plural)* high-quality glass
▶ *crystal wine glasses*
3 a regular shape that forms naturally when some MINERAL substances become solid ▶ *crystals of ice*
▶ *salt crystals*

cub /kʌb/ *noun*
a young bear, lion, tiger, or fox

cube /kjuːb/ *noun*
a solid shape with six equal square sides

cubicle /ˈkjuːbɪkəl/ *noun*
a small room for one person, especially for changing their clothes in ▶ *the changing cubicles at the swimming pool*

cuckoo /ˈkʊkuː/ *noun*
a bird that has a call which sounds like its name

cucumber /ˈkjuːkʌmbəʳ/ *noun*
a long, thin, green vegetable which is usually eaten without being cooked

cuddle /ˈkʌdl/ *verb (present participle* ***cuddling****, past* ***cuddled****)*
to put your arms around someone ▶ *She cuddled her little boy.*
SAME MEANING: **hug**

cue /kjuː/ *noun*
1 a long, thin stick used for hitting the ball in games such as SNOOKER
2 an action or event that is a sign for something else to happen ▶ *His girlfriend's arrival was our cue to leave.*

cuff /kʌf/ *noun*
the end of an arm of a shirt, dress, etc.

cul-de-sac /ˈkʌl də ˌsæk/ *noun*
a street which is closed at one end

culminate /ˈkʌlmɪneɪt/ *verb (present participle* ***culminating****, past* ***culminated****)*
culminate in something to have something as an important final result ▶ *a series of arguments that culminated in a divorce*

culprit /ˈkʌlprɪt/ *noun*
a person who has done something wrong or who is guilty of a crime ▶ *The man whose car was damaged was determined to find the culprits.*

cult /kʌlt/ *noun*
a small religion whose members have unusual views ▶ *a member of an extreme religious cult*

cultivate /ˈkʌltɪveɪt/ *verb (present participle* ***cultivating****, past* ***cultivated****)*
to grow plants on land that has been specially prepared

cultivation /ˌkʌltɪˈveɪʃən/ *noun (no plural)*
the growing of plants or crops

cultural /ˈkʌltʃərəl/ *adjective*
1 connected with a particular society and its beliefs, customs, and way of life ▶ *the cultural differences between England and Pakistan*
2 related to art, literature, music, etc. ▶ *There aren't many cultural events in this town.*

culture /ˈkʌltʃəʳ/ *noun*
1 the beliefs, customs, and way of life of a particular society
2 *(no plural)* art, literature, music, etc. ▶ *Paris is full of culture.*

cultured /ˈkʌltʃəd/ *adjective*
knowing a lot about art, literature, music, etc.

cumbersome /ˈkʌmbəsəm/ *adjective*
heavy and difficult to move or use ▶ *a large, cumbersome bag*

cunning /ˈkʌnɪŋ/ *adjective*
clever at making people believe things that are not true

cup /kʌp/ *noun*
1 a container, usually with a handle, that you can drink from
2 the drink inside the cup ▶ *a cup* ***of*** *tea*
3 a prize, shaped like a bowl, usually made of silver or gold

cupboard /ˈkʌbəd/ *noun*
a piece of furniture with shelves and a door, in which you keep clothes, plates, food, etc.

curb /kɜːb/ *verb*
to control or limit something ▶ *You must curb your spending.*

cure[1] /kjʊəʳ/ *verb (present participle* ***curing****, past* ***cured****)*
to make someone better when they have been ill ▶ *I hope the doctor can cure the pain in my shoulder.*

C

cure² *noun*
a way of making someone better when they have been ill ▶ *a cure for an illness*

curiosity /ˌkjʊəriˈɒsətɪ/ *noun* *(no plural)*
the desire to know something or learn about something ▶ *He is full of curiosity.*

curious /ˈkjʊərɪəs/ *adjective*
1 wanting to know about things or people ▶ *I'm very curious **about** our new neighbours.*
2 odd or strange ▶ *We heard a curious noise upstairs.*

curiously /ˈkjʊərɪəslɪ/ *adverb*
in a way that seems odd or strange

curl¹ /kɜːl/ *verb*
1 to roll or bend in a round or curved shape ▶ *The snake curled round the branch.* ▶ *She curled her hair.*
2 curl up to lie comfortably with your arms and legs drawn close to your body ▶ *She curled up in front of the fire.*

curl² *noun*
a piece of hair that curves around

curly /ˈkɜːlɪ/ *adjective* ***(curlier, curliest)***
(used about hair) bending round and round

currant /ˈkʌrənt/ *noun*
1 a small, dried fruit
2 a small black, red, or white fruit that grows on bushes

currency /ˈkʌrənsɪ/ *noun (plural **currencies**)*
the money used in a country ▶ *Can I pay in British currency on the boat?*

current¹ /ˈkʌrənt/ *adjective*
happening or being used right now ▶ *Why does he want to change his current job?*

current² *noun*
a flow of water, electricity, etc. ▶ *Don't swim in the river; the current is very fast.*

curriculum /kəˈrɪkjʊləm/ *noun* *(plural **curricula** /-lə/ or **curriculums**)*
all of the subjects that are taught at a school, college, etc.

curried /ˈkʌrɪd/ *adjective*
(used about food) cooked in a hot-tasting liquid

curry /ˈkʌrɪ/ *noun (plural **curries**)*
an Indian food of meat, vegetables, or fish, cooked in a thick, hot-tasting liquid and usually eaten with rice ▶ *I'll have a chicken curry, please.*

curse¹ /kɜːs/ *verb (present participle **cursing**, past **cursed**)*
1 to wish that something unpleasant will happen to someone ▶ *He cursed the person who had stolen his money.*
2 to speak angry words ▶ *He cursed when he hit his head on the shelf.*

curse² *noun*
1 something that you say which expresses anger or hate, or which uses swearwords
2 put a curse on someone to make a wish that, with the help of God or some magical power, something unpleasant will happen to someone ▶ *In the story, the old woman put a curse on the beautiful princess.*

cursor /ˈkɜːsəʳ/ *noun*
a small mark on a computer screen that moves to show where you are writing

curtain /ˈkɜːtn/ *noun*
a piece of hanging cloth that can be pulled across to cover a window or door
COMPARE: **blind**

curve¹ /kɜːv/ *noun*
a line of which no part is straight; a bend ▶ *a curve in the road*

curve² *verb (present participle **curving**, past **curved**)*
to make a line which is not straight ▶ *The river curved round the hill.*

curved /kɜːvd/ *adjective*
having the shape of a curve ▶ *a Japanese sword with a curved blade*

cushion /ˈkʊʃən/ *noun*
a bag filled with soft material to sit on or rest against
COMPARE: **pillow**

cushy /ˈkʊʃɪ/ *adjective (**cushier, cushiest**)*
very easy ▶ *Teaching is not a cushy job.*

custard /ˈkʌstəd/ *noun (no plural)*
a thick, sweet, yellow liquid that you pour over some fruit and sweet foods

custody /ˈkʌstədɪ/ *noun (no plural)*
the right to take care of a child, given by a law court when the child's parents are legally separated ▶ *My ex-wife has custody of the kids.*

custom /ˈkʌstəm/ *noun*
a special way of doing something that a person or group of people has

customary /ˈkʌstəmərɪ/ *adjective*
usual or normal ▶ *It is customary to cover your head in the temple.*

customer /ˈkʌstəməʳ/ *noun*
a person who buys things from a shop

customs /ˈkʌstəmz/ *plural noun*
a place where your cases can be searched when you leave or enter a country, and where you have to pay tax on certain goods

cut¹ /kʌt/ *verb (present participle **cutting**, past **cut**)*
1 to break or damage something with a knife or something sharp ▶ *He cut the apple in half.* ▶ *He has cut his leg, and it is bleeding.*
2 to make something shorter ▶ *Could you cut my hair for me?*
3 to remove one part from something bigger ▶ *She cut a piece of cake.*
4 cut down to make something fall to the ground by cutting it ▶ *We'll have to cut down that tree.*
5 cut off (**a**) to stop or disconnect something ▶ *They've cut the gas off!* (**b**) to separate a person or place from the other people or places near them ▶ *Snow has cut off many villages.*
6 cut something up to cut something into pieces ▶ *Could you cut up the chicken?*
7 cut something out to remove something by cutting it ▶ *She cut a picture out of the newspaper.*

cut² *noun*
an opening or wound made by something sharp ▶ *a cut on the leg*

cute /kjuːt/ *adjective*
pretty or attractive ▶ *her cute little nose*

cutlery /ˈkʌtlərɪ/ *noun (no plural)*
knives, forks, and spoons used for eating

cut-price /ˌkʌt ˈpraɪs/ *adjective*
cheaper than normal ▶ *a shop selling cut-price books*

cutting¹ /ˈkʌtɪŋ/ *noun*
1 a stem or leaf that is cut from a plant to be grown into a new plant
2 a piece of writing that is cut from a newspaper or magazine

cutting² *adjective*
unkind and intended to upset someone ▶ *a cutting remark*

cutting edge /ˌkʌtɪŋ ˈedʒ/ *noun*
be at/on the cutting edge to be involved in the most recent and most exciting part of the development of something

CV /ˌsiː ˈviː/ *noun*
CURRICULUM VITAE; a document that describes your education and the jobs that you have done, used when you are trying to get a new job

cyberspace /ˈsaɪbəspeɪs/ *noun (no plural)*
a place that is not real, used for describing where electronic messages go when they travel from

one computer to another ▶ *The e-mail was lost somewhere in cyberspace.*

cycle¹ /'saɪkəl/ *noun*
a bicycle
SAME MEANING: **bicycle, bike**

cycle² *verb (present participle* ***cycling****, past* ***cycled****)*
to ride a bicycle ▶ *He cycles to school every day.*

cycling /'saɪklɪŋ/ *noun (no plural)*
the sport of riding a bicycle

D

cyclist /'saɪklɪst/ *noun*
a person who rides a bicycle

cyclone /'saɪkləʊn/ *noun*
a very strong wind that moves in a circle

cylinder /'sɪlɪndəʳ/ *noun*
a long, round shape like a tube or a pencil

cymbal /'sɪmbəl/ *noun*
a round, metal plate that you hit with another metal plate or a stick to make a musical sound

cynic /'sɪnɪk/ *noun*
a person who believes that no one does things for good or honest reasons ▶ *Don't be such a cynic!*

cynical /'sɪnɪkəl/ *adjective*
believing that no one does things for good or honest reasons ▶ *I'm rather cynical about journalists who claim to be helping the public.*

Dd

'd /d/
1 had ▶ *He'd* (=he had) *eaten all the cake.*
2 would ▶ *I'd* (=I would) *buy a new car if I had enough money.*

dab¹ /dæb/ *verb (present participle* ***dabbing****, past* ***dabbed****)*
to lightly touch something several times in order to dry it or put something on it ▶ *He dabbed at the mark on his trousers.*

dab² *noun*
a small amount of a liquid, cream, etc. ▶ *a dab of paint*

dad /dæd/ *noun*
father

daddy /'dædɪ/ *noun (plural* ***daddies****)*
(used by and to small children) father

daffodil /'dæfədɪl/ *noun*
a yellow flower which appears in the spring

daft /dɑːft/ *adjective*
foolish or silly ▶ *a daft idea*

dagger /'dægəʳ/ *noun*
a short knife used as a weapon
COMPARE: **sword**

daily /'deɪlɪ/ *adjective, adverb*
happening every day ▶ *Take the medicine twice daily.*

dairy /'deərɪ/ *noun (plural* ***dairies****)*
a place where milk is kept and foods are made from milk

daisy /'deɪzɪ/ *noun (plural* ***daisies****)*
a small wild flower that is white with a yellow centre

dalmatian /dæl'meɪʃən/ *noun*
a white dog with black spots

dam¹ /dæm/ *noun*
a wall built to hold back water

dam² *verb (present participle* ***damming****, past* ***dammed****)*
to put a dam across something ▶ *to dam a river*

damage¹ /'dæmɪdʒ/ *noun (no plural)*
harm done to something

damage² *verb (present participle* ***damaging****, past* ***damaged****)*
to harm something ▶ *The cars were badly damaged in the accident.*

damn¹ /dæm/ *(also* ***damned*** */dæmd/) adverb, adjective*
used to emphasize something in a

rude way, especially when you are annoyed ▶ *Don't be so damn stupid!* ▶ *The damned thing's broken again.*

damn[2] *interjection*
used when you are annoyed or disappointed ▶ *Damn! I forgot to bring my wallet!*

damp /dæmp/ *adjective*
rather wet ▶ *damp clothes*

dance[1] /dɑːns/ *verb (present participle* ***dancing****, past* ***danced****)*
to move to music

dance[2] *noun*
1 a set of movements you do to music ▶ *to learn a new dance*
2 a party where there is dancing ▶ *Are you going to the dance?*

dancer /ˈdɑːnsəʳ/ *noun*
a person who is dancing, or someone who dances as their job

dancing /ˈdɑːnsɪŋ/ *noun (no plural)*
moving to music

dandelion /ˈdændɪlaɪən/ *noun*
a yellow flower which grows wild

dandruff /ˈdændrʌf/ *noun (no plural)*
very small, white pieces of loose skin in a person's hair

danger /ˈdeɪndʒəʳ/ *noun*
1 *(no plural)* the possibility of harm ▶ *Danger! Do not enter* (=written on a notice). ▶ *You are not* ***in*** *any danger here* (=there is no danger here).
2 something that can cause harm ▶ *the dangers of smoking*

dangerous /ˈdeɪndʒərəs/ *adjective*
likely to harm people ▶ *a dangerous driver* ▶ *dangerous drugs*

dangle /ˈdæŋgəl/ *verb (present participle* ***dangling****, past* ***dangled****)*
to hang or swing from something ▶ *The keys were dangling from his belt.*

dare /deəʳ/ *verb (present participle* ***daring****, past* ***dared****)*
1 to be brave enough to do something ▶ *I daren't refuse.*
2 dare someone to do something to try to make someone do something to prove they are not afraid
3 don't you dare a phrase used when you are angry with someone and are telling them not to do something ▶ *Don't you dare touch that!*
4 how dare you a phrase used when you are angry with someone because they have done something ▶ *How dare you speak to me like that!*

daren't /deənt/
dare not ▶ *I daren't talk to him.*

daring /ˈdeərɪŋ/ *adjective*
1 willing to do dangerous things ▶ *a daring rescue attempt*
2 new or unusual in a slightly shocking way ▶ *a daring evening dress*

dark[1] /dɑːk/ *adjective*
1 like night; not light or bright ▶ *It was getting dark, so we hurried home.*
2 of a deep colour, nearer black than white ▶ *She has dark hair.* ▶ *He wore a dark suit.*

dark[2] *noun (no plural)*
the lack of light ▶ *We could not see in the dark.* ▶ *Make sure you are home before dark* (=before it is night).

darken /ˈdɑːkən/ *verb*
to become darker, or to make something darker ▶ *The sky darkened very quickly.*

darkness /ˈdɑːknəs/ *noun (no plural)*
lack of light ▶ *The room was in darkness* (=was dark).

darling /ˈdɑːlɪŋ/ *noun, adjective*
a name you call someone you love ▶ *Come on darling, or we'll be late.*

dart /dɑːt/ *verb*
to move suddenly and quickly ▶ *A mouse darted across the floor.*

darts /dɑːts/ *noun (no plural)*
a game in which you throw small

D

objects with sharp points at a board with numbers on it

dash¹ /dæʃ/ *verb*
to move quickly ▶ *She dashed out of the room.*

dash² *noun (plural* ***dashes****)*
the sign (–) used in writing, to show a short space, or to separate two parts of a sentence

dashboard /ˈdæʃbɔːd/ *noun*
the part at the front of a car that has the controls on it

D

data /ˈdeɪtə, ˈdɑːtə/ *noun (no plural)*
facts and information

database /ˈdeɪtəˌbeɪs/ *noun*
a large amount of information stored in a computer system

date /deɪt/ *noun*
1 the day of the month, or the year ▶ *"What date is your birthday?" "It's April 2nd."* ▶ *The date was 1857.* ▶ *Please write today's date.*
2 an arrangement to meet a boyfriend or girlfriend ▶ *I've got a date tonight.*
3 a small, sweet, brown fruit
4 out of date not fashionable any more
5 up to date modern

dated /ˈdeɪtɪd/ *adjective*
no longer fashionable or modern ▶ *dated ideas*

daughter /ˈdɔːtəʳ/ *noun*
your female child ▶ *They have three daughters and one son.*

daughter-in-law /ˈdɔːtər ɪn lɔː/ *noun (plural* ***daughters-in-law****)*
the wife of your son

daunted /ˈdɔːntɪd/ *adjective*
afraid or worried about something you have to do ▶ *He felt daunted* ***by*** *the size of the job.*

daunting /ˈdɔːntɪŋ/ *adjective*
frightening or worrying ▶ *Being captain of the team is a daunting responsibility.*

dawn /dɔːn/ *noun*
the start of the day when the sun rises
SAME MEANING: **daybreak**

day /deɪ/ *noun*
1 *(no plural)* the time when it is light
OPPOSITE: **night**
2 24 hours ▶ *It hasn't stopped raining for days.* ▶ *"What day is it today?" "It's Tuesday."*
3 one day, some day at some time in the future ▶ *Some day I'll be rich.*
4 the other day a few days ago ▶ *I went there the other day.*
5 these days at the present time ▶ *Everyone seems so busy these days.*

daybreak /ˈdeɪbreɪk/ *noun (no plural)*
the start of the day when the light first appears
SAME MEANING: **dawn**

daydream /ˈdeɪdriːm/ *verb*
to imagine nice things, especially things you would like to happen in the future

daylight /ˈdeɪlaɪt/ *noun (no plural)*
the light of the day ▶ *We want to travel in daylight* (=before it gets dark).

day off /ˌdeɪ ˈɒf/ *noun (plural* ***days off****)*
a day when you do not have to go to work or school ▶ *She's having a day off.*

daytime /ˈdeɪtaɪm/ *noun (no plural)*
the time when it is light
OPPOSITE: **nighttime**

day-to-day /ˌdeɪ tə ˈdeɪ/ *adjective*
happening every day as a regular part of your life ▶ *the day-to-day running of the office*

daze /deɪz/ *noun*
in a daze unable to think clearly ▶ *He wandered around in a daze.*

dazed /deɪzd/ *adjective*
unable to think clearly, usually

because you are shocked or have been in an accident ▶ *The news left him feeling dazed.*

dazzle /'dæzəl/ *verb (present participle **dazzling**, past **dazzled**)*
if a light dazzles you, it is so bright that you cannot see clearly for a short time

dead¹ /ded/ *adjective*
not living ▶ *My grandfather has been dead for ten years.*
OPPOSITE: **alive, living**

dead² *plural noun*
the dead dead people ▶ *After the battle, they counted the dead.*
OPPOSITE: **the living**

dead end /ˌded 'end/ *noun*
a street with no way out at one end

dead heat /ˌded 'hiːt/ *noun*
the result of a race in which two people finish at exactly the same time ▶ *The race ended in a dead heat.*

deadline /'dedlaɪn/ *noun*
a date or time by which you must finish something ▶ *Do you think we'll be able to meet the deadline?*

deadlock /'dedlɒk/ *noun (no plural)*
a situation in which groups or countries cannot agree ▶ *The talks ended in deadlock.*

deadly /'dedlɪ/ *adjective (**deadlier, deadliest**)*
likely to cause death ▶ *a deadly poison*
COMPARE: **fatal**

deaf /def/ *adjective*
not able to hear because you have something wrong with your ears

deafen /'defən/ *verb*
if a noise deafens you, it is so loud that it is difficult for you to hear anything ▶ *The music deafened us.*

deal¹ /diːl/ *noun*
1 a business arrangement ▶ *Let's make a deal.* ▶ *a deal between the two governments*
2 a good deal, a great deal a lot ▶ *There's a good deal **of** work to do.*

deal² *verb (past **dealt** /delt/)*
1 deal with someone to do business with someone
2 deal with something to do what is necessary for something ▶ *I will deal with your questions now* (=answer them).

dealer /'diːləʳ/ *noun*
a person whose job is to buy and sell a certain thing ▶ *a dealer **in** old cars*

dealt /delt/
the PAST TENSE and PAST PARTICIPLE of the verb **deal**

dear¹ /dɪəʳ/ *adjective*
1 loved ▶ *a dear friend*
2 used at the start of a letter to someone ▶ *Dear Sue* ▶ *Dear Sir*
3 costing a lot of money
SAME MEANING (3): **costly, expensive**

dear² *interjection*
oh dear an expression you use when you are surprised, annoyed, or disappointed ▶ *Oh dear! I've forgotten my purse.*

death /deθ/ *noun*
the state of being dead, or the act of dying ▶ *the death of his father*

death penalty /'deθ ˌpenltɪ/ *noun (plural **death penalties**)*
the death penalty the legal punishment of killing someone who is guilty of a crime ▶ *He was convicted of the murder and given the death penalty.*

debatable /dɪ'beɪtəbəl/ *adjective*
(used about facts, decisions, etc.) not certain ▶ *It is debatable whether the peace will last.*

debate¹ /dɪ'beɪt/ *noun*
a public talk at which people give opinions about a subject

debate² *verb (present participle **debating**, past **debated**)*
to talk about something important

▶ *The government is debating the education laws.*

debit[1] /'debɪt/ *noun*
an amount of money that you take out of your bank account ▶ *Your bank statement shows all your debits and credits.*

debit[2] *verb*
to take money out of a bank account ▶ *The sum of £50 has been debited from your account.*
OPPOSITE: **credit**

D

debris /'debri:/ *noun (no plural)*
pieces of material that are left after something has been destroyed ▶ *The road was covered with debris from the crash.*

debt /det/ *noun*
1 money owed ▶ *a debt of £500*
2 be in debt to owe money to someone

debut /'deɪbju:/ *noun*
the first time that an actor, sports player, etc. performs in public ▶ *the band's debut album*

decade /'dekeɪd/ *noun*
a period of ten years

decaffeinated /di:'kæfɪneɪtɪd/ *adjective*
(used about drinks) not containing CAFFEINE (=a substance that makes you feel more awake) ▶ *a cup of decaffeinated coffee*

decay[1] /dɪ'keɪ/ *verb*
to be destroyed slowly; to go bad
SAME MEANING: **rot**

decay[2] *noun (no plural)*
the state of being bad ▶ *tooth decay*

deceit /dɪ'si:t/ *noun (no plural)*
making someone believe something that is not true

deceive /dɪ'si:v/ *verb (present participle **deceiving**, past **deceived**)*
to make someone believe something that is not true ▶ *He had managed to deceive us all.*

December /dɪ'sembəʳ/ *noun*
the 12th month of the year

decent /'di:sənt/ *adjective*
good ▶ *Make sure you eat a decent breakfast.* ▶ *a decent job*

deceptive /dɪ'septɪv/ *adjective*
something that is deceptive seems very different from how it really is ▶ *She seems very calm, but appearances can be deceptive.* *(adverb: **deceptively**)*

decide /dɪ'saɪd/ *verb (present participle **deciding**, past **decided**)*
to think that you will do something; to choose what to do ▶ *I decided to go home.* ▶ *She could not decide which dress to buy.*

decidedly /dɪ'saɪdɪdlɪ/ *adverb*
very, in a way that is easy to notice ▶ *Her boss was decidedly unsympathetic.*

decimal /'desɪməl/ *noun*
a number less than one, that is shown by a point (.) followed by numbers. For example, a quarter is shown by the decimal 0.25.

decision /dɪ'sɪʒən/ *noun*
a choice ▶ *They couldn't make a decision about where to go on holiday.*

decisive /dɪ'saɪsɪv/ *adjective*
1 having an important effect on the result of something ▶ *a decisive moment in his career*
2 good at making decisions quickly and firmly ▶ *a strong, decisive leader*
OPPOSITE (**2**): **indecisive**
*(adverb: **decisively**)*

deck /dek/ *noun*
a part of a ship, bus, etc. where passengers sit or stand ▶ *the top deck of a bus*

deckchair /'dek,tʃeəʳ/ *noun*
a type of chair that you can fold until it is flat, and that people sit on outside, especially by the sea

declaration /ˌdekləˈreɪʃən/ *noun*
an official statement ▶ *a declaration **of** war*

declare /dɪˈkleəʳ/ *verb (present participle **declaring**, past **declared**)*
to say in public what you think or decide ▶ *to declare war on a country* (=to say that your country will fight another country)

decline¹ /dɪˈklaɪn/ *verb (present participle **declining**, past **declined**)*
1 to become less in number or quality ▶ *The number of teachers has declined in recent years.*
2 to refuse to do something ▶ *He declined to answer*

decline² *noun*
a decrease in the number or quality of something

décor /ˈdeɪkɔːʳ/ *noun (no plural)*
the way that a room looks, and the colours, kind of furniture, etc. in it ▶ *The restaurant had changed its décor.*

decorate /ˈdekəreɪt/ *verb (present participle **decorating**, past **decorated**)*
1 to put paint or paper on the walls of a house ▶ *We're decorating the bathroom.*
2 to make something look more attractive by adding things to it ▶ *to decorate a cake*

decoration /ˌdekəˈreɪʃən/ *noun*
an attractive thing that is added to something to improve its appearance

decorative /ˈdekərətɪv/ *adjective*
pretty and used to decorate something ▶ *a decorative vase*

decorator /ˈdekəreɪtəʳ/ *noun*
a person whose job is to put paint or paper on the inside of houses

decrease¹ /dɪˈkriːs/ *verb (present participle **decreasing**, past **decreased**)*
to get less or fewer ▶ *The number of children in the school has decreased this year.*
OPPOSITE: **increase**

decrease² /ˈdiːkriːs/ *noun (no plural)*
getting less or fewer ▶ *a decrease in the number of pupils*
OPPOSITE: **increase**

decree /dɪˈkriː/ *noun*
an official order that a ruler or government makes

decrepit /dɪˈkrepɪt/ *adjective*
old and in bad condition ▶ *a decrepit old car*

dedicate /ˈdedɪkeɪt/ *verb (present participle **dedicating**, past **dedicated**)*
to say that a book, film, song, etc. has been written or made for someone, to show that you respect or love them ▶ *The book is dedicated to his mother.*

dedicated /ˈdedɪkeɪtɪd/ *adjective*
working very hard at doing something because you think it is important ▶ *The nurses are all very dedicated.*

dedication /ˌdedɪˈkeɪʃən/ *noun (no plural)*
the act of working very hard because you believe that what you are doing is important ▶ *I was impressed by the dedication of the school staff.*

deduce /dɪˈdjuːs/ *verb (present participle **deducing**, past **deduced**)*
to decide that something is true, using the information that you have ▶ *From his accent, I deduced that he was not English.*

deduct /dɪˈdʌkt/ *verb*
to take one amount away from another larger amount ▶ *The tax is deducted from your salary each month.*

deed /diːd/ *noun*
an action ▶ *to do a good deed* (=to do something to help someone)

D

deep /diːp/ *adjective*
1 going down a long way ▶ *a deep river* ▶ *How deep is the river?*
OPPOSITE: **shallow**
2 having a low sound ▶ *a deep voice*
3 strong or dark in colour ▶ *deep brown eyes*
4 felt strongly ▶ *a deep love*

deepen /ˈdiːpən/ *verb*
to become worse, or make something become worse ▶ *The crisis deepened.*

deep freeze /ˌdiːp ˈfriːz/ *noun*
a large container in which you can freeze food and keep it for a long time

deeply /ˈdiːplɪ/ *adverb*
very strongly ▶ *I care deeply about this problem.* ▶ *deeply in love*

deer /dɪəʳ/ *noun (plural **deer**)*
an animal that can run fast. The male usually has horns.

defeat[1] /dɪˈfiːt/ *verb*
to beat an opponent in a war, game, etc.

defeat[2] *noun*
an experience or event in which you are beaten by an opponent ▶ *The football team suffered a defeat.*
OPPOSITE: **victory**

defect /dɪˈfekt/ *noun*
a fault in something that stops it working properly ▶ *a defect in the plane engine* ▶ *He's had a hearing defect since he was a child.*

defence /dɪˈfens/ *noun (no plural)*
1 protecting someone or something from an attack ▶ *the defence of your country*
2 the defence the lawyers who are trying to prove that someone is not guilty of a crime in a law court ▶ *Is the defence ready to call the first witness?*
OPPOSITE: **prosecution**

defenceless /dɪˈfensləs/ *adjective*
unable to protect yourself ▶ *a defenceless old woman*

D

defend /dɪˈfend/ *verb*
to fight in order to protect someone or something
COMPARE: **attack**

defendant /dɪˈfendənt/ *noun*
the person in a law court who the police say is guilty of a crime

defensive /dɪˈfensɪv/ *adjective*
1 used for protection against an attack ▶ *defensive weapons*
2 behaving in a way that shows you think someone is criticizing you ▶ *She got really defensive when I asked her why she hadn't finished.*

defiant /dɪˈfaɪənt/ *adjective*
bold and not obedient ▶ *defiant behaviour*

deficiency /dɪˈfɪʃənsɪ/ *noun (plural **deficiencies**)*
1 a lack of something ▶ *a vitamin deficiency*
2 a fault that makes something not good enough ▶ *the deficiencies of the public transport system*

define /dɪˈfaɪn/ *verb (present participle **defining**, past **defined**)*
to say exactly what a word means or what something is

definite /ˈdefɪnət/ *adjective*
clear; sure ▶ *Let's fix a definite date for the next meeting.*

definite article /ˌdefɪnət ˈɑːtɪkəl/ *noun*
in English, the word **the**
COMPARE: **indefinite article**

definitely /ˈdefɪnətlɪ/ *adverb*
certainly; without any doubt ▶ *I'm definitely going to come.*

definition /ˌdefɪˈnɪʃən/ *noun*
an explanation of what a word means, which you find in a dictionary

deflect /dɪˈflekt/ *verb*
to make something move in a different direction, or to change directions in this way ▶ *The ball hit the post and was deflected for a corner.*

deforestation /diːˌfɒrəˈsteɪʃən/ *noun (no plural)*
cutting down or destroying all the trees in an area

deformed /dɪˈfɔːmd/ *adjective*
not having a normal shape
▶ *Mothers who took the drug gave birth to deformed babies.*

defrost /ˌdiːˈfrɒst/ *verb*
if frozen food defrosts, or if you defrost it, it slowly stops being frozen until you can cook or eat it
▶ *Defrost the chicken thoroughly before cooking.*

deft /deft/ *adjective*
quick and skilful ▶ *Katherine drew a picture with a few deft strokes of her pen.*

defy /dɪˈfaɪ/ *verb (past* ***defied****)*
to refuse to obey someone and show no respect for them ▶ *to defy your parents*

degrading /dɪˈgreɪdɪŋ/ *adjective*
making you lose respect for yourself
▶ *A lot of people say housework is degrading.*

degree /dɪˈgriː/ *noun*
1 a measurement used for temperatures or angles ▶ *an angle of 45 degrees (45°)* ▶ *a temperature of 80 degrees (80°)*
2 a QUALIFICATION that a person gets after studying and taking examinations, usually at university or college ▶ *a history degree*

dehydrated /ˌdiːhaɪˈdreɪtɪd/ *adjective*
ill or weak because you do not have enough water in your body

delay¹ /dɪˈleɪ/ *noun*
a time of waiting before something can happen ▶ *We are sorry about the delay.*

delay² *verb*
to make something late ▶ *The train has been delayed.*

delegate¹ /ˈdelɪgət/ *noun*
a person that a country or an organization chooses to do something for it, such as speak or vote at a meeting ▶ *UN delegates*

delegate² /ˈdelɪgeɪt/ *verb (present participle* ***delegating****, past* ***delegated****)*
to give part of your work to someone in a lower position than you ▶ *You must learn to delegate more.*

delegation /ˌdelɪˈgeɪʃən/ *noun*
a small group of people that a country or an organization sends to do something for it, such as vote or find out about something

delete /dɪˈliːt/ *verb (present participle* ***deleting****, past* ***deleted****)*
to remove a piece of information from a computer ▶ *Are you sure you want to delete this file?*

deliberate /dɪˈlɪbərət/ *adjective*
planned or done on purpose

deliberately /dɪˈlɪbərətlɪ/ *adverb*
on purpose ▶ *I didn't do it deliberately – it was an accident.*

delicacy /ˈdelɪkəsɪ/ *noun (plural* ***delicacies****)*
a rare or an expensive food that is especially nice to eat

delicate /ˈdelɪkət/ *adjective*
easily harmed, damaged, or broken
▶ *a delicate glass* ▶ *a delicate child who is often ill*

delicatessen /ˌdelɪkəˈtesən/ *noun*
a shop that sells special or unusual food, especially food from foreign countries

delicious /dɪˈlɪʃəs/ *adjective*
good to eat ▶ *a delicious meal*

delight¹ /dɪˈlaɪt/ *noun (no plural)*
great happiness ▶ *to laugh with delight*

delight² *verb*
to give great happiness to someone

D

delighted /dɪˈlaɪtɪd/ *adjective*
very pleased ▶ *We are delighted with the news.*

delightful /dɪˈlaɪtfəl/ *adjective*
very nice or attractive ▶ *What a delightful idea!* ▶ *a delightful child*

delirious /dɪˈlɪrɪəs/ *adjective*
unable to think clearly because you are ill

deliver /dɪˈlɪvəʳ/ *verb*
1 to take something to the place where it should go ▶ *to deliver a letter*
2 to help a baby come out of its mother's body ▶ *to deliver a baby*

D

delivery /dɪˈlɪvərɪ/ *noun (plural* ***deliveries****)*
the taking of something to the place where it should go

delta /ˈdeltə/ *noun*
a low area of land where a river separates into many smaller rivers flowing towards the sea ▶ *the Mississippi Delta*

deluge /ˈdeljuːdʒ/ *noun*
1 a large flood, or a period of time when it rains continuously
2 a large amount of something such as letters, questions, etc. that someone receives all at the same time

de luxe /dɪˈlʌks/ *adjective*
(used about a hotel, car, etc.) costing more money than others of the same kind because it is better ▶ *We had a de luxe room with a balcony.*

delve /delv/ *verb (present participle* ***delving****, past* ***delved****)*
to put your hand deep inside a bag, box, etc. in order to find something ▶ *He delved* ***into*** *his pockets to find his key.*

demand¹ /dɪˈmɑːnd/ *verb*
to say in a very strong and firm way that you want something ▶ *"Give me my book at once!" she demanded.*

demand² *noun*
1 a very strong request ▶ *a demand* ***for*** *more money*
2 in demand wanted by a lot of people

demanding /dɪˈmɑːndɪŋ/ *adjective*
needing a lot of your time, effort, skill, etc. ▶ *a very demanding job*

democracy /dɪˈmɒkrəsɪ/ *noun (plural* ***democracies****)*
a government or country where everyone has an equal right to choose their leaders, by voting

democrat /ˈdeməkræt/ *noun*
a person who believes in or supports democracy

democratic /ˌdeməˈkrætɪk/ *adjective*
(used about a country, company, etc.) letting everyone have the right to choose their government by voting

demolish /dɪˈmɒlɪʃ/ *verb*
to destroy a building on purpose, in a controlled way

demolition /ˌdeməˈlɪʃən/ *noun (no plural)*
the destroying of a building on purpose, in a controlled way

demon /ˈdiːmən/ *noun*
an evil spirit

demonstrate /ˈdemənstreɪt/ *verb (present participle* ***demonstrating****, past* ***demonstrated****)*
1 to show something clearly ▶ *He demonstrated how to use the new machine.*
2 to walk through the streets in a group to show that you are angry about something or do not agree with something

demonstration /ˌdemənˈstreɪʃən/ *noun*
1 showing how to do something ▶ *a cookery demonstration*
2 a group of people walking through the streets to show that they are angry about something or do not agree with something

demonstrator /'demənstreɪtəʳ/ *noun*
a person who takes part in a demonstration

demoralized /dɪ'mɒrəlaɪzd/ *adjective*
feeling less confident and hopeful than before because of bad things that have happened ► *After a year in the job, I felt totally demoralized.*

demoralizing /dɪ'mɒrəlaɪzɪŋ/ *adjective*
making you feel less confident and hopeful than before ► *The announcement had a demoralizing effect on the staff.*

den /den/ *noun*
a place in which a wild animal lives

denial /dɪ'naɪəl/ *noun*
a statement that something is not true ► *his denial of guilt*

denim /'denɪm/ *noun (no plural)*
a strong cloth, usually blue in colour, which is used to make JEANS

dense /dens/ *adjective*
thick ► *a dense forest*

dent¹ /dent/ *noun*
a hollow place in the surface of something where it has been hit or pressed ► *a big dent in the car*

dent² *verb*
to hit or press something, making a hollow place in its surface

dental /'dentl/ *adjective*
of or about teeth ► *dental problems*

dentist /'dentɪst/ *noun*
a doctor who looks after people's teeth

dentures /'dentʃəz/ *plural noun*
false teeth worn by people who have lost their real teeth

deny /dɪ'naɪ/ *verb (past* ***denied****)*
to say that something someone has said about you is not true
OPPOSITE: **admit**

deodorant /diː'əʊdərənt/ *noun (no plural)*
a substance that people put under their arms, to stop their body smelling bad

depart /dɪ'pɑːt/ *verb*
to leave; to go away ► *The York train will depart from platform 2.*
OPPOSITE: **arrive**

department /dɪ'pɑːtmənt/ *noun*
a part of a business, company, government, etc.

department store /dɪ'pɑːtmənt ˌstɔːʳ/ *noun*
a type of shop that is divided into several parts, each of which sells a different kind of goods

departure /dɪ'pɑːtʃəʳ/ *noun*
an act of leaving a place ► *the day of his departure*
OPPOSITE: **arrival**

depend /dɪ'pend/ *verb*
1 it depends a phrase used when you are not sure about something ► *"How long will the journey take?" "I don't know; it depends."*
2 depend on someone to need someone very much

dependable /dɪ'pendəbəl/ *adjective*
able to be trusted ► *a dependable employee*

dependant /dɪ'pendənt/ *noun*
a person who depends on someone for money, e.g. children who depend on their parents

dependent /dɪ'pendənt/ *adjective*
needing someone or something to support you
OPPOSITE: **independent**

deport /dɪ'pɔːt/ *verb*
to force someone to leave a country and return to the country they came from

depose /dɪ'pəʊz/ *verb (present participle* ***deposing****, past* ***deposed****)*
to remove a leader from their position

D

of power ▶ *an attempt to depose the king*

deposit[1] /dɪˈpɒzɪt/ *verb*
1 to put something down and leave it
2 to put money, etc. into a bank

deposit[2] *noun*
1 part of the cost of something that you pay at once so that the thing will not be sold to anyone else before you pay the rest of the money
2 money that you pay when you rent something and which is returned to you if you do not cause any damage

D

depot /ˈdepəʊ/ *noun*
a place where goods or vehicles are stored

depress /dɪˈpres/ *verb*
to make someone feel very sad

depressed /dɪˈprest/ *adjective*
very sad ▶ *She's depressed.*

depressing /dɪˈpresɪŋ/ *adjective*
causing you to feel very sad
▶ *depressing news*

depression /dɪˈpreʃən/ *noun (no plural)*
a feeling of great sadness

deprive /dɪˈpraɪv/ *verb (present participle* ***depriving,*** *past* ***deprived****)*
to stop someone having something that they need or that they normally have ▶ *They deprived the prisoners* ***of*** *food.*

deprived /dɪˈpraɪvd/ *adjective*
not having enough of the things that are necessary for a normal, happy life
▶ *a deprived childhood*

depth /depθ/ *noun*
the distance to the bottom of something ▶ *the depth* ***of*** *the river*

deputy /ˈdepjʊtɪ/ *noun (plural* ***deputies****)*
a person who is second in importance to the head of a business, a school, etc.

derelict /ˈderɪlɪkt/ *adjective*
(used about buildings or land) in bad condition because no one has used it for a long time ▶ *derelict factories*

descend /dɪˈsend/ *verb*
to go down ▶ *to descend the stairs*
OPPOSITE: **ascend**

descendant /dɪˈsendənt/ *noun*
a person in your family who is born a long time after you are dead
COMPARE: **ancestor**

descent /dɪˈsent/ *noun*
1 the act of going down to a lower place ▶ *The plane began its descent.*
OPPOSITE: **ascent**
2 *(no plural)* your family origins, especially the country that they came from ▶ *Tara's family is* ***of*** *Irish descent.*

describe /dɪˈskraɪb/ *verb*
(present participle ***describing,*** *past* ***described****)*
to say what someone or something is like

description /dɪˈskrɪpʃən/ *noun*
an account of what someone or something is like

desert /ˈdezət/ *noun*
a large, empty, usually very dry, place where almost nothing grows

deserted /dɪˈzɜːtɪd/ *adjective*
empty of people ▶ *a deserted street*

desert island /ˌdezət ˈaɪlənd/ *noun*
an island with no people living on it

deserve /dɪˈzɜːv/ *verb*
(present participle ***deserving,*** *past* ***deserved****)*
to be worthy of something ▶ *You deserve a holiday after all your hard work.*

design[1] /dɪˈzaɪn/ *noun*
1 a pattern ▶ *a design of blue flowers*
2 a drawing of how to make something ▶ *designs for a new house*

design[2] *verb*
to make a drawing as a plan for something ▶ *to design a building*

designer /dɪ'zaɪnəʳ/ *noun*
a person whose job is to think of ideas for making things and then draw them

desirable /dɪ'zaɪərəbəl/ *adjective*
good or useful, and wanted by many people ▶ *a desirable apartment in the centre of the city*

desire[1] /dɪ'zaɪəʳ/ *noun*
a strong wish ▶ *a desire **for** power*

desire[2] *verb (present participle **desiring**, past **desired**)*
to want something very much

desk /desk/ *noun*
a table for writing on, often with space inside it for keeping books, pens, etc.

despair[1] /dɪ'speəʳ/ *noun (no plural)*
a feeling of great sadness and loss of hope

despair[2] *verb*
to have no hope

despatch /dɪ'spætʃ/ *verb*
another word for **dispatch**

desperate /'despərət/ *adjective*
wanting or needing something very much ▶ *to be desperate **for** money*

despise /dɪ'spaɪz/ *verb*
*(present participle **despising**, past **despised**)*
to hate a person or thing because you think they are not worth anything

despite /dɪ'spaɪt/ *preposition*
although something is true ▶ *Despite the bad weather, we enjoyed our holiday.*

dessert /dɪ'zɜːt/ *noun*
a sweet dish that you eat at the end of a meal
SAME MEANING: **pudding, sweet**

destination /ˌdestɪ'neɪʃən/ *noun*
the place you are travelling to
▶ *What is your destination?*

destined /'destɪnd/ *adjective*
certain to do or become something in the future ▶ *She was destined **to** become her country's first woman Prime Minister.*

destiny /'destɪnɪ/ *noun (plural **destinies**)*
the things that will happen to someone in the future ▶ *Do you think we can control our own destinies?*

destroy /dɪ'strɔɪ/ *verb*
to break or ruin something completely ▶ *The building was destroyed by fire.*

destruction /dɪ'strʌkʃən/ *noun (no plural)*
the breaking of something completely

detach /dɪ'tætʃ/ *verb*
to remove a part of something, especially a part that is designed to be removed ▶ *Detach the bottom half of the page by tearing along the dotted line.*

detached /dɪ'tætʃt/ *adjective*
(used about houses) not joined to another house

detail /'diːteɪl/ *noun*
1 one of the small points that makes up the whole of something ▶ *Please could you send me details of the conference?*
2 in detail thoroughly; paying attention to all the facts ▶ *We must talk about it in detail.*

detailed /'diːteɪld/ *adjective*
including a lot of information or facts
▶ *a detailed analysis of the text*

detain /dɪ'teɪn/ *verb*
(used about the police) to keep someone somewhere and not allow them to leave

detect /dɪ'tekt/ *verb*
to discover or notice something

detective /dɪ'tektɪv/ *noun*
a special police officer who tries to discover who has carried out a crime

detector /dɪ'tektəʳ/ *noun*
a piece of equipment that tells you if

there is a particular substance somewhere ▶ *a smoke detector*

detention /dɪ'tenʃən/ *noun (no plural)*
1 the act of keeping someone in prison because the police think that they have done something illegal
2 a punishment in which pupils have to stay at school after the other pupils have left

deter /dɪ'tɜːʳ/ *verb (present participle **deterring**, past **deterred**)*
to make someone less likely to do something by making it difficult for them to do it ▶ *security measures aimed at deterring shoplifters*

detergent /dɪ'tɜːdʒənt/ *noun*
soap in the form of powder or liquid for washing clothes, dishes, etc.

deteriorate /dɪ'tɪərɪəreɪt/ *verb (present participle **deteriorating**, past **deteriorated**)*
to get worse ▶ *Her health has deteriorated.*

determination /dɪˌtɜːmɪ'neɪʃən/ *noun (no plural)*
a strong wish to succeed in doing something ▶ *her determination to win*

determined /dɪ'tɜːmɪnd/ *adjective*
wanting to do something very much so that nothing can stop you ▶ *I'm determined to win.*

determiner /dɪ'tɜːmɪnəʳ/ *noun*
in grammar, a word used before a noun or an adjective to show which thing you mean. In the phrases "the car" and "some new cars", "the" and "some" are determiners.

detest /dɪ'test/ *verb*
to hate someone or something

detonate /'detəneɪt/ *verb (present participle **detonating**, past **detonated**)*
to explode, or to make a bomb explode ▶ *Nuclear bombs were detonated in tests in the desert.*

D

detour /'diːtʊəʳ/ *noun*
a way of going from one place to another that is longer than the usual way

devastate /'devəsteɪt/ *verb (present participle **devastating**, past **devastated**)*
to damage a place very badly ▶ *Bombing raids devastated the city of Dresden.*

devastated /'devəsteɪtɪd/ *adjective*
very sad and shocked ▶ *Ellen was devastated **by** the news.*

devastating /'devəsteɪtɪŋ/ *adjective*
1 causing a lot of damage ▶ *Chemical pollution has had a devastating effect on the environment.*
2 making you feel extremely sad and shocked ▶ *Losing your job can be a devastating experience.*

develop /dɪ'veləp/ *verb*
1 to grow ▶ *The fighting could develop into a war.* ▶ *an insect which develops wings*
2 to make something grow or improve ▶ *plans to develop industry in the area*
3 to treat the film from a camera with special chemicals so that you can see the picture ▶ *to develop a photograph*

developing country /dɪˌveləpɪŋ 'kʌntrɪ/ *noun (plural **developing countries**)*
a country which is just starting to have modern industries

development /dɪ'veləpmənt/ *noun*
1 the latest in a number of real or imaginary events
2 *(no plural)* growth ▶ *a child's development* ▶ *the development of industry in the area*

device /dɪ'vaɪs/ *noun*
a thing that you use for a particular purpose ▶ *a device for opening bottles*

Devil /'devəl/ *noun*
the Devil an evil spirit that is God's powerful enemy in some religions

devious /'diːvɪəs/ *adjective*
dishonest in a clever way ▶ *a devious scheme for making money*

devise /dɪ'vaɪz/ *verb (present participle* ***devising****, past* ***devised****)*
to plan or think of a new way of doing something ▶ *software that allows you to devise your own computer games*

devote /dɪ'vəʊt/ *verb (present participle* ***devoting****, past* ***devoted****)*
devote yourself to something to give all your time or thoughts to something ▶ *She devoted herself to her work.*

devoted /dɪ'vəʊtɪd/ *adjective*
caring about or loving someone or something a lot ▶ *He is devoted* ***to*** *his family.*

devotion /dɪ'vəʊʃən/ *noun (no plural)*
the state of caring about or loving someone or something a lot ▶ *her devotion* ***to*** *her job*

devour /dɪ'vaʊəʳ/ *verb*
to eat something quickly ▶ *Tony had already devoured half a pizza.*

devout /dɪ'vaʊt/ *adjective*
very religious ▶ *a devout Catholic*

dew /djuː/ *noun (no plural)*
small drops of water that form on the ground or on plants during the night

diabetes /ˌdaɪə'biːtiːz/ *noun (no plural)*
a disease in which there is too much sugar in your blood

diabetic /ˌdaɪə'betɪk/ *noun*
a person who has diabetes
▶ *Diabetics cannot eat a lot of sweet food.*

diabolical /ˌdaɪə'bɒlɪkəl/ *adjective*
very bad ▶ *This film is diabolical.*

diagnose /'daɪəgnəʊz/ *verb (present participle* ***diagnosing****, past* ***diagnosed****)*
to find out what illness someone has
▶ *His doctor diagnosed cancer.*

diagnosis /ˌdaɪəg'nəʊsɪs/ *noun (plural* ***diagnoses*** */-siːz/)*
a statement about what illness someone has ▶ *The doctor's diagnosis was wrong.*

diagonal /daɪ'ægənəl/ *noun*
a straight line that goes between the opposite corners of a square or other shape, dividing it into two parts

diagram /'daɪəgræm/ *noun*
a plan or picture drawn to explain an idea, or to show how something works

dial[1] /'daɪəl/ *noun*
a round part of a machine or an instrument, often with numbers on it
▶ *a telephone dial* ▶ *the dial of a clock*

dial[2] *verb (present participle* ***dialling****, past* ***dialled****)*
to make a telephone call by moving the DIAL to get the right numbers ▶ *to dial a number*

dialect /'daɪəlekt/ *noun*
a form of a particular language that has different words and different sounds and is spoken in only a small area
COMPARE: **accent**

dialling code /'daɪəlɪŋ ˌkəʊd/ *noun*
the part of a telephone number that you have to add when you are telephoning a different town or country
SAME MEANING: **area code**

dialogue /'daɪəlɒg/ *noun*
a conversation between people in a book, film, or play

diameter /daɪ'æmɪtəʳ/ *noun*
a straight line that divides a circle in half

D

diamond /'daɪəmənd/ *noun*
a very hard, bright, clear stone that is worth a lot of money and is set in jewellery

diarrhoea /ˌdaɪə'riːə/ *noun (no plural)*
an illness in which waste from your body is not solid and comes out often ▶ *Too much fruit can give you diarrhoea.*

diary /'daɪərɪ/ *noun (plural **diaries**)*
a book in which you write about the things that happen or will happen to you each day

dice /daɪs/ *noun (plural **dice**)*
a small, square block with a different number of spots on each side (from 1 to 6) which is used in games

dictate /dɪk'teɪt/ *verb (present participle **dictating**, past **dictated**)*
to say something for someone else to write down ▶ *I dictated a letter to my secretary.*

dictation /dɪk'teɪʃən/ *noun*
a language test in which you must write the words someone says without making mistakes

dictator /dɪk'teɪtəʳ/ *noun*
a very strong ruler, especially one who is not fair and who uses soldiers to control people

dictatorship /dɪk'teɪtəʃɪp/ *noun*
a political system in which a dictator controls a country

dictionary /'dɪkʃənərɪ/ *noun (plural **dictionaries**)*
a book that tells you what words mean and how to spell them

did /dɪd/ *verb*
the PAST TENSE of the verb **do**
▶ *"Did you go out today?" "Yes, I did."*

didn't /'dɪdnt/
did not ▶ *I didn't enjoy the film; did you?*

die /daɪ/ *verb (present participle **dying**, past **died**)*
1 to stop living ▶ *She died last year.* ▶ *to die **of** an illness*
2 **be dying for something** to want something very much ▶ *I'm dying for a cup of tea.*

diesel /'diːzəl/ *noun (no plural)*
a type of FUEL used in some engines

diet /'daɪət/ *noun*
1 the food that you eat ▶ *She has a healthy diet* (=she usually eats healthy food).
2 the things you eat when you are controlling the type of food you have, e.g. because you are too fat or because you are ill ▶ *You are not allowed to eat sugar on this diet.*
3 **go on a diet** to eat less food than usual, or different types of food, because you are too fat and want to become thinner

differ /'dɪfəʳ/ *verb*
1 to be different ▶ *This book differs **from** his other novels.*
2 to have different opinions ▶ *My father and I differ **on** many subjects.*

difference /'dɪfrəns/ *noun*
1 a way in which things are not the same ▶ *a difference **in** size* ▶ *a difference in price* ▶ *There isn't much difference **between** them.*
OPPOSITE: **similarity**
2 **make no difference** to have no importance or effect ▶ *It makes no difference to me what you say; I've already decided.*

different /'dɪfrənt/ *adjective*
not the same ▶ *I don't like that dress. Do you have any different ones?* ▶ *My ideas are different **from** yours.*
OPPOSITE: **same**

difficult /'dɪfɪkəlt/ *adjective*
hard to do or understand ▶ *a difficult question* ▶ *a difficult test*
OPPOSITE: **easy, simple**

difficulty /'dɪfɪkəltɪ/ *noun (plural **difficulties**)*
a problem

dig /dɪg/ *verb (present participle* ***digging,*** *past* ***dug*** */dʌg/)*
to make a hole in the ground by moving earth ▶ *He is digging the garden.* ▶ *to dig a hole*

digest /daɪ'dʒest/ *verb*
to break down food in your stomach so that your body can use it

digestion /daɪ'dʒestʃən/ *noun (no plural)*
the process of digesting food ▶ *He has problems with his digestion.*

digit /'dɪdʒɪt/ *noun*
a single number ▶ *a seven-digit phone number*

digital /'dɪdʒɪtl/ *adjective*
1 using a system in which information is shown in the form of changing electrical signals ▶ *a digital recording*
2 giving information in the form of numbers ▶ *a digital watch*

dignified /'dɪgnɪfaɪd/ *adjective*
proud and calm

dignity /'dɪgnɪtɪ/ *noun (no plural)*
a person's feeling that they are worth as much as other people ▶ *Although she is very poor, she has not lost her dignity.*

dilapidated /dɪ'læpɪdeɪtɪd/ *adjective*
(used about buildings and vehicles) old and in bad condition

dilemma /dɪ'lemə/ *noun*
a situation in which you find it difficult to choose between two possible actions ▶ *He's in a dilemma about whether to go to college or not.*

diligent /'dɪlɪdʒənt/ *adjective*
working very hard ▶ *Mary is a very diligent student.*

dilute /daɪ'luːt/ *verb (present participle* ***diluting,*** *past* ***diluted****)*
to make a liquid weaker or thinner by mixing another liquid with it
▶ *Dilute the orange juice with water.*

dim /dɪm/ *adjective (****dimmer, dimmest****)*
not very bright ▶ *a dim light*
(adverb: ***dimly****)*

dimensions /daɪ'menʃənz/ *plural noun*
the size of something, including its length, width, and height ▶ *Prices vary according to the dimensions of the room.*

diminish /dɪ'mɪnɪʃ/ *verb*
to become smaller or less important
▶ *The problem diminished as time passed.*

dimple /'dɪmpəl/ *noun*
a small, hollow place on your cheek or chin ▶ *She gets two little dimples when she smiles.*

din /dɪn/ *noun (no plural)*
loud noise ▶ *What a din the children are making!*

dingy /'dɪndʒɪ/ *adjective (****dingier, dingiest****)*
dirty, dark, and unpleasant ▶ *The room was small and dingy.*

dining room /'daɪnɪŋ rʊm/ *noun*
a room with a table where you can eat meals

dinner /'dɪnəʳ/ *noun*
the largest meal of the day, eaten in the evening or in the middle of the day
COMPARE: **lunch, supper, tea**

dinner jacket /'dɪnə ˌdʒækɪt/ *noun*
a jacket that men wear on formal occasions

dinosaur /'daɪnəsɔː/ *noun*
a large REPTILE that lived in very ancient times and no longer exists

dip /dɪp/ *verb (present participle* ***dipping,*** *past* ***dipped****)*
to put something into a liquid and then take it out again ▶ *She dipped her hand in the water.*

diploma /dɪ'pləʊmə/ *noun*
a piece of paper given to someone to

D

prove that they have passed an examination

diplomat /ˈdɪpləmæt/ *noun*
a person employed by a government to live in another country and make sure that their own country is listened to, its citizens are treated correctly, etc.

diplomatic /ˌdɪpləˈmætɪk/ *adjective*
1 of or about political relations between countries ▶ *Feingold plans to join the diplomatic service.*
2 good at dealing with people in a way that does not offend them ▶ *He won't give you a thing unless you're very diplomatic.*
(adverb: ***diplomatically****)*

D

dire /daɪəʳ/ *adjective*
very serious or terrible ▶ *They were in dire trouble.*

direct[1] /daɪˈrekt, dɪ-/ *adjective*
going straight towards a person, place, etc. ▶ *Which is the most direct way to the station?* ▶ *a direct flight to Paris*
OPPOSITE: **indirect**

direct[2] *verb*
to tell someone the way to go or what to do ▶ *Can you direct me to the station?*

direction /dɪˈrekʃən, daɪ-/ *noun*
the way that someone or something is going or pointing

directly /dɪˈrektlɪ, daɪ-/ *adverb*
1 straight towards a person, place, etc.
2 very soon ▶ *I'll be there directly.*

direct object /ˌdaɪrekt ˈɒbdʒɪkt/ *noun*
the person or thing that is directly affected by the verb in a sentence. In the sentence "Joe ate a sandwich", the direct object is "sandwich"
COMPARE: **indirect object**

director /dɪˈrektəʳ, daɪ-/ *noun*
a person who controls a business ▶ *He is one of the directors of the company.*

directory /dɪˈrektərɪ, daɪ-/ *noun (plural* ***directories****)*
a book that tells you where people live or what their telephone numbers are ▶ *a telephone directory*

direct speech /ˌdaɪrekt ˈspiːtʃ/ *noun*
the style used in writing to report what someone said, by repeating the actual words. The sentence *"I don't want to go," said Julia* is an example of direct speech
COMPARE: **reported speech**

dirt /dɜːt/ *noun (no plural)*
anything that stops something being clean ▶ *He had dirt all over his face.*

dirty /ˈdɜːtɪ/ *adjective (****dirtier, dirtiest****)*
having dirt on ▶ *My shoes were dirty.*
OPPOSITE: **clean**

disability /ˌdɪsəˈbɪlətɪ/ *noun (plural* ***disabilities****)*
a physical or mental condition that makes it difficult for someone to do things that most people do easily, such as walk or see ▶ *children with learning disabilities*

disabled /dɪsˈeɪbəld/ *adjective*
not being able to move or use a part of your body properly because of some illness or wound

disadvantage /ˌdɪsədˈvɑːntɪdʒ/ *noun*
something that makes things more difficult for you ▶ *the disadvantages of not having a car*
OPPOSITE: **advantage**

disagree /ˌdɪsəˈgriː/ *verb (past* ***disagreed****)*
not to agree with someone; to have different opinions ▶ *I'm afraid I disagree* ***with*** *you.*
OPPOSITE: **agree**

disagreement /ˌdɪsəˈgriːmənt/ *noun*
an argument or a lack of agreement ▶ *a disagreement* ***over*** *money*
OPPOSITE: **agreement**

disappear /ˌdɪsəˈpɪəʳ/ *verb*

to go away or go out of sight suddenly ▶ *The boy disappeared round the corner.*
OPPOSITE: **appear**

disappoint /ˌdɪsəˈpɔɪnt/ *verb*
to be less good or less nice than you expected, and so make you sad

disappointed /ˌdɪsəˈpɔɪntɪd/ *adjective*
sad because something is not as good or as nice as you expected ▶ *We were disappointed by the result.*

disappointing /ˌdɪsəˈpɔɪntɪŋ/ *adjective*
not as good or as nice as you expected ▶ *a disappointing film*

disappointment /ˌdɪsəˈpɔɪntmənt/ *noun*
the sad feeling of being disappointed

disapproval /ˌdɪsəˈpruːvəl/ *noun (no plural)*
the judgement or opinion that some-one or something is bad or wrong
OPPOSITE: **approval**

disapprove /ˌdɪsəˈpruːv/ *verb (present participle **disapproving**, past **disapproved**)*
not to like someone or something because you think they are bad or wrong ▶ *My mother disapproves **of** my friends.*
OPPOSITE: **approve**

disarmament /dɪsˈɑːməmənt/ *noun (no plural)*
the reduction of the number of soldiers and weapons that a country has ▶ *nuclear disarmament*

disarray /ˌdɪsəˈreɪ/ *noun*
be in disarray to be very untidy or not organized ▶ *After the party, the room was in total disarray.*

disaster /dɪˈzɑːstəʳ/ *noun*
something very bad, especially something that happens to a lot of people and causes damage or harm

disastrous /dɪˈzɑːstrəs/ *adjective*
very bad, or ending in complete failure ▶ *It will be disastrous if we lose.*

disbelief /ˌdɪsbɪˈliːf/ *noun (no plural)*
a feeling that something is not true or does not exist ▶ *He stared at the broken window in disbelief.*

disc /dɪsk/ *noun*
1 any round, flat thing
2 a record (for playing music)

discard /dɪˈskɑːd/ *verb*
to throw something away because you no longer need it ▶ *They were collecting the boxes that others had discarded.*

discharge /dɪsˈtʃɑːdʒ/ *verb (present participle **discharging**, past **discharged**)*
to officially allow someone to leave a place or an organization ▶ *They discharged him **from** hospital yesterday.*

discipline /ˈdɪsɪplɪn/ *noun (no plural)*
the training of people so that they will obey orders and control their own feelings and behaviour ▶ *Soldiers have to learn discipline in the army.*

disc jockey /ˈdɪsk ˌdʒɒkɪ/ *noun*
a person whose job is to play records on the radio, or at parties, etc.

disco /ˈdɪskəʊ/ *(also **discotheque**) noun*
a place where people, especially young people, go to dance in the evenings

discomfort /dɪsˈkʌmfət/ *noun (no plural)*
slight pain, or a feeling of being physically uncomfortable ▶ *Your injury isn't serious, but it may cause some discomfort.*

disconcerting /ˌdɪskənˈsɜːtɪŋ/ *adjective*
making you feel slightly embarrassed, confused, or worried

D

► *It's disconcerting when someone keeps staring at you.*

disconnect /ˌdɪskəˈnekt/ *verb*
to take out the wire, pipe, etc. that connects a machine or piece of equipment to something ► *Have you disconnected the phone?*
OPPOSITE: **connect**

discontented /ˌdɪskənˈtentɪd/ *adjective*
unhappy or not satisfied
OPPOSITE: **contented**

D

discotheque /ˈdɪskətek/ *noun*
another word for **disco**

discount /ˈdɪskaʊnt/ *noun*
an amount of money taken away from the price of something ► *a discount of £5 for students*

discourage /dɪsˈkʌrɪdʒ/ *verb (present participle* ***discouraging****, past* ***discouraged****)*
to try to stop someone doing something ► *We discourage smoking in our offices.*
OPPOSITE: **encourage**

discouraged /dɪsˈkʌrɪdʒd/ *adjective*
no longer having the confidence to continue doing something ► *She gets discouraged when she doesn't win.*

discover /dɪsˈkʌvəʳ/ *verb*
to find something, or to learn about something for the first time
► *Columbus discovered America.* ► *to discover the truth about something*

discovery /dɪsˈkʌvərɪ/ *noun (plural* ***discoveries****)*
something discovered ► *a new discovery in medical science*

discreet /dɪˈskriːt/ *adjective*
careful about what you say or do, so that you do not embarrass or upset people ► *It wasn't very discreet of you to call me at the office. (adverb:* ***discreetly****)*

discrepancy /dɪˈskrepənsɪ/ *noun (plural* ***discrepancies****)*
a difference between two things that should be the same ► *There were discrepancies* ***between*** *the two sets of results.*

discretion /dɪˈskreʃən/ *noun (no plural)*
1 the freedom to decide what is the right thing to do in a situation
► *Promotions are left to the discretion of the manager.* ► *Tipping is entirely at the customer's discretion.*
2 the act of being careful about what you say or do, so that you do not upset or embarrass people ► *This situation must be handled with discretion.*

discriminate /dɪˈskrɪmɪneɪt/ *verb (present participle* ***discriminating****, past* ***discriminated****)*
to treat one person or group differently from another in a way that is unfair ► *It is illegal to discriminate* ***against*** *people because of their sex.*

discrimination /dɪˌskrɪmɪˈneɪʃən/ *noun (no plural)*
unfair treatment of people because of the colour of their skin, where they come from, their sex, age, etc.

discus /ˈdɪskəs/ *noun (plural* ***discuses****)*
a flat, heavy, circular object that you throw as a sport

discuss /dɪˈskʌs/ *verb*
to talk about something ► *I want to discuss your work with you.*

discussion /dɪˈskʌʃən/ *noun*
a talk about something ► *a discussion about work*

disease /dɪˈziːz/ *noun*
an illness, especially a serious one that lasts a long time

disenchanted /ˌdɪsɪnˈtʃɑːntɪd/ *adjective*
no longer believing that something is good or important ► *She has become very disenchanted* ***with*** *her job.*

disfigure /dɪsˈfɪɡəʳ/ *verb (present participle **disfiguring**, past **disfigured**)*
to damage someone's appearance
► *His face was disfigured in the fire.*

disgrace /dɪsˈɡreɪs/ *noun (no plural)*
the loss of other people's good opinion of you

disgraceful /dɪsˈɡreɪsfəl/ *adjective*
very bad and wrong ► *disgraceful behaviour*

disguise[1] /dɪsˈɡaɪz/ *verb (present participle **disguising**, past **disguised**)*
to make yourself look like someone else so that people do not know who you are

disguise[2] *noun*
something that you wear to make you look like someone else so that people do not know who you are ► *wearing glasses as a disguise*

disgust[1] /dɪsˈɡʌst/ *verb*
to make you feel that something is very bad or unpleasant ► *Your behaviour disgusts me.*

disgust[2] *noun (no plural)*
a strong feeling of not liking something or finding it unpleasant

disgusted /dɪsˈɡʌstɪd/ *adjective*
feeling strong dislike or disapproval
► *I'm disgusted at the way we were treated.*

disgusting /dɪsˈɡʌstɪŋ/ *adjective*
very bad and unpleasant ► *a disgusting smell*
SAME MEANING: **revolting**

dish /dɪʃ/ *noun (plural **dishes**)*
1 a container like a large bowl, used for cooking or serving food
2 do the dishes to wash the dirty plates, etc. after a meal

dishcloth /ˈdɪʃklɒθ/ *noun*
a cloth that you use for washing dirty plates, etc.

disheartened /dɪsˈhɑːtnd/ *adjective*
unhappy because you do not think you will achieve something you have been hoping for ► *Don't get disheartened if they don't accept your first offer.*

dishevelled /dɪˈʃevəld/ *adjective*
(used about clothes, hair, etc.) untidy
► *She looked tired and dishevelled.*

dishonest /dɪsˈɒnɪst/ *adjective*
not honest
OPPOSITE: **honest**

dishonesty /dɪsˈɒnɪstɪ/ *noun (no plural)*
behaviour in which someone tells lies, steals, or cheats ► *They accused me of dishonesty.*
OPPOSITE: **honesty**

dishonour /dɪsˈɒnəʳ/ *noun (no plural)*
a lack of respect for someone because of something bad they have done ► *You have brought dishonour on your family.*
OPPOSITE: **honour**

dishwasher /ˈdɪʃˌwɒʃəʳ/ *noun*
a machine that washes dirty plates, etc.

disillusioned /ˌdɪsɪˈluːʒənd/ *adjective*
unhappy because you have lost your belief that someone or something is good or right ► *He became disillusioned **with** religion.*

disinfect /ˌdɪsɪnˈfekt/ *verb*
to clean something with a chemical that destroys BACTERIA (=small creatures that spread disease)
► *They disinfected all the surfaces.*

disinfectant /ˌdɪsɪnˈfektənt/ *noun (no plural)*
a chemical used to clean things thoroughly, which destroys BACTERIA (=small creatures that spread disease)

disintegrate /dɪsˈɪntɪɡreɪt/ *verb (present participle **disintegrating**, past **disintegrated**)*

D

to break up into small pieces ▶ *The plane just disintegrated in midair.*

disk /dɪsk/ *noun*
a small, flat piece of plastic which is round or square and is used in a computer for keeping information

disk drive /ˈdɪsk draɪv/ *noun*
a piece of equipment in a computer that is used to pass information to or from a disk

dislike[1] /dɪsˈlaɪk/ *verb (present participle* ***disliking****, past* ***disliked****)*
not to like someone or something
OPPOSITE: **like**

The verb **dislike** is not often used in ordinary conversation because it is rather formal. People usually say that they **don't like** something, rather than they **dislike** it: *I don't like her.* ▶ *He doesn't like swimming.*

dislike[2] *noun*
a feeling of not liking someone or something

dislocate /ˈdɪsləkeɪt/ *verb (present participle* ***dislocating****, past* ***dislocated****)*
to put a bone in your body out of its normal place because of an accident ▶ *He's dislocated his shoulder.*

disloyal /dɪsˈlɔɪəl/ *adjective*
not faithful or true to someone
OPPOSITE: **loyal**

disloyalty /dɪsˈlɔɪəltɪ/ *noun (no plural)*
behaviour in which you do not support your friends, family, country, etc., or you do things that may harm them ▶ *He was accused of disloyalty to his country.*
OPPOSITE: **loyalty**

dismal /ˈdɪzməl/ *adjective*
dull or sad; not bright or happy ▶ *dismal weather*

dismay /dɪsˈmeɪ/ *noun (no plural)*
a feeling of surprise and disappointment

dismiss /dɪsˈmɪs/ *verb*
1 to send someone away
2 to tell someone they must leave their job because they have done something wrong

disobedience /ˌdɪsəˈbiːdɪəns/ *noun (no plural)*
the act of refusing to obey someone
OPPOSITE: **obedience**

disobedient /ˌdɪsəˈbiːdɪənt/ *adjective*
not willing to obey ▶ *a disobedient child*
OPPOSITE: **obedient**

disobey /ˌdɪsəˈbeɪ/ *verb*
not to do what someone tells you to do ▶ *to disobey your parents*
OPPOSITE: **obey**

disorder /dɪsˈɔːdəʳ/ *noun*
1 *(no plural)* the state of being very untidy ▶ *The classroom was in a state of disorder.*
OPPOSITE: **order**
2 an illness that stops part of your body working properly ▶ *She has a rare blood disorder.*

disorderly /dɪsˈɔːdəlɪ/ *adjective*
untidy or uncontrolled ▶ *The papers were in a disorderly mess.*
OPPOSITE: **orderly**

disorganized /dɪsˈɔːgənaɪzd/ *adjective*
1 not tidy
2 not able to plan or arrange things well
OPPOSITE (**1** and **2**): **organized**

disoriented /dɪsˈɔːrɪəntɪd/ *(also* ***disorientated*** /dɪsˈɔːrɪənteɪtɪd/*)* *adjective*
confused and not knowing what is happening or where you are ▶ *She felt disoriented after the accident.*

dispatch *(also* ***despatch****)* /dɪˈspætʃ/ *verb*
1 to send someone to a place as part of their job ▶ *UN troops are being dispatched to protect the airport.*

2 to send a letter, package, etc. to someone ▸ *Father dispatched an angry letter immediately.*

dispense /dɪ'spens/ *verb (present participle **dispensing**, past **dispensed**)*
1 dispense with something to not use or do something because it is no longer necessary ▸ *Your new computer dispenses with the need for a secretary.*
2 to give or provide people with something ▸ *The machines in the hall dispense drinks.*

dispenser /dɪ'spensəʳ/ *noun*
a machine that you can get things such as drinks or money from ▸ *I got a coffee from the drinks dispenser.* ▸ *a cash dispenser*

disperse /dɪ'spɜːs/ *verb (present participle **dispersing**, past **dispersed**)*
to go in different directions, or to make things or people go in different directions ▸ *The police finally managed to disperse the crowd.*

dispirited /dɪ'spɪrɪtɪd/ *adjective*
sad and without hope ▸ *After their defeat, the team felt dispirited.*

display¹ /dɪ'spleɪ/ *verb*
to show something so that many people can see it ▸ *The children's pictures were displayed on the wall.*

display² *noun*
1 a show of something ▸ *a display of the children's work* ▸ *a dancing display*
2 on display being shown for many people to see

disposable /dɪ'spəʊzəbəl/ *adjective*
intended to be used once or for a short time and then thrown away ▸ *a disposable toothbrush*

disposal /dɪ'spəʊzəl/ *noun (no plural)*
the act of getting rid of something

dispose /dɪ'spəʊz/ *verb (present participle **disposing**, past **disposed**)*
dispose of something to get rid of something

disposition /ˌdɪspə'zɪʃən/ *noun*
a person's usual character ▸ *a warm and friendly disposition*

disprove /dɪs'pruːv/ *verb (present participle **disproving**, past **disproved**)*
to show that something is false ▸ *He set out to disprove my theory.*
OPPOSITE: **prove**

dispute /dɪ'spjuːt/ *noun*
a quarrel ▸ *a pay dispute* (=a quarrel about pay)

disqualify /dɪs'kwɒlɪfaɪ/ *verb (past **disqualified**)*
to stop someone taking part in an activity or a competition because they have done something wrong ▸ *The judges disqualified him for taking drugs.*

disregard /ˌdɪsrɪ'gɑːd/ *verb*
to ignore something, especially because you do not think it is important ▸ *The judge ordered us to disregard the witness's last statement.*

disrupt /dɪs'rʌpt/ *verb*
to stop a situation or an event from continuing normally ▸ *Traffic will be severely disrupted by road works.*

disruption /dɪs'rʌpʃən/ *noun*
a situation in which someone or something stops a situation or an event from continuing normally ▸ *After the brief disruption, the game continued.*

dissatisfied /dɪ'sætɪsfaɪd/ *adjective*
not content or pleased enough with something ▸ *We were very dissatisfied **with** the food at the restaurant.*
OPPOSITE: **satisfied**

dissect /dɪ'sekt/ *verb*
to cut up a plant or an animal in order

to study it ▶ *In biology, we dissected a rat.*

dissertation /ˌdɪsəˈteɪʃən/ *noun*
a long piece of writing about a subject, especially one that you write as part of a university degree
▶ *She wrote her dissertation on the Romantic poets.*

dissident /ˈdɪsɪdənt/ *noun*
a person who publicly criticizes their government

D

dissolve /dɪˈzɒlv/ *verb (present participle* ***dissolving****, past* ***dissolved****)*
to mix completely with a liquid
▶ *Sugar dissolves* ***in*** *water.* ▶ *Dissolve the powder in water.*

distance /ˈdɪstəns/ *noun*
1 the amount of space between two places ▶ *What's the distance between London and Paris?* ▶ *a long distance*
2 in the distance far away

distant /ˈdɪstənt/ *adjective*
far away ▶ *a distant country* ▶ *the distant past*

distaste /dɪsˈteɪst/ *noun (no plural)*
a strong dislike of something ▶ *He has a great distaste for foreign films.*

distil /dɪˈstɪl/ *verb (present participle* ***distilling****, past* ***distilled****)*
to turn a liquid into gas and then turn the gas into liquid again, in order to make it purer or stronger ▶ *distilled water*

distinct /dɪˈstɪŋkt/ *adjective*
1 clear; easily seen or heard ▶ *the distinct sound of fighting*
2 separate; different ▶ *There are several distinct languages in every African country.*

distinction /dɪˈstɪŋkʃən/ *noun*
1 a clear difference between things
▶ *The author draws a distinction* ***between*** *"crime" and "sin".*
2 a special honour given to someone
▶ *Sol had the distinction of leading the delegation.*

distinctive /dɪˈstɪŋktɪv/ *adjective*
different from others and easy to recognize ▶ *She has a distinctive style of writing.*

distinctly /dɪˈstɪŋktlɪ/ *adverb*
very clearly ▶ *I distinctly remember telling you.*

distinguish /dɪˈstɪŋgwɪʃ/ *verb*
1 to see the difference between things ▶ *to distinguish good* ***from*** *bad* ▶ *to distinguish* ***between*** *good and bad*
2 to be able to see, hear, or taste something even though it is difficult to do this ▶ *It was dark and I could just distinguish their faces.*

distinguished /dɪˈstɪŋgwɪʃt/ *adjective*
famous and respected by many people ▶ *a distinguished scientist*

distort /dɪˈstɔːt/ *verb*
1 to change the shape or sound of something so that it is strange or unclear ▶ *The heat had distorted the doll's face.*
2 to tell people about a fact, statement, etc. in a way that changes its meaning ▶ *Journalists distorted what he actually said.*

distract /dɪˈstrækt/ *verb*
to take someone's attention away from what they are doing ▶ *Don't distract me while I'm driving!*
▶ *Charles is easily distracted* ***from*** *his studies.*

distracted /dɪˈstræktɪd/ *adjective*
anxious and not able to think clearly about what is happening around you ▶ *You seem a little distracted.*

distraction /dɪˈstrækʃən/ *noun*
something that takes your attention away from what you are doing
▶ *I can't work at home – there are too many distractions.*

distraught /dɪ'strɔːt/ *adjective*
very anxious or upset ▶ *She looked distraught.*

distress¹ /dɪ'stres/ *noun (no plural)*
a feeling of sadness, pain, or trouble

distress² *verb*
to make someone sad or upset

distressing /dɪ'stresɪŋ/ *adjective*
making you feel sad or upset
▶ *distressing news*

distribute /dɪ'strɪbjuːt/ *verb (present participle* ***distributing****, past* ***distributed****)*
to give or send something to different people or places ▶ *The teacher distributed the books to the children.*

district /'dɪstrɪkt/ *noun*
a part of a country, city, etc.

distrust /dɪs'trʌst/ *noun (no plural)*
a feeling that you cannot trust someone ▶ *There's a certain distrust* ***of*** *technology among older people.*

disturb /dɪ'stɜːb/ *verb*
1 to interrupt someone and stop them working, thinking, sleeping, etc.
▶ *Please don't disturb me while I'm working.*
2 to make someone feel worried or upset ▶ *We were very disturbed by these events.*
3 to change or move something
▶ *Someone had disturbed the papers on his desk.*

disturbance /dɪ'stɜːbəns/ *noun*
a noisy event in which people fight or cause trouble ▶ *There has been a disturbance in the street.*

disturbing /dɪ'stɜːbɪŋ/ *adjective*
making you feel worried or upset
▶ *disturbing news*

disused /ˌdɪs'juːzd/ *adjective*
(used about a place) not used any more ▶ *a disused factory*

ditch /dɪtʃ/ *noun (plural* ***ditches****)*
a deep, narrow place for water to go along, especially by the side of a road or field

ditto /'dɪtəʊ/ *noun*
two small marks („)that you write under a word in a list so that you do not have to write the same word again

dive /daɪv/ *verb (present participle* ***diving****, past* ***dived****)*
to jump into water with your head and arms first ▶ *He dived into the lake.* ▶ *She dived to the bottom of the river.*

diver /'daɪvəʳ/ *noun*
a person who works underwater and wears special equipment to help them breathe

diverse /daɪ'vɜːs/ *adjective*
very different from each other
▶ *London is home to people of many diverse cultures.*

diversion /daɪ'vɜːʃən/ *noun*
1 something that takes your attention away from something else ▶ *The prisoners created a diversion so the others could escape.*
2 a situation in which traffic has to use a different road because the usual way is blocked

divert /daɪ'vɜːt/ *verb*
1 to change the direction of something ▶ *Traffic is being diverted to avoid the scene of the accident.*
2 divert attention from something to stop people giving their attention to something ▶ *The government is trying to divert attention from its mistakes.*

divide /dɪ'vaɪd/ *verb (present participle* ***dividing****, past* ***divided****)*
1 to split into pieces or parts ▶ *The road divided into three.*
2 to share something ▶ *We divided the money between us.*
3 to find how many times a number will go into a bigger number ▶ *If you*

divide 39 by 3, the answer is 13.
COMPARE: **multiply**

divine /dɪˈvaɪn/ *adjective*
from a god or like a god

diving /ˈdaɪvɪŋ/ *noun (no plural)*
1 the activity of swimming underwater, using special equipment to help you breathe
2 the activity or sport of jumping into water with your head and arms first

diving board /ˈdaɪvɪŋ ˌbɔːd/ *noun*
a special board, often high above the ground, that you stand on before jumping or diving (DIVE) into water

divisible /dɪˈvɪzɪbəl/ *adjective*
able to be divided by another number exactly ▶ *15 is divisible **by** 3 and 5.*

division /dɪˈvɪʒən/ *noun*
1 *(no plural)* sums in which you find how many times a number will go into a bigger number
2 a part of something ▶ *Which division **of** the company do you work in?*

divorce¹ /dɪˈvɔːs/ *verb (present participle **divorcing**, past **divorced**)*
to arrange by law for a marriage to end ▶ *They're getting divorced.*

divorce² *noun*
the ending of a marriage according to the law

DIY /ˌdiː aɪ ˈwaɪ/ *noun (no plural)*
DO-IT-YOURSELF; painting or building things in your house yourself instead of paying a painter, builder, etc. to do it for you

dizzy /ˈdɪzɪ/ *adjective (**dizzier**, **dizziest**)*
feeling as if you are going to fall and as if things are moving when they are not ▶ *I feel dizzy when I look out of a high window.*

DJ /ˌdiː ˈdʒeɪ/ *noun*
DISC JOCKEY; a person whose job it is to play records on the radio or at parties, etc.

do¹ /duː/ *verb*

present tense

singular	*plural*
I **do**	We **do**
You **do**	You **do**
He/She/It **does**	They **do**

past tense

singular	*plural*
I **did**	We **did**
You **did**	You **did**
He/She/It **did**	They **did**

present participle	**doing**
past participle	**done**
negative short forms	**don't, doesn't, didn't**

(you can find each of these words in its own place in the dictionary)

1 to carry out an action ▶ *I must do some work.* ▶ *What are you doing?* ▶ *We're doing* (=learning) *French at school.*
2 **do as you are told** to do what someone, e.g. a parent, tells you to do
3 **do someone good** to make someone feel better or more healthy ▶ *A holiday will do you good.*
4 **do something up** to fasten something ▶ *Do up your coat.*
5 **do well** to be a success
6 **could do with** to want or need something ▶ *I could do with some sleep.*
7 **to do with** about or concerning someone or something ▶ *Her job's to do with looking after old people.*
8 **do without something** to live or continue without a particular thing ▶ *I couldn't do without your help.*
9 **How do you do?** something you say as a polite greeting when you meet

someone for the first time. The reply is also "How do you do?" ▶ *"Mother, this is Doctor Jones." "How do you do, Doctor Jones?" "How do you do?"*
10 What do you do? What is your job?
11 What have you done with ...? Where is ...?/Where have you put ...? ▶ *What have you done with my book?*

Compare the verbs **do** and **make.** Use **do** when you are talking about an action or activity: *to do some work* ▶ *to do the shopping.* Use **make** when you are talking about producing something or producing a result: *to make a cake* ▶ *to make a noise.* You also use **make** when you are talking about plans or decisions: *to make a plan* ▶ *to make a choice* ▶ *to make an appointment.*

do² *verb*
1 used with **not** before another verb, to say that something is not so ▶ *I don't* (=do not) *agree.* ▶ *He doesn't* (=does not) *have a car.*
2 used with another verb, to ask a question ▶ *Do you like dancing?* ▶ *Did you find the answer?*
3 used with **not**, to tell someone not to do something ▶ *Do not lean out of the window.* ▶ *Don't* (=do not) *do that!*
4 used to make the meaning of another verb stronger ▶ *You do talk a lot!* ▶ *You do believe me, don't you?*

docile /ˈdəʊsaɪl/ *adjective*
quiet and easy to control ▶ *The horse was very docile.*

dock¹ /dɒk/ *noun*
a place where goods are taken on and off ships

dock² *verb*
(used about a ship) to come into a dock

doctor /ˈdɒktəʳ/ *noun*
a person who looks after people's health

document /ˈdɒkjʊmənt/ *noun*
a piece of paper with something official written on it

documentary /ˌdɒkjʊˈmentrɪ/ *noun* *(plural **documentaries**)*
a film giving information and facts about something

documentation /ˌdɒkjʊmənˈteɪʃən/ *noun (no plural)*
documents that provide a record of something or show that something is true ▶ *Have you got any documentation to prove who you are?*

dodge /dɒdʒ/ *verb (present participle **dodging**, past **dodged**)*
1 to move quickly to one side to avoid something
2 to avoid something you should not avoid ▶ *to dodge payment of tax*

dodgy /ˈdɒdʒɪ/ *adjective* ***(dodgier, dodgiest)***
dishonest or unable to be trusted ▶ *His friend looked a bit dodgy to me.*

does /dəz; *strong* dʌz/ *verb*
the part of the verb **do** that is used with **he, she** and **it** ▶ *Does she have a job?*

doesn't /ˈdʌzənt/
does not ▶ *She doesn't like school.*

dog /dɒg/ *noun*
an animal with four legs and a tail, that eats meat and is sometimes used to protect buildings. Many people keep dogs as pets.

dogmatic /dɒgˈmætɪk/ *adjective*
having strong beliefs which you are not willing to change ▶ *He is very dogmatic about how languages should be taught.*

doing¹ /ˈduːɪŋ/ *noun (no plural)*
1 be sb's (own) doing to be someone's fault ▶ *His bad luck was all his own doing.*
2 take some doing to be hard work ▶ *Getting the place clean is going to take some doing.*

doing[2]
the PRESENT PARTICIPLE of the verb **do**

do-it-yourself /ˌduː ɪt jɔːˈself/ *(also **DIY**) noun (no plural)*
painting or building things in your house yourself instead of paying a painter, builder, etc. to do it for you

dole /dəʊl/ *noun (no plural)*
be on the dole to have no job and receive money from the government to help you buy food, clothes, etc. ▶ *He left school at 16, and now he's on the dole.*

D

doll /dɒl/ *noun*
a toy made to look like a person, especially a baby, woman, or girl

dollar /ˈdɒləʳ/ *noun*
the money used in America and some other countries

dolphin /ˈdɒlfɪn/ *noun*
a large sea animal that swims about in a group

dome /dəʊm/ *noun*
a high, round roof

domestic /dəˈmestɪk/ *adjective*
1 in the home or about the home ▶ *domestic jobs like cleaning and cooking*
2 not wild ▶ *Cattle are domestic animals.*

dominant /ˈdɒmɪnənt/ *adjective*
strongest, most important, or most noticeable ▶ *TV news is the dominant source of information in our society.*

dominate /ˈdɒmɪneɪt/ *verb (present participle **dominating**, past **dominated**)*
to have power and control over someone or something

domineering /ˌdɒmɪˈnɪərɪŋ/ *adjective*
trying to control other people without considering their feelings ▶ *a domineering father*

domino /ˈdɒmɪnəʊ/ *noun (plural **dominoes**)*
1 one of a set of small pieces of wood or plastic, with spots on, used for playing a game
2 dominoes *(no plural)* the game played using dominoes

donate /dəʊˈneɪt/ *verb (present participle **donating**, past **donated**)*
to give something to an organization that helps people, such as a hospital ▶ *to donate money*

donation /dəʊˈneɪʃən/ *noun*
a gift made to an organization that helps people ▶ *a donation of money to the hospital*

done[1] /dʌn/
the PAST PARTICIPLE of the verb **do**

done[2] *adjective*
finished ▶ *The work is nearly done.*

donkey /ˈdɒŋkɪ/ *noun*
an animal like a small horse with long ears

donor /ˈdəʊnəʳ/ *noun*
someone who gives something ▶ *She is a blood donor* (=she gives her blood to be used in the hospital).

don't /dəʊnt/
do not ▶ *I don't want to go.* ▶ *Don't touch that!*

doom /duːm/ *noun (no plural)*
something bad in the future that you cannot avoid ▶ *I had an awful sense of doom before the exam.*

doomed /duːmd/ *adjective*
certain to fail ▶ *Our relationship was doomed from the beginning.*

door /dɔːʳ/ *noun*
1 the flat piece of wood, metal, etc. that shuts the entrance to a building or room ▶ *Please open the door for me.*
2 the entrance to a building or room ▶ *Will you wait at the door?*
3 answer the door to open the door when someone knocks
4 door to door going from one house or building to another ▶ *to sell things door to door*

5 next door to in the building or room next to a place ▶ *He lives next door to my parents* (=in the house next to theirs).
6 out of doors outside ▶ *to work out of doors*

doorbell /'dɔːbel/ *noun*
a bell that you ring when you want someone to open a door, especially at the entrance to a house or building ▶ *to ring a doorbell*

doorknob /'dɔːnɒb/ *noun*
a round handle on a door that you use when you open and close it

doormat /'dɔːmæt/ *noun*
a small mat at the door of a house which you walk on to clean your shoes after you have been outside

doorstep /'dɔːstep/ *noun*
1 a step in front of the door of a house
2 on your doorstep very close to where you live

doorway /'dɔːweɪ/ *noun*
an opening where there is a door ▶ *He stood in the doorway.*

dormice /'dɔːmaɪs/
the plural of **dormouse**

dormitory /'dɔːmɪtrɪ/ *noun (plural **dormitories**)*
a large room with beds for people to sleep in ▶ *the school dormitory*

dormouse /'dɔːmaʊs/ *noun (plural **dormice** /'dɔːmaɪs/)*
a small mouse that lives in fields and sleeps in the winter

dose /dəʊs/ *noun*
the amount of a medicine that you should take at one time ▶ *The dose is two spoonfuls every four hours.*

dot /dɒt/ *noun*
a small, round mark ▶ *On the map, towns were marked by a red dot.* ▶ *A small "i" has a dot on it.*

doting /'dəʊtɪŋ/ *adjective*
loving someone very much, in a way that seems silly to other people ▶ *His doting parents let him do whatever he likes.*

double[1] /'dʌbəl/ *adjective, adverb, noun*
1 twice as much ▶ *I'll pay you double if you finish the work quickly.*
2 (used before a number or letter) happening twice ▶ *My telephone number is 65588 (six, double five, double eight).*
3 with two parts ▶ *a double door*
4 made for two people ▶ *a double bed*
COMPARE: **single**

double[2] *verb (present participle **doubling**, past **doubled**)*
1 to become twice as big or twice as much as before ▶ *Sales of our new car have doubled.*
2 to make something twice as big or twice as much as before ▶ *We have doubled sales of our new car.*

double bass /ˌdʌbəl 'beɪs/ *noun (plural **double basses**)*
a very large musical instrument, shaped like a VIOLIN, that you play standing up

double-check /ˌdʌbəl 'tʃek/ *verb*
to check something again so that you are completely sure about it ▶ *Could you just double-check that the door is locked?*

double-decker /ˌdʌbəl 'dekəʳ/ *noun*
a bus with two levels

doubles /'dʌbəlz/ *noun*
a game of tennis played by two teams of two people ▶ *I prefer playing doubles.*

doubly /'dʌblɪ/ *adverb*
twice as much ▶ *The job was doubly difficult because of the rain.*

doubt[1] /daʊt/ *verb*
to be not sure whether something is true or will happen ▶ *I doubt if he will pass the examinations.* ▶ *I doubt that they will come.*

doubt[2] *noun*
1 a reason for not being sure about something ▶ *I have doubts about whether he is the best man for the job.* ▶ *There is no doubt he is guilty* (=he certainly is guilty).
2 no doubt almost certainly ▶ *No doubt we'll see you again soon.*

doubtful /'daʊtfəl/ *adjective*
not likely ▶ *It's doubtful whether she'll succeed.*

D

doubtless /'daʊtləs/ *adverb*
certainly; without a doubt ▶ *He will doubtless arrive on the next train.*

dough /dəʊ/ *noun (no plural)*
a soft mixture of flour, water, and YEAST that is cooked to make bread

doughnut /'dəʊnʌt/ *noun*
a small, round, sweet cake that is cooked in oil

dove /dʌv/ *noun*
a white bird that people think of as a sign of peace

dowdy /'daʊdɪ/ *adjective (**dowdier, dowdiest**)*
(used about people or clothes) dull and not interesting

down[1] /daʊn/ *adverb, preposition*
1 in or to a lower place ▶ *Sit down, please.* ▶ *The children ran down the hill.* ▶ *I must put these bags down.*
2 showing a decrease ▶ *Our sales have gone down this year.*
OPPOSITE (**1** and **2**): **up**
3 written on paper ▶ *to put something down in writing* ▶ *to write something down*
4 down the road, down the street along the road, along the street

down[2] *adjective*
1 sad ▶ *Andrew was feeling down.*
2 behind in a game by a particular number of points ▶ *We were down by six points halfway through the game.*
3 (used about a computer) not working

downfall /'daʊnfɔːl/ *noun*
a situation in which you suddenly stop being successful, rich, or important ▶ *Greed will be his downfall.*

downhill /ˌdaʊn'hɪl/ *adjective, adverb*
to or towards the bottom of a hill ▶ *to walk downhill*
OPPOSITE: **uphill**

download /ˌdaʊn'ləʊd/ *verb*
to move information from one part of a computer system to another, especially from the INTERNET to a computer ▶ *I downloaded the anti-virus update from their website this morning.*

downpour /'daʊnpɔːʳ/ *noun*
a lot of rain falling in a short time

downright /'daʊnraɪt/ *adverb*
completely ▶ *It was downright stupid to go there on your own.*

downside /'daʊnsaɪd/ *noun*
the downside a bad feature of something that is good in other ways ▶ *The downside of the job is you have to work at weekends.*

downstairs /ˌdaʊn'steəz/ *adjective, adverb*
in or towards the part of a house which is on the same level as the ground ▶ *The bathroom is downstairs.* ▶ *a downstairs bathroom* ▶ *to walk downstairs*
OPPOSITE: **upstairs**

downstream /ˌdaʊn'striːm/ *adverb*
in the same direction that a river or stream is flowing ▶ *The boat floated downstream.*

down-to-earth /ˌdaʊn tʊ 'ɜːθ/ *adjective*
sensible and practical ▶ *For a famous pop star, she's very down-to-earth.*

downwards /'daʊnwədz/ *adverb*
from a higher to a lower place; towards the ground or floor
OPPOSITE: **upwards**

doze[1] /dəʊz/ *verb (present participle **dozing**, past **dozed**)*
1 to sleep lightly for some time
SAME MEANING: **snooze**
2 **doze off** to go to sleep without meaning to ► *I dozed off watching television.*

doze[2] *noun*
a short sleep ► *to have a doze*
SAME MEANING: **nap**

dozen /'dʌzən/ *noun*
1 twelve ► *a dozen eggs*
2 **dozens** very many ► *There were dozens **of** people there.*

Dr
a short way of writing the word **doctor** when you are writing someone's name ► *Dr Brown*

drab /dræb/ *adjective (**drabber, drabbest**)*
not bright or interesting ► *The room was painted a drab brown.*

draft[1] /drɑːft/ *noun*
a drawing, plan, or piece of writing that you have not finished yet ► *This is just a first draft of my essay.*

draft[2] *verb*
to write a plan, letter, report, etc. that you will need to change before it is finished ► *She drafted a letter of complaint.*

drag /dræg/ *verb (present participle **dragging**, past **dragged**)*
to pull something heavy along behind you

dragon /'drægən/ *noun*
a fierce animal in stories that has fire coming out of its mouth

drain[1] /dreɪn/ *noun*
a pipe that takes dirty water away

drain[2] *verb*
to flow away; to make water flow away ► *The water drained away slowly.*

drained /dreɪnd/ *adjective*
very tired ► *I felt completely drained after they had all gone home.*

draining board /'dreɪnɪŋ bɔːd/ *noun*
the place next to the SINK in a kitchen, where plates, etc. are left to dry after they have been washed

drainpipe /'dreɪnpaɪp/ *noun*
a pipe on the outside of a building that takes away dirty water or water from the roof

drama /'drɑːmə/ *noun (no plural)*
1 acting and plays ► *She's studying drama.*
2 excitement ► *I like the drama of a big storm.*

dramatic /drə'mætɪk/ *adjective*
exciting ► *a dramatic event*

dramatist /'dræmətɪst/ *noun*
a person who writes plays

dramatize /'dræmətaɪz/ *verb (present participle **dramatizing**, past **dramatized**)*
1 to use a real event or a story from a book to write a play ► *They are dramatizing her life story for TV.*
2 to make an event seem more exciting than it really is ► *She tends to dramatize things.*

drank /dræŋk/
the PAST TENSE of the verb **drink**

drastic /'dræstɪk/ *adjective*
sudden, and having a big effect ► *The new school principal is planning to make drastic changes. (adverb: **drastically**)*

draught /drɑːft/ *noun*
cold air blowing into a room ► *a cold draught under the door*

draughts /drɑːfts/ *noun (no plural)*
a game played by two people using 24 round pieces on a board of black and white squares

draughty /'drɑːftɪ/ *adjective (**draughtier, draughtiest**)*
(used about rooms, buildings, etc.) having cold air blowing through

draw¹ /drɔː/ *verb (past tense* ***drew*** */druː/, past participle* ***drawn*** */drɔːn/)*
1 to make a picture, especially with a pencil or pen ▶ *I like drawing.*
▶ *to draw a picture*
2 to take something out of a place
▶ *He drew a gun from his pocket.*
▶ *to draw money out of a bank*
3 to end a game or match with an equal result so that nobody wins
▶ *We drew with the London team.*
▶ *to draw a match*
4 draw back to move away from someone or something
5 draw near to move towards someone or something
6 draw the curtains to pull curtains across so that they cover a window
7 draw up (used about a car) to stop

draw² *noun*
a game or a result where nobody wins because both sides are equal
▶ *The match was a draw.* ▶ *The game ended in a draw.*

drawback /ˈdrɔːbæk/ *noun*
something that might be a problem or disadvantage ▶ *The only drawback to living in London is the cost.*

drawer /drɔːʳ/ *noun*
a part of a piece of furniture, used for keeping things in, which has handles so that it can be pulled out and pushed in

drawing /ˈdrɔːɪŋ/ *noun*
1 *(no plural)* the making of pictures with pencils or pens ▶ *I like to do some drawing in my spare time.*
2 a picture done by pen or pencil
▶ *She had done a drawing* ***of*** *her mother.*

drawing pin /ˈdrɔːɪŋ pɪn/ *noun*
a small pin with a round, flat top which is used for fixing things to a wall

drawl /drɔːl/ *verb*
to speak slowly with long vowel sounds ▶ *"Hi there," he drawled.*

drawn /drɔːn/
the PAST PARTICIPLE of the verb **draw**

dread /dred/ *verb*
to feel very worried about something that is going to happen ▶ *I'm really dreading the interview tomorrow.*
▶ *I always used to dread going to the dentist's.*

dreadful /ˈdredfəl/ *adjective*
very bad or unpleasant ▶ *There's been a dreadful accident.* ▶ *I've had a dreadful day – everything seems to have gone wrong.*
SAME MEANING: **awful, dreadful, horrible**

dreadfully /ˈdredfəlɪ/ *adverb*
1 very badly ▶ *The children behaved dreadfully.*
2 very ▶ *She was dreadfully upset.*

dream¹ /driːm/ *verb (past* ***dreamt*** */dremt/ or* ***dreamed****)*
1 to imagine things while you are asleep ▶ *I dreamt about you last night.*
2 to imagine something nice ▶ *He dreamt of becoming famous.*

dream² *noun*
1 something that you imagine while you are asleep
2 something nice that you imagine or that you want to do ▶ *It is their dream to visit Australia.*

dreamt /dremt/
the PAST TENSE and PAST PARTICIPLE of the verb **dream**

dreary /ˈdrɪərɪ/ *adjective (****drearier, dreariest****)*
very dull, and making you feel sad
▶ *a dreary afternoon*

drench /drentʃ/ *verb*
to make someone or something completely wet ▶ *I was drenched in the storm.*

dress¹ /dres/ *verb*
1 to put on and wear clothes ▶ *She washed and dressed, and ate her*

breakfast. ▶ *He dresses well* (=he wears nice clothes).
2 to put clothes on someone ▶ *to dress oneself*
OPPOSITE (**1** and **2**): **undress**
3 be dressed to be wearing clothes ▶ *They arrived before I was dressed.* ▶ *She was dressed in red* (=wearing red clothes).
4 get dressed to put on clothes ▶ *It will only take a minute to get dressed.*
5 dress up (**a**) to put on special clothes for an important occasion (**b**) (used about children) to wear someone else's clothes or to wear a DISGUISE as a game

dress² *noun*
1 *(plural* ***dresses****)* a piece of clothing covering the body and legs that is worn by women and girls
2 *(no plural)* clothes of a certain type or for a particular purpose ▶ *evening dress*

dresser /'dresəʳ/ *noun*
a piece of furniture with shelves for showing plates

dressing /'dresɪŋ/ *noun (no plural)*
a cold liquid made with oil and put on SALADS

dressing gown /'dresɪŋ ˌgaʊn/ *noun*
a piece of clothing like a coat that you wear only in the house, often on top of the clothes you wear to sleep in

dressing room /'dresɪŋ rʊm/ *noun*
a room where an actor gets ready before going on stage or on television

dressing table /'dresɪŋ ˌteɪbəl/ *noun*
a table with a mirror on top, used for sitting at while you brush your hair, etc.

dressmaker /'dresˌmeɪkəʳ/ *noun*
a woman whose job is to sew clothes for other women
COMPARE: **tailor**

drew /druː/
the PAST TENSE of the verb **draw**

dribble /'drɪbəl/ *verb (present participle* ***dribbling****, past* ***dribbled****)*
1 if you dribble, liquid in your mouth comes out onto your chin ▶ *The baby's dribbling on your jacket.*
2 to move a ball forward by kicking or BOUNCING it several times in football or BASKETBALL

dried /draɪd/
the PAST TENSE and PAST PARTICIPLE of the verb **dry**

drier /'draɪəʳ/ *noun*
another word for **dryer**

drift /drɪft/ *verb*
to float along or be moved by water or wind ▶ *leaves drifting in the wind*

drill¹ /drɪl/ *verb*
to make a hole in something with a special machine ▶ *to drill a hole in the wall*

drill² *noun*
a machine for making holes

drink¹ /drɪŋk/ *verb (past tense* ***drank*** */dræŋk/, past participle* ***drunk*** */drʌŋk/)*
to take liquid into your mouth and swallow it ▶ *Would you like something to drink?* ▶ *He drank some coffee.*

drink² *noun*
a liquid which you can swallow ▶ *Can I have a drink?* ▶ *a drink of water*

drip /drɪp/ *verb (present participle* ***dripping****, past* ***dripped****)*
1 (used about a liquid) to fall in drops
2 to have a liquid dripping from it ▶ *The tap was dripping.*

drive¹ /draɪv/ *verb (present participle* ***driving****, past tense* ***drove*** */drəʊv/, past participle* ***driven*** */'drɪvən/)*
to make a vehicle move in the direction you want ▶ *Can you drive?* ▶ *I drove to town yesterday.* ▶ *to drive a car*

drive² *noun*
1 a journey in a road vehicle ▶ *It is a short drive to the village.*

2 a short road that goes to one house only ► *He left his car in the drive.*
3 a system in a computer that can read or store information ► *disk drive* ► *hard drive*

drive-in /ˈdraɪv ɪn/ *adjective*
(used about restaurants, cinemas, etc.) that you can use without getting out of your car

drivel /ˈdrɪvəl/ *noun (no plural)*
nonsense ► *Don't talk drivel!*

D

driven /ˈdrɪvən/
the PAST PARTICIPLE of the verb **drive**

driver /ˈdraɪvəʳ/ *noun*
a person whose job is to drive a bus, train, etc. ► *a train driver*

drive-through /ˈdraɪv θruː/ *adjective*
(used about restaurants, banks, etc.) that you can use without getting out of your car

driveway /ˈdraɪvweɪ/ *noun*
a short road that goes to one house only ► *There is room to park two cars in his driveway.*

driving¹ /ˈdraɪvɪŋ/ *noun (no plural)*
the activity or skill of driving a car ► *I love driving.* ► *His driving is terrible sometimes.*

driving² *adjective*
(used about rain or snow) falling very heavily and at an angle

driving licence /ˈdraɪvɪŋ ˌlaɪsəns/ *noun*
an official piece of paper that shows you are allowed to drive a car

driving test /ˈdraɪvɪŋ ˌtest/ *noun*
an examination that you must pass before you are allowed to drive a car

drizzle /ˈdrɪzəl/ *verb*
be drizzling to be raining very lightly ► *It was only drizzling, so I didn't take an umbrella.*

drool /druːl/ *verb*
1 if you drool, the liquid in your mouth comes out onto your chin ► *At the sight of food, the dog began to drool.*
2 to show in a silly way that you like someone or something a lot ► *Sarah was drooling **over** the lead singer through the whole concert!*

droop /druːp/ *verb*
to hang down ► *The flowers drooped because they had no water.*

drop¹ /drɒp/ *verb (present participle **dropping**, past **dropped**)*
1 to fall or let something fall ► *The plate dropped from her hands.* ► *She dropped the plate.*
2 drop in on someone to visit someone when they are not expecting you

drop² *noun*
a small amount of liquid ► *drops **of** rain*

dropout /ˈdrɒpaʊt/ *noun*
1 a person who does not want a job or possessions because they do not want to work or live in the usual way
2 a person who leaves school or college without completing their course

drought /draʊt/ *noun*
a time when no rain falls and the land becomes very dry

drove /drəʊv/
the PAST TENSE of the verb **drive**

drown /draʊn/ *verb*
to die underwater because you cannot breathe

drowsy /ˈdraʊzɪ/ *adjective (**drowsier, drowsiest**)*
wanting to sleep ► *to feel drowsy*

drug /drʌg/ *noun*
1 a medicine
2 something that people take to change the way they feel or behave. Many drugs are not allowed by law.

drum¹ /drʌm/ *noun*
1 a musical instrument made of a round, hollow box with skin stretched

tightly over it, which you hit to make a sound
2 a metal container for oil, water, etc.

drum² *verb (present participle **drumming**, past **drummed**)*
to make music on a drum by hitting it

drummer /ˈdrʌməʳ/ *noun*
a person who plays the drums ▶ *The band has a great new drummer.*

drunk¹ /drʌŋk/ *adjective*
having had too much alcohol and so not able to behave properly ▶ *You're drunk! You can't even walk in a straight line!*
OPPOSITE: **sober**

drunk²
the PAST PARTICIPLE of the verb **drink**

drunken /ˈdrʌŋkən/ *adjective*
caused by too much alcohol ▶ *drunken behaviour*

dry¹ /draɪ/ *adjective (**drier, driest**)*
1 not containing water or not covered in water ▶ *This coat will keep you dry in the rain.*
2 without any rain ▶ *a dry day*
OPPOSITE (**1** and **2**): **wet**

dry² *verb (past **dried**)*
1 to become dry ▶ *The clothes dried quickly outside.*
2 to make something dry ▶ *to dry your hair*
OPPOSITE (**2**): **wet**

dry-clean /ˌdraɪ ˈkliːn/ *verb*
to clean clothes with chemicals instead of water

dry-cleaner's /ˌdraɪ ˈkliːnəz/ *noun*
a shop that cleans clothes in a special way using chemicals not water

dryer *(also **drier**)* /ˈdraɪəʳ/ *noun*
a machine that dries things, especially clothes or hair ▶ *Put the washing in the dryer.*

dual /ˈdjuːəl/ *adjective*
having two of something ▶ *The car has dual controls.*

dual carriageway /ˌdjuːəl ˈkærɪdʒweɪ/ *noun*
a wide road on which cars travelling in opposite directions are kept apart by a narrow piece of land

dubious /ˈdjuːbɪəs/ *adjective*
1 be dubious about something to have doubts about whether something is good or true ▶ *I'm very dubious about the quality of food in this restaurant.*
2 not seeming honest, safe, or true ▶ *a dubious character*

duchess /ˈdʌtʃəs/ *noun (plural **duchesses**)*
the title of a woman from a very important family in Britain ▶ *the Duchess of York*
COMPARE: **duke**

duck¹ /dʌk/ *noun*
a bird that swims on water and can be kept by people for its eggs and meat

duck² *verb*
to suddenly move your head or body down because you want to avoid being hit by something or seen by someone

duckling /ˈdʌklɪŋ/ *noun*
a young duck

due /djuː/ *adjective*
1 expected ▶ *The train is due at 5 o'clock.* ▶ *When is the baby due* (=expected to be born)?
2 needing to be paid ▶ *The rent is due at the end of the month.*
3 owing to someone ▶ *Our thanks are due to you for all your help.*
4 due to because of ▶ *This shop is closed due to illness.*
5 be due for something to be expecting to have something soon ▶ *I'm due for a holiday.*
6 be due to do something to be going to do something ▶ *We're due to leave on the 17th.*

duet /djuːˈet/ *noun*
a song or piece of music for two people

dug /dʌg/
the PAST TENSE and PAST PARTICIPLE of the verb **dig**

duke /djuːk/ *noun*
the title of a man from a very important family in Britain ▶ *the Duke of York*
COMPARE: **duchess**

dull /dʌl/ *adjective*
1 not bright or light ▶ *a dull, cloudy day* ▶ *a dull brown colour*
2 not interesting or clever ▶ *a dull speech* ▶ *a dull man*
SAME MEANING (**2**): **boring**

dumb /dʌm/ *adjective*
not able to speak because you have a problem with your voice

dummy /ˈdʌmɪ/ *noun (plural **dummies**)*
a small, rubber object that you put in a baby's mouth to stop it crying

dump[1] /dʌmp/ *verb*
1 to drop something and leave it ▶ *We dumped our bags on the floor.*
2 to throw something away or get rid of it

dump[2] *noun*
a place where things can be left when people do not want them any more

dune /djuːn/ *noun*
a hill of sand

dung /dʌŋ/ *noun (no plural)*
solid waste from animals, especially large animals ▶ *cow dung*

dungarees /ˌdʌŋgəˈriːz/ *plural noun*
trousers with a piece of material at the top which covers your chest

dungeon /ˈdʌndʒən/ *noun*
a dark PRISON underneath a castle

dunk /dʌŋk/ *verb*
to quickly put food into a liquid and then take it out again ▶ *He dunked his biscuit in his coffee.*

dunno /ˈdʌnəʊ/
an informal way of saying "I don't know" ▶ *"Where's Lucy?" "Dunno."*

dupe /djuːp/ *verb (present participle **duping**, past **duped**)*
to tell lies in order to make someone believe or do something ▶ *She was duped into giving the robbers her car keys.*

duplicate[1] /ˈdjuːplɪkət/ *adjective*
made to be exactly the same as something else ▶ *a duplicate key*

duplicate[2] /ˈdjuːplɪkeɪt/ *verb (present participle **duplicating**, past **duplicated**)*
to copy or repeat something exactly ▶ *Scientists were unable to duplicate the results in a laboratory.*

duration /djʊˈreɪʃən/ *noun (no plural)*
the length of time that something continues ▶ *They moved to America for the duration of the war.*

during /ˈdjʊərɪŋ/ *preposition*
1 all the time that something is going on ▶ *They swim every day during the holidays.*
2 at some time while something else is happening ▶ *He fell asleep during the lesson.*

dusk /dʌsk/ *noun (no plural)*
the time in the evening when the sun has just gone down

dust[1] /dʌst/ *noun (no plural)*
fine powder or dirt, carried in the air

dust[2] *verb*
to clean dust from something ▶ *I dust in the living room every morning.* ▶ *She dusted the table.*

dustbin /ˈdʌstbɪn/ *noun*
a large metal or plastic container that people keep outside their houses and in which they put things they want to get rid of
COMPARE: **bin**

duster /ˈdʌstəʳ/ *noun*
a cloth you use to clean DUST from furniture

dust jacket /ˈdʌst ˌdʒækɪt/ *noun*
the loose cover of a book

dustman /ˈdʌstmən/ *noun (plural* ***dustmen*** /-mən/*)*
a person whose job is to take away the things inside DUSTBINS

dustpan /ˈdʌstpæn/ *noun*
a flat container that you use to carry away dust after you have swept the floor

dusty /ˈdʌstɪ/ *adjective (****dustier, dustiest****)*
covered in dust

duty /ˈdjuːtɪ/ *noun (plural* ***duties****)*
1 something you must do because it is right ▶ *You have a duty to look after your family.* ▶ *Everyone has a duty to pay taxes.*
2 off duty (used about people with certain jobs, such as doctors, policemen, or soldiers) not at work or working ▶ *She's off duty tomorrow.*
3 on duty (used about people with certain jobs, such as doctors, policemen, or soldiers) at work or working

duvet /ˈdjuːveɪ/ *noun*
a thick, warm cover with feathers inside it, that you put on a bed
COMPARE: **bedspread**

DVD /ˌdiː viː ˈdiː/ *noun*
DIGITAL VIDEO DISC; a small, round piece of hard plastic that pictures and sounds are recorded on like a CD

dwarf /dwɔːf/ *noun*
a person, a plant, or an animal that is much smaller than usual

dwell /dwel/ *verb (past* ***dwelt*** */dwelt/ or* ***dwelled****)*
dwell on something to think or talk for too long about something unpleasant ▶ *I don't want to dwell on all the details of the accident.*

dye[1] /daɪ/ *verb (present participle* ***dyeing****, past* ***dyed****)*
to give a different colour to something ▶ *She dyed her hair black.*

dye[2] *noun*
a liquid or powder that is used to change the colour of things

dying /daɪ-ɪŋ/
the PRESENT PARTICIPLE of the verb **die**

dynamic /daɪˈnæmɪk/ *adjective*
full of energy and ideas ▶ *The new teacher is very dynamic.*

dynamite /ˈdaɪnəmaɪt/ *noun (no plural)*
a substance used to make explosions

dynasty /ˈdɪnəstɪ/ *noun (plural* ***dynasties****)*
in the past, a family of rulers who controlled a country for a long time ▶ *The Ming dynasty ruled China for 300 years.*

Ee

E
a short way of writing the words **east** or **eastern**

each /iːtʃ/ *adjective, pronoun*
1 every one separately ▶ *Each child has an exercise book to work in.* ▶ *Father Christmas gave a present to each of the children.*
2 each other used to show that two people do the same thing one to the other ▶ *The two brothers help each other* (=each brother helps the other).

eager /ˈiːgəʳ/ *adjective*
very keen to do something ▶ *The girl was eager to show me her photographs. (adverb:* ***eagerly****)*

eagle /ˈiːgəl/ *noun*
a large bird that lives in mountain areas and kills small animals for food

ear /ɪəʳ/ *noun*
1 one of the parts of your body with which you hear

E

2 the part of a plant where the seed is ▶ *an ear of corn*

earache /ˈɪəreɪk/ *noun*
a pain inside your ear

early /ˈɜːlɪ/ *adjective, adverb (**earlier, earliest**)*
1 before the usual or agreed time ▶ *We agreed to meet at 7 o'clock, but I was early; I arrived at 6.30.* ▶ *The bus arrived early.*
2 near the beginning of the day or a period of time ▶ *It often rains in the early morning.* ▶ *Do you get up early?*
OPPOSITE (**1** and **2**): **late**
LOOK AT: **soon**

E

earn /ɜːn/ *verb*
1 to get money for work you do ▶ *She earns a lot of money.*
2 to get something that you deserve because you have worked hard ▶ *You've earned a good rest.*

earnings /ˈɜːnɪŋz/ *plural noun*
money that you get when you work ▶ *Average earnings in Europe have risen by 3%.*

earplug /ˈɪəplʌg/ *noun*
one of two small pieces of rubber, WAX, etc. that you put into your ears to keep out noise

earring /ˈɪərɪŋ/ *noun*
a piece of jewellery you wear on your ear

earshot /ˈɪəʃɒt/ *noun*
within earshot, out of earshot near enough or not near enough to hear what someone is saying ▶ *Make sure the kids are out of earshot before you tell her.*

earth /ɜːθ/ *noun (no plural)*
1 *(also **Earth**)* the world in which we live ▶ *The Earth goes round the sun once a year.* ▶ *the longest river on earth*
2 the substance on the ground in which plants can grow ▶ *She planted the seeds in the wet earth.*

earthquake /ˈɜːθˌkweɪk/ *noun*
a strong and sudden shaking of the ground

ease¹ /iːz/ *noun (no plural)*
1 lack of difficulty ▶ *He passed the examination with ease.*
2 at ease feeling comfortable and sure of yourself ▶ *She felt at ease in her new school.*

ease² *verb (present participle **easing**, past **eased**)*
to make something better ▶ *The medicine eased the pain.*

easel /ˈiːzəl/ *noun*
a wooden frame to hold a BLACKBOARD or a picture that is being painted

easily /ˈiːzɪlɪ/ *adverb*
1 without difficulty ▶ *This recipe can be made quickly and easily.*
2 easily the best, biggest, most stupid, etc. definitely the best, biggest, most stupid, etc. ▶ *She is easily the most intelligent girl in the class.*

east /iːst/ *noun, adjective, adverb*
1 the direction from which the sun comes up ▶ *Our house faces east.* ▶ *Norwich is in the east of England.* ▶ *the east coast* ▶ *living east of London*
2 an east wind a wind that comes from the east

eastbound /ˈiːstbaʊnd/ *adjective*
travelling or leading towards the east ▶ *An accident on the eastbound section of the motorway is blocking traffic.*

Easter /ˈiːstəʳ/ *noun*
a special Sunday in March or April when Christians remember Christ's death and His return to life

Easter egg /ˈiːstər eg/ *noun*
a chocolate egg eaten at Easter

easterly /ˈiːstəlɪ/ *adjective*
1 towards the east ▶ *The plane was heading in an easterly direction.*

2 (used about wind) blowing from the east

eastern /ˈiːstən/ *adjective*
in or of the east

eastward /ˈiːstwəd/ *adjective*
towards the east ▶ *We drove in an eastward direction.*

eastwards /ˈiːstwədz/ *adverb*
towards the east ▶ *to travel eastwards*

easy /ˈiːzɪ/ *adjective (**easier, easiest**)*
not difficult; done with no trouble ▶ *It was an easy job and we did it quickly.*
OPPOSITE: **difficult, hard**

easygoing /ˌiːzɪˈgəʊɪŋ/ *adjective*
relaxed and calm, and not often angry or upset ▶ *The boss is very easygoing.*

eat /iːt/ *verb (past tense **ate** /et, eɪt/, past participle **eaten** /ˈiːtn/)*
1 to put food into your mouth and swallow it ▶ *Have you eaten your breakfast yet?*
2 to have a meal ▶ *What time did you eat?*

eccentric /ɪkˈsentrɪk/ *adjective*
behaving in a way that is unusual but amusing ▶ *an eccentric old woman (adverb: **eccentrically**)*

echo¹ /ˈekəʊ/ *verb*
(used about a sound) to come back again ▶ *Our voices echoed in the empty room.*

echo² *noun (plural **echoes**)*
a sound that comes back to you and that you can hear again ▶ *the echo of our voices in the cave*

eclipse /ɪˈklɪps/ *noun*
a time when the light from the sun or moon is blocked by the moon or Earth

ecological /ˌiːkəˈlɒdʒɪkəl/ *adjective*
relating to the way that plants, animals, and people affect their environment ▶ *ecological problems caused by the huge oil spill* ▶ *an ecological study (adverb: **ecologically**)*

ecologist /ɪˈkɒlədʒɪst/ *noun*
a person who studies ecology

ecology /ɪˈkɒlədʒɪ/ *noun (no plural)*
the relationship between plants, animals, people, and the environment, or the study of this relationship ▶ *The ecology of the forest has been damaged by farming.*

economic /ˌiːkəˈnɒmɪk, ˌekə-/ *adjective*
connected with industry and trade ▶ *the country's economic problems*

economical /ˌiːkəˈnɒmɪkəl, ˌekə-/ *adjective*
cheap ▶ *Going by train is more economical than going by plane.*

economics /ˌiːkəˈnɒmɪks, ˌekə-/ *noun (no plural)*
the study of the way in which money, goods, and services are produced and used

economist /ɪˈkɒnəmɪst/ *noun*
a person who studies economics

economize /ɪˈkɒnəmaɪz/ *verb (present participle **economizing**, past **economized**)*
to try to spend less money, or to use a smaller amount of something ▶ *Try to economize **on** water during this dry period.*

economy /ɪˈkɒnəmɪ/ *noun (plural **economies**)*
the system by which a country's industry and trade are controlled ▶ *The country's economy depends on the amount of goods it sells abroad.*

economy class /ɪˈkɒnəmɪ ˌklɑːs/ *noun (no plural)*
the cheaper seats on a plane or the cheaper rooms on a ship ▶ *They travelled to America in economy class.* ▶ *an economy class ticket*

ecstasy /ˈekstəsɪ/ *noun (no plural)*
a feeling of great happiness ▶ *He had a look of ecstasy on his face.*

ecstatic /ɪkˈstætɪk/ *adjective*
feeling very happy and excited ▶ *an ecstatic welcome from thousands of people (adverb: **ecstatically**)*

edge /edʒ/ *noun*
1 the outside end of something; the part which is furthest from the middle ▶ *the edge of a plate* ▶ *the water's edge*
2 the sharp, cutting part of a knife or tool
3 on edge nervous and worried

edible /ˈedɪbəl/ *adjective*
able to be eaten, or safe to eat ▶ *edible mushrooms*

E

edit /ˈedɪt/ *verb*
to prepare a book, film, etc. by correcting mistakes and deciding which parts to keep

edition /ɪˈdɪʃən/ *noun*
a book or newspaper brought out at a particular time

editor /ˈedɪtəʳ/ *noun*
a person who prepares books or newspapers before they are printed

educate /ˈedjʊkeɪt/ *verb (present participle **educating**, past **educated**)*
to teach someone, especially in a school or a college ▶ *He was educated in Scotland.* ▶ *Children should be educated about the dangers of smoking.*

educated /ˈedjʊkeɪtɪd/ *adjective*
having a high standard of knowledge and education ▶ *She is a highly educated woman.*

education /ˌedjʊˈkeɪʃən/ *noun (no plural)*
teaching and learning ▶ *The government believes in the importance of education.*

educational /ˌedjʊˈkeɪʃənəl/ *adjective*
helping you to learn ▶ *an educational toy*

eel /iːl/ *noun*
a long fish shaped like a snake

effect /ɪˈfekt/ *noun*
a result ▶ *Eating too many sweets can have a bad effect **on** your teeth.*

effective /ɪˈfektɪv/ *adjective*
getting the result you want ▶ *These pills are an effective cure for a headache.*
OPPOSITE: **ineffective**

effectively /ɪˈfektɪvlɪ/ *adverb*
in a way that gets the results that you want ▶ *She controlled the class very effectively.*

efficient /ɪˈfɪʃənt/ *adjective*
working well, quickly, and without waste ▶ *an efficient secretary* ▶ *an efficient central heating system (adverb: **efficiently**)*
OPPOSITE: **inefficient**

effluent /ˈefluənt/ *noun (no plural)*
liquid waste that flows out from a factory, etc., usually into the sea or a river

effort /ˈefət/ *noun*
the use of strength or determination in trying to do something ▶ *With a great effort, he pushed open the door.* ▶ *Please put more effort into your school work.*

effortless /ˈefətləs/ *adjective*
done skilfully in a way that seems easy ▶ *She swam with smooth, effortless strokes. (adverb: **effortlessly**)*

EFL /ˌiː ef ˈel/ *noun (no plural)*
ENGLISH AS A FOREIGN LANGUAGE; the teaching of English to people who speak a different language

e.g. /ˌiː ˈdʒiː/
a short way of writing or saying the words **for example** ▶ *You can try many different sports on this holiday, e.g. sailing, tennis and swimming.*

egg /eg/ *noun*
a round object with a hard shell, from which baby birds, snakes, fish, or insects come; eggs are often eaten as food ▶ *We had eggs for breakfast.*

ego /ˈiːgəʊ/ *noun*
the opinion that you have about yourself ▶ *Her remarks were not very good for my ego.*

eh /eɪ/ *interjection*
used to ask someone in an informal way to say something again ▶ *"You need a modem." "Eh?"*

eight /eɪt/ *adjective, noun*
the number 8

eighteen /eɪˈtiːn/ *adjective, noun*
the number 18

eighteenth /eɪˈtiːnθ/ *adjective*
18th

eighth /eɪtθ/ *adjective, noun*
1 8th
2 one of eight equal parts

eightieth /ˈeɪtɪ-əθ/ *adjective*
80th

eighty /ˈeɪtɪ/ *adjective, noun*
the number 80

either /ˈaɪðəʳ, ˈiːðəʳ/ *conjunction, adverb*
1 one or the other of two people or things ▶ *Either the father or one of his sons drives the truck.*
2 used in sentences with not, when you add another idea ▶ *I haven't been to America, or to England either.*

eject /ɪˈdʒekt/ *verb*
1 to make something come out of a machine by pressing a button ▶ *Eject the tape and turn it over.*
2 to make someone leave a place, using force ▶ *A few people were ejected from the club for fighting.*

elaborate /ɪˈlæbərət/ *adjective*
full of detail, with a large number of parts

elastic[1] /ɪˈlæstɪk/ *adjective*
able to go back into shape after being stretched or pulled ▶ *Rubber is an elastic substance.*

elastic[2] *noun*
a material which is elastic ▶ *a belt made of elastic*

elastic band /ɪˌlæstɪk ˈbænd/ *noun*
a thin piece of elastic that is used to hold things together

elbow /ˈelbəʊ/ *noun*
the part of your arm which bends it in the middle

elder /ˈeldəʳ/ *adjective*
older of two people ▶ *Which brother did you see – the elder one or the younger one?*

elderly /ˈeldəlɪ/ *adjective*
old ▶ *My aunt is rather elderly and needs a lot of care.*

eldest /ˈeldɪst/ *adjective*
oldest of three or more people ▶ *his eldest sister*

elect /ɪˈlekt/ *verb*
to choose someone for an official position, usually by voting ▶ *She was elected **as** chairman of the committee.*

election /ɪˈlekʃən/ *noun*
a time when people are chosen for official positions by voting ▶ *His party won the last election.* ▶ *She's standing for election.*

electric /ɪˈlektrɪk/ *adjective*
working by electricity
▶ *an electric cooker*

electrical /ɪˈlektrɪkəl/ *adjective*
concerning or using electricity
▶ *The cooker isn't working because of an electrical fault.*

electrician /ɪˌlekˈtrɪʃən, ˌelɪk-/ *noun*
a person whose job is to fit and repair electrical machinery

electricity /ɪˌlekˈtrɪsətɪ, ˌelɪk-/ *noun (no plural)*
power that is sent through wires and is used for lighting, heating, and making machines work

electric shock /ɪˌlektrɪk ˈʃɒk/ *noun*
a sudden, painful feeling you get if you accidentally touch electricity ▶ *I got an electric shock from my hairdryer.*

E

electrocute /ɪ'lektrəkjuːt/ *verb (present participle* ***electrocuting,*** *past* ***electrocuted)***
to kill someone by passing electricity through their body ▶ *He accidentally electrocuted himself when he touched the damaged wiring.* ▶ *He was electrocuted for the murder of two children.*

electronic /ɪˌlek'trɒnɪk, ˌelɪk-/ *adjective*
using electricity and MICROCHIPS ▶ *"E-mail" stands for "electronic mail".* ▶ *He likes electronic music. (adverb:* ***electronically)***

E

electronics /ɪˌlek'trɒnɪks, ˌelɪk-/ *noun (no plural)*
the study of making machinery such as radios, televisions, and computers

elegant /'elɪgent/ *adjective*
pleasing and graceful ▶ *elegant clothes (adverb:* ***elegantly)***

element /'elɪmənt/ *noun*
1 one of the very simple substances from which everything is made ▶ *Gold and iron are elements.*
2 a part of a whole ▶ *an important element* ***of*** *the job*

elementary /ˌelɪ'mentrɪ/ *adjective*
simple and easy ▶ *elementary exercises for the piano*

elephant /'elɪfənt/ *noun*
a very large, grey animal with a long nose, which lives in hot countries

eleven /ɪ'levən/ *adjective, noun*
the number 11

eleventh /ɪ'levənθ/ *adjective*
11th

elf /elf/ *noun (plural* ***elves*** */elvz/)*
a small fairy with pointed ears

eligible /'elɪdʒəbəl/ *adjective*
1 having the right to do or receive something ▶ *Students are eligible* ***for*** *financial support.* ▶ *Are you eligible* ***to*** *vote?*
2 (used about men) rich, attractive, and not yet married, and therefore desirable as a husband ▶ *an eligible bachelor*

eliminate /ɪ'lɪmɪneɪt/ *verb (present participle* ***eliminating,*** *past* ***eliminated)***
1 to completely destroy or get rid of something so that it no longer exists ▶ *We can never eliminate crime from our society.*
2 be eliminated to be defeated in a sports competition, so that you can no longer take part in it ▶ *We were eliminated in the very first game.*

else /els/ *adverb*
1 other; different; instead ▶ *If you don't like eggs, I can cook something else.*
2 more; as well ▶ *Would you like something else to eat?*
3 used in some questions and phrases ▶ *It's not here; where else can we look?* ▶ *If the train has gone, how else can we get home?* ▶ *Hold the bottle in both hands, or else* (=if not) *you'll drop it.*

elsewhere /els'weəʳ/ *adverb*
in or to some other place ▶ *They left the village and went elsewhere.*

ELT /ˌiː el 'tiː/ *noun (no plural)*
ENGLISH LANGUAGE TEACHING; the teaching of English to people whose first language is not English

elves /elvz/
the plural of **elf**

e-mail¹ *(also* ***email)*** /'iː meɪl/ *noun*
1 *(no plural)* ELECTRONIC MAIL; a system for sending messages by computer ▶ *Send the file by e-mail.*
2 a message sent by computer ▶ *I got an e-mail from Josie.*

e-mail² *(also* ***email)*** *verb*
to send a message to someone using e-mail ▶ *He e-mailed me about his visit yesterday.*

embark /ɪm'bɑːk/ *verb*
1 to get on a ship

2 embark on something to start something new or difficult ▶ *She left school to embark on a career as a model.*

embarrass /ɪmˈbærəs/ *verb*
to make someone feel uncomfortable, nervous, or silly in front of other people

embarrassed /ɪmˈbærəst/ *adjective*
nervous or uncomfortable in front of other people ▶ *I feel so embarrassed when I think of how I behaved.*

> **1** People feel **embarrassed** about small things that they have done which make them appear silly to other people, such as forgetting someone's name or going to a party in the wrong type of clothes. If someone is sorry because they have done something very bad and important, they feel **ashamed**, not **embarrassed**.
> **2** Do not confuse **embarrassed** (=feeling uncomfortable and nervous) and **embarrassing** (=making someone feel like this): *It was an embarrassing mistake.* ▶ *We all felt very embarrassed.*

embarrassing /ɪmˈbærəsɪŋ/ *adjective*
making you feel nervous or uncomfortable ▶ *an embarrassing moment*
LOOK AT: **embarrassed**

embarrassment /ɪmˈbærəsmənt/ *noun (no plural)*
the feeling of being nervous or uncomfortable in front of other people

embassy /ˈembəsɪ/ *noun (plural* ***embassies****)*
a place where people work for their government, to represent their own country in another country

embrace¹ /ɪmˈbreɪs/ *verb (present participle* ***embracing****, past* ***embraced****)*
to hold someone in your arms to show that you love them ▶ *The child embraced his parents.* ▶ *The couple embraced.*

embrace² *noun*
holding someone in your arms as a sign of love

embroider /ɪmˈbrɔɪdəʳ/ *verb*
to sew beautiful patterns with a needle on cloth ▶ *to embroider a dress*

embroidery /ɪmˈbrɔɪdərɪ/ *noun (no plural)*
beautiful patterns sewn with a needle on cloth ▶ *a dress covered with embroidery*

embryo /ˈembrɪəʊ/ *noun*
an animal or a human that has just begun to develop inside its mother's body

emerald¹ /ˈemərəld/ *adjective, noun*
a bright green colour

emerald² *noun*
a bright green stone which is very valuable

emerge /ɪˈmɜːdʒ/ *verb (present participle* ***emerging****, past* ***emerged****)*
to come or appear from somewhere hidden ▶ *The baby birds emerged from their eggs.*

emergency /ɪˈmɜːdʒənsɪ/ *noun (plural* ***emergencies****)*
a sudden dangerous event that needs to be dealt with very quickly ▶ *The hospital has to treat emergencies such as car accidents.* ▶ *In an emergency, phone the police.*

emergency services /ɪˈmɜːdʒənsɪ ˌsɜːvɪsɪz/ *plural noun*
the emergency services official organizations, such as the police, that deal with crimes, fires, or helping people who are badly hurt or very ill

emigrant /ˈemɪgrənt/ *noun*
a person who leaves their own country in order to live in another country
COMPARE: **immigrant**

E

emigrate /ˈemɪgreɪt/ *verb (present participle **emigrating,** past **emigrated**)* to leave your own country to go and live in another country ▶ *Her family emigrated to Australia.*

emigration /ˌemɪˈgreɪʃən/ *noun (no plural)* the act of leaving your own country to go and live in another country COMPARE: **immigration**

eminent /ˈemɪnənt/ *adjective* famous and respected ▶ *an eminent professor*

eminently /ˈemɪnəntlɪ/ *adverb* very ▶ *He is eminently qualified to do the job.*

E

emotion /ɪˈməʊʃən/ *noun* a strong feeling ▶ *Anger and love are very powerful emotions.*

emotional /ɪˈməʊʃənəl/ *adjective* having strong feelings that you show, sometimes by crying

emotive /ɪˈməʊtɪv/ *adjective* making people have strong feelings ▶ *Abortion is an emotive issue.*

emperor /ˈempərəʳ/ *noun* a ruler of a big country or several countries

emphasis /ˈemfəsɪs/ *noun (plural **emphases** /-siːz/)* the special importance that you give to something ▶ *Most schools do not place enough emphasis on health education.*

emphasize /ˈemfəsaɪz/ *verb (present participle **emphasizing,** past **emphasized**)* to show that something is important ▶ *He emphasized the need for hard work.* SAME MEANING: **stress**

emphatic /ɪmˈfætɪk/ *adjective* said in a strong way that shows you are certain about something ▶ *His answer was an emphatic "No." (adverb: **emphatically**)*

empire /ˈempaɪəʳ/ *noun* a group of countries ruled by one government ▶ *the British Empire*

employ /ɪmˈplɔɪ/ *verb* to give someone a job ▶ *She is employed as a teacher.* ▶ *The hospital employs hundreds of people.*

employee /ɪmˈplɔɪ-iː/ *noun* a person who works for someone else ▶ *There are ten employees in his firm.*

employer /ɪmˈplɔɪəʳ/ *noun* a person or group that pays people to work for them

employment /ɪmˈplɔɪmənt/ *noun (no plural)* the state of having paid work ▶ *She's looking for employment.* OPPOSITE: **unemployment**

empress /ˈemprəs/ *noun (plural **empresses**)* a female ruler of a country or several countries; the wife of an EMPEROR

empty[1] /ˈemptɪ/ *adjective (**emptier, emptiest**)* having nothing inside ▶ *The house is empty; no one is living there.* OPPOSITE: **full**

empty[2] *verb (past **emptied**)* to take everything out of something ▶ *He emptied the bottle.* OPPOSITE: **fill**

empty-handed /ˌemptɪ ˈhændɪd/ *adjective* without getting anything ▶ *The thieves fled the building empty-handed.*

enable /ɪˈneɪbəl/ *verb (present participle **enabling,** past **enabled**)* to make someone able to do something ▶ *The new machines enable us to cut and tie up our wheat quickly.*

enchanting /ɪnˈtʃɑːntɪŋ/ *adjective* very beautiful ▶ *She looked enchanting.*

enclose /ɪn'kləʊz/ *verb (present participle* ***enclosing****, past* ***enclosed****)*
1 to surround something completely ▶ *The football field is enclosed by a wall.*
2 to put something in an envelope with a letter ▶ *I enclose a copy of my CV for your attention.*

enclosure /ɪn'kləʊʒəʳ/ *noun*
an area that has a wall or fence all the way around it ▶ *The animals are kept in a large enclosure.*

encore /'ɒŋkɔːʳ/ *noun*
a piece of music that performers add at the end of a performance because people ask for more ▶ *The band played one of their old hits as an encore.*

encounter¹ /ɪn'kaʊntəʳ/ *verb*
1 to experience something that causes difficulty ▶ *The engineers encountered more problems when the rainy season began.*
2 to meet someone or something, especially when you are not expecting to meet them ▶ *I was just 12 years old when I first encountered him.*

encounter² *noun*
a meeting, especially one that is dangerous or not expected ▶ *a chance encounter with the famous actor, Wilfred Lawson*

encourage /ɪn'kʌrɪdʒ/ *verb (present participle* ***encouraging****, past* ***encouraged****)*
to give praise and support to someone so that they will do something ▶ *I encouraged her to start playing tennis.*
OPPOSITE: **discourage**

encouragement /ɪn'kʌrɪdʒmənt/ *noun (no plural)*
praise and support given to someone so that they will do something ▶ *Her parents gave her lots of encouragement.*

encouraging /ɪn'kʌrɪdʒɪŋ/ *adjective*
making you feel hopeful and sure of yourself ▶ *encouraging news*

encyclopaedia /ɪnˌsaɪklə'piːdɪə/ *noun*
a book that gives you knowledge about a lot of things and is usually arranged in alphabetical order

end¹ /end/ *noun*
1 the point where something finishes ▶ *When you get to the end of this road, turn right.* ▶ *At the end of the lesson, we went home.* ▶ *at the end of August*
OPPOSITE: **beginning**
2 in the end at last ▶ *We walked for hours, but we found the house in the end.*

end² *verb*
1 to finish ▶ *The party ended at midnight.*
OPPOSITE: **begin**
2 end up to finish in a particular way or place although you did not want to ▶ *We ended up going by bus.*

endanger /ɪn'deɪndʒəʳ/ *verb*
to put someone or something in a dangerous or harmful situation ▶ *Pollution is endangering our planet.*

ending /'endɪŋ/ *noun*
the point where a story, film, or play finishes ▶ *a happy ending*

endless /'endləs/ *adjective*
not pleasant and seeming never to end ▶ *There is endless work to do when you have children in the house.*

endure /ɪn'djʊəʳ/ *verb (present participle* ***enduring****, past* ***endured****)*
to patiently suffer pain or deal with a difficult situation for a long time ▶ *The prisoners had to endure months of hunger.*

enemy /'enəmɪ/ *noun (plural* ***enemies****)*
a person or country that is not friendly to you or wants to harm you ▶ *He's made a lot of enemies at school.*

energetic /ˌenəˈdʒetɪk/ *adjective*
very active ▶ *an energetic tennis player*

energy /ˈenədʒɪ/ *noun (no plural)*
1 the ability to be active and do a lot without feeling tired ▶ *I have no energy left after playing football.*
2 the power that makes machines work or gives heat ▶ *Coal provides energy for lighting the factory.*

enforce /ɪnˈfɔːs/ *verb (present participle* ***enforcing****, past* ***enforced****)*
to make people obey a rule or law ▶ *We are finding it difficult to enforce the "no smoking" rule.*

E

engaged /ɪnˈgeɪdʒd/ *adjective*
1 busy or being used ▶ *The telephone number you want is engaged; try again in a few minutes.*
2 having promised to marry someone ▶ *My brother is engaged* ***to*** *Anne, and they are getting married next year.*

engagement /ɪnˈgeɪdʒmənt/ *noun*
1 a promise to marry someone ▶ *My brother has just told me about his engagement to Anne.*
2 an arrangement to go somewhere or meet someone ▶ *I'm unable to come because I have another engagement.*

engine /ˈendʒɪn/ *noun*
a machine that uses petrol, oil, gas, electricity, or steam and makes things work or move ▶ *a car engine*

engine driver /ˈendʒɪn ˌdraɪvəʳ/ *noun*
a person who drives a train

engineer /ˌendʒɪˈnɪəʳ/ *noun*
a person who is trained to plan and build machines, roads, bridges, etc.

engineering /ˌendʒɪˈnɪərɪŋ/ *noun (no plural)*
the science or job of an engineer ▶ *He is studying engineering at college.*

English[1] /ˈɪŋglɪʃ/ *noun (no plural)*
the language that is spoken in Great Britain, the United States, Canada, Australia, etc.

English[2] *adjective*
1 connected with the English language ▶ *an English course*
2 of, about, or from England ▶ *the English countryside*

engrave /ɪnˈgreɪv/ *verb (present participle* ***engraving****, past* ***engraved****)*
to cut words or pictures into metal, stone, or glass ▶ *a silver mug engraved with his name*

engrossed /ɪnˈgrəʊst/ *adjective*
so interested in something that you do not think of anything else ▶ *He was so engrossed* ***in*** *his work that he forgot about lunch.*

enjoy /ɪnˈdʒɔɪ/ *verb*
1 to get pleasure and happiness from something ▶ *She enjoys listening to music.*
2 enjoy yourself to have a good time ▶ *Did you enjoy yourself at the wedding?*

enjoyable /ɪnˈdʒɔɪəbəl/ *adjective*
giving pleasure or happiness ▶ *an enjoyable weekend*

enjoyment /ɪnˈdʒɔɪmənt/ *noun (no plural)*
pleasure ▶ *I get a lot of enjoyment from my job.*

enlarge /ɪnˈlɑːdʒ/ *verb (present participle* ***enlarging****, past* ***enlarged****)*
to make something bigger ▶ *to enlarge a photograph*

enormous /ɪˈnɔːməs/ *adjective*
very large ▶ *an enormous plate of food*
SAME MEANING: **gigantic, huge, vast**

enormously /ɪˈnɔːməslɪ/ *adverb*
very much ▶ *I like Jane enormously.*

enough /ɪˈnʌf/ *adjective, adverb, noun*
as much as is needed ▶ *There isn't enough paper to finish my letter.*

▶ *I've used six eggs, but are you sure that's enough?* ▶ *The water isn't warm enough to swim in.*
COMPARE: **ample**

enquire /ɪn'kwaɪəʳ/ *verb (present participle **enquiring**, past **enquired**)*
another word for **inquire**

enquiring /ɪn'kwaɪərɪŋ/ *adjective*
another word for **inquiring**

enquiry /ɪn'kwaɪərɪ/ *noun (plural **enquiries**)*
another word for **inquiry**

enrol /ɪn'rəʊl/ *verb (present participle **enrolling**, past **enrolled**)*
to become a member of a particular school, college, class, etc. ▶ *I decided to enrol **on** the chemistry course.*

enrolment /ɪn'rəʊlmənt/ *noun*
the process of becoming a member of a particular school, college, class, etc.

en route /ˌɒn 'ruːt/ *adverb*
on the way to somewhere ▶ *We bought a bottle of wine en route **to** the party.*

ensure /ɪn'ʃʊəʳ/ *verb (present participle **ensuring**, past **ensured**)*
to make certain that something happens ▶ *Please ensure that you sign the form.*

enter /'entəʳ/ *verb*
1 to go or come into a particular place ▶ *He entered the room quietly.*
2 to become part of a profession or an organization ▶ *He decided to enter the law.*
3 to say that you want to take part in something ▶ *She entered the race and won.*
4 to write down information or include it on a computer ▶ *Please enter your name on this list.*

enterprise /'entəpraɪz/ *noun*
1 *(no plural)* the ability to think of and try new things, especially in business ▶ *He showed a lot of enterprise in the way he solved the problem.*
2 a company or business ▶ *She got a loan to set up her new enterprise.*

enterprising /'entəpraɪzɪŋ/ *adjective*
able and willing to do things that are new or difficult ▶ *One enterprising young man started his own radio station.*

entertain /ˌentə'teɪn/ *verb*
1 to do something to amuse or interest people ▶ *He entertained us with stories about life abroad.*
2 to give food and drink to guests ▶ *We entertain a lot at weekends.*

entertainer /ˌentə'teɪnəʳ/ *noun*
a person whose job is to amuse others, for example by telling jokes

entertaining /ˌentə'teɪnɪŋ/ *adjective*
amusing and interesting

entertainment /ˌentə'teɪnmənt/ *noun (no plural)*
activities which amuse or interest people ▶ *For entertainment, we watch television.*

enthral /ɪn'θrɔːl/ *verb (present participle **enthralling**, past **enthralled**)*
to keep someone's attention and interest completely ▶ *The kids were absolutely enthralled by the stories.*

enthusiasm /ɪn'θjuːzɪæzəm/ *noun (no plural)*
a strong feeling of being interested in something or wanting to do something ▶ *He is full of enthusiasm for his job.*

enthusiast /ɪn'θjuːzɪæst/ *noun*
a person who is very interested in a particular subject or activity ▶ *My brother is a motorbike enthusiast.*

enthusiastic /ɪnˌθjuːzɪ'æstɪk/ *adjective*
very keen on something or interested in it

entice /ɪn'taɪs/ *verb (present participle **enticing**, past **enticed**)*
to persuade someone to do something by offering them something nice ▶ *The shops are already enticing customers **with** low prices.*

entire /ɪn'taɪəʳ/ *adjective*
whole; complete ▶ *The entire class will be there. (adverb: **entirely**)*

entitle /ɪn'taɪtl/ *verb*
be entitled to something to have the right to do or have something ▶ *You are entitled to have your money back if you are not satisfied.*

E

entrance /'entrəns/ *noun*
1 a place where you go into a building ▶ *Where's the entrance **to** the hospital?*
2 the arrival or coming in of a person ▶ *She made a dramatic entrance down the grand staircase.*

entranced /ɪn'trɑːnst/ *adjective*
feeling great pleasure because of something very beautiful which has taken all your attention ▶ *We were entranced by her singing.*

entrance examination /'entrəns ɪgzæmɪˌneɪʃən/ *noun*
an examination you have to pass before you can go to a particular school or college

entrant /'entrənt/ *noun*
a person who enters a competition, university, or profession

entrepreneur /ˌɒntrəprə'nɜːʳ/ *noun*
a person who starts a company

entrust /ɪn'trʌst/ *verb*
to make someone responsible for something ▶ *I was entrusted **with** the task of looking after the money.*

entry /'entrɪ/ *noun*
1 *(no plural)* the right to enter a building or country ▶ *The sign says "No Entry".*
2 *(plural **entries**)* a person or thing entered for a race or competition ▶ *The winning entry was a beautiful photo.*

envelope /'envələʊp, 'ɒn-/ *noun*
a folded paper cover for a letter

envious /'envɪəs/ *adjective*
wishing you had something that belongs to someone else ▶ *He was envious **of** my new car.*
SAME MEANING: **jealous**

environment /ɪn'vaɪərənmənt/ *noun*
1 the conditions in which you live and work, that affect your life ▶ *Children need a happy home environment.*
2 the world of land, sea, and air that you live in ▶ *Cutting down too many trees destroys the environment.*

environmental /ɪnˌvaɪərən'mentl/ *adjective*
relating to the world of land, sea, and air that you live in ▶ *environmental pollution*

environmentalist /ɪnˌvaɪərən-'mentəlɪst/ *noun*
a person who tries to protect the environment

environmentally friendly /ɪnˌvaɪərənmentəlɪ 'frendlɪ/ *adjective*
(used about products) not containing things that will harm the environment

envisage /ɪn'vɪzɪdʒ/ *verb (present participle **envisaging**, past **envisaged**)*
to think that something is likely to happen in the future ▶ *I don't envisage any major problems.*

envy[1] /'envɪ/ *noun (no plural)*
a feeling of anger or bitterness because you want something that someone else has got ▶ *He was filled with envy because Richard passed the examination and he did not.*
SAME MEANING: **jealousy**

envy[2] *verb (past **envied**)*
to wish that you had what someone else has got ▶ *I envied his success.*

epic¹ /ˈepɪk/ *adjective*
very long, exciting, or impressive ▶ *an epic journey in the Himalayas* ▶ *an epic novel*

epic² *noun*
a long book, poem, or film containing exciting adventures ▶ *Homer's epic, "The Odyssey"*

epidemic /ˌepɪˈdemɪk/ *noun*
an illness that spreads quickly to a lot of people

episode /ˈepɪsəʊd/ *noun*
one of the parts of a television or radio story that is broadcast separately ▶ *Tonight's episode of Star Trek starts at 6.30.*

epitaph /ˈepɪtɑːf/ *noun*
something written about a dead person, often on the stone over their GRAVE ▶ *"He did his best" would be my epitaph.*

equal¹ /ˈiːkwəl/ *adjective*
the same in size, number, or value ▶ *Divide the cake into four equal parts.* ▶ *Women want equal pay to men.*

equal² *noun*
a person who has the same ability and rights as someone else ▶ *All people should be treated as equals by the law.*

equal³ *verb (present participle **equalling**, past **equalled**)*
1 to be the same as something else in number or amount ▶ *Three plus five equals eight* (3 + 5 = 8).
2 to be as good as someone or something else ▶ *None of us can equal Sarah – she's always top of the class.*

equality /ɪˈkwɒlətɪ/ *noun (no plural)*
having the same ability and rights ▶ *Women want equality with men.*

equalize /ˈiːkwəlaɪz/ *verb (present participle **equalizing**, past **equalized**)*
to get a point or goal in a game so that you have the same number of points or goals as your opponents ▶ *Spain equalized in the 75th minute.*

equally /ˈiːkwəlɪ/ *adverb*
1 just as much ▶ *Both teams are equally capable of winning.*
2 in equal parts or amounts ▶ *We'll divide the work equally.*
3 in a way that is fair ▶ *We have to try to treat everyone equally.*

equation /ɪˈkweɪʒən/ *noun*
a statement in mathematics showing that two quantities are equal, for example 2y + 4 = 10

equator /ɪˈkweɪtəʳ/ *noun*
an imaginary line that runs round the middle of the Earth and divides it into north and south

equip /ɪˈkwɪp/ *verb (present participle **equipping**, past **equipped**)*
to give someone things that are useful for doing something ▶ *Our school is equipped **with** a radio.*

equipment /ɪˈkwɪpmənt/ *noun (no plural)*
the things which are used for a particular activity ▶ *office equipment*

equivalent¹ /ɪˈkwɪvələnt/ *adjective*
equal in amount, value, or rank to something or someone else ▶ *The workers received a bonus equivalent **to** two months' pay.*

equivalent² *noun*
something that has the same value, size, meaning, etc. as something else ▶ *Some French words have no equivalent in English.*

era /ˈɪərə/ *noun*
a period of time in history that is different from other periods ▶ *the post-war era*

eradicate /ɪˈrædɪkeɪt/ *verb (present participle **eradicating**, past **eradicated**)*
to completely get rid of something such as an illness or a social problem

E

► *We want to eradicate nuclear weapons by 2030.*

erase /ɪ'reɪz/ *verb (present participle **erasing**, past **erased**)*
to completely remove written or recorded information ► *I erased the file from the computer.*

erect[1] /ɪ'rekt/ *adjective*
upright; standing straight ► *He stood erect and saluted the general.*

erect[2] *verb*
to fit something together and make it stand up ► *They erected the tent.*

erode /ɪ'rəʊd/ *verb (present participle **eroding**, past **eroded**)*
(used about land) to wear, or be gradually worn away, due to water or the weather ► *The coastline is being eroded by the sea.*

erosion /ɪ'rəʊʒən/ *noun (no plural)*
the gradual destruction of land by the weather or by water ► *Planting trees will help prevent soil erosion.*

erotic /ɪ'rɒtɪk/ *adjective*
involving or causing feelings of sexual desire ► *an erotic dream (adverb: **erotically**)*

errand /'erənd/ *noun*
a short journey made to do something useful or to buy something

erratic /ɪ'rætɪk/ *adjective*
changing often without any reason, or moving in an irregular way ► *the England team's rather erratic performance in the World Cup (adverb: **erratically**)*

error /'erəʳ/ *noun*
a mistake ► *The doctor's error was very serious.*

erupt /ɪ'rʌpt/ *verb*
(used about a VOLCANO) to explode and throw out fire, ash, and smoke

eruption /ɪ'rʌpʃən/ *noun*
a situation in which a VOLCANO explodes and throws out fire, ash, and smoke

escalator /'eskəleɪtəʳ/ *noun*
a set of moving stairs that can take you up or down without you having to walk

escape[1] /ɪ'skeɪp/ *verb (present participle **escaping**, past **escaped**)*
1 to get free from a place where you are kept by force ► *He escaped **from** prison.*
2 to get out of a hole or crack in a container ► *Gas escaped **from** the pipes.*

escape[2] *noun*
the act of escaping ► *The prisoner made his escape at night.*

escort[1] /ɪ'skɔːt/ *verb*
to go with someone in order to protect them ► *A group of soldiers escorted the President.*

escort[2] /'eskɔːt/ *noun*
people, cars, planes, etc. that travel with someone to protect them ► *an escort of soldiers*

ESL /ˌiː es 'el/ *noun (no plural)*
ENGLISH AS A SECOND LANGUAGE; the teaching of English to students whose first language is not English, but who live in an English-speaking country

especially /ɪ'speʃəlɪ/ *adverb*
1 very; more than usual ► *She is especially good at science*
2 most of all ► *I would like a bicycle, especially a blue one.*

essay /'eseɪ/ *noun*
a piece of writing on a subject ► *She wrote an essay **on** "My Family".*

essential /ɪ'senʃəl/ *adjective*
necessary; very important ► *If you travel abroad, it is essential that you have the right papers.*

essentials /ɪ'senʃəlz/ *plural noun*
things that are important or necessary ► *We only have enough money for essentials like food and clothing.*

establish /ɪ'stæblɪʃ/ *verb*
1 to start a company, an organization, etc., especially one that will exist for a long time ▶ *He established the business in 1999.*
2 to find out facts or prove that something is true ▶ *We have been unable to establish the cause of the accident.*

establishment /ɪ'stæblɪʃmənt/ *noun*
a place for education, training, or RESEARCH ▶ *an educational establishment*

estate /ɪ'steɪt/ *noun*
a large piece of land, usually with a house or group of buildings on it

estate agent /ɪ'steɪt ˌeɪdʒənt/ *noun*
a person whose job is to arrange the buying and selling of houses and land

estate car /ɪ'steɪt ˌkɑːʳ/ *noun*
a large car with a door at the back

estimate[1] /'estɪmeɪt/ *verb* *(present participle **estimating**, past **estimated**)*
to make a reasonable guess about the size or amount of something ▶ *They estimated that the house cost £95,000.*

estimate[2] /'estɪmət/ *noun*
a guess about the size or amount of something

etc. /et'setərə/ *adverb*
a short way of writing **etcetera**; and so on ▶ *There are lots of things to buy – tea, sugar, bread, etc.*

eternal /ɪ'tɜːnəl/ *adjective*
continuing for ever ▶ *eternal love* *(adverb: **eternally**)*

eternity /ɪ'tɜːnɪti/ *noun*
1 *(no plural)* time that does not end, especially the time after you die
2 an eternity a very long time ▶ *It was an eternity before the phone rang.*

ethical /'eθɪkəl/ *adjective*
connected with principles of what is right and wrong ▶ *Research on animals raises difficult ethical questions.* *(adverb: **ethically**)*

ethics /'eθɪks/ *plural noun*
rules of behaviour used to decide what is right and wrong ▶ *the ethics of scientific research*

ethnic /'eθnɪk/ *adjective*
relating to a particular race of people ▶ *an ethnic minority*

etiquette /'etɪket/ *noun (no plural)*
the rules of polite behaviour

EU /ˌiː 'juː/ *noun*
the EU the EUROPEAN UNION

euphemism /'juːfəmɪzəm/ *noun*
a polite word or phrase that you use to avoid saying something that might offend people ▶ *"Passed away" is often used as a euphemism for "died".*

euro /'jʊərəʊ/ *noun*
a unit of money intended to be used by all the European Union countries

European[1] /ˌjʊərə'piːən/ *adjective*
from or connected with a country in Europe

European[2] *noun*
a person from a country in Europe

European Union /ˌjʊərəpiːən 'juːnjən/ *noun*
the European Union a political and economic organization of European countries

euthanasia /ˌjuːθə'neɪzɪə/ *noun (no plural)*
the practice of killing very old or ill people in a painless way, so that they will not suffer any more ▶ *Euthanasia is illegal in most countries.*

evacuate /ɪ'vækjʊeɪt/ *verb (present participle **evacuating**, past **evacuated**)*
to move people from a dangerous place to a safer place

evacuation /ɪˌvækjʊ'eɪʃən/ *noun*
the act of moving people from a dangerous place to a safer place
▶ *the evacuation of children from the war zone*

evaluate /ɪ'væljʊeɪt/ *verb*
(present participle ***evaluating****, past* ***evaluated****)*
to carefully consider something or someone in order to decide how good or bad they are ▶ *Teachers meet regularly to evaluate the progress of each student.*

evaporate /ɪ'væpəreɪt/ *verb*
(present participle ***evaporating****, past* ***evaporated****)*
if a liquid evaporates, or if something evaporates it, it changes into steam
▶ *Salt is produced by evaporating sea water.*

evaporation /ɪ'væpə'reɪʃən/ *noun*
(no plural)
the process of removing water from something, usually by heating it

eve /iːv/ *noun*
the night or day before a religious holiday or important event
▶ *Christmas Eve* ▶ *There were demonstrations on the eve of the election.*

even[1] /'iːvən/ *adjective*
1 flat and smooth ▶ *an even surface*
OPPOSITE: **uneven**
2 equal ▶ *He won the first game and I won the second, so we're even.*
3 even number a number that can be divided exactly by two – for example, 2, 4, and 6

even[2] *adverb*
1 used to show when something is surprising or unusual ▶ *Even Peter helped us, and he's usually very busy.*
2 used when you are comparing two things to make the second seem stronger ▶ *Yesterday it rained hard, and today it's raining even harder.*

evening /'iːvnɪŋ/ *noun*
the end of the afternoon and the early part of night

evenly /'iːvənlɪ/ *adverb*
equally ▶ *Divide the sweets evenly among the three boys* (=give the same number to each boy).

event /ɪ'vent/ *noun*
something that happens, often something important or unusual
▶ *What events do you remember from your schooldays?*

eventful /ɪ'ventfəl/ *adjective*
full of interesting or important events
▶ *an eventful holiday*

eventually /ɪ'ventʃəlɪ/ *adverb*
at last; in the end ▶ *I looked everywhere for my glasses, and eventually found them under my chair.*

ever /'evəʳ/ *adverb*
1 at any time ▶ *Have you ever been abroad?* ▶ *She used to sing well, but now she sings better than ever.*
2 ever since since a particular time long ago ▶ *I have lived here ever since I was a child.*

every /'evrɪ/ *adjective*
each one; not missing out one ▶ *I have read every book on the shelf.*

everybody /'evrɪbɒdɪ/ *(also* ***everyone****)* *pronoun*
every person ▶ *Everybody wants to watch the match.*

> Remember that **everybody** and **everyone** are singular words, like **he** or **she**, so you must use them with a singular verb ending: *Everyone knows that sugar is bad for your teeth.*

everyday /ˌevrɪ'deɪ/ *adjective*
usual or ordinary ▶ *Worries are just part of everyday life.*

everyone /'evrɪwʌn/ *(also* ***everybody****)* *pronoun*
every person ▶ *She likes everyone in her class.* ▶ *Everyone agreed that*

the concert was a success.
LOOK AT: **everybody**

everything /ˈevrɪθɪŋ/ *pronoun*
all things ▶ *I got everything I needed at the market.*

everywhere /ˈevrɪweəʳ/ *adverb*
in or to every place ▶ *I looked everywhere for my watch, but I couldn't find it.*

evidence /ˈevɪdəns/ *noun (no plural)*
words or things that prove something ▶ *What evidence do you have to support your theory?*

evident /ˈevɪdənt/ *adjective*
plain or clear ▶ *Her love of animals is evident. (adverb: **evidently**)*
SAME MEANING: **obvious**

evil /ˈiːvəl/ *adjective*
wicked and causing harm ▶ *In the film, the good queen saves her from an evil enemy.*

evolution /ˌiːvəˈluːʃən/ *noun (no plural)*
the gradual development of something over a long period of time, especially types of plant and animal ▶ *the evolution of man*

evolve /ɪˈvɒlv/ *verb (present participle **evolving**, past **evolved**)*
to develop gradually over a long period of time ▶ *a political system that has evolved over several centuries*

exact /ɪgˈzækt/ *adjective*
completely correct ▶ *Can you tell me the exact time?*

exactly /ɪgˈzæktlɪ/ *adverb*
1 with complete correctness ▶ *Where exactly do you live?*
2 used to agree with someone ▶ *"So you think the school will have to close?" "Exactly."*
SAME MEANING (**1** and **2**): **precisely**

exaggerate /ɪgˈzædʒəreɪt/ *verb (present participle **exaggerating**, past **exaggerated**)*
to make something seem bigger, better, worse, etc. than it really is
▶ *He exaggerated when he said the dog was the size of a horse.*

exaggeration /ɪgˌzædʒəˈreɪʃən/ *noun*
a statement saying that something is bigger, better, worse, etc. than it really is ▶ *It would be an exaggeration to call it a disaster.*

exam /ɪgˈzæm/ *noun*
an examination ▶ *Well done for passing your science exam!*

examination /ɪgˌzæmɪˈneɪʃən/ *noun*
1 an official test of knowledge in a subject ▶ *Please arrive on time for all examinations.*
2 a careful look at someone or something ▶ *a medical examination*

examine /ɪgˈzæmɪn/ *verb (present participle **examining**, past **examined**)*
1 to look at someone or something closely and carefully ▶ *The doctor examined my ears.*
2 to ask someone questions to be sure that they know something ▶ *The teacher will examine the students on everything they have studied this year.*

example /ɪgˈzɑːmpəl/ *noun*
1 one thing taken from a number of things of the same kind to show what the other things are like ▶ *I showed my new employer some examples of my work.*
2 for example used to give an example of something which makes your meaning clearer ▶ *Heavy rains cause many problems – for example, flooding the roads.*

exasperate /ɪgˈzɑːspəreɪt/ *verb (present participle **exasperating**, past **exasperated**)*
to annoy someone or make them angry

exasperation /ɪgˈzɑːspəˈreɪʃən/ *noun (no plural)*

E

a feeling of great annoyance or anger ▶ *She hit the computer in exasperation.*

excavate /ˈekskəveɪt/ *verb (present participle **excavating**, past **excavated**)*
to dig up the ground, especially in order to find things from the past ▶ *archaeologists excavating an ancient city*

excavation /ˌekskəˈveɪʃən/ *noun*
the activity of digging up the ground, especially in order to find things from the past ▶ *the archaeological excavation of an ancient city*

E

exceed /ɪkˈsiːd/ *verb*
to be more than a particular amount ▶ *Lorries which exceed this weight cannot cross the bridge.*

excel /ɪkˈsel/ *verb (present participle **excelling**, past **excelled**)*
1 to do something very well, or much better than most people ▶ *I never excelled **at** sport.*
2 excel yourself to do something even better than usual

excellence /ˈeksələns/ *noun (no plural)*
the quality of being very good at doing something ▶ *She won a prize for sporting excellence.*

excellent /ˈeksələnt/ *adjective*
very good ▶ *This is excellent work, Peter. (adverb: **excellently**)*
SAME MEANING: **outstanding**

except /ɪkˈsept/ *preposition*
apart from; not including ▶ *I washed all your clothes except your new shirt.*

exception /ɪkˈsepʃən/ *noun*
1 something that is different from what is usually expected ▶ *Most children like sweets, but she is the exception – she hates them!*
2 with the exception of apart from ▶ *They'd all been there before, with the exception of Jim.*

exceptional /ɪkˈsepʃənəl/ *adjective*
of unusually high ability ▶ *an exceptional pupil*

exceptionally /ɪkˈsepʃənəlɪ/ *adverb*
unusually or especially ▶ *an exceptionally cold winter*

excess /ˈekses/ *noun, adjective (plural **excesses**)*
more than is usual or allowed ▶ *You have to pay for excess luggage on a plane.*

excessive /ɪkˈsesɪv/ *adjective*
too much or too great ▶ *Excessive dieting can be very harmful. (adverb: **excessively**)*

exchange[1] /ɪksˈtʃeɪndʒ/ *verb (present participle **exchanging**, past **exchanged**)*
to give something to someone in return for something else ▶ *This skirt is too small. Maybe the shop will exchange it.*

exchange[2] *noun*
1 the giving of something in return for something else ▶ *an exchange of prisoners between two countries*
2 in exchange for in place of something that you give to someone ▶ *I gave him the book in exchange for a record.*

exchange rate /ɪksˈtʃeɪndʒ ˌreɪt/ *noun*
the value of the money of one country compared to that of another country

excite /ɪkˈsaɪt/ *verb (present participle **exciting**, past **excited**)*
to make someone feel strong feelings of enjoyment or pleasure ▶ *The games excited the children and they all started to shout.*

excited /ɪkˈsaɪtɪd/ *adjective*
having strong feelings of enjoyment or pleasure; not calm

excitement /ɪkˈsaɪtmənt/ *noun (no plural)*

the condition of being excited ▶ *The crowd's excitement grew as the match drew to a close* (=got near the end).

exciting /ɪk'saɪtɪŋ/ *adjective*
able to make someone excited
▶ *exciting news*

exclaim /ɪk'skleɪm/ *verb*
to speak loudly and suddenly in surprise ▶ *"Look – there's James on the television!" exclaimed Peter.*

exclamation /ˌekskləˈmeɪʃən/ *noun*
words showing a sudden, strong feeling

exclamation mark /ˌekskləˈmeɪʃən mɑːk/ *noun*
the sign (!) used in writing to show a strong feeling like surprise, or when calling someone ▶ *Come here!* ▶ *I don't believe it!*

exclude /ɪk'skluːd/ *verb (present participle* ***excluding****, past* ***excluded****)*
to stop someone or something from doing something or joining something ▶ *We had to exclude John from the team because he hurt his leg.*
OPPOSITE: **include**

excluding /ɪk'skluːdɪŋ/ *preposition*
not including ▶ *The shop is open every day, excluding Sundays.*
OPPOSITE: **including**

exclusive[1] /ɪk'skluːsɪv/ *adjective*
1 expensive and only available to certain people ▶ *an exclusive London club*
2 used or done by only one person or group, and not shared ▶ *an exclusive interview with President Mandela*

exclusive[2] *noun*
a news story that is only in one newspaper, magazine, etc.

exclusively /ɪk'skluːsɪvlɪ/ *adverb*
only ▶ *This offer is exclusively available to club members.*

excursion /ɪk'skɜːʃən/ *noun*
a short journey made for pleasure
▶ *We went on an excursion to the sea.*

excuse[1] /ɪk'skjuːz/ *verb (present participle* ***excusing****, past* ***excused****)*
1 to forgive ▶ *Please excuse this untidy room.*
2 to give someone permission not to do something, or permission to leave
▶ *The teacher excused her from going to the school's sports day.*
3 Excuse me used to get someone's attention, leave a group of people, or say sorry for doing something slightly rude ▶ *Excuse me, but have you got the time, please?* ▶ *Excuse me, I didn't mean to step on your foot!*

excuse[2] /ɪk'skjuːs/ *noun*
a reason given when you ask someone to forgive you for a mistake or bad behaviour ▶ *Have you any excuse for not finishing the work on time?*

execute /'eksɪkjuːt/ *verb (present participle* ***executing****, past* ***executed****)*
to kill someone as a punishment decided by law

execution /ˌeksɪ'kjuːʃən/ *noun*
a killing which is a punishment decided by law

executive /ɪg'zekjʊtɪv/ *noun*
an important manager in a company
▶ *a sales executive*

exercise[1] /'eksəsaɪz/ *noun*
1 *(no plural)* the use of your body to make it stronger or more healthy
▶ *Running is good exercise.*
2 a movement of your body which you do again and again in order to get fit or practise a skill ▶ *Have you done your exercises yet?*
3 a set of questions given in school to help students practise something
▶ *Please do Exercise 3 on page 4.*

exercise[2] *verb (present participle* ***exercising****, past* ***exercised****)*

E

to use your body or part of it in order to be healthy ▶ *The doctor told him to exercise more.*

exercise book /'eksəsaɪz ˌbʊk/ *noun* a book with empty pages in which pupils do their work for school

exhaust[1] /ɪg'zɔːst/ *verb* to make someone very tired ▶ *The long journey exhausted her.*

exhaust[2] *noun*
1 *(no plural)* burnt gas that comes out from the back of a car
2 a pipe that lets burnt gas out of the back of a car

exhausted /ɪg'zɔːstɪd/ *adjective* very tired ▶ *I'm exhausted after that walk.*

E

exhausting /ɪg'zɔːstɪŋ/ *adjective* making you very tired ▶ *Looking after babies is exhausting.*

exhibit /ɪg'zɪbɪt/ *verb* to show objects, e.g. paintings, in public ▶ *She exhibited her paintings at our school.*

exhibition /ˌeksɪ'bɪʃən/ *noun* a public show of objects, e.g. paintings ▶ *an art exhibition*

exhilarated /ɪg'zɪləreɪtɪd/ *adjective* feeling very happy and excited ▶ *The team were exhilarated at their success.*

exhilarating /ɪg'zɪləreɪtɪŋ/ *adjective* making you feel very happy and excited ▶ *an exhilarating helicopter ride*

exile[1] /'eksaɪl/ *noun* a person who, as a punishment, often for political reasons, is not allowed to live in their own country

exile[2] *verb (present participle* ***exiling****, past* ***exiled****)* to send a person away from their own country as a punishment

exist /ɪg'zɪst/ *verb* to be ▶ *The house where I was born no longer exists.*

existence /ɪg'zɪstəns/ *noun (no plural)* the state of being ▶ *The elephant is the largest land animal in existence.*

existing /ɪg'zɪstɪŋ/ *adjective* being used now ▶ *The existing computer network is out of date.*

exit /'eksɪt/ *noun* a door through which you can leave a place ▶ *Where is the exit?*
SAME MEANING: **way out**

exotic /ɪg'zɒtɪk/ *adjective* unusual and exciting, especially because of a connection with a distant country ▶ *an exotic flower from Africa*

expand /ɪk'spænd/ *verb* to become larger or make something larger ▶ *The business has expanded from having one office to having ten.*

expansion /ɪk'spænʃən/ *noun* an increase in size

expect /ɪk'spekt/ *verb*
1 to think that something will happen ▶ *"Do you expect to win the race?" "Yes, I expect I will win."*
2 be expecting someone or something to feel sure that someone or something will arrive, often because you have arranged it ▶ *We're expecting them for lunch.*
3 be expecting (a baby) to be going to have a baby
4 to ask strongly for certain behaviour ▶ *Visitors to the hospital are expected not to smoke.*

expectant /ɪk'spektənt/ *adjective* hoping that something good will happen ▶ *Hundreds of expectant fans waited for him to appear. (adverb:* ***expectantly****)*

expectation /ˌekspek'teɪʃən/ *noun* a strong belief or hope that something will happen ▶ *He had no expectation* ***of*** *passing the exam.* ▶ *Many refugees arrive in the country with high expectations.*

expedition /ˌekspəˈdɪʃən/ *noun*
a long, difficult journey, usually to find out something ▶ *an expedition to find where the River Nile starts*

expel /ɪkˈspel/ *verb (present participle* ***expelling****, past* ***expelled****)*
to force someone to leave a place, especially a school ▶ *The pupils were expelled for stealing.*

expense /ɪkˈspens/ *noun*
money spent on something ▶ *travelling expenses* ▶ *Having a car is a big expense.*

expensive /ɪkˈspensɪv/ *adjective*
costing a lot of money ▶ *It is expensive to travel by plane.*
OPPOSITE: **cheap, inexpensive**
SAME MEANING: **costly, dear**

experience[1] /ɪkˈspɪəriəns/ *noun*
1 something that happens to you ▶ *The accident was an experience she will never forget.*
2 *(no plural)* work you have done before of the same sort ▶ *a teacher with five years' experience*

experience[2] *verb (present participle* ***experiencing****, past* ***experienced****)*
to have something happen to you ▶ *to experience fear*

experienced /ɪkˈspɪəriənst/ *adjective*
good at something because you have done it before ▶ *an experienced doctor*
OPPOSITE: **inexperienced**

experiment[1] /ɪkˈsperɪmənt/ *noun*
a careful test done to see whether something is true ▶ *a scientific experiment*

experiment[2] /ɪkˈsperɪment/ *verb*
to do a careful test to see if something is true ▶ *We experimented by putting oil and water together, and we saw that they did not mix.*

expert[1] /ˈekspɜːt/ *noun*
a person who has special skill in something or knowledge of something ▶ *an expert* ***on*** *Stone Age pottery* ▶ *a cookery expert*

expert[2] *adjective*
having special skill in something or knowledge of something ▶ *expert advice* ▶ *an expert cook*

expertise /ˌekspɜːˈtiːz/ *noun (no plural)*
special skills or knowledge ▶ *legal expertise*

expire /ɪkˈspaɪəʳ/ *verb (present participle* ***expiring****, past* ***expired****)*
(used about something which lasts for a period of time) to be unable to be used any longer ▶ *My passport expires in two weeks.*

explain /ɪkˈspleɪn/ *verb*
to make something clear or give the reason for something ▶ *Can you explain what this word means?* ▶ *I explained to him that I'd missed the bus.*

explanation /ˌekspləˈneɪʃən/ *noun*
something that makes something clear or gives the reason for it ▶ *What is your explanation* ***for*** *being late?*

explicit /ɪkˈsplɪsɪt/ *adjective*
1 very clear and easy to understand ▶ *Could you be more explicit?*
2 showing or describing all the details of sex or violence ▶ *explicit love scenes*
(adverb: ***explicitly****)*

explode /ɪkˈspləʊd/ *verb (present participle* ***exploding****, past* ***exploded****)*
to burst with a loud noise and force ▶ *A bomb exploded there last night.*

exploit /ɪkˈsplɔɪt/ *verb*
to unfairly use someone's ideas, time, work, etc. without rewarding them for it ▶ *The company was accused of exploiting workers.*

exploits /ˈeksplɔɪts/ *plural noun*
brave or interesting things that someone has done ▶ *My father loved telling us about his exploits in the army.*

exploration /ˌekspləˈreɪʃən/ *noun*
a journey through a place to learn about it

explore /ɪkˈsplɔːʳ/ *verb (present participle **exploring**, past **explored**)*
to find out about a place by travelling through it ▶ *Have you really explored your nearest town?*

explorer /ɪkˈsplɔːrəʳ/ *noun*
a person who travels into an unknown area to find out about it

explosion /ɪkˈspləʊʒən/ *noun*
a sudden, loud noise caused, for example, by a bomb ▶ *The explosion was caused by a burst gas pipe.*

E

explosive¹ /ɪkˈspləʊsɪv/ *adjective*
1 likely to cause an explosion ▶ *an explosive mixture of gases*
2 likely to make people become violent or angry ▶ *an explosive situation*

explosive² *noun*
a substance that can cause an explosion

export¹ /ɪkˈspɔːt/ *verb*
to send things out of the country to be sold abroad ▶ *India exports cloth.*
COMPARE: **import**

export² /ˈekspɔːt/ *noun*
something that is sent to another country to be sold ▶ *Fruit is one of South Africa's exports.*
COMPARE: **import**

exporter /ɪkˈspɔːtəʳ/ *noun*
a person or company that sells things to other countries
COMPARE: **importer**

expose /ɪkˈspəʊz/ *verb (present participle **exposing**, past **exposed**)*
to uncover something ▶ *You shouldn't expose your skin to the sun.*

exposure /ɪkˈspəʊʒəʳ/ *noun*
1 *(no plural)* the act of putting someone into a harmful situation without any protection ▶ *Exposure **to** tobacco smoke can harm children.*
2 *(no plural)* the harmful effects of staying outside for a long time when the weather is extremely cold ▶ *Three climbers died of exposure.*
3 the amount of film that is used each time you take a photograph ▶ *This roll has 36 exposures.*

express¹ /ɪkˈspres/ *verb*
to show a feeling or thought by saying or doing something ▶ *He wanted to express his thanks, but he could not think of the best words.*

express² *noun (plural **expresses**)*
a fast train that makes only a few stops on its journey

express³ *adjective*
going or sent quickly ▶ *express mail*

expression /ɪkˈspreʃən/ *noun*
1 a word or group of words with a particular meaning ▶ *You shouldn't use that expression – it's not polite.*
2 the look on someone's face ▶ *a sad expression*

expressive /ɪkˈspresɪv/ *adjective*
showing what someone thinks or feels ▶ *She had expressive brown eyes.*

exquisite /ɪkˈskwɪzɪt/ *adjective*
very beautiful or delicate ▶ *an exquisite piece of jewellery*

extend /ɪkˈstend/ *verb*
1 to make something larger or longer ▶ *The headmaster extended our holiday by four days.*
2 to reach or stretch over an area ▶ *The garden extends all the way to the river.*

extension /ɪkˈstenʃən/ *noun*
a part added to make something longer or bigger ▶ *We built an extension onto the school, so now we have two more classrooms.*

extensive /ɪkˈstensɪv/ *adjective*
spreading over a large area ▶ *The school has extensive playing fields.*

extent /ɪk'stent/ *noun*
the size or limit of something ▶ *The extent **of** the North Pole is not fully known.*

exterior[1] /ɪk'stɪərɪəʳ/ *adjective*
on the outside of something ▶ *the exterior walls of the house*
OPPOSITE: **interior**

exterior[2] *noun*
the outside part of something ▶ *the exterior of the building*
OPPOSITE: **interior**

external /ɪk'stɜːnl/ *adjective*
1 outside a place, person, or thing ▶ *external walls*
OPPOSITE: **internal**
2 **for external use only** not to be eaten or drunk

extinct /ɪk'stɪŋkt/ *adjective*
1 (used about animals or plants) no longer existing
2 (used about VOLCANOES) no longer active

extinction /ɪk'stɪŋkʃən/ *noun (no plural)*
a situation in which a type of animal or plant no longer exists ▶ *The white tiger is facing extinction.*

extinguish /ɪk'stɪŋgwɪʃ/ *verb*
to put out a light or fire

extinguisher /ɪk'stɪŋgwɪʃəʳ/ *noun*
a container of chemicals that will put out a fire quickly

extra /'ekstrə/ *adjective, adverb, noun*
more than usual, necessary, or expected ▶ *Can I have extra time to finish my work?* ▶ *This hotel charges extra for a room with a view.*

extract[1] /ɪk'strækt/ *verb*
1 to make someone give you information, money, etc. that they do not want to give ▶ *The police failed to extract any information **from** him.*
2 to remove something ▶ *gaps in her mouth where teeth had been extracted*

extract[2] /'ekstrækt/ *noun*
a small part of a story, poem, song, etc. ▶ *an extract from "A Midsummer Night's Dream"*

extracurricular /ˌekstrəkə'rɪkjʊləʳ/ *adjective*
not part of the lessons or work that students have to do in school or college ▶ *extracurricular activities*

extraordinary /ɪk'strɔːdənərɪ/ *adjective*
very unusual or strange ▶ *I heard an extraordinary story the other day.*

extravagance /ɪk'strævəgəns/ *noun*
the spending of too much money

extravagant /ɪk'strævəgənt/ *adjective*
spending too much money ▶ *She's very extravagant – she spends all her money on clothes. (adverb: **extravagantly**)*

extreme /ɪk'striːm/ *adjective*
1 at the furthest end or edge of something ▶ *the extreme south*
2 very great ▶ *extreme danger*

extremely /ɪk'striːmlɪ/ *adverb*
very ▶ *I'm extremely grateful for your help.*

extrovert /'ekstrəvɜːt/ *noun*
a person who is confident and enjoys being with other people
OPPOSITE: **introvert**

eye /aɪ/ *noun*
1 the part of your head with which you see
2 a small hole at one end of a needle
3 **in someone's eyes** in someone's opinion ▶ *In her eyes, he's perfect.*
4 **keep an eye on** to watch people or things to make sure that they are safe ▶ *Will you keep an eye on my house while I'm away?*
5 **see eye to eye** to agree with someone completely ▶ *My father and I have never seen eye to eye.*

E

eyebrow /ˈaɪbraʊ/ *noun*
the hairy line above your eye

eyelash /ˈaɪlæʃ/ *noun (plural **eyelashes**)*
one of the hairs growing on the part of your eye which shuts

eyelid /ˈaɪlɪd/ *noun*
either of the pieces of skin which shut over your eye

eye-shadow /ˈaɪ ʃædəʊ/ *noun (no plural)*
a coloured substance that women put on their eyelids

eyesight /ˈaɪsaɪt/ *noun (no plural)*
your ability to see ▶ *If your eyesight is very bad, you won't get a driving licence.*

eyesore /ˈaɪsɔːʳ/ *noun*
a building or an area that is very ugly ▶ *The glass factory is a real eyesore.*

F

Ff

F
a short way of writing the word **Fahrenheit** ▶ 32°F (=32 degrees FAHRENHEIT)

fable /ˈfeɪbəl/ *noun*
a story that teaches people a lesson about how to behave

fabric /ˈfæbrɪk/ *noun*
material made by weaving; cloth ▶ *a metre of fabric* ▶ *a woollen fabric*

fabulous /ˈfæbjʊləs/ *adjective*
very good or nice ▶ *a fabulous holiday* ▶ *a fabulous meal*
SAME MEANING: **wonderful**

face[1] /feɪs/ *noun*
1 the front part of your head, with your eyes, nose, and mouth
2 the part of a clock or watch that has numbers on it

face[2] *verb (present participle **facing**, past **faced**)*
1 to have the front towards something; to look towards something ▶ *Our house faces the park.*
2 to deal with someone or something you are afraid of or do not like ▶ *I knew he was angry, and could not face him.* ▶ *You must face the fact that you are ill.*

facecloth /ˈfeɪsklɒθ/ *noun*
a cloth that you use to wash yourself with

facelift /ˈfeɪslɪft/ *noun*
a medical operation to make your face look younger by removing loose skin

face value /ˌfeɪs ˈvæljuː/ *noun*
take something at face value to accept something without thinking that it might not be as good or true as it seems

facilities /fəˈsɪlətɪz/ *plural noun*
things for you to use, especially in a public place ▶ *sports facilities* (=places and equipment for playing sport)

fact /fækt/ *noun*
1 something that you know is true; something that you know has happened ▶ *It is a fact that plants need water.* ▶ *historical facts*
2 in fact something you say when you are telling someone that something is true even if it does not seem likely ▶ *I don't know him very well – in fact, I've only met him once.*

factor /ˈfæktəʳ/ *noun*
one of several things that affect or cause a situation ▶ *The bad weather was an important factor **in** the crash.*

factory /ˈfæktərɪ/ *noun (plural **factories**)*
a place where things are made by machines ▶ *a car factory* (=a place where cars are made)

factual /ˈfæktʃʊəl/ *adjective*
based on facts ▶ *He gave us a factual account of what happened.*

faculty /ˈfækəltɪ/ *noun (plural* ***faculties****)*
a group of university departments ▶ *the Faculty of Engineering*

fad /fæd/ *noun*
something that you are interested in or that is popular for only a short time ▶ *Most of her special diets are just fads.*

fade /feɪd/ *verb (present participle* ***fading****, past* ***faded****)*
(used about a colour) to become less bright ▶ *If you leave that photograph in the sun, it will fade.*

Fahrenheit /ˈfærənhaɪt/ *noun*
a system for measuring temperature, in which water freezes at 32° and boils at 212°

fail /feɪl/ *verb*
1 not to succeed ▶ *Their attempt to cross the desert failed.* ▶ *The crops have failed because of lack of rain.*
2 not to pass an examination ▶ *He failed his English test.*
3 fail to do something not to do something that people expect ▶ *Our train failed to arrive* (=did not arrive).

failing¹ /ˈfeɪlɪŋ/ *noun*
a fault or weakness ▶ *He loved her in spite of her failings.*

failing² *preposition*
failing that used to say that if one thing is not possible or available there is another one you could try ▶ *You could try phoning but, failing that, a letter only takes a few days.*

failure /ˈfeɪljəʳ/ *noun*
someone or something that does not succeed ▶ *The plan was a failure.*
OPPOSITE: **success**

faint¹ /feɪnt/ *adjective*
not strong or clear ▶ *a faint sound* ▶ *a faint light* ▶ *a faint hope*

faint² *verb*
to suddenly become unconscious for a short time

fair¹ /feəʳ/ *adjective*
1 equally good to everyone ▶ *I try to be fair* ***to*** *all my children.* ▶ *It's not fair – I want one too!*
OPPOSITE: **unfair**
2 quite good, but not very good ▶ *His writing is good, but his reading is only fair.*
3 pale ▶ *Danish people usually have fair skin and fair hair.*
OPPOSITE (3): **dark**

fair² *noun*
a place where people, especially children, go and pay money to ride on special machines and play games in order to win prizes

fairly /ˈfeəlɪ/ *adverb*
a little bit, but not very ▶ *I'm fairly happy with the result.*
SAME MEANING: **quite**

fairy /ˈfeərɪ/ *noun (plural* ***fairies****)*
(in stories) a very small person with wings who can do magic things

fairy tale /ˈfeərɪ teɪl/ *noun*
a story for children about magic people or events

faith /feɪθ/ *noun*
1 *(no plural)* belief in something or someone ▶ *I have faith* ***in*** *you; I am sure you will do well.*
2 a religion

faithful /ˈfeɪθfəl/ *adjective*
able to be trusted ▶ *a faithful friend*

faithfully /ˈfeɪθfəlɪ/ *adverb*
Yours faithfully something you put at the end of a business letter, or a letter to someone you do not know, before you write your name ▶ *Dear Sir ... Yours faithfully, B. Wilson*

fake¹ /feɪk/ *noun*
a copy of something valuable that is intended to deceive people ▶ *We thought it was a Picasso, but it was a fake.*

F

fake[2] *adjective*
made to look like a real object or real material in order to deceive people ▶ *fake fur*

fake[3] *verb (present participle* ***faking****, past* ***faked****)*
1 to pretend to be ill, interested, pleased, etc. when you are not ▶ *I thought he was really hurt, but he was just faking it.*
2 to make an exact copy of something in order to deceive people ▶ *He faked his uncle's signature on the note.*

fall[1] /fɔːl/ *verb (past tense* ***fell*** */fel/, past participle* ***fallen*** */'fɔːlən/)*
1 to drop to a lower place ▶ *The leaves are falling off the trees.* ▶ *Rain was falling.* ▶ *She fell down the stairs.* ▶ *I fell off my bicycle.* ▶ *Be careful or you'll fall!*
2 to become less in amount; to decrease ▶ *House prices are falling.*
3 fall apart to break into pieces ▶ *These old shoes are falling apart.*
4 fall asleep to start to sleep ▶ *I fell asleep in front of the fire.*
5 fall for someone to start to feel love for someone ▶ *She's fallen for a boy in her class.*
6 fall in love with someone to start to feel love for someone
7 fall out with someone to quarrel with someone ▶ *They're always falling out with each other.*
8 fall over to fall to the ground ▶ *I fell over on the ice.*
9 fall to pieces to break into pieces ▶ *When I sat down, the old chair fell to pieces.*

fall[2] *noun*
1 an act of falling to the ground ▶ *He had a bad fall and hurt himself.*
2 a decrease ▶ *a fall* ***in*** *prices*

fallen /'fɔːlən/
the PAST PARTICIPLE of the verb **fall**

false /fɔːls/ *adjective*
1 not true ▶ *Is this statement true or false?*
2 not real ▶ *false teeth*

fame /feɪm/ *noun (no plural)*
the state of being known and admired by a lot of people

familiar /fə'mɪlɪəʳ/ *adjective*
1 well known to you ▶ *This song sounds familiar.*
OPPOSITE: **unfamiliar**
2 be familiar with something to know something ▶ *Are you familiar with that story?*

familiarity /fəˌmɪlɪ'ærətɪ/ *noun (no plural)*
a good knowledge of something ▶ *a familiarity* ***with*** *Russian poetry*

family /'fæməlɪ/ *noun (plural* ***families****)*
a group of relatives including parents and their children, and sometimes also aunts, uncles, grandmothers, grandfathers and COUSINS ▶ *a family of four* (=with four people in it)

family tree /ˌfæməlɪ 'triː/ *noun*
a drawing that shows how all the people in a family are related to each other

famine /'fæmɪn/ *noun*
a time when there is not enough food for people to eat

famous /'feɪməs/ *adjective*
well-known and admired ▶ *This town is famous* ***for*** *its beautiful buildings.* ▶ *a famous singer*

fan[1] /fæn/ *noun*
1 an instrument for moving the air around you to make you cooler
2 someone who likes a particular person or thing very much ▶ *I'm a fan* ***of*** *his music.* ▶ *a football fan*

fan[2] *verb (present participle* ***fanning****, past* ***fanned****)*
to make the air around you move ▶ *She fanned herself with the newspaper* (=to cool her face).

fanatic /fə'nætɪk/ *noun*
1 a person who has very strong and

unreasonable beliefs about religion or politics
2 a person who likes something very much ▶ *a football fanatic*

fancy¹ /ˈfænsɪ/ *adjective (**fancier, fanciest**)*
not ordinary or plain ▶ *fancy clothes*

fancy² *verb (past **fancied**)*
1 to want something ▶ *Do you fancy fish for dinner?* ▶ *I fancy a walk.*
2 to be attracted to someone in a sexual way ▶ *I've always fancied his brother.*

fancy dress /ˌfænsɪ ˈdres/ *noun (no plural)*
strange clothes that you wear for fun at a party ▶ *a fancy dress party* (=a party where people wear fancy dress)

fanfare /ˈfænfeəʳ/ *noun*
a short piece of music played loudly on a TRUMPET to introduce an important person or event

fang /fæŋ/ *noun*
a long, sharp tooth of an animal such as a dog or snake

fantasize /ˈfæntəsaɪz/ *verb (present participle **fantasizing**, past **fantasized**)*
to imagine that something pleasant is happening to you ▶ *We all fantasize **about** winning the lottery.*

fantastic /fænˈtæstɪk/ *adjective*
very good ▶ *You look fantastic in that dress.* ▶ *a fantastic idea*
SAME MEANING: **great**

fantasy /ˈfæntəsɪ/ *noun (plural **fantasies**)*
something that you think about that is pleasant but unlikely to happen ▶ *I had fantasies **about** becoming a famous actress.*

far¹ /fɑːʳ/ *adverb (**farther** /ˈfɑːðəʳ/ or **further** /ˈfɜːðəʳ/, **farthest** /ˈfɑːðɪst/ or **furthest** /ˈfɜːðɪst/)*
1 distant from a place ▶ *How far is it to London?* ▶ *We didn't walk very far.*
OPPOSITE: **near**

> Use **far** in questions, in NEGATIVE sentences, and after **too**, **as**, and **so**: *How far is it to your house?* ▶ *It isn't far.* ▶ *It's too far to walk.* ▶ *We drove as far as the next town.* ▶ *We didn't mean to walk so far.* In other types of sentences, use **a long way**: *We walked a long way.* ▶ *It's a long way from the school to my house.*

2 very much ▶ *I'm far too tired to go out.* ▶ *a far better idea*
3 as far as to a place ▶ *He only drove as far as the end of the road.*
4 far away distant from a place
5 so far until now

far² *adjective*
not near; distant ▶ *the far side of town*
OPPOSITE: **near**

farce /fɑːs/ *noun*
1 an event or a situation that is very badly organized
2 a funny play in which a lot of silly things happen

fare /feəʳ/ *noun*
the amount of money that you have to pay to travel on a bus, train, plane, etc. ▶ *a taxi fare*

farewell /feəˈwel/ *noun*
goodbye

far-fetched /ˌfɑː ˈfetʃt/ *adjective*
very strange and not likely to be true ▶ *I thought her story was pretty far-fetched.*

farm /fɑːm/ *noun*
land on which people grow food or keep animals

farmer /ˈfɑːməʳ/ *noun*
a person who owns or works on a farm

farmhouse /ˈfɑːmhaʊs/ *noun (plural **farmhouses** /-haʊzɪz/)*
the house on a farm where the farmer lives

farming /ˈfɑːmɪŋ/ *noun (no plural)*
the job of growing food or keeping animals

farmyard /ˈfɑːmjɑːd/ *noun*
the piece of ground next to a farmhouse

farther /ˈfɑːðəʳ/
the COMPARATIVE of **far**

farthest /ˈfɑːðɪst/
the SUPERLATIVE of **far**

fascinate /ˈfæsɪneɪt/ *verb (present participle **fascinating**, past **fascinated**)*
to interest someone very much

fascinating /ˈfæsɪneɪtɪŋ/ *adjective*
extremely interesting, especially because you are learning something new ▶ *a fascinating subject*

fascination /ˌfæsɪˈneɪʃən/ *noun (no plural)*
very strong interest in something

fascism /ˈfæʃɪzəm/ *noun (no plural)*
an extreme political system in which the state has complete power and controls everything

F

fascist /ˈfæʃɪst/ *noun*
a person who supports fascism

fashion /ˈfæʃən/ *noun*
1 the way of dressing or doing something that is liked by many people at a particular time ▶ *the fashion for short skirts*
2 **in fashion** liked by many people now ▶ *These ideas are in fashion.*
3 **out of fashion** no longer liked by many people

fashionable /ˈfæʃənəbəl/ *adjective*
liked by many people at a particular time ▶ *fashionable clothes*
OPPOSITE: **unfashionable**

fast[1] /fɑːst/ *adjective*
1 quick; not slow ▶ *He is a fast runner.*
2 (used about a clock or watch) showing a time that is later than the real time
OPPOSITE (**1** and **2**): **slow**
3 firmly fixed

fast[2] *adverb*
1 quickly ▶ *to run fast*
OPPOSITE: **slowly**
2 firmly; tightly ▶ *The boat stuck fast in the mud.*
3 **fast asleep** sleeping very well

fast[3] *verb*
to eat no food, usually for religious reasons
COMPARE: **starve**

fasten /ˈfɑːsən/ *verb*
to fix something firmly; to join or tie together ▶ *She fastened her coat.*
OPPOSITE: **unfasten**

fastener /ˈfɑːsənəʳ/ *noun*
something used to join or tie things together

fastening /ˈfɑːsənɪŋ/ *noun*
something that you use to hold another thing closed

fast food /ˈfɑːst fuːd/ *noun (no plural)*
cooked food, e.g. HAMBURGERS and CHIPS, that you buy from special shops to eat there or to take away with you

fast-forward /ˌfɑːst ˈfɔːwəd/ *verb*
to wind a TAPE forward quickly without playing it

fat[1] /fæt/ *adjective (**fatter, fattest**)*
having a wide, round body ▶ *I think he's too fat.*
OPPOSITE: **thin**

fat[2] *noun*
an oily substance, especially the oil that comes from meat when it is cooked

fatal /ˈfeɪtl/ *adjective*
causing someone to die ▶ *a fatal car accident (adverb: **fatally**)*
COMPARE: **deadly**

fate /feɪt/ *noun (no plural)*
a power which some people believe causes things to happen to you during your life

father /ˈfɑːðəʳ/ *noun*
your male parent ▶ *my mother and father*

Father Christmas /ˌfɑːðə ˈkrɪsməs/ *noun*

an old man who children think brings them presents at Christmas, and who wears red clothes and has a long, white beard
SAME MEANING: **Santa Claus**

father-in-law /ˈfɑːðər ɪn lɔː/ *noun (plural **fathers-in-law**)*
the father of your wife or husband

fatigue /fəˈtiːg/ *noun (no plural)*
extreme tiredness

fattening /ˈfætn-ɪŋ/ *adjective*
(used about food) likely to make you fat ▶ *Those cakes look fattening.*

fatty /ˈfætɪ/ *adjective (**fattier, fattiest**)*
(used about food) containing a lot of fat

fault /fɔːlt/ *noun*
1 something that is wrong; a mistake or problem ▶ *a fault in the engine*
2 the fact of being responsible for something bad ▶ *I'm sorry – it's all my fault.*

faultless /ˈfɔːltləs/ *adjective*
having no faults; perfect ▶ *faultless work*

faulty /ˈfɔːltɪ/ *adjective*
having a mistake or something wrong ▶ *a faulty machine*

favour /ˈfeɪvəʳ/ *noun*
1 something kind done for someone ▶ *May I ask you a favour?* ▶ *Will you do me a favour* (=do something for me) *and lend me some money?*
2 be in favour of something to think something is a good idea; to support something ▶ *I'm not in favour of the plan.* ▶ *Are you in favour of changing the law?*

favourable /ˈfeɪvərəbəl/ *adjective*
good and suitable ▶ *favourable weather for working outside*
OPPOSITE: **unfavourable**

favourite /ˈfeɪvərɪt/ *adjective*
liked best of all ▶ *Orange is my favourite colour.*

favouritism /ˈfeɪvərɪtɪzəm/ *noun (no plural)*
the act of unfairly treating one person or group better than others because you like them more

fax /fæks/ *noun (plural **faxes**)*
a machine, joined to a telephone, which you use for sending copies of letters or pictures to another place

fear¹ /fɪəʳ/ *verb*
1 to be afraid of someone or something
2 to worry because you think that something bad has happened or is going to happen ▶ *We feared an accident.*

fear² *noun*
1 the feeling of being afraid ▶ *a fear of dogs* ▶ *He was shaking with fear.*
2 a feeling of being worried in case something bad has happened or is going to happen ▶ *fears of an accident*

fearful /ˈfɪəfəl/ *adjective*
causing fear; very bad ▶ *a fearful sound*

fearless /ˈfɪələs/ *adjective*
never showing fear; never afraid ▶ *a fearless soldier*
SAME MEANING: **brave**

feasible /ˈfiːzəbəl/ *adjective*
possible, and likely to work or be true ▶ *Her story sounds quite feasible.*

feast¹ /fiːst/ *noun*
a large meal of good food for a special reason

feast² *verb*
to eat a large meal of good food

feat /fiːt/ *noun*
something that someone does that shows a lot of strength or skill ▶ *an amazing feat **of** engineering*

feather /ˈfeðəʳ/ *noun*
one of the things that covers a bird, like a thin stick with soft hairs

feature /ˈfiːtʃəʳ/ *noun*
1 a part of your face, especially your eyes, nose, or mouth
2 one part of something that you notice especially, or that is typical of it

February /ˈfebrʊərɪ/ *noun*
the second month of the year

fed /fed/
the PAST TENSE and PAST PARTICIPLE of the verb **feed**

federal /ˈfedərəl/ *adjective*
having several states or countries that are joined under one government, but which also decide certain things on their own ▶ *a federal system*

fed up /ˌfed ˈʌp/ *adjective*
not happy because you have had too much of something or because you are annoyed with someone ▶ *I'm fed up **with** staying at home all day.*
COMPARE: **bored**

fee /fiː/ *noun*
money that you pay to a doctor, lawyer, school, etc.

feeble /ˈfiːbəl/ *adjective*
very weak

feed /fiːd/ *verb (past **fed** /fed/)*
to give food to a person or an animal ▶ *Have you fed the cat?*

feedback /ˈfiːdbæk/ *noun (no plural)*
advice or criticism about how well or badly you have done something ▶ *We are still waiting for feedback **on** the report.*

feel /fiːl/ *verb (past **felt** /felt/)*
1 to be ▶ *to feel happy* ▶ *to feel ill*
2 to touch something with your fingers to see what it is like
3 to experience something touching you ▶ *to feel the wind in your hair*
4 to think or believe something ▶ *I feel sure she will agree.*
5 feel like something to want something ▶ *I feel like something to eat.* ▶ *I feel like staying in tonight.*

feeling /ˈfiːlɪŋ/ *noun*
1 something that you experience in your body or your mind ▶ *feelings **of** love* ▶ *a feeling **of** pain*
2 hurt someone's feelings to upset someone

feet /fiːt/
1 the plural of **foot**
2 on your feet standing up ▶ *I've been on my feet all day.*
3 put your feet up to rest

fell /fel/
the PAST TENSE of the verb **fall**

fellow¹ /ˈfeləʊ/ *noun*
a man

fellow² *adjective*
very like you or from the same place as you ▶ *your fellow students*

felt /felt/
the PAST TENSE and PAST PARTICIPLE of the verb **feel**

felt tip /ˈfelt tɪp/ *noun*
a type of thick, coloured pen, used especially by children

female¹ /ˈfiːmeɪl/ *adjective*
belonging to the sex that gives birth to young ones
OPPOSITE: **male**

female² *noun*
a girl or woman; an animal of the sex that gives birth to young ones
OPPOSITE: **male**

feminine /ˈfemɪnɪn/ *adjective*
like a woman or typical of a woman
OPPOSITE: **masculine**

feminism /ˈfemɪnɪzəm/ *noun (no plural)*
the belief that women should have the same rights and opportunities as men

feminist /ˈfemɪnɪst/ *noun*
a person who believes that women should have the same rights and opportunities as men

fence¹ /fens/ *noun*
a wooden or wire wall round something

fence² *verb (present participle* ***fencing****, past* ***fenced****)*
fence something off to put a wooden or wire wall around something ▶ *to fence off some land*

fencing /ˈfensɪŋ/ *noun (no plural)*
a sport in which people fight with long, thin swords

fend /fend/ *verb*
fend for yourself to look after yourself without help from other people ▶ *The children had to fend for themselves while their parents were at work.*

fern /fɜːn/ *noun*
a green plant that has no flowers and grows in places that are wet and dark

ferocious /fəˈrəʊʃəs/ *adjective*
very fierce ▶ *a ferocious animal*

ferry /ˈferɪ/ *noun (plural* ***ferries****)*
a boat that takes people or things across a stretch of water ▶ *A ferry crosses the river every hour.*

fertile /ˈfɜːtaɪl/ *adjective*
(used about land, earth, etc.) able to grow plants and seeds very well ▶ *His farm is on fertile land.*
OPPOSITE: **infertile**

fertilize /ˈfɜːtɪlaɪz/ *verb (present participle* ***fertilizing****, past* ***fertilized****)*
(used about an egg) to become joined with a SPERM so that a new animal or baby can start to develop

fertilizer /ˈfɜːtɪlaɪzəʳ/ *noun (no plural)*
something that you put on the land to make your crops grow better

festival /ˈfestɪvəl/ *noun*
1 a period of time when there are many special events of a particular type ▶ *a film festival* ▶ *a festival of music*
2 a time when everyone has a holiday from work to enjoy something such as a religious event

festive /ˈfestɪv/ *adjective*
happy or cheerful because people are celebrating something ▶ *a festive occasion*

festivities /feˈstɪvətɪz/ *plural noun*
an occasion when people eat, drink, or dance to celebrate something

fetch /fetʃ/ *verb*
to go somewhere and bring someone or something back with you ▶ *Will you fetch some water?*

> Compare the verbs **fetch** and **bring**. If you **bring** something to a place, you have it with you when you go there. If you **fetch** something, you go and get it from somewhere else and then have it with you when you come back: *Please bring a bottle of wine to the party* (=come to the party with a bottle of wine). ▶ *Can you fetch me some milk when you go to the shop* (=go and get it and come back with it)*?*

fete /feɪt/ *noun*
a special market with games, competitions, and things for sale, arranged by people who want to get money to help a church, a school, or some other organization

feud /fjuːd/ *noun*
an angry argument between two people or groups that continues for a long time ▶ *There has been a feud between the two families for many years.*

fever /ˈfiːvəʳ/ *noun*
an increase of heat in your body, caused by illness ▶ *to have a fever*

feverish /ˈfiːvərɪʃ/ *adjective*
feeling hot because of a fever ▶ *He was pale and feverish.*

few /fjuː/ *adjective, pronoun*
1 not many ▶ *He has few friends.* ▶ *Few people would agree with you.*
OPPOSITE: **many**

2 a few a small number of ▶ *Can I ask you a few questions?* ▶ *a few days*
3 quite a few quite a lot ▶ *There were quite a few people at the party.*

fiancé /fɪˈɒnseɪ/ *noun*
a man who has promised to marry a particular woman ▶ *Her fiancé is called George.*

fiancée /fɪˈɒnseɪ/ *noun*
a woman who has promised to marry a particular man ▶ *His fiancée is called Susan.*

fiasco /fɪˈæskəʊ/ *noun*
an event that is so unsuccessful that people feel embarrassed about it ▶ *The evening was a total fiasco from start to finish.*

fib /fɪb/ *noun*
a lie; not the truth ▶ *to tell a fib*

F

fibre /ˈfaɪbəʳ/ *noun*
a thin thread of a plant or animal substance

fiction /ˈfɪkʃən/ *noun (no plural)*
books and stories about people and events that are not real ▶ *Most children enjoy reading fiction.*
OPPOSITE: **nonfiction**

fictional /ˈfɪkʃənəl/ *adjective*
(used about people or events) from a book or story that is not real

fiddle¹ /ˈfɪdl/ *verb (present participle* ***fiddling****, past* ***fiddled****)*
1 to dishonestly take money out of an organization by cheating it in small ways ▶ *His boss found out that he'd been fiddling his expenses.*
2 fiddle (around) with something to keep moving something around with your hands, especially because you are bored or nervous ▶ *I wish he'd stop fiddling with his keys.*

fiddle² *noun*
1 a VIOLIN
2 a dishonest way of getting money ▶ *an insurance fiddle*

fiddly /ˈfɪdlɪ/ *adjective*
difficult to use or do because you have to move very small objects ▶ *a very fiddly job*

fidget /ˈfɪdʒɪt/ *verb*
to keep moving your hands or feet, because you are bored, uncomfortable, or nervous ▶ *The audience were starting to fidget.*

field /fiːld/ *noun*
a piece of ground, usually with a fence or wall round it, used for growing crops or keeping animals ▶ *a field of wheat*

fielder /ˈfiːldəʳ/ *noun*
one of the players who tries to catch the ball in BASEBALL or CRICKET

field trip /ˈfiːld trɪp/ *noun*
a trip in which students go somewhere to learn about a subject ▶ *a geography field trip*

fierce /fɪəs/ *adjective*
violent and angry ▶ *a fierce dog* ▶ *a fierce storm*

fiery /ˈfaɪərɪ/ *adjective*
full of strong or angry emotion ▶ *John has a fiery temper.*

fifteen /fɪfˈtiːn/ *adjective, noun*
the number 15

fifteenth /fɪfˈtiːnθ/ *adjective*
15th

fifth /fɪfθ/ *adjective, noun*
1 5th
2 one of five equal parts

fiftieth /ˈfɪftɪ-əθ/ *adjective*
50th

fifty /ˈfɪftɪ/ *adjective, noun*
the number 50

fifty-fifty /ˌfɪftɪ ˈfɪftɪ/ *adjective, adverb*
1 divided or shared equally between two people ▶ *I think we should divide the profits fifty-fifty.*
2 a fifty-fifty chance an equal chance that something will happen or will not happen ▶ *The operation has a fifty-fifty chance of success.*

fig /fɪg/ *noun*
a sweet fruit which is full of small seeds

fight[1] /faɪt/ *verb (past **fought** /fɔːt/)*
1 to use your body or weapons to try and hurt or kill someone ▶ *He fought in the war.* ▶ *to fight an enemy* ▶ *to fight a battle*
2 to quarrel with someone

fight[2] *noun*
an act of fighting ▶ *The two boys had a fight.*

figure /ˈfɪgəʳ/ *noun*
1 a written number such as 3 or 8
2 a shape, especially the shape of a human body ▶ *I could see a tall figure near the door.* ▶ *She has a good figure* (=her body is an attractive shape).

file[1] /faɪl/ *noun*
1 a cardboard cover or container for papers
2 a tool with a rough edge that you use for making things smooth ▶ *a nail file*
3 in single file walking one behind the other in a line ▶ *Please walk in single file.*

file[2] *verb (present participle **filing**, past **filed**)*
1 to put papers into a file ▶ *to file letters*
2 to make something smooth using a file ▶ *to file your nails*
3 to walk in a line one behind the other ▶ *The children filed into the classroom.*

filing cabinet /ˈfaɪlɪŋ ˌkæbɪnət/ *noun*
a tall, narrow piece of furniture with drawers, where important papers are kept

fill /fɪl/ *verb*
1 to put something into something until no more will fit in ▶ *to fill a glass with water*
2 to become full ▶ *The streets filled with people.*
OPPOSITE (**1** and **2**): **empty**
3 fill something in to give the written information you are asked for on an official piece of paper ▶ *Fill in the answers to these questions.*
4 fill something up to fill something completely ▶ *to fill up a car with petrol*

fillet[1] /ˈfɪlɪt/ *noun*
a piece of meat or fish without any bones

fillet[2] *verb*
to remove the bones from a piece of meat or fish

filling /ˈfɪlɪŋ/ *noun*
a substance that a DENTIST puts in a hole in your tooth

filling station /ˈfɪlɪŋ ˌsteɪʃən/ *noun*
a place where you go to buy petrol for your car

film[1] /fɪlm/ *noun*
1 a story shown in a cinema or on television ▶ *a Charlie Chaplin film*
2 the thing you put into a camera, on which photographs are made

film[2] *verb*
to make a film of something ▶ *He filmed the football match.*

film star /ˈfɪlm stɑːʳ/ *noun*
a famous actor or actress who acts in films

filter[1] /ˈfɪltəʳ/ *noun*
a thing that removes substances that you do not want from a liquid or gas as the liquid or gas flows through it ▶ *the oil filter in a car*

filter[2] *verb*
to clean a liquid or gas using a filter ▶ *I filter all my drinking water*

filth /fɪlθ/ *noun (no plural)*
unpleasant dirt ▶ *The old bicycle was completely covered in filth.*

filthy /ˈfɪlθɪ/ *adjective (**filthier**, **filthiest**)*
very dirty ▶ *filthy clothes*

fin /fɪn/ *noun*
a part on the side of a fish that helps it to swim

final[1] /ˈfaɪnl/ *adjective*
coming at the end; last ▶ *the final part of the story*

final[2] *noun*
the last and most important game in a competition, to decide who will win

finalist /ˈfaɪnəlɪst/ *noun*
one of the people or teams that reach the last part of a competition

finalize /ˈfaɪnəl-aɪz/ *verb (present participle **finalizing**, past **finalized**)*
to finish the last part of a plan, business agreement, etc. ▶ *Can we finalize the details of the deal tomorrow?*

finally /ˈfaɪnəlɪ/ *adverb*
1 after a long delay ▶ *When she finally arrived, it was too late.*
2 a word you use when you come to the last thing you want to say about a subject you have been speaking or writing about ▶ *Finally, let me thank you all for your help in this matter.*
3 a word you use when you are giving the last of a number of instructions ▶ *Finally, bake the cake for 30 minutes.*

finance[1] /ˈfaɪnæns, fɪˈnæns/ *noun (no plural)*
the controlling of large sums of money, e.g. by a bank, a company, or a government

finance[2] *verb (present participle **financing**, past **financed**)*
to give someone the money for something ▶ *The government will finance the building of the new roads.*

financial /faɪˈnænʃəl/ *adjective*
connected with money ▶ *financial advice*

find /faɪnd/ *verb (past **found** /faʊnd/)*
1 to see or get something after you have been looking for it ▶ *I can't find my keys.* ▶ *to find a job*
OPPOSITE: **lose**
2 to learn or discover something ▶ *to find the answer to a question*
3 find someone guilty to say that someone is guilty of a crime ▶ *The court found him guilty **of** murder.*
4 find something out to discover the facts about something ▶ *to find out the truth about something*

findings /ˈfaɪndɪŋz/ *plural noun*
the things that people have learned as the result of an official study ▶ *They reported their findings to the Health Minister.*

fine[1] /faɪn/ *adjective*
1 very nice or good ▶ *a fine building*
2 good enough ▶ *"How is your meal?" "Fine, thanks."*
3 very well or happy ▶ *"How are you?" "Fine, thank you."*
4 sunny and without rain ▶ *a fine day* ▶ *fine weather*
5 very thin ▶ *fine lines*

fine[2] *noun*
money that you pay as a punishment after doing something wrong

fine[3] *verb (present participle **fining**, past **fined**)*
to make someone pay money as a punishment after they have done something wrong ▶ *The man was fined £100 by the court.*

finely /ˈfaɪnlɪ/ *adverb*
into very small pieces ▶ *Chop the onion finely.*

finger /ˈfɪŋgəʳ/ *noun*
one of the five long parts on your hand

fingernail /ˈfɪŋgəneɪl/ *noun*
one of the hard, flat things that grow at the end of your fingers

fingerprint /ˈfɪŋgəprɪnt/ *noun*
a mark made by the lines on the end of your fingers, used by the police to IDENTIFY people

fingertip /ˈfɪŋgətɪp/ *noun*
the end of one of your fingers

finish[1] /ˈfɪnɪʃ/ *noun*
the end of something
OPPOSITE: **start**

finish[2] *verb*
1 to end ▶ *the game finished at 4 o'clock*
2 to complete something or to stop doing something ▶ *I finish work at 5 o'clock.* ▶ *I've finished reading the newspaper.*
OPPOSITE (**1** and **2**): **start**
3 finish something off to complete something ▶ *I'm just finishing off a letter.*
4 finish with something to stop using something because you no longer need it ▶ *Have you finished with that pen?*

finished /ˈfɪnɪʃt/ *adjective*
1 completed ▶ *The finished building will be 200 feet high.*
OPPOSITE: **unfinished**
2 no longer able to be successful ▶ *Most top footballers are finished by the time they are 30.*

fir /fɜːʳ/ *noun*
a tree that grows especially in cold countries and keeps its leaves in winter

fire[1] /faɪəʳ/ *noun*
1 heat and flames which burn and destroy things ▶ *a forest fire* (=a fire which destroys a forest) ▶ *a building destroyed by fire*
2 a mass of burning coal or wood, or a piece of apparatus heated by gas or electricity, used to make a room warm ▶ *to sit in front of the fire* ▶ *a gas fire*
3 catch fire to begin to burn
4 on fire burning ▶ *The house is on fire.*
5 set fire to something to make something burn

fire[2] *verb (present participle* ***firing****, past* ***fired****)*
to shoot with a gun

fire alarm /ˈfaɪər əˌlɑːm/ *noun*
a bell that rings to warn you when a building starts to burn

firearm /ˈfaɪərɑːm/ *noun*
a gun

fire brigade /ˈfaɪə brɪˌgeɪd/ *noun*
a group of people whose job is to stop dangerous fires

fire engine /ˈfaɪər ˌendʒɪn/ *noun*
a vehicle used by the FIRE BRIGADE, which has water and special apparatus for stopping fires

fire escape /ˈfaɪər ɪˌskeɪp/ *noun*
a set of stairs on the outside of a building that you use to escape when there is a fire

fire extinguisher /ˈfaɪər ɪkˌstɪŋgwɪʃəʳ/ *noun*
a metal container with water or chemicals inside for putting on a fire to stop it burning

firefighter /ˈfaɪəˌfaɪtəʳ/ *noun*
a person whose job is to stop dangerous fires

fireman /ˈfaɪəmən/ *noun (plural* ***firemen*** */-mən/)*
a man whose job is to stop dangerous fires

fireplace /ˈfaɪəpleɪs/ *noun*
the part of the wall of a room where you have a fire

fire station /ˈfaɪə ˌsteɪʃən/ *noun*
the building where firemen (FIREMAN) are and where the FIRE ENGINE is kept

firewood /ˈfaɪəwʊd/ *noun (no plural)*
wood for burning on a fire

firework /ˈfaɪəwɜːk/ *noun*
a cardboard tube filled with special chemicals, which burns with a loud noise and makes bright lights in the air

firm[1] /fɜːm/ *adjective*
1 not soft ▶ *firm ground*
2 having strong control; not weak ▶ *The teacher was firm with the children.*

firm² *noun*
a group of people who work together in a business; a company

firmly /ˈfɜːmlɪ/ *adverb*
in a way that shows strong control ▶ *She told him firmly that he must wait.*

first /fɜːst/ *adjective, adverb*
1 coming before all the others; earliest ▶ *It's his first year at school.* ▶ *She came first in the competition.* ▶ *We can talk later, but first* (=before that) *we must finish our work.* ▶ *the first day of the month*
2 for the first time; before all the other times ▶ *I first visited America two years ago.*
OPPOSITE (**1** and **2**): **last**
3 first of all (**a**) before doing anything else ▶ *First of all, can you tell me your name, sir?*
(**b**) used when you are talking about something which happened before a lot of other things ▶ *First of all we had dinner, then we went to the cinema, and then we went home.*
4 at first at the start of something ▶ *At first I didn't enjoy my job, but now I like it.*
LOOK AT: **firstly**

first aid /ˌfɜːst ˈeɪd/ *noun (no plural)*
simple help that you give to an ill or a wounded person before the doctor comes

first aid box /ˌfɜːst ˈeɪd bɒks/ *noun (plural **first aid boxes**)*
a box containing medicines, etc. to give to someone who is ill or has an accident

first-class /ˌfɜːst ˈklɑːs/ *adjective*
of the best or most expensive type ▶ *a first-class train ticket*

first floor /ˌfɜːst ˈflɔːʳ/ *noun*
the floor of a building on top of the one which is level with the ground

firsthand /ˌfɜːstˈhænd/ *adjective, adverb*
learned, discovered, etc. directly, not from being told by other people ▶ *officers with firsthand experience of war* ▶ *He saw firsthand the conditions the poorest people were living in.*

firstly /ˈfɜːstlɪ/ *adverb*
a word you use when you are making the first of several points ▶ *Firstly, let me thank everyone for coming here this evening.*
OPPOSITE: **lastly**

> **Firstly** does NOT mean "in the beginning". Use **at first** instead: *At first I didn't like my new job, but then I started to enjoy it.*

first name /ˈfɜːst neɪm/ *noun*
the name that comes before your family name ▶ *"What is your first name, Mrs Jones?" "It's Anne; I'm Mrs Anne Jones."*
COMPARE: **surname**

first person /ˌfɜːst ˈpɜːsən/ *noun*
the first person the form of a verb that you use with "I" and "we"

fish¹ /fɪʃ/ *noun (plural **fish** or **fishes**)*
a creature that lives in water and can swim, and which people eat as food

fish² *verb*
1 to try to catch fish
2 go fishing to go to a place to try and catch fish

fisherman /ˈfɪʃəmən/ *noun (plural **fishermen** /-mən/)*
a person who catches fish for sport or as a job

fishing /ˈfɪʃɪŋ/ *noun (no plural)*
the sport or job of catching fish ▶ *Fishing is an important source of income in this area.*

fishing rod /ˈfɪʃɪŋ ˌrɒd/ *noun*
a long stick with string at the end, used for catching fish

fishmonger /ˈfɪʃmʌŋgəʳ/ *noun*
1 a person who owns or works in a shop that sells fish
2 fishmonger's a shop that sells fish

F

fishy /ˈfɪʃɪ/ *adjective (**fishier, fishiest**)*
seeming bad or dishonest ▶ *The deal sounds a bit fishy to me.*

fist /fɪst/ *noun*
a hand with the fingers closed tightly together ▶ *She shook her fist angrily.*

fit[1] /fɪt/ *adjective*
1 not ill; well and able to be active as a result of doing sport
2 good enough ▶ *This food is not fit **for** your visitors*
OPPOSITE (**1** and **2**): **unfit**

fit[2] *verb (present participle **fitting**, past **fitted**)*
1 to be the right size for someone or something ▶ *The trousers don't fit him; they are too small.*
2 to find space to put someone or something ▶ *We can't fit any more people in here.*
3 to fix something in place ▶ *He fitted a new lock on the door.*

Do not confuse the verbs **fit** (=to be the right size for someone or something) and **suit** (=to be right or suitable for someone or something). Compare *That dress doesn't fit you* (=it's too big/too small) and *That dress doesn't suit you* (=it doesn't look nice).

fitness /ˈfɪtnəs/ *noun (no plural)*
the condition of being healthy and able to run or do physical work for a long time ▶ *He started to go running to improve his fitness.*

five /faɪv/ *adjective, noun*
the number 5

fix /fɪks/ *verb*
1 to put something in place firmly ▶ *He fixed a picture to the wall.*
2 to mend something ▶ *Can you fix my bicycle?*
3 to arrange something ▶ *We have fixed a date for the meeting.* ▶ *to fix a price* (=to agree what it should be)

fixture /ˈfɪkstʃəʳ/ *noun*
1 a piece of furniture or equipment that is fastened inside a house and is sold as part of the house ▶ *bathroom fixtures*
2 a sports event that has been arranged

fizz /fɪz/ *verb*
to make the sound of bubbles of gas bursting ▶ *She uncorked the champagne and it came fizzing out of the bottle.*

fizzle /ˈfɪzəl/ *verb (present participle **fizzling**, past **fizzled**)*
fizzle out to gradually end in a weak or disappointing way ▶ *Their relationship just fizzled out.*

fizzy /ˈfɪzɪ/ *adjective (**fizzier, fizziest**)*
(used about a drink) containing gas ▶ *fizzy water*

flabbergasted /ˈflæbəˌgɑːstɪd/ *adjective*
extremely surprised or shocked

flabby /ˈflæbɪ/ *adjective (**flabbier, flabbiest**)*
having too much soft, loose fat ▶ *I've been getting all flabby since I stopped swimming.*

flag /flæg/ *noun*
a piece of cloth with a special pattern on it, used as the sign of a country, club, etc.

flagpole /ˈflægpəʊl/ *noun*
a tall pole at the top of which you hang a flag

flair /fleəʳ/ *noun (no plural)*
1 a natural ability to do something very well ▶ *Carla's always had a flair **for** languages.*
2 the exciting quality that someone has who does things in an interesting way ▶ *Bates' advertising campaigns showed flair and imagination.*

flak /flæk/ *noun (no plural)*
criticism ▶ *She got a lot of flak for her decision to move abroad.*

flake /fleɪk/ *noun*
a small, thin piece of something that has broken off a larger piece

flame /fleɪm/ *noun*
1 a bright piece of burning gas that you see in a fire
2 in flames burning ▶ *The house was in flames.*

flan /flæn/ *noun*
a PIE with no lid that is filled with fruit, cheese, etc.

flannel /ˈflænl/ *noun*
1 a piece of cloth that you use to wash yourself
2 *(no plural)* a type of soft cloth that is warm ▶ *flannel sheets*

flap[1] /flæp/ *verb (present participle* ***flapping****, past* ***flapped****)*
to move up and down ▶ *The bird flapped its wings.*

flap[2] *noun*
a piece of something that hangs down over an opening ▶ *a flap on a pocket*

flare[1] /fleəʳ/ *(also* ***flare up****) verb (present participle* ***flaring****, past* ***flared****)*
to suddenly start, or become more violent ▶ *Fighting has flared up again in the city.*

flare[2] *noun*
a thing that produces a bright light, used as a sign that someone needs help

flared /fleəd/ *adjective*
(used about trousers or skirts) becoming wider towards the bottom

flash[1] /flæʃ/ *noun (plural* ***flashes****)*
1 a sudden bright light ▶ *a flash of lightning*
2 a light on a camera that you use when you take a photograph inside a building
3 in a flash very quickly ▶ *The ambulance arrived in a flash.*

flash[2] *verb*
(used about a light) to shine for a moment

flashback /ˈflæʃbæk/ *noun*
a part of a film, play, book, etc. that shows something that happened earlier in the story

flashy /ˈflæʃɪ/ *adjective (****flashier****, ****flashiest****)*
too big, bright, or expensive, in a way that you disapprove of ▶ *She was showing off her flashy engagement ring.*

flask /flɑːsk/ *(also* ***vacuum flask****) noun*
a special type of bottle for keeping hot drinks hot, or cold drinks cold ▶ *a flask of coffee*

flat[1] /flæt/ *adjective (****flatter****, ****flattest****)*
1 without hills; not sloping ▶ *flat land* ▶ *a flat roof*
2 (used about tyres) having no air inside

flat[2] *noun*
a number of rooms on one floor of a building, used as a home
SAME MEANING: **apartment**

flat[3] *adverb*
in a straight position along a flat surface ▶ *I have to lie flat on my back to sleep.*

flatly /ˈflætlɪ/ *adverb*
flatly refuse, flatly deny to refuse or deny something in a very firm, strong way ▶ *She flatly refused to let me borrow her car.*

flatmate /ˈflætmeɪt/ *noun*
a person who shares a flat with another person but is not a member of their family

flatten /ˈflætn/ *verb*
to make something flat ▶ *The rain flattened the corn.*

flatter /ˈflætəʳ/ *verb*
to say that someone is better, nicer, etc. than they really are because you are trying to please them

flattering /ˈflætərɪŋ/ *adjective*
making you look more attractive ▶ *a flattering dress*

flattery /ˈflætərɪ/ *noun (no plural)*
nice things that you say to someone because you are trying to please them

flaunt /flɔːnt/ *verb*
to show your wealth, success, beauty, etc. in order to make other people notice it and admire you for it ▶ *I don't like the way he flaunts his money.*

flavour /ˈfleɪvəʳ/ *noun*
a taste ▶ *coffee with a strong flavour*

flavouring /ˈfleɪvərɪŋ/ *noun*
something used to give food or drink a particular taste ▶ *This drink contains artificial flavourings.*

flaw /flɔː/ *noun*
a mistake, mark, or weakness that stops something from being perfect ▶ *She took the material back to the shop because there was a flaw in it.*

flawed /flɔːd/ *adjective*
not perfect because of mistakes, marks, or weaknesses ▶ *a flawed experiment*

flea /fliː/ *noun*
a very small, jumping insect that drinks blood from animals and people

flee /fliː/ *verb (past* ***fled*** */fled/)*
to run away; to escape

fleece /fliːs/ *noun*
the wool of a sheep

fleet /fliːt/ *noun*
a lot of ships or boats together ▶ *a fleet* ***of*** *fishing boats*

flesh /fleʃ/ *noun (no plural)*
the soft part of your body that covers your bones
COMPARE: **skin**

flew /fluː/
the PAST TENSE of the verb **fly**

flexible /ˈfleksəbəl/ *adjective*
1 able to change or be changed easily ▶ *One good thing about the job is the flexible working hours.*
2 easy to bend ▶ *a flexible plastic tube*
OPPOSITE (**1** and **2**): **inflexible**

flick /flɪk/ *verb*
1 to make something small and light go through the air with a quick movement of your finger or hand ▶ *He flicked the fly off his sleeve.*
2 flick something on/off to press a SWITCH in order to start or stop electrical equipment ▶ *I flicked on the TV.*
3 flick through something to look at a book, magazine, etc. quickly ▶ *She was flicking through a magazine.*

flicker /ˈflɪkəʳ/ *verb*
to burn or shine with an unsteady light ▶ *flickering candles*

flight /flaɪt/ *noun*
1 a journey on a plane ▶ *a flight from New York to Paris*
2 a flight of stairs a set of stairs

flight attendant /ˈflaɪt əˌtendənt/ *noun*
a person whose job is to look after passengers on a plane

flimsy /ˈflɪmzɪ/ *adjective (****flimsier, flimsiest****)*
1 not strong, and easily damaged ▶ *Their flimsy boats were destroyed in the storm.*
2 (used about arguments, excuses, etc.) not good or strong enough for you to believe ▶ *The evidence against him is very flimsy.*

flinch /flɪntʃ/ *verb*
to make a sudden, small, backward movement because you are afraid, hurt, or shocked ▶ *The boy flinched when she tried to clean his cuts.*

fling /flɪŋ/ *verb (past* ***flung*** */flʌŋ/)*
to throw something with force

F

flip /flɪp/ *verb (present participle* ***flipping****, past* ***flipped****)*
1 flip over to turn over quickly ▶ *The boat went too fast and flipped over.*
2 *(also* ***flip out****)* to suddenly become very angry ▶ *I just suggested a few changes, and he flipped.*
3 flip something on/off to press a SWITCH in order to start or stop electrical equipment ▶ *He flipped on the light.*
4 flip through something to look at a book, magazine, etc. quickly ▶ *He flipped through his diary to find a free day.*

flip chart /ˈflɪp tʃɑːt/ *noun*
large sheets of paper on a board, used to write things on in a meeting or class

F

flip-flop /ˈflɪp flɒp/ *noun*
a light, open shoe with a V-shaped band to hold your foot

flippant /ˈflɪpənt/ *adjective*
not serious enough about something, in a way that shows a lack of respect ▶ *He was rather flippant* ***about*** *her problems.* ▶ *Don't get flippant with me, young man!*
(adverb: ***flippantly****)*

flipper /ˈflɪpəʳ/ *noun*
1 a broad, flat part of the body which some sea animals have and which helps them to swim
2 a kind of broad, flat, plastic shoe that you wear to help you swim fast underwater

flirt /flɜːt/ *verb*
to behave in a way that is intended to attract sexual attention ▶ *He flirts* ***with*** *all the women.*

float /fləʊt/ *verb*
to stay on the surface of a liquid ▶ *The branch of a tree floated by.*
OPPOSITE: **sink**

flock /flɒk/ *noun*
a group of sheep, goats, or birds
COMPARE: **herd**

flog /flɒg/ *verb (present participle* ***flogging****, past* ***flogged****)*
to beat someone with a whip or stick as a punishment

flood[1] /flʌd/ *noun*
a great quantity of water covering a place that is usually dry ▶ *The floods destroyed many homes.*

flood[2] *verb*
to cover a place with water ▶ *The river flooded the fields.*

flooding /ˈflʌdɪŋ/ *noun (no plural)*
a situation in which an area that is usually dry becomes covered with water ▶ *The heavy rain has caused more flooding.*

floodlight /ˈflʌdlaɪt/ *noun*
a very strong light used at night to show the outside of buildings, or at sports events

floodlit /ˈflʌdlɪt/ *adjective*
lit by floodlights ▶ *floodlit tennis courts*

floor /flɔːʳ/ *noun*
1 the part of a room that you walk on ▶ *a wooden floor*
2 all the rooms on the same level of a building ▶ *We live on the third floor* (=three floors above the ground).

floorboard /ˈflɔːbɔːd/ *noun*
a long, narrow piece of wood used to make floors

flooring /ˈflɔːrɪŋ/ *noun (no plural)*
a material used to make or cover floors ▶ *They chose wooden flooring for the kitchen.*

flop[1] /flɒp/ *verb (present participle* ***flopping****, past* ***flopped****)*
1 to sit or fall down quickly, especially because you are tired ▶ *Sarah flopped down into an armchair.*
2 (used about films, plays, plans, etc.) to be unsuccessful ▶ *The musical flopped on Broadway.*
3 to hang down loosely ▶ *Her hair flopped across her face.*

flop² *noun*
something that is unsuccessful ▶ *The show's first series was a complete flop.*

floppy /ˈflɒpɪ/ *adjective* (***floppier, floppiest***)
soft and hanging loosely down ▶ *a dog with long, floppy ears*

floppy disk /ˌflɒpɪ ˈdɪsk/ *noun*
a piece of plastic that you can put into a computer and on which information can be stored
COMPARE: **hard disk**

floral /ˈflɔːrəl/ *adjective*
made of flowers, or decorated with flowers ▶ *floral wallpaper*

florist /ˈflɒrɪst/ *noun*
1 a person who sells flowers
2 florist's a shop that sells flowers

flounder /ˈflaʊndəʳ/ *verb*
to have great difficulty doing something, especially because you do not know what to do ▶ *Some of the younger students seemed to be floundering a bit.*

flour /flaʊəʳ/ *noun (no plural)*
fine powder made from wheat, used for making bread, etc.

flourish /ˈflʌrɪʃ/ *verb*
to grow well ▶ *The garden is flourishing.*

flow¹ /fləʊ/ *verb*
(used about liquids) to move along ▶ *The river flows through York before it reaches the sea.*

flow² *noun (no plural)*
a smooth movement ▶ *a flow of air*

flower /ˈflaʊəʳ/ *noun*
the part of a plant which holds the seeds and which is usually pretty and brightly coloured ▶ *a vase of flowers*

flowerbed /ˈflaʊəbed/ *noun*
an area of earth with flowers planted in it

flowerpot /ˈflaʊəpɒt/ *noun*
a container in which you grow plants

flowery /ˈflaʊərɪ/ *adjective*
decorated with pictures of flowers ▶ *a flowery pattern*

flown /fləʊn/
the PAST PARTICIPLE of the verb **fly**

flu /fluː/ *(also **influenza**) noun (no plural)*
a common illness of the nose and throat which is like a bad cold but is more serious ▶ *The whole team has got flu.*

fluctuate /ˈflʌktʃʊeɪt/ *verb (present participle **fluctuating**, past **fluctuated**)*
to change very often, especially from a high level to a low level and back again ▶ *The price of copper fluctuated wildly.*

fluency /ˈfluːənsɪ/ *noun (no plural)*
the ability to speak a language very well

fluent /ˈfluːənt/ *adjective*
speaking a language very well ▶ *He is fluent in English. (adverb: **fluently**)*

fluff /flʌf/ *noun (no plural)*
soft, fine bits that come off animals, wool, etc.

fluffy /ˈflʌfɪ/ *adjective* (***fluffier, fluffiest***)
made of or covered with something soft such as fur ▶ *a fluffy toy*

fluid¹ /ˈfluːɪd/ *noun*
a liquid

fluid² *adjective*
liquid; not solid; able to flow

fluke /fluːk/ *noun*
something that only happens because of luck ▶ *The goal was a complete fluke.*

flung /flʌŋ/
the PAST TENSE and PAST PARTICIPLE of the verb **fling**

fluorescent /flʊəˈresənt/ *adjective*
1 fluorescent light a light that consists of a long, glass tube containing a special gas

F

2 (used about colours) very bright

fluoride /ˈflʊəraɪd/ *noun (no plural)*
a chemical that is added to water and TOOTHPASTE to help protect people's teeth

flush /flʌʃ/ *verb*
1 to clean a TOILET by making water go down it ▶ *to flush a toilet*
2 to become red in the face because you are ashamed, angry, etc. ▶ *He flushed at her suggestion.*

flushed /flʌʃt/ *adjective*
having a red face ▶ *She looked hot and flushed.*

flustered /ˈflʌstəd/ *adjective*
confused because you are nervous or trying to do things too quickly ▶ *She got flustered and dropped her papers.*

F

flute /fluːt/ *noun*
a musical instrument like a pipe, that you hold to one side of your mouth and blow

flutter /ˈflʌtəʳ/ *verb*
to move in the air quickly and in different directions ▶ *dead leaves fluttering to the ground* ▶ *a flag fluttering in the wind*

fly[1] /flaɪ/ *verb (past tense **flew** /fluː/, past participle **flown** /fləʊn/)*
1 to move through the air ▶ *Birds were flying above the houses.* ▶ *The plane flew from Paris to Rome.*
2 to go quickly ▶ *She flew* (=ran) *out of the house.*

fly[2] *noun (plural **flies**)*
a small, flying insect

flying /ˈflaɪ-ɪŋ/ *noun (no plural)*
the activity of travelling by plane or being a pilot ▶ *fear of flying*

flying saucer /ˌflaɪ-ɪŋ ˈsɔːsəʳ/ *noun*
a SPACESHIP which is round and flat and is shown in pictures and stories

flyover /ˈflaɪəʊvəʳ/ *noun*
a part of a road that goes up and crosses over another road

FM /ˌef ˈem/ *noun (no plural)*
FREQUENCY MODULATION; a system used for broadcasting radio programmes

foal /fəʊl/ *noun*
a baby horse

foam /fəʊm/ *noun (no plural)*
the white substance that you sometimes see on top of water

focus[1] /ˈfəʊkəs/ *verb (present participle **focusing** or **focussing**, past **focused** or **focussed**)*
1 to give all your attention to a particular thing ▶ *In his speech he focused **on** the economy.*
2 to turn the LENS on a camera, TELESCOPE, etc. so that you can see something clearly

focus[2] *noun*
1 *(no plural)* the person or subject that gets most attention ▶ *traditional education, with its focus **on** basic reading and writing skills* ▶ *She loves being the focus of attention.*
2 in focus (used about photographs) clear
3 out of focus (used about photographs) not clear

foetus /ˈfiːtəs/ *noun (plural **foetuses**)*
a human or an animal that is growing inside its mother

fog /fɒg/ *noun (no plural)*
thick cloud close to the ground that makes it difficult to see
COMPARE: **mist**

foggy /ˈfɒgɪ/ *adjective (**foggier**, **foggiest**)*
having a lot of thick cloud close to the ground so that you cannot see very well ▶ *a foggy day*
COMPARE: **misty**

foil /fɔɪl/ *noun (no plural)*
very thin metal used for covering and wrapping food

fold[1] /fəʊld/ *verb*
1 to turn part of something over another part ▶ *She folded the letter*

so that it would fit into her bag.
OPPOSITE: **unfold**
2 fold your arms to cross your arms over your chest so that one hand rests on top of one arm and the other hand rests underneath the other arm
3 fold something up to fold something several times so that it becomes smaller ▶ *She folded up the sheets.*

fold² *noun*
a part of something that has been folded over another part

folder /ˈfəʊldəʳ/ *noun*
a cardboard cover, like the cover of a book, for holding papers, etc.

foliage /ˈfəʊli-ɪdʒ/ *noun (no plural)*
the leaves of a plant ▶ *She arranged the flowers and foliage in a vase.*

folk¹ /fəʊk/ *plural noun*
people ▶ *The old folk sat and talked.*

folk² *adjective*
typical of the ordinary people of a particular country or area ▶ *folk music* ▶ *a folk song*

folks /fəʊks/ *plural noun*
1 your parents or family ▶ *My girlfriend has never met my folks.*
2 used to talk to a group of people in an informal and friendly way ▶ *Hi, folks – it's good to see you all.*

follow /ˈfɒləʊ/ *verb*
1 to come or go after someone or something ▶ *He left the room, and I followed.* ▶ *Follow me.* ▶ *Their success follows years of hard work.*
2 to go in the same direction as a road, river, etc. ▶ *Follow the road as far as the church.*
3 to understand something ▶ *I didn't follow what you were saying.*
4 to do what someone tells you to do ▶ *to follow instructions*
5 follow in someone's footsteps to do the same as someone else did in the past ▶ *He's following in his father's footsteps and training to be a doctor.*

follower /ˈfɒləʊəʳ/ *noun*
a person who supports someone or believes in something ▶ *a follower of Karl Marx*

following /ˈfɒləʊɪŋ/ *adjective*
the following day, week, year, etc. the next day, week, year, etc. ▶ *We leave on Friday and return the following Monday.*

fond of /ˈfɒnd ɒv/ *adjective*
liking someone or something ▶ *I'm very fond of you* (=I like you very much).

food /fuːd/ *noun (no plural)*
things that you eat ▶ *He had had no food for two days.*

food poisoning /ˈfuːd ˌpɔɪzənɪŋ/ *noun (no plural)*
an illness that is caused by eating food containing harmful BACTERIA (=small creatures that spread disease) ▶ *I got food poisoning from eating a beefburger.*

fool¹ /fuːl/ *noun*
1 a silly or stupid person
SAME MEANING: **idiot**
2 make a fool of yourself to behave in a way which makes other people think you are silly

fool² *verb*
1 to trick or deceive someone ▶ *He fooled me into giving him money.*
2 fool about to behave in a silly way ▶ *Stop fooling about!*

foolish /ˈfuːlɪʃ/ *adjective*
not reasonable; silly ▶ *foolish behaviour*

foolproof /ˈfuːlpruːf/ *adjective*
certain to be successful ▶ *a foolproof plan*

foot /fʊt/ *noun (plural **feet** /fiːt/)*
1 the part of your body that you stand on
2 the bottom of something ▶ *the foot of a hill*
3 a measure of length equal to 12 inches ▶ *The man was 6 feet tall.*

4 on foot walking ▶ *They made the journey on foot.*

football /ˈfʊtbɔːl/ *noun*
1 *(no plural)* a game played by two teams who each try to kick a ball into a net
2 a ball filled with air, used for playing the game of football

footballer /ˈfʊtbɔːləʳ/ *noun*
a person whose job is to play football

football pitch /ˈfʊtbɔːl ˌpɪtʃ/ *noun (plural* ***football pitches****)*
a piece of land where people play the game of football

footnote /ˈfʊtnəʊt/ *noun*
a note at the bottom of a page in a book, that gives more information about something on that page

F

footpath /ˈfʊtpɑːθ/ *noun (plural* ***footpaths*** */ˈfʊtpɑːðz/)*
a narrow path for people to walk on, especially in the country

footprint /ˈfʊtprɪnt/ *noun*
the mark left by a person's foot ▶ *footprints in the snow*

footstep /ˈfʊtstep/ *noun*
the sound of someone walking ▶ *I heard footsteps behind me.*

footwear /ˈfʊtweəʳ/ *noun (no plural)*
things that you wear on your feet, such as shoes or boots ▶ *The store has a big footwear department.*

for /fəʳ; *strong* fɔːʳ/ *preposition*
1 meant to be used in this way ▶ *a knife for cutting bread*
2 meant to be given to or used by someone or something ▶ *Here's a letter for you.* ▶ *I'm making some curtains for the bedroom.* ▶ *a school for girls*
3 showing how far or how long ▶ *She has lived in this town for many years.* ▶ *I waited for three hours.*
LOOK AT: **since**
4 towards a place ▶ *the train for London*
5 at a price of ▶ *She bought the dress for £5.*
6 with the meaning of ▶ *What is the word for "tree" in your language?*
7 in favour of someone or something ▶ *The government is for the plan.*
8 by or at a particular time ▶ *We'll be home for Christmas.*
9 used to show the reason for something ▶ *He won a prize for singing.* ▶ *The government is working for peace.* ▶ *They were punished for their bad behaviour.*
10 used to show who is helped by someone or something ▶ *She did some work for her father.*
11 used to show who a feeling is about ▶ *I'm very pleased for you.*

forbid /fəˈbɪd/ *verb (present participle* ***forbidding****, past tense* ***forbade*** */fəˈbæd/, past participle* ***forbidden*** */fəˈbɪdn/)*
to tell someone they must not do something ▶ *You are forbidden to smoke in school.*
OPPOSITE: **allow**
COMPARE: **ban**

force¹ /fɔːs/ *verb (present participle* ***forcing****, past* ***forced****)*
1 to make someone do something they do not want to do ▶ *He forced me to see a doctor.*
2 to use your strength to make something move ▶ *to force a door open* (=make it open by pushing or pulling)

force² *noun*
1 *(no plural)* power or strength ▶ *to use force to make someone do something* ▶ *the force of an explosion*
2 a group of people like the army, etc. who are trained to fight or work together ▶ *enemy forces* ▶ *the police force*
3 by force using violence, power, or strength

forced /fɔːst/ *adjective*
1 (used about a smile or laugh) given because you feel it is necessary, and not because you really mean it
2 done suddenly because a situation makes it necessary ▶ *The plane had to make a forced landing in a field.*

forceful /ˈfɔːsfəl/ *adjective*
powerful and strong ▶ *a forceful personality* ▶ *forceful arguments (adverb:* ***forcefully****)*

forearm /ˈfɔːrɑːm/ *noun*
the part of your arm between your hand and your elbow ▶ *She has a cut on her left forearm.*

forecast /ˈfɔːkɑːst/ *noun*
something that says what you think will happen in future ▶ *a weather forecast*

forefather /ˈfɔːˌfɑːðəʳ/ *noun*
a person in your family who lived a long time before you were born ▶ *the time when our forefathers arrived in America*

forefront /ˈfɔːfrʌnt/ *noun*
be at the forefront of something to do more than other people in developing something new ▶ *a British company that was at the forefront of computer design*

foregone conclusion /ˌfɔːgɒn kənˈkluːʒən/ *noun*
a situation where the result is certain ▶ *The election result was a foregone conclusion.*

foreground /ˈfɔːgraʊnd/ *noun*
the foreground the part of a picture, photograph, etc. nearest to you

forehead /ˈfɔːhed, ˈfɒrəd/ *noun*
the top part of your face, above your eyes but below your hair

foreign /ˈfɒrɪn/ *adjective*
of or from a country that is not your country ▶ *a foreign language*

foreigner /ˈfɒrɪnəʳ/ *noun*
a person who comes from a country that is not your country

foreman /ˈfɔːmən/ *noun (plural* ***foremen*** */-mən/)*
a man whose job is to tell a group of workers what to do

foremost /ˈfɔːməʊst/ *adjective*
the most famous or important ▶ *the foremost scientist of his generation*

forensic /fəˈrensɪk/ *adjective*
connected with the use of scientific methods to solve crimes ▶ *forensic evidence*

foresee /fɔːˈsiː/ *verb (past tense* ***foresaw*** */-ˈsɔː/, past participle* ***foreseen*** */-ˈsiːn/)*
to expect that something will happen in the future ▶ *I don't foresee any problems with the new system.*

foresight /ˈfɔːsaɪt/ *noun (no plural)*
the ability to imagine what might happen in the future, and consider this in your plans ▶ *Lucy was glad she had had the foresight to keep her money separate from her passport.*

forest /ˈfɒrɪst/ *noun*
an area where a lot of trees grow together

forever /fərˈevəʳ/ *adverb*
always; for all time in the future ▶ *I shall love you forever.*

foreword /ˈfɔːwɜːd/ *noun*
a short piece of writing, at the beginning of a book, about the book or its writer

forgave /fəˈgeɪv/
the PAST TENSE of the verb **forgive**

forge /fɔːdʒ/ *verb (present participle* ***forging****, past* ***forged****)*
to make a copy of something in order to deceive people ▶ *He was sent to prison for forging money.*

forgery /ˈfɔːdʒərɪ/ *noun*
1 *(no plural)* the crime of making a copy of something in order to deceive people ▶ *to go to prison for forgery*
2 *(plural* ***forgeries****)* a copy which is intended to deceive people

F

forget /fə'get/ *verb (present participle **forgetting**, past tense **forgot** /fə'gɒt/, past participle **forgotten** /fə'gɒtn/)*
not to remember something ► *"Did you post the letter?" "No, I forgot."* ► *She forgot to post the letter.*
OPPOSITE: **remember**

> If you want to say **where** you have left something, always use **leave**, not **forget**: *Oh no! I've forgotten my bag!* ► *I've left my bag on the bus.*

forgetful /fə'getfəl/ *adjective*
often forgetting things

forgive /fə'gɪv/ *verb (present participle **forgiving**, past tense **forgave** /fə'geɪv/, past participle **forgiven** /fə'gɪvən/)*
to stop being angry with someone ► *Please forgive me – I didn't mean to be rude.*

forgot /fə'gɒt/
the PAST TENSE of the verb **forget**

forgotten /fə'gɒtn/
the PAST PARTICIPLE of the verb **forget**

fork¹ /fɔːk/ *noun*
1 an instrument with a handle and two or more points at the end, which you use to eat food
2 a place where a road or a river divides into two ► *a fork **in** the road*

fork² *verb*
(used about a road or river) to divide into two

forlorn /fə'lɔːn/ *adjective*
sad and lonely ► *a forlorn figure sitting on a park bench*

form¹ /fɔːm/ *noun*
1 a school class ► *Which form are you in?* ► *the sixth form*
2 a shape ► *a birthday cake in the form of the number 18*
3 a type of something ► *a new form **of** government*
4 a piece of printed paper on which you have to write things or answer questions about yourself

form² *verb*
1 to start to appear or exist ► *These rocks were formed 4000 million years ago.*
2 to make or produce something ► *to form a plan*
3 to make a particular shape ► *The children formed a circle* (=stood together in the shape of a circle).
4 to start an organization or group ► *to form a club*

formal /'fɔːməl/ *adjective*
suitable for an official or important occasion ► *a formal letter* ► *formal clothes*
OPPOSITE: **informal**

formality /fɔː'mælətɪ/ *noun (plural **formalities**)*
an official part of a process ► *After going through the usual formalities, we got on the plane.*

format¹ /'fɔːmæt/ *noun*
the way that something is organized or designed ► *This week the show has a new format.*

format² *verb (present participle **formatting**, past **formatted**)*
to organize the space on a computer DISK so that you can store information on it

formation /fɔː'meɪʃən/ *noun (no plural)*
the process during which something starts to exist or develop ► *the formation of ice crystals*

former¹ /'fɔːməʳ/ *noun*
the former the first of two people or things which have just been mentioned ► *Britain has agreements with both Germany and Italy, but its agreement with the former* (=Germany) *will soon change.*
OPPOSITE: **the latter**

former² *adjective*
at an earlier time but not any more

▶ *the former president of the United States* ▶ *her former husband (adverb: **formerly**)*

formidable /ˈfɔːmɪdəbəl/ *adjective*
powerful and slightly frightening ▶ *a formidable opponent*

formula /ˈfɔːmjʊlə/ *noun (plural **formulas** or **formulae** /ˈfɔːmjʊliː/)*
a list of the substances used to make something ▶ *the secret formula for the new drug*

formulate /ˈfɔːmjʊleɪt/ *verb (present participle **formulating**, past **formulated**)*
to develop a plan and decide all the details ▶ *He soon formulated a plan of escape.*

fort /fɔːt/ *noun*
a strong building where soldiers lived in the past and where people could go to be safe from attack

forthcoming /ˌfɔːθˈkʌmɪŋ/ *adjective*
1 happening soon ▶ *the forthcoming election*
2 given or offered to someone ▶ *If more money is not forthcoming, we'll have to close the theatre.*
3 willing to give information ▶ *Michael wasn't very forthcoming **about** his plans.*

forthright /ˈfɔːθraɪt/ *adjective*
saying what you think honestly and directly ▶ *Bill answered in his usual forthright manner.*

fortieth /ˈfɔːtɪ-əθ/ *adjective*
40th

fortnight /ˈfɔːtnaɪt/ *noun*
two weeks ▶ *We're going on holiday for a fortnight* (=we will be away for two weeks). ▶ *We're going on holiday in a fortnight* (=we leave two weeks after today).
LOOK AT: **time**

fortnightly /ˈfɔːtnaɪtlɪ/ *adverb*
happening once every two weeks

fortress /ˈfɔːtrəs/ *noun (plural **fortresses**)*
a big, strong building that people use for defending a place

fortunate /ˈfɔːtʃənət/ *adjective*
lucky *(adverb: **fortunately**)*
OPPOSITE: **unfortunate**

fortune /ˈfɔːtʃən/ *noun*
1 *(no plural)* luck or chance ▶ *to have good fortune* (=to be lucky)
2 a very large amount of money ▶ *He made a fortune by selling houses.*
3 tell someone's fortune to tell someone what is going to happen to them in the future

forty /ˈfɔːtɪ/ *adjective, noun*
the number 40

forward /ˈfɔːwəd/ *adjective*
1 in the direction that is in front of you ▶ *a forward movement*
OPPOSITE: **backward**
2 look forward to something to think about something that is going to happen and feel pleased about it ▶ *I'm looking forward to meeting you.*

forwards /ˈfɔːwədz/ *adverb*
in the direction that is in front of you ▶ *to move forwards*
OPPOSITE: **backwards**

fossil /ˈfɒsəl/ *noun*
a part of an animal or a plant that lived thousands of years ago and that has turned hard like rock

foster[1] /ˈfɒstəʳ/ *verb*
1 to encourage a feeling or skill to develop ▶ *We want to foster a friendly atmosphere in the office.*
2 to take care of someone else's child for a period of time, without becoming the child's legal parent ▶ *They fostered two children for nearly a year.*

foster[2] *adjective*
1 foster parents people who foster someone else's child
2 foster children children who are fostered

F

fought /fɔːt/
the PAST TENSE and PAST PARTICIPLE of the verb **fight**

foul /faʊl/ *adjective*
unpleasant and dirty ▶ *a foul smell*

found[1] /faʊnd/
the PAST TENSE and PAST PARTICIPLE of the verb **find**

found[2] *verb*
to start ▶ *He founded the school in 1954.*

foundation /faʊnˈdeɪʃən/ *noun*
1 something basic or important on which something else is based ▶ *Reading and writing are the foundations **of** learning.*
2 an organization that gives money for special purposes ▶ *The kit was paid for by the AIDS Foundation.*

F

foundations /faʊnˈdeɪʃənz/ *plural noun*
the parts of the walls of a building that are under the ground

founder /ˈfaʊndəʳ/ *noun*
a person who starts an organization ▶ *one of the original founders of the company*

fountain /ˈfaʊntən/ *noun*
water thrown high into the air from a pipe, e.g. in a garden or park

fountain pen /ˈfaʊntən pen/ *noun*
a pen that is filled with ink

four /fɔːʳ/ *adjective, noun*
the number 4

fourteen /fɔːˈtiːn/ *adjective, noun*
the number 14

fourteenth /fɔːˈtiːnθ/ *adjective*
14th

fourth /fɔːθ/ *adjective*
4th

fowl /faʊl/ *noun*
a bird, usually one that is kept for food

fox /fɒks/ *noun (plural **foxes**)*
a wild animal like a dog, with a thick tail

foyer /ˈfɔɪeɪ/ *noun*
a room at the entrance to a hotel, a theatre, or some other large building ▶ *I'll meet you in the foyer of the nightclub.*

fraction /ˈfrækʃən/ *noun*
a division or part of a number, e.g. $^1/_4$, $^1/_2$

fracture[1] /ˈfræktʃəʳ/ *verb (present participle **fracturing**, past **fractured**)*
to crack or break ▶ *to fracture your skull*

fracture[2] *noun*
a crack or break

fragile /ˈfrædʒaɪl/ *adjective*
able to be broken easily

fragment /ˈfrægmənt/ *noun*
a small piece broken off something ▶ *a fragment **of** glass*

fragrance /ˈfreɪgrəns/ *noun*
a sweet or pleasant smell ▶ *the fragrance of flowers*
SAME MEANING: **perfume**

fragrant /ˈfreɪgrənt/ *adjective*
having a sweet or pleasant smell
COMPARE: **smelly**

frail /freɪl/ *adjective*
weak and not healthy

frame[1] /freɪm/ *noun*
1 the bars around which a building, car, etc. is made ▶ *a building with a steel frame* (=with steel supports inside it) ▶ *a tent frame*
2 a piece of wood or metal round the edges of a picture, window, mirror, etc.

frame[2] *verb (present participle **framing**, past **framed**)*
to put a wooden or metal frame around the edges of a picture

frames /freɪmz/ *plural noun*
the part of a pair of glasses that holds the two pieces of glass ▶ *He sat on my glasses and broke the frames.*

framework /ˈfreɪmwɜːk/ *noun*
1 a set of rules, facts, or beliefs that people use to make plans or decisions ▶ *We must work within the framework of the existing budget.*
2 the bars around which a building, car, etc. is made

frank /fræŋk/ *adjective*
honest and not afraid to say what is true ▶ *a frank talk*

frankly /ˈfræŋklɪ/ *adverb*
1 used when you want to show that you are giving your true opinion about something, even if you know other people will think you are wrong ▶ *Frankly, I think you are wasting your time.*
2 in an honest way ▶ *They talked very frankly.*

frantic /ˈfræntɪk/ *adjective*
1 hurrying in a way that is not organized ▶ *There was a frantic rush for tickets.*
2 very anxious or upset ▶ *We've been frantic with worry – where have you been?*
*(adverb: **frantically**)*

fraud /frɔːd/ *noun (no plural)*
the crime of deceiving people, especially in order to get money

fraught /frɔːt/ *adjective*
1 fraught with problems/difficulty/danger full of problems, difficulty, or danger
2 very anxious or worried ▶ *The survivors were met at the airport by fraught relatives.*

frayed /freɪd/ *adjective*
(used about clothes or material) having loose threads at the edges ▶ *a frayed dress*

freak /friːk/ *noun*
a person or an animal that is very strange

freckle /ˈfrekəl/ *noun*
a very small, brown spot on a person's skin

free[1] /friː/ *adjective*
1 able to do what you like ▶ *You are free to leave at any time.*
2 not in prison
3 not working or busy ▶ *Are you free this evening?*
4 not costing any money ▶ *a free ticket*
5 free of charge not costing any money ▶ *Our help is free of charge.*
6 free time time when you are not busy or working and can do what you want
7 set someone free to allow someone to leave a prison

free[2] *verb (past **freed**)*
to let a person or an animal leave a place where they have been kept as a prisoner ▶ *They freed the birds from the cages.*

free[3] *adverb*
1 without having to pay any money ▶ *Children under 12 travel free.*
2 not controlled by someone or held in a particular position ▶ *He held my arm, but I pulled it free.*

freedom /ˈfriːdəm/ *noun (no plural)*
being able to do what you want without being a prisoner and without being under another person's control

freelance /ˈfriːlɑːns/ *adjective, adverb*
working independently for several different organizations ▶ *a freelance journalist* ▶ *How long have you been working freelance?*

freely /ˈfriːlɪ/ *adverb*
1 without anyone trying to control you or prevent you from doing something ▶ *We encourage our students to speak freely.* ▶ *People can now travel freely across the border.*
2 freely admit/acknowledge to agree that something is true ▶ *I freely admit I made a bad choice.*

free speech /ˌfriː ˈspiːtʃ/ *noun (no plural)*

the right to express your opinions ▶ *If the government believes in free speech, why does it try to stop us protesting?*

freeze /friːz/ *verb (present participle* ***freezing****, past tense* ***froze*** */frəʊz/, past participle* ***frozen*** */ˈfrəʊzən/)*
to become very cold and change from a liquid into a solid ▶ *When water freezes, it becomes ice.*

freezer /ˈfriːzəʳ/ *noun*
a machine that keeps food very cold, so that it stays fresh for a long time

freezing /ˈfriːzɪŋ/ *adjective*
very cold ▶ *I'm freezing!* ▶ *It's freezing outside.*

freezing point /ˈfriːzɪŋ ˌpɔɪnt/ *noun (no plural)*
the temperature at which water changes to become ice

F

freight /freɪt/ *noun (no plural)*
goods that are being taken from one place to another by train, road, plane, or ship ▶ *a freight train*

French fry /ˌfrentʃ ˈfraɪ/ *noun (plural* ***French fries****)*
a long, thin piece of potato cooked in oil
SAME MEANING: **chip**

frenzy /ˈfrenzɪ/ *noun (no plural)*
a situation in which you are so anxious, excited, etc. that you are unable to control your behaviour ▶ *In a frenzy, Brady began kicking and punching the police officers.*

frequency /ˈfriːkwənsɪ/ *noun*
1 *(no plural)* the number of times that something happens, or the fact that it happens a lot ▶ *Her headaches have increased in frequency.*
2 *(plural* ***frequencies****)* the rate at which a sound or light WAVE is repeated ▶ *The human ear cannot hear sounds of very high frequency.*

frequent /ˈfriːkwənt/ *adjective*
happening often ▶ *They make frequent trips abroad. (adverb:* ***frequently****)*
OPPOSITE: **infrequent**

fresh /freʃ/ *adjective*
1 (used about food) in good condition because of being picked, killed, etc. a short time ago ▶ *fresh fish* ▶ *fresh vegetables*
2 new and different ▶ *Write your answer on a fresh sheet of paper.*
3 fresh air pleasant, cool air outside, not in a building ▶ *I'm going for a walk to get some fresh air.*

freshly /ˈfreʃlɪ/ *adverb*
very recently ▶ *the smell of freshly baked bread*

friction /ˈfrɪkʃən/ *noun (no plural)*
1 a situation in which people disagree with each other and argue in an unfriendly way ▶ *There seemed to be some friction between Joe and Pete.*
2 the action of one surface rubbing against another ▶ *Friction produces heat.*

Friday /ˈfraɪdeɪ, -dɪ/ *noun*
the sixth day of the week

fridge /frɪdʒ/ *(also* ***refrigerator****) noun*
a type of electric cupboard that you keep in your kitchen and use for keeping food cool and fresh

fried[1] /fraɪd/
the PAST TENSE of the verb **fry**

fried[2] *adjective*
cooked in hot oil ▶ *fried eggs*

friend /frend/ *noun*
1 a person who you know well and who you like and trust ▶ *He is my friend.* ▶ *He is a friend of mine.* ▶ *We are friends.*
COMPARE: **acquaintance**
2 make friends with someone to start to know someone and be their friend

friendly /ˈfrendlɪ/ *adjective (****friendlier, friendliest****)*
behaving in a nice, kind way like a friend
OPPOSITE: **unfriendly**

friendship /ˈfrendʃɪp/ *noun*
the state of being friends ► *The boys have had a long friendship.*

fries /fraɪz/ *plural noun*
French fries ► *I'll have a cheeseburger and fries.*
SAME MEANING: **chips**

fright /fraɪt/ *noun (no plural)*
1 a feeling of fear
2 give someone a fright to make someone feel afraid suddenly

frighten /ˈfraɪtn/ *verb*
to make someone afraid ► *The noise frightened me.*
SAME MEANING: **scare**

frightened /ˈfraɪtnd/ *adjective*
afraid ► *He's frightened **of** dogs.*
SAME MEANING: **scared**

frightening /ˈfraɪtnɪŋ/ *adjective*
making you afraid ► *a frightening film*

frill /frɪl/ *noun*
a decoration on the edge of a piece of cloth, made from another piece of cloth with many small folds in it

frilly /ˈfrɪlɪ/ *adjective (**frillier, frilliest**)*
decorated with many folds of cloth around the edges ► *a frilly blouse*

fringe /frɪndʒ/ *noun*
1 hair that goes in a line across the top of your face, above your eyes
2 threads that hang in a straight line around the edge of something

frivolity /frɪˈvɒlətɪ/ *noun (plural **frivolities**)*
behaviour that is not serious or sensible ► *My father disapproves of frivolity.*

frivolous /ˈfrɪvələs/ *adjective*
behaving in a silly way when you should be serious or sensible ► *She kept making frivolous comments.*

frizzy /ˈfrɪzɪ/ *adjective (**frizzier, frizziest**)*
(used about hair) curled very tightly ► *My hair's gone all frizzy.*

fro /frəʊ/ *adverb*
to and fro first in one direction and then in the opposite direction ► *He was walking to and fro in front of the house.*

frock /frɒk/ *noun*
a dress for a girl or woman

frog /frɒg/ *noun*
a small brown or green jumping animal that lives in water and on land

frogman /ˈfrɒgmən/ *noun (plural **frogmen** /-mən/)*
a person whose job is to work underwater wearing a rubber suit and special equipment for breathing ► *Frogmen are searching for the body in the river.*

from /frəm; *strong* frɒm/ *preposition*
1 starting at or coming from a place; starting at a time ► *The train goes from Paris to Rome.* ► *He's from Spain.* ► *from Monday to Friday*
2 given or sent by someone ► *This letter is from my uncle.*
3 used to show how far away something is ► *a town 10 miles from here*
4 out of a place ► *books from the cupboard*
5 away ► *Her children were taken from her.*
6 using something ► *Bread is made from flour.*
7 because of something ► *She was crying from the pain.*

front[1] /frʌnt/ *noun*
1 the side opposite the back ► *sitting at the front **of** the class*
OPPOSITE: **back, rear**
2 in front of at the front of someone or something ► *I'll meet you in front of the cinema.*

front[2] *adjective*
at the front of something ► *the front seat of a car*
OPPOSITE: **back**

front door /ˌfrʌnt ˈdɔːʳ/ *noun*
the door at the front of the house, that you use when you go in

F

frontier /ˈfrʌntɪəʳ/ *noun*
the dividing line between two countries
SAME MEANING: **border**

frost /frɒst/ *noun (no plural)*
frozen water that stays on every outdoor surface in cold weather
▶ *The trees were white with frost.*

frostbite /ˈfrɒstbaɪt/ *noun (no plural)*
a medical condition in which your fingers or toes become frozen and badly damaged

frosty /ˈfrɒstɪ/ *adjective (**frostier, frostiest**)*
very cold or covered with FROST ▶ *It was a frosty morning.*

froth /frɒθ/ *noun (no plural)*
a lot of small BUBBLES on top of a liquid ▶ *He blew the froth off his coffee.*

frown /fraʊn/ *verb*
to look as if you are angry or thinking very hard by bringing your EYEBROWS together so that lines appear at the top of your face

froze /frəʊz/
the PAST TENSE of the verb **freeze**

frozen[1] /ˈfrəʊzən/
the PAST PARTICIPLE of the verb **freeze**

frozen[2] *adjective*
preserved by being kept very cold ▶ *I bought a bag of frozen peas.*

frozen food /ˌfrəʊzən ˈfuːd/ *noun (no plural)*
food that you buy after it has been frozen, and which you keep in a FREEZER

fruit /fruːt/ *noun (no plural)*
the part of a plant that carries the seeds; it is often sweet and good to eat ▶ *Would you like some fruit – an apple or an orange?* ▶ *a bowl of fruit*

fruitful /ˈfruːtfəl/ *adjective*
producing good results ▶ *Was it a fruitful meeting?*

fruit juice /ˈfruːt dʒuːs/ *noun (no plural)*
a drink made by pressing fruit and getting liquid from it

fruitless /ˈfruːtləs/ *adjective*
failing to produce good results, especially after much effort ▶ *They spent three fruitless weeks looking for the body.*

fruity /ˈfruːtɪ/ *adjective (**fruitier, fruitiest**)*
tasting or smelling strongly of fruit
▶ *This wine has a fruity smell.*

frustrate /frʌˈstreɪt/ *verb (present participle **frustrating**, past **frustrated**)*
to make you feel impatient or angry because you are unable to do what you want to do ▶ *It frustrates me when she doesn't listen.*

frustrating /frʌˈstreɪtɪŋ/ *adjective*
making you feel impatient or angry because you are unable to do what you want to do ▶ *They keep sending me the wrong forms – it's very frustrating.*

frustration /frʌˈstreɪʃən/ *noun*
the feeling of being impatient or angry because you are unable to do what you want to do ▶ *She threw her pen on the floor in frustration.*

fry /fraɪ/ *verb (past **fried**)*
to cook something in hot oil ▶ *to fry an egg*

frying pan /ˈfraɪ-ɪŋ ˌpæn/ *noun*
a wide, flat pan used for cooking food in hot oil

ft
a short way of writing the words **foot** or **feet** when they are used for measuring things ▶ *He's 6ft* (=6 feet) *tall.*

fuel /ˈfjuːəl/ *noun*
a substance that burns to give heat, light, or power ▶ *Gas and coal are fuels.*

fugitive /ˈfjuːdʒɪtɪv/ *noun*
a person who has escaped and is trying to avoid being caught, especially by the police ► *a fugitive from justice*

fulfil /fʊlˈfɪl/ *verb (present participle* ***fulfilling****, past* ***fulfilled****)*
to do what you have promised or are expected to do ► *to fulfil a promise* ► *to fulfil an ambition*

fulfilled /fʊlˈfɪld/ *adjective*
completely satisfied with your life or your job ► *It is important to feel fulfilled in your work.*

fulfilling /fʊlˈfɪlɪŋ/ *adjective*
making you feel satisfied ► *Is your relationship a fulfilling one?*

full /fʊl/ *adjective*
1 containing as much as possible ► *My cup is full.*
OPPOSITE: **empty**
2 having had as much as you want to eat ► *I couldn't eat any more – I'm full.*
3 complete or whole ► *What's your full address?*
4 **be full of something** to contain a lot of something ► *The streets were full of people.*
5 **full up** (used about a place or thing) containing as much of something, or as many people, as possible ► *The restaurant is full up.*

full-blown /ˌfʊl ˈbləʊn/ *adjective*
fully developed ► *full-blown AIDS*

full-grown /ˌfʊl ˈgrəʊn/ *(also* ***fully-grown****) adjective*
(used about an animal, a plant, or a person) having developed completely, or grown to its full size ► *A full-grown blue whale can weigh 30 tons.*

full-length /ˌfʊl ˈleŋθ/ *adjective*
not shorter than the normal length ► *I've seen the full-length version of the film.*

full moon /ˌfʊl ˈmuːn/ *noun*
the moon when it looks completely round ► *There's going to be a full moon tonight.*

full-scale /ˌfʊl ˈskeɪl/ *adjective*
1 using all possible powers or forces ► *a full-scale nuclear war* ► *a full-scale inquiry into the disaster*
2 (used about a model, copy, picture, etc.) that is the same size as the thing it represents

full stop /ˌfʊl ˈstɒp/ *noun*
the sign (.) used in writing, to show the end of a sentence, or after a short form of a word such as **Mr.** or **ft.**

full-time /ˌfʊl ˈtaɪm/ *adverb, adjective*
working or studying, or giving work or study, all day during the whole working week ► *I'm looking for a full-time job.*
COMPARE: **part-time**

fully /ˈfʊlɪ/ *adverb*
completely ► *I am fully aware of the situation.*

fully-grown /ˌfʊlɪ ˈgrəʊn/ *adjective*
another word for **full-grown**

fumble /ˈfʌmbəl/ *verb (present participle* ***fumbling****, past* ***fumbled****)*
to try with difficulty to find, move, or hold something, using your hands in an awkward way ► *She fumbled in her bag* ***for*** *her keys.*

fume /fjuːm/ *verb*
be fuming to be very angry ► *I was an hour late coming home, and my mother was fuming.*

fumes /fjuːmz/ *plural noun*
gas or smoke that has a strong smell and is unpleasant to breathe ► *They had breathed in poisonous fumes.*

fun /fʌn/ *noun (no plural)*
1 amusement, enjoyment, or pleasure ► *That was really good fun.*
2 **have fun** to enjoy yourself ► *The children all had a lot of fun.*

3 make fun of someone to laugh at someone in a cruel way or to make other people laugh at them ▶ *You shouldn't make fun of him just because he's fat.*

function[1] /ˈfʌŋkʃən/ *noun*
the purpose of someone or something, or the job that they do

function[2] *verb*
to work ▶ *He functions as her deputy when she's away.*

fund /fʌnd/ *noun*
an amount of money collected for a particular reason ▶ *a fund to build a new church*

fundamental /ˌfʌndəˈmentl/ *adjective*
relating to the most basic and important parts of something ▶ *fundamental changes to the education system (adverb: **fundamentally**)*

fund-raising /ˈfʌnd ˌreɪzɪŋ/ *noun (no plural)*
the activity of collecting money for a particular purpose ▶ *concerts and other fund-raising activities*

funeral /ˈfjuːnərəl/ *noun*
a ceremony in which the body of a dead person is burned or put into the ground

funfair /ˈfʌnfeəʳ/ *noun*
a place where people go to enjoy themselves by paying to ride on special machines and by playing games for small prizes

fungus /ˈfʌŋgəs/ *noun (plural **fungi** /ˈfʌŋgaɪ, -dʒaɪ/)*
a plant such as a MUSHROOM which has no leaves or flowers

funky /ˈfʌŋkɪ/ *adjective (**funkier, funkiest**)*
(used about music) having a strong beat and enjoyable to listen to

funnel /ˈfʌnl/ *noun*
1 a tube which is wide at the top and narrow at the bottom, used for pouring things into a narrow opening
2 a pipe through which smoke leaves a ship or an engine

funny /ˈfʌnɪ/ *adjective (**funnier, funniest**)*
1 making you laugh; amusing ▶ *a funny joke*
2 strange; unusual ▶ *What's that funny smell?*

fur /fɜːʳ/ *noun (no plural)*
the soft hair on some animals such as cats and rabbits ▶ *a fur coat* (=a coat made of animal fur)

furious /ˈfjʊərɪəs/ *adjective*
very angry

furnace /ˈfɜːnɪs/ *noun*
a large, covered fire for heating metals

furnish /ˈfɜːnɪʃ/ *verb*
to put furniture in a place ▶ *to furnish a house*

furnished /ˈfɜːnɪʃt/ *adjective*
having furniture in ▶ *a furnished room*

furniture /ˈfɜːnɪtʃəʳ/ *noun (no plural)*
things used in a house, like beds, tables, and chairs

furry /ˈfɜːrɪ/ *adjective (**furrier, furriest**)*
covered in soft hairs ▶ *a furry animal*
COMPARE: **hairy**

further /ˈfɜːðəʳ/
the COMPARATIVE of **far**

further education /ˌfɜːðər edjʊˈkeɪʃən/ *noun (no plural)*
study that you do after leaving school, but not at a university ▶ *a college of further education*
COMPARE: **higher education**

furthest /ˈfɜːðɪst/
the SUPERLATIVE of **far**

furtive /ˈfɜːtɪv/ *adjective*
behaving as if you want to keep something secret ▶ *She gave him a furtive smile. (adverb: **furtively**)*

F

fury /ˈfjʊərɪ/ *noun (no plural)*
very great anger
SAME MEANING: **rage**

fuse[1] /fjuːz/ *noun*
a short wire inside a piece of electrical equipment that melts if too much electricity passes through it
▶ *This plug needs a new fuse.*

fuse[2] *verb (present participle **fusing**, past **fused**)*
1 to join together and become one thing, or to join two things together
▶ *The bones of the spine had become fused together.*
2 if an electrical system fuses, or if you fuse it, it stops working because the fuse has melted ▶ *The lights had fused.*

fuss[1] /fʌs/ *noun (no plural)*
1 worry or excitement about something which is not important
▶ *What's all the fuss about?*
2 make a fuss to cause trouble, especially by complaining ▶ *He was making a fuss because the waitress had forgotten him.*
3 make a fuss of someone to be very kind to someone and give them a lot of attention ▶ *My grandparents always make a fuss of me when I visit.*

fuss[2] *verb*
to worry too much about things that are not important, or to give too much attention to them

fussy /ˈfʌsɪ/ *adjective (**fussier, fussiest**)*
thinking too much about small things that are not important

futile /ˈfjuːtaɪl/ *adjective*
certain not to be effective or successful ▶ *The police made a futile attempt to rescue him.*

future /ˈfjuːtʃəʳ/ *noun (no plural)*
1 the future time that will come; things that have not happened yet
▶ *Do you have any plans for the future?*
COMPARE: **past**
2 in future after now ▶ *In future, please be more careful* (=in the past, you were not careful enough).

future tense /ˌfjuːtʃə ˈtens/ *noun*
the form of a verb that you use when you are talking about the future, e.g. in English, "I will go" is in a future tense

fuzzy /ˈfʌzɪ/ *adjective (**fuzzier, fuzziest**)*
unclear ▶ *The TV picture's gone fuzzy.*

Gg

g
a short way of writing the words **gram** or **grams** ▶ *500g*

gabble /ˈgæbəl/ *verb (present participle **gabbling**, past **gabbled**)*
to speak so quickly that people cannot understand you

gadget /ˈgædʒɪt/ *noun*
a machine or tool that is small but useful ▶ *a clever little gadget for cutting bread*

gag[1] /gæg/ *verb (present participle **gagging**, past **gagged**)*
to cover someone's mouth with a piece of cloth so that they cannot make any noise ▶ *The robbers tied him up and gagged him.*

gag[2] *noun*
a piece of cloth used to cover someone's mouth so that they cannot make any noise

gain /geɪn/ *verb*
1 to increase in something ▶ *The baby's gaining weight.*
2 to get something useful ▶ *What will you gain from doing the course?*
▶ *She's gaining good experience in the job.*

gala /ˈgɑːlə/ *noun*
a special public performance of sports, etc. ▶ *a swimming gala*

galaxy /ˈgæləksɪ/ *noun (plural* ***galaxies****)*
a very big group of stars in space ▶ *One day, people might be able to travel to other galaxies.*

gale /geɪl/ *noun*
a very strong wind

gall /gɔːl/ *noun*
have the gall to do something to do something that is rude without caring what other people think ▶ *She had the gall to say I was being childish!*

gallery /ˈgælərɪ/ *noun (plural* ***galleries****)*
a building or a large, long room where paintings, photographs, etc. are shown to the public ▶ *an art gallery*

gallon /ˈgælən/ *noun*
a measure of liquid equal to 8 pints

G

gallop[1] /ˈgæləp/ *verb*
(used about a horse) to run very fast

gallop[2] *noun*
the very fast run of a horse

gamble[1] /ˈgæmbəl/ *noun*
something you do in which you take a risk because you hope to get something ▶ *The doctors say the operation is a bit of a gamble which may not succeed.*

gamble[2] *verb (present participle* ***gambling****, past* ***gambled****)*
1 to try to win money on card games, horse races, etc. ▶ *He lost a lot of money by gambling.*
COMPARE: **bet**
2 to take a risk because you hope to get something

gambler /ˈgæmbləʳ/ *noun*
a person who tries to win money on card games, horse races, etc.

gambling /ˈgæmblɪŋ/ *noun (no plural)*
the activity of trying to win money by guessing the result of card games, horse races, etc. ▶ *Many more people are now using the Internet for gambling.*

game[1] /geɪm/ *noun*
1 an activity in which you follow certain rules in order to get points and defeat another person or team ▶ *Football is a team game.* ▶ *a game of cards*
2 a secret plan that is usually not honest ▶ *I don't know what his game is, but he's up to something.*
3 give the game away to tell people something that should be a secret
4 games *plural noun* sports in which people compete ▶ *The winter games were very exciting.*

game[2] *noun (no plural)*
wild animals or birds that people hunt for food or sport

Gameboy /ˈgeɪmbɔɪ/ *noun*
trademark
a small computer on which you play games

game show /ˈgeɪm ʃəʊ/ *noun*
a television programme in which people play games to win money or prizes

gang[1] /gæŋ/ *noun*
1 a group of people working together, e.g. building workers or criminals
2 a group of young people who cause trouble

gang[2] *verb*
gang up to get together in a group and behave badly to someone ▶ *The older children ganged up against the younger ones.*

gangster /ˈgæŋstəʳ/ *noun*
a member of a group of violent criminals

gaol /dʒeɪl/ *noun*
another word for **jail**

gap /gæp/ *noun*
1 a space between two things or between two parts of something ▶ *He*

has a gap ***between*** *his two front teeth.* ▶ *There was a small gap* ***in*** *the fence.*
2 a difference between two groups, amounts, or situations ▶ *the gap* ***between*** *rich and poor*
3 something that is missing in a situation, so that the situation is not complete ▶ *There's been a gap* ***in*** *my life since my father died.*
4 a period of time when nothing happens or is said ▶ *a gap* ***in*** *the conversation*

gape /geɪp/ *verb (present participle* ***gaping****, past* ***gaped****)*
to look at something or someone in surprise, with your mouth open ▶ *He just stood there gaping* ***at*** *the mess.*

gaping /ˈgeɪpɪŋ/ *adjective*
open very wide ▶ *The crash left a gaping hole in the wall.* ▶ *a gaping wound*

garage /ˈgærɑːʒ/ *noun*
1 a place where cars, buses, etc. are kept
2 a place where you can buy petrol or have your car repaired

garbled /ˈgɑːbəld/ *adjective*
mixed up and difficult to understand ▶ *She left a garbled message about being late.*

garden /ˈgɑːdn/ *noun*
a piece of land where trees, flowers, or vegetables are grown, round a house or in a public place

gardener /ˈgɑːdnəʳ/ *noun*
a person who works in a garden, for pleasure or as a job

gardening /ˈgɑːdnɪŋ/ *noun (no plural)*
work in a garden ▶ *He enjoys gardening.*

gargle /ˈgɑːgəl/ *verb (present participle* ***gargling****, past* ***gargled****)*
to clean your throat with water or a special liquid that you do not swallow ▶ *If you have a sore throat, try gargling with salt water.*

garish /ˈgeərɪʃ/ *adjective*
very brightly coloured and unpleasant to look at ▶ *The curtains are very garish.*

garland /ˈgɑːlənd/ *noun*
a ring of flowers or leaves, worn for decoration

garlic /ˈgɑːlɪk/ *noun (no plural)*
a plant used in cooking to give a strong taste

garment /ˈgɑːmənt/ *noun*
a piece of clothing ▶ *This garment should be washed by hand.*

garnish /ˈgɑːnɪʃ/ *verb*
to decorate food with small pieces of fruit or vegetables ▶ *I garnished the meat with some herbs.*

gas /gæs/ *noun*
1 *(plural* ***gases****)* any substance like air that is not liquid or solid
2 *(no plural)* a substance like air, that is used in the home to give heat and light ▶ *She cooks with gas.*

gash /gæʃ/ *noun (plural* ***gashes****)*
a deep cut in something ▶ *She had a deep gash in her leg.*

gasp[1] /gɑːsp/ *verb*
to take a quick, short breath ▶ *I gasped as I jumped into the cold river.*

gasp[2] *noun*
the sound of a quick, short breath ▶ *a gasp of surprise*

gate /geɪt/ *noun*
1 a door which closes an opening in a wall or fence
2 an entrance or way out at an airport

gâteau /ˈgætəʊ/ *noun (plural* ***gâteaux*** */-təʊz/)*
a large cake, often filled and decorated with cream and fruit ▶ *a piece of chocolate gâteau*

gatecrash /ˈgeɪtkræʃ/ *verb*
to go to a party or an event that you have not been invited to ▶ *People always gatecrash my parties.*

G

gateway /ˈgeɪtweɪ/ *noun*
an opening in a fence or in an outside wall that can be closed with a gate

gather /ˈgæðəʳ/ *verb*
1 to come together in a group ▶ *A crowd soon gathered to see what had happened.*
2 to collect flowers or crops ▶ *In the summer, the farmers gather the fruit.*
SAME MEANING **(2)**: **pick**

gathering /ˈgæðərɪŋ/ *noun*
a meeting or coming together of a lot of people in one place

gaudy /ˈgɔːdɪ/ *adjective (**gaudier, gaudiest**)*
very bright, in a way that is unpleasant ▶ *He was wearing a gaudy tie.*

gauge /geɪdʒ/ *noun*
an instrument that measures the amount of something ▶ *A petrol gauge shows the amount of petrol left in a car.*

G

gaunt /gɔːnt/ *adjective*
very thin and pale, especially because of illness ▶ *He was looking sick and gaunt.*

gave /geɪv/
the PAST TENSE of the verb **give**

gay /geɪ/ *adjective*
1 sexually attracted to people of the same sex; HOMOSEXUAL
2 bright and attractive ▶ *gay colours*

gaze /geɪz/ *verb (present participle **gazing**, past **gazed**)*
to look steadily at something for a long time ▶ *The child gazed **at** the toys in the shop window.*

GCSE /ˌdʒiː siː es ˈiː/ *noun*
GENERAL CERTIFICATE OF SECONDARY EDUCATION; an examination in a choice of subjects taken in British schools by pupils who are 15 or 16 years old

gear /gɪəʳ/ *noun*
1 a set of wheels with teeth in an engine, which work together to make the wheels of a car go faster or more slowly ▶ *The lorry driver changed gear to go up the hill.*
2 *(no plural)* the special clothes or things you need for a particular sport ▶ *tennis gear*

geese /giːs/
the plural of **goose**

gel /dʒel/ *noun (no plural)*
a thick liquid that you put on your hair to make it stay in the right position

gem /dʒem/ *noun*
any sort of stone which is worth a lot of money and is used as jewellery

gender /ˈdʒendəʳ/ *noun*
(used about a person) the state of being male or female

gene /dʒiːn/ *noun*
the part of a cell of a living thing that controls its development, and which is passed from the parent to the young child, animal, or plant ▶ *Brothers and sisters share some of the same genes.*

general[1] /ˈdʒenərəl/ *adjective*
1 concerning most people or places ▶ *How soon will the drug be available for general use?*
2 concerning the whole of something, rather than its parts ▶ *The house's general condition is good, although it needs painting.*
3 in general in most cases ▶ *In general, I like the people I work with.*

general[2] *noun*
a very important officer in the army

general election /ˌdʒenərəl ɪˈlekʃən/ *noun*
a time when the people of a country vote to choose their government

generalization /ˌdʒenərəlaɪˈzeɪʃən/ *noun*
a statement about all people or things of a particular kind, which may not be true about every one ▶ *It is*

silly to make generalizations about all students.

general knowledge /ˌdʒenərəl ˈnɒlɪdʒ/ *noun (no plural)*
knowledge about many different subjects

generally /ˈdʒenərəlɪ/ *adverb*
usually ▶ *Children in England generally start school when they are five.*

generate /ˈdʒenəreɪt/ *verb (present participle* ***generating****, past* ***generated****)*
to make heat or power ▶ *We use coal to generate electricity.*

generation /ˌdʒenəˈreɪʃən/ *noun*
the people born at a certain time ▶ *My parents and I belong to different generations.*

generator /ˈdʒenəreɪtəʳ/ *noun*
a machine that makes electricity

generosity /ˌdʒenəˈrɒsətɪ/ *noun (no plural)*
the willingness to give money, help, or presents ▶ *a card thanking him for his generosity*

generous /ˈdʒenərəs/ *adjective*
willing to give money, help, or presents ▶ *How generous of you to lend us your car!*
OPPOSITE: **mean**

genetic /dʒɪˈnetɪk/ *adjective*
relating to or caused by GENES ▶ *genetic diseases*

genetically modified /dʒɪˌnetɪklɪ ˈmɒdɪfaɪd/ *adjective*
(used about plants) having received GENES from another plant in a scientific process ▶ *These burgers contain genetically modified soya.*

genetics /dʒɪˈnetɪks/ *noun (no plural)*
the study of how the development and form of living things are affected by their GENES

genitals /ˈdʒenɪtlz/ *plural noun*
the parts on the outside of your body that are used for having sex and producing babies

genius /ˈdʒiːnɪəs/ *noun (plural* ***geniuses****)*
a person who is very, very clever

gentle /ˈdʒentl/ *adjective*
kind and calm; not rough or violent ▶ *Be gentle with the baby.* ▶ *a gentle voice (adverb:* ***gently****)*

gentleman /ˈdʒentlmən/ *noun (plural* ***gentlemen*** */-mən/)*
1 a kind man who behaves well towards other people
2 a polite word for a man ▶ *This gentleman has been waiting for an hour.*

Gents /dʒents/ *noun*
the Gents the men's TOILET ▶ *He's gone to the Gents.*
COMPARE: **Ladies**

genuine /ˈdʒenjʊɪn/ *adjective*
real and true ▶ *This ring is genuine gold. (adverb:* ***genuinely****)*

geography /dʒɪˈɒgrəfɪ/ *noun (no plural)*
the study of the countries of the world and things like seas, mountains, and weather

geology /dʒɪˈɒlədʒɪ/ *noun (no plural)*
the study of rocks, and how they were made

geometric /ˌdʒiːəˈmetrɪk/ *(also* ***geometrical*** */ˌdʒiːəˈmetrɪkəl/) adjective*
1 having regular shapes and lines ▶ *The rugs have geometric designs.*
2 of or about geometry

geometry /dʒɪˈɒmətrɪ/ *noun (no plural)*
the study of measuring shapes, lines, etc.

germ /dʒɜːm/ *noun*
a very small, living thing that grows in dirty places and makes people ill

G

German measles /ˌdʒɜːmən ˈmiːzəlz/ *noun (no plural)*
a disease that causes red spots on your body ▶ *Sam's got German measles.*

germinate /ˈdʒɜːmɪneɪt/ *verb (present participle* ***germinating****, past* ***germinated****)*
(used about seeds) to begin to grow

gerund /ˈdʒerənd/ *noun*
a noun with the same form as the PRESENT PARTICIPLE of a verb – for example, "reading" in the sentence "He enjoys reading."

gesture[1] /ˈdʒestʃəʳ/ *noun*
a movement of your hands, head, etc. done to express something

gesture[2] *verb (present participle* ***gesturing****, past* ***gestured****)*
to move your head, hands, etc. in order to express something ▶ *He gestured angrily at me.*

G

get /get/ *verb (present participle* ***getting****, past* ***got*** */gɒt/)*
1 to obtain something ▶ *I must get a birthday present for my mother.* ▶ *Can I get you a drink?*
2 to have or receive something ▶ *I got a real shock when I heard the news.* ▶ *The boy got a bicycle from his aunt.* ▶ *I don't get much time for reading.*
3 to become ▶ *She got very cross with me.* ▶ *The weather is getting colder.*
4 to bring or fetch something ▶ *Could you get me a glass of water, please?* ▶ *She went to get the children from school.*
5 get away to escape from a place ▶ *Four prisoners got away.*
6 get back to return, usually to your home ▶ *When did you get back from your holiday?*
7 get off to climb down from something such as a bus, train, or horse ▶ *The train stopped and he got off.* ▶ *She got off her bicycle.*
8 get on to climb onto something such as a bus, train, or horse ▶ *I got on at the library.* ▶ *She got on her bike and rode home.*
9 get on with someone to be friendly with someone ▶ *Do you get on well with your neighbours?*
10 get up to rise from a lying or sitting position, especially from your bed after sleeping ▶ *What time do you usually get up on Sundays?*

getaway /ˈgetəweɪ/ *noun*
make a getaway to escape quickly from a place, especially after doing something illegal ▶ *The robbers made a quick getaway after stealing the money.*

get-together /ˈget təˌgeðəʳ/ *noun*
a friendly, informal meeting or party ▶ *We're having a family get-together tomorrow.*

ghastly /ˈgɑːstlɪ/ *adjective*
very bad ▶ *ghastly news* ▶ *ghastly food*
SAME MEANING: **awful**

ghetto /ˈgetəʊ/ *noun (plural* ***ghettoes****)*
a part of a city where a lot of very poor people live

ghost /gəʊst/ *noun*
the form of a dead person that some people believe can be seen

ghostly /ˈgəʊstlɪ/ *adjective (****ghostlier, ghostliest****)*
making people afraid, as if there were ghosts ▶ *a ghostly light.*

giant[1] /ˈdʒaɪənt/ *noun*
a very large, strong man in children's stories

giant[2] *adjective*
very large

gibberish /ˈdʒɪbərɪʃ/ *noun (no plural)*
things someone says or writes that have no meaning or are difficult to understand ▶ *I tried to read the*

instruction book, but it was all gibberish.

gibe /dʒaɪb/ *noun*
another word for **jibe**

giddy /ˈgɪdɪ/ *adjective (**giddier, giddiest**)*
having a sick feeling that everything is moving around you ▶ *She felt giddy when she looked down from the high bridge.*

gift /gɪft/ *noun*
1 a present ▶ *a gift shop*
2 a special ability to do something ▶ *a gift **for** languages*

gifted /ˈgɪftɪd/ *adjective*
very intelligent or having a natural ability to do something very well ▶ *a school for gifted children* ▶ *Paul's a very gifted artist.*

gig /gɪg/ *noun*
a popular music or JAZZ concert

gigantic /dʒaɪˈgæntɪk/ *adjective*
very big
SAME MEANING: **enormous**

giggle /ˈgɪgəl/ *verb (present participle **giggling**, past **giggled**)*
to laugh in a silly way ▶ *The girls were giggling in class.*

gills /gɪlz/ *plural noun*
the part of a fish, near its head, through which it breathes

gimmick /ˈgɪmɪk/ *noun*
something unusual that is used to make people interested in something ▶ *The news story was just a gimmick to sell more tickets.*

gin /dʒɪn/ *noun*
1 *(no plural)* a strong alcoholic drink that has no colour ▶ *Her favourite drink is gin and tonic.*
2 a glass of this drink ▶ *Can I have two gins, please?*

ginger[1] /ˈdʒɪndʒəʳ/ *noun (no plural)*
1 a plant with a root which can be used to give food a strong taste
2 a colour between orange and brown

ginger[2] *adjective*
with a colour between orange and brown ▶ *ginger hair* ▶ *a ginger cat* ▶ *a man with a ginger beard*

gingerly /ˈdʒɪndʒəlɪ/ *adverb*
slowly, carefully, and gently ▶ *She crept gingerly into the room.*

gipsy *(also **gypsy**)* /ˈdʒɪpsɪ/ *noun (plural **gipsies**)*
one of a race of people who travel around in CARAVANS, earning money by selling flowers, etc.

giraffe /dʒɪˈrɑːf/ *noun*
a tall African animal with a very long neck, very long legs, and large, brown spots on its coat

girder /ˈgɜːdəʳ/ *noun*
a long, thick piece of iron or steel, used to build bridges or buildings ▶ *Huge iron girders held up the roof.*

girl /gɜːl/ *noun*
a female child ▶ *She has two children: a girl and a boy.* ▶ *There are four girls in our class.*

girlfriend /ˈgɜːlfrend/ *noun*
a girl or woman you have a romantic relationship with

Girl Guide /ˌgɜːl ˈgaɪd/ *noun*
a member of a special club for girls

gist /dʒɪst/ *noun*
the main points or general meaning of what someone says or writes ▶ *I understood the gist **of** what he was saying.*

give /gɪv/ *verb (present participle **giving**, past tense **gave** /geɪv/, past participle **given** /ˈgɪvən/)*
1 to hand or pass something to someone for them to use, or as a present ▶ *Please give that back to me when you've finished.* ▶ *His uncle gave him a toy train for his birthday.*
2 to let or make someone have something ▶ *That child has given us a lot of trouble.* ▶ *Can I give you some advice?*

G

3 to perform an action ▶ *She gave a cry of anger when she heard the news.* ▶ *He gave us a talk about the history of the city.*
4 give way to allow other cars, etc. to go before you when you are driving ▶ *You have to give way to traffic coming from the left.*
5 give something away (**a**) to make known something that is secret ▶ *She begged him not to give away her secret to anyone.*
(**b**) to let someone keep something of yours, usually because you do not want it any more ▶ *I'm giving away all the clothes that are too small for the children.*
6 give something back to return something to its owner ▶ *I'll give you back your CDs next week.*
7 give something in to hand something to the person in charge ▶ *Give your exam papers in as you leave the room.*
8 give something out to give something to each of several other people ▶ *The teacher gave out the books.*
9 give something up to stop having or doing something ▶ *She's trying to give up smoking.*

G

giveaway /ˈɡɪvəweɪ/ *noun*
be a (dead) giveaway to make it very easy for someone to guess something ▶ *Vince was lying. His red face was a dead giveaway.*

given¹ /ˈɡɪvən/
the PAST PARTICIPLE of the verb **give**

given² *adjective*
1 (used about times, dates, etc.) previously arranged ▶ *All claims have to be made by a given date.*
2 any given ..., a given ... a particular time or thing that can be used as an example of what you are talking about ▶ *There are thousands of homeless people in London at any given time.*

given³ *preposition*
if you consider ▶ *Given the circumstances, you've coped well.*

glacier /ˈɡlæsɪəʳ/ *noun*
a very large mass of ice in the mountains that moves very slowly along the ground

glad /ɡlæd/ *adjective (**gladder, gladdest**)*
pleased and happy ▶ *I am glad to see you. (adverb: **gladly**)*

glamorous /ˈɡlæmərəs/ *adjective*
attractive and exciting, especially because of being connected with wealth or success

glamour /ˈɡlæməʳ/ *noun (no plural)*
the quality of being attractive and exciting, and connected with wealth or success ▶ *I love the glamour of Hollywood.*

glance¹ /ɡlɑːns/ *verb (present participle **glancing**, past **glanced**)*
to look quickly at someone or something ▶ *She glanced **at** her watch.*

glance² *noun*
a quick, short look

gland /ɡlænd/ *noun*
a small organ in the body that produces a liquid, such as SWEAT or SALIVA ▶ *The glands in her neck are swollen.*

glare¹ /ɡleəʳ/ *verb (present participle **glaring**, past **glared**)*
1 to shine with an unpleasantly bright light ▶ *The sun glared down.*
2 to look at someone angrily ▶ *She glared **at** me and then walked away.*

glare² *noun*
1 an angry look
2 unpleasant brightness ▶ *The glare of the sun made her eyes hurt.*

glaring /ˈɡleərɪŋ/ *adjective*
1 (used about lights) very bright, making your eyes hurt if you look at them ▶ *the car's glaring headlights*

2 (used about a mistake) very bad and very noticeable

glass /glɑːs/ *noun*
1 *(no plural)* a clear, hard substance used for windows and bottles
2 *(plural **glasses**)* a cup made of glass, without a handle
3 glasses *plural noun* specially shaped pieces of glass or plastic that you wear in front of your eyes to help you see better

glaze /gleɪz/ *(also **glaze over**) verb (present participle **glazing**, past **glazed**)*
(used about eyes) to show no expression because you are bored or tired ▶ *As soon as he mentioned football, her eyes started to glaze over.*

gleam /gliːm/ *verb*
to shine ▶ *The river gleamed in the moonlight.*

glean /gliːn/ *verb*
to find out information slowly and with difficulty ▶ *It's difficult to glean any information **from** Dan.*

glide /glaɪd/ *verb (present participle **gliding**, past **glided**)*
to move forward smoothly

glider /ˈglaɪdəʳ/ *noun*
an aircraft without an engine

glimmer¹ /ˈglɪməʳ/ *verb*
to give a faint light ▶ *lights glimmering in the distance*

glimmer² *noun*
a faint light

glimpse¹ /glɪmps/ *noun*
a very quick look ▶ *I only caught a glimpse of the thief's face, so I can't describe it.*

glimpse² *verb (present participle **glimpsing**, past **glimpsed**)*
to see something very quickly and usually by chance

glint /glɪnt/ *verb*
to give out small flashes of light ▶ *His glasses glinted in the sun.*

glisten /ˈglɪsən/ *verb*
to shine as if wet ▶ *eyes glistening with tears*

glitter¹ /ˈglɪtəʳ/ *verb*
to shine brightly with flashes of light ▶ *The sea glittered in the sun.*

glitter² *noun*
a bright light that seems to flash

gloat /gləʊt/ *verb*
to show in an annoying way that you are happy about your success or about someone else's failure ▶ *Dick was still gloating over his team's win.*

global /ˈgləʊbəl/ *adjective*
affecting or including the whole world ▶ *global environmental issues (adverb: **globally**)*

global warming /ˌgləʊbəl ˈwɔːmɪŋ/ *noun (no plural)*
an increase in temperatures around the world, because gases caused by POLLUTION trap the sun's heat

globe /gləʊb/ *noun*
1 a ball with a map of the world on it
2 the Earth ▶ *She's travelled all over the globe.*

gloom /gluːm/ *noun (no plural)*
1 almost complete darkness ▶ *He could just make out a distant figure in the gloom.*
2 a strong feeling of sadness and having no hope ▶ *News of her arrest filled them with gloom.*

gloomy /ˈgluːmɪ/ *adjective (**gloomier, gloomiest**)*
1 rather dark ▶ *a gloomy day*
2 sad and having little hope ▶ *a gloomy expression on his face (adverb: **gloomily**)*

glorious /ˈglɔːrɪəs/ *adjective*
1 having great honour ▶ *the country's glorious history*
2 very pleasant ▶ *a glorious holiday*

glory /ˈglɔːrɪ/ *noun (no plural)*
fame and respect that is given to someone who has done something great

glossary /ˈglɒsərɪ/ *noun (plural* ***glossaries****)*
a list of technical or unusual words and what they mean, printed at the end of a book ▶ *a glossary of technical terms*

glossy /ˈglɒsɪ/ *adjective (****glossier, glossiest****)*
1 shiny and smooth ▶ *a small dog with glossy, black fur*
2 (used about magazines, photographs, etc.) printed on good-quality paper that is shiny

glove /glʌv/ *noun*
a piece of clothing that you wear on your hand, with separate parts for all your fingers

glow[1] /gləʊ/ *verb*
to shine with a dull light ▶ *The fire glowed in the dark.*

glow[2] *noun*
a soft, warm light ▶ *the glow of a sunset*

G

glower /ˈglaʊəʳ/ *verb*
to look at someone in an angry way ▶ *I started to speak, but Chris glowered* ***at*** *me so I stopped.*

glowing /ˈgləʊɪŋ/ *adjective*
praising someone or something a lot ▶ *The play got a glowing review.*

glue[1] /gluː/ *noun (no plural)*
a substance used for sticking things together ▶ *She stuck the handle onto the cup with glue.*

glue[2] *verb (present participle* ***glueing*** *or* ***gluing****, past* ***glued****)*
to stick something with glue ▶ *She glued the pieces together.*

glum /glʌm/ *adjective (****glummer, glummest****)*
sad *(adverb:* ***glumly****)*

glut /glʌt/ *noun*
too many things of the same kind that exist or are available at the same time ▶ *There's a glut of violent American films around at the moment.*

gm
a short way of writing the words **gram** or **grams**

GM /ˌdʒiː ˈem/ *adjective*
GENETICALLY MODIFIED; used to describe foods which contain GENES that have been artificially changed

GMT /ˌdʒiː em ˈtiː/ *noun (no plural)*
GREENWICH MEAN TIME; the time in London, used as an international measure

gnaw /nɔː/ *verb*
to bite on something for a long time ▶ *The rat gnawed a hole in the wooden box.*

go[1] /gəʊ/ *verb (past tense* ***went*** */went/, past participle* ***gone*** */gɒn/)*
1 to move towards a place ▶ *She went into the kitchen.* ▶ *This car is going too fast.*
2 to leave a place ▶ *The train goes in five minutes.*
LOOK AT: **gone**
3 to travel somewhere, usually in order to do something ▶ *They've gone shopping.*
4 to become ▶ *His hair is going grey.*
5 (used about a machine) to work properly ▶ *My watch won't go since it fell in the bath.*
6 be going to used to say that something will happen in the future ▶ *I think it's going to snow.* ▶ *I'm going to buy that bicycle.*
7 go well to be successful ▶ *The game went very well for my team.*
8 go away to leave ▶ *She's gone away for a few months.*
9 go out to leave a building ▶ *She took her bag and went out.*
10 go up to increase ▶ *Prices have really gone up this year.*

go[2] *noun (plural* ***goes****)*
a try ▶ *Can I have a go at mending the bicycle?*

go-ahead /ˈgəʊ əˌhed/ *noun*
give someone the go-ahead to give someone official permission to start

doing something ▶ *The council gave them the go-ahead to build the new stadium.*

goal /gəʊl/ *noun*
1 the space between two posts, into which you try to hit or kick the ball in games like football
2 a point that you win when the ball goes into the goal ▶ *Our team won by three goals to one.*
3 an aim ▶ *My goal is to go to college.*

goalie /ˈgəʊlɪ/ *noun*
a GOALKEEPER

goalkeeper /ˈgəʊlkiːpəʳ/ *noun*
the player in games like football who tries to stop the ball before it goes into the GOAL

goalpost /ˈgəʊlpəʊst/ *noun*
one of the two posts on each side of the GOAL in games such as football

goat /gəʊt/ *noun*
an animal like a sheep that is kept for milk and for its hairy coat

gobble /ˈgɒbəl/ *(also* ***gobble up****)* *verb (present participle* ***gobbling****, past* ***gobbled****)*
to eat something very quickly ▶ *Matt gobbled up his dinner and ran back outside.*

goblin /ˈgɒblɪn/ *noun*
a small, ugly creature in children's stories, who often does bad things

god /gɒd/ *noun*
any being to whom people pray, and who is believed to control the world

God /gɒd/ *noun*
the being who, especially in the Christian, Muslim, and Jewish religions, is believed to be the maker and ruler of the world ▶ *to pray to God*

godchild /ˈgɒdtʃaɪld/ *noun (plural* ***godchildren*** */-ˌtʃɪldrən/)*
in the Christian religion, a person's godchild is a child whose religious education that person has promised at a religious ceremony to be responsible for

goddess /ˈgɒdes/ *noun (plural* ***goddesses****)*
a female god

godfather /ˈgɒdˌfɑːðəʳ/ *noun*
in the Christian religion, a man who promises at a religious ceremony to be responsible for a child's religious education

godmother /ˈgɒdˌmʌðəʳ/ *noun*
in the Christian religion, a woman who promises at a religious ceremony to be responsible for a child's religious education

godparent /ˈgɒdˌpeərənt/ *noun*
in the Christian religion, a person who promises at a religious ceremony to be responsible for a child's religious education

goes /gəʊz/
the THIRD PERSON SINGULAR of the PRESENT TENSE of the verb **go**

goggles /ˈgɒgəlz/ *plural noun*
large, round glasses that you wear to keep your eyes safe, e.g. when swimming or working with dangerous chemicals, fire, etc.

going[1] /ˈgəʊɪŋ/ *noun (no plural)*
the speed at which you travel or work ▶ *We got there in four hours, which wasn't bad going.*

going[2] *adjective*
the going rate the usual amount that you have to pay for a service or that you get for doing a job ▶ *What's the going rate for private lessons at the moment?*

goings-on /ˌgəʊɪŋz ˈɒn/ *plural noun*
things that happen which are strange or interesting ▶ *There have been some interesting goings-on at the house next door.*

go-kart /ˈgəʊ kɑːt/ *noun*
a low vehicle with no roof and a small

G

engine that people drive in races for pleasure

gold /gəʊld/ *noun (no plural)*
1 a yellow metal that costs a lot of money ▶ *a ring made of gold*
2 the colour of this metal

golden /ˈgəʊldən/ *adjective*
like gold or made of gold ▶ *a golden sky* ▶ *a golden plate*

goldfish /ˈgəʊldfɪʃ/ *noun (plural* ***goldfish****)*
a small, orange fish, usually kept as a pet

golf /gɒlf/ *noun (no plural)*
a game in which a small, hard ball is hit into a number of holes in the ground using special sticks

golf course /ˈgɒlf kɔːs/ *noun*
an area of land where people play golf

gone /gɒn/
the PAST PARTICIPLE of the verb **go**

> Look at the difference between **been** and **gone**. If you have **been** to a place, you have travelled there and returned. If you have **gone** to a place, you have travelled there and have not yet returned: *Liz has gone to Spain* (=she is in Spain now). ▶ *Liz has been to Spain* (=she went there and now she has returned).

gong /gɒŋ/ *noun*
a flat piece of metal that is hung up and hit with a stick to make a noise

gonna /ˈgɒnə/
an informal way of saying "going to" ▶ *We're gonna spend the evening in Bar Rita.*

good[1] /gʊd/ *adjective (****better*** /ˈbetəʳ/, ***best*** /best/*)*
1 of a high standard or quality ▶ *a good school* ▶ *a very good memory*
2 pleasant or favourable ▶ *Have a good time.* ▶ *a good party*
3 skilful or successful at something ▶ *She's good* ***at*** *languages.* ▶ *He's good with babies.*
4 right for a particular purpose ▶ *This music is good* ***for*** *dancing.*
5 (used about children) well-behaved ▶ *She's got very good children.*
6 kind ▶ *He's been very good* ***to*** *me.*
7 healthy and strong ▶ *good teeth*
OPPOSITE (**1** to **7**): **bad**
8 Good for you! used to show you approve of what someone has done ▶ *"I've passed all my exams." "Good for you!"*

good[2] *noun (no plural)*
1 advantage ▶ *What's the good of having a car if you can't drive?*
2 for good for ever ▶ *She's left her job for good.*
3 do someone good to do something that will make someone feel well ▶ *A walk will do you good.*

good afternoon /gʊd ˌɑːftəˈnuːn/ *interjection*
an expression you use to greet someone in the afternoon

goodbye /gʊdˈbaɪ/ *interjection*
a word you use when you leave someone or someone leaves you
COMPARE: **hello**

good evening /gʊd ˈiːvnɪŋ/ *interjection*
an expression you use to greet someone in the evening

Good Friday /gʊd ˈfraɪdeɪ, -dɪ/ *noun*
the Friday before EASTER, a Christian religious holiday

good-looking /gʊd ˈlʊkɪŋ/ *adjective*
(used about a person) attractive ▶ *He's very good-looking.*

good morning /gʊd ˈmɔːnɪŋ/ *interjection*
an expression you use to greet someone in the morning

goodness[1] /ˈgʊdnəs/ *noun (no plural)*
kindness

goodness[2] *interjection*
a word used in expressions which show you are surprised or annoyed ▶ *Goodness me!*

goodnight /gʊd'naɪt/ *interjection*
an expression you use when you are going home at night or before you go to bed

goods /gʊdz/ *plural noun*
things like food or clothes that are bought and sold

gooey /'guːɪ/ *adjective (**gooier, gooiest**)*
sticky, soft, and usually sweet ▶ *a gooey chocolate cake*

goose /guːs/ *noun (plural **geese** /giːs/)*
a white bird that looks like a large duck

gorge /gɔːdʒ/ *noun*
a very narrow valley with steep sides ▶ *The railway runs through a beautiful gorge.*

gorgeous /'gɔːdʒəs/ *adjective*
very nice or beautiful ▶ *a gorgeous dress*
SAME MEANING: **lovely**

gorilla /gə'rɪlə/ *noun*
a very large, strong animal that looks like a very large monkey

gory /'gɔːrɪ/ *adjective (**gorier, goriest**)*
(used about films, stories, etc.) involving a lot of violence and blood ▶ *The ending was too gory for me.*

gosh /gɒʃ/ *interjection*
something you say when you are surprised ▶ *Gosh! What are you doing here?*

gossip[1] /'gɒsɪp/ *noun*
1 *(no plural)* unkind talk about people's private lives ▶ *You shouldn't listen to gossip.*
2 a person who talks unkindly about other people's private lives

gossip[2] *verb*
to talk unkindly about other people's private lives

got /gɒt/
the PAST TENSE and PAST PARTICIPLE of the verb **get**
LOOK AT: **have**

gourmet[1] /'gʊəmeɪ/ *adjective*
relating to good food and drink ▶ *a gourmet restaurant*

gourmet[2] *noun*
a person who enjoys and knows a lot about good food and drink

govern /'gʌvən/ *verb*
to control and rule a country and its people ▶ *a country governed by the army*

government /'gʌvəmənt/ *noun*
the people who control what happens in a country

governor /'gʌvənəʳ/ *noun*
a person who controls a state or prison

gown /gaʊn/ *noun*
a long dress for a woman ▶ *a beautiful evening gown*

GP /ˌdʒiː 'piː/ *noun*
a GENERAL PRACTITIONER; a doctor who treats people for ordinary health problems

grab /græb/ *verb (present participle **grabbing**, past **grabbed**)*
to take hold of something quickly and roughly ▶ *The thief grabbed my bag.*
SAME MEANING: **snatch**

grace /greɪs/ *noun (no plural)*
1 an attractive way of moving ▶ *She dances with such grace.*
2 a short prayer before or after a meal ▶ *Who is going to say grace?*

graceful /'greɪsfəl/ *adjective*
attractive and smooth in movement *(adverb: **gracefully**)*

gracious /'greɪʃəs/ *adjective*
1 kind, polite, and pleasant ▶ *a gracious smile*
2 Gracious!, Good Gracious! a phrase used when you are surprised ▶ *Gracious! What are you doing here?*

grade[1] /greɪd/ *noun*
1 a level, size, or quality ▶ *We sell three grades of egg.*
2 a mark you get for an examination or piece of work at school

grade[2] *verb (present participle **grading**, past **graded**)*
to put things into groups according to size, quality, etc. ▶ *The farmers graded the apples into several sizes.*

gradient /ˈgreɪdɪənt/ *noun*
a measurement of how steep a slope is, especially on a road or railway ▶ *Ringstead Road was on a steep gradient.*

gradual /ˈgrædʒʊəl/ *adjective*
happening slowly ▶ *a gradual improvement in his work (adverb: **gradually**)*

graduate[1] /ˈgrædʒʊeɪt/ *verb (present participle **graduating**, past **graduated**)*
to take and pass the last examination at a university ▶ *She graduated from a French university.* ▶ *She graduated in history.*

graduate[2] /ˈgrædʒʊət/ *noun*
a person who has passed the last examination at a university

graduation /ˌgrædʒʊˈeɪʃən/ *noun*
the act of completing a university degree, or the ceremony at which you receive your degree ▶ *After graduation, Sally trained as a teacher.*

graffiti /græˈfiːtɪ/ *noun (no plural)*
writing and pictures that people draw illegally in public places ▶ *The school walls were covered with graffiti.*

grain /greɪn/ *noun*
1 *(no plural)* a crop like wheat, maize, or rice that has seeds which we eat ▶ *Grain is used for making flour.*
2 a seed, or small, hard piece of something ▶ *a few grains **of** salt*

gram *(also **gramme**)* /græm/ *noun*
a measure of weight. There are 1,000 grams in a kilogram ▶ *500 grams* (=500g)

grammar /ˈgræməʳ/ *noun (no plural)*
the rules of a language ▶ *English grammar*

grammar school /ˈgræmə skuːl/ *noun*
a school in Britain, especially in the past, for clever children between the ages of 11 and 18
COMPARE: **comprehensive school**

grammatical /grəˈmætɪkəl/ *adjective*
correct according to the rules of language ▶ *"I aren't" is not grammatical.*

gramme /græm/ *noun*
another word for **gram**

gramophone /ˈgræməfəʊn/ *noun*
a machine on which records can be played, so that you can hear the music or words

gran /græn/ *noun*
a grandmother

grand /grænd/ *adjective*
very large and fine ▶ *He lives in a rather grand house.*

grandchild /ˈgræntʃaɪld/ *noun (plural **grandchildren** /-ˌtʃɪldrən/)*
the child of your son or daughter

granddad /ˈgrændæd/ *noun*
a grandfather

granddaughter /ˈgrændɔːtəʳ/ *noun*
the daughter of your son or daughter

grandfather /ˈgrænfɑːðəʳ/ *noun*
the father of one of your parents

grandma /ˈgrænmɑː/ *noun*
a grandmother

grandmother /ˈgrænmʌðəʳ/ *noun*
the mother of one of your parents

grandpa /ˈgrænpɑː/ *noun*
a grandfather

grandparent /ˈgrænpeərənt/ *noun*
the parent of your mother or father

grandson /ˈgrænsʌn/ *noun*
the son of your son or daughter

granny /'grænɪ/ *noun (plural* ***grannies)***
(used by children) a grandmother

grant¹ /grɑːnt/ *verb*
to give or allow someone something, often officially ▶ *The children were granted a holiday from school.*

grant² *noun*
an allowed sum of money ▶ *The government gave us a grant to build another classroom.*

granule /'grænjuːl/ *noun*
a very small, hard piece of something, especially dried coffee ▶ *instant coffee granules*

grape /greɪp/ *noun*
a small, round, juicy fruit that grows in bunches and is used to make wine

grapefruit /'greɪpfruːt/ *noun*
a large, round, yellow fruit that is like an orange but not as sweet

graph /grɑːf/ *noun*
a drawing that shows how two or more sets of measurements are related to each other ▶ *They made a graph of how hot the weather was every day for a month.*

graphic /'græfɪk/*adjective*
very clear and giving a lot of details ▶ *She gave a graphic description of the accident.*

graphic design /ˌgræfɪk dɪ'zaɪn/ *noun (no plural)*
the job or art of combining pictures with the writing in books, magazines, etc.

graphics /'græfɪks/ *plural noun*
drawings or pictures, especially the ones that a computer produces ▶ *The new version of the software has brilliant graphics.*

graph paper /'grɑːf peɪpəʳ/ *noun (no plural)*
paper with squares on it for making GRAPHS

grasp /grɑːsp/ *verb*
1 to take hold of something firmly ▶ *He grasped the rope and pulled himself up.*
2 to understand something ▶ *I could not grasp what the teacher said.*

grass /grɑːs/ *noun (no plural)*
a common plant with thin leaves that covers fields and gardens ▶ *We sat on the grass to have our picnic.*

grasshopper /'grɑːsˌhɒpəʳ/ *noun*
an insect with strong back legs for jumping

grassy /'grɑːsɪ/ *adjective (****grassier, grassiest****)*
covered with grass

grate¹ /greɪt/ *noun*
a metal frame put in front of a fire

grate² *verb (present participle* ***grating****, past* ***grated****)*
to cut food into small, thin pieces by rubbing it against an instrument with a rough surface ▶ *to grate cheese*

grateful /'greɪtfəl/ *adjective*
feeling that you want to thank someone ▶ *I am grateful* ***to*** *you* ***for*** *helping me. (adverb:* ***gratefully****)*
OPPOSITE: **ungrateful**

grater /'greɪtəʳ/ *noun*
a kitchen tool used for grating food

gratitude /'grætɪtjuːd/ *noun (no plural)*
the feeling of wanting to thank someone ▶ *He expressed his gratitude to everyone involved.*
OPPOSITE: **ingratitude**

gratuitous /grə'tjuːɪtəs/ *adjective*
done without a good reason, in a way that offends people ▶ *There is too much gratuitous violence on television.*

grave¹ /greɪv/ *noun*
a hole in the ground where a dead body is buried

G

grave² *adjective*
serious ▶ *a grave accident (adverb: **gravely**)*

gravel /ˈgrævəl/ *noun (no plural)*
a mixture of small stones and sand, used on the surfaces of roads and paths

gravestone /ˈgreɪvstəʊn/ *noun*
a stone put up over a grave, with the name of the dead person on it

graveyard /ˈgreɪvjɑːd/ *noun*
a piece of ground where people are buried

gravity /ˈgrævətɪ/ *noun (no plural)*
the force that makes things fall to the ground when they are dropped

gravy /ˈgreɪvɪ/ *noun (no plural)*
a liquid that is made with meat juices and poured over meat and other food

graze¹ /greɪz/ *verb (present participle **grazing**, past **grazed**)*
1 to eat grass ▶ *Cattle were grazing in the field.*
2 to cut the surface of your skin by rubbing it against something ▶ *He grazed his knee when he fell.*

graze² *noun*
a small wound on the surface of your skin

grease¹ /griːs/ *noun (no plural)*
oil or fat ▶ *You put grease on a wheel to make it turn more easily.*

grease² *verb (present participle **greasing**, past **greased**)*
to put oil or fat on something

greasy /ˈgriːsɪ/ *adjective (**greasier**, **greasiest**)*
covered with oil or fat

great /greɪt/ *adjective*
1 large in size or amount ▶ *She had great difficulty in doing her homework.* ▶ *a great big dog*
2 important or famous ▶ *one of our greatest poets*
3 very good ▶ *It was a great party.* ▶ *I feel great.*
SAME MEANING (3): **fantastic, marvellous**

great-grandchild /ˌgreɪt ˈgræntʃaɪld/ *noun (plural **great-grandchildren** /-ˌtʃɪldrən/)*
the son or daughter of your GRANDCHILD

great-granddaughter /ˌgreɪt ˈgrændɔːtəʳ/ *noun*
the daughter of your GRANDCHILD

great-grandfather /ˌgreɪt ˈgrænfɑːðəʳ/ *noun*
the father of your grandmother or grandfather

great-grandmother /ˌgreɪt ˈgrænmʌðəʳ/ *noun*
the mother of your grandmother or grandfather

great-grandson /ˌgreɪt ˈgrænsʌn/ *noun*
the son of your GRANDCHILD

greatly /ˈgreɪtlɪ/ *adverb*
very much ▶ *She greatly admired his poems.*

greed /griːd/ *noun (no plural)*
the feeling that you want more than enough food, money, or power

greedy /ˈgriːdɪ/ *adjective (**greedier**, **greediest**)*
wanting too much of something ▶ *He's so greedy he ate all our sweets.*

green¹ /griːn/ *adjective*
1 the colour of growing leaves and grass ▶ *She wore a green dress.*
2 covered with grass and trees ▶ *Cities need more green areas.*

green² *noun*
1 the colour of leaves and grass ▶ *She was dressed in green.*
2 an area of grass in the middle of an English village

green card /ˈgriːn kɑːd/ *noun*
an official piece of paper that allows you to live and work in America, although you are not American

greengrocer /ˈgriːnˌgrəʊsəʳ/ *noun*
1 a person who has a shop selling fruit and vegetables
2 greengrocer's a shop selling fruit and vegetables

greenhouse /ˈgriːnhaʊs/ *noun (plural* ***greenhouses*** */-haʊzɪz/)*
a glass building in which you grow plants

greenhouse effect /ˈgriːnhaʊs ɪˌfekt/ *noun*
the greenhouse effect a problem caused by POLLUTION, which stops the sun's heat from escaping and causes the air around the Earth to become warmer

greenhouse gas /ˈgriːnhaʊs gæs/ *noun (plural* ***greenhouse gases****)*
gases, caused by POLLUTION, which trap the sun's heat and make the Earth's temperature rise

greet /griːt/ *verb*
to welcome someone with words or actions ▶ *He greeted her with a smile.*

greeting /ˈgriːtɪŋ/ *noun*
words you say or write when you meet someone or send them good wishes ▶ *a friendly greeting* ▶ *Christmas greetings*

grenade /grɪˈneɪd/ *noun*
a small bomb that can be thrown or fired from a gun

grew /gruː/
the PAST TENSE of the verb **grow**

grey /greɪ/ *adjective, noun*
the colour of rain clouds; a mixture of black and white ▶ *She wore a grey dress.* ▶ *She was dressed in grey.*

grid /grɪd/ *noun*
a pattern of straight lines that cross each other and form squares

gridlock /ˈgrɪdlɒk/ *noun (no plural)*
a situation when the roads are so full of traffic that nothing can move

grief /griːf/ *noun (no plural)*
great sadness, usually because someone you love has died ▶ *She did not show her grief when her son died.*

grievance /ˈgriːvəns/ *noun*
something that you think is unfair and that you complain about, especially to someone in authority ▶ *The manager called a meeting to try and deal with our grievances.*

grieve /griːv/ *verb (present participle* ***grieving****, past* ***grieved****)*
to feel very sad, usually because someone you love has died

grill¹ /grɪl/ *verb*
to cook meat, fish, etc. under direct heat

grill² *noun*
a metal frame under direct heat, on which you can cook things

grim /grɪm/ *adjective (****grimmer, grimmest****)*
1 serious and worrying ▶ *grim news*
2 (used about a place) not pleasant or attractive

grimace /grɪˈmeɪs/ *verb (present participle* ***grimacing****, past* ***grimaced****)*
to twist your face in an ugly way because something is hurting you or because you do not like something ▶ *Trevor was grimacing with pain.*

grime /graɪm/ *noun (no plural)*
thick, black dirt ▶ *The factory walls were covered in grime.*

grimy /ˈgraɪmɪ/ *adjective (****grimier, grimiest****)*
covered in thick, black dirt ▶ *a row of grimy houses near the railway*

grin¹ /grɪn/ *verb (present participle* ***grinning****, past* ***grinned****)*
to smile widely, showing your teeth ▶ *He grinned with pleasure when we gave him the money.*

grin² *noun*
a wide smile ▶ *She had a big grin on her face.*

grind /graɪnd/ *verb (past* ***ground*** */graʊnd/)*

G

to crush something so that it becomes powder ▶ *We grind grain to make flour.*

grip[1] /grɪp/ *verb (past participle **gripping**, past **gripped**)*
to hold something very tightly ▶ *She gripped his hand in fear.*
SAME MEANING: **clasp**

grip[2] *noun*
a tight hold ▶ *She kept a firm grip **on** the bag.*

grisly /ˈgrɪzlɪ/ *adjective (**grislier, grisliest**)*
extremely unpleasant and connected with violence or death ▶ *the grisly discovery of a body in the cellar*

grit[1] /grɪt/ *noun (no plural)*
very small pieces of stone ▶ *I had a piece of grit stuck in my shoe.*

grit[2] *verb (present participle **gritting**, past **gritted**)*
grit your teeth to use all your determination to continue doing something in a difficult or painful situation ▶ *He gritted his teeth against the pain.*

groan[1] /grəʊn/ *noun*
a low noise of pain or unhappiness ▶ *There was a groan from the class when the teacher gave them the test.*
SAME MEANING: **moan**

groan[2] *verb*
to make a low noise of pain or unhappiness ▶ *He groaned with pain.*
SAME MEANING: **moan**

grocer /ˈgrəʊsəʳ/ *noun*
1 a person who sells foods like sugar, tea, and rice
2 grocer's a shop selling foods like sugar, tea, and rice

groceries /ˈgrəʊsərɪz/ *plural noun*
foods like sugar, tea, and rice which you can buy in a grocery

grocery /ˈgrəʊsərɪ/ *noun (plural **groceries**)*
a shop where you can buy foods like sugar, tea, and rice

groggy /ˈgrɒgɪ/ *adjective (**groggier, groggiest**)*
feeling weak and ill or tired ▶ *The injection made him feel groggy.*

groin /grɔɪn/ *noun*
the place where your legs join at the front of your body ▶ *a groin injury*

groom /gruːm/ *noun*
a man who is getting married ▶ *The groom wore a dark blue suit.*
SAME MEANING: **bridegroom**

groove /gruːv/ *noun*
a line cut into the surface of something ▶ *a pattern of deep grooves*

grope /grəʊp/ *verb (present participle **groping**, past **groped**)*
to use your hands to look for something that you cannot see ▶ *He groped **for** his matches in the dark.*

gross /grəʊs/ *adjective*
1 very unpleasant to look at or think about ▶ *His jokes are really gross.*
2 gross amount the total amount of money before taxes or costs have been taken away ▶ *Our gross profit was £50,000.*
3 very serious ▶ *children suffering from gross neglect*

grossly /ˈgrəʊslɪ/ *adverb*
very much ▶ *He is grossly overweight.*

grotesque /grəʊˈtesk/ *adjective*
ugly or strange in a way that is unpleasant or frightening

grouchy /ˈgraʊtʃɪ/ *adjective (**grouchier, grouchiest**)*
feeling annoyed and complaining a lot ▶ *Dad's always grouchy in the morning.*

ground[1] /graʊnd/ *noun*
1 *(no plural)* the surface of the earth ▶ *an apple fell to the ground.*
2 *(no plural)* soil or land ▶ *The ground was too hard to plant seeds in.*
3 a piece of land used for a particular purpose ▶ *a football ground*
4 grounds *plural noun* the land around a large building

ground²
the PAST TENSE and PAST PARTICIPLE of the verb **grind**

ground floor /ˌgraʊnd ˈflɔːʳ/ *noun*
the floor of a building on the same level as the ground

groundnut /ˈgraʊndnʌt/ *noun*
a nut that grows in a soft shell under the ground ► *groundnut oil*
SAME MEANING: **peanut**

group /gruːp/ *noun*
1 a number of people or things together ► *A group **of** girls was waiting by the school.*
2 a small number of people who sing and play popular music together

grovel /ˈgrɒvəl/ *verb (present participle **grovelling**, past **grovelled**)*
to try very hard to please someone, because you are frightened of them or you have upset them ► *I don't care how important she is; I'm not going to grovel to her.*

grow /grəʊ/ *verb (past tense **grew** /gruː/, past participle **grown** /grəʊn/)*
1 to get bigger, taller, etc. ► *Some plants grow very quickly.*
2 to care for plants and help them to grow ► *The farmer is growing potatoes.*
3 to let your hair get longer ► *Jack is growing a beard.*
4 to become ► *My uncle is growing old.*
5 grow out of something to become too big or too old for something ► *My daughter's grown out of all her dresses.*
6 grow up to change from being a child to a man or a woman ► *He grew up on a farm.*

growl¹ /graʊl/ *verb*
(used about a dog) to make a low, angry noise in the throat ► *The dog growled at the visitors.*

growl² *noun*
the low, angry noise made by a dog

grown /grəʊn/
the PAST PARTICIPLE of the verb **grow**

grown-up¹ /ˌgrəʊn ˈʌp/ *adjective*
old enough to be a man or woman, not a child ► *Her children are all grown-up now.*

grown-up² *noun*
a man or woman, not a child ► *"Be quiet – the grown-ups are coming," said the little girl.*
SAME MEANING: **adult**

growth /grəʊθ/ *noun (no plural)*
the act of getting bigger or developing ► *the growth of the company* ► *a tree's growth*

grub /grʌb/ *noun*
the young form of an insect, without wings

grubby /ˈgrʌbɪ/ *adjective (**grubbier, grubbiest**)*
rather dirty ► *Those shorts look a bit grubby.*

grudge /grʌdʒ/ *noun*
an unfriendly or angry feeling that you have towards someone because of something they said or did in the past ► *He always had a grudge **against** me after I beat him in the race.*

gruelling /ˈgruːəlɪŋ/ *adjective*
very difficult and tiring ► *a gruelling 10-mile run*

gruesome /ˈgruːsəm/ *adjective*
very unpleasant and connected with violence or death ► *This castle has a gruesome history.*

grumble¹ /ˈgrʌmbəl/ *verb (past participle **grumbling**, past **grumbled**)*
to complain in a quiet but cross way ► *She was grumbling about the cost of the food.*

grumble² *noun*
a complaint ► *You're full of grumbles today!*

grumpy /ˈgrʌmpɪ/ *adjective (**grumpier, grumpiest**)*

bad-tempered ▶ *a tired and grumpy child*

grunt¹ /grʌnt/ *verb*
to make a short, low noise like a pig

grunt² *noun*
a short, low noise like the noise made by a pig

guarantee¹ /ˌgærən'tiː/ *noun*
1 a promise ▶ *There's no guarantee that they will repair the car today.*
2 a written promise by the maker of an article to repair it or give you another one if it goes wrong within a certain time ▶ *a watch with a two-year guarantee*

guarantee² *verb (past* ***guaranteed****)*
1 to promise ▶ *He guaranteed that he would do it today.*
2 to promise to repair an article if it goes wrong within a certain time ▶ *This radio is guaranteed for three years.*

G

guard¹ /gɑːd/ *verb*
1 to keep something safe from danger by watching it carefully ▶ *The dog guards the house when we go out.*
2 to watch a prisoner so that they do not escape

guard² *noun*
1 a person who watches over someone or something to prevent danger or escape ▶ *a prison guard*
2 be on guard, stand guard to stand near a building ready to protect it ▶ *There was a policeman on guard outside.*

guardian /'gɑːdɪən/ *noun*
a person who looks after a child because the child's parents are dead or away

guava /'gwɑːvə/ *noun*
a pink, round fruit with a yellow skin

guerrilla /gə'rɪlə/ *noun*
a member of an unofficial military group that is fighting for political reasons ▶ *guerrilla warfare*

guess¹ /ges/ *verb*
to give an answer that you feel may be right although you are not sure ▶ *I didn't know where she was from, but I could guess.* ▶ *Can you guess my age?*

guess² *noun (plural* ***guesses****)*
an answer that you think is right, although you do not know for sure ▶ *If you don't know the answer, make a guess.*

guest /gest/ *noun*
1 a visitor to someone's house ▶ *We have three guests for dinner tonight.*
2 a person who is staying in a hotel

guidance /'gaɪdns/ *noun (no plural)*
help and advice ▶ *With my teacher's guidance, I finished the work.*

guide¹ /gaɪd/ *verb (present participle* ***guiding****, past* ***guided****)*
to lead or show the way to someone ▶ *He guided the old woman across the busy street.*

guide² *noun*
1 a person who shows you round a place of interest or helps you to travel in a dangerous area ▶ *They had a guide to show them the city.* ▶ *a mountain guide*
2 a book that teaches you about something ▶ *a guide for parents*

guide book /'gaɪd bʊk/ *noun*
a book that gives tourists information about a place

guide dog /'gaɪd dɒg/ *noun*
a dog that is specially trained to guide a blind person

guidelines /'gaɪdlaɪnz/ *plural noun*
official advice about how to do something ▶ *guidelines* ***on*** *health and safety at work*

guilt /gɪlt/ *noun (no plural)*
1 the unhappy feeling you have when you know you have done something wrong ▶ *She doesn't seem to feel any guilt for her bad behaviour.*

2 the fact of having broken the law ▶ *The court was sure of his guilt.*
OPPOSITE (**1** and **2**): **innocence**

guilty /ˈgɪltɪ/ *adjective (**guiltier, guiltiest**)*
1 showing or feeling unhappiness because you have done something wrong ▶ *a guilty look*
2 having broken a law ▶ *He was guilty **of** stealing the money.*
OPPOSITE (**1** and **2**): **innocent**

guinea pig /ˈgɪnɪ pɪg/ *noun*
a small, furry animal that looks like a rat without a tail and is sometimes kept as a pet

guitar /gɪˈtɑːʳ/ *noun*
a musical instrument with six strings, a long neck, and a wooden or plastic body

guitarist /gɪˈtɑːrɪst/ *noun*
a person who plays the guitar ▶ *the guitarist, Jimi Hendrix*

gulf /gʌlf/ *noun*
a narrow piece of sea with land on three sides of it ▶ *the Persian Gulf*

gull /gʌl/ *noun*
a seagull

gullible /ˈgʌlɪbəl/ *adjective*
easily tricked as a result of always trusting other people ▶ *I was angry with myself for being so gullible.*

gulp¹ /gʌlp/ *verb*
to swallow food or drink quickly ▶ *He gulped down the water.*

gulp² *noun*
a swallow ▶ *He drank it in one gulp.*

gum /gʌm/ *noun*
1 *(no plural)* a sticky substance used for joining things together
2 gums *plural noun* the pink part of your mouth in which your teeth grow
3 CHEWING GUM

gun /gʌn/ *noun*
a weapon that sends out bullets and is used for hurting or killing animals or people

gunfire /ˈgʌnfaɪəʳ/ *noun (no plural)*
the repeated firing of guns ▶ *The sound of gunfire shattered the peace of this normally quiet town.*

gunman /ˈgʌnmæn/ *noun (plural **gunmen** /-men/)*
a person who shoots another person

gunpoint /ˈgʌnpɔɪnt/ *noun*
at gunpoint under the threat of being shot, or while threatening to shoot you ▶ *The victims were held at gunpoint while the thief stole their car.* ▶ *The man kidnapped her at gunpoint.*

gunpowder /ˈgʌnpaʊdəʳ/ *noun (no plural)*
a substance that explodes easily and is used in guns

gunshot /ˈgʌnʃɒt/ *noun*
1 the sound made when a gun is fired ▶ *We heard three gunshots.*
2 *(no plural)* the bullets fired from a gun ▶ *a gunshot wound*

gurgle /ˈgɜːgəl/ *verb (present participle **gurgling**, past **gurgled**)*
to make a sound like flowing water ▶ *The baby gurgled with pleasure.*

guru /ˈgʊruː/ *noun*
1 a person that people respect because they are very wise or skilful in a particular subject ▶ *a top management guru*
2 a Hindu religious teacher

gush /gʌʃ/ *verb*
to flow quickly in large quantities ▶ *Blood gushed from the cut in his leg.*

gust /gʌst/ *noun*
a sudden, strong wind ▶ *A gust of wind blew the leaves along.*

gut¹ /gʌt/ *adjective*
gut feeling, gut reaction a feeling that something is right, although you cannot say why you are sure ▶ *My gut reaction was to refuse.*

G

gut² *noun*
1 *(also **guts**)* the tube in your body that food passes through after it leaves your stomach ▶ *I had a pain in my gut.*
2 guts *plural noun* courage and determination to do something difficult ▶ *Have you got the guts to ask for a pay rise?*

gut³ *verb (present participle **gutting**, past **gutted**)*
1 to destroy the inside of a building completely ▶ *The school was completely gutted by fire.*
2 to remove the organs from inside a fish or an animal in order to prepare it for cooking

gutted /ˈgʌtɪd/ *adjective*
very disappointed ▶ *The team were gutted when they lost.*

gutter /ˈgʌtəʳ/ *noun*
an open pipe along the edge of a roof, or a narrow ditch on the side of the road, which carries away rain water

guy /gaɪ/ *noun*
a man ▶ *What a nice guy!*

H

guzzle /ˈgʌzəl/ *verb (present participle **guzzling**, past **guzzled**)*
to drink or eat a lot very quickly ▶ *The children were guzzling lemonade.*

gym /dʒɪm/ *noun*
1 a large room that is used for doing exercises or training
2 *(also **gymnastics**) (no plural)* exercises for your body that make you strong and able to move easily ▶ *a gym class*

gymnasium /dʒɪmˈneɪzɪəm/ *noun*
a GYM

gymnast /ˈdʒɪmnæst/ *noun*
a person who is trained in gymnastics

gymnastics /dʒɪmˈnæstɪks/ *noun (no plural)*
another word for **gym** (**2**)

gypsy /ˈdʒɪpsɪ/ *noun (plural **gypsies**)*
another word for **gipsy**

Hh

habit /ˈhæbɪt/ *noun*
something that you always do, often without thinking about it ▶ *She has a habit of biting her fingernails.*

habitat /ˈhæbɪtæt/ *noun*
the natural environment in which a plant grows or an animal lives ▶ *Pollution is damaging many wildlife habitats.*

habitual /həˈbɪtʃʊəl/ *adjective*
1 typical or happening often ▶ *Jane was in her habitual bad temper this morning.*
2 doing something often because it is a habit ▶ *a habitual smoker*
*(adverb: **habitually**)*

hack /hæk/ *verb*
hack into to use a computer to enter someone else's computer system ▶ *John managed to hack into the company's computer network.*

had /d, əd, həd; *strong* hæd/
the PAST TENSE and PAST PARTICIPLE of the verb **have**

haddock /ˈhædək/ *noun (plural **haddock**)*
a sea fish used for food

hadn't /ˈhædnt/
had not ▶ *I hadn't finished making dinner when everyone arrived.*

hag /hæg/ *noun*
an ugly or unpleasant old woman

haggard /ˈhægəd/ *adjective*
looking tired, thin, and ill ▶ *His face looked haggard and pale.*

haggle /ˈhægəl/ *verb (present participle **haggling**, past **haggled**)* to argue about the amount that you will pay for something ▶ *We were haggling* ***over*** *the price for an hour.*

hail¹ /heɪl/ *noun (no plural)*
drops of hard, icy rain ▶ *We had a hail storm yesterday.*

hail² *verb*
to rain with hard, icy drops ▶ *It's hailing.*

hailstone /ˈheɪlstəʊn/ *noun*
a hard, icy drop of rain

hair /heəʳ/ *noun*
1 one of the fine threads that grow on the head and skin of people and animals ▶ *There's a hair in my soup!*
2 *(no plural)* a lot of these threads together, for example on your head ▶ *I must get my hair cut.*
3 make your hair stand on end to make you feel very afraid

hairbrush /ˈheəbrʌʃ/ *noun (plural* ***hairbrushes)***
a brush for keeping your hair tidy

haircut /ˈheəkʌt/ *noun*
1 the style in which your hair is cut ▶ *I like your new haircut.*
2 have a haircut to have your hair cut ▶ *I must have a haircut.*

hairdresser /ˈheəˌdresəʳ/ *noun*
1 a person whose job is to wash, cut, and shape your hair
COMPARE: **barber**
2 hairdresser's a shop where you go to get your hair cut

hairdryer /ˈheəˌdraɪəʳ/ *noun*
a machine that you use to dry your hair after washing it

hairgrip /ˈheəgrɪp/ *noun*
a thin piece of metal, used to hold hair in place

hair-raising /ˈheə ˌreɪzɪŋ/ *adjective*
frightening but exciting ▶ *a hair-raising fairground ride*

hairstyle /ˈheəstaɪl/ *noun*
the style in which your hair is cut or arranged ▶ *I like your new hairstyle.*

hairy /ˈheərɪ/ *adjective (****hairier, hairiest****)*
(used about a part of your body) covered with a lot of hairs ▶ *a man with a hairy chest*
COMPARE: **furry**

half /hɑːf/ *noun (plural* ***halves*** */hɑːvz/)*
1 one of the two parts of something ▶ *I gave half the apple to my brother.* ▶ *We had half each.*
2 in half into two equal pieces ▶ *I cut the apple in half.*
3 half past 30 minutes after an hour ▶ *It's half past ten* (=30 minutes after 10 o'clock).

half-brother /ˈhɑːf ˌbrʌðəʳ/ *noun*
a brother who has either the same mother or father as you, but not both

half-hearted /ˌhɑːf ˈhɑːtɪd/ *adjective*
done without any real effort or interest ▶ *He made a half-hearted attempt to talk to me.*

half-price /ˌhɑːf ˈpraɪs/ *adjective*
costing half the usual amount ▶ *half-price tickets*

half-sister /ˈhɑːf ˌsɪstəʳ/ *noun*
a sister who has either the same mother or father as you, but not both

half term /ˌhɑːf ˈtɜːm/ *noun (no plural)*
a short holiday in the middle of a school term

half time /ˌhɑːf ˈtaɪm/ *noun (no plural)*
the middle point in a game or match when the players stop to rest

halfway /ˌhɑːfˈweɪ/ *adverb*
in the middle between two places or things ▶ *I live halfway* ***between*** *London and Guildford.*

hall /hɔːl/ *noun*
1 a large room or building ▶ *The children were in the school hall.*
2 the room just inside the front door of a house ▶ *Hang your coat in the hall.*

hallo *(also* ***hello, hullo****)* /həˈləʊ/ *interjection*
the usual word that you say when you meet someone or talk on the telephone ▶ *Hallo John.* ▶ *Hallo. My name's Anne.*

hall of residence /ˌhɔːl əv ˈrezɪdəns/ *noun (plural* ***halls of residence****)*
a college or university building where students live

Hallowe'en /ˌhæləʊˈiːn/ *noun*
the last night in October, when children dress in strange clothes, and visit people's houses to ask for sweets or to play tricks on them

hallucinate /həˈluːsɪneɪt/ *verb (present participle* ***hallucinating,*** *past* ***hallucinated****)*
to see, feel, or hear something that is not really there ▶ *Jim started hallucinating after he took the drugs.*

hallucination /həˌluːsɪˈneɪʃən/ *noun*
something you see, feel, or hear that is not really there ▶ *They suffered from strange hallucinations.*

hallway /ˈhɔːlweɪ/ *noun*
a HALL in a house

H

halo /ˈheɪləʊ/ *noun*
in paintings, a golden circle above the head of a holy person ▶ *The angel had wings and a halo.*

halt¹ /hɔːlt/ *verb*
to stop ▶ *The policemen halted all the traffic.* ▶ *The car halted by the house.*

halt² *noun (no plural)*
a stop ▶ *The car came to a halt.*

halve /hɑːv/ *verb (present participle* ***halving,*** *past* ***halved****)*
to divide something into two pieces ▶ *James and I halved the apple* (=we each had half of it).

halves /hɑːvz/
the plural of **half**

ham /hæm/ *noun (no plural)*
meat from a pig's leg that has had salt added to stop it going bad
COMPARE: **bacon**

hamburger /ˈhæmbɜːgəʳ/ *noun*
meat that has been cut into very small pieces and then made into a round, flat shape before being cooked
SAME MEANING: **beefburger**

hammer¹ /ˈhæməʳ/ *noun*
a tool with a metal head and a wooden handle, used for knocking nails into things or for breaking things

hammer² *verb*
to hit something with a hammer

hammock /ˈhæmək/ *noun*
a large net or piece of material that hangs between two trees or poles, used for sleeping on

hamper¹ /ˈhæmpəʳ/ *verb*
to make it difficult for someone to do something ▶ *Storms hampered our attempts to reach the crash victims.* ▶ *Shearer was hampered by a leg injury.*

hamper² *noun*
a large basket with a lid, used for carrying food somewhere ▶ *a picnic hamper*

hamster /ˈhæmstəʳ/ *noun*
a small animal like a mouse, which keeps its food in its cheeks and which children sometimes keep as a pet

hand¹ /hænd/ *noun*
1 the part of your body at the end of your arm, with which you hold things
2 by hand not by machine ▶ *This toy was made by hand.*
3 give someone a hand to help someone ▶ *Will you give me a hand* ***with*** *the cleaning?*
4 hand in hand holding each other by the hand ▶ *They were walking hand in hand.*
5 hold hands (with somebody) if two people hold hands, they hold each other by the hand ▶ *They sat there, holding hands throughout the entire film.*

6 the part of a clock that moves to show the time ▶ *When the minute hand points to 12 and the hour hand points to 3, it's 3 o'clock.*

hand² *verb*
1 to give something to someone using your hands ▶ *Hand me that plate, please.* ▶ *She handed the letter to John.*
2 hand something in to give something to someone, usually to a teacher ▶ *Please hand in your books at the end of the lesson.*
3 hand things out to give one thing to each person ▶ *Could you hand out the forms, please?*

handbag /'hændbæg/ *noun*
a woman's bag for keeping money and small things in, carried in her hand or over her shoulder

handbook /'hændbʊk/ *noun*
a small book with instructions and information about a particular subject ▶ *an employee handbook*

handbrake /'hændbreɪk/ *noun*
the part of a car that you pull up with your hand to stop the car from moving

handcuffs /'hændkʌfs/ *plural noun*
two metal rings joined together and put round a prisoner's wrists

handful /'hændfʊl/ *noun*
1 a small number or amount ▶ *a handful **of** people*
2 the amount that you can hold in your hand ▶ *a handful **of** rice*

handicap¹ /'hændɪkæp/ *noun*
something that makes it difficult for you to do something ▶ *His sore leg will be a handicap in the race.*

handicap² *verb (present participle **handicapping**, past **handicapped**)*
to make it difficult for someone to do something ▶ *She has been handicapped by her illness.*

handicapped /'hændɪkæpt/ *adjective*
not able to use a part of your body or mind normally because it has been damaged ▶ *schools for mentally handicapped children*

handkerchief /'hæŋkətʃɪf/ *noun*
a square piece of cloth for cleaning your nose

handle¹ /'hændl/ *noun*
the part of a tool or an instrument that you hold in your hand

handle² *verb (present participle **handling**, past **handled**)*
1 to hold or touch something ▶ *Please don't handle the fruit.*
2 to control someone or something ▶ *He doesn't handle the children very well.*

handlebars /'hændlˌbɑːz/ *plural noun*
the parts of a bicycle that you hold when you ride it

handler /'hændləʳ/ *noun*
used in job titles to show what someone works with ▶ *airport baggage handlers* ▶ *a police dog handler*

handmade /ˌhænd'meɪd/ *adjective*
made by a person, not a machine ▶ *handmade furniture*

handout /'hændaʊt/ *noun*
1 money or food that is given to someone, usually because they are poor
2 a piece of paper with information on it that a speaker gives to the people in a class or a meeting

handshake /'hændʃeɪk/ *noun*
an action in which two people hold each other's right hand and move it up and down when they meet or leave each other ▶ *a firm handshake*

handsome /'hænsəm/ *adjective*
(used about men) attractive to look at
SAME MEANING: **good-looking**
LOOK AT: **beautiful**

hands-on /'hændz ɒn/ *adjective*
(used about experience or training) obtained from doing something rather than studying it

H

handwriting /ˈhændˌraɪtɪŋ/ *noun (no plural)*
1 writing done by hand with a pen or pencil
2 the style of someone's writing

handy /ˈhændɪ/ *adjective (**handier, handiest**)*
1 near ▶ *This house is handy for the market.*
2 useful ▶ *It's very handy having a car.*

hang /hæŋ/ *verb*
1 *(past **hung** /hʌŋ/)* to fix something at the top so that the lower part is free ▶ *I hung my coat up on a hook.*
2 *(past **hanged**)* to kill someone, usually as a punishment, by holding them above the ground with a rope around their neck
3 hang about to stand and do nothing or to wait around without any reason ▶ *He was hanging about outside my house.*
4 hang on to wait ▶ *Hang on – I want to talk to you.*
5 hang on to something to hold something tightly ▶ *Hang on everybody! The road's very bumpy.*

H

hangar /ˈhæŋəʳ/ *noun*
a large building where aircraft are kept

hanger /ˈhæŋəʳ/ *noun*
a specially shaped piece of wire or wood for hanging clothes on

hangover /ˈhæŋəʊvəʳ/ *noun*
have a hangover to feel sick because you have drunk too much alcohol the evening before

hankie *(also **hanky**)* /ˈhæŋkɪ/ *noun (plural **hankies**)*
a handkerchief

haphazard /hæpˈhæzəd/ *adjective*
not planned or organized ▶ *We work in a very haphazard way. (adverb: **haphazardly**)*

happen /ˈhæpən/ *verb*
1 to take place ▶ *The accident happened outside my house.*

If an event **occurs** or **happens**, it is not planned: *The explosion happened on Friday evening.* If an event **takes place**, it is the result of a plan or an arrangement: *The wedding will take place on June 6th.*

2 happen to do something to do something by chance ▶ *If you happen to see her, will you give her a message?*

happening /ˈhæpənɪŋ/ *noun*
an event ▶ *a strange happening*

happily /ˈhæpɪlɪ/ *adverb*
in a pleased or cheerful way ▶ *They were laughing happily.*
OPPOSITE: **unhappily**

happiness /ˈhæpɪnəs/ *noun (no plural)*
pleasure ▶ *They've had years of happiness together.*

happy /ˈhæpɪ/ *adjective (**happier, happiest**)*
very pleased ▶ *I am happy to see you again.* ▶ *Happy Birthday* ▶ *Happy New Year* (=said or written to someone to wish them happiness on those occasions)
OPPOSITE: **unhappy**

harass /ˈhærəs/ *verb*
to deliberately annoy or threaten someone, often over a long period of time ▶ *They claim that they are being harassed by the police.*

harassment /ˈhærəsmənt/ *noun (no plural)*
behaviour that threatens or offends someone ▶ *racial harassment*

harbour /ˈhɑːbəʳ/ *noun*
a place on the shore where ships can shelter safely

hard¹ /hɑːd/ *adjective*
1 not moving or soft when touched; firm like rock or metal ▶ *This ground is too hard to dig.*
OPPOSITE: **soft**

2 difficult to do or understand ▶ *a hard exam*
OPPOSITE (**2**): **easy**

hard² *adverb*
a lot; very much ▶ *It's raining hard.* ▶ *Are you working hard?*

hard-and-fast /ˌhɑːd ən ˈfɑːst/ *adjective*
hard-and-fast rules rules that cannot be changed ▶ *There are no hard-and-fast rules for success.*

hardback /ˈhɑːdbæk/ *noun*
a book that has a strong, stiff cover
COMPARE: **paperback**

hard-boiled /ˌhɑːd ˈbɔɪld/ *adjective*
(used about eggs) boiled until the yellow part becomes solid

hard disk /ˌhɑːd ˈdɪsk/ *noun*
a part fixed inside a computer on which you can store information
COMPARE: **floppy disk**

harden /ˈhɑːdn/ *verb*
to become firm

hard-headed /ˌhɑːd ˈhedɪd/ *adjective*
able to make difficult decisions without being influenced by your emotions

hard-hearted /ˌhɑːd ˈhɑːtɪd/ *adjective*
not kind to other people ▶ *She's a very hard-hearted woman.*
OPPOSITE: **kind-hearted**

hardly /ˈhɑːdlɪ/ *adverb*
almost not at all; only just ▶ *It was so dark that I could hardly see.* ▶ *He hardly ever* (=almost never) *eats meat.*
SAME MEANING: **barely**

hard-nosed /ˌhɑːd ˈnəʊzd/ *adjective*
not affected by your emotions, and determined to get what you want ▶ *a hard-nosed negotiator*

hardship /ˈhɑːdʃɪp/ *noun*
something that makes your life unpleasant, especially not having enough money ▶ *The family suffered years of poverty and hardship.* ▶ *the hardships of war*

hard shoulder /ˌhɑːd ˈʃəʊldəʳ/ *noun*
the area at the side of a big road where you are allowed to stop if you have a problem with your car

hard-up /ˌhɑːd ˈʌp/ *adjective*
not having enough money ▶ *We were very hard-up when I was young.*

hardware /ˈhɑːdweəʳ/ *noun (no plural)*
1 computer machinery and equipment
COMPARE: **software**
2 equipment and tools you use in your home and garden ▶ *a hardware store*

hard-working /ˌhɑːd ˈwɜːkɪŋ/ *adjective*
working with a lot of effort ▶ *a hard-working student*

hardy /ˈhɑːdɪ/ *adjective (**hardier, hardiest**)*
strong and able to exist in difficult conditions ▶ *hardy plants*

hare /heəʳ/ *noun*
an animal like a large rabbit that has long ears and long back legs

harm¹ /hɑːm/ *noun (no plural)*
1 hurt ▶ *Modern farming methods do a lot of harm to the environment.*
2 come to no harm to not be hurt or damaged ▶ *We left the dog outside last night, but she came to no harm.*
3 there's no harm in ... there is nothing bad in ... ▶ *There's no harm in asking him for a job.*

harm² *verb*
to hurt someone or something ▶ *Our dog won't harm you.*

harmful /ˈhɑːmfəl/ *adjective*
dangerous ▶ *Smoking is harmful to your health.*

harmless /ˈhɑːmləs/ *adjective*
not dangerous ▶ *a harmless snake*

H

harmonica /hɑːˈmɒnɪkə/ *noun*
a small musical instrument with holes along the side that you blow into and move from side to side

harmony /ˈhɑːmənɪ/ *noun*
1 *(no plural)* the state of not arguing or fighting ▶ *Why can't people live in harmony?*
2 *(plural **harmonies**)* musical notes that sound good together

harness[1] /ˈhɑːnɪs/ *noun (plural **harnesses**)*
1 a set of bands that you put round a horse so that you can control it or it can pull a vehicle
2 a set of bands that hold someone or stop them from falling ▶ *The climbers used safety harnesses.*

harness[2] *verb*
to use the energy from something ▶ *ways of harnessing the sun's energy*

harp[1] /hɑːp/ *noun*
a large musical instrument with strings stretched on a frame with three corners

harp[2] *verb*
harp on about something to talk about something all the time, in a way that is annoying or boring ▶ *I wish he'd stop harping on about his bad back.*

harsh /hɑːʃ/ *adjective*
very unpleasant; cruel ▶ *a harsh punishment (adverb: **harshly**)*

harvest[1] /ˈhɑːvɪst/ *noun*
1 the time when the crops are gathered ▶ *I hope it doesn't rain much during the harvest.*
2 the amount of food collected during the harvest ▶ *The harvest was good this year.*

harvest[2] *verb*
to gather a crop

has /z, əz, s, həz; *strong* hæz/
the part of the verb **have** that we use with **he, she**, and **it** ▶ *She has three children.*

has-been /ˈhæz biːn/ *noun*
a person who is no longer important or popular

hash /hæʃ/ *noun*
make a hash of something to do something very badly

hasn't /ˈhæzənt/
has not ▶ *Hasn't he finished yet?*

hassle[1] /ˈhæsəl/ *noun*
something that is annoying because it takes a lot of time or effort ▶ *I didn't want the hassle of moving house again.*

hassle[2] *verb (present participle **hassling**, past **hassled**)*
to continuously ask someone to do something, in a way that is annoying ▶ *He keeps hassling me about the money I owe him.*

haste /heɪst/ *noun (no plural)*
quick movement or action often done without care ▶ *In my haste I forgot my coat.*

hasten /ˈheɪsən/ *verb*
1 to make something happen sooner ▶ *The accident hastened his death.*
2 hasten to do something to do or say something quickly ▶ *Gina hastened to assure him that everything was fine.*

hasty /ˈheɪstɪ/ *adjective (**hastier, hastiest**)*
done in a hurry ▶ *He ate a hasty lunch. (adverb: **hastily**)*

hat /hæt/ *noun*
a piece of clothing that you wear on your head

hatch /hætʃ/ *verb*
to come out of an egg ▶ *The chickens hatched this morning.*

hatchet /ˈhætʃɪt/ *noun*
a small tool like an AXE that you use to cut wood into small pieces

hate /heɪt/ *verb (present participle **hating**, past **hated**)*

not to like someone or something at all ▶ *I hate snakes.*
OPPOSITE: **love**

hatred /'heɪtrɪd/ *(also **hate**) noun (no plural)*
a very strong feeling of not liking someone or something ▶ *She looked at me with an expression of hatred.*
OPPOSITE: **love**

hat trick /'hæt trɪk/ *noun*
three GOALS that are SCORED by the same player in one game of football or HOCKEY

haul /hɔːl/ *verb*
to lift or pull something with difficulty ▶ *They hauled the boat up onto the shore.*
SAME MEANING: **heave**

haunt /hɔːnt/ *verb*
(used about the spirits of dead people) to visit or be in a place ▶ *People say that the spirit of his dead wife haunts the house.*

haunted /'hɔːntɪd/ *adjective*
visited by the spirits of dead people ▶ *The old church is haunted.*

haunting /'hɔːntɪŋ/ *adjective*
beautiful, sad, and staying in your thoughts for a long time ▶ *haunting landscapes*

have /v, əv, həv; *strong* hæv/ *verb*

present tense

singular	*plural*
I **have** (I**'ve**)	We **have** (We**'ve**)
You **have** (You**'ve**)	You **have** (You**'ve**)
He/She/It **has** (He**'s**/She**'s**/It**'s**)	They **have** (They**'ve**)

past tense

singular	*plural*
I **had** (I**'d**)	We **had** (We**'d**)
You **had** (You**'d**)	You **had** (You**'d**)
He/She/It **had** (He**'d**/She**'d**/It**'d**)	They **had** (They**'d**)

present participle	**having**
past participle	**had**
negative short forms	**haven't, hasn't, hadn't**

(you can find each of these words in its own place in the dictionary)

1 a word that helps another word to say that something happened in the past: *We have been to the shops.* ▶ *When I arrived, she had already gone away.*
2 to own; to hold; to keep: *Do you have a car?* ▶ *She has blue eyes.* ▶ *I haven't any money.* ▶ *He has two sisters.* ▶ *I have a good job.* You can use **have got** instead of **have** with this meaning of the verb: *Have you got a car?* ▶ *I haven't got any money.* ▶ *She's got blue eyes.* ▶ *He's got two sisters.* ▶ *I've got a good job.*
3 to feel or experience something (especially a pain): *She has a headache.* You can use **have got** instead of **have** with this meaning of the verb: *She's got a headache.*
4 to do something: *I usually have my breakfast at 8 o'clock.* ▶ *I think I'll have a swim.*

haven't /'hævənt/
have not ▶ *I haven't seen that film.*

have to /'hæv tuː/ *(also **have got to** /həv 'gɒt tuː/) verb*
must ▶ *We have to leave now, if we want to catch the bus.* ▶ *We've got to be there by 6 o'clock.*

havoc /'hævək/ *noun (no plural)*
a situation in which there is a lot of confusion ▶ *The failure of the airport's computer system caused havoc.*

hawk /hɔːk/ *noun*
a large bird that kills small animals and birds for food

hay /heɪ/ *noun (no plural)*
dry grass fed to cattle

H

hay fever /ˈheɪ ˌfiːvəʳ/ *noun (no plural)*
a medical condition like a bad COLD, caused by breathing in dust from plants

hazard /ˈhæzəd/ *noun*
a danger ▶ *There are many hazards in a journey across Africa.*

hazardous /ˈhæzədəs/ *adjective*
dangerous ▶ *hazardous chemicals*

haze /heɪz/ *noun (no plural)*
fine clouds which stop you seeing clearly

hazy /ˈheɪzɪ/ *adjective (**hazier, haziest**)*
not clear ▶ *Since it was hazy, we couldn't see the mountains.*

he /ɪ, hɪ; *strong* hiː/ *pronoun (plural **they** /ðeɪ/)*
the male person or animal that the sentence is about ▶ *He is my brother.* ▶ *Be careful of that dog – he bites.*

head¹ /hed/ *noun*
1 the top part of your body, where your brain, eyes, ears, and mouth are
2 your brain ▶ *His head's full of ideas.*
3 the most important position of something ▶ *She sat at the head **of** the table.*
4 someone who is in charge of a group of people ▶ *the head **of** a large firm*
5 the front ▶ *At the head **of** the queue of cars was a bus.*
6 the teacher in charge of a school
7 keep your head to stay calm
8 lose your head to do things without thinking because you are too afraid or angry

head² *verb*
1 to be at the front or the top of something ▶ *The list was headed "Things to do".*
2 to hit a ball with your head
3 head for something to go towards something ▶ *I'm heading for home.*

headache /ˈhedeɪk/ *noun*
a pain in your head ▶ *I've got a headache.*

headfirst /ˌhedˈfɜːst/ *adverb*
with your head in front and the rest of your body following ▶ *He fell headfirst into the lake.*

heading /ˈhedɪŋ/ *noun*
something written at the top of a piece of writing

headlight /ˈhedlaɪt/ *(also **headlamp** /ˈhedlæmp/) noun*
one of the big lights at the front of a car

headline /ˈhedlaɪn/ *noun*
words printed in large letters at the top of a newspaper story

headlong /ˈhedlɒŋ/ *adverb*
1 rush headlong into something to do something important without thinking carefully about it first ▶ *Fran isn't the type to rush headlong into marriage.*
2 with your head going first ▶ *Ben went tumbling headlong down the hill.*

headmaster /hedˈmɑːstəʳ/ *noun*
the man who is in charge of a school

headmistress /hedˈmɪstrəs/ *noun (plural **headmistresses**)*
the woman who is in charge of a school

head-on /ˌhed ˈɒn/ *adverb, adjective*
(used about two vehicles) with the front part of one vehicle hitting the front part of the other ▶ *A car and a truck had collided head-on.* ▶ *a head-on crash*

headphones /ˈhedfəʊnz/ *plural noun*
things that fit over your head and ears and are used for listening to music

headquarters /hedˈkwɔːtəz/ *plural noun*
the main office of a business or of some other group

head start /ˌhed 'stɑːt/ *noun*
an advantage that helps you to be successful ▶ *His education gave him a head start.*

headteacher /hed'tiːtʃəʳ/ *noun*
the teacher in charge of a school

headway /'hedweɪ/ *noun*
make headway to make progress ▶ *We have made little headway towards a solution.*

heal /hiːl/ *verb*
to make something healthy again or become healthy again ▶ *The wound on my arm has healed.*

health /helθ/ *noun (no plural)*
how well your body is ▶ *His health is not good* (=he is often ill).

health club /'helθ klʌb/ *noun*
a place where you pay to use equipment to do physical exercises

health food /'helθ fuːd/ *noun (no plural)*
food that contains only natural substances ▶ *a health food shop*

healthy /'helθɪ/ *adjective (**healthier, healthiest**)*
1 strong and well in your body ▶ *healthy children* ▶ *a healthy plant*
2 good for your body ▶ *It is healthy to eat fruit.*
OPPOSITE (1 and 2): **unhealthy**

heap¹ /hiːp/ *noun*
a number of things put untidily on top of each other ▶ *A heap **of** old clothes was lying in the corner.*
SAME MEANING: **pile**

heap² *verb*
to put a lot of things on top of each other ▶ *He heaped his plate with food.*
SAME MEANING: **pile**

hear /hɪəʳ/ *verb (past **heard** /hɜːd/)*
1 to notice sounds through your ears ▶ *I heard the rain on the roof.*
2 to be given information about something ▶ *I heard that he was ill.*
3 **hear from someone** to get news of someone ▶ *Have you heard from John recently?*
4 **have heard of someone or something** to know about someone or something ▶ *I've never heard of her.*

hearing /'hɪərɪŋ/ *noun (no plural)*
your ability to hear ▶ *My hearing is getting worse.*

hearing aid /'hɪərɪŋ ˌeɪd/ *noun*
a small object that makes sounds louder and is put in your ear so that you can hear better

hearse /hɜːs/ *noun*
a large car for carrying a dead body in a COFFIN at a funeral

heart /hɑːt/ *noun*
1 the part of your body in your chest that pumps the blood round your body
2 your feelings ▶ *He has a kind heart.*
3 the middle ▶ *in the heart **of** the forest*
4 a shape like the shape of a heart
5 **break someone's heart** to make someone very unhappy
6 **by heart** so that you can remember something perfectly
7 **lose heart** to have less courage and hope ▶ *We had hoped they were still alive, but we're losing heart now.*
8 **take heart** to be encouraged and more hopeful about something
9 **with a heavy heart** sadly
10 **with all your heart** with deep feeling ▶ *I love you with all my heart.*

heart attack /'hɑːt əˌtæk/ *noun*
a serious medical condition in which a person's heart suddenly stops beating normally or regularly, sometimes causing death

heartbeat /'hɑːtbiːt/ *noun*
the movement or sound of someone's heart

heartbreaking /'hɑːtˌbreɪkɪŋ/ *adjective*

H

making you feel very sad
▶ *heartbreaking pictures of starving children*

heartbroken /ˈhɑːtˌbrəʊkən/ *adjective*
very unhappy

heartfelt /ˈhɑːtfelt/ *adjective*
honest and sincere ▶ *a heartfelt apology*

hearth /hɑːθ/ *noun*
the part of the floor around a FIREPLACE

heartily /ˈhɑːtɪlɪ/ *adverb*
1 loudly and cheerfully ▶ *He laughed heartily.*
2 very much or completely ▶ *I heartily agree.*

heartless /ˈhɑːtləs/ *adjective*
not kind; cruel

heartwarming /ˈhɑːtˌwɔːmɪŋ/ *adjective*
making you feel happy and hopeful
▶ *a heartwarming story*

hearty /ˈhɑːtɪ/ *adjective (**heartier, heartiest**)*
1 very cheerful and friendly ▶ *We were given a hearty welcome.*
2 (used about meals) very large

heat¹ /hiːt/ *noun*
1 *(no plural)* the feeling of something hot ▶ *The heat of the sun made her feel ill.*
2 a race run earlier than the main race, to decide who will run in the main race
3 *(no plural)* hot weather ▶ *I hate the heat.*
OPPOSITE (**3**): **cold**

heat² *verb*
to make something hot ▶ *It's expensive to heat big rooms.*

heated /ˈhiːtɪd/ *adjective*
1 kept warm by using a heater
▶ *a heated swimming pool*
2 (used about arguments, discussions, etc.) causing people to become very angry and excited

heater /ˈhiːtəʳ/ *noun*
a machine that makes things hot

heather /ˈheðəʳ/ *noun*
a small bush with purple or white flowers that grows on hills

heating /ˈhiːtɪŋ/ *noun (no plural)*
a system for keeping rooms warm

heatwave /ˈhiːtweɪv/ *noun*
a period of unusually hot weather

heave /hiːv/ *verb (present participle **heaving**, past **heaved**)*
to lift or pull something with difficulty
▶ *I heaved the heavy box up the steps.*
SAME MEANING: **haul**

heaven /ˈhevən/ *noun (no plural)*
a place where people think God or the gods live, and good people will go after they die
COMPARE: **hell**

heavily /ˈhevɪlɪ/ *adverb*
very much or a lot ▶ *It was still raining heavily.* ▶ *They rely heavily on government aid.*

heavy /ˈhevɪ/ *adjective (**heavier, heaviest**)*
1 weighing a lot ▶ *This bag is too heavy to carry.*
2 great in amount ▶ *heavy rain*
▶ *heavy traffic*
OPPOSITE (**1** and **2**): **light**
3 a heavy sleeper someone who sleeps deeply
4 a heavy smoker someone who smokes a lot

heavy-handed /ˌhevɪ ˈhændɪd/ *adjective*
1 not considering people's feelings
▶ *He dealt with the problem in a heavy-handed way.*
2 using too much force ▶ *They were criticized for their heavy-handed treatment of the crowds.*

heavy metal /ˌhevɪ ˈmetl/ *noun (no plural)*
a type of rock music played on electric instruments and drums

heavyweight /ˈhevɪweɪt/ *noun*
1 a person who has a lot of power and importance ▶ *one of the heavyweights of the film industry*
2 a BOXER from the heaviest weight group

heck /hek/ *noun*
used when you are annoyed, surprised, etc. ▶ *Where the heck have you been?* ▶ *Moving all that furniture will be a heck of a job.*

hectare /ˈhektɑːʳ, ˈhekteəʳ/ *noun*
a measure of land, equal to 10,000 square metres

hectic /ˈhektɪk/ *adjective*
very busy or full of activity ▶ *It's been a really hectic week.*

he'd /hiːd/
1 he had ▶ *He'd met her before.*
2 he would ▶ *He said he'd tell me tomorrow.*

hedge /hedʒ/ *noun*
a row of small trees planted between fields or along roads to make a wall

hedgehog /ˈhedʒhɒg/ *noun*
a small animal whose body is covered in sharp points

heel /hiːl/ *noun*
1 the back part of your foot below your ankle
2 the part of a shoe or sock under your heel

hefty /ˈheftɪ/ *adjective (**heftier, heftiest**)*
1 large ▶ *She had to pay a hefty fine.*
2 heavy and slightly fat ▶ *He used to be quite hefty before he started jogging.*

height /haɪt/ *noun*
how tall or far from the ground something is ▶ *He measured the height of the bridge.*

heighten /ˈhaɪtn/ *verb*
to increase, or make something increase ▶ *The film has heightened public awareness of AIDS.*

heir /eəʳ/ *noun*
a person who gets money or goods when someone dies

heiress /ˈeərəs/ *noun (plural **heiresses**)*
a woman who gets money or goods when someone dies

heirloom /ˈeəluːm/ *noun*
a valuable object that the same family has owned for many years ▶ *Carrie's ring is a family heirloom.*

held /held/
the PAST TENSE and PAST PARTICIPLE of the verb **hold**

helicopter /ˈhelɪkɒptəʳ/ *noun*
a flying machine with blades which go round on its top

helium /ˈhiːlɪəm/ *noun (no plural)*
a gas that is lighter than air

hell /hel/ *noun (no plural)*
a place where people think that the Devil lives and where bad people will go after they die
COMPARE: **heaven**

he'll /hiːl/
he will ▶ *He'll be here soon.*

hello *(also **hallo, hullo**)* /həˈləʊ/ *interjection*
the usual word that you say when you meet someone or talk on the telephone ▶ *Hello, Jane!*
COMPARE: **goodbye**

helmet /ˈhelmɪt/ *noun*
a hard hat that you wear to stop your head being hurt

help[1] /help/ *verb*
1 to do something for someone ▶ *Could you help me move this box?*
2 cannot help something cannot stop or control something ▶ *I couldn't help laughing when I saw his funny hat.*
3 help yourself to take what you want ▶ *Help yourself **to** a drink.*

help[2] *noun*
someone or something that makes things easier or better for someone

else ▶ *If you want any help, just ask me.*

helpful /'helpfəl/ *adjective*
doing something to help someone else ▶ *She's so kind and helpful.*
OPPOSITE: **unhelpful**

helping /'helpɪŋ/ *noun*
the amount of food on a plate ▶ *Would you like another helping **of** soup?*

helpless /'helpləs/ *adjective*
not able to do things for yourself ▶ *a helpless child*

hem /hem/ *noun*
the bottom edge of a skirt, shirt, etc. when turned under ▶ *I'll let down the hem of that dress for you.*

hemisphere /'hemɪsfɪəʳ/ *noun*
one of the two halves of the Earth ▶ *the northern hemisphere*

hen /hen/ *noun*
a female chicken

hence /hens/ *adverb*
for this reason ▶ *The department is short of money: hence the need to reduce spending.*

her /əʳ, həʳ; *strong* hɜːʳ/ *pronoun, adjective*
1 a woman or girl (used in sentences like this) ▶ *I saw her last week.* ▶ *Give her the book.* ▶ *I had a letter from her.*
2 belonging to a woman or girl ▶ *Her baby is two months old now.*

herb /hɜːb/ *noun*
a plant used for medicine or for giving a special taste to food

herbal /'hɜːbəl/ *adjective*
made from herbs ▶ *herbal medicine*

herd¹ /hɜːd/ *noun*
a group of animals of the same kind ▶ *a herd **of** cattle*
COMPARE: **flock**

herd² *verb*
to make a group of people or animals move in a certain direction

here /hɪəʳ/ *adverb*
1 at or to this place ▶ *Come here and sit beside me.*
COMPARE: **there**
2 here and there in different places ▶ *There were a few colourful boats here and there on the water.*
3 Here you are a phrase used when you are giving someone something that they want

hereditary /hə'redɪtərɪ/ *adjective*
(used about qualities or diseases) passed to a child by its parents

heresy /'herəsɪ/ *noun (plural **heresies**)*
a belief that a religious or political group thinks is wrong

heritage /'herɪtɪdʒ/ *noun (no plural)*
things that have been in a society for a long time, especially things that people think are valuable ▶ *We must protect our musical heritage.*

hero /'hɪərəʊ/ *noun (plural **heroes**)*
1 a man who does something great or brave
2 a person you admire very much ▶ *Robbie Williams is my hero.*

heroic /hɪ'rəʊɪk/ *adjective*
very brave

heroin /'herəʊɪn/ *noun (no plural)*
a very strong, illegal drug

heroine /'herəʊɪn/ *noun*
a woman who does something great or brave

heroism /'herəʊɪzəm/ *noun (no plural)*
great courage

hers /hɜːz/ *pronoun*
something belonging to a woman or girl ▶ *My hand touched hers.*

herself /ə'self; *strong* hə'self/ *pronoun (plural **themselves** /ðəm'selvz/)*
1 the same girl or woman as the subject of the sentence ▶ *The woman dressed herself in her best clothes.*

2 used to give the word "she" a stronger meaning ▶ *She gave me some money, although she didn't have much herself.*
3 by herself alone; without help ▶ *She went for a walk by herself.* ▶ *She prepared that wonderful meal all by herself.*

he's /hiːz/
he is ▶ *He's a doctor.*

hesitant /ˈhezɪtənt/ *adjective*
slow to do something because you are nervous or uncertain ▶ *a hesitant smile (adverb: **hesitantly**)*

hesitate /ˈhezɪteɪt/ *verb (present participle **hesitating**, past **hesitated**)*
to stop what you are doing for a short time ▶ *He hesitated before he answered because he didn't know what to say.*

hesitation /ˌhezɪˈteɪʃən/ *noun*
a short stop or wait before you do something, because you feel uncertain

heterosexual /ˌhetərəˈsekʃʊəl/ *adjective*
sexually attracted to people of the opposite sex

hexagon /ˈheksəgən/ *noun*
a flat shape with six sides

hey /heɪ/ *interjection*
used to get someone's attention, or to show someone you are surprised or annoyed ▶ *Hey! Look who's here!*

hi /haɪ/ *interjection*
a friendly word that you use when you meet other people

hibernate /ˈhaɪbəneɪt/ *verb (present participle **hibernating**, past **hibernated**)*
(used about animals) to sleep all the time during winter

hiccup¹ /ˈhɪkʌp/ *noun*
1 hiccups *plural noun* sudden, loud sounds in your throat that you sometimes make after eating or drinking too quickly
2 a small problem ▶ *There were a few small hiccups before the concert began.*

hiccup² *verb*
to make sudden, loud sounds in your throat after eating or drinking too quickly

hid /hɪd/
the PAST TENSE of the verb **hide**

hidden¹ /ˈhɪdn/
the PAST PARTICIPLE of the verb **hide**

hidden² *adjective*
difficult to see, find, or notice ▶ *They were filmed with hidden cameras.*

hide¹ /haɪd/ *verb (present participle **hiding**, past tense **hid** /hɪd/, past participle **hidden** /ˈhɪdn/)*
1 to put something in a place where no one can see it or find it ▶ *Where did you hide the money?*
2 to go to a place where no one can see or find you ▶ *I hid behind the door, so that no one would see me.*
3 to not tell people about something ▶ *She hid her feelings.*
4 hide and seek a children's game in which one child hides and the others have to find him or her

hide² *noun*
the skin of an animal

hideous /ˈhɪdɪəs/ *adjective*
very ugly or unpleasant ▶ *a hideous yellow and purple dress*

hiding /ˈhaɪdɪŋ/ *noun*
be in hiding to be hiding somewhere because you are in danger or you have done something wrong ▶ *The couple have been in hiding since the allegations were made public.*

hi-fi /ˌhaɪ ˈfaɪ/ *noun*
a machine that plays records or CDS and TAPES

high /haɪ/ *adjective*
1 tall, or far from the ground ▶ *The highest mountain in Africa is Mount Kilimanjaro.* ▶ *It is nearly 20,000 feet high.*

H

2 stronger, greater, or larger than usual ▶ *a high wind* ▶ *travelling at high speed* ▶ *high prices*
3 near the top of a set of sounds that the ear can hear ▶ *a high voice*
OPPOSITE (**1, 2** and **3**): **low**

high-class /ˌhaɪ ˈklɑːs/ *adjective*
of good quality and style, and usually expensive ▶ *a high-class restaurant*

higher education /ˌhaɪər edjʊˈkeɪʃən/ *noun (no plural)*
study after you have left school, for example at university or college
COMPARE: **further education**

high jump /ˈhaɪ dʒʌmp/ *noun*
the high jump a sport in which you run and jump over a bar that is raised higher after each successful jump

highlands /ˈhaɪləndz/ *plural noun*
land which has a lot of hills, or is high up in the hills

highlight[1] /ˈhaɪlaɪt/ *verb*
1 to make something the main subject or problem that people pay attention to ▶ *In his speech, the President highlighted the issue of crime.*
2 to cover written words with a line or block of colour, so that you can see them more easily

highlight[2] *noun*
the most important, interesting, or enjoyable part of something ▶ *You can see highlights of today's game after the news.*

highly /ˈhaɪlɪ/ *adverb*
1 very ▶ *a highly intelligent girl*
2 think highly of someone to respect and admire someone a lot ▶ *His employees think very highly of him.*

Highness /ˈhaɪnəs/ *noun (plural* ***Highnesses****)*
a way of talking to or about certain royal people ▶ *His Royal Highness the Prince of Wales*

high-pitched /ˌhaɪ ˈpɪtʃt/ *adjective*
high and sharp, and unpleasant to hear ▶ *a high-pitched scream*

high-powered /ˌhaɪ ˈpaʊəd/ *adjective*
1 (used about machines) very powerful ▶ *a high-powered speedboat*
2 having an important job with a lot of responsibility ▶ *a high-powered executive*

high-rise /ˈhaɪ raɪz/ *adjective*
(used about buildings) very tall and modern ▶ *high-rise apartment blocks*

high school /ˈhaɪ skuːl/ *noun*
a school for children between 11 and 18 years old

high street /ˈhaɪ striːt/ *noun*
the main road in a town, where all the shops are

high-tech *(also* ***hi-tech****)* /ˌhaɪ ˈtek/ *adjective*
using the most modern and advanced ways of doing things in business and industry ▶ *a new, high-tech camera*

high tide /ˌhaɪ ˈtaɪd/ *noun*
the time when the sea is very high up the shore
OPPOSITE: **low tide**

highway /ˈhaɪweɪ/ *noun*
a main road

hijack /ˈhaɪdʒæk/ *verb*
to force the driver of a plane, lorry, etc. to take you somewhere

hijacker /ˈhaɪdʒækəʳ/ *noun*
a person who forces the driver of a plane, lorry, etc. to take them somewhere

hike[1] /haɪk/ *verb (present participle* ***hiking****, past* ***hiked****)*
to take a long walk in the countryside or mountains for pleasure ▶ *The Lake District is a great place to go hiking.*

hike[2] *noun*
a long walk in the countryside or mountains for pleasure ▶ *The*

weather was too bad for us to go for a hike.

hilarious /hɪ'leərɪəs/ *adjective*
very funny ▶ *a hilarious film*

hill /hɪl/ *noun*
a piece of ground higher than usual; a small mountain

hillside /'hɪlsaɪd/ *noun*
the sloping side of a hill ▶ *a hotel built high on the hillside*

hilly /'hɪlɪ/ *adjective (**hillier, hilliest**)*
with a lot of hills ▶ *The surrounding countryside was very hilly.*

him /ɪm; *strong* hɪm/ *pronoun*
a man or boy (used in sentences like this) ▶ *I saw him last week.* ▶ *Give him the book.* ▶ *I had a letter from him.*

himself /ɪm'self; *strong* hɪm'self/ *pronoun (plural **themselves** /ðəm'selvz/)*
1 the same man or boy as the subject of the sentence ▶ *Peter bought himself some new clothes.*
2 used to give the word "he" a stronger meaning ▶ *He told me so himself.*
3 by himself alone; without help ▶ *He stayed at home by himself.* ▶ *He repaired the roof all by himself.*

hinder /'hɪndə^r^/ *verb*
to make it more difficult for someone to do something

hindsight /'haɪndsaɪt/ *noun (no plural)*
the ability to understand or judge an event only after it has happened ▶ *With hindsight, I should never have let her use my car.*

Hindu /'hɪnduː/ *noun*
a person who follows the main religion of India

Hinduism /'hɪnduːɪzəm/ *noun (no plural)*
the main religion of India

hinge /hɪndʒ/ *noun*
a piece of metal that joins two things together so that one of them can swing freely ▶ *We need a new hinge on that door.*

hint¹ /hɪnt/ *verb*
to say something in a way that is not direct ▶ *He hinted that he was looking for another job.*

hint² *noun*
1 something said in a way that is not direct ▶ *When she said she was tired, it was a hint that she wanted us to go.*
2 a piece of useful advice ▶ *helpful hints for cleaning children's clothes*

hip /hɪp/ *noun*
the part of your body where your legs join your bottom

hippie *(also **hippy**)* /'hɪpɪ/ *noun*
a person who deliberately does not live or dress like ordinary people and who believes in love and peace. People first started becoming hippies in the 1960s

hippopotamus /ˌhɪpə'pɒtəməs/ *noun (plural **hippopotamuses**)*
a large, African animal with short legs and thick, hairless skin, that lives near rivers

hippy /'hɪpɪ/ *noun (plural **hippies**)*
another word for **hippie**

hire¹ /haɪə^r^/ *verb (present participle **hiring**, past **hired**)*
to pay for the use of something or for someone's help ▶ *He hired a car for two days.*

> Use **hire** only when you are talking about paying to use something for a short time: *We hired a car for a few days.* Compare **rent**, which is used when talking about longer periods of time, e.g. you rent a house to live in; you do not hire it.

hire² *noun (no plural)*
the use of something for a certain amount of money ▶ *Boats for hire.*

H

his /ɪz; *strong* hɪz/ *adjective, pronoun*
1 belonging to a man or boy ▶ *He sat drinking his coffee.*
2 something belonging to a man or boy ▶ *My hand touched his.*

Hispanic /hɪˈspænɪk/ *adjective*
of or from a country where Spanish or Portuguese is spoken

hiss[1] /hɪs/ *verb*
to make a sound like a continuous "s" by forcing air out through your teeth or mouth ▶ *The snake hissed angrily.*

hiss[2] *noun (plural* ***hisses****)*
a sound like a continuous "s"

historian /hɪˈstɔːrɪən/ *noun*
a person who studies or writes about history

historic /hɪˈstɒrɪk/ *adjective*
important in the past ▶ *a historic meeting between the two leaders*

historical /hɪˈstɒrɪkəl/ *adjective*
in or about the past ▶ *historical facts*

history /ˈhɪstərɪ/ *noun (no plural)*
1 things that happened in the past
2 the study of things that happened in the past ▶ *a history lesson*

hit[1] /hɪt/ *verb (present participle* ***hitting****, past* ***hit****)*
to touch something suddenly and with a lot of force ▶ *He hit me in the stomach.* ▶ *She hit her head on the low roof.*

hit[2] *noun*
1 an act of touching something suddenly and forcefully ▶ *I got a direct hit with my first shot.*
2 a song or film that is popular and successful ▶ *That song was a hit last year.*

hit-and-run /ˌhɪt ən ˈrʌn/ *adjective*
hit-and-run accident an accident in which a car driver hits someone and then drives away without stopping to help

hitch[1] /hɪtʃ/ *verb*
1 to stand beside a road and ask for free rides in other people's cars ▶ *We tried to hitch a ride into Manchester.*
2 to fasten one thing to another ▶ *Dad hitched the boat to the back of the car.*

hitch[2] *noun (plural* ***hitches****)*
a small problem that causes a delay ▶ *The presentation went off without a hitch.*

hitchhike /ˈhɪtʃhaɪk/ *verb (present participle* ***hitchhiking****, past* ***hitchhiked****)*
to stand beside a road and ask for free rides in other people's cars

hitchhiker /ˈhɪtʃˌhaɪkəʳ/ *noun*
a person who stands beside a road and asks for free rides in other people's cars

hi-tech /ˌhaɪ ˈtek/ *adjective*
another word for **high-tech**

HIV /ˌeɪtʃ aɪ ˈviː/ *noun (no plural)*
1 HUMAN IMMUNODEFICIENCY VIRUS; a type of infection that enters the body through the blood or sexual activity, and can cause AIDS
2 be HIV positive to have the HIV infection in your blood

hive /haɪv/ *(also* ***beehive****) noun*
a wooden box made for bees to live in

h'm *(also* ***hmm****)* /m, hm/ *interjection*
a sound that you make when you are thinking what to say or do

hoard[1] /hɔːd/ *verb*
to collect and store things but not use them ▶ *squirrels hoarding nuts for the winter*

hoard[2] *noun*
a large amount of something that has been stored ▶ *a hoard of gold coins*

hoarse /hɔːs/ *adjective*
(used about a person's voice) rough, as when your throat is sore and dry ▶ *His voice was hoarse after speaking for an hour.*

hoax /həʊks/ *noun (plural **hoaxes**)* an attempt to make people believe something that is not true ▶ *The bomb threat turned out to be a hoax.*

hob /hɒb/ *noun* the flat surface on the top of a COOKER where you cook food in pans

hobble /ˈhɒbəl/ *verb (present participle **hobbling**, past **hobbled**)* to walk slowly and with difficulty ▶ *I had to hobble after I hurt my leg.*

hobby /ˈhɒbɪ/ *noun (plural **hobbies**)* an activity that you enjoy doing in your free time ▶ *He works in a bank, but his hobby is building model boats.*

hockey /ˈhɒkɪ/ *noun (no plural)* a game played by two teams who use curved sticks to hit a ball into a net

hoe /həʊ/ *noun* a tool used to loosen the ground in your garden

hog¹ /hɒg/ *noun* **go the whole hog** to do something thoroughly or completely ▶ *Why don't we go the whole hog and get champagne?*

hog² *verb (present participle **hogging**, past **hogged**)* to keep or use all of something for yourself ▶ *Katie always hogs the duvet.*

hoist /hɔɪst/ *verb* to pull something up or raise it to a high place, often using ropes

hold¹ /həʊld/ *verb (past **held** /held/)*
1 to have something in your hand or arms ▶ *The little girl held the toy tightly in her arms.*
2 to keep something in a particular position ▶ *Can you hold the picture up for a minute, please?*
3 to have something inside ▶ *This bottle holds one litre.*
4 to arrange and make something happen ▶ *The meeting will be held next week.*
5 to have something ▶ *He holds an important position at the bank.*
6 hold someone back to stop someone from moving forwards ▶ *The police tried to hold the crowd back.*
7 hold a conversation to talk to someone
8 hold your breath to stop breathing for a short time ▶ *You have to hold your breath underwater.*
9 hold the line to wait for a short time when you are talking on the telephone ▶ *Hold the line. I'll see if I can find the manager.*
10 hold on to wait for a short time ▶ *Could you hold on, please? I'll see if he's in.*

hold² *noun*
1 the place on a ship where goods are stored
2 get hold of, take hold of to take something in your hand and keep it there ▶ *He took hold of the rope and pulled.*

holdall /ˈhəʊldɔːl/ *noun* a bag used for carrying clothes, tools, etc.

holder /ˈhəʊldəʳ/ *noun*
1 used to show that someone has a particular position, place, or thing ▶ *the Olympic record holder* ▶ *UK passport holders*
2 something that holds or contains something else ▶ *a leather chequebook holder*

hold-up /ˈhəʊld ʌp/ *noun*
1 a delay ▶ *I'm sorry I'm late, but there was a hold-up near the bridge.*
2 an occasion when robbers use guns to persuade other people to give them money ▶ *a hold-up in a bank*

hole /həʊl/ *noun* an empty space or opening in something ▶ *a hole in the road*

holiday /ˈhɒlɪdeɪ, -dɪ/ *noun*
1 a time when you do not work or go to school ▶ *Next Friday is a holiday.*

H

2 on holiday not at school or work ▶ *I'm on holiday next week.*
3 go on holiday to go to another place for a short time to have a rest from school or work

hollow /'hɒləʊ/ *adjective*
having an empty space inside ▶ *a hollow tree*
OPPOSITE: **solid**

holly /'hɒlɪ/ *noun (no plural)*
a small tree with dark green, prickly leaves and red berries

hologram /'hɒləgræm/ *noun*
a picture made in a special way so that the image looks as if it is real, because you can see the sides as well as the front of it

holy /'həʊlɪ/ *adjective (**holier, holiest**)*
1 concerning God or religion ▶ *the holy city of Mecca*
2 very good and pure; religious ▶ *a holy man*

home[1] /həʊm/ *noun*
1 the place where someone lives ▶ *Her home is in Wales.*
2 a place where a particular group of people or animals are cared for ▶ *a children's home*
3 at home in your own house ▶ *I stayed at home to read.*

home[2] *adjective*
1 of or being the place where someone or something lives or is based ▶ *my home town*
2 playing on your own sports field and not that of the other team ▶ *the home team*

home[3] *adverb*
to or at your own house ▶ *Let's go home.*

homeland /'həʊmlænd/ *noun*
the country where you were born ▶ *She returned to her homeland, Somalia.*

homeless /'həʊmləs/ *adjective*
having nowhere to live

homely /'həʊmlɪ/ *adjective (**homelier, homeliest**)*
ordinary and comfortable in a way that makes you feel relaxed ▶ *a small, family hotel with a homely atmosphere*

homemade /ˌhəʊm'meɪd/ *adjective*
made at home and not bought from a shop ▶ *homemade jam*

homeopathy /ˌhəʊmɪ'ɒpəθɪ/ *noun (no plural)*
a method of treating illness that involves using very small amounts of natural substances

home page /'həʊm peɪdʒ/ *noun*
a place on the INTERNET where you can find information about a person, company, etc. ▶ *Visit our home page for more information and links to other sites.*

homesick /'həʊmsɪk/ *adjective*
sad because you are away from home ▶ *I felt homesick living in Paris by myself.*

homeward /'həʊmwəd/ *adjective*
going towards home ▶ *my homeward journey*

homework /'həʊmwɜːk/ *noun (no plural)*
work that a teacher gives you to do at home

homicide /'hɒmɪsaɪd/ *noun*
the crime of murder

homosexual /ˌhəʊmə'sekʃʊəl/ *adjective*
sexually attracted to people of the same sex

honest /'ɒnɪst/ *adjective*
not likely to lie, steal, or cheat; truthful ▶ *an honest face*
OPPOSITE: **dishonest**

honestly /'ɒnɪstlɪ/ *adverb*
1 without lying, stealing, or cheating ▶ *If I can't get the money honestly, I'll have to think of something else.*

2 speaking truthfully ▶ *I honestly don't mind working late tonight.*
3 Honestly! a word used to express annoyance ▶ *Honestly! What a stupid thing to do.*

honesty /ˈɒnɪstɪ/ *noun (no plural)*
behaviour in which you tell the truth, and do not lie, steal, or cheat ▶ *He was praised for his honesty when he returned the money.*
OPPOSITE: **dishonesty**

honey /ˈhʌnɪ/ *noun (no plural)*
a sweet, sticky liquid that is made by bees and that people can eat

honeymoon /ˈhʌnɪmuːn/ *noun*
a holiday taken by a man and a woman who have just got married

honk /hɒŋk/ *verb*
to make a loud noise using a car HORN ▶ *A taxi driver honked his horn behind her.*

honour /ˈɒnəʳ/ *noun (no plural)*
1 great respect ▶ *The things that he has done have brought honour to our country.*
OPPOSITE: **dishonour**
2 in honour of someone, in someone's honour done to show respect for someone ▶ *a ceremony in honour of the soldiers who died*

honourable /ˈɒnərəbəl/ *adjective*
behaving in a way that people think is morally right, which makes them respect you ▶ *an honourable man (adverb:* ***honourably****)*

hood /hʊd/ *noun*
1 a piece of cloth on a coat or other piece of clothing that you can pull up to cover your head and neck
2 the covering of an open car ▶ *It's raining. Put the hood up.*

hoof /huːf/ *noun (plural* ***hooves*** */huːvz/)*
the foot of a horse, cow, sheep, or goat

hook /hʊk/ *noun*
1 a bent piece of metal or hard plastic for hanging something on or for catching something ▶ *He hung his coat on the hook behind the door.* ▶ *a fish hook*
2 off the hook having the telephone receiver lifted so that the telephone will not ring

hooked /hʊkt/ *adjective*
1 be hooked on something to like something a lot and not want to stop doing it or using it ▶ *Thousands of children are hooked on computer games.*
2 shaped like a hook ▶ *a hooked nose*

hooligan /ˈhuːlɪgən/ *noun*
a noisy, violent young person who causes trouble by fighting and breaking things

hoop /huːp/ *noun*
a round band of wood, plastic, or metal

hooray /hʊˈreɪ/ *interjection*
another word for **hurray**

hoot[1] /huːt/ *verb*
to make a loud noise like the noise of a car's horn ▶ *The bus driver hooted at the man who stepped onto the road.*

hoot[2] *noun*
1 the sound made by a car's horn
2 the sound made by an OWL
3 a shout of laughter

hoover /ˈhuːvəʳ/ *verb*
to clean the floor using a machine that sucks up dirt ▶ *Most days I hoover the floor after breakfast.*
SAME MEANING: **vacuum**

Hoover /ˈhuːvəʳ/ *noun trademark*
a VACUUM CLEANER
SAME MEANING: **vacuum**

hooves /huːvz/
the plural of **hoof**

hop[1] /hɒp/ *verb (present participle* ***hopping****, past* ***hopped****)*
1 (used about people) to jump on one foot

2 (used about small birds and animals) to jump with both legs together

hop[2] *noun*
1 a small jump
2 a short aircraft flight ▶ *We'll do the final hop from Cairo to Luxor tomorrow.*

hope[1] /həʊp/ *verb (present participle* ***hoping****, past* ***hoped****)*
to want something to happen and to think it probably will happen ▶ *I hope to go to college.* ▶ *Is she coming? I hope so.* ▶ *I hope not.*

hope[2] *noun*
1 an idea that something will happen as you want it to ▶ *Hopes of reaching an agreement are fading.*
2 someone or something that could make everything happen as you want it to ▶ *You're my last hope.*
3 give up hope, lose hope to stop thinking that everything will happen as you want it to ▶ *Don't lose hope.*
4 hope for the best to hope that everything will be all right in the end

hopeful /ˈhəʊpfəl/ *adjective*
feeling quite sure about something ▶ *I am hopeful that she will come tomorrow.*

hopefully /ˈhəʊpfəlɪ/ *adverb*
1 in a hopeful way ▶ *The dog waited hopefully beside the table for some food.*
2 if everything goes well ▶ *Hopefully, we'll be there by dinner time.*

hopeless /ˈhəʊpləs/ *adjective*
1 with no sign of something getting better ▶ *a hopeless situation*
2 very bad or lacking in skill ▶ *I am hopeless* ***at*** *science.*
(adverb: ***hopelessly****)*

horde /hɔːd/ *noun*
a very large crowd ▶ *Hordes of reporters were waiting at the airport.*

horizon /həˈraɪzən/ *noun*
the line between the land or sea and the sky ▶ *I could see a ship on the horizon.*

horizontal /ˌhɒrɪˈzɒntl/ *adjective*
in a flat position, along or parallel to the ground ▶ *a horizontal surface*
COMPARE: **vertical**

hormone /ˈhɔːməʊn/ *noun*
a substance produced by your body, which helps it to grow or causes it to change in some other way

horn /hɔːn/ *noun*
1 one of the two hard pieces sticking out from the heads of some animals
2 an instrument on a car, bus, etc. that gives a short, loud sound as a warning ▶ *He sounded his horn at the car in front.*
3 a musical instrument that you blow into

horoscope /ˈhɒrəskəʊp/ *noun*
a description of your character and things that will happen to you in the future, based on the position of the stars and PLANETS when you were born

horrendous /hɒˈrendəs/ *adjective*
very bad or unpleasant ▶ *The traffic was horrendous.*
(adverb: ***horrendously****)*

horrible /ˈhɒrəbəl/ *adjective*
very unpleasant ▶ *There was a horrible accident here yesterday.*
SAME MEANING: **terrible, dreadful**

horrid /ˈhɒrɪd/ *adjective*
unpleasant ▶ *horrid food*

horrific /hɒˈrɪfɪk/ *adjective*
very shocking and unpleasant ▶ *That was a horrific accident.*

horrify /ˈhɒrɪfaɪ/ *verb (past* ***horrified****)*
to shock someone or make them feel fear ▶ *I was horrified by the news.*

horror /ˈhɒrəʳ/ *noun (no plural)*
great fear and shock ▶ *I watched in horror as the cars crashed into each other.*

horse /hɔːs/ *noun*
a large animal that people ride on and use for pulling heavy things

horseback /ˈhɔːsbæk/ *noun*
on horseback riding on a horse

horse-riding /ˈhɔːsˌraɪdɪŋ/ *noun (no plural)*
the sport of riding horses

horseshoe /ˈhɔːsʃuː/ *noun*
a piece of iron shaped like a half-circle, which is nailed to a horse's foot to protect it

hose /həʊz/ *noun*
a long piece of tube that bends easily, used for getting water from one place to another

hospitable /ˈhɒspɪtəbəl/ *adjective*
friendly and generous to someone who is visiting you ▶ *Greek people are very hospitable.*

hospital /ˈhɒspɪtl/ *noun*
a building where doctors and nurses care for people who are ill

hospitality /ˌhɒspɪˈtæləti/ *noun (no plural)*
kind attention given to visitors ▶ *The people of your village showed me great hospitality.*

host /həʊst/ *noun*
a person who has invited other people to their house for a social event

hostage /ˈhɒstɪdʒ/ *noun*
a person taken and kept as a prisoner by someone to force other people to do something, e.g. pay money

hostel /ˈhɒstl/ *noun*
a building where students, or other people living away from home, can eat and sleep cheaply

hostess /ˈhəʊstɪs/ *noun (plural **hostesses**)*
a woman who has invited people to her house for a social event

hostile /ˈhɒstaɪl/ *adjective*
not friendly ▶ *a hostile crowd*

hostility /hɒˈstɪlɪti/ *noun (no plural)*
unfriendly and angry feelings or behaviour ▶ *There has always been hostility between the two countries.*

hot /hɒt/ *adjective (**hotter, hottest**)*
1 having a lot of heat ▶ *the hottest day of the year* ▶ *The soup's really hot.*
OPPOSITE: **cold**
2 having a strong, burning taste ▶ *a hot curry*
OPPOSITE: **mild**

hot dog /ˌhɒt ˈdɒg/ *noun*
a special sort of long, red SAUSAGE eaten in a long piece of bread

hotel /həʊˈtel/ *noun*
a building where people can pay for a room to sleep in and for meals

hotline /ˈhɒtlaɪn/ *noun*
a special telephone number that people can call for information or advice

hound /haʊnd/ *noun*
a dog used for hunting or racing

hour /aʊəʳ/ *noun*
1 a measure of time; 60 minutes ▶ *There are 24 hours in a day.*
2 a particular time of day or night ▶ *There won't be any trains at this hour.*
3 a time when you usually do a particular thing ▶ *Our business hours are 9.30 to 5.30.* ▶ *my lunch hour*
4 for hours for a long time ▶ *I've been waiting here for hours.*
5 in an hour after one hour has passed ▶ *I'll meet you in an hour.*
6 on the hour at 1 o'clock, 2 o'clock, etc. ▶ *The trains leave on the hour.*

hourly /ˈaʊəli/ *adjective*
happening every hour ▶ *There are hourly trains to London.*

house /haʊs/ *noun (plural **houses** /ˈhaʊzɪz/)*
a building that people live in

housebound /ˈhaʊsbaʊnd/ *adjective*
unable to leave your house, because you are ill or cannot walk far

household /ˈhaʊsˌhəʊld/ *noun*
all the people who live in a house together

H

housekeeper /ˈhaʊsˌkiːpəʳ/ *noun*
someone who is paid to clean, cook, and look after your house for you

houseproud /ˈhaʊspraʊd/ *adjective*
spending a lot of time cleaning and taking care of your home

house-to-house /ˌhaʊs tə ˈhaʊs/ *adjective*
visiting every house in an area ▶ *The police are making house-to-house enquiries.*

housewarming /ˈhaʊsˌwɔːmɪŋ/ *noun*
a party to celebrate moving into a new house

housewife /ˈhaʊswaɪf/ *noun (plural* ***housewives*** */-waɪvz/)*
a married woman who works in the house for her family

housework /ˈhaʊswɜːk/ *noun (no plural)*
work that you do at home, such as cleaning, washing, etc. ▶ *I usually do the housework at weekends.*

housing /ˈhaʊzɪŋ/ *noun (no plural)*
houses for people to live in ▶ *More money is needed for housing, education, and health.*

hover /ˈhɒvəʳ/ *verb*
to stay in the air in one place ▶ *The great bird hovered above the field, looking for a mouse.*

hovercraft /ˈhɒvəkrɑːft/ *noun*
a sort of boat that travels over land or water by floating on air that is pushed out by its engines

how /haʊ/ *adverb*
1 in what way ▶ *How do you open this box?*
2 used in questions about time, amount, or size ▶ *How much did you pay?* ▶ *How many children do you have?* ▶ *How old are you?*
3 How is ...?, How are ...? used to ask about someone's health ▶ *How is your mother?* ▶ *How are you?*
4 How do you do? an expression used as a greeting when you first meet someone
5 used to make something you say stronger ▶ *How nice of you to remember my birthday!*

however /haʊˈevəʳ/ *adverb*
1 in whatever way; it does not matter how ▶ *She goes swimming every day, however cold it is.*
2 but ▶ *I don't think we can do it – however, we'll try.*

howl[1] /haʊl/ *verb*
to make a long, loud crying sound ▶ *The dog howled when it was shut in the house.* ▶ *Wind howled round the house.*

howl[2] *noun*
a long, loud cry

HQ /ˌeɪtʃ ˈkjuː/ *noun*
the HEADQUARTERS of a business or of some other group

hr
a short way of writing the word **hour**

huddle /ˈhʌdl/ *verb (present participle* ***huddling****, past* ***huddled****)*
to move close to the other people in a small group ▶ *We huddled round the fire to keep warm.*

huff[1] /hʌf/ *noun*
in a huff angry because someone has offended you ▶ *Ray walked out in a huff.*

huff[2] *verb*
huff and puff to breathe in a noisy way, especially because you are doing something tiring ▶ *When we got to the top of the hill, we were all huffing and puffing.*

hug[1] /hʌg/ *verb (present participle* ***hugging****, past* ***hugged****)*
to put your arms round someone and hold them because you love them ▶ *He hugged his daughter and tried to comfort her.*
SAME MEANING: **cuddle**

hug² *noun*
an act of holding someone close to you in your arms ▶ *He gave her a hug.*
SAME MEANING: **cuddle**

huge /hjuːdʒ/ *adjective*
very large ▶ *a huge amount of food (adverb: **hugely**)*
SAME MEANING: **enormous, massive, vast**

hull /hʌl/ *noun*
the main part of a ship

hullo *(also **hallo, hello**)* /həˈləʊ/ *interjection*
the usual word you say when you meet someone or talk on the telephone

hum /hʌm/ *verb (present participle **humming**, past **hummed**)*
1 to make a low, steady noise like a bee
2 to sing with your lips closed

human /ˈhjuːmən/ *adjective*
of or like a person ▶ *the human voice*

human being /ˌhjuːmən ˈbiːɪŋ/ *noun*
a man, woman, or child, not an animal

humane /hjuːˈmeɪn/ *adjective*
kind; not cruel ▶ *the humane treatment of animals (adverb: **humanely**)*
OPPOSITE: **inhumane**

humanitarian /hjuːˌmænɪˈteərɪən/ *adjective*
concerned with trying to help people who are ill, hungry, etc. ▶ *The UN has sent humanitarian aid to help the refugees.*

humanity /hjuːˈmænətɪ/ *noun (no plural)*
1 kindness, respect, and sympathy towards other people ▶ *a man of great humanity*
2 people in general ▶ *the danger to humanity caused by pollution*

human race /ˌhjuːmən ˈreɪs/ *noun*
the human race all people, rather than animals or other types of life ▶ *There are many things that threaten the survival of the human race.*

human rights /ˌhjuːmən ˈraɪts/ *plural noun*
the basic rights that everyone has to be free and to be treated fairly, especially by their government

humble /ˈhʌmbəl/ *adjective*
1 thinking that you are not better or more important than other people; not proud ▶ *She was always humble about her work, although she helped many people.*
2 simple or poor ▶ *a humble home*

humid /ˈhjuːmɪd/ *adjective*
very warm and wet in an unpleasant way ▶ *Florida is extremely humid in the summer.*

humiliate /hjuːˈmɪlɪeɪt/ *verb (present participle **humiliating**, past **humiliated**)*
to make someone feel stupid or weak ▶ *He often humiliated other people in meetings.*

humorous /ˈhuːmərəs/ *adjective*
funny; making you laugh ▶ *a humorous book*

humour /ˈhjuːməʳ/ *noun (no plural)*
the ability to laugh at things or to make others laugh ▶ *He doesn't have a sense of humour.*

hump /hʌmp/ *noun*
1 a large lump, for example on a camel's back
2 a small hill or raised part in a road

hunch /hʌntʃ/ *noun*
have a hunch to have a feeling that something is true or will happen, even though you have no definite information about it ▶ *I had a hunch that something would go wrong.*

hunched /hʌntʃt/ *adjective*
sitting or standing with your back and shoulders bent forwards ▶ *He was sitting in his study, hunched over his books.*

hundred /ˈhʌndrəd/ *adjective, noun*
1 *(plural* ***hundred****)* the number 100 ▶ *a hundred years ago* ▶ *three hundred people*
2 **hundreds** a very large number of people or things ▶ *We received hundreds of letters after mum died.*

hundredth /ˈhʌndrədθ/ *adjective*
100th

hung /hʌŋ/
the PAST TENSE and PAST PARTICIPLE of the verb **hang**

hunger /ˈhʌŋgəʳ/ *noun (no plural)*
the feeling of wanting or needing to eat
COMPARE: **thirst**

hungry /ˈhʌŋgrɪ/ *adjective (****hungrier, hungriest****)*
wanting or needing food ▶ *Can I have an apple? I'm hungry.*
COMPARE: **thirsty**

hunk /hʌŋk/ *noun*
1 an attractive man who has a strong body
2 a thick piece of something, especially food ▶ *a hunk of bread*

hunt /hʌnt/ *verb*
1 to chase and kill wild animals or birds for food or sport
2 **hunt for something** to try to find something ▶ *I hunted everywhere for that book.*

hunter /ˈhʌntəʳ/ *noun*
a person who chases and kills wild animals or birds, usually for food

hunting /ˈhʌntɪŋ/ *noun (no plural)*
the activity of chasing wild animals or birds in order to catch and kill them ▶ *Is fox-hunting cruel?*

hurdle /ˈhɜːdl/ *noun*
1 a small fence that a person or horse jumps over during a race ▶ *the 100-metre hurdles*
2 a problem or difficulty that you have to deal with ▶ *Exams are a hurdle that everyone has to face.*

hurl /hɜːl/ *verb*
to throw something with force ▶ *He hurled the brick through the window.*

hurray *(also* ***hooray****)* /hʊˈreɪ/ *interjection*
a shout of joy or approval ▶ *We've won! Hurray!*

hurricane /ˈhʌrɪkən/ *noun*
a bad storm with a very strong wind
COMPARE: **blizzard**

hurried /ˈhʌrɪd/ *adjective*
done more quickly than usual, especially because there is not much time ▶ *He said a hurried goodbye and ran for the bus. (adverb:* ***hurriedly****)*

hurry¹ /ˈhʌrɪ/ *verb (past* ***hurried****)*
1 to move quickly or do something quickly ▶ *You'll catch the train if you hurry.*
2 **hurry up** to do something more quickly ▶ *I wish you'd hurry up!*

hurry² *noun*
be in a hurry to try to do things quickly because you do not have much time ▶ *You always seem to be in a hurry.*

hurt¹ /hɜːt/ *verb (past* ***hurt****)*
1 to damage part of a person's body or bring pain to them ▶ *I fell over and hurt myself.* ▶ *Sorry – did I hurt you?*
2 to cause you pain ▶ *My feet hurt.*
3 to make someone unhappy ▶ *I tried not to hurt her feelings.*

hurt² *adjective*
1 damaged or feeling pain ▶ *He was badly hurt.*
2 unhappy ▶ *She's hurt because you haven't visited her.*

hurtful /ˈhɜːtfəl/ *adjective*
making you feel upset or unhappy ▶ *a hurtful remark*

hurtle /ˈhɜːtl/ *verb (present participle* ***hurtling****, past* ***hurtled****)*
to move very fast ▶ *We hurtled down the road at 100km an hour.*

husband /ˈhʌzbənd/ *noun*
the man to whom a woman is married
COMPARE: **wife**

hush /hʌʃ/ *noun (no plural)*
a peaceful silence

husky /ˈhʌskɪ/ *adjective (**huskier, huskiest**)*
(used about voices) deep and sounding rough but attractive

hustle[1] /ˈhʌsəl/ *verb (present participle **hustling**, past **hustled**)*
to make someone move somewhere quickly, often by pushing them
▶ *Steve hustled his son into the house and shut the door.*

hustle[2] *noun (no plural)*
hustle and bustle busy and noisy activity

hut /hʌt/ *noun*
a small building often made of wood

hutch /hʌtʃ/ *noun (plural **hutches**)*
a wooden box that people keep rabbits in

hydraulic /haɪˈdrɒlɪk/ *adjective*
moved or operated by the pressure of water or another liquid ▶ *a hydraulic pump*

hydroelectric /ˌhaɪdrəʊ-ɪˈlektrɪk/ *adjective*
using water power to produce electricity ▶ *The hydroelectric plant provides the town with energy.*

hydrogen /ˈhaɪdrədʒən/ *noun (no plural)*
a very light, colourless gas

hyena /haɪˈiːnə/ *noun*
a wild animal like a large dog

hygiene /ˈhaɪdʒiːn/ *noun (no plural)*
the practice of keeping yourself and the things around you clean in order to prevent diseases ▶ *The children are taught the importance of personal hygiene.*

hygienic /haɪˈdʒiːnɪk/ *adjective*
clean and likely to stop diseases from spreading

hymn /hɪm/ *noun*
a religious song

hype /haɪp/ *noun (no plural)*
talking about something on television, in newspapers, etc. to make it sound good or important
▶ *The media hype surrounding the event is incredible.*

hypermarket /ˈhaɪpəˌmɑːkɪt/ *noun*
a very large shop outside a town, that sells many different kinds of food and other things

hyphen /ˈhaɪfən/ *noun*
the sign (-) used to join two words or parts of words ▶ *half-price*

hypnosis /hɪpˈnəʊsɪs/ *noun (no plural)*
a method of putting someone into a state like a deep sleep, so that you can influence what they think or do
▶ *Under hypnosis, Jean was able to remember exactly what had happened that day.*

hypnotize /ˈhɪpnətaɪz/ *verb (present participle **hypnotizing**, past **hypnotized**)*
to make someone go into a state like a deep sleep, so that you can influence what they think or do

hypocrisy /hɪˈpɒkrəsɪ/ *noun (no plural)*
the practice of pretending to have particular feelings or opinions, but then behaving in a way that shows that you do not really have them
▶ *The government was accused of hypocrisy.*

hypocrite /ˈhɪpəkrɪt/ *noun*
a person who says that they have particular feelings or opinions, but then behaves in a way that shows that they do not really have them
▶ *He's such a hypocrite!*

hysterical /hɪˈsterɪkəl/ *adjective*
1 very upset, afraid, or excited, and not able to control yourself ▶ *She was so hysterical that no one could stop her screaming*

2 very funny ▶ *The play was hysterical!* *(adverb:* ***hysterically)***

Ii

I /aɪ/ *pronoun (plural* **we** /wɪ; *strong* wiː/)
the person who is speaking ▶ *I want to go home.* ▶ *My friend and I went to the cinema.* ▶ ***I'm*** (=I am) *very glad to see you.* ▶ ***I've*** (=I have) *been waiting a long time.* ▶ ***I'll*** (=I will or I shall) *wait a little longer.* ▶ *When* ***I'd*** (=I had) *written the story, I read it to my friend.* ▶ *I thought that* ***I'd*** (=I would) *miss the bus, but I didn't.*

ice /aɪs/ *noun (no plural)*
water which is so cold that it has become hard ▶ *He put some ice in his drink.* ▶ *There was ice on the roads this morning.*

iceberg /ˈaɪsbɜːg/ *noun*
a very large piece of ice floating in the sea

ice-cold /ˌaɪs ˈkəʊld/ *adjective*
very cold ▶ *an ice-cold drink*

ice cream /ˌaɪs ˈkriːm/ *noun (no plural)*
a sweet food made from milk which has been frozen ▶ *a bowl of chocolate ice cream*

ice cube /ˈaɪs kjuːb/ *noun*
a small, square piece of ice that you put in a drink to make it cold

ice hockey /ˈaɪs ˌhɒkɪ/ *noun (no plural)*
a game played on ice, in which two teams of players use long, curved sticks to hit a hard, flat object into a GOAL

ice skate[1] /ˈaɪs skeɪt/ *noun*
a special shoe that you wear for moving or dancing on ice

ice-skate[2] *verb (present participle* ***ice-skating****, past* ***ice-skated)***
to move or dance on ice wearing special shoes ▶ *to go ice-skating*

ice-skating /ˈaɪs skeɪtɪŋ/ *noun (no plural)*
the sport of moving or dancing on ice wearing special shoes

icicle /ˈaɪsɪkəl/ *noun*
a long, thin piece of ice that hangs down from something ▶ *There were icicles hanging from the edge of the roof.*

icing /ˈaɪsɪŋ/ *noun (no plural)*
a mixture of sugar and water, or sugar and butter, put on top of cakes

icon /ˈaɪkɒn/ *noun*
1 a small picture on a computer SCREEN that you choose in order to make the computer do something ▶ *Select the print icon, using the right-hand mouse button.*
2 a person or thing that many people admire and connect with an important idea ▶ *a feminist icon*

icy /ˈaɪsɪ/ *adjective* ***(icier, iciest)***
1 very cold ▶ *an icy wind*
2 covered with ice ▶ *icy roads*

ID /ˌaɪ ˈdiː/ *noun (no plural)*
a document that shows your name, address, etc., usually with a photograph ▶ *Do you have any ID?*

I'd /aɪd/
1 I had ▶ *I'd already left by the time she arrived.*
2 I would ▶ *I'd like a cup of coffee, please.*

idea /aɪˈdɪə/ *noun*
1 a thought or plan that you form in your mind ▶ *I've got an idea – why don't we have a party?* ▶ *What a good idea!*
2 **have no idea** not to know something ▶ *"What time is it?" "I've no idea."* ▶ *I had no idea that you had a brother.*

I

ideal /aɪˈdɪəl/ *adjective*
the best possible ▶ *This book is an ideal Christmas present.*

idealistic /aɪˌdɪəˈlɪstɪk/ *adjective*
believing in principles and high standards, even if they cannot be achieved in real life

ideally /aɪˈdɪəlɪ/ *adverb*
1 used to say how you would like things to be, even if it is not possible ▶ *Ideally, we would like an extra month to finish this project.*
2 very well ▶ *The hotel is ideally located.*

identical /aɪˈdentɪkəl/ *adjective*
exactly the same ▶ *identical twins* (=looking the same)

identification /aɪˌdentɪfɪˈkeɪʃən/ *noun (no plural)*
something which shows who someone is or what something is ▶ *Have you any identification with you?*

identify /aɪˈdentɪfaɪ/ *verb (past* ***identified****)*
to say who someone is or what something is ▶ *Can you identify the man in the picture?*

identity /aɪˈdentətɪ/ *noun (plural* ***identities****)*
who someone is or what something is ▶ *The police do not know the identity of the dead man* (=do not know his name).

ideology /ˌaɪdɪˈɒlədʒɪ/ *noun (plural* ***ideologies****)*
a set of beliefs or ideas, especially political beliefs ▶ *socialist ideology*

idiom /ˈɪdɪəm/ *noun*
a group of words which have a special meaning when they are used together ▶ *To have cold feet about something is an English idiom which means to be worried or nervous about doing something.*

idiomatic /ˌɪdɪəˈmætɪk/ *adjective*
(used about language) containing idioms, and typical of the way people usually talk and write

idiot /ˈɪdɪət/ *noun*
a silly or stupid person
SAME MEANING: **fool**

idiotic /ˌɪdɪˈɒtɪk/ *adjective*
very stupid ▶ *Don't ask idiotic questions.*

idle /ˈaɪdl/ *adjective*
1 (used about a machine) doing no work ▶ *idle machines in a factory*
2 (used about a person) lazy

idol /ˈaɪdl/ *noun*
1 a famous person who is loved and admired by many people
2 something such as a STATUE which people worship as a god

idolize /ˈaɪdəl-aɪz/ *verb (present participle* ***idolizing****, past* ***idolized****)*
to admire someone so much that you think they are perfect ▶ *Herman idolized his father.*

i.e. /ˌaɪ ˈiː/
a short way of writing or saying **that is,** used when you want to give more information to show what you mean by something ▶ *The total cost of the holiday, I.e. including hotel, food, and travel, is £500.*

if /ɪf/ *conjunction*
1 on condition that ▶ *You can catch the bus if you go now.*
2 whether ▶ *I don't know if he will come or not.*
3 whenever ▶ *I always visit them if I go to the city.*
4 as if like; used when you are describing something ▶ *It looks as if it is going to rain.* ▶ *He talks to me as if I'm stupid.*
5 if I were you ... a phrase used when you are giving advice to someone ▶ *If I were you, I'd buy a cheaper car.*
6 Do you mind if ...? a polite way of asking someone if you can do something ▶ *Do you mind if I smoke?*

ignite /ɪg'naɪt/ *verb (present participle **igniting**, past **ignited**)*
to start burning, or to make something start burning

ignition /ɪg'nɪʃən/ *noun*
the electrical part of a car engine that starts the engine ▶ *He put the key in the ignition.*

ignorance /'ɪgnərəns/ *noun (no plural)*
the state of being without knowledge or education

ignorant /'ɪgnərənt/ *adjective*
not knowing very much; not educated ▶ *She is very ignorant **about** her own country.*

ignore /ɪg'nɔːʳ/ *verb (present participle **ignoring**, past **ignored**)*
to take no notice of someone or something; to pretend that someone or something is not there ▶ *I tried to tell her, but she ignored me.*

ill /ɪl/ *adjective*
1 not feeling healthy; unwell ▶ *She can't go to work because she is ill.*
2 be taken ill to become ill suddenly ▶ *He was taken ill last night.*

I'll /aɪl/
I will; I shall ▶ *I'll come with you.*

I

illegal /ɪ'liːgəl/ *adjective*
not allowed by law ▶ *It is illegal to park here. (adverb: **illegally**)*
OPPOSITE: **legal**

illegible /ɪ'ledʒəbəl/ *adjective*
not able to be read ▶ *illegible writing*
OPPOSITE: **legible**

illegitimate /ˌɪlɪ'dʒɪtɪmət/ *adjective*
having parents who are not married ▶ *an illegitimate child*

illiterate /ɪ'lɪtərət/ *adjective*
(used especially about men or women, not children) not able to read or write

illness /'ɪlnəs/ *noun*
1 *(plural **illnesses**)* a disease ▶ *to have an illness*
2 *(no plural)* a time of being not healthy or well ▶ *She has suffered years of illness.*

illogical /ɪ'lɒdʒɪkəl/ *adjective*
not reasonable ▶ *I have an illogical fear of the dark.*
OPPOSITE: **logical**

illuminate /ɪ'luːmɪneɪt/ *verb (present participle **illuminating**, past **illuminated**)*
to light something ▶ *The room was illuminated by a single lamp.*

illusion /ɪ'luːʒən/ *noun*
something that seems to be true or real but is not ▶ *In expensive cars, you get the illusion that you are floating on air.* ▶ *Terry is under the illusion that we are paying for him.*

illustrate /'ɪləstreɪt/ *verb (present participle **illustrating**, past **illustrated**)*
to add pictures to a book or magazine ▶ *The book was illustrated with colour photographs.*

illustration /ˌɪlə'streɪʃən/ *noun*
a picture in a book or magazine

I'm /aɪm/
I am ▶ *I'm very pleased to meet you.*

image /'ɪmɪdʒ/ *noun*
1 a picture of someone or something which you have in your mind
2 the way a person or an organization appears to other people ▶ *You need to have a more modern image* (=wear more modern clothes, etc.).
3 be the image of someone to look exactly like someone ▶ *He's the image of his father.*

imaginary /ɪ'mædʒɪnərɪ/ *adjective*
not real; existing only in your mind ▶ *a story about an imaginary king*

imagination /ɪˌmædʒɪ'neɪʃən/ *noun (no plural)*
the ability that you have to form pictures or ideas in your mind ▶ *You didn't really see it – it was just your imagination.*

imaginative /ɪ'mædʒɪnətɪv/ *adjective*
1 able to think of new and interesting ideas ▶ *an imaginative writer*
2 containing new and interesting ideas ▶ *an imaginative story*
*(adverb: **imaginatively**)*

imagine /ɪ'mædʒɪn/ *verb (present participle **imagining**, past **imagined**)*
1 to make a picture in your mind of someone or something ▶ *I tried to imagine what life was like a hundred years ago.*
2 to think or believe something ▶ *John imagines that we don't like him, but it isn't true.*

imitate /'ɪmɪteɪt/ *verb (present participle **imitating**, past **imitated**)*
to copy someone ▶ *She imitated the way her teacher talked.*

imitation /ˌɪmɪ'teɪʃən/ *noun*
a copy ▶ *This isn't a real gun; it's only an imitation.*

immature /ˌɪmə'tjʊəʳ/ *adjective*
(used about a man or woman) rather silly and behaving in a way which is only suitable for someone much younger
OPPOSITE: **mature**

immediate /ɪ'miːdɪət/ *adjective*
happening at once ▶ *I need an immediate answer.*

immediately /ɪ'miːdɪətlɪ/ *adverb*
1 without any delay ▶ *Open this door immediately!*
2 next to something in position, or just before or after something in time ▶ *They live immediately above us.*

immense /ɪ'mens/ *adjective*
very large ▶ *He made an immense amount of money in business.*
SAME MEANING: **enormous**

immensely /ɪ'menslɪ/ *adverb*
very much ▶ *I enjoyed the concert immensely.*

immerse /ɪ'mɜːs/ *verb (present participle **immersing**, past **immersed**)*
1 be immersed in something, immerse yourself in something to be completely involved in something ▶ *Grant is completely immersed in his work.*
2 to put something in a liquid so that the liquid covers it completely ▶ *Immerse the fabric in the dye and leave for two hours.*

immigrant /'ɪmɪgrənt/ *noun*
a person from another country who comes to your country to live
COMPARE: **emigrant**

immigration /ˌɪmɪ'greɪʃən/ *noun (no plural)*
coming to live in a foreign country ▶ *The government wants to control immigration.*
COMPARE: **emigration**

immoral /ɪ'mɒrəl/ *adjective*
bad or wicked ▶ *immoral behaviour*
OPPOSITE: **moral**

immortal /ɪ'mɔːtl/ *adjective*
living or continuing for ever ▶ *man's immortal soul* ▶ *Nobody is immortal.*

immune /ɪ'mjuːn/ *adjective*
1 not affected by a disease ▶ *Only a few people are immune **to** tuberculosis.*
2 not affected by problems, criticisms, etc. that affect other people ▶ *Their business seems to be immune **to** economic pressures.*

immunization /ˌɪmjʊnaɪ'zeɪʃən/ *noun*
the act of immunizing someone ▶ *immunization **against** polio*

immunize /'ɪmjʊnaɪz/ *verb (present participle **immunizing**, past **immunized**)*
to put an amount of a substance that causes an illness into a person's body, usually by using a special needle, so that the person will not catch that illness in the future

impact[1] /'ɪmpækt/ *noun*
1 the effect something or someone has ▶ *Paul has had a positive impact **on** my life.*

I

2 *(no plural)* the force of one object hitting another ▶ *The impact of the crash made her car turn over.* ▶ *missiles that explode on impact*

impact² /ɪm'pækt/ *verb*
impact on something to have a noticeable effect on something ▶ *The closure of the airport will seriously impact on the city's economy.*

impaired /ɪm'peəd/ *adjective*
1 damaged or made weaker ▶ *Radio reception had been impaired by the storm.*
2 visually impaired, hearing impaired unable to see or hear very well

impartial /ɪm'pɑːʃəl/ *adjective*
not supporting or preferring one person, group, or opinion rather than another ▶ *We offer impartial help and advice.*

impassive /ɪm'pæsɪv/ *adjective*
not showing any emotions ▶ *His face was impassive as the judge spoke.*

impatience /ɪm'peɪʃəns/ *noun (no plural)*
feelings of anger because you have to wait for something
OPPOSITE: **patience**

impatient /ɪm'peɪʃənt/ *adjective*
not being able to wait calmly for something to happen because you want it to happen now ▶ *After an hour's delay, the passengers were starting to get impatient. (adverb: **impatiently**)*
OPPOSITE: **patient**

impeccable /ɪm'pekəbəl/ *adjective*
perfect and without any mistakes ▶ *Her English is impeccable. (adverb: **impeccably**)*

impediment /ɪm'pedɪmənt/ *noun*
speech impediment, hearing impediment a problem that makes speaking or hearing difficult

impending /ɪm'pendɪŋ/ *adjective*
going to happen very soon ▶ *He sensed the impending danger.*

imperative /ɪm'perətɪv/ *noun, adjective*
the form of a verb that you use when you are telling someone to do something ▶ *In the sentence "Come here!", "come" is in the imperative.*

imperfect¹ /ɪm'pɜːfɪkt/ *adjective*
not completely perfect ▶ *It's an imperfect world.*

imperfect² *noun*
the form of a verb that shows an incomplete action in the past. In "We were walking down the road", the verb "were walking" is in the imperfect.

impersonal /ɪm'pɜːsənəl/ *adjective*
not showing any feelings of kindness, friendliness, etc. ▶ *Sue complained about the doctor's impersonal manner.*

impersonate /ɪm'pɜːsəneɪt/ *verb (present participle **impersonating**, past **impersonated**)*
to copy the way someone talks, behaves, etc., in order to trick people or make them laugh ▶ *They were arrested for impersonating police officers.*

impertinent /ɪm'pɜːtɪnənt/ *adjective*
rude, especially to older people or people you should respect ▶ *She scolded her son for being impertinent.* ▶ *an impertinent remark*

impetuous /ɪm'petʃʊəs/ *adjective*
doing things quickly, without thinking ▶ *They are young and impetuous.*

implausible /ɪm'plɔːzəbəl/ *adjective*
not likely to be true ▶ *His excuse is totally implausible.*
OPPOSITE: **plausible**

implement¹ /'ɪmplɪment/ *verb*
to begin to use a plan or system ▶ *The company has until next year to implement the new safety recommendations.*

implement² /'ɪmplɪmənt/ *noun*
a tool ▶ *farming implements*

implicate /'ɪmplɪkeɪt/ *verb (present participle* ***implicating,*** *past* ***implicated)***
to show or suggest that someone is involved in something bad or illegal ▶ *Howard was implicated* ***in*** *the crime.*

implication /ˌɪmplɪ'keɪʃən/ *noun*
a possible result of a plan, an action, etc. ▶ *This research has many important implications.*

imply /ɪm'plaɪ/ *verb (past* ***implied)***
to suggest that something is true without saying or showing it directly ▶ *He implied that the money had been stolen rather than lost.*

impolite /ˌɪmpə'laɪt/ *adjective*
rather rude in the way you speak or behave towards other people
OPPOSITE: **polite**

import¹ /ɪm'pɔːt/ *verb*
to bring goods into a country for use there ▶ *We import machinery that we cannot make in our country.*
COMPARE: **export**

import² /'ɪmpɔːt/ *noun*
something that is imported
▶ *Machinery is one of our biggest imports.*
COMPARE: **export**

importance /ɪm'pɔːtəns/ *noun (no plural)*
great value or power ▶ *the importance* ***of*** *a good education*

important /ɪm'pɔːtənt/ *adjective*
1 very useful or valuable ▶ *an important meeting*
2 having power ▶ *an important person*
OPPOSITE: **unimportant**

importer /ɪm'pɔːtəʳ/ *noun*
a person or an organization whose business is to bring goods into a country for use there ▶ *a wine importer*
COMPARE: **exporter**

impose /ɪm'pəʊz/ *verb (present participle* ***imposing,*** *past* ***imposed)***
to force people to accept a rule, a tax, beliefs, etc. ▶ *The king imposed his authority* ***on*** *the whole country.*

imposing /ɪm'pəʊzɪŋ/ *adjective*
large and impressive ▶ *an imposing building*

impossible /ɪm'pɒsəbəl/ *adjective*
not possible; not able to happen
▶ *I can't come today; it's impossible.*
OPPOSITE: **possible**

impostor *(also* ***imposter)*** /ɪm'pɒstəʳ/ *noun*
a person who pretends to be someone else in order to trick people

impractical /ɪm'præktɪkəl/ *adjective*
not sensible ▶ *an impractical suggestion*
OPPOSITE: **practical**

imprecise /ˌɪmprɪ'saɪs/ *adjective*
not exact ▶ *Our measurements were imprecise.*
OPPOSITE: **precise**

impress /ɪm'pres/ *verb*
to make someone feel admiration
▶ *He was trying to impress me.*

impressed /ɪm'prest/ *adjective*
feeling admiration for someone or something ▶ *I was really impressed* ***by*** *how well the team played in its first game.*

impression /ɪm'preʃən/ *noun*
1 the way something seems to you
▶ *My impression is that she is not telling the truth.*
2 make an impression on someone to make someone remember you, usually with admiration

impressionable /ɪm'preʃənəbəl/ *adjective*
easy to influence ▶ *The children are at an impressionable age.*

impressive /ɪm'presɪv/ *adjective*
very good and so causing admiration
▶ *His work was very impressive.*

imprint[1] /ˈɪmprɪnt/ *noun*
the mark left by an object that has been pressed onto something
▶ *Fossils are rocks that have imprints of animals on them.*

imprint[2] /ɪmˈprɪnt/ *verb*
be imprinted on your mind/memory to make you unable to forget something ▶ *The whole conversation is imprinted on my memory.*

imprison /ɪmˈprɪzən/ *verb*
to put someone in prison ▶ *He was imprisoned for two years.*

imprisonment /ɪmˈprɪzənmənt/ *noun (no plural)*
the state of being in prison ▶ *He was given two years' imprisonment.*

improper /ɪmˈprɒpəʳ/ *adjective*
not correct according to moral, social, or professional rules *(adverb: **improperly**)*

improve /ɪmˈpruːv/ *verb*
*(present participle **improving**, past **improved**)*
1 to become better ▶ *My tennis is improving.*
2 to make something better ▶ *I want to improve my tennis.*

improvement /ɪmˈpruːvmənt/ *noun*
1 a change which makes something better ▶ *to make improvements **to** your house*
2 a change which shows that something is becoming better
▶ *There has been an improvement **in** trade.* ▶ *Her health is showing signs of improvement.*

improvise /ˈɪmprəvaɪz/ *verb*
*(present participle **improvising**, past **improvised**)*
to do or make something without preparing first, using whatever you have got ▶ *If you do not have a screwdriver, you will have to improvise and use the end of a knife.*

impulse /ˈɪmpʌls/ *noun*
a sudden wish to do something ▶ *She had an impulse to buy a new dress.*
▶ *She bought the dress **on** impulse.*

impulsive /ɪmˈpʌlsɪv/ *adjective*
doing things without thinking about them carefully first ▶ *an impulsive decision*

in /ɪn/ *preposition, adverb*
1 inside a place or thing ▶ *They were sitting in the kitchen.* ▶ *She opened the washing machine and put the clothes in.*
2 at a place ▶ *We live in the country.*
▶ *We stayed at a hotel in London.*
3 surrounded by something ▶ *to walk in the rain*
4 during a period of time ▶ *The house was built in 1950.* ▶ *It's his birthday in June.*
5 after a period of time ▶ *I'll be ready in a few minutes.*
6 at home or in the place where you work ▶ *I'm afraid Mrs Jones is not in at the moment.*
OPPOSITE **(6)**: **out**
7 using ▶ *She spoke in a quiet voice.*
▶ *The words were written in pencil.*
▶ *They were talking in French.*
8 wearing ▶ *Who's the woman in the black dress?*
9 in all in total ▶ *It will cost you £50 in all.*

inability /ˌɪnəˈbɪlətɪ/ *noun (no plural)*
the state of not being able to do something ▶ *They were worried about their son's inability to make friends.*
OPPOSITE: **ability**

inaccurate /ɪnˈækjʊrət/ *adjective*
not correct; having mistakes in it
▶ *an inaccurate news report*
OPPOSITE: **accurate**

inactive /ɪnˈæktɪv/ *adjective*
not doing anything or not working
▶ *An inactive lifestyle can lead to health problems.*
OPPOSITE: **active**

inadequate /ɪnˈædɪkwət/ *adjective*
not enough or not good enough ▶ *inadequate health care services*
OPPOSITE: **adequate**

inadvertently /ˌɪnədˈvɜːtəntli/ *adverb*
without intending to do something ▶ *She inadvertently knocked his arm.*

inanimate /ɪnˈænɪmət/ *adjective*
not living ▶ *an inanimate object such as a stone*

inappropriate /ˌɪnəˈprəʊpriət/ *adjective*
not suitable or right ▶ *Those clothes are inappropriate* **for** *work.* (*adverb:* ***inappropriately***)
OPPOSITE: **appropriate**

inaugurate /ɪˈnɔːgjʊreɪt/ *verb* (*present participle* ***inaugurating***, *past* ***inaugurated***)
to have a formal ceremony in order to show that someone new has an important job, or that a new building is open ▶ *The President was inaugurated in January.*

incapable /ɪnˈkeɪpəbəl/ *adjective*
not able to do something ▶ *Since her accident, she has been incapable* ***of*** *working.*
OPPOSITE: **capable**

incarcerate /ɪnˈkɑːsəreɪt/ *verb* (*present participle* ***incarcerating***, *past* ***incarcerated***)
to put someone in prison

incense /ˈɪnsens/ *noun* (*no plural*)
a substance that has a pleasant smell when you burn it

incentive /ɪnˈsentɪv/ *noun*
something that encourages you to work harder, or to start something new ▶ *Money is a good incentive for hard work.*

incessant /ɪnˈsesənt/ *adjective*
never stopping ▶ *Incessant rain caused floods and mudslides.* (*adverb:* ***incessantly***)

inch /ɪntʃ/ *noun* (*plural* ***inches***)
a measure of length, equal to 2.5 CENTIMETRES ▶ *There are 12 inches* (=12 ins) *in a foot.*

incident /ˈɪnsɪdənt/ *noun*
an event or something that happens

incidentally /ˌɪnsɪˈdentli/ *adverb*
a word which you use when you are adding more information to something you have just said, or when you have just remembered an interesting fact ▶ *I saw Peter the other day. Incidentally, he's invited us to lunch next week.*

incite /ɪnˈsaɪt/ *verb* (*present participle* ***inciting***, *past* ***incited***)
to deliberately make someone feel so angry or excited that they do something bad ▶ *One man was jailed for inciting a riot.*

inclination /ˌɪŋklɪˈneɪʃən/ *noun*
the desire to do something ▶ *His first inclination was to laugh at Jean's mistake.*

incline /ɪnˈklaɪn/ *verb*
be inclined to do something to be likely to do something, or to tend to do something ▶ *I am inclined to be lazy sometimes.*

include /ɪnˈkluːd/ *verb* (*present participle* ***including***, *past* ***included***)
1 to have something as part of a whole ▶ *The price of the holiday includes meals.* ▶ *The group included several women.*
OPPOSITE: **exclude**
2 to count someone or something as part of a whole ▶ *I included my uncle in my list of people to invite.*

including /ɪnˈkluːdɪŋ/ *preposition*
a word used to show that some people or things are part of a larger group ▶ *All the family is going, including the children* (=they are going too).
OPPOSITE: **excluding**

I

inclusion /ɪn'klu:ʒən/ *noun (no plural)*
the act of including someone or something in a larger group ▶ *There were never any doubts about her inclusion in the team.*

inclusive /ɪn'klu:sɪv/ *adjective*
1 including a particular thing, especially the price of something ▶ *The cost is £600, inclusive* ***of*** *insurance.*
2 including the first and last number, letter, etc. you say, plus all those in between ▶ *He will be on holiday from March 22nd to 24th inclusive.*

income /'ɪŋkʌm, -kəm/ *noun*
all the money you receive ▶ *What is your annual income?*

income tax /'ɪŋkəm ˌtæks/ *noun (no plural)*
money taken by the government from what people earn

incompatible /ˌɪnkəm'pætəbəl/ *adjective*
1 having different ideas or interests, and not able to have a good relationship
2 not able to exist or be used together without problems ▶ *Some software may be incompatible* ***with*** *your computer.*
OPPOSITE (**1** and **2**): **compatible**

incompetence /ɪn'kɒmpɪtəns/ *noun (no plural)*
the lack of ability or skill to do a job correctly
OPPOSITE: **competence**

incompetent /ɪn'kɒmpɪtənt/ *adjective*
lacking the ability or skill to do a job correctly ▶ *Airlines need to get rid of incompetent pilots.*
OPPOSITE: **competent**

incomplete /ˌɪnkəm'pli:t/ *adjective*
not finished ▶ *The work is incomplete.*
OPPOSITE: **complete**

incomprehensible /ɪnˌkɒmprɪ'hensəbəl/ *adjective*
impossible to understand ▶ *The instructions were incomprehensible.*

inconclusive /ˌɪnkən'klu:sɪv/ *adjective*
not leading to any decision or result ▶ *The medical tests were inconclusive.*
OPPOSITE: **conclusive**

inconsiderate /ˌɪnkən'sɪdərət/ *adjective*
not thinking about other people's feelings or needs ▶ *Inconsiderate drivers can cause accidents.*
OPPOSITE: **considerate**

inconsistency /ˌɪnkən'sɪstənsɪ/ *noun*
1 *(plural* ***inconsistencies****)* something in a report, an argument, etc. that cannot be true if something else in the report or argument is also true ▶ *the inconsistencies in her statement*
2 *(no plural)* the act of changing your ideas too often or of doing something differently each time, so that people do not know what you think or want ▶ *There's too much inconsistency in the way the rules are applied.*
OPPOSITE (**1** and **2**): **consistency**

inconsistent /ˌɪnkən'sɪstənt/ *adjective*
1 not doing things in the same way each time, or not following an expected principle ▶ *Children get confused if parents are inconsistent.*
2 be inconsistent with something to say different things or follow different principles ▶ *His story was inconsistent with the evidence.*
OPPOSITE (**1** and **2**): **consistent**

inconvenience¹ /ˌɪnkən'vi:nɪəns/ *noun*
difficulty ▶ *I hope that the delay won't cause you any inconvenience.*

inconvenience² *verb (present participle* ***inconveniencing****, past* ***inconvenienced****)* to make things difficult for someone ▶ *I hope I'm not inconveniencing you by staying here.*

inconvenient /ˌɪnkən'viːnɪənt/ *adjective*
not suitable; causing difficulty ▶ *I hope this isn't an inconvenient time for me to visit you.*
OPPOSITE: **convenient**

incorporate /ɪn'kɔːpəreɪt/ *verb (present participle* ***incorporating****, past* ***incorporated****)*
to include something as part of a group, system, etc. ▶ *This style of karate incorporates kicks and punches.*

incorrect /ˌɪnkə'rekt/ *adjective*
not right; wrong ▶ *incorrect spelling (adverb:* ***incorrectly****)*
OPPOSITE: **correct**

increase¹ /ɪn'kriːs/ *verb (present participle* ***increasing****, past* ***increased****)*
1 to become more in amount or number ▶ *My wages have increased this year.* ▶ *The noise suddenly increased.*
2 to make something more in amount or number ▶ *My employer has increased my wages.*
OPPOSITE (**1** and **2**): **decrease**

increase² /'ɪŋkriːs/ *noun*
a rise in amount ▶ *an increase* ***in*** *your wages* ▶ *a price increase* ***of*** *10%*
OPPOSITE: **decrease**

increasingly /ɪn'kriːsɪŋlɪ/ *adverb*
more and more ▶ *It's becoming increasingly difficult to find work.*

incredible /ɪn'kredəbəl/ *adjective*
1 very good ▶ *What incredible luck!*
2 very large in amount ▶ *an incredible sum of money*
3 very strange or unusual ▶ *an incredible story*
SAME MEANING (**1**, **2**, and **3**): **amazing**

incredibly /ɪn'kredəblɪ/ *adverb*
1 very ▶ *The show is incredibly popular among teenagers.*
2 in a way that is difficult to believe ▶ *Incredibly, no one was hurt in the crash.*

incubator /'ɪŋkjʊbeɪtəʳ/ *noun*
a machine used in hospitals to keep weak babies alive

incur /ɪn'kɜːʳ/ *verb (present participle* ***incurring****, past* ***incurred****)*
to have to deal with something unpleasant because of something you have done ▶ *If the amount is not paid within seven days, you will incur a charge of £15.*

incurable /ɪn'kjʊərəbəl/ *adjective*
impossible to cure ▶ *an incurable disease*

indecent /ɪn'diːsənt/ *adjective*
likely to offend or shock people because of being related to sex ▶ *indecent photographs*

indecisive /ˌɪndɪ'saɪsɪv/ *adjective*
not able to make decisions ▶ *a weak, indecisive leader*
OPPOSITE: **decisive**

indeed /ɪn'diːd/ *adverb*
1 used in answers to questions when you want to say **yes** or **no** very strongly ▶ *"Did he really say that?" "He did indeed."*
2 used when you want to make the meaning of **very** even stronger ▶ *He runs very fast indeed.*

indefinite /ɪn'defɪnət/ *adjective*
not clear or fixed ▶ *I am staying for an indefinite length of time* (=I'm not sure how long I will stay). *(adverb:* ***indefinitely****)*

indefinite article /ɪnˌdefɪnət 'ɑːtɪkəl/ *noun*
in English, the word **a** or **an**
COMPARE: **definite article**

independence /ˌɪndɪ'pendəns/ *noun (no plural)*
1 the quality of being able to look after yourself ▶ *Old people want to keep their independence.*

I

2 the state of being free from the control of another country ▶ *the American War of Independence* ▶ *India gained its independence in 1947.*

independent /ˌɪndɪ'pendənt/ *adjective*
1 able to look after yourself; not needing help and support from other people ▶ *Although she is young, she is very independent.*
OPPOSITE: **dependent**
2 free; not controlled or governed by another country ▶ *India became independent from Britain in 1947.*

in-depth /'ɪn depθ/ *adjective* considering all the details ▶ *an in-depth interview with the prime minister*

index /'ɪndeks/ *noun (plural **indexes** or **indices** /'ɪndɪsiːz/)* a list in a book which tells you what can be found in the book, and on what page

index finger /'ɪndeks ˌfɪŋgəʳ/ *noun* the finger which is next to your thumb

Indian /'ɪndɪən/ *adjective* of or from India ▶ *Do you like Indian food?*

Indian summer /ˌɪndɪən 'sʌməʳ/ *noun* a period of warm weather in the autumn

indicate /'ɪndɪkeɪt/ *verb (present participle **indicating**, past **indicated**)* to show someone something ▶ *Please indicate your choice on the form provided.*

indication /ˌɪndɪ'keɪʃən/ *noun* a sign that tells you that something may be true or may happen ▶ *Did he give you any indication of when the work will be finished?*

indicative /ɪn'dɪkətɪv/ *adjective*
1 be indicative of something to show that something exists or is likely to be true ▶ *They've lost a few games, but this is not really indicative of the team's ability.*
2 indicative verb a verb that expresses a fact or an action

indicator /'ɪndɪkeɪtəʳ/ *noun* one of the two lights on a car that are used to show that the car is going to turn left or right

indices /'ɪndɪsiːz/ a plural of **index**

indifference /ɪn'dɪfərəns/ *noun (no plural)* the state of not being interested in or not caring about something or someone ▶ *The factory's indifference **to** safety rules led to several injuries.*

indifferent /ɪn'dɪfərənt/ *adjective* not interested in or not caring about something or someone ▶ *How could a father be so indifferent **to** his own children?*

indigestion /ˌɪndɪ'dʒestʃən/ *noun (no plural)* an uncomfortable pain in your stomach that you get when you eat too much or too fast

indignant /ɪn'dɪgnənt/ *adjective* angry and surprised because of something that appears wrong *(adverb: **indignantly**)*

indignity /ɪn'dɪgnətɪ/ *noun (plural **indignities**)* a situation that makes you feel very ashamed, unimportant, and not respected ▶ *I suffered the final indignity of being taken to the police station.*

indirect /ˌɪndɪ'rekt/ *adjective* not going straight towards a person, place, etc. ▶ *an indirect route* *(adverb: **indirectly**)*
OPPOSITE: **direct**

indirect object /ˌɪndɪrekt 'ɒbdʒɪkt/ *noun* the person or thing that receives something as a result of the action of

the verb. In the sentence "Joe gave her a sandwich", "her" is the indirect object
COMPARE: **direct object**

indirect speech /ˌɪndɪrekt 'spiːtʃ/ *noun (no plural)*
REPORTED SPEECH
COMPARE: **direct speech**

indiscriminate /ˌɪndɪ'skrɪmɪnət/ *adjective*
done without considering who will be affected or harmed
▶ *indiscriminate killings by teenage gangs*

indispensable /ˌɪndɪ'spensəbəl/ *adjective*
too important or useful to manage without ▶ *The information he provided was indispensable to our research.*

indistinguishable /ˌɪndɪ'stɪŋgwɪʃəbəl/ *adjective*
so similar that you cannot see any difference ▶ *The copy was almost indistinguishable **from** the original.*

individual[1] /ˌɪndɪ'vɪdʒʊəl/ *noun*
a person, not a group ▶ *something which happens in the life of each individual*

individual[2] *adjective*
single; for one person only ▶ *The children had individual desks.*

individuality /ˌɪndɪvɪdʒʊ'ælətɪ/ *noun (no plural)*
the quality that makes someone different from everyone else ▶ *work that allows children to express their individuality*

individually /ˌɪndɪ'vɪdʒʊəlɪ/ *adverb*
separately, not together in a group
▶ *The children were taught individually.*

indoor /'ɪndɔːʳ/ *adjective*
inside a building ▶ *If it rains, we play indoor games.*
OPPOSITE: **outdoor**

indoors /ɪn'dɔːz/ *adverb*
inside a building ▶ *Let's stay indoors out of the rain.*
OPPOSITE: **outdoors**

induce /ɪn'djuːs/ *verb (present participle **inducing**, past **induced**)*
to cause someone to do something, or cause something to happen ▶ *Can too much exercise induce illness?*

indulge /ɪn'dʌldʒ/ *verb (present participle **indulging**, past **indulged**)*
to let yourself do something that you enjoy, especially something that you should not do ▶ *I often indulge myself with chocolates.*

indulgent /ɪn'dʌldʒənt/ *adjective*
willing to let someone have whatever they want, even if it is bad for them
▶ *an indulgent grandparent*

industrial /ɪn'dʌstrɪəl/ *adjective*
having a lot of factories ▶ *an industrial town*

industrialized /ɪn'dʌstrɪəlaɪzd/ *adjective*
with a lot of industry ▶ *industrialized nations*

industry /'ɪndəstrɪ/ *noun (plural **industries**)*
the making of things in factories
▶ *What are the important industries in the town?* ▶ *Our town has a lot of heavy industry.*

ineffective /ˌɪnɪ'fektɪv/ *adjective*
not getting the result you want ▶ *The drug has been ineffective against this disease.*
OPPOSITE: **effective**

inefficient /ˌɪnɪ'fɪʃənt/ *adjective*
not working well, and wasting time, money, or energy ▶ *We have an inefficient railway system. (adverb: **inefficiently**)*
OPPOSITE: **efficient**

inequality /ˌɪnɪ'kwɒlətɪ/ *noun (plural **inequalities**)*
an unfair situation in which some

groups in society have less money, fewer opportunities, etc. than others ▶ *the many inequalities in our legal system*

inevitable /ɪ'nevɪtəbəl/ *adjective* definitely going to happen ▶ *Getting older is inevitable.*

inexcusable /ˌɪnɪk'skjuːzəbəl/ *adjective* (used about behaviour) too bad or too rude to be forgiven

inexpensive /ˌɪnɪk'spensɪv/ *adjective* not costing a lot of money, but good ▶ *an inexpensive holiday*
OPPOSITE: **expensive**

inexperienced /ˌɪnɪk'spɪərɪənst/ *adjective* not having much experience of something ▶ *The team had a number of young, inexperienced players.*
OPPOSITE: **experienced**

inexplicable /ˌɪnɪk'splɪkəbəl/ *adjective* very strange, and impossible to explain or understand ▶ *For some inexplicable reason, he started to laugh.*

infallible /ɪn'fæləbəl/ *adjective* never wrong ▶ *Scientists are not infallible.*

infancy /'ɪnfənsɪ/ *noun (no plural)* the period when you are a baby or young child

infant /'ɪnfənt/ *noun* a baby or young child

infantry /'ɪnfəntrɪ/ *noun (no plural)* soldiers who fight on foot, not on horses or in vehicles

infatuated /ɪn'fætʃʊeɪtɪd/ *adjective* having unreasonably strong feelings of romantic or sexual love for someone ▶ *He's been infatuated **with** Clare for a couple of years.*

infect /ɪn'fekt/ *verb* to give an illness to someone ▶ *One of the women at work had a cold and infected everyone else.*

infected /ɪn'fektɪd/ *adjective* containing harmful BACTERIA ▶ *This cut has become infected.*

infection /ɪn'fekʃən/ *noun* an illness ▶ *a throat infection*

infectious /ɪn'fekʃəs/ *adjective* (used about an illness) able to be given to other people ▶ *an infectious disease*

inferior /ɪn'fɪərɪəʳ/ *adjective* not as good as someone or something else ▶ *Luke had a way of looking at me that always made me feel inferior.* ▶ *Larry's work is inferior **to** Ben's.*
OPPOSITE: **superior**

infertile /ɪn'fɜːtaɪl/ *adjective* (used about land, earth, etc.) not able to grow plants and seeds very well ▶ *infertile, stony soil*
OPPOSITE: **fertile**

infidelity /ˌɪnfɪ'delətɪ/ *noun* the act of having sex with someone when you are already having a serious relationship with someone else

infiltrate /'ɪnfɪltreɪt/ *verb (present participle **infiltrating**, past **infiltrated**)* to become part of a group, an organization, etc., especially a criminal one, in order to get information about it ▶ *Trent was ordered to try and infiltrate the terrorists' group.*

infinite /'ɪnfɪnət/ *adjective* very large or great and seeming to have no limit ▶ *a teacher with infinite patience*

infinitely /'ɪnfɪnətlɪ/ *adverb* very much ▶ *I feel infinitely better after my holiday.*

infinitive /ɪn'fɪnɪtɪv/ *noun* the part of a verb which is used with the word **to** ▶ *In the sentence "I want to go", "to go" is an infinitive.*

infinity /ɪnˈfɪnətɪ/ *noun (no plural)*
space or time that has no end or limit ▶ *It's difficult to understand the idea of infinity.*

inflamed /ɪnˈfleɪmd/ *adjective*
red, painful, and SWOLLEN ▶ *an inflamed throat*

inflammable /ɪnˈflæməbəl/ *adjective*
that will burn very easily ▶ *inflammable gases*
OPPOSITE: **nonflammable**

inflammation /ˌɪnfləˈmeɪʃən/ *noun*
redness, pain, and swelling on or in a part of the body ▶ *inflammation **of** the knee*

inflatable /ɪnˈfleɪtəbəl/ *adjective*
needing to be filled with air before being used ▶ *an inflatable boat*

inflate /ɪnˈfleɪt/ *verb (present participle **inflating**, past **inflated**)*
to fill something with air ▶ *to inflate a tyre*

inflated /ɪnˈfleɪtɪd/ *adjective*
1 (used about prices, figures, etc.) higher than is reasonable or usual ▶ *Fans are prepared to pay hugely inflated prices for the tickets.*
2 filled with air or gas ▶ *an inflated life jacket*

inflation /ɪnˈfleɪʃən/ *noun (no plural)*
the continuing increase in prices, or the rate at which prices increase ▶ *the Mexican government's efforts to control inflation*

inflection *(also **inflexion**)* /ɪnˈflekʃən/ *noun*
the way the ending of a word changes to show that it is plural, in the past tense, etc.

inflexible /ɪnˈfleksəbəl/ *adjective*
1 not able to change or be changed easily ▶ *As we get older our attitudes become more inflexible.*
2 not easy to bend
OPPOSITE (**1** and **2**): **flexible**

inflexion /ɪnˈflekʃən/ *noun*
another word for **inflection**

inflict /ɪnˈflɪkt/ *verb*
to make a person, place, etc. suffer something unpleasant ▶ *The earthquake inflicted an enormous amount of damage **on** the whole area.*

influence¹ /ˈɪnfluəns/ *noun*
1 have an influence on someone to have the power to change what a person thinks or does ▶ *Her parents have a strong influence on her.*
2 be a bad influence on someone to make someone behave badly because you yourself behave badly
3 be a good influence on someone to make someone behave in a better way than usual because you yourself behave well

influence² *verb (present participle **influencing**, past **influenced**)*
to change what happens ▶ *My teacher influenced my decision to study science* (=made me decide to do it).

influential /ˌɪnfluˈenʃəl/ *adjective*
important and having the power to change people or things ▶ *an influential politician* ▶ *an influential speech*

influenza /ˌɪnfluˈenzə/ *noun (no plural)*
another word for **flu**

info /ˈɪnfəʊ/ *noun (no plural)*
information

inform /ɪnˈfɔːm/ *verb*
to tell someone something ▶ *The teacher informed us that the school would be closed for one day next week.* ▶ *I will inform you **of** my decision.*

informal /ɪnˈfɔːməl/ *adjective*
happening or done in an easy, friendly way and not according to rules ▶ *an informal meeting* ▶ *an informal party*
OPPOSITE: **formal**

I

information /ˌɪnfəˈmeɪʃən/ *noun (no plural)*
facts; knowledge ▶ *Could you give me some information* ***about*** *the times of the buses?* ▶ *I need to find information* ***on*** *the car industry.* ▶ *a tourist information office* (=a place where tourists go to ask about things they want to know)

information superhighway /ˌɪnfəmeɪʃən ˌsuːpəˈhaɪweɪ/ *noun*
the information superhighway the INTERNET

information technology /ɪnfəˈmeɪʃən tekˌnɒlədʒɪ/ *noun (no plural)*
the use of computers to store and manage information

informative /ɪnˈfɔːmətɪv/ *adjective*
providing useful information or ideas ▶ *a very informative book*

informed /ɪnˈfɔːmd/ *adjective*
having plenty of knowledge and information about something ▶ *It is important for everyone to keep well informed about what's going on in the world.*

informer /ɪnˈfɔːməʳ/ *noun*
a person who helps the police by secretly giving them information about crimes and criminals

I

infrequent /ɪnˈfriːkwənt/ *adjective*
not happening often ▶ *one of our infrequent visits to Uncle Edwin's house (adverb:* ***infrequently****)*
OPPOSITE: **frequent**

infuriate /ɪnˈfjʊərɪeɪt/ *verb (present participle* ***infuriating****, past* ***infuriated****)*
to make someone very angry ▶ *It infuriates me when she behaves so badly.*

infuriating /ɪnˈfjʊərɪeɪtɪŋ/ *adjective*
making someone very angry ▶ *He can be infuriating at times.*

ingenious /ɪnˈdʒiːnɪəs/ *adjective*
very clever ▶ *What an ingenious idea!*

ingratitude /ɪnˈgrætɪtjuːd/ *noun (no plural)*
the state of not being grateful for something when you should be
OPPOSITE: **gratitude**

ingredient /ɪnˈgriːdɪənt/ *noun*
something that you add when you are making something, especially in cooking ▶ *Flour, butter, eggs, and sugar are the main ingredients.*

inhabit /ɪnˈhæbɪt/ *verb*
1 to live in a place ▶ *a country inhabited by 20 million people*
2 be inhabited to have people living there ▶ *The island is not inhabited.*

inhabitant /ɪnˈhæbɪtənt/ *noun*
a person who lives in a place ▶ *the inhabitants* ***of*** *the village*

inhale /ɪnˈheɪl/ *verb (present participle* ***inhaling****, past* ***inhaled****)*
to breathe air, smoke, or gas into your lungs ▶ *Percy lit a cigarette and inhaled deeply.*

inherit /ɪnˈherɪt/ *verb*
to get something from someone when they die ▶ *He inherited the farm from his parents.*

inheritance /ɪnˈherɪtəns/ *noun*
money or other things that you receive from a person after they have died

inhospitable /ˌɪnhɒˈspɪtəbəl/ *adjective*
1 (used about places) difficult to live in because of the heat, cold, etc. ▶ *an inhospitable climate*
2 unfriendly to people who are visiting you ▶ *There was no need to be quite so inhospitable.*

inhuman /ɪnˈhjuːmən/ *adjective*
very cruel ▶ *inhuman acts of violence and terrorism*

inhumane /ˌɪnhjuːˈmeɪn/ *adjective*
treating people or animals in a cruel and unacceptable way ▶ *inhumane living conditions*
OPPOSITE: **humane**

initial[1] /ɪ'nɪʃəl/ *noun*
the first letter of a name, used to represent the name ▶ *His name is John Smith, so his initials are J. S.*

initial[2] *adjective*
first; at the beginning ▶ *The initial plan was to build a new hospital, but now the council has decided to repair the old hospital instead. (adverb: **initially**)*

initiative /ɪ'nɪʃətɪv/ *noun (no plural)*
the ability to make decisions and take action without waiting for someone to tell you what to do ▶ *I was impressed by the initiative she showed.*

inject /ɪn'dʒekt/ *verb*
to give someone medicine by using a special needle to go through their skin

injection /ɪn'dʒekʃən/ *noun*
an act of giving someone medicine by using a special needle to go through their skin ▶ *to have an injection* ▶ *an injection **against** a disease*

injure /'ɪndʒəʳ/ *verb (present participle **injuring**, past **injured**)*
to harm or wound a person or an animal ▶ *Two people were injured in the accident.* ▶ *I injured myself playing football.*
SAME MEANING: **hurt**

injury /'ɪndʒərɪ/ *noun (plural **injuries**)*
a wound ▶ *The people in the accident had serious injuries.*

injustice /ɪn'dʒʌstɪs/ *noun*
1 *(no plural)* the fact of being unfair ▶ *the injustice of the situation*
OPPOSITE: **justice**
2 something unfair ▶ *a great injustice*
3 **do someone an injustice** to judge someone in an unfair way by thinking something bad about them which is not true

ink /ɪŋk/ *noun (no plural)*
a coloured liquid used for writing or printing

inland[1] /'ɪnlənd/ *adjective*
not near the sea ▶ *an inland town*

inland[2] /ɪn'lænd/ *adverb*
away from the sea ▶ *We travelled 20 kilometres inland.*

in-laws /'ɪn lɔːz/ *plural noun*
the parents of your husband or wife, or other members of their family ▶ *We're spending Christmas with my in-laws this year.*

inn /ɪn/ *noun*
a place that sells drinks and food, and is sometimes a hotel as well ▶ *The travellers stopped to eat at a small inn.*

inner /'ɪnəʳ/ *adjective*
further in, or in the middle ▶ *the inner ear* (=the part inside your head)

inner city /ˌɪnə 'sɪtɪ/ *noun (plural **inner cities**)*
the part of a city that is near the centre, especially the part where the buildings are in a bad condition and the people are poor ▶ *the problem of crime in our inner cities*

inning /'ɪnɪŋ/ *noun*
one of the nine periods of play in a game of BASEBALL

innings /'ɪnɪŋz/ *noun (plural **innings**)*
one of the periods of play in a game of CRICKET

innocence /'ɪnəsəns/ *noun (no plural)*
the fact of having done nothing bad or wrong
OPPOSITE: **guilt**

innocent /'ɪnəsənt/ *adjective*
having done nothing bad or wrong ▶ *to be innocent **of** a crime*
OPPOSITE: **guilty**

innocuous /ɪ'nɒkjʊəs/ *adjective*
not likely to harm anyone or cause trouble ▶ *It seemed like a fairly innocuous thing to say.*

innovation /ˌɪnə'veɪʃən/ *noun*
an exciting new idea or method that people are using for the first time

▶ *scientific and technological innovations*

input /ˈɪnpʊt/ *noun (no plural)*
ideas, advice, money, or effort that you put into a job, meeting, etc. in order to help it succeed ▶ *At the start of a project, everyone's input is very welcome.* ▶ *Thanks for coming to the meeting, Julie – we value your input.*

inquest /ˈɪŋkwest/ *noun*
an official process to try and discover why someone has died suddenly

inquire *(also **enquire**)* /ɪnˈkwaɪəʳ/ *verb (present participle **inquiring**, past **inquired**)*
to ask for information about something ▶ *He inquired **about** the times of trains to London.*

inquiring *(also **enquiring**)* /ɪnˈkwaɪərɪŋ/ *adjective*
always wanting to find out new things ▶ *a lively boy with a very inquiring mind*

inquiry *(also **enquiry**)* /ɪnˈkwaɪərɪ/ *noun (plural **inquiries**)*
1 a question asking for information about something ▶ *an inquiry **about** a job*
2 make inquiries to ask for information ▶ *to make inquiries **about** someone*

inquisitive /ɪnˈkwɪzɪtɪv/ *adjective*
wanting to know too many things, especially about other people

ins
a short way of writing the words **inch** or **inches** ▶ *6ins*

insane /ɪnˈseɪn/ *adjective*
mad ▶ *He must be insane to go out with her!*
OPPOSITE: **sane**

insect /ˈɪnsekt/ *noun*
a very small creature that has six legs ▶ *Bees and ants are insects.*

insecure /ˌɪnsɪˈkjʊəʳ/ *adjective*
not feeling confident about yourself, your abilities, your relationships, etc. ▶ *I was young, very shy, and insecure.*

insensitive /ɪnˈsensɪtɪv/ *adjective*
not noticing other people's feelings and often doing or saying things that will make them unhappy ▶ *He can be rude and insensitive.* ▶ *insensitive remarks about religion*

inseparable /ɪnˈsepərəbəl/ *adjective*
always together and very friendly ▶ *As children, my brother and I were inseparable.*

insert /ɪnˈsɜːt/ *verb*
to put something into something else ▶ *to insert a key in a lock*

inside¹ /ɪnˈsaɪd/ *noun*
the part that is in the middle of something or contained by something ▶ *Have you seen the inside of the house?*
OPPOSITE: **outside**

inside² /ɪnˈsaɪd/ *preposition, adverb*
in or onto something ▶ *She put the money inside her bag.* ▶ *Don't stand out there in the sun; come inside* (=into the house).
OPPOSITE: **outside**

inside³ /ˈɪnsaɪd/ *adjective*
in the middle of something or contained by something ▶ *the inside walls of a house*
OPPOSITE: **outside**

inside out /ˌɪnsaɪd ˈaʊt/ *adverb*
with the parts that are usually inside on the outside ▶ *You're wearing your socks inside out.*

insight /ˈɪnsaɪt/ *noun*
the ability to understand something clearly because you have done it, studied it, etc. ▶ *The museum gave us a real insight **into** how people used to live.*

insignificant /ˌɪnsɪgˈnɪfɪkənt/ *adjective*
too small or unimportant to think or worry about ▶ *I felt small and*

insignificant beside all those important people.
OPPOSITE: **significant**

insincere /ˌɪnsɪnˈsɪəʳ/ *adjective*
pretending to be pleased, sympathetic, etc., but not really meaning what you say or do ▶ *an insincere smile (adverb:* ***insincerely****)*
OPPOSITE: **sincere**

insist /ɪnˈsɪst/ *verb*
to say that something must happen or be done ▶ *I insist that you stop doing that.* ▶ *She insisted* ***on*** *seeing the manager.*

insistence /ɪnˈsɪstəns/ *noun (no plural)*
the act of demanding that something must happen or be done ▶ *My parents' insistence on good manners was a very good thing.*

insistent /ɪnˈsɪstənt/ *adjective*
saying very firmly that something must happen or be done ▶ *He was insistent that you call him back.*

insolent /ˈɪnsələnt/ *adjective*
rude and not showing someone respect ▶ *an insolent smile*

insoluble /ɪnˈsɒljʊbəl/ *adjective*
not disappearing when mixed with water ▶ *Sand is insoluble.*

insomnia /ɪnˈsɒmnɪə/ *noun (no plural)*
the problem you have when you regularly cannot sleep ▶ *Dad's suffered from insomnia for years.*

inspect /ɪnˈspekt/ *verb*
to look at something carefully, to see if there is anything wrong ▶ *He inspected the car carefully before he bought it.*

inspection /ɪnˈspekʃən/ *noun*
a careful look to see if there is anything wrong with something

inspector /ɪnˈspektəʳ/ *noun*
1 an official whose job is to visit places and see if there is anything wrong with them ▶ *a school inspector*
2 a police officer

inspiration /ˌɪnspɪˈreɪʃən/ *noun*
new ideas about what to do, or the feeling that you can do something ▶ *These gardening programmes give people inspiration for their own homes.*

inspire /ɪnˈspaɪəʳ/ *verb (present participle* ***inspiring****, past* ***inspired****)*
to make someone want to do something, especially by giving them new ideas ▶ *He inspired me to write a poem.*

inspired /ɪnˈspaɪəd/ *adjective*
very skilful ▶ *It was an inspired piece of football.*

install /ɪnˈstɔːl/ *verb*
to put in new machinery, etc. ▶ *We have installed a new computer system at work.*

instalment /ɪnˈstɔːlmənt/ *noun*
1 one of several payments that you make over a period of time in order to buy something ▶ *She paid for her car in instalments.*
2 one part of a long story which is told in several parts on television, in a magazine, etc.

instance /ˈɪnstəns/ *noun*
for instance for example ▶ *She's totally unreliable – for instance, she often leaves the children alone.*

instant¹ /ˈɪnstənt/ *adjective*
1 happening or working at once ▶ *The new shop was an instant success.*
2 very quick to prepare ▶ *instant coffee*

instant² *noun*
a moment ▶ *He waited for an instant before answering the question.*

instantaneous /ˌɪnstənˈteɪnɪəs/ *adjective*
happening immediately ▶ *The effect of the drug was instantaneous. (adverb:* ***instantaneously****)*

I

instantly /ˈɪnstəntlɪ/ *adverb*
at once

instead /ɪnˈsted/ *adverb*
in place of someone or something else ▶ *I didn't have a pen, so I used a pencil instead.*

instead of /ɪnˈsted ɒv/ *preposition*
in place of someone or something else ▶ *Can you come on Saturday instead of Sunday?* ▶ *Instead of going shopping, why don't we go for a walk?*

instil /ɪnˈstɪl/ *verb (present participle **instilling**, past **instilled**)*
to make someone think, feel, or behave in a particular way ▶ *It's my job to instil confidence **into** the team.*

instinct /ˈɪnstɪŋkt/ *noun*
a force or ability that makes you do things without thinking about them or learning them ▶ *Cats kill birds by instinct.*

institute /ˈɪnstɪtjuːt/ *noun*
a group of people who study a special thing, or the building used by such a group

institution /ˌɪnstɪˈtjuːʃən/ *noun*
a large organization such as a school, a hospital, or a bank

instruct /ɪnˈstrʌkt/ *verb*
1 to teach someone something
2 instruct someone to do something to tell someone that they must do something ▶ *I've been instructed to wait here.*

instruction /ɪnˈstrʌkʃən/ *noun*
a piece of information that tells you how to do something ▶ *Read the instructions before you use the machine.*

instructor /ɪnˈstrʌktəʳ/ *noun*
a person who teaches a skill or an activity ▶ *a sports instructor*

instrument /ˈɪnstrʊmənt/ *noun*
1 a tool used for doing a particular thing ▶ *medieval writing instruments*
2 an object used for making music ▶ *A piano is a musical instrument.*

instrumental /ˌɪnstrʊˈmentl/ *adjective*
1 be instrumental in doing something to be the thing or person that makes something happen ▶ *a clue that was instrumental in solving the mystery*
2 (used about music) played on instruments, not sung by people

insufficient /ˌɪnsəˈfɪʃənt/ *adjective*
not enough ▶ *The people here have insufficient food and water.*
OPPOSITE: **sufficient**

insulate /ˈɪnsjʊleɪt/ *verb (present participle **insulating**, past **insulated**)*
to cover something with a material that stops electricity, sound, heat, etc. getting in or out ▶ *Make sure you insulate your pipes before winter.*

insulin /ˈɪnsjʊlɪn/ *noun (no plural)*
a substance that your body produces so that it can use sugar for energy

insult[1] /ɪnˈsʌlt/ *verb*
to be rude to someone and offend them

insult[2] /ˈɪnsʌlt/ *noun*
something rude said to offend someone ▶ *He shouted insults at the boys.*

insurance /ɪnˈʃʊərəns/ *noun (no plural)*
money you pay to a company which then agrees to pay an amount of money if something bad happens to you or your property

insure /ɪnˈʃʊəʳ/ *verb (present participle **insuring**, past **insured**)*
to pay money regularly to a company so that it will give you an amount of money if something bad happens to you or your property ▶ *to insure your house **against** fire*

intact /ɪnˈtækt/ *adjective*
not broken or damaged
▶ *The package arrived intact.*

intake /ˈɪnteɪk/ *noun*
1 the amount of food, liquid, etc. that you eat or drink ▶ *If you're on a diet, you should reduce your sugar intake.*
2 the number of people that join a school, profession, etc. at a particular time ▶ *The school has an intake of about 100 children each year.*

integral /ˈɪntɪgrəl/ *adjective*
forming a necessary part of something ▶ *Training is an integral part of any team's preparation.*

integrate /ˈɪntɪgreɪt/ *verb (present participle* ***integrating****, past* ***integrated****)*
to become part of a group or a society, or to help someone do this ▶ *Our neighbours have never really integrated* ***into*** *the local community.*

integrity /ɪnˈtegrətɪ/ *noun (no plural)*
the quality of being honest and having high moral standards ▶ *a man of integrity*

intellect /ˈɪntɪlekt/ *noun*
the ability to understand things and think in an intelligent way ▶ *a woman of superior intellect*

intellectual /ˌɪntɪˈlektʃuəl/ *adjective*
related to the ability to think and understand ideas and information ▶ *the intellectual development of children*

intelligence /ɪnˈtelɪdʒəns/ *noun (no plural)*
the ability to learn and understand things ▶ *a creature of low intelligence*

intelligent /ɪnˈtelɪdʒənt/ *adjective*
quick to learn and understand things; clever

intelligible /ɪnˈtelɪdʒəbəl/ *adjective*
easy to understand

intend /ɪnˈtend/ *verb*
to plan to do something ▶ *What do you intend to do today?*
COMPARE: **aim**

intense /ɪnˈtens/ *adjective*
very strong ▶ *He had an intense love of music.* ▶ *The pain in my leg was intense.*

intensify /ɪnˈtensɪfaɪ/ *verb (past* ***intensified****)*
to increase in strength, size, or amount, or to make something do this ▶ *The pressure at work had slowly intensified.*

intensive /ɪnˈtensɪv/ *adjective*
involving a lot of work or effort in a short time ▶ *an intensive advertising campaign*

intent /ɪnˈtent/ *adjective*
be intent on doing something to be determined to do something ▶ *She was intent on making a good impression.*

intention /ɪnˈtenʃən/ *noun*
a plan ▶ *What are your intentions?* ▶ *I have no intention of going there.*

intentional /ɪnˈtenʃənəl/ *adjective*
done deliberately ▶ *I'm sorry if I upset you – it wasn't intentional.* *(adverb:* ***intentionally****)*

interact /ˌɪntərˈækt/ *verb*
to talk to people and make friends with them ▶ *Children need to learn to interact* ***with*** *each other at an early age.*

interactive /ˌɪntərˈæktɪv/ *adjective*
involving communication between a computer, television, etc. and the person who is using it ▶ *interactive CD-ROMs* ▶ *interactive video materials*

intercept /ˌɪntəˈsept/ *verb*
to stop someone or something that is moving from one place to another ▶ *The aircraft was intercepted and shot down.*

intercom /ˈɪntəkɒm/ *noun*
a system that people in a large building use to speak to other people in different parts of the building

I

▶ *They made the announcement over the intercom.*

interest[1] /'ɪntrəst/ *noun*
1 a wish to know more about something ▶ *to take an interest* ***in*** *something*
2 something you do or study because you enjoy it; a HOBBY ▶ *Her interests are music and sport.*

interest[2] *verb*
to make someone want to know more about something ▶ *Her story interested me.*

interested /'ɪntrəstɪd/ *adjective*
wanting to do something or know more about something ▶ *He's very interested* ***in*** *history.* ▶ *Are you interested in coming with us?*

interesting /'ɪntrəstɪŋ/ *adjective*
making you want to pay attention ▶ *an interesting story* ▶ *an interesting idea*
OPPOSITE: **boring, uninteresting**

interfere /ˌɪntə'fɪəʳ/ *verb*
(present participle ***interfering,*** *past* ***interfered****)*
1 to annoy another person by giving your opinions about things which have nothing to do with you, or by trying to take part in things where you are not wanted ▶ *Just go away and stop interfering!*
2 to prevent something or to make something different ▶ *The rain interfered* ***with*** *our plans to go out.*

interference /ˌɪntə'fɪərəns/ *noun (no plural)*
1 the act of interfering in something ▶ *I resented his interference in my personal life.*
2 noise caused by bad weather or an electrical problem that makes it difficult to hear a radio signal or see a television programme

interior[1] /ɪn'tɪərɪəʳ/ *noun*
the inside ▶ *the interior* ***of*** *a house*
OPPOSITE: **exterior**

interior[2] *adjective*
on the inside of something ▶ *the interior walls of a house*
OPPOSITE: **exterior**

interjection /ˌɪntə'dʒekʃən/ *noun*
a word or phrase that is used to express surprise, shock, pain, etc. In the sentence "Ouch! That hurts!", "Ouch!" is an interjection

intermediate /ˌɪntə'miːdɪət/ *adjective*
(used about a student or a class) of the middle level

intermission /ˌɪntə'mɪʃən/ *noun*
a period of time when a play, film, game, etc. stops for a short time before starting again ▶ *We had an ice cream during the intermission.*
SAME MEANING: **interval**

internal /ɪn'tɜːnl/ *adjective*
of or on the inside ▶ *an internal injury*
OPPOSITE: **external**

international /ˌɪntə'næʃənəl/ *adjective*
for or by many countries ▶ *an international agreement* ▶ *an international airport*

Internet /'ɪntənet/ *noun*
the Internet a system that allows people using computers around the world to send and receive information ▶ *You can find all the latest information* ***on*** *the Internet.*

interpret /ɪn'tɜːprɪt/ *verb*
1 to put the words of one language into the words of another language by talking ▶ *to interpret from French into English*
COMPARE: **translate**
2 to explain or understand information, someone's actions, etc. ▶ *His silence was interpreted as guilt.*

interpretation /ɪnˌtɜːprɪ'teɪʃən/ *noun*
a way of explaining or understanding information, someone's actions, etc. ▶ *Their interpretation* ***of*** *the evidence was very different from ours.*

interpreter /ɪn'tɜːprɪtəʳ/ *noun*
a person whose job is to put the words of one language into the words of another language by talking

interrogate /ɪn'terəgeɪt/ *verb* *(present participle **interrogating**, past **interrogated**)*
to ask someone a lot of questions, often in an unpleasant way ▶ *Forty people were arrested and interrogated by military police.*

interrogative /ˌɪntə'rɒgətɪv/ *noun*
a word or sentence that asks a question

interrogator /ɪn'terəgeɪtəʳ/ *noun*
a person who tries to get information by asking lots of questions, often in an unpleasant way ▶ *She managed to trick her interrogators and escape.*

interrupt /ˌɪntə'rʌpt/ *verb*
to say something when someone else is already speaking, and cause them to stop ▶ *It is rude to interrupt.* ▶ *Don't interrupt me!*

interruption /ˌɪntə'rʌpʃən/ *noun*
something which stops you from continuing what you are doing for a while ▶ *I couldn't work because there were so many interruptions.*

intersection /'ɪntəˌsekʃən/ *noun*
a place where two roads, lines, etc meet, especially where they cross each other ▶ *Meet me at the intersection of Main Street and Queen Street.*

interval /'ɪntəvəl/ *noun*
1 a time or space between things ▶ *an interval between the first part and the second part of a film*
2 at intervals happening regularly, with a period of time or space between ▶ *There were trees at intervals along the road.*

intervene /ˌɪntə'viːn/ *verb* *(present participle **intervening**, past **intervened**)*
to do something to try to stop an argument, a problem, a war, etc. ▶ *Police eventually had to intervene in the dispute.*

interview¹ /'ɪntəvjuː/ *noun*
1 a meeting to decide if a person is suitable for a job ▶ *to go for an interview*
2 a meeting at which a person, usually someone famous, is asked about their opinions or their life, e.g. for a newspaper, or on television or radio

interview² *verb*
1 to talk to someone to see if they are suitable for a job
2 to ask someone questions for a newspaper, etc., or on television or radio

interviewer /'ɪntəvjuːəʳ/ *noun*
a person whose job is to interview people, especially famous people, on television or radio

intestine /ɪn'testɪn/ *noun*
the long tube in your body that carries food away from your stomach

intimate /'ɪntɪmət/ *adjective*
very private or personal ▶ *She wrote all her most intimate thoughts in her diary.*

intimidate /ɪn'tɪmɪdeɪt/ *verb* *(present participle **intimidating**, past **intimidated**)*
to frighten someone, especially so that they do what you want ▶ *Some of the older boys were trying to intimidate him into giving them money.*

into /'ɪntə; *strong* 'ɪntuː/ *preposition*
1 so as to be inside or in something ▶ *They went into the house.*
2 used to show how something changes ▶ *She made the material into a dress.* ▶ *He cut the cake into six pieces.*
3 used when dividing one number by another number ▶ *5 into 20 goes 4 times.*

I

intolerable /ɪn'tɒlərəbəl/ *adjective* very unpleasant or painful ▶ *In the middle of the day, the heat was intolerable.*

intolerant /ɪn'tɒlərənt/ *adjective* not willing to accept ways of thinking and behaving that are different from your own
OPPOSITE: **tolerant**

intranet /'ɪntrənet/ *noun* a system, which is similar to the INTERNET but smaller, for sending computer messages between people who work for the same company or organization

intransitive /ɪn'trænsətɪv/ *adjective* (used about a verb) not taking an object; where the action is not done to a person or thing ▶ *In the sentence "When he had finished, he sat down", "finish" and "sit" are intransitive verbs.*
COMPARE: **transitive**

intricate /'ɪntrɪkət/ *adjective* containing a lot of details or different parts ▶ *intricate carved statues*

intrigue /ɪn'tri:g/ *verb (present participle* ***intriguing****, past* ***intrigued****)* to interest someone a lot, especially by being strange or mysterious ▶ *I was intrigued by the story of the young girl who used to live in the house.*

introduce /ˌɪntrə'dju:s/ *verb (present participle* ***introducing****, past* ***introduced****)*
1 to cause two people to meet each other for the first time, and tell each person the name of the other person ▶ *He introduced his friend to me.*
2 to bring in a new thing ▶ *to introduce a new subject in a school*

introduction /ˌɪntrə'dʌkʃən/ *noun*
1 *(no plural)* the bringing in of something new for the first time ▶ *the introduction of a new law*
2 a piece of writing at the beginning of a book, which tells you what the rest of the book is about

introductory /ˌɪntrə'dʌktərɪ/ *adjective*
1 coming at the beginning of something and introducing the subject ▶ *an introductory lesson in Arabic*
2 available for a short time when something new is being sold ▶ *The software is available at an introductory price of £175.*

introvert /'ɪntrəvɜ:t/ *noun* a person who is quiet and shy and does not like to be with other people
OPPOSITE: **extrovert**

introverted /'ɪntrəvɜ:tɪd/ *adjective* quiet and shy ▶ *Jake has always been a bit introverted.*

intrude /ɪn'tru:d/ *verb (present participle* ***intruding****, past* ***intruded****)* to go into a place or become involved in a situation where you are not wanted ▶ *I'm sorry to intrude, but I need to talk to you.*

intruder /ɪn'tru:dəʳ/ *noun* a person who enters a building or an area without permission ▶ *The alarm will go off if there's an intruder.*

intuition /ˌɪntjʊ'ɪʃən/ *noun* the feeling that you know something is correct or true, although you do not have any definite facts ▶ *My intuition told me not to trust him.*

invade /ɪn'veɪd/ *verb (present participle* ***invading****, past* ***invaded****)* to attack and enter a country or place with an army ▶ *The army invaded the town.*

invalid /'ɪnvəlɪd/ *noun* a person who is weak because they are ill ▶ *He helps to look after his grandfather who is an invalid.*

invaluable /ɪn'væljʊəbəl/ *adjective* very useful ▶ *I gained invaluable experience while I was working abroad.*

I

invariably /ɪnˈveəriəbli/ *adverb*
almost always ▶ *The trains are invariably late in the morning.*

invasion /ɪnˈveɪʒən/ *noun*
the act of an army attacking and entering a country or place in order to control it ▶ *an enemy invasion*

invent /ɪnˈvent/ *verb*
to think of and plan something completely new that did not exist before ▶ *Who invented the telephone?*

invention /ɪnˈvenʃən/ *noun*
1 *(no plural)* the thinking of a new idea and making of something that did not exist before ▶ *the invention of the telephone*
2 something completely new that has just been thought of and made ▶ *This machine is their latest invention.*

inventive /ɪnˈventɪv/ *adjective*
good at thinking of new and interesting ideas ▶ *Ed's a very inventive cook.*

inventor /ɪnˈventəʳ/ *noun*
a person who thinks of and plans something completely new ▶ *the inventor of the telephone*

inverted commas /ɪnˌvɜːtɪd ˈkɒməz/ *plural noun*
the signs (' ') or (" "), used in writing to show what somebody says
SAME MEANING: **speech marks**

invest /ɪnˈvest/ *verb*
to give money to a bank, business, etc. so that you can get a profit later

investigate /ɪnˈvestɪgeɪt/ *verb (present participle* ***investigating****, past* ***investigated****)*
to search for information about someone or something by looking, asking questions, etc. ▶ *The police are investigating the crime.*

investigation /ɪnˌvestɪˈgeɪʃən/ *noun*
a search for information about someone or something ▶ *a police investigation into the crime*

investment /ɪnˈvestmənt/ *noun*
1 *(no plural)* the act of putting money in a bank or buying something, in order to get a profit later ▶ *We need more investment in small businesses.*
2 something that you buy because it will be more valuable or useful later ▶ *We bought the house as an investment.*

invisible /ɪnˈvɪzəbəl/ *adjective*
not able to be seen ▶ *Air is invisible.*
OPPOSITE: **visible**

invitation /ˌɪnvɪˈteɪʃən/ *noun*
an offer, in words or writing, of a chance to do something or to go somewhere ▶ *a party invitation* ▶ *an invitation* ***to*** *a party*

invite /ɪnˈvaɪt/ *verb (present participle* ***inviting****, past* ***invited****)*
to ask someone to come to your house, to go out with you, etc. ▶ *She invited us* ***to*** *her party.*

> People do not use the verb **invite** when they are asking you if you want to go somewhere or do something. Instead they say things like *Would you like to come to dinner at my house?* or *Do you want to come to a party tonight?* (Never say *I invite you ...*)

inviting /ɪnˈvaɪtɪŋ/ *adjective*
attractive and making you want to have, enjoy, or use something ▶ *The swimming pool looked very inviting.*

invoice /ˈɪnvɔɪs/ *noun*
a list showing how much money you must pay for things you have received or work that has been done ▶ *You haven't paid these invoices.*

involve /ɪnˈvɒlv/ *verb (present participle* ***involving****, past* ***involved****)*
1 to make a person or thing be a part of something ▶ *Don't involve me* ***in*** *your argument.*
2 to make something necessary ▶ *The job will involve a lot of hard work.*

I

3 be involved in something, be involved with something to take part in something ► *She's involved in politics.*

involvement /ɪn'vɒlvmənt/ *noun (no plural)*
the act of taking part in something ► *They thanked us for our involvement in the project.*

inward /'ɪnwəd/ *adjective*
1 towards the middle or the inside of something
OPPOSITE: **outward**
2 (used about a thought or feeling) not shown to other people ► *an inward feeling of happiness*

inwards /'ɪnwədz/ *adverb*
towards the middle or the inside of something ► *The walls fell inwards.*
OPPOSITE: **outwards**

IPA /ˌaɪ piː 'eɪ/ *noun (no plural)*
INTERNATIONAL PHONETIC ALPHABET; a system of signs showing the sounds made in speech

irate /ˌaɪ'reɪt/ *adjective*
very angry ► *An irate customer complained to the manager.*

irk /ɜːk/ *verb*
to annoy someone ► *It irks me how he never helps his mother.*

I

iron[1] /'aɪən/ *noun*
1 *(no plural)* a hard, grey metal
2 an instrument that is heated and then used to make clothes smooth

iron[2] *verb*
to press clothes with a hot iron to make them smooth ► *to iron a shirt*

iron[3] *adjective*
made of the metal iron ► *an iron gate*

ironic /aɪ'rɒnɪk/ *adjective*
using words that are different from what you really mean, in order to be amusing or show that you are annoyed ► *I think when he said "Thanks a lot" he was being ironic.* *(adverb:* ***ironically****)*

ironing /'aɪənɪŋ/ *noun (no plural)*
do the ironing to press clothes with a hot iron to make them smooth

ironing board /'aɪənɪŋ ˌbɔːd/ *noun*
a narrow table on which you iron clothes

irony /'aɪərənɪ/ *noun (no plural)*
1 the part of a situation that is strange or amusing because what happens is completely different from what you expected ► *The irony was that the more the media criticized the film, the more the audiences liked it.*
2 the use of words that are different from what you really mean, in order to be amusing or show that you are annoyed ► *The author uses irony to convey his true feelings about the government.*

irrational /ɪ'ræʃənəl/ *adjective*
not sensible or reasonable ► *She has an irrational fear of mice.*
OPPOSITE: **rational**

irregular /ɪ'regjʊləʳ/ *adjective*
(used about nouns, verbs, etc.) not following the usual rules of grammar ► *"To go" is an irregular verb.*
OPPOSITE: **regular**

irrelevant /ɪ'reləvənt/ *adjective*
not important and having no effect in a particular situation ► *She thinks my opinion is irrelevant.*
OPPOSITE: **relevant**

irresistible /ˌɪrɪ'zɪstəbəl/ *adjective*
impossible not to want, like, enjoy, etc. ► *The chocolate cake was irresistible.*

irresponsible /ˌɪrɪ'spɒnsəbəl/ *adjective*
behaving in a careless way, without thinking of the bad results you might cause ► *It's irresponsible to leave small children alone.*
OPPOSITE: **responsible**

irreversible /ˌɪrɪ'vɜːsəbəl/ *adjective*
impossible to change back to the

previous state ▶ *irreversible brain damage*
OPPOSITE: **reversible**

irrigate /ˈɪrɪgeɪt/ *verb (present participle* ***irrigating****, past* ***irrigated****)*
to make water flow onto dry land so that crops can grow

irrigation /ˌɪrɪˈgeɪʃən/ *noun (no plural)*
the supplying of water to dry land so that crops can grow

irritable /ˈɪrɪtəbəl/ *adjective*
easily annoyed ▶ *He's always irritable in the morning.*

irritate /ˈɪrɪteɪt/ *verb (present participle* ***irritating****, past* ***irritated****)*
1 to annoy someone ▶ *The noise the children were making was irritating me.*
2 to make a part of your body sore ▶ *The sun irritates my eyes.*

is /s, z, əz; *strong* ɪz/ *verb*
the part of the verb **be** that you use with **he, she**, and **it** ▶ *She is Peter's sister.* ▶ *He's* (=he is) *her brother.* ▶ *That boy's* (=boy is) *in my class.* ▶ *He's not* (=he is not) *very clever.* ▶ *She isn't* (=she is not) *my friend.*

Islam /ˈɪzlɑːm/ *noun (no plural)*
the religion of the Muslims

Islamic /ɪzˈlæmɪk/ *adjective*
of or about Islam ▶ *Islamic traditions* ▶ *the Islamic faith*

island /ˈaɪlənd/ *noun*
a piece of land surrounded by water

isle /aɪl/ *noun*
used in the names of some islands ▶ *Jersey is one of the Channel Isles.*

isn't /ˈɪzənt/
is not ▶ *She isn't coming.* ▶ *It's a lovely day, isn't it?*

isolate /ˈaɪsəleɪt/ *verb (present participle* ***isolating****, past* ***isolated****)*
to keep one person or thing separate from others ▶ *We isolate dangerous prisoners in another part of the prison*

isolated /ˈaɪsəˌleɪtɪd/ *adjective*
far from other houses, towns, etc. ▶ *an isolated house* ▶ *an isolated village*

isolation /ˌaɪsəˈleɪʃən/ *noun (no plural)*
1 a feeling of being lonely ▶ *Moving to a new town can lead to a sense of isolation.*
2 in isolation happening or existing separately from other things ▶ *These events cannot be examined in isolation from one another.*

issue[1] /ˈɪʃuː/ *verb (present participle* ***issuing****, past* ***issued****)*
to supply someone with something ▶ *The teacher issued paper and pencils to all the children.*

issue[2] *noun*
1 a subject that many people think is important ▶ *new government policy on the issue* ***of*** *health*
2 something that is printed in large numbers and sold at one time ▶ *today's issue of the newspaper*

it /ɪt/ *pronoun (plural* ***they*** */ðeɪ/)*
1 the thing or animal that the sentence is about ▶ *I've lost my book, and I can't find it anywhere.* ▶ *It's* (=it is) *not in my room.* ▶ *It was an interesting film.*
2 used when you are talking about the weather, time, and date ▶ *It is very hot today.* ▶ *It's nearly 4 o'clock.* ▶ *It is Thursday, September 2nd.*
3 used when you are talking about a happening or a fact ▶ *It's a long way to the town.* ▶ *"What's that noise?" "It's a car."*
4 used when you are asking or saying who is there ▶ *"Who is it?"* ▶ *"It's me – Peter."*

IT /ˌaɪ ˈtiː/ *noun (no plural)*
INFORMATION TECHNOLOGY

italics /ɪˈtælɪks/ *plural noun*
a style of printed letters that slope to

I

the right ▶ *The examples in this dictionary are written in italics.*

itch[1] /ɪtʃ/ *verb*
(used about your skin) to be sore and making you want to rub it ▶ *The insect bite itched all night.*

itch[2] *noun (plural **itches**)*
a sore and annoying feeling on your skin that makes you want to rub it

itchy /'ɪtʃɪ/ *adjective (**itchier, itchiest**)*
(used about a part of your body) making you want to rub it ▶ *itchy skin*

it'd /'ɪtəd/
1 it would ▶ *It'd be lovely to see you.*
2 it had ▶ *It'd taken us two hours to get there.*

item /'aɪtəm/ *noun*
a thing ▶ *There was an interesting item in the newspaper today.* ▶ *On the desk there were two books, a pen, and some other items.*

itinerary /aɪ'tɪnərərɪ/ *noun (plural **itineraries**)*
a plan or list of the places you will visit on a trip ▶ *The first stop on our itinerary is Rome.*

it'll /'ɪtl/
it will ▶ *It'll soon be the holidays.*

its /ɪts/ *adjective*
of it; belonging to it ▶ *She gave the cat its food.* ▶ *The dog hurt its foot.*

Do not confuse **its** (=belonging to it) with **it's** (=it is or it has) which is spelt with (').

J

it's /ɪts/
1 it is ▶ *It's very nice to meet you.*
2 it has ▶ *It's stopped raining.*
LOOK AT: **its**

itself /ɪt'self/ *pronoun (plural **themselves** /ðəm'selvz/)*
the same thing or animal as the one that the sentence is about
▶ *The house stands by itself* (=alone) *outside the village.*

I've /aɪv/
I have ▶ *I've got two sisters.*

ivory /'aɪvərɪ/ *noun (no plural)*
the hard, yellow substance taken from the TUSKS (=long teeth) of elephants

ivy /'aɪvɪ/ *noun*
a plant with dark green, shiny leaves that grows on the walls of buildings ▶ *The cottage was covered in ivy.*

Jj

jab[1] /dʒæb/ *verb (present participle **jabbing**, past **jabbed**)*
to push something long or sharp forward with a lot of force ▶ *I jabbed the needle into my finger.* ▶ *He kept jabbing his finger into my back until I turned round.*

jab[2] *noun*
a quick, sharp push ▶ *I felt a jab in my back.*

jack[1] /dʒæk/ *noun*
1 a piece of equipment used for lifting something heavy, such as a car
2 a playing card with a picture of a young man on it

jack[2] *verb*
jack something in to stop doing something, such as your job or a course of study ▶ *I'd love to jack in my job.*

jackal /'dʒækɔːl/ *noun*
a wild animal like a small dog

jacket /'dʒækɪt/ *noun*
1 a short coat
2 the loose cover of a book

jackpot /'dʒækpɒt/ *noun*
a large amount of money that you can win ▶ *The lottery jackpot is £3 million.*

jaded /'dʒeɪdɪd/ *adjective*
no longer feeling excited about something because you are tired of it

or it no longer interests you ▶ *She felt jaded after the long journey.*

jagged /ˈdʒægɪd/ *adjective*
having a rough, uneven edge with many sharp points ▶ *I cut myself on the jagged edge of the tin.* ▶ *jagged rocks*

jaguar /ˈdʒægjʊəʳ/ *noun*
a large, wild cat with spots

jail *(also* ***gaol****)* /dʒeɪl/ *noun*
a place where criminals are kept locked up as a punishment ▶ *The man was sent to jail.*
SAME MEANING: **prison**

jam¹ /dʒæm/ *verb (present participle* ***jamming****, past* ***jammed****)*
1 to press things or people tightly together into a place ▶ *I jammed all my clothes into a case.*
2 to make something unable to move ▶ *I've jammed the lock and I can't open the door.*
3 to become stuck and unable to move ▶ *I can't ride my bicycle because the brakes have jammed.*

jam² *noun*
1 a lot of people or things pressed so tightly together that movement is stopped ▶ *a traffic jam*
2 *(no plural)* a sweet food made of fruit boiled with sugar, usually eaten with bread

jangle /ˈdʒæŋgəl/ *verb (present participle* ***jangling****, past* ***jangled****)*
to make a sharp noise like metal hitting metal ▶ *She jangled her keys in her pocket.*

January /ˈdʒænjʊərɪ/ *noun*
the first month of the year

jar /dʒɑːʳ/ *noun*
a container like a bottle with a short neck and a wide opening ▶ *a jam jar*

jargon /ˈdʒɑːgən/ *noun (no plural)*
words and phrases that are used by people doing the same type of work, and that other people find difficult to understand ▶ *legal jargon*

javelin /ˈdʒævəlɪn/ *noun*
a light spear which is thrown as a sport

jaw /dʒɔː/ *noun*
either of the two bony parts of your face which hold your teeth

jazz /dʒæz/ *noun (no plural)*
a kind of music with a strong beat ▶ *Do you like listening to jazz?*

jealous /ˈdʒeləs/ *adjective*
1 unhappy because you want something that someone else has ▶ *I was very jealous* ***of*** *Linda's new bicycle.*
SAME MEANING: **envious**
2 afraid that you will lose someone's love because they seem to love another person more ▶ *Her husband gets jealous if she talks to other men. (adverb:* ***jealously****)*

jealousy /ˈdʒeləsɪ/ *noun (no plural)*
1 the unhappiness that you feel when you want something that someone else has
SAME MEANING: **envy**
2 the fear that you feel when you think you will lose someone's love because they seem to love another person more

jeans /dʒiːnz/ *plural noun*
trousers made of a strong, cotton cloth, usually blue ▶ *a pair of jeans*

Jeep /dʒiːp/ *noun trademark*
a car that has a strong engine and can be used on rough roads

jeer /dʒɪəʳ/ *verb*
to laugh rudely at someone or shout unkind remarks ▶ *The crowd jeered* ***at*** *the politician.*

jeers /dʒɪəz/ *plural noun*
rude laughter; unkind remarks

jelly /ˈdʒelɪ/ *noun*
1 *(plural* ***jellies****)* a sweet, soft DESSERT made with fruit and sugar
2 *(no plural)* any substance that is between liquid and solid

J

jellyfish /ˈdʒelɪˌfɪʃ/ *noun (plural **jellyfish** or **jellyfishes**)*
a soft sea creature that is nearly transparent and can sting

jerk[1] /dʒɜːk/ *verb*
1 to pull something suddenly and quickly ▶ *She jerked the rope, but it wouldn't move.*
2 to move with a sudden movement ▶ *Her hand jerked as she dropped her drink.*

jerk[2] *noun*
a short, hard pull or sudden movement ▶ *The old bus started with a jerk.*

jerky /ˈdʒɜːkɪ/ *adjective (**jerkier, jerkiest**)*
rough and sudden, not smooth ▶ *We had a very jerky ride in his car.*

jersey /ˈdʒɜːzɪ/ *noun*
a piece of clothing, usually made of wool, that covers the top part of your body.
SAME MEANING: **jumper, pullover, sweater**

Jesus /ˈdʒiːzəs/ *(also **Jesus Christ** /ˌdʒiːzəs ˈkraɪst/) noun*
the man on whose life and teaching Christianity is based

jet /dʒet/ *noun*
1 a narrow stream of gas, air, or liquid that comes out of a small hole ▶ *The fireman sent jets of water into the burning house.*
2 a kind of aircraft that can go very fast ▶ *a jet engine*

jet lag /ˈdʒet læg/ *noun (no plural)*
the feeling of being very tired after a long journey on a plane ▶ *Do you get jet lag after a long flight?*

jetty /ˈdʒetɪ/ *noun (plural **jetties**)*
a kind of wall built out into water, used for getting on and off boats

Jew /dʒuː/ *noun*
a person who follows the religion of Judaism

jewel /ˈdʒuːəl/ *noun*
a stone that is worth a lot of money and worn as an ornament ▶ *She wore beautiful jewels round her neck.*

jeweller /ˈdʒuːələʳ/ *noun*
a person who sells or makes jewellery ▶ *The jeweller fixed my watch.*

jewellery /ˈdʒuːəlrɪ/ *noun (no plural)*
things such as rings, etc. that people wear as ornaments

Jewish /ˈdʒjuːɪʃ/ *adjective*
belonging to a group of people whose religion is Judaism

jibe *(also **gibe**)* /dʒaɪb/ *noun*
something that you say that criticizes someone or makes them seem silly ▶ *She's always making jibes about my weight.*

jigsaw puzzle /ˈdʒɪgsɔː ˌpʌzəl/ *(also **jigsaw**) noun*
a game in which you must fit together many small pieces to make one big picture ▶ *Let's do a jigsaw puzzle.*

jilt /dʒɪlt/ *verb*
to suddenly end a romantic relationship with someone ▶ *She jilted him the day before their wedding.*

jingle /ˈdʒɪŋgəl/ *verb (present participle **jingling**, past **jingled**)*
to make a ringing noise, like little bells ▶ *The coins jingled in his pocket.*

jittery /ˈdʒɪtərɪ/ *adjective*
worried and nervous ▶ *I get very jittery about going to the dentist.*

job /dʒɒb/ *noun*
1 a piece of work that must be done ▶ *My mother does all the jobs about the house.*
SAME MEANING: **task**
2 work that you are paid to do ▶ *"What is your job?" "I'm a teacher."*
LOOK AT: **work**
3 a good job a phrase used when you think it is lucky or a good thing that

something has happened ▶ *It's a good job* (=it's lucky) *you were here to help me.*

jockey /ˈdʒɒkɪ/ *noun*
a person who rides in horse races

jog¹ /dʒɒg/ *verb (present participle* ***jogging****, past* ***jogged****)*
to run slowly, usually for exercise ▶ *She jogs every morning.*

jog² *noun*
a slow, steady run, which you do as exercise ▶ *Let's go for a jog.*

jogger /ˈdʒɒgəʳ/ *noun*
a person who goes running as a form of exercise

jogging /ˈdʒɒgɪŋ/ *noun (no plural)*
the activity of running for exercise ▶ *I love jogging.*

join¹ /dʒɔɪn/ *verb*
1 to put or bring two or more things together ▶ *Join the two pieces of rope with a strong knot.* ▶ *This road joins the two villages.*
2 to come together; to meet ▶ *Where do the two roads join?*
3 to go and be with someone, usually so that you can do something together ▶ *Will you join me for a drink* (=will you have a drink with me)*?* ▶ *I am joining my family for Christmas.*
4 to become a member of something ▶ *He joined the army in 1939.*
5 join hands to hold each other's hands ▶ *We all joined hands and danced round in a circle.*
6 join in to take part in an activity, a game, etc. ▶ *We all joined in the singing.* ▶ *We're going to play football; do you want to join in?*

join² *noun*
a place where two things have been joined together ▶ *There's a join in this piece of material.*

joint¹ /dʒɔɪnt/ *noun*
1 a place where two bones in your body meet
2 a place where two things are joined together
3 a large piece of meat for cooking, usually with a bone in it

joint² *adjective*
shared by two or more people ▶ *We wrote it together; it was a joint effort.* ▶ *His sons are joint owners of the business.* ▶ *We have a joint bank account.* (adverb: ***jointly***)

joke¹ /dʒəʊk/ *noun*
1 something that you say or do to make people laugh ▶ *Our teacher told us a funny joke.* ▶ *Do you know any jokes?*
2 play a joke on someone to do something funny to someone to make other people laugh ▶ *Let's play a joke on Michael.*
3 practical joke a trick played on someone to make them look silly and to make other people laugh

joke² *verb (present participle* ***joking****, past* ***joked****)*
to say things to make people laugh ▶ *I didn't mean that seriously – I was only joking.*

jolly¹ /ˈdʒɒlɪ/ *adjective (****jollier****,* ***jolliest****)*
happy; pleasant ▶ *a jolly person*

jolly² *adverb*
very ▶ *You were jolly lucky!*

jolt¹ /dʒəʊlt/ *noun*
1 a sudden shake or movement ▶ *The lorry started with a jolt.*
2 a shock or surprise ▶ *The telephone rang in the middle of the night and gave me a bit of a jolt.*

jolt² *verb*
to move with sudden, rough shakes ▶ *The bus jolted along the mountain road.*

jostle /ˈdʒɒsəl/ *verb (present participle* ***jostling****, past* ***jostled****)*
to push against other people in a crowd ▶ *Spectators jostled for a better view.*

jot /dʒɒt/ *verb (present participle* ***jotting****, past* ***jotted****)*
jot something down to write something down quickly ▶ *I jotted down her address on my newspaper.*

journal /ˈdʒɜːnl/ *noun*
1 a serious newspaper or magazine for a special subject ▶ *a medical journal*
2 a record of the things you do each day

journalism /ˈdʒɜːnl-ɪzəm/ *noun (no plural)*
the job of writing for a newspaper or magazine

journalist /ˈdʒɜːnl-ɪst/ *noun*
a person who writes for a newspaper or magazine

journey /ˈdʒɜːnɪ/ *noun*
a trip, usually a long one ▶ *How long is the journey to the coast?*

joy /dʒɔɪ/ *noun*
1 something that gives great happiness ▶ *Her child was a joy to her.*
2 *(no plural)* great happiness ▶ *She cried with joy when her son was born.*

joyful /ˈdʒɔɪfəl/ *adjective*
full of great happiness ▶ *a joyful occasion (adverb:* ***joyfully****)*

joyrider /ˈdʒɔɪˌraɪdəʳ/ *noun*
a person who steals a car and drives it in a fast and dangerous way

joyriding /ˈdʒɔɪˌraɪdɪŋ/ *noun (no plural)*
the activity of stealing a car and driving it in a fast and dangerous way ▶ *He was arrested for joyriding.*

joystick /ˈdʒɔɪˌstɪk/ *noun*
a handle that you use to control something in a computer game

Judaism /ˈdʒuːdeɪ-ɪzəm/ *noun (no plural)*
the religion of the Jews

judge[1] /dʒʌdʒ/ *noun*
1 a person who can decide questions of law in a court ▶ *The judge decided to send the man to prison for two years.*
2 a person who decides who is the winner of a competition

judge[2] *verb (present participle* ***judging****, past* ***judged****)*
1 to form an opinion about something or someone, especially after you have thought carefully ▶ *How can you judge which dictionary to buy?*
2 to decide who or what is the winner of a competition ▶ *Who is judging the poetry competition?*
COMPARE: **decide**

judgement /ˈdʒʌdʒmənt/ *noun*
1 the decision made by a judge in a court of law
2 *(no plural)* what you decide after thinking about something carefully ▶ *I think John is lying, but you will have to make your own judgement.*

judo /ˈdʒuːdəʊ/ *noun (no plural)*
a fighting sport in which you try to throw the other person to the ground

jug /dʒʌg/ *noun*
a container with a handle, for holding and pouring liquids ▶ *a jug of water*

juggle /ˈdʒʌgəl/ *verb (present participle* ***juggling****, past* ***juggled****)*
to throw several things into the air and keep them moving by throwing and catching them many times, as a trick

juggler /ˈdʒʌgləʳ/ *noun*
a person who does juggling tricks for people to watch

juice /dʒuːs/ *noun (no plural)*
the liquid that comes out of fruit or vegetables ▶ *a glass of orange juice*

juicy /ˈdʒuːsɪ/ *adjective (****juicier, juiciest****)*
having a lot of juice ▶ *a juicy orange*

July /dʒʊˈlaɪ/ *noun*
the seventh month of the year

jumble[1] /ˈdʒʌmbəl/ *noun (no plural)*
1 a lot of things which are mixed together in an untidy way

J

2 a lot of different, old things, usually which you do not want to keep any more

jumble[2] *verb (present participle **jumbling**, past **jumbled**)*
to mix things together in an untidy way ▶ *The clothes were all jumbled up in the drawer.*

jumble sale /ˈdʒʌmbəl ˌseɪl/ *noun*
an event where people sell a lot of different, old things, usually to make money to help people

jumbo /ˈdʒʌmbəʊ/ *adjective*
larger than other things of the same type ▶ *jumbo sausages*

jumbo jet /ˈdʒʌmbəʊ ˌdʒet/ *noun*
a large aircraft that can carry a lot of passengers

jump[1] /dʒʌmp/ *verb*
1 to push yourself up in the air or over something, using your legs ▶ *The children jumped up and down with excitement.* ▶ *The horse jumped over the fence.*
2 to move suddenly because of fear or surprise ▶ *That noise made me jump.*
3 jump to your feet to get up quickly, especially to go and do something ▶ *She jumped to her feet when the post arrived.*

jump[2] *noun*
the act of pushing yourself up in the air or over something, using your legs ▶ *He got over the fence in one jump.*

jumper /ˈdʒʌmpəʳ/ *noun*
a piece of clothing, usually made of wool, that covers the top part of your body
SAME MEANING: **jersey, pullover, sweater**

junction /ˈdʒʌŋkʃən/ *noun*
a place where two or more things join or meet ▶ *Turn left at the junction.*

June /dʒuːn/ *noun*
the sixth month of the year

jungle /ˈdʒʌŋgəl/ *noun*
a thick forest in hot countries

junior /ˈdʒuːnjəʳ/ *adjective*
1 younger ▶ *a junior school* (=a school for young children)
2 low in importance or position ▶ *a junior member of the company*
OPPOSITE (**1** and **2**): **senior**

junior school /ˈdʒuːnjə ˌskuːl/ *noun*
a school for children who are between seven and eleven years old

junk /dʒʌŋk/ *noun (no plural)*
useless things that you do not want ▶ *That room is full of junk.*
COMPARE: **rubbish**

junk food /ˈdʒʌŋk fuːd/ *noun (no plural)*
food that is not healthy because it contains a lot of fat or sugar ▶ *You eat too much junk food.*

junk mail /ˈdʒʌŋk meɪl/ *noun (no plural)*
letters that companies send to your house to tell you about the things they sell ▶ *I get far too much junk mail, and most of it goes in the bin.*

juror /ˈdʒʊərəʳ/ *noun*
a member of a jury ▶ *The jurors must decide whether or not he is guilty.*

jury /ˈdʒʊərɪ/ *noun (plural **juries**)*
a group of people who decide if a person is guilty or not in a law court ▶ *The jury decided the man was guilty and he was sent to prison.*

just[1] /dʒʌst/ *adverb*
1 a very short time ago ▶ *I've just got home.*

> **Just** (**1**), **already**, and **yet** are usually used with the PRESENT PERFECT tense (=the tense formed with **have** + the PAST PARTICIPLE) and not with the simple past tense: *He had just heard the news.* ▶ *I've already seen that film.* ▶ *Have you finished yet?*

2 by a very short time ▶ *You just missed the bus.*

J

3 at the moment; now ▶ *The telephone rang just as I was leaving.* ▶ *I'm just making some coffee – would you like some?*
4 exactly at a particular time or place ▶ *I'm not hungry just yet* (=right now). ▶ *I live just here.*
5 the exact amount; not more, not less ▶ *I've got just enough money to get home.*
6 only ▶ *I rang just to say hello.*
7 **just a minute, just a moment** a phrase used when you want to ask someone to wait a little bit until you can help them ▶ *"Can I speak to Mr Jones?" "Just a minute, please. I'll find him for you."*
8 **just now** at the moment ▶ *I'm busy just now, but I can help you later.*

just² *adjective*
fair and right ▶ *a just punishment*
OPPOSITE: **unjust**

justice /'dʒʌstɪs/ *noun (no plural)*
1 treatment of people which is fair and right ▶ *to fight for justice*
OPPOSITE: **injustice**
2 the system of law in a country

justifiable /'dʒʌstɪfaɪəbəl/ *adjective*
able to be justified ▶ *a justifiable decision*

justification /ˌdʒʌstɪfɪ'keɪʃən/ *noun (no plural)*
a good reason for doing something ▶ *There's no justification for violence.*

justified /'dʒʌstɪfaɪd/ *adjective*
fair and done for good reasons ▶ *Her criticism is justified.*

justify /'dʒʌstɪfaɪ/ *verb (past* ***justified****)*
to give a good reason for doing something that other people think is not reasonable ▶ *He keeps trying to justify his bad behaviour.*

juvenile /'dʒuːvənaɪl/ *adjective*
of or about young people ▶ *There has been an increase in juvenile crime.*

Kk

kangaroo /ˌkæŋgə'ruː/ *noun*
an Australian animal that jumps along on its large back legs and keeps its young in a special pocket

karate /kə'rɑːtɪ/ *noun (no plural)*
a Japanese sport in which you fight using your hands and legs

keen /kiːn/ *adjective*
eager to do something; having a strong interest and liking for something ▶ *He was keen to see the new film.* ▶ *Are you keen* ***on*** *swimming? (adverb:* ***keenly****)*

keep¹ /kiːp/ *verb (past* ***kept*** */kept/)*
1 to continue to have something which you do not need to give to anyone ▶ *You can keep it. I don't need it any more.*
2 to store something in a particular place so that you can find it easily ▶ *Where do you keep the tea?*
3 to make someone or something stay in a place or state ▶ *Keep still while I take your photo!* ▶ *They kept her in hospital for a week.*
4 to stay fresh ▶ *Milk only keeps for a few days.*
5 **keep doing something** to do something again and again ▶ *I kept making the same mistake.*
6 **keep a secret** not to tell a secret
7 **keep off** to stay off or away from a place ▶ *Please keep off the grass.*
8 **keep someone up** to make someone stay awake and out of bed ▶ *I'm sorry I kept you up so late last night.*
9 **keep up** to move as fast as a person or thing so that you stay the same ▶ *I can't keep up* ***with*** *you when you walk so fast.*

keep² *noun (no plural)*
the cost of someone's food, clothes,

etc. ▶ *He earns his keep by working with his uncle.*

keeper /ˈkiːpəʳ/ *noun*
the person who takes care of the animals in a zoo

kennel /ˈkenl/ *noun*
a small house for a dog to sleep in

kept /kept/
the PAST TENSE and PAST PARTICIPLE of the verb **keep**

kerb /kɜːb/ *noun*
a line of raised stones separating the path at the side of a road from the road itself

ketchup /ˈketʃʌp/ *noun (no plural)*
a thick liquid made from TOMATOES, eaten with food to give a pleasant taste

kettle /ˈketl/ *noun*
a metal pot with a lid, a handle, and a long, narrow mouth for pouring; it is used for boiling water ▶ *Let's put the kettle on and make some tea.*

key /kiː/ *noun*
1 a shaped piece of metal used for locking and unlocking things ▶ *car keys* ▶ *the keys for the cupboard*
2 a button on a computer or TYPEWRITER that you press when you use it
3 one of the narrow black and white bars that you press to make music on some musical instruments ▶ *the keys of a piano*
4 a set of answers to a test or exercise ▶ *See if your answers are right by looking in the key at the back of the book.*

keyboard /ˈkiːbɔːd/ *noun*
a set of keys on a computer or a musical instrument such as a piano, that you press to produce letters or sounds

keyhole /ˈkiːhəʊl/ *noun*
the part of a lock that a key fits into

key ring /ˈkiː rɪŋ/ *noun*
a ring on which you can keep keys

kg
a short way of writing the words **kilogram** or **kilograms**

khaki /ˈkɑːkɪ/ *adjective, noun (no plural)*
a yellow-brown colour; a strong, cotton cloth of this colour

kick¹ /kɪk/ *verb*
1 to hit someone or something with your foot ▶ *He kicked the ball over the fence.*
2 to move your legs strongly ▶ *The baby kicked happily.*
3 kick off to start a football match
4 kick someone out to force someone to leave a place

kick² *noun*
1 a strong movement of your leg or foot ▶ *If the door won't open, give it a kick.*
2 a feeling of pleasure or excitement ▶ *I get a kick* ***out of*** *driving fast.*

kickoff /ˈkɪkɒf/ *noun*
the time when a game of football begins ▶ *Kickoff is at 3 o'clock.*

kid /kɪd/ *noun*
1 a child
2 a young goat

kidnap /ˈkɪdnæp/ *verb (present participle* ***kidnapping****, past* ***kidnapped****)*
to take someone away and ask for money in return for bringing them back safely

kidnapper /ˈkɪdnæpəʳ/ *noun*
a person who KIDNAPS someone

kidney /ˈkɪdnɪ/ *noun*
one of the two parts inside your body which remove waste liquid from your blood

kill /kɪl/ *verb*
to make a plant, an animal, or a person die ▶ *Ten people were killed in the train crash.* ▶ *The cat killed the bird.*
COMPARE: **murder**

killer /ˈkɪləʳ/ *noun*
a person, an animal, or a thing that kills ▶ *The police are searching for the killer.*
COMPARE: **murderer**

killing /ˈkɪlɪŋ/ *noun*
a murder ▶ *The killing took place outside a nightclub.*

kilo /ˈkiːləʊ/ *noun*
a kilogram ▶ *a kilo of sugar*

kilobyte /ˈkɪləbaɪt/ *noun*
a unit for measuring computer information

kilogram *(also **kilogramme**)* /ˈkɪləgræm/ *noun*
a measure of weight; 1,000 grams ▶ *3 kilograms* (=3kg)

kilometre /ˈkɪləmiːtəʳ, kɪˈlɒmɪtəʳ/ *noun*
a measure of length; 1,000 metres ▶ *500 kilometres* (=500km)

kilt /kɪlt/ *noun*
a skirt traditionally worn by Scottish men

kin /kɪn/ *noun (no plural)*
people in your family ▶ *The dead man's next of kin* (=his closest relative) *was told about his death.*

kind[1] /kaɪnd/ *noun*
a type or group which is different from other groups ▶ *She is the kind **of** woman who helps people.* ▶ *What kind of car has he got?*
SAME MEANING: **type, sort**

kind[2] *adjective*
helpful, caring, and wanting to do things that make other people happy ▶ *She was kind **to** me when I was unhappy.* ▶ *It's very kind of you to help me.*
OPPOSITE: **unkind**

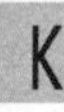

kindergarten /ˈkɪndəgɑːtn/ *noun*
a school for children aged between two and five

kind-hearted /ˌkaɪnd ˈhɑːtɪd/ *adjective*
caring and sympathetic ▶ *a kind-hearted person*
OPPOSITE: **hard-hearted**

kindly /ˈkaɪndlɪ/ *adverb*
1 used when someone has done something kind or generous ▶ *Mr Thomas has kindly offered to let us use his car.*
2 in a kind way ▶ *Miss Havisham looked kindly at Joe.*

kindness /ˈkaɪndnəs/ *noun (no plural)*
the quality of being kind ▶ *Thank you very much for your kindness.*

king /kɪŋ/ *noun*
1 a male ruler of a country, especially one who comes from a family of rulers ▶ *the King **of** Spain*
2 a playing card with a picture of a king on it
COMPARE: **queen**

kingdom /ˈkɪŋdəm/ *noun*
a country ruled by a king or queen

kiosk /ˈkiːɒsk/ *noun*
a small shop where you can buy things such as newspapers or tickets through a window

kipper /ˈkɪpəʳ/ *noun*
a dried fish kept in salt

kiss[1] /kɪs/ *verb*
to touch someone with your lips, as a sign of love or greeting ▶ *He kissed his wife goodbye.*

kiss[2] *noun (plural **kisses**)*
a touch with your lips ▶ *He gave his daughter a kiss.*

kit /kɪt/ *noun*
1 *(no plural)* all the things that you need for doing a particular sport ▶ *I've forgotten my football kit.*
2 a set of small pieces from which to make something ▶ *We made a model plane out of a kit.*

kitchen /ˈkɪtʃɪn/ *noun*
a room used for preparing and cooking food

kite /kaɪt/ *noun*
a toy with a light frame covered with plastic or cloth, which flies in the air on the end of a long string

kitten /ˈkɪtn/ *noun*
a young cat

kitty /ˈkɪti/ *noun*
money that a group of people have collected and saved for something

kiwi fruit /ˈkiːwiː fruːt/ *noun (plural* ***kiwi fruit*** *or* ***kiwi fruits****)*
a small, round, green fruit with a rough skin

Kleenex /ˈkliːneks/ *noun trademark (plural* ***Kleenex*** *or* ***Kleenexes****)*
a piece of soft, thin paper used especially for cleaning your nose

km
a short way of writing the words **kilometre** or **kilometres**

knack /næk/ *noun*
the ability to do something well ► *She has a real knack for writing memorable songs.*

knead /niːd/ *verb*
to make and press a mixture of flour and water etc. with your hands so that it becomes ready to cook

knee /niː/ *noun*
1 the joint in the middle of your leg where the leg bends
2 on your knee on the top part of your leg when you are sitting down ► *The baby sat on my knee.*

kneecap /ˈniːkæp/ *noun*
the bone at the front of your knee

knee-deep /ˌniː ˈdiːp/ *adjective*
be knee-deep in something to be standing in something that is deep enough to reach your knees ► *We were knee-deep in water.*

knee-high /ˌniː ˈhaɪ/ *adjective*
tall enough to reach your knees ► *a pair of knee-high boots*

kneel /niːl/ *verb (past* ***knelt*** */nelt/)*
to bend your legs and rest on your knees ► *She knelt down to pray.*

knew /njuː/
the PAST TENSE of the verb **know**

knickers /ˈnɪkəz/ *plural noun*
a piece of clothing for women and girls, for the lower part of the body, worn under skirts or trousers, not covering the legs
SAME MEANING: **pants**

knife /naɪf/ *noun (plural* ***knives*** */naɪvz/)*
a blade with a handle, used for cutting things or as a weapon

knight /naɪt/ *noun*
1 a man who is given a title by the king or queen in Britain, and whose name then has "Sir" in front of it
2 a noble soldier of the Middle Ages, trained to fight on his horse

knighthood /ˈnaɪthʊd/ *noun*
a special title that is given to a man by the king or queen in Britain

knit /nɪt/ *verb (present participle* ***knitting****, past* ***knitted*** *or* ***knit****)*
to make clothes by joining wool or another thread with long needles or on a special machine ► *She's knitting some clothes for her baby.*
COMPARE: **sew**

knitting /ˈnɪtɪŋ/ *noun (no plural)*
the activity of making things by knitting; a piece of knitted work

knitting needle /ˈnɪtɪŋ ˌniːdl/ *noun*
a long, thin stick that you use for knitting

knives /naɪvz/
the plural of **knife**

knob /nɒb/ *noun*
1 a round handle on a door or a drawer
2 a round control button on a machine

knobbly /ˈnɒbli/ *adjective (****knobblier, knobbliest****)*
not smooth, with hard parts sticking out ► *knobbly knees*

knock[1] /nɒk/ *verb*
1 to make a noise by hitting something several times ▶ *I knocked **on** the door.*
2 to hit something hard so that it moves or falls ▶ *He knocked the glass off the table.*
3 knock something down to destroy or remove a building ▶ *They knocked down the houses to build a shopping centre.*
4 knock someone down to hit someone with a car, bus, etc. so that they fall to the ground ▶ *She was knocked down by a bus.*
5 knock someone out to make someone go to sleep or become unconscious ▶ *Those sleeping pills really knocked me out.*

knock[2] *noun*
the sound made by hitting something ▶ *a knock **on** the door*

knockout /'nɒk-aʊt/ *noun*
a situation in which a BOXER hits another boxer so that he falls on the ground and cannot get up ▶ *Tyson won in 15 minutes with a knockout.*

knot[1] /nɒt/ *noun*
1 a fastening made by tying two ends of string or rope together ▶ *She tied a knot in her belt.*
2 a measure of the speed of a ship, about 1,853 metres per hour

knot[2] *verb (present participle **knotting**, past **knotted**)*
to tie something with a knot

know /nəʊ/ *verb (past tense **knew** /nju:/, past participle **known** /nəʊn/)*
1 to have something in your mind which you are sure is true ▶ *Do you know where they went?* ▶ *They don't know your address.*
2 to have learned and be able to use a language or skill ▶ *Do you know French?* ▶ *She knows how to cook.*
3 to have learned about something from studying or experience ▶ *I don't know anything about history.*

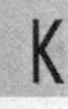

Compare **know**, **learn**, and **teach**. If you **know** something, you already have the facts or information about it: *She knows a lot about computers.* If you **learn** something, you discover facts about it, or discover how to do it, either on your own or with a teacher: *He's learning to drive.* ▶ *The children are learning maths at school.* If you **teach** someone something, you make them learn it by giving them help and information: *He is teaching me to drive.* ▶ *She teaches maths to the first years* (=the children in the first year at school).

4 to be familiar with a person or a place ▶ *I know Mary well.* ▶ *Do you know London?*
5 I know a phrase used to show you agree with someone ▶ *"It's a bad idea." "I know."*
6 you know a phrase used when you want to explain something more clearly ▶ *It's the building on the left. You know – the new one.*

know-all /'nəʊ ɔ:l/ *noun*
an annoying person who thinks they know more than everyone else

know-how /'nəʊ haʊ/ *noun (no plural)*
knowledge that you need to do something ▶ *We don't have the know-how to build our own house.*

knowingly /'nəʊɪŋlɪ/ *adverb*
if you knowingly do something wrong, you do it even though you know that it is wrong ▶ *He claimed he'd never knowingly sold alcohol to teenagers.*

knowledge /'nɒlɪdʒ/ *noun (no plural)*
information or understanding that you have in your mind ▶ *His knowledge **of** languages is excellent.*

knowledgeable /'nɒlɪdʒəbəl/ *adjective*

having a lot of information or understanding about something ▶ *She's very knowledgeable **about** that subject*

known /nəʊn/
the PAST PARTICIPLE of the verb **know**

knuckle /ˈnʌkəl/ *noun*
one of the joints in your fingers ▶ *Our fingers bend at the knuckles.*

koala /kəʊˈɑːlə/ *noun*
an Australian animal like a small bear

Koran /kɔːˈrɑːn/ *noun*
the Koran the holy book of the MUSLIMS

kosher /ˈkəʊʃəʳ/ *adjective*
(used about food) prepared according to JEWISH law

kung fu /ˌkʌŋ ˈfuː/ *noun (no plural)*
a Chinese sport in which people fight with their hands and feet

kw
a short way of writing the words **kilowatt** or **kilowatts**

Ll

l
a short way of writing the words **litre** or **litres** ▶ *a 2l bottle of beer*

lab /læb/ *noun*
a LABORATORY

label¹ /ˈleɪbəl/ *noun*
a piece of paper fixed to something which gives you information about it ▶ *Put a label on the box – then we'll know what's inside.*

label² *verb (present participle **labelling**, past **labelled**)*
to put or fix a label on something ▶ *The parcel wasn't labelled, so it got lost.*

laboratory /ləˈbɒrətərɪ/ *noun (plural **laboratories**)*
a room or building in which scientific work is done

laborious /ləˈbɔːrɪəs/ *adjective*
needing a lot of time and effort to do ▶ *the laborious process of examining all the data*

labour¹ /ˈleɪbəʳ/ *noun (no plural)*
1 hard work that you do with your hands ▶ *Her beautiful home was the result of many years of labour.*
2 the workers in a country or factory ▶ *There is a shortage of skilled labour in the region.*

labour² *verb*
to work hard ▶ *We laboured all day to finish the job.*

labourer /ˈleɪbərəʳ/ *noun*
a person who does hard work with their hands ▶ *a farm labourer*
COMPARE: **worker**

lace¹ /leɪs/ *noun*
1 a piece of string for fastening a shoe ▶ *I need some new laces for my shoes.*
2 *(no plural)* ornamental cloth with holes in it, made from fine thread ▶ *My dress has lots of pretty lace around the neck and sleeves.*

lace² *verb (present participle **lacing**, past **laced**)*
lace something up to tie something with a lace ▶ *Lace your shoes up.*

lack¹ /læk/ *verb*
to have none or too little of something ▶ *He lacked the strength to lift the box.*

lack² *noun (no plural)*
not having something, or not having enough of it ▶ *The plants died through lack **of** water.*

lad /læd/ *noun*
a boy ▶ *He moved here when he was a young lad.*

ladder /ˈlædəʳ/ *noun*
two long pieces of wood or metal, joined together by shorter pieces that form steps for climbing ▶ *I need a ladder to reach the roof.*

laden /'leɪdn/ *adjective*
carrying something, especially a large amount ▶ *The lorry was laden* ***with*** *boxes of fruit.*

Ladies /'leɪdɪz/
the Ladies the women's TOILET ▶ *She's gone to the Ladies.*
COMPARE: **Gents**

ladle /'leɪdl/ *noun*
a big, deep spoon with a long handle, used for serving soup

lady /'leɪdɪ/ *noun (plural* ***ladies****)*
1 a polite word for a woman ▶ *the lady in the shop* ▶ *a lady doctor*
2 a title given to certain women who have done important things in British public life ▶ *Lady Thatcher*
3 a noble woman or the wife of a lord
4 Ladies and Gentlemen a way to start a formal talk to a group of people

ladybird /'leɪdɪbɜːd/ *noun*
a small, round insect that is red with black spots

lag /læg/ *verb (present participle* ***lagging****, past* ***lagged****)*
lag behind to move or develop more slowly than other people ▶ *Gina lagged behind, waiting for Rob.* ▶ *My daughter is lagging behind in her studies.*

lager /'lɑːgəʳ/ *noun*
1 *(no plural)* a kind of light beer
2 a glass or bottle of light beer ▶ *Two lagers, please.*

lagoon /lə'guːn/ *noun*
an area of sea water that is separated from the sea by sand

laid /leɪd/
the PAST TENSE and PAST PARTICIPLE of the verb **lay**
LOOK AT: **lay**[1]

laid-back /ˌleɪd 'bæk/ *adjective*
relaxed and not worried about anything ▶ *She seems very laid-back about her exams.*

lain /leɪn/
the PAST PARTICIPLE of the verb **lie**
LOOK AT: **lay**[1]

lake /leɪk/ *noun*
a big pool of water with land all round it
COMPARE: **pond**

lamb /læm/ *noun*
a young sheep

lame /leɪm/ *adjective*
not able to walk easily, usually because of a hurt leg or foot ▶ *My horse is lame – I can't ride her.*

lamp /læmp/ *noun*
a small light which you have on a table, etc. ▶ *a bedside lamp*

lamppost /'læmp-pəʊst/ *noun*
a tall post in the street with a light at the top

lampshade /'læmpʃeɪd/ *noun*
a cover put over a lamp to soften its light or make it look nice

land[1] /lænd/ *noun*
1 *(no plural)* ground that people own ▶ *The big farmers own most of the land.*
2 *(no plural)* ground for farming ▶ *excellent land for wheat*
3 *(no plural)* the dry part of the Earth not covered by the sea ▶ *They reached land after six weeks at sea.*
4 a country ▶ *foreign lands*

land[2] *verb*
to arrive somewhere after a journey by plane ▶ *We landed in Rome at 6 in the evening.*
OPPOSITE: **take off**

landing /'lændɪŋ/ *noun*
1 the space at the top of a set of stairs in a building ▶ *The bedroom opens onto the landing.*
2 the action of a plane coming down from the air onto the ground ▶ *The plane made a safe landing.*

landlady /'lændˌleɪdɪ/ *noun (plural* ***landladies****)* a woman who owns a building which she lets other people use or live in, in return for money

landlord /ˈlændlɔːd/ *noun*
a man who owns a building which he lets other people use or live in, in return for money

landmark /ˈlændmɑːk/ *noun*
1 something that helps you recognize where you are, such as a famous building ▶ *The Eiffel Tower is a well-known landmark in Paris.*
2 a very important event, change, or discovery in the development of something ▶ *a landmark in the history of aviation*

landowner /ˈlændˌəʊnəʳ/ *noun*
a person who owns a lot of land

landscape /ˈlændˌskeɪp/ *noun (no plural)*
the way an area of land looks ▶ *a landscape of mountains and lakes*

landslide /ˈlændslaɪd/ *noun*
1 soil and rocks falling down the side of a hill or mountain ▶ *The village was destroyed in a landslide.*
2 a situation in which a person or political party wins a lot more votes than the others in an election ▶ *It was a landslide victory for the Labour Party.*

lane /leɪn/ *noun*
a narrow road ▶ *We walked down the lane past the farm*

language /ˈlæŋgwɪdʒ/ *noun*
the words that people use in speaking and writing ▶ *a foreign language* ▶ *the English language* ▶ *business language*

lantern /ˈlæntən/ *noun*
a lamp in a glass case, often with a handle for carrying it

lap¹ /læp/ *noun*
1 the flat surface formed by the upper parts of your legs when you are sitting down ▶ *Her little girl sat on her lap.*
2 the distance once around the track in a race ▶ *a six-lap race*

lap² *verb (present participle **lapping**, past **lapped**)*
to drink liquid with the tongue, like a dog ▶ *The cat lapped its milk.*

lapel /ləˈpel/ *noun*
one of the parts at the front of a coat or JACKET that is joined to the collar and folds back on each side

lapse¹ /læps/ *noun*
1 the act of forgetting something or not paying attention to something for a short time ▶ *a lapse of concentration*
2 the act of making a mistake or behaving badly, in a way that does not seem typical ▶ *Apart from the occasional lapse, her work seems quite good.*

lapse² *verb (present participle **lapsing**, past **lapsed**)*
to end, especially because the official period when something is allowed to continue has ended ▶ *Your membership of the tennis club has lapsed.*

laptop /ˈlæptɒp/ *noun*
a small computer that you can carry with you

larder /ˈlɑːdəʳ/ *noun*
a cupboard or small room in which food is kept

large /lɑːdʒ/ *adjective*
big ▶ *They need a large house because they have nine children.*
OPPOSITE: **small**

largely /ˈlɑːdʒlɪ/ *adverb*
mostly or mainly ▶ *The delay was largely due to bad weather.*

large-scale /ˌlɑːdʒ ˈskeɪl/ *adjective*
happening over a large area or involving a lot of people ▶ *large-scale unemployment*

laser /ˈleɪzəʳ/ *noun*
an apparatus with a very strong, very

narrow beam of light, used in some machines or in medical operations ▶ *a laser printer*

lash /læʃ/ *noun (plural* ***lashes****)*
one of the hairs that grow round your eye

last[1] /lɑːst/ *adjective, adverb*
1 coming after all others ▶ *The last girl who came in was Mary.* ▶ *Who came in last?*
OPPOSITE: **first**
2 happening just before this time; the time before now ▶ *I saw my friend last week, but I haven't seen him since.* ▶ *I haven't seen his sister since last July* (=July of last year). ▶ *When did you last read an exciting book?*
3 at last in the end, when you are getting tired of waiting ▶ *The bus came at last.*

last[2] *verb*
1 to continue to happen for a period of time ▶ *Our holiday lasted ten days.*
2 to stay in good condition or unchanged ▶ *Good shoes last longer.* ▶ *She was very angry yesterday, but it didn't last.*
3 to be enough for a certain time ▶ *Two loaves of bread will last us for two days.*

lasting /ˈlɑːstɪŋ/ *adjective*
continuing for a long time ▶ *We want to have a lasting relationship.*

lastly /ˈlɑːstlɪ/ *adverb*
a word you use when you are making several points and you come to the last one ▶ *Lastly, I would like to thank everyone who has worked to make the new school such a success.*
OPPOSITE: **firstly**

last-minute /ˌlɑːst ˈmɪnɪt/ *adjective*
happening or done very late within a period of time ▶ *last-minute Christmas shopping*

last name /ˈlɑːst neɪm/ *noun*
your family's name which, in English, comes after your other names
SAME MEANING: **surname**

latch /lætʃ/ *noun (plural* ***latches****)*
a fastening for a door, gate, or window

late /leɪt/ *adjective, adverb*
1 after the usual or agreed time ▶ *I missed the meeting because I got up late.*
2 near the end (of a day, year, etc.) ▶ *It's very late – I should be in bed. He began the work in late May.*
OPPOSITE (**1** and **2**): **early**

lately /ˈleɪtlɪ/ *adverb*
in the recent past ▶ *Have you seen him lately?*

later /ˈleɪtəʳ/ *adverb*
1 after some time ▶ *I can't do it now, but I'll do it later.*
2 later on after some time ▶ *I can't do it now, but I'll do it later on.*

latest /ˈleɪtɪst/ *adjective*
most recent ▶ *Have you heard the latest news?* ▶ *Please arrive by 9 o'clock at the latest* (=and no later).

Latin /ˈlætɪn/ *noun (no plural)*
the language of the ancient Romans ▶ *A few children still study Latin at school.*

latitude /ˈlætɪtjuːd/ *noun (no plural)*
a position on the Earth shown on maps by lines (lines of latitude) that go from east to west
COMPARE: **longitude**

latter /ˈlætəʳ/ *noun*
the latter the second of two people or things which have just been mentioned ▶ *Britain has agreements with both Germany and Italy, but its agreement with the latter* (=Italy) *has been more successful.*
OPPOSITE: **the former**

laugh[1] /lɑːf/ *verb*
1 to make a sound that shows you are pleased, happy, or think something is funny ▶ *It was so funny we couldn't stop laughing.*

L

2 laugh at someone or something to treat a person or thing as very foolish, or make jokes about them ▶ *They'll laugh at you if you wear that awful coat.*

laugh² *noun*
the sound you make when you find something funny ▶ *We had a good laugh at his mistake.*

laughter /ˈlɑːftəʳ/ *noun (no plural)*
the act or sound of laughing

launch¹ /lɔːntʃ/ *noun (plural **launches**)*
a small boat driven by an engine

launch² *verb*
to put a ship into the water or to send a spaceship into space

launderette /ˌlɔːndəˈret/ *noun*
a shop where you pay to wash your clothes and sheets etc. in a machine

laundry /ˈlɔːndrɪ/ *noun*
1 *(plural **laundries**)* a place where clothes and sheets etc. are washed
2 *(no plural)* clothes and sheets etc. that need washing or have just been washed

lava /ˈlɑːvə/ *noun (no plural)*
very hot, liquid rock that comes out of the top of a VOLCANO

lavatory /ˈlævətrɪ/ *noun (plural **lavatories**)*
1 a container joined to a waste pipe, used for taking away body waste
2 a room with this in it ▶ *Where is the ladies' lavatory, please?*
SAME MEANING (**1** and **2**): **toilet, loo**

law /lɔː/ *noun*
1 a rule made by the government that all people must obey ▶ *a law **against** drinking and driving*
2 the law the whole system of laws in a country
3 against the law not allowed by the law ▶ *Driving without a seat belt is against the law.*

lawful /ˈlɔːfəl/ *adjective*
allowed by the law
SAME MEANING: **legal**

lawn /lɔːn/ *noun*
an area of short grass outside a house or in a park

lawnmower /ˈlɔːnˌməʊəʳ/ *noun*
a machine for cutting the grass in a garden or park

lawyer /ˈlɔːjəʳ/ *noun*
a person who advises people about the law, and speaks for them in court

lay¹ /leɪ/ *verb (past **laid** /leɪd/)*
1 to put something down ▶ *She laid her coat over a chair.*
2 lay the table to arrange knives, forks, plates, and other things on a table ready for a meal
3 to make eggs and send them out of the body ▶ *The hen laid three eggs.*

> Do not confuse the verb **lay** (PAST TENSE and PAST PARTICIPLE **laid**) with the verb **lie** (past tense **lay**, PAST PARTICIPLE **lain**). **Lay¹** means "to put something down" and is **always** used with an object: *She laid the clothes on the bed.* **Lie** means "to have your body flat on something", and is **never** used with an object: *She lay on her bed.* There is another verb **lie** (PAST TENSE and PAST PARTICIPLE **lied**), which means "to say something which is not true" and which is also used without an object.

lay²
the PAST TENSE of the verb **lie**

lay-by /ˈleɪ baɪ/ *noun*
an area at the side of a road, where vehicles can stop ▶ *We pulled into a lay-by for a rest.*

layer /ˈleɪəʳ/ *noun*
a covering that is spread on top of something or in between two things ▶ *This cake has got a layer of chocolate in the middle.*

layout /ˈleɪaʊt/ *noun*
the way in which rooms or objects are arranged ▶ *a picture showing the layout of Buckingham Palace*

laze /leɪz/ *(also **laze around**) verb (present participle **lazing**, past **lazed**)*
to relax and not do very much ▶ *two cats lazing in the sun*

lazy /ˈleɪzɪ/ *adjective (**lazier, laziest**)*
not wanting to work ▶ *He won't work; he's just too lazy.*

lb *(plural **lbs**)*
a short way of writing the words **pound** or **pounds**, when used about weight ▶ *1lb flour* ▶ *3lbs potatoes*

lead[1] /liːd/ *verb (past **led** /led/)*
1 to show someone the way, usually by going in front ▶ *You lead and we'll follow.* ▶ *She led us to the town centre.*
2 to go to a place ▶ *This path leads to the church.*
3 to be the chief person doing a thing; to be first or at the front, especially in a race or competition ▶ *He's going to lead the climb up Mount Everest.* ▶ *The English team was leading at half time.*
4 lead a ... life to experience a particular kind of life ▶ *She led a very lonely life.*

lead[2] /liːd/ *noun*
1 a position in front of the others ▶ *The Spanish runner now has a lead of 50 metres.*
2 be in the lead to be winning in a game or competition
3 a piece of rope, leather, etc. for holding an animal ▶ *Please keep your dog on a lead.*
SAME MEANING (**3**): **leash**

lead[3] /led/ *noun*
1 *(no plural)* a heavy, soft, grey metal ▶ *as heavy as lead* ▶ *old lead pipes* ▶ *a lead roof*
2 the part inside a pencil that you write with

leader /ˈliːdəʳ/ *noun*
a person who leads other people ▶ *the team leader* ▶ *leaders **of** the world's richest nations*

leadership /ˈliːdəʃɪp/ *noun (no plural)*
1 the position of leader ▶ *the leadership of the Labour Party*
2 the qualities necessary in a leader

leading /ˈliːdɪŋ/ *adjective*
most important ▶ *the world's leading sports people*
SAME MEANING: **top**

leaf /liːf/ *noun (plural **leaves** /liːvz/)*
one of the green, flat parts of a plant or tree that grow out of branches or stems ▶ *Some plants have leaves that grow straight out of the ground*

leaflet /ˈliːflɪt/ *noun*
a piece of paper with a notice or an advertisement printed on it

league /liːg/ *noun*
1 a group of people or teams that play against each other in a competition ▶ *the Football League*
2 a group of people or countries who have joined together to work for a special aim

leak[1] /liːk/ *noun*
a hole or crack through which gas or liquid may pass in or out ▶ *There's a leak in the roof.*

leak[2] *verb*
(used about gas or liquid) to escape through a hole or crack ▶ *The roof leaks and the rain's coming in.*

leaky /ˈliːkɪ/ *adjective (**leakier, leakiest**)*
having a leak ▶ *The roof is leaky and the rain comes in.*

lean[1] /liːn/ *verb (past **leaned** or **leant** /lent/)*
1 to bend forwards, sideways, or backwards ▶ *Don't lean out of the window – you might fall.*
2 to put something against another thing to support it ▶ *She leant her bicycle **against** the wall.*

3 to rest your body against something to support it

lean² *adjective*
not containing very much fat ▶ *lean meat* ▶ *lean cattle*

leant /lent/
the PAST TENSE and PAST PARTICIPLE of the verb **lean**

leap¹ /liːp/ *verb (past* ***leaped*** *or* ***leapt*** */lept/)*
1 to jump very high or a long way ▶ *The dog leapt over the fence.*
2 to increase suddenly ▶ *Prices have leapt up recently.*

leap² *noun*
1 a sudden jump which goes very high or a long way ▶ *With a great leap, she crossed the stream.*
2 a sudden, large increase ▶ *a leap* ***in*** *oil prices*

leap year /ˈliːp jɪəʳ/ *noun*
a year, once every four years, in which February has 29 days instead of 28 days ▶ *The years 1996 and 2000 were leap years.*

learn /lɜːn/ *verb (past* ***learned*** *or* ***learnt*** */lɜːnt/)*
1 to get knowledge of something or the ability to do something ▶ *Have you learnt to swim?* ▶ *I am learning English.*
2 to fix something in the memory ▶ *She learnt the whole poem so that she could repeat it the next day.*
LOOK AT: **know**

learner /ˈlɜːnəʳ/ *noun*
a person who is learning ▶ *She's a slow learner.* ▶ *a learner driver*

learning /ˈlɜːnɪŋ/ *noun (no plural)*
knowledge that you get by reading and studying, or the activity of reading and studying ▶ *Learning should be fun.*

learnt /lɜːnt/
the PAST TENSE and PAST PARTICIPLE of the verb **learn**

leash /liːʃ/ *noun (plural* ***leashes****)*
a piece of rope, leather, etc. used for holding an animal ▶ *I have to keep my dog on a leash.*
SAME MEANING: **lead³**

least¹ /liːst/ *adverb*
1 the smallest amount or number ▶ *the least expensive one* (=the cheapest one). ▶ *They arrived when I least expected them* (=when I did not expect them at all).
2 less than all the others ▶ *Of all your friends, I like him the least.*
OPPOSITE (**1** and **2**): **most**
3 at least not less than and probably more than a certain amount ▶ *He's going away for at least a week* (=a week or longer).
4 least of all especially not ▶ *I don't like any of them, least of all Debbie.*
5 not in the least not at all ▶ *I'm not in the least interested in what she says.*

least² *adjective, pronoun*
the smallest amount or number ▶ *Buy the one that costs the least.* ▶ *Do it the way that takes the least time.*
OPPOSITE: **most**

leather /ˈleðəʳ/ *noun (no plural)*
the skin of dead animals used for making things such as shoes and bags ▶ *a leather belt*

leave¹ /liːv/ *verb (present participle* ***leaving****, past* ***left*** */left/)*
1 to go away from a place or person ▶ *The train leaves in five minutes.* ▶ *She left Australia for Britain in 1963.* ▶ *He left his wife.*
2 to let a thing stay in a place ▶ *I left my bag in the office.*
LOOK AT: **forget**
3 to let things stay as they are ▶ *Leave the dishes – I'll wash them later.*
4 to give something to someone after your death ▶ *My aunt left me her house.*

5 leave someone or something alone not to touch, move, worry, or annoy a person or thing ▶ *Leave the dog alone.* ▶ *Leave those cakes alone or there won't be enough for tea.*
6 leave off to stop ▶ *Let's start from where we left off yesterday.*
7 leave someone or something out to fail to include a person or thing ▶ *I left out a really important idea.* ▶ *They left me out of the team.*

leave² *noun (no plural)*
a period of time away from work ▶ *The soldiers had six weeks' leave.*

leaves /liːvz/
the plural of **leaf**

lecture¹ /ˈlektʃəʳ/ *noun*
a talk given to a group of people about a particular subject ▶ *The students have lectures every day.*

lecture² *verb*
to talk to a group of people about a particular subject ▶ *She lectures **on** Shakespeare at Edinburgh University.*

lecturer /ˈlektʃərəʳ/ *noun*
a person who teaches at a university or college or who gives talks to a group of people about a particular subject ▶ *a chemistry lecturer*

led /led/
the PAST TENSE and PAST PARTICIPLE of the verb **lead**

ledge /ledʒ/ *noun*
1 a narrow shelf, such as the one at the bottom of a window
2 a narrow, flat piece on the side of a rock or cliff

leek /liːk/ *noun*
a long, green and white vegetable that tastes like onion

left¹ /left/
the PAST TENSE and PAST PARTICIPLE of the verb **leave**

left² *noun (no plural)*
the opposite side to the hand that most people write with ▶ *The school is to the left of the church.*
OPPOSITE: **right**

left³ *adjective, adverb*
on or towards the left ▶ *Turn left at the corner.*
OPPOSITE: **right**

left-hand /ˌleft ˈhænd/ *adjective*
on the left side of something ▶ *The house is on the left-hand side of the street.*

left-handed /ˌleft ˈhændɪd/ *adjective*
using your left hand more than your right hand
OPPOSITE: **right-handed**

left luggage office /ˌleft ˈlʌgɪdʒ ˌɒfɪs/ *noun*
a place at a station or an airport where you can leave your case for a period of time

leftover /ˈleftəʊvəʳ/ *adjective*
remaining after you have used what you need ▶ *leftover food*

leftovers /ˈleftəʊvəz/ *plural noun*
food that has not been eaten during a meal

left-wing /ˌleft ˈwɪŋ/ *adjective*
supporting the political ideas of groups such as Socialists and Communists ▶ *left-wing voters*

leg /leg/ *noun*
1 one of the two parts of your body that you use for walking ▶ *She broke her leg skiing last year.*
2 one of the parts on which chairs, tables, etc. stand ▶ *a chair with a broken leg*

legal /ˈliːgəl/ *adjective*
allowed by the law ▶ *Drinking alcohol is legal in Britain (adverb: **legally**)*
OPPOSITE: **illegal**
SAME MEANING: **lawful**

legalize /ˈliːgəlaɪz/ *verb (present participle **legalizing**, past **legalized**)*
to change the law so that something is made legal ▶ *They want the government to legalize the drug.*

legend /ˈledʒənd/ *noun*

1 a story about people who lived in the past, which may not be true
2 a very famous person ▸ *Elvis Presley was a legend in his lifetime.*

legendary /ˈledʒəndərɪ/ *adjective*
very famous and admired ▸ *the legendary singer, Frank Sinatra*

leggings /ˈlegɪŋz/ *plural noun*
a piece of women's clothing that fits closely around the legs ▸ *She wore a pair of red leggings.*

legible /ˈledʒəbəl/ *adjective*
clear enough to read ▸ *legible writing*
OPPOSITE: **illegible**

legitimate /lɪˈdʒɪtɪmət/ *adjective*
1 not illegal ▸ *legitimate business activities*
2 fair and reasonable ▸ *a legitimate question*

leisure /ˈleʒəʳ/ *noun (no plural)*
the time when you are not at work and can do things that you enjoy ▸ *What do you do in your leisure time?*

leisure centre /ˈleʒə ˌsentəʳ/ *noun*
a place where people can go and do a large number of different sports

leisurely /ˈleʒəlɪ/ *adjective*
done in a relaxed way because you do not have to hurry ▸ *a leisurely walk around the park*

lemon /ˈlemən/ *noun*
a yellow fruit with a sour taste, which grows on trees in hot places

lemonade /ˌleməˈneɪd/ *noun (no plural)*
a sweet drink made from lemons

lemon juice /ˈlemən ˌdʒuːs/ *noun (no plural)*
the liquid from lemons

lend /lend/ *verb (past* **lent** */lent/)*
to let someone use or have something for a time, after which they must give it back ▸ *Can you lend me that book for a few days?*
LOOK AT: **borrow**

length /leŋθ/ *noun (no plural)*
the distance from one end of something to the other; how long something is ▸ *The room is 4 metres in length.*

lengthen /ˈleŋθən/ *verb*
to make something longer ▸ *to lengthen a dress*
OPPOSITE: **shorten**

lengthways /ˈleŋθweɪz/ *(also* ***lengthwise*** */-waɪz)/ adverb*
in the direction of the longest side ▸ *Cut the carrots lengthways.*

lengthy /ˈleŋθɪ/ *adjective (**lengthier, lengthiest**)*
too long ▸ *a lengthy speech*

lens /lenz/ *noun (plural* **lenses***)*
one of the shaped pieces of glass used to bend light in an instrument for seeing things clearly, like a pair of glasses, a camera, or a microscope

lent /lent/
the PAST TENSE and PAST PARTICIPLE of the verb **lend**

Lent /lent/ *noun (no plural)*
the 40 days before Easter, when some Christians stop eating particular foods or doing other things which they enjoy

lentil /ˈlentəl/ *noun*
a round orange, green, or brown seed that can be cooked and eaten

leopard /ˈlepəd/ *noun*
a big cat with a spotted coat which lives in Africa or Asia

leotard /ˈliːətɑːd/ *noun*
a piece of women's clothing like a SWIMSUIT, used for dancing or exercising

lesbian /ˈlezbɪən/ *noun*
a woman who is sexually attracted to other women ▸ *lesbian and gay rights*

less¹ /les/ *adverb*
1 not as; not so much ▸ *This one is less expensive.* ▸ *I definitely walk*

less since I've had the car. ▶ *The next train was less crowded* **than** *the first one.*
OPPOSITE: **more**
2 less and less gradually becoming smaller in amount or degree ▶ *He comes here less and less.* ▶ *Our trips became less and less frequent.*
OPPOSITE: **more and more**

less[2] *adjective, pronoun*
a smaller amount (of something) ▶ *You ought to eat less salt.* ▶ *Most single parents earn £100 a week or less.* ▶ *She spends less* **of** *her time abroad now.* ▶ *I live less* **than** *a mile from here.*
OPPOSITE: **more**

lessen /ˈlesən/ *verb*
1 to make something less ▶ *The medicine will lessen the pain.*
2 to become less ▶ *The pain lessened.*

lesson /ˈlesən/ *noun*
something you must learn; a time when you learn things in school ▶ *We have four history lessons a week.*

let /let/ *verb (present participle* ***letting****, past* ***let****)*
1 to allow ▶ *My mother wouldn't let me go to the film.* ▶ *They won't let people in without a ticket.*
2 to allow someone to use a house or some land in return for money ▶ *They let their house to another family when they went away.*
3 Let's a word used when you ask someone to do something with you ▶ *Let's go down to the river and have a swim.*
4 let go to stop holding something ▶ *Hold the ladder for me and don't let go.*
5 let someone know to tell someone about something ▶ *Let me know what time you'll be arriving.*
6 let someone down to cause someone to be disappointed when you do not do what you should do ▶ *You've let us down by not working for your exam.*

letdown /ˈletdaʊn/ *noun*
something that disappoints you as it is not as good as you expected ▶ *That film was a real letdown.*

lethal /ˈliːθəl/ *adjective*
able to kill you ▶ *a lethal dose of heroin*

letter /ˈletəʳ/ *noun*
1 one of the signs we use to write words ▶ *A, B, C, and D are the first four letters in the alphabet.*
2 a written message sent to someone by post ▶ *I got a letter from my dad this morning.*
LOOK AT: **yours**

letterbox /ˈletəbɒks/ *noun (plural* ***letterboxes****)*
1 a box in the street or post office in which letters are put when you are sending them
SAME MEANING: **postbox**
2 a hole or box in the front of a building, into which letters are delivered

lettuce /ˈletɪs/ *noun*
a vegetable with large, soft, green leaves which are eaten without being cooked

level[1] /ˈlevəl/ *adjective*
1 flat; without higher or lower places ▶ *We need a level piece of ground to plant the tree.*
2 at the same height or position as something else ▶ *He bent down so that his face was level with the little boy's* (=the little boy's face).

level[2] *noun*
a place or position of a particular height ▶ *The house was built on two levels.*

level[3] *verb (present participle* ***levelling****, past* ***levelled****)*
to make something flat ▶ *They levelled the piece of ground so that we could play football on it.*

level crossing /ˌlevəl 'krɒsɪŋ/ *noun*
a place where a railway crosses a road, and traffic has to wait for trains to pass

level-headed /ˌlevəl 'hedɪd/ *adjective*
calm and sensible ▶ *He's a firm and level-headed leader.*

lever[1] /'liːvə^r/ *noun*
1 a long bar for lifting or moving heavy things
2 a handle on a machine, which you push or pull to work the machine

lever[2] *verb*
to move something with a lever ▶ *I levered the lid off the box with a stick.*

liability /ˌlaɪə'bɪlətɪ/ *noun (no plural)*
legal responsibility for something ▶ *We accept no liability for cars that are left here overnight.*

liable /'laɪəbəl/ *adjective*
likely ▶ *He's liable to get angry if people keep him waiting.*

liar /'laɪə^r/ *noun*
someone who tells lies

liberal /'lɪbərəl/ *adjective*
willing to understand and accept the different behaviour or ideas of other people

liberate /'lɪbəreɪt/ *verb (present participle **liberating**, past **liberated**)*
to free someone from a situation or place that they could not get out of ▶ *US soldiers liberated the prisoners.*

liberation /ˌlɪbə'reɪʃən/ *noun (no plural)*
the act of freeing people from a situation or place that they could not get out of ▶ *the black liberation movement*

liberty /'lɪbətɪ/ *noun (no plural)*
the state in which you are free and do not have to do what other people order ▶ *They fought for their liberty.*

librarian /laɪ'breərɪən/ *noun*
a person who works in a library

library /'laɪbrərɪ/ *noun (plural **libraries**)*
a collection of books that people can borrow, or a room or building in which they are kept ▶ *There's a very good library in the next town.*

lice /laɪs/
the plural of **louse**

licence /'laɪsəns/ *noun*
a piece of paper showing that the law allows you to do something, like drive a car ▶ *The policeman asked to see my driving licence.*

license /'laɪsəns/ *verb (present participle **licensing**, past **licensed**)*
to give someone a licence ▶ *a licensed restaurant* ▶ *a hall licensed for music*

lick /lɪk/ *verb*
to touch something with your tongue ▶ *She licked the stamps and stuck them on the letter.*

lid /lɪd/ *noun*
a cover for a box, pan, or other container, which can be taken off
SAME MEANING: **top**

lie[1] /laɪ/ *verb (present participle **lying**, past tense **lay** /leɪ/, past participle **lain** /leɪn/)*
to have your body flat on something or to get into this position ▶ *He was lying in the shade of the tree.* ▶ *She lay down on her bed.*
LOOK AT: **lay**

lie[2] *verb (present participle **lying**, past **lied**)*
to say things that are not true ▶ *She lied to him **about** her age.*
LOOK AT: **lay**

lie[3] *noun (plural **lies**)*
something said which is not true ▶ *Why did he tell her a lie?*

lieutenant /lef'tenənt/ *noun*
an officer of low rank in the army or the navy

L

life /laɪf/ *noun*
1 *(no plural)* the ability that we have to grow and feel ▶ *a baby's first moments of life*
2 *(plural **lives** /laɪvz/)* the time during which someone is alive ▶ *She had lived in the same village all her life.*
3 *(plural **lives**)* the way in which someone lives or spends their time ▶ *He leads a happy life in the country.*
4 *(no plural)* activity and cheerfulness ▶ *She was four years old and full of life.*

lifeboat /ˈlaɪfbəʊt/ *noun*
a boat used for saving people who are in danger at sea

lifeguard /ˈlaɪfgɑːd/ *noun*
a person whose job is to help swimmers who are in danger at the beach or at a swimming pool

life jacket /ˈlaɪf ˌdʒækɪt/ *noun*
a special piece of clothing that you wear round your chest to make you float in water

lifelike /ˈlaɪflaɪk/ *adjective*
looking very much like a real person or thing ▶ *The statue is quite lifelike.*

lifelong /ˈlaɪflɒŋ/ *adjective*
continuing all through your life ▶ *She was my mother's lifelong friend.*

life-size /ˈlaɪf saɪz/ *adjective*
(used about a picture or model) being the same size as the real thing ▶ *She painted a life-size picture of her dog.*

lifestyle /ˈlaɪfstaɪl/ *noun*
the way in which you live, including the conditions you live in, the things you own, and the things you do ▶ *a healthy lifestyle*

lifetime /ˈlaɪftaɪm/ *noun*
the time for which someone is alive ▶ *In my father's lifetime, there have been many changes in the village.*

lift[1] /lɪft/ *verb*
to pick something up ▶ *Can you lift the other end of the table?* ▶ *"Lift me up so I can see over the fence," said the little girl.*

lift[2] *noun*
1 a machine that carries people or things between the floors of a tall building
2 a free ride in a vehicle ▶ *He drives to the station, and he sometimes gives me a lift.*

lift-off /ˈlɪft ɒf/ *noun*
the moment when a space vehicle rises up into the air at the beginning of its journey

light[1] /laɪt/ *noun*
1 *(no plural)* the force from the sun that allows our eyes to see ▶ *There's more light near the window.*
2 a thing that gives out light ▶ *Turn off the lights when you go to bed.*

light[2] *adjective*
1 not dark in colour; pale ▶ *a light blue shirt*
OPPOSITE: **dark**
2 easy to lift; not heavy ▶ *The basket is very light – I can easily carry it myself.*
3 not great in amount ▶ *The traffic was very light this evening.*
OPPOSITE (**2** and **3**): **heavy**

light[3] *verb (past **lit** /lɪt/ or **lighted**)*
to make a thing like a lamp, fire, or cigarette burn or give out light ▶ *Will you light the fire for me?*

light bulb /ˈlaɪt bʌlb/ *(also **bulb**)* *noun*
the glass part of an electric lamp that gives out light

lighten /ˈlaɪtn/ *verb*
to make something light or lighter in weight or colour

lighter /ˈlaɪtəʳ/ *noun*
an instrument for lighting a cigarette

lighthouse /ˈlaɪthaʊs/ *noun (plural **lighthouses** /-haʊzɪz/)*
a tall building with a powerful flashing light that guides ships or warns them of dangerous rocks